SEX AND GENDER IN THE
LEGAL PROCESS

SEX AND GENDER IN THE
LEGAL PROCESS

Susan S. M. Edwards

BA, MA, PhD, LLM

University of Buckingham, School of Law

BLACKSTONE
PRESS LIMITED

This edition published in Great Britain 1996 by Blackstone Press Limited, 9-15 Aldine Street, London W12 8AW. Telephone: 0181-740 1173

© Susan S. M. Edwards, 1996

ISBN: 1 85431 507 2

Typeset by Montage Studios Limited, Tonbridge, Kent
Printed by Ashford Colour Press, Gosport, Hampshire

Contents

Preface

For their support, influence and inspiration I am enormously grateful to many friends and colleagues who, in their several ways, have been instrumental in supporting me during the researching and writing of this book. I would like to thank especially Father James Alcock; the late Morayo Atoki; Professor Kathleen Barry; Jamie Bogle, barrister; Tony Bowyer; Frank Brown; Sir Ralph Kilner Brown; Professor Jill Bystydzienski; Francis Coleman; Susan Coombs; Abdul-Redha Dashti; Professor Donald Denman; Professor Andrew Durand; Andrea Dworkin; Patricia Easteal; Lynn Ferguson; Evelina Giobbe; Bill Godwin; Ann Halpern, barrister; Michael Hames, formerly head of the Obscene Publications Department; John Hatchard; PC Kevin Ives; Helena Kennedy QC; His Honour Alan King-Hamilton QC; Dorchen Leidholt; Sybil Lloyd-Morris, solicitor; the late Kathleen McCormack; Sheena McMurtrie; Richard Newell; His Honour Aron Owen; Professor Hal Pepinsky; Professor Jan Raymond; DCI Jim Reynolds; Professor Douglas Sanders; Professor Jacqueline Savornin; Dame Barbara Shenfield; Nigel Spencer-Knott; Dr Lenore Walker; Dr Mary Welstead; Sheila Wilyman and PC Len Yeoll, and Nadia and Shadia Edwards-Dashti.

I am also as ever grateful to the Metropolitan Police for their guidance and understanding on policing matters pertaining to pornography and to the Obscene Publications Department (now the Paedophile Unit, part of the Organised Crime Group) for providing me with considerable hospitality and friendship. I would like to thank the Home Office Statistical Department, the Lord Chancellor's Department, and the Department of Health for providing statistical information. The Pornography and Violence Research Trust not only provided a grant enabling me to conduct research into pornography law and prosecutions which is the subject of Chapter Three but gave me sound advice and support. The producer of Channel 4's 'Till Death Us Do Part' documentary made available research materials on spousal homicide which informed some of my thinking for Chapter Eight on Homicide.

I am grateful to all students of Family Law, Criminal Law and Criminology and Criminal Justice with whom I worked for tolerating my embryonic ideas, but it is students of Sex and Gender in the Legal Process from whom I gained especially, as we explored together the vicissitudes of the law's frame of sex and gender.

Susan Edwards
April 1996

'The question is . . . which is to be master — that's all.'

Lewis Carroll, *Through the Looking-Glass*

Table of Cases

Introduction

Law makes claims to neutrality, to objectivity, and to universality. Law speaks to us all and for us all, so Ronald Dworkin assures us. We are, in his words, 'all subjects of law's empire'; by that he means we are all 'liegemen to its methods and ideals, bound in spirit ...' (1986, p. vii). It is assumed that in law's allegiance to the scientific method, the inexorable social facts from which law is drawn and hewed can be rendered 'value free' in this inductive process. The law's very clay, and its exteriority is made and distilled from individual facts. In the application of scientific method to law is the false premise that all subjectivity and partiality will be washed away. This is the promise of law's baptism. Law's language befitting the discourse of reason and science camouflages its discretion. Judges in constructing and construing law, 'rule' and 'judge', arriving at these self evident truths by applying the 'law to the facts'. The logic of induction is founded on 'particulars', which pass when tried and tested into universal statements (Popper 1968, p. 27). The logic of law is similarly a disciple of induction founded on 'particulars' which by contrast are not of necessity tried and tested. As Thayer (1890, p. 287) wrote, 'In conducting a process of judicial reasoning, as of other reasoning, not a step can be taken without assuming something which has not been proved'. But in this extrapolation of laws, of rules and principles from 'particulars', what, if any, consideration is given to the selective process by which some particulars remain particulars, whilst others become law's universal truths? There are, instead, many competing 'particulars' which, if permitted, become universal to the class of particular from which they are drawn. Indeed the rule of *ejusdem generis* rests on this principle. Exclusion is achieved by differentiating between those particulars that fit the general rule and those that do not, through the process of distinguishing, silencing often, and for ever, equally valid alternate realities. As MacKinnon (1982, p. 515) argues, method 'organises the apprehension of truth; it determines what counts as evidence and defines what is taken as verification'. But which facts, and whose facts receive this divine blessing? And, in this process of largely invisible legal reasoning, how can we know whether the objective path is trod or whether reason from cause to effect is applied, or instead are decisions reached spontaneously and then rationalised *de facto*?

Once the grand achievement of universal law is crafted law then turns on its head in camera obscura from induction to deduction, and the general principle exerts its coercive power and becomes a means by which particular phenomena are explained by nomothetic proposition.

What if the process of legal reasoning is sophistry, and what if discretion, prejudice, opinion and sentiment are an inevitable part? Oliver Wendell Holmes wrote that 'prejudices which judges share with their fellow men' have more to do with interpreting the law than logic (see Monahan and Walker 1994, p. 2). If law is truly objective, then what sense can be made, for example, of the 'lurking doubt' test which exercises an influence on whether an appeal against conviction succeeds; a 'judgment' arrived at via the judicial viscera rather than the judicial cerebra. How is it then that the House of Lords, and the Supreme Court are frequently 'split' at the root when applying the law to the facts (see *Gillick* v *West Norfolk and Wisbech Area Health Authority* [1986] AC 112, *Brown* [1993] 2 All ER 75, *Roth* v *United States*, 1 L Ed 2d 1498 (1957)), or reach the same decision via different routes (see *Richards* v *Richards* [1984] AC 174). Lee (1989, p. 43) asks 'how can it be so simple?', and shows that it is not, since much law is not settled and is itself the subject of dispute.

At the heart of this logic is an allegiance to the very mechanics of the law — the doctrine of precedent. Precedent is the universalised particular, applied over and over again to future particulars. Judges in 'doing' law feel obliged to give a 'gravitational force' (Dworkin, p. viii) to past decisions. In this implacable allegiance to history, law's constancy, its immutability denies competing claims and equally compelling realities. The doctrine of precedent has a negativing effect on modernity. Precedent becomes law's 'halting place', rather than law's 'stepping stone', resistant to social change. Precedent obfuscates any challenge to bad law, leading to the hopeless application of laws that are manifestly unjust. In this cruel and unintended snare, judges respond on occasion with courage and tenacity, breaking rank and rule and discreetly abandoning law altogether. In *Ahluwalia* [1992] 4 All ER 889, and in *Thornton (No. 2)* [1995] *The Times*, 14 December, judges put away law's game in 'the interests of justice' and quashed these convictions for murder when the law had irrevocably failed.

But what if these universal truths were derived from particular facts belonging to the individual experience of one person, e.g., the King and master, and not the common 'man', who was claiming to speak for us all. Would his voice be truly 'ours'? Would his interests be mine? Would I be subsumed within him, absorbed, imbibed, assimilated? Would I share his needs and experience? Whose voice is chosen and who decides who will speak? (see Mossman 1986). As Minow argues, 'Judges and lawyers in the contemporary legal system . . ., like managers in other systems of knowledge and control, treat their own points of reference as natural and necessary' (1988, p. 47). The construct of the 'reasonable man' lies at the heart of this specious absorption and is the very gravitas of legal decision making. Forell (1992, p. 2) writes, 'Indeed, it is considered the very expression of the law's fairness and objectivity'. It is said, so we are told, that reasonable *man* means the reasonable *woman*, just simply by saying so, even though the experiences of women are otherwise immaterial, otherwise irrelevant, and unlike the male experience are rarely authenticated or given law's divine blessing. If such experiences are authenticated, they remain specific to women without universal applicability. In the same way, the Interpretation Acts were founded on the same precept, i.e., that by saying 'Words importing male persons include female persons ...' it would make the difference; (see Ritchie 1975 for an analysis of gender and the Interpretation Acts).

It is said that somewhere deep within the reasonable man we all have a voice and through and in that concept we all have a place, thereby eschewing the hegemony (see Unikel 1992, Cahn 1992, Lahey 1991). This claim is refuted as absurd. How, for example, can the partial defence of provocation founded on what reasonable men do in the face of adversity truly absorb reasonable women and their reaction to adversity? Thus, what men do when wives take lovers, is what any reasonable man would do if presented with the same circumstances and is common knowledge and experience. Yet, what battered women do when abused and threatened by violent husbands, is not within the ken of the reasonable man concept; it is instead 'distinguished' it is within a specialised domain of knowledge and calls for experts to speak to it. Subjectivity, which lies at the heart of the reasonable man, is constituted as universal and rests on particular and highly selective facts. The normative is male (Thornton 1989). As Poulain de la Barre (a little known feminist of the seventeenth century) said, 'All that has been written about women by men should be suspect, for the men are at once the judge and party to the lawsuit' (cited in de Beauvoir 1974, p. 21). Or as a prostitute expressed it, 'It is men, men only men, from the first to the last, that we have to do with! To please a man I did wrong first, then I was flung about from man to man. Men police lay hands on us. By men we are examined, handled, doctored and messed about with. We are had up before magistrates who are men, and we never get out of the hands of men' (*Shield*, 9 May 1870).

It has been the task of post modernism to challenge the law's claim to ontology and to contest laws reification. But deconstructionism does not of necessity embrace feminism, neither does all feminism embrace the varieties of women's experience and challenge to law, nor is all feminism alive to its own pitfall of reductionism. The first step is to expose the falsehood of law's claims. Ronald Dworkin argues that legal reasoning is an exercise in constructive interpretation. Deconstructionism is an exercise in exposing the unassailable truths as myth. Philosophers, social scientists and jurisprudents have deconstructed the social, and deconstructed law. For the philosopher and the social scientist law is no more or less redolent with social meaning, no more or less a product of social constructionism. It is not a discrete domain as its practitioners would have us believe, which somehow in the process of evolution has been inoculated and immunised from the effect of social construction. In law, as elsewhere, concepts are given a significance and authorised as a priori valid. Post modernism's gripe is with the acceptance of the everyday and the legal world as ontologically given. Post modernism as a critical discourse has assumed a discrete significance within legal circles, creating excitement and *frisson* as if a new discovery. The legal scholar lays claim to the precepts of post modernism and thereby endorses the enterprise as a valid part of the legal critique. Much of what gave post modernism its identity was the very gravitas of phenomenology and social constructionism and the very mainstay of the sociological enterprise. If the new terminology brings these precious and valuable insights to law's domain and makes them relevant, so much the better. There is, however, no single post modernism (Frug 1992, p. 1045, Cain 1989–90, p. 204), nor is a feminist exegesis, guaranteed within it.

It has been the task of contemporary feminism to challenge the law's claims to neutrality, objectivity and universality and the several resonances of this partiality for the lives of women and the consequence for heterosexuality and homosexuality within culture and law. Indeed, some of the essential tenets of social constructionism and post modernism overlap with feminism's long standing critique of law. Feminist jurisprudence is a challenge to the essentialism of law. Frug argues, 'Most feminists are committed to the position that however "natural" and common sense sex difference may seem, the differences between women and men are not biologically compelled; they are, rather, "socially constructed"' (p. 1048). The critique has developed on three fronts. Preoccupation in the past has been with the differential application of the law on the basis of sex, gender, race and class. Feminists have challenged the patriarchy of law (Rhode 1994, p. 1193), and the dichotomy of public and private (O'Donovan 1985) around which some laws are built and some institutions of society are structured. This hallowed, revered and protected divide has left women exposed and unprotected against male brutality where State intervention has been determinedly absent in observance of the cardinal sanctity of the 'private' (Fiss 1994). Feminists have asked how it is that all manner of abuses are perpetrated against women and children where the 'privacy' issue at both the level of the family institution and the personal sphere, reigns.

Feminist debate has engaged with law at the level of examining the symbolic function of law, either its absence as in the protection of women from violence, or its presence, and the function of law in exercising control as an ideological State apparatus, and as a powerful symbolic statement of what forms of conduct are permissible and impermissible (Althusser 1971). Feminist jurisprudence in recent years has turned to examine the structural basis of the law and to make known what is taken for granted and what is considered the norm, not merely by employing techniques of reflexivity but by analysing the inherent power base, thereby appraising, decentring and destabilising this dominant discourse. Precedent authorises and thereby situates the male experience within the morphology of the law. Statutory interpretation allows for masculine individualism to creep in.

The interest that the law protects must be considered. The project of writers like Smart 1989, Mossman 1986, Cain 1989–90, Grbich 1991, Lacey 1989, Lahey 1991 and Abrams 1991, has been a challenge to law's method. Here the endeavour is to examine law's claims, law's essentialism, law's masculinism and exclusion of women (Spelman 1988, Orff 1995). Part of this recent assessment has drawn on the inspiration of the feminist critique in disciplines which are considered to be outside the law but which nevertheless act on it (see

Fuss 1989). The aim has been to discern whether there is a feminist legal method that makes feminist critique distinct. The concern with extrapolation of a different method has been a central concern of the feminist enterprise in its search for validating its version of reality. Some say that there is a distinct method (Bartlett 1990, p. 831, Cain 1989–90, p. 195). Do we need to lay claims to a distinctive method in order to validate a distinctive consciousness, experience and voice? I am sceptical and I prefer to think of a feminist perspective as grounded in feminist experience, insights and knowledge. There are also many faces of feminist jurisprudence: it cannot speak for all women (see Minow 1988, Cain 1989–90, p. 203).

There are also internal conflicts over the interpretation of the oracle of law in defining women's lives. Intense conflict rages between sexual liberals and feminists especially in the approach to pornography law. Segal writes, 'opposing attitudes to heterosexuality and to the significance of male violence blew apart the women's movement of the seventies' (1988, p. 69). Issues centring on the construction of homosexuality and the role which lesbian jurisprudence might have in this critique are also central to these conflicts (Cain 1989–90), as are issues of race (Joseph 1981, Rice 1990, Cahn 1992, p. 1415–16, Guillaumin 1995) and who will speak for and to the experience of black women. All women cannot be simply absorbed within one feminist jurisprudence lest the preciousness of the critique lapses too into homogeneity and reductionism. As Guillaumin (1985) points out, black women may have more in common with black men than white women. This reality is most apparent where black women are victims of domestic violence, caught between loyalties, fighting personally against violence and publicly against racism. As Southall Black Sisters concede (1989, p. 40), 'We are forced to make demands of the police to protect our lives from the very same men along whose side we fight in anti-racist struggles'. There is conflict too over the problem of whether in highlighting women's difference and distinctiveness we bring an a priori essentialism, or instead an a posteriori experience. This debate is of supreme significance when considering the relevance of battered women's syndrome to defences (Schneider 1992, p. 531). Feminist critiques of law, whatever their specific exegesis, have been marginalised, regarded as anarchy and as attacks from 'without' the legal enterprise.

This allows law's protectors to deny some real problems within their edifice. Such critiques have been trivialised. Arguably, one of the most important jurisprudential critiques, its opponents claim, is that feminism is trying to introduce a killing licence for women. However what is in situ is a male licence to kill and when the rules binding the legal construction of homicide are dissected, the masculinist hegemony is all too visible. And, without a parallel recognition of the inherent masculinism in law, feminist attempts to engage with law to expose its myths and secrets are met with the rebuff that women want to usurp law's universality and replace these truths with a women's perspective. The integration of a feminist jurisprudence into the study of law suffers indelibly from the prosthesis problem. Mossman talks of 'tacking on' feminist jurisprudence (Mossman 1986, p. 46). In other areas of the social sciences the feminist critique has met with a similar marginalisation. In the criminological enterprise, Heidensohn (1985) talks of feminist criminology as having a 'lean-to' role, as mainstream, male criminology continues on its ejaculatory trajectory (see Carrington 1994). The same is true of political science (Pateman 1989) and of psychology (Gilligan 1982). And so the contribution of feminist jurisprudence promises to be an 'other' perspective. Woman's voice has been silenced: for Dworkin 'she cannot speak', for MacKinnon 'his foot is on her throat'. For de Beauvoir (1974, p. 19) 'They have no past, no history, no religion of their own'.

Part of the collective task is to make the masculinism of these several enterprises visible to men (see Scraton's critique of criminology 1990, Collier's critique of law teaching 1991). This task beset the women's movement and whilst women engaged in consciousness raising, men remained wedded to partriarchy, male power, domination, sexism and racism. Only through notions of civil liberty could they be free from the orthodoxy, but civil liberties may not always be congruous with feminism and so the problem remained. The intellectual unevenness is explored in relation to pornography. Dworkin writes:

> The intellectual defences of pornography have leftist origins. They are not quite accurately characterised as 'defences' either – because with rare exceptions the intellectual left has advocated pornography as crucial to liberation. Leftist writers from Abbie Hoffman to Gore Vidal to leftwing investigative journalists publish in pornography magazines and the actual producers of pornography are men, not exclusively but in shocking numbers, who were active in the anti-war movement, who were roughly my age, who were my political comrades (Dworkin 1982, p. 28).

We must render masculinity, masculinism, structures of patriarchy — heterosexism as accountable and open to challenge. The empire of law is masculinist, the application of legal rules have been recognised as masculinist, but the argument that the method of law itself is masculinist is not so readily conceded. It has been the endeavour of more recent legal feminism to explore the relationship of gender to law beyond the extra- or para-legal application by agents operating the law, and to look within to the form and structure itself.

This book is a contribution to this enterprise and aims to address the several levels of engagement which have characterised scholarship in examination of the legal method underlying the law, the content of the law, the application of law by judges and by the process of applying the law, and the symbolic function of law not merely as a product of social construction and power relations but in the authentication of these relations and the formation of the institutions of patriarchy and heterosexuality with which they are enmeshed.

Feminist writers are both optimistic and pessimistic about what can be achieved with regard to reform and reconstruction of law. Smart (1989) is pessimistic. Many feminists have argued that engaging with law is no solution. Martin argues that gender biases are 'more often transformed than terminated' (1992, p. 740). Dorie Klein in an interview with Andriesson in 1982 remarked, 'The women's movement, at least in this country, has, according to me, made the mistake to believe that the criminal justice system could be transformed into a vigorous feminist instrument'. Like it or not, law is the most powerful tool we have at our disposal and efforts to reveal its genderedness and also to challenge the significance which is given to law as ultimate truth and ultimate justice and to transform it, are neither futile nor doomed. But the inexorable fact remains that *inter alia* law is holistically, root and branch, viscerally, temporally male. Do we have a choice not to challenge, engage and transform it, if we value our 'existence'?

ONE

Transsexuals: in legal exile

Garfinkel opens his chapter on Agnes, '*Passing and the managed achievement of sex status in an "intersexed" person*' thus:

> Every society exerts close controls over the transfers of persons from one status to another. Where transfers of sexual statuses are concerned, these controls are particularly restrictive and rigorously enforced. Only upon highly ceremonialized occasions are changes permitted and then such transfers are characteristically regarded as 'temporary' and 'playful' variations on what the person 'after all', and 'really' is. Thereby societies exercise close controls over the ways in which the sex composition of their own populations are constituted and changed. (1967, p. 116.)

Or to put it another way, 'Perceptual capacities are tied, then, to conceptual capacities and membership categories' (Coulter 1973, p. 116). The question arises how far these perceptual categories are monistically determined by what are considered to be biological 'givens' or how far these perceptual categories emerge in a reflexive process, the interplay of biology, psyche and social constructionism? The law has its own particular response to these categories. The human body in law is, for the most part, biologically determined.

The law is a body of authority of consuetude, which regulates and organises social conduct, social relationships and the institution of the family through the application of rules and sanctions, conferring meaning, not merely on conduct or relationships *in abstracto*, but regulating action in relation to the sex of a specific actor.

> It is no new thing for the law to be drawing the line between biological and social events, choosing the moment when a foetus is enough of a person to require legal protection, deciding when a marriage has been physically consummated, deciding on the definitions of death, rape, cruelty, indecency, a standard of living above starvation. (Douglas 1973, p. 113.)

In *Corbett* v *Corbett* (otherwise Ashley) [1970] 2 All ER 33, 48 (discussed below), Ormrod J stated:

> The fundamental purpose of law is the regulation of the relations between persons, and between persons and the State or community. For the limited purposes of this case, legal relations can be classified into those in which the sex of the individual concerned is either irrelevant, relevant or an essential determinant of the nature of the relationship.

Clearly, it is not always the action in itself, *per se*, which is at the centre of the prohibition. It is instead, and perhaps illogically, who is doing what, and to whom? This definition of action, in relation to specific actors, is nowhere more apparent than in the law as it circumscribes sex offenders, and sex offences in particular. The law organises and regulates familial relationships around the primacy of biology and regulates the gender roles of men and women into masculine and feminine as if naturally predicated on biological dimorphism as a requirement of parenting. The 'rights' conferred are not propitious gifts, but must be earned through conformity to biological sex and gender role, together with allegiance to the accepted model of heterosexuality. The result of such demands for conformity creates discrimination and differential treatment between these two categories of male and female and renders transsexuals legal exiles, conundrums, contradictions who remain, *de jure*, belonging to one category and, *de facto*, to another.

The problem arises that for the transsexual there is no concept in everyday language to give credence and thereby existential sanction, *ipso facto*. The transsexual does not exist in social or even less in legal language. The modern transsexual remains an enigma, regarded by and large as a 'sexual' deviant, bent on distorting and challenging a natural body form. The transsexual is regarded too as a political deviant challenging the very bedrock and orthodoxy of institutions of marriage, of procreation, and of parenthood which are inexorably founded on sexual dimorphism. Androgyny, natally occurring, by contrast has a place in culture, history and language. The hermaphrodite is perceived as the 'victim' of some mutant and malignant process and is considered as a disordered pathology. The androgyne is accorded a status not as a third sex but as either the first or second sex in order to conform to social convention (see Foucault's *Herculine Barbin* 1978). The third sex, natally male or female, instead pleads to have penis or breasts, uterus and ovaries removed in order to achieve an androgynous state, in fact, if not in law. The constructed androgyne once regarded as severely mentally ill, is by contrast regarded as the ultimate deviant, a sex/gender anarchist. Yet arguably, it is the surgically constructed androgyne who is truly liberated from the male or female and its suffocating presumptions of ascribed gender roles. In contrast to the surgically constructed androgyne, transsexuals seek validation in conformity in their new rôle by pursuing the conservative male or female role models. In this sense, there can be scarcely anything more oppressive.

In a world where there is no concept of the transsexual, the hermaphrodite or third sex, the desires, motives and realisations and, in essence, being of the transsexual remain silent. The social and legal organisation of sex and gender roles in wife/husband, mother/father is a confirmation that anatomy is destiny without possibility of change or transcendence.

If biology is political destiny, then women might want to be men. It is the social construction of the body and its meaning that is the primary source of enslavement. Simone de Beavoir wrote on women, 'Woman is determined not by her hormones or by mysterious instincts, but by the manner in which her body and her relation to the world are modified through the action of others than herself' (see Roszak and Roszak 1969, p. 151). It is what the body has come to signify, it is these meanings and not its flesh that must be challenged. The need for a concept to define transsexualism is overwhelming, for without language to define the transsexual then they are lost. The significance of social constructionism is explained by Berger and Luckmann (1971, p. 53):

> Language provides . . . a ready-made possibility for the ongoing objectification of my unfolding experience . . . (53) . . . and builds up semantic fields or zones of meaning that are linguistically circumscribed. Vocabulary, grammar and syntax are geared to the organization of these semantic fields. Thus language builds up classification schemes to differentiate objects by 'gender' (a quite different matter from sex, of course) . . . (55) . . . By virtue of this accumulation a social stock of knowledge is constituted, which is transmitted from generation to generation (56).

On the matter of sex and gender, Berger and Luckmann write:

> At the same time, of course, human sexuality is directed, sometimes rigidly structured, in every particular culture. Every culture has a distinctive sexual configuration, with its own specialized patterns of sexual conduct and its own 'anthropological' assumptions in the sexual area. The empirical relativity of these configurations, their immense variety and luxurious inventiveness, indicate that they are the product of man's own socio-cultural formations rather than of a biologically fixed human nature (67).

Biology is regarded as an unassailable truth, a monist determinant of relationships in the social world. In this essentialist framework biology is a coercive fact, which assumes a 'thing like facticity' *sui generis* (Durkheim 1966) determining all other conduct in its wake. It is not plastic, pliable or malleable, but is deterministic, moulding and shaping gender role in its own image. The biological body dictates the social ascription of gender from birth to the grave from which the transsexual psyche struggles to be free. And yet in a society built on biological sex the only freedom is in congruity and in altering the flesh to conform with the psyche, seeking as the solution the finality of body transformation. It is language and mental concepts which determine meaning and biological meaning. It is language which validates or invalidates human experience. Phenomenological critique of determinism, especially of the biological as given, is offered by Merleau-Ponty who writes:

I am not the outcome or the meeting point of numerous causal agencies which determine my bodily or psychological make-up. I cannot conceive myself as nothing but a bit of the world, a mere object of biological, psychological or sociological investigation. I cannot shut myself up in the realm of science. All my knowledge of the world, even my scientific knowledge, is gained from my own particular point of view, or from some experience of the world without which the symbols of science would be meaningless. The whole universe of science is built upon the world as directly experienced (1967, p. 365).

Scheler (1960) emphasised that the 'relative-natural world view (*relativnatur-liche Weltanschauung*) whilst it appears to the individual as the natural and obvious way of looking at the world, is indeed a product of social construction-ism. Is it then possible to reformulate and reconstruct biology?

Through a different philosophical route, Grbich (1991) explores the epistemological status of the body and challenges.

The theory of the subject questions the origins of knowledge and directs attention to social practices which contain and confine what subjects know. It places our recognition of what is 'natural' as an effect of power — whether the naturalness of femininity or the naturalness of legal institutions (62).

She explores the way in which language and legal language is a system of signification which gives authorisation to certain experiences. From within the bowels of post modernism and its emphasis on social constructionism, emerges the possibility of challenging law's biological determinism and the precept that the subject is a programmed and ontologically given biological being. In this discussion I will explore the several ways in which the transsexual is that immutable ontological given and programmed individual and the ways in which the legal validation of quintessentially social institutions validates this essentialism. I will explore the way in which the legal organisation of sexual dimorphism and the gender roles attaching to it create the surgeons prepared to operate on transexuals and thereby the transsexual. The law as the ultimate form of validation or invalidation of social rules and meanings is incongruous and widely out of step with developments that have taken place in medical science which enable transsexers to undergo 'sex-change' operations allowing them to take on the role of the opposite sex. Yet, once surgically transformed, the transsexual inhabits a legal 'no man's land', a barren terrain of sexual statelessness, where the only rights, obligations and duties are those pertaining to the former sex, the sex renounced, the sex erased, leaving the transsexual in a state of 'exile'. The desire for legal recognition in the constructed sex is denied and the designated sex at birth, all semblance which has been obliterated, continues inexorably and cruelly to define the legal sexual status. Those who identify as a 'third sex', androgynous, neither male nor female are similarly despised and misunderstood, outcasts in a society, whose credo is the social and legal organisation and maintenance of sex difference and the reproduction of institutions premised on biological essentialism.

In this debate there are those who argue that the transsexual should be accorded legal sexual status congruent with the post-operative sex. On the humanitarian front alone it seems that the law should accede to the demands of the transsexual lobby and accept that it can no longer impose meaning on a state which no longer exists. On the other hand, perhaps, the demands for legal recognition of the transsexual in their post operative/psychical status should not be acceded to, not because of some right-wing moralism or aversion to what is considered by many to be a grotesque physical realisation of a specific psychological disturbance, but, instead, on the basis, as experience has shown, that the hopes and aspirations of those seeking 'sex-change' operations, through a suspect medical mutilation, i.e., some congruency with their perceived psychical/sexual identity, is not necessarily a guaranteed outcome. Whilst the law has left unexplored and untrammelled certain questions of the medico-legal ethics of surgical or psychotherapeutic intervention, its central concern has been to order rights, duties, remedies around the gender of citizens rather than around citizens *per se*. It is precisely the organisation of sex differences on biological essentialist criteria, and the rigidity of the legal construction of sex determination and indeed sex designation itself, which functions to exclude transsexuals.

The transsexual body is being pulled and pushed by countervailing forces. Law presses on with its strict allegiance to the hegemony of the determinism of the nascent body: equally it is the application of law that is beginning to abandon and break with this tradition. These competing realities are being played out on the world's legal stage. The polarities have never been more apparent. Posner J, in the United States, clings to a biologically essentialist view of social order as natural, whilst Australian judges recognise the old law as decrepit and anachronistic as the body of the transsexual shrieks of incongruity. The social constructionism of Martens J, in a dissenting judgment in *Cossey* in the European Court of Justice has now come to constitute the prevailing order and opinion in New Zealand. In the judgment of Ellis J, in *Attorney-General* v *Otahuhu Family Court* [1995] 1 NZLR 603, the final death blow is dealt to the biological hegemony of the *Corbett* ruling on sex for marriage purposes, and law's biological heterosexual empire falls.

The way forward in recognising the transsexual phenomenon, may be to limit surgical intervention and find alternate means of treatment. The silence of the law on the question of surgical intervention is of itself indicative of the marginalisation and disempowerment of the rights of this group to health care and the lack of informed discussion of the limits to surgical intervention. It is not the question of transsexuality *per se* that creates the obstacle to the recognition of their civil rights, but transsexuality in its relation to other sexual-legal, and gender-legal constructed relationships and/or institutions, as in marriage and family relationships (such as parenthood and employment) and discrete areas of criminal law and liability. Surgical intervention achieves the semblance of the desired sex, only to be invalidated by the law as the post-operative transsexual attempts to live in the new gendered role. Society, the medical profession, its surgeons and sculptors, should be under a duty to inform those who seek solutions to their dysphoria, and incongruency in the promise of 'sex-change' surgery, of the inevitability of legal invalidation. Legal invalidation for the person in the chosen sex is replete with personal consequences such as mental illness, suicide attempts, all as drastic in their implications as the unhappiness that compels pre-operative transsexuals to search for salvation at the mercy of the surgeon's scalpel. This discussion proceeds with a consideration of the extent of the transsexuals' asynchronism in law, the law's sex/gender recalcitrance in both the private and the public arena.

THE TRANSSEXUAL IN FAMILY LAW: QUESTIONS OF MARRIAGE AND PARENTING

The transsexual's problem is traditionally considered to be confined exclusively to the marriage question. The Universal Declaration of Human Rights, Article 16(1) recognises 'Men and women of full age, without any limitation due to race, nationality or religion, have the right to marry and to found a family' (Ghandhi 1995, pp. 21, 23). Whilst, in some jurisdictions, marriage between persons of the same sex (as in homosexual unions), and persons of the same sex at birth (as in unions involving transsexuals) has been formally recognised, namely in Sweden in 1972, in Germany in 1980, and in Austria, Turkey, Denmark, Holland and South Africa and some Canadian and US states, such unions are not recognised in the United Kingdom (see McMullan and Whittle 1994, p. 105). A House of Commons meeting on 2 February 1995 convened on 'Transsexualism', considered an Act drafted and proposed by Steven Whittle, entitled 'Births Marriages and Deaths Registration Act 1995', which would allow for changes to the birth certificate and thereby facilitate marriage for the transsexual. Alex Carlile MP's 'Gender Identity (Registration and Civil Status)' Bill, received its second reading on 2 February 1996. It provides for the issue of a recognition certificate for transsexuals who have undergone sex reassignment treatment which will allow for the issue of a new certificate and thereby allow marriage between a transsexual and non-transsexual.

With regard to the legal regulation of the family and the institution of marriage, it is perhaps convenient to start with the judgment of Wilde J, (later Lord Penzance) in *Hyde* v *Hyde* [1861-73] All ER 175 (1866). The question before the court was, whether a marriage by Mormons in Salt Lake City was a marriage that the English Matrimonial Court would recognise for the purposes of the English divorce legislation, Wilde J formulated the classic definition of a marriage for those purposes (177), 'I conceive that marriage, as understood in Christendom, may for this purpose be defined as the voluntary union for life of one man and one woman, to the exclusion of all others.'. The history of the consideration of this question and indeed all others pertaining to the sexual status of the transsexual in common law jurisdictions begins with the celebrated English case of *Corbett* v *Corbett (otherwise Ashley)* [1971] P 83, which was the first time that the matter of sexuality, i.e., masculinity and femininity, manhood and womanhood, for the purposes of marriage fell to be decided. The petitioner, Arthur Corbett and the respondent, April Ashley, went through a ceremony of marriage in September 1963. The petitioner knew that the respondent had been registered a male at birth and had subsequently undergone a 'sex-change' operation. The marriage was not a success, neither party finding any peace or happiness. Arthur Corbett brought to the 'marriage' his own particular cocktail of sexual and emotional difficulties, including a desire to dress up in women's clothes and his increasing involvement in the world of transvestism (92–94). In December 1963, the petitioner filed for a declaration that the marriage was null and void, since both of the parties were of the male sex, or, if that failed, then for a decree of nullity on the basis of the respondent's incapacity or wilful refusal to consummate. The respondent, April Ashley, contested and prayed for a decree of nullity on the grounds of the petitioner's incapacity or wilful refusal and not on the grounds that she was of the male sex. Ormrod J, in deciding the question of sex for the purposes of marriage said:

> Since marriage is essentially a relationship between man and woman, the validity of the marriage in this case depends, in my judgment, upon whether the respondent is or is not a woman. . . . The question then becomes, what is meant by the word 'woman' in the context of a marriage, for I am not concerned to determine the 'legal sex' of the respondent at large. Having regard to the essentially heterosexual character of the relationship which is called marriage, the criteria must, in my judgment, be biological, for even the most extreme degree of transsexualism in a male or the most severe hormonal imbalance which can exist in a person with male chromosomes, male gonads and male genitalia cannot reproduce a person who is naturally capable of performing the essential role of a woman in marriage (106B–D).

Ormrod J concluded that '. . . the law should adopt in the first place, the first three of the doctors' criteria, i.e., the chromosomal, gonadal and genital tests, and if all three are congruent, determine the sex for the purpose of marriage accordingly, and ignore any operative intervention' (106D). The judgment clearly relegated the psychological component of sexual identity to a secondary consideration in declaring the marriage void.

The paramountcy of biological essentialism in sex determination was widely followed and applied when courts in other common law jurisdictions were called upon to consider the marriage question. The dictum in *Corbett* was followed in the New Zealand case of *Re T* (1975) 2 NZLR 449 (a declaration case), where McMullin J, in the Supreme Court in Auckland, dismissed the applicant's motion for an order 'determining and declaring' his sex, where a male had undergone sex change surgery. In 1973, the applicant sought to effect a change in the registration of the details of his birth and show his sex as female (450). This application was declined. The court ruled, 'Only a legislative enactment in this country can provide the means whereby the applicant can secure a declaration of the kind he seeks' (453). In Canada, in the case of *M v M(A)* 42 RFL (2d) 55 (1985) (a marriage case) the Supreme Court of Prince Edward Island, Family Division, annulled the marriage of the parties following the wife's intention to undergo a sex change operation. The court ruled that the capacity for natural heterosexual intercourse is an essential element of marriage (59). McQuaid J considered *Corbett* and concluded that there existed 'a latent physical incapacity for natural heterosexual intercourse' (59–60). In South Africa in *W* v *W* (1976) 2 SALR 308 (a marriage case), the court followed *Corbett* in a case where the plaintiff, prior to the marriage ceremony, underwent a sex change operation and the marriage was annulled. Nestadt J said, 'My conclusion is that the plaintiff was a male prior to her operation and that, in the absence of proof that such operation changed her sex, she has failed to prove that the marriage to the defendant was valid'. In *Re Ladrach* 513 NE 2d 828, (1987), a US case, the issue for the consideration of the court was whether a post-operative male to female transsexual is permitted under Ohio law to marry a male. A declaratory judgment action was brought seeking issuance of a marriage licence to allow a post operative male to female transsexual to marry. The court cited *Corbett* with approval in its denial of the application.

Whilst the transsexual has been barred from marriage, the nascent intersex or hermaphrodite seems not to have fared any better. In this regard the courts have similarly disregarded psychological and social factors often to the point of absurdity. In *C* and *D* (1979) 6 FLR 636, the respondent had been diagnosed an hermaphrodite at the age of 21. He married a woman, who some 12 years later filed a petition for a decree of nullity. Perhaps one of the most disquieting aspects of the judgment was when the court ruled that the person was neither male nor female, where the chromosome pattern was female, where the person had been reared as male, and where he possessed both a short penis, a rudimentary vagina, a tiny uterus and breasts. Following surgery, breasts were removed and the penis reconstructed. Although the operation and surgery seemed successful, according to the wife's evidence at trial, the husband was unable to consummate the marriage. In the words of Bell J, 'She did not in fact marry a male but a combination of both male and female and notwithstanding that the husband exhibited as a male, he was in fact not ... and the wife was mistaken as to the identity of her husband and the ground under the Matrimonial Causes Act is made out' (639), (Finlay 1980, p. 117). The court went on to declare the marriage a nullity. This ruling was made in respect of a marriage of some 12 years' duration where there were two children of that marriage (one adopted and one fathered by another man) and the couple had held themselves out as a married couple for all this period of time, even though the marriage had not been physically consummated. The effect of the ruling was not only to discount the marriage relationship which had subsisted for all that time, but also to render the man unable to marry at all. The court ruled, 'I am satisfied as to the evidence that the husband was neither man nor woman but was a combination of both.'.

Notwithstanding this measure of support and allegiance, the *Corbett* judgment has also been the subject of considerable criticism, not only because of the primacy given to biology in sex determination and the relegation of the psyche to the legal boundaries, but also because of the presumption of consummation as of quintessential importance to the viability of marriage itself (see Finlay 1989, Bradney 1987, Taitz 1988). Both these aspects have in more recent years been deemed to be immaterial to the contracting of a valid marriage under

Australian law (see the Sex Reassignment Act 1988). In the New Jersey case of
MT v *JT* 355 A 2d 204 (1976), the issue, for the consideration of the court, was
whether a marriage between a male to female transsexual was a lawful marriage
'between a male and a post operative transsexual, who has surgically changed
her external sexual anatomy from male to female' (208). The court expressly
rejected *Corbett*, 'we cannot join the reasoning of the *Corbett* case', replacing the
hegemony of the biology at birth test, with a dual test embracing both anatomy
and gender:

> Our departure from the *Corbett* thesis is not a matter of semantics. It stems
> from fundamentally different understanding of what is meant by 'sex' for
> marital purposes.... The evidence and authority which we have examined,
> however, shows that a person's sex or sexuality embraces an individual's
> gender, that is, one's self-image, the deep psychological or emotional sense
> of sexual identity and character ... we are impelled to the conclusion that for
> marital purposes if the anatomical or genital features of a genuine transsexual
> are made to conform to the person's gender, psyche or psychological sex,
> then identity by sex must be governed by the congruence of these standards
> ... if sex re-assignment surgery is successful ... we perceive no legal barrier,
> cognisable sexual taboo, or reason grounded in public policy to prevent that
> person's identification, at least for purposes of marriage, to the final sex
> indicated (210–211).

It is worthy of note that a court in Switzerland in 1945 had ruled that an
essential component of a person's sex was his psyche:

> Now that the patient's psychic association with the female sex is strongly
> supported by anatomical changes it appears to us impossible to go back. It
> would therefore be advisable to recognize legally a state which the law did not
> prevent from coming into existence.... This aversion (to male clothing,
> genitalia etc.) may even lead to self-mutilation ... or to castration. It is clear
> that it is not an ordinary vice ... the subject must be driven ... by inner forces
> beyond his control. This inclines us to attribute to the psychic element, in the
> determination of sex, an importance at least equal to that of the physical
> element.... In granting him the civic status of a woman we are satisfying the
> most profound desire of his being while consolidating his psychic and moral
> equilibrium; at the same time we are facilitating his social adaptation by
> permitting him to lead a more normal type of life than heretofore. The
> personal interest which urges him to ask for a change of civic status is thus
> not opposed to the interest of public order and morality — quite the contrary
> (see Smith 1971, p. 963).

The edifice of biological essentialism as the monist determinant of the marriage
question is foundering. In New Zealand, in *Attorney-General* v *Otahuhu Family
Court* [1995] 1 NZLR 603, where two persons of the same genetic sex applied
to enter into a valid marriage, the Attorney-General applied, on behalf of the
Registrar of Marriage, for clarification and the court had to decide the

definition of 'a man' and 'a woman' for the purpose of marriage. Ellis J, in the High Court, delivered a judgment from which it is worth quoting extensively:

> In my view the law of New Zealand has changed to recognise a shift away from sexual activity and more emphasis being placed on psychological and social aspects of sex, sometimes referred to as gender issues. This shift has been recognised by jurisdictions outside England and the approach of Ormrod J in *Corbett's* case has not always been accepted. In our own Family Court in *M* v *M* and in the Appellate Division of the Superior Court of New Jersey in *MT* v *JT*. . . . Judges have held that post-operative transsexual male to female persons have been able to marry, or more precisely that their marriages to a male husband were not void. Added to these is the powerful majority decision of the New South Wales Court of Appeal in *R* v *Harris* (1988) 17 NSWLR 158, a criminal case where the sex of the alleged offender was in issue. These cases and the others that bear on the matter are fully analysed in Ms Ullrich's submissions. I find the reasoning in these three cases to be compelling, and I find myself unable to accept the decision in *Corbett's* case as governing the outcome of the present application. I think it is important to emphasise (as was emphasised in the cases) that the declaration sought is to resolve the capacity to marry and is not intended to resolve questions that arise in other branches of the law such as the criminal law, and the law of succession. I recognise of course that in such cases the considerations may have much in common. Some persons have a compelling desire to be recognised and be able to behave as persons of the opposite sex. If society allows such persons to undergo therapy and surgery in order to fulfil that desire, then it ought also to allow such persons to function as fully as possible in their reassigned sex, and this must include the capacity to marry. Where two persons present themselves as having the apparent genitals of a man or a woman, they should not have to establish that each can function sexually. Once a transsexual has undergone surgery, he or she is no longer able to operate in his or her original sex. A male to female transsexual will have had the penis and testes removed, and have had a vagina-like cavity constructed, and — possibly breast implants, and can never appear unclothed as a male, or enter into a sexual relationship as a male, or procreate. A female to male transsexual will have had the uterus and ovaries and breasts removed, have a beard growth, a deeper voice, and possibly constructed penis and can no longer appear unclothed as a woman, or enter into a sexual relationship as a woman, or procreate. There is no social advantage in the law not recognising the validity of the marriage of a transsexual in the sex of reassignment. It would merely confirm the factual reality. If the law insists that genetic sex is the predeterminant for entry into a valid marriage, then a male to female transsexual can contract a valid marriage with a woman and a female to male transsexual can contract a valid marriage with a man. To all outward appearances, such would be same sex marriages. As I have said, I find the arguments in Ms Ullrich's submissions compelling, and the preceding two paragraphs are adapted from them. I can see no socially adverse effects from allowing such transsexuals to marry in

their adopted sex, I cannot see any harm to others, children in particular, that is not properly proscribed and manageable in accordance with the existing framework of the law. I refer for example to my decision on a proposed adoption by two women of the child of one of them: *Re T* (High Court, Wellington, AP 55/89, 10 April 1992), where the best interests of the child were determinative. In this I find myself of the same persuasion as the Court of Appeal of New Jersey in *MT* v *JT* and the majority of the Court of Criminal Appeal of New South Wales in *Harris*. Further, I find myself of the same view as Judge Aubin in *M* v *M*, the case that prompted this application. The form of the declaration was the subject of careful submissions also. In the Births, Deaths, and Marriages Registration Bill 1989 as originally introduced, provision was made in cl 29 to allow changes to be made to the sex shown on birth certificates of persons who had 'undergone surgical and medical procedures that have effectively given the person the physical conformation of a person of a specified sex'. I consider that this somatic test is an adequate test. It is formulated on the basis of the undisputed evidence that persons who have undertaken such procedures will have already had the social and psychological disposition of the chosen sex. Declaration. I therefore make a declaration that for the purposes of s. 23 of the Marriage Act 1955 where a person has undergone surgical and medical procedures that have effectively given that person the physical conformation of a person of a specified sex, there is no lawful impediment to that person marrying as a person of that sex (606–608). By contrast, the position in the UK remains that a transsexual cannot marry in his or her post operative sex. Although two transsexuals, one male to female the other female to male may contract a lawful marriage given the law's allegiance to biological sex (B.S.D.) as the sole basis for marriage.

See further, *Registrar General for England and Wales, ex parte P, Same* v *Same, ex parte G, The Times*, 27 March 1996.

On the question of parenting, access and custody

The socio-legal construction of the family, the roles, duties and obligations of its prospective members are determined in accordance with biological and gender essentialism, thereby excluding from the heterosexual family the transsexual parent. Within the domain of the family, the law has constructed rights and entitlements around reproductive genderised relationships of females to their offspring in the legal construction of motherhood and males in relation to their offspring in the legal role of fatherhood. Historically, the father had sole rights and entitlement to the child, representing one of the last vestiges of the application of the ideology of natural law to patriarchal effect. In *Re Agar-Ellis* (1883) 24 Ch D 317, a father's rights were considered sacred rights, natural, immutable, sacrosanct, impenetrable. Paternal authority remained the underlying principle of family law until the Guardianship of Infants Act 1973. Parental rights have now been transformed into responsibilities, the parental right being 'a dwindling one' (see *Hewar* v *Bryant* [1970] 1 QB 357, *J* v *C* [1970] AC 668, *Gillick* v *West Norfolk and Wisbech Health Authority* [1986] AC

112). The position of the unmarried father has been revolutionised, his right no longer axiomatic. In accordance with the Children Act 1989 s. 4 he must now seek legal authentication of that hitherto pre-ordained entitlement through making an application to the court. The mother, by contrast, had no legal right to guardianship or custody until 1973. Her more recent realisation of rights have similarly been reconstituted and redefined as responsibilities toward the child, but for her they are axiomatic. Since the Children Act 1989 s. 1(3)(a) the child's welfare is paramount and the duty to consider the child's wishes is enshrined as a legal obligation. It is into this heterosexual taxonomy of the legal organisation of family life, parental rights and responsibilities and children's rights that the transsexual parent must negotiate a new place. The transsexual parent as mother or father is soon to find that sex change denies him/her entitlements where access to offspring is considered inappropriate.

There are two sites of conflict for the transsexual in this highly organised terrain of biologically ordered familial relationships. One emerges as a result of the exercise of discretion and the application both of the principle of 'best interests of the child', and of the Children Act 1989, s. 1(3)(a), in considering the child's welfare in custody and access arrangements. The other emerges as a result of express legal rules which exclude transsexuals from parenthood or, more precisely, the acquisition of parental responsibility by virtue of their sexual status at birth.

In exploring the first site of conflict in struggles over custody and access (Children Act 1975, s. 33(1)), and residence and contact arrangements (Children Act 1989, s. 8), the courts have assessed and ruled on the suitability of the transsexual parent to dispense the duties of parenting. The welfare of the child is the paramount consideration of the court, operating with a presumption that harm and distress is caused to the child by this parental transfiguration. Yet, the ability of a person to give love, support and care to their child is not dependent upon sexual orientation (heterosexual, homosexual or lesbian), or indeed their gender preference, as in the case of transvestites and pre and post operative transsexuals. Nevertheless, the courts have denied access or contact on the basis of the incongruity of transsexuals with the idealised and proscribed parenting mould. Rights to parenthood depend quintessentially on heterosexuality, on subscribing to fixed codes of sexual conduct and gender orientation within that gender role, requirements which are, arguably, social conventions unrelated to the caring function. For the transsexual parent who undergoes 'sex-change' surgery during the childhood of the offspring, his/her capacity for caring and love does not alter or diminish as a consequence of surgery, nor because of the ingestion of oestrogens or progesterones or the wearing of different attire or the wish to be known and treated as of a different gender. Capacity for loving and nurturing may of course be altered and diminished, because of mental distress attributable to gender dysphoria. This being the case, it could be argued that the post operative transsexual is likely to dispense with parenting functions more adequately having resolved the dysphoric confusion causing the mental disturbance.

In disputes over custody and access, the transsexual has been regarded as a 'wholly unfit' parent. Decisions to grant access with conditions, or to deny access altogether follow on from the application of the principle of what is in the 'best interests of the child'; a determination predicated on the subjective view of 'powerful' others with little consideration of the interests of the child who is, after all, at the centre of the struggle itself. In the UK, it is not transsexuality *per se* but its visible expression and outward display that continues to be regarded as central to custody/access decisions. Where the transsexual parent applies for custody/access, residence/contact, the court seeks to control and circumscribe the outward appearance of the transsexual, presumably in the name of the child's best interests. In 1981, in an unreported case in which Professor Richard Green was called as expert witness to testify to the effects of transsexual parents on children (see Green 1992, p. 114), a High Court judge ruled that access would only be permitted when the father, a male to female transsexual, dressed as a man. The Court of Appeal overturned this stringent requirement, tempering it, and putting instead, its own 'liberal' stipulation, that C should not dress in a 'bizarre or aggressively feminine way' (see Crane 1982, p. 193). Similarly, in *G* v *G* (1981) (unreported), a court made an order for access, for a male to female transsexual father, on the condition of an undertaking that, on access visits 'she' would wear male orientated attire, no jewelry or cosmetics (see McMullan and Whittle 1994, p. 77).

It is only in the most exceptional circumstances that a transsexual will be awarded custody (residence) of the children of the family. In *Re H-S (minors: protection of identity)* [1994] 3 All ER 390, a male to female transsexual obtained custody of 'her' children. The wife was granted a divorce on the grounds of unreasonable behaviour and was subsequently granted custody of their three children. In 1987, she suffered a nervous breakdown following the transsexuality of her former husband, which resulted in the children being placed in care. The county court granted custody to the father (now a female), subject to local authority supervision. During this time the father took part in a television programme on 'Transsexualism', as a result of which the children were identified and experienced some difficulties at school. The petitioner sought a variation of the custody order and applied for an injunction in the High Court restraining the transsexual parent from exposing the children to further publicity. In a reserved judgment, the Court of Appeal refused to remove the injunction, and confirmed that the injunction would last until 2001. On appeal, the court held that the injunction was drawn too widely and the appeal was allowed. However, the terms of the order were to be varied, by restricting the respondent's dealings with the media and preventing any dealing with the media from the property at which the respondent and the children lived or any such dealing in their presence (391).

Some US states, in grappling with similar access/custody disputes in determining 'the best interests and welfare of the child', have boldly taken the view that, '. . . the court shall not consider conduct of a proposed custodian that does not affect his relationship with the child' (Colorado Rev. Stat 46-1-24 (2) 1963 and Supp. 1971). Thus in *Christian* v *Randall* 516 P 2d 132 (1973), where a father applied for custody of his four teenage daughters who were with their mother a female to male transsexual, and who had subsequently remarried a woman, the Colorado Court of Appeals found that the mother's transsexuality did not adversely affect '. . . "her" (*sic*) relationship with the children or impair their emotional development' (133). 'The record contains no evidence that the respondent's home in Colorado endangered the children's physical health or impaired their emotional development. On the contrary, the evidence shows that the children were happy, healthy, well-adjusted children who were doing well in school and who were active in community activities' (133) (see Haag and Sullinger 1982, p. 351–2).

In considering the principle of the 'best interests of children' the matter of a parent's transsexualism has been the basis for an ouster injunction. In *Briscoe* v *Briscoe* (unreported) (Court of Appeal, 12 April 1984, Lexis transcript), in applying the factors which must be taken into account in an application under the Matrimonial Homes Act 1983 (chapter entitled, All in the Name of Privacy — Domestic Violence for further discussion on this point), the judge ordered a husband respondent to leave the matrimonial home to enable the wife and son to return to it. The pre operative transsexual husband had an ouster made against him under the Matrimonial Homes Act 1983, as a result of cross-dressing and the possible effect on the child of the marriage. The Court of Appeal dismissed the appeal against this decision.

The second major site of conflict and exclusion for the transsexual emerges with relation to specific legal rules governing parenthood predicated on biological essentialist criteria. The issues raised by the application of X, Y and Z to the European Court of Human Rights has succeeded in the first stage of hearing before the Commission. This case is instructive, involving X, a female to male transsexual currently living with Y, a female partner who has had a child Z, the result of artificial insemination by a donor. The complaint to the Court relates to the refusal of the UK Government to recognise the female to male transsexual as the 'father' of the child for the purposes of the Children Act 1989, s. 4. When Y, the second applicant, went for treatment for artificial insemination, the first applicant, X, was asked to acknowledge himself to be the father of the child within the meaning of the Human Fertility and Embryology Act 1990, s. 28(3). Advances in *in vitro* fertilisation, where embryo or eggs, or sperm are implanted in the woman and where the sperm donor is not the partner, are circumstances governing ss. 27, 28. Section 27 states that, '. . . the woman who is carrying or has carried a child as a result of the placing in her of an embryo or of a sperm and eggs, and no other woman is to be treated as the mother of the child', providing legal expression to the recommendations of the *Warnock Report* (1984, para. 6.8). However, where a child is born to a married woman as a result of artificial insemination, if the husband consented to the insemination then he is to be treated as the father of the child. The position of the unmarried couple and *in vitro* fertilisation has meant that where, 'in the course of treatment services provided for her and a man together', the male party is then regarded in law as the child's father (1990 Act, s. 28(3)), he can subsequently apply for parental rights under the Children Act 1989, s. 4(1) (see Hoggett 1993, p. 49). The application to the Registrar General to have X registered as the father was met with objection. The Registrar General sought legal advice from the Department of Health and was advised that only a biological male could be registered as the father. The applicant family complained to the European Court of Human Rights that as a result they had been denied respect for their family and private life and invoked Articles 8, 12, 13 and 14 of the Convention for the Protection of Human Rights and Fundamental Freedoms (1950), which they argued have been breached. The British Government's response, regarding Article 8, was that 'no family relationships' exist, since X is a male. In respect of the third applicant, Z the Government submitted that Article 8 did not extend beyond recognising relationships of blood, marriage and adoption. The Commission in reply accepted the admissibility of the claim under Articles 8 and 14. Although it by no means follows that the trial judgment of the European Court of Human Rights will accord with that of the Commission. Article 8 states:

(1) Everyone has the right to respect for his private and family life, his home and his correspondence.

(2) There shall be no interference by a public authority with the exercise of this right except as in accordance with the law and as necessary in a democratic society in the interests of national security, public safety or the economic well-being of the country, for the prevention of disorder or crime, for the protection of health or morals, or for the protection of the rights and freedoms of others (Ghandi 1995, p. 127).

Article 14 which is concerned with the prohibition of discrimination, states:

The enjoyment of the rights and freedoms set forth in this Convention shall be secured without discrimination on any ground such as sex, race, colour, language, religion, political or other opinion, national or social origin, association with a national minority, property, birth or other status (Ghandi, p. 128).

Following *Rees* v *United Kingdom* (1987) 9 EHRR 56 and *Cossey* v *United Kingdom* (1991) 13 EHRR 622, discussed below, the Commission did not accept the complaint under Article 12, in respect of the right to marry. Article 12 states, 'Men and women of marriageable age have the right to marry and to found a family, according to the national laws governing the exercise of this right.'. The Commission also rejected a claim under Article 13 on the right to an effective remedy. Article 13 states that,

Everyone whose rights and freedoms are set forth in this Convention shall be secured without discrimination on any ground such as sex, race, colour, language, religion, political or other opinion, national or social origin, association with a national minority, property, birth or other status (Ghandi, p. 128).

However, the decision of the court in *Re L (Contact: Transsexual Applicant)* [1995] 2 FLR 438, 443, suggests that the courts are prepared to accede to a s. 4 Children Act 1989, application for parental responsibility where the transsexual is male at birth. In this case where a male to female transsexual sought such an order, the court found no basis upon which it could refuse. 'After all this was a natural parent who was closely involved in S's nurture and upbringing for the all-important early years of her life. There is a commitment. That has been demonstrated historically and for the time present'.

Nobody's child: the child of the transsexual family

What rights or say does the child in the transsexual family have? The Children Act 1989, s. 10(1)(a)(ii), (2), (8) makes provision for children who wish to make applications for orders in respect of residence and contact and other matters in their own right (Bainham 1993, p. 289, Lyon and Parton 1995). The Children Act 1989, s. 1(3)(a) enshrines in statute the principle emergent in earlier case law which regards the child's interests as paramount, replacing the 'best interest' principle. This development follows a line of case law authority commencing with the case of *J* v *C* [1970] AC 668, where the welfare of the child was held to be paramount outweighing the fact that his parents were unimpeachable (see *Re K (Minors) Wardship* [1977] Fam 179; *Gillick* v *West Norfolk and Wisbech Health Authority* [1986] AC 112). At the heart of *Gillick* was established the '*Gillick* competence' principle which raised the question as to when the child was competent to give consent or express its wishes. Lord Scarman asserted, 'the parental right yields to the child's right to make his own decision when he reaches a sufficient understanding and intelligence to be capable of making up his own mind on the matter requiring decision'. Case law indicates the reluctance of the courts to accede to the child's wishes even where the child is deemed competent and the courts' willingness to use their power to override a ward's decision (see *Re R (A Minor) (Wardship: Consent to Treatment)*, *The Independent*, 25 July 1991; *Re R* [1992] 4 All ER 177, *Re W* [1992] 3 WLR 758).

In residence and contact matters, unless adoption is under consideration, having regard to all the circumstances 'first consideration' will be given to the need to safeguard and promote the child's welfare. Case law reveals that where there is a conflict between the 'best interests' principle, which in practice is judicial paternalism, and the wishes and feelings of the child, the child's wishes are invariably overruled, on the basis that either the child is not '*Gillick* competent' or, if competent, the *parens patriae* jurisdiction may prevail to overrule the child's wishes. The principle of letting the child's wishes prevail has been unevenly applied. In *Birmingham CC* v *H (No. 2)* [1993] 1 FLR 883, where there was a conflict between mother and son, the Court of Appeal held that neither mother nor son should be given priority. From the child's perspective, in cases where children have expressed a wish to have 'no contact' with a parent, even though the child is considered competent, this wish has rarely been granted.

Considering the transsexual parent, where the parent is known to the child in the pre operative state, as male or female, and then undergoes sexual reassignment, and, as a result of this change, the child has expressed a wish not to have contact, then, exceptionally, the court has, or so it appears, accepted the child's wishes. It is likely, however, in such cases that the views of the child merely mirror what the court would have decided anyway. In *Re F (Minors)*

(Denial of Contact) [1993] 2 FLR 677, where a father left the family home and began to live his life as a male to female transsexual, the two children of the marriage did not want to see their father dressed as a woman, although the welfare officer and mother expressed the wish that the children should keep in contact with the father. The court upheld the children's wishes and made a no contact order although it is not clear whether the children had expressed a wish not to see their father at all or merely not to see him dressed as a woman. The judge in considering the wishes and interests of the children (s. 1(3)(a)) made 'no order' as to contact. In applying s. 1(5) in considering whether to make an order, the court must decide whether it is better to make no order at all (see the chapter entitled, A Betrayal of Trust — The Sexual Abuse of Children).

Where the child is already being reared by a transsexual parent and knows and has known that parent only in the post operative identity, that child is denied the right to the validation of that carer, as a specific gendered parent and all that this validation implies for privacy and the preservation of the right to a normal childhood and a normal family life. The application of *Z* (see *X*, *Y*, and *Z* above) to the European Court of Human Rights, raises further fundamental issues affecting children's rights to a parent and arguably to a transsexual parent. *Z* had a birth certificate which had a nil entry for the father, and yet knew *X* to be its father. *X* had assumed the role of parental responsibility for the child *de jure* although acquiring legal rights of fatherhood were prohibited *de jure*. The child is then being denied the benefits of a father and of a family life through the intransigence of the law to recognise and validate what would, after all, break the law's pact with biological essentialism in family relationships. Parental responsibility includes, in s. 1 of the Act, all the rights, duties, powers, responsibilities and authority which by law a parent of a child has in relation to the child and his property. The Children Act provides in s. 3(5), 'A person who (a) does not have parental responsibility for a particular child; but (b) has care of the child may (subject to the provisions of this Act) do what is reasonable in all the circumstances of the case for the purpose of safeguarding or promoting the child's welfare.'. The child's welfare is being thwarted by the resolute refusal to recognise a *de facto* transsexual father as the father *de jure*.

The ruling of the European Commission in this first stage is extremely encouraging. By 13 votes to 5, the Commission concluded that there had been a violation of Article 8 of the Convention (1995, para. 71 *Report of the Commission Ruling*). In the view of the Commission they made out an extremely strong argument for recognising the semblance of a family unity *in situ*:

> To all appearances, the Commission notes that the first applicant is the third applicant's father (para. 54). The Commission finds that the relationships enjoyed by the applicants fulfil both the appearance and substance of 'family life'. The only element which detracts from this is the fact that the first applicant was registered at birth as being of the female sex with the consequence, inter alia, that he is under a legal incapacity to marry the child's mother or register on the child's birth certificate as father (para. 57). The Commission is of the opinion that this element, whether seen as biological or historical, cannot outweigh the reality of the applicant's situation, which is

otherwise indistinguishable from the traditional notion of 'family life' (para. 58).

Clearly with the advent of new reproductive technology the age old assumptions of parentage are being challenged. If it is now no longer self-evident how we describe a mother where, for example, one egg is removed from a female fertilised *in vitro* and placed in another woman for gestation, we must also be open to the transsexual parent as mother in surrogacy arrangements and father in arrangements such as *X, Y* and *Z*.

THE CRIMINAL LIABILITY OF THE TRANSSEXUAL

Although Ormrod J in *Corbett* was clear in limiting the application of his judgment and his definition of biological sex to the marriage question, the repercussions have infected areas of law outside marriage, especially for the criminal liability of the transsexual in respect of sex offences throughout the common law jurisdictions where sex offences are gender specific in law. It was not until the Australian case of *Harris and McGuiness* (1988) 35 A Crim L 146, that the Ormrod legacy was finally abandoned and regarded as having been misapplied in cases outside marriage. The transsexual in the UK faces particular difficulties in discrete areas of criminal law which are sex specific. First, in respect to offences where criminal liability is predicated on biological sex, and secondly where transsexuals may also fall foul of the law merely by being transsexual; by being charged either with insulting a female or with a breach of the peace. McMullan and Whittle (1994, p. 34), report a case of a man who was fined £50 by Aberdeen Crown Court on the grounds that his wearing of women's clothes in a red light district was, 'conduct likely to cause breach of the peace'. In considering the question of the transsexual sex offender, it is not possible to rely on reported cases, since the courts have not had to consider a case of a transsexual charged with rape, or attempted rape. This does not, however, preclude the possibility of indecent assault charges being brought (see Saunders below). In the event of such an allegation being made it is likely that no charge will be brought, or if a charge is brought, the offence might well be reduced to one of a gender neutral 'indecent assault', to obviate any legal difficulties which may otherwise result in the case being dismissed for want of jurisdiction. Notwithstanding the legal dilemma, the consequences for the victim of rape, perpetrated by a female to male transsexual, remain the same, whether penetrated by an artificially constructed or a 'real' penis. In the arena of rape and attempted rape, until the Criminal Justice and Public Order Act 1994, s. 142, the law regulating sexual offences was predicated on the sex specificity of the *actus reus* which depended on the nascent maleness of the accused and the femaleness of the victim rather than on an *actus reus* and *mens rea* stripped of gender.

Criminal liability: the female to male sex offender

Given the sex specific offences created by UK statute, the problem arises that a female to male transsexual could not in law be charged with rape, buggery, indecent exposure or forced fellatio on a female. So far as rape is concerned, 'It is a felony for a man to rape a woman' (Sexual Offences Act 1956, s. 1(1)), attempted rape is committed by a man on a woman (Sexual Offences Act 1956, s. 37(4)). The Criminal Justice and Public Order Act 1994, now substitutes the following section for s. 1 of the Sexual Offences Act 1956, '(1) It is an offence for a man to rape a woman or another man. (2) A man commits rape if (a) he has sexual intercourse (whether vaginal or anal) with a person who at the time of the intercourse does not consent to it.'. Although drafted with the intention of recognising homosexual rape it remains a matter for statutory interpretation as to the criminal liability of a female to male transsexual (see Sharpe 1995). The case of *Saunders* (1990) (unreported) (McMullan and Whittle 1994, p. 39), is instructive of the approach of the courts to pre operative female to male transsexuals. Here the appellant, a pre operative female to male transsexual, was charged with an indecent assault under the Sexual Offences Act 1956, s. 14 (indecent assault on a woman). Saunders had had two affairs with two separate women and used an attachable penis to have sexual intercourse. The women consented to intercourse, although claimed that they would not have done so had they known that Saunders was in fact a woman. Saunders was convicted of indecent assault and sentenced to six years imprisonment, reduced on appeal to a nine month suspended sentence. Although sexual intercourse had taken place so far as the complainants were concerned, as a charge of rape depended on the maleness of the perpetrator, since Saunders was not a male then rape could not appear on the indictment, and since the consent of the complainants was obtained by fraud then consent was negated, although it is not altogether clear how a charge of indecent assault was sustained where the woman consented. Crabtree J, in passing sentence, said that the two women would have been '. . . better able to cope if they had been raped by a man' (*sic*).

Transsexuals who do not disclose their previous sexual status to their partner may well face prosecution. Tully (1992, p. 206), in his study of transsexuals reveals the problems encountered by the female to male transsexual in sexual relations and outlines the obvious difficulties that this will pose:

I would tell girlfriends that I cared for them and nothing else mattered. Now when they feel like that towards me, that was the time to tell them the details. I have never miscalculated this. I remember Laura put her arms around my neck and expressed her admiration. . . . Recently I told Cathy my present girlfriend about myself. I hadn't told her that I have a problem with my genitals as I used to cover those parts. I used a false penis which I wore all the time. I told her this was me but it had a lot of scars and it wasn't quite as it should be . . . Cathy didn't know about my prosthesis even when it was used for sex over a couple of years. She was very embarrassed, but she wasn't really very angry, rather, hurt.

The law, however, has not been as sympathetic as Cathy!

The male to female transsexual prostitute

The criminal liability of the male to female transsexual is dependent upon the determination of the liability of males for sexual offences. The major legal conundrum arises in respect of the male to female transsexual prostitute. Although not expressly provided for in statute, statutory interpretation has resulted in a sex specific construction of the law of prostitution. The Street Offences Act 1959, s. 1(1) states, 'It shall be an offence for a common prostitute to loiter or solicit in a street or public place for the purpose of prostitution, and there is a presumption in law that the offence is committed by women only. The Sexual Offences Act 1956, s. 32 states , 'It is an offence for a man persistently to solicit or importune in a public place for immoral purposes' and this presumes that when men solicit they are importuning other men.

Prostitution: importuning or loitering and soliciting   In the UK, for several decades, the experience of magistrates has been replete with the dilemma of the male to female transsexual prostitute appearing before the bench on charges of loitering and soliciting before the natal sex status is discerned. My own empirical research and interest in this particular aspect of criminal liability began in 1980 at Manchester magistrates' court, where within a period of one year I met several male to female transsexuals proceeded against on charges of homosexual soliciting/importuning (Sexual Offences Act 1956, s. 32 see above) and/or loitering and soliciting for the purpose of prostitution (Street Offences Act 1959, s. 1(1) see above). The following case is instructive and illustrative of the way in which physical boundaries are drawn according to rules and meanings and then given a particular significance within the legal domain. In *Stella Greer* (1991) (unreported, 10 March) the charge of importuning was dismissed by the magistrates for want of evidence, the ambiguity over the sex of the defendant notwithstanding.

Court Clerk   'You have previously stated that you want the matter dealt with summarily.'

Defendant   'Yes.'

Court Clerk   'The charge is that on 10th March 1981 that being a man you did persistently importune for an immoral purpose in a public place, namely Canal Street.'

Defendant   'Not Guilty.'

Prosecuting Solicitor   'You've heard the charge and will see that the prosecution have to prove certain elements. Firstly, that the defendant is a man and, secondly, that he was importuning. For the first element I refer to you to the case of *Corbett v Corbett*, the defendant otherwise known as April Ashley. The decision in that case was "once a man always a man". I will bring before the court evidence to prove that this person is a man and therefore he remains a man. The second part of the charge is quite easy to prove. Plain clothes detectives will give evidence to prove they saw the defendant standing in the doorway of the Union Hotel. They saw him move over to a car, get into it and start shouting across to lone males, "Hey, do you want to have a good time?"'

The trial continued and the prosecution went to great lengths to prove that the defendant was not a female. Whilst the magistrates were convinced of this fact they did not consider that the prosecution had discharged the burden of proof on the question of importuning and dismissed the case. It is clear that when transsexuals come under police suspicion it is as female loitering and soliciting for the purpose of prostitution. The evidence then collected by police is to support a charge of loitering and soliciting where the evidential requirement is one of a single act of solicitation.

Transsexuals arrested for female prostitution find that at some stage in the prosecution process, often before charging, when their sex is made known, they are charged with the homosexual offence under s. 32 of the Sexual Offences Act 1956 of importuning, where the evidential requirement, as expressly indicated in the statutory provision, is that of persistence. A transsexual might initially be charged with the offences of both loitering and soliciting and also with importuning, as an alternative, as in a case observed by the author where the proceedings were adjourned for 'matters to be sorted out'. At a later hearing the prosecution decided to offer no evidence on the loitering charge and proceeded with the charge of importuning. The post operative male to female transsexual, in a state of shock and bewilderment, palpably distressed by the reference to her as male, on the advice of counsel pleaded guilty (see Edwards 1984, p. 43). Research on how the courts deal with this question took me to Knightsbridge Crown Court, London. Here Lisa Williams, who had undergone sex change surgery some years previously and had also gone through a ceremony of marriage in 1976, was charged and convicted of importuning. Evidence against her tendered by police was that she approached men in cars. The police officer who approached her said in his statement that this conversation took place between them.

Police officer   'What are you doing?'

Defendant   'I do nothing, I not a street walker.'

Police officer   'Who said anything about that?'

Defendant   'I do nothing. Why were you talking? I not ...'

Police officer   'You are a man, aren't you?'

Defendant   'I am what I am.'

By 1988, if the British courts remained manacled to biological hegemony in respect of the sex specificity of offences of loitering and soliciting, and in respect of the determination of the post operative transsexual according to the pre operative status at birth, in strict allegiance to the Ormrod direction, Australian courts were not of like mind. In the case of *Harris and McGuiness* (1988) A Crim R 146 (Street CJ, Mathews J and Carruthers J, dissenting), the Supreme Court of Australia rejected the biological prerogative of sex at birth for the purposes of prostitution and the present determination of sex. Both defendants were loitering and soliciting for the purposes of prostitution. Vice squad officers were approached and solicited. Both defendants were considered by the police to be males at birth and were charged with offences of homosexual soliciting. Harris, at the age of 18, had undergone full sexual reassignment surgery from male to female and was a post operative male to female transsexual. McGuiness who had not undergone sexual reassignment surgery was living as a woman and was a pre operative transsexual. Both Harris and McGuiness were charged with attempting to procure the commission of an act of indecency under the Crimes Act 1900, s. 81A (repealed in 1984), 'Whosoever, being a male person, in public or private, commits, or is a party to the commission of, or procures or attempts to procure the commission by any male person of, any act of indecency with another male person shall be liable to imprisonment for two years.' (see Edwards 1984, p. 46). Both defendants were convicted in 1982 and sent to prison. On appeal, after hearing submissions; the judge indicated his intention to dismiss the appeal. The judge was then asked on behalf of the appellants to state a case for the opinion of the Court. The questions of law that were stated were these. First, is the test of *Corbett* the only test to be applied in determining the words 'a male person' for the purpose of s. 81A ? Secondly, in respect of the appellant Harris, can a third sex exist for the purpose of legislation?

In delivering the principal judgment of the court on the question of the authority of *Corbett*, Mathews J held that *Corbett* does not provide a test of relevance to be applied in this case. Street CJ concurred (159). Mathews J declared:

It is not easy to perceive the legitimate interest of the State in probing behind the physical attributes of an individual, who is to all intents and purposes a woman, with a view to having her clinically classified as a male person for the purpose of fixing her with guilt under a section such as s. 81A. It is often said that the law takes people as it finds them. On the night of this alleged offence it found Lee Harris with the physical attributes of a woman. I am satisfied that this precludes it being held that she was 'a male person' (161). The time has come when the beacon of *Corbett* will have to give place to more modern navigational guides to voyages on the seas of problems thrown up by human sexuality (161–162).

Carruthers J in the dissenting judgment relied rigidly on the decision in *Corbett* in reaching his decision and took the view that it was for Parliament and not the courts to correct any such problem, and found *Corbett*, and the application of *Corbett* in *Tan* (below), sound (170). The true issue in his view which had been overlooked is a question of fact. Whether she looked like a female, considered herself to be so, or was accepted by society as female (171) was not in his view material.

It was precisely this issue of fact which was raised by Mr Lyon MP in the Nullity of Marriage Bill in the UK in 1970 following the *Corbett* direction. He said:

> The way that a judge decides the sex of a particular person is and always will remain a question of fact. It will be a question of fact which will change with the change in medical opinion. . . . If medical opinion were that the mere sex change operation was enough to change a person from a man to a woman or a woman to a man, that would be the end of the case. . . . If in the end medical opinion is able to state with greater certainty who is a male and who is female on tests which were not applied in the *Corbett* case, then some new court can apply those tests because the evidence will have changed and the question of fact, therefore, will also have changed. (*Hansard* Vol 814, 5th Series HC 1970-71, 1832-1833.)

Turning to consider the criminal liability of Harris, the courts decided that the appellant possessed the external genitalia of a female, was not psychologically male and therefore could not be treated as a male person. In interpreting the Crimes Act 1990, Mathews J asserted:

> The fundamental purpose of the law, as Ormrod J himself said, is the regulation of the relations between persons, and between persons and the state or community: *Corbett* (at 105). Within this context, the criminal law is concerned with the regulation of behaviour. It is the relevant circumstances at the time of the behaviour to which we must have regard. And I cannot see that the state of a person's chromosomes can or should be a relevant circumstance in the determination of his or her criminal liability. It is equally unrealistic, in my view, to treat as relevant the fact that the person has acquired his or her external attributes as a result of operative procedure. After all, sexual offences — with which we are particularly concerned here — frequently involve the use of the external genitalia. How can the law sensibly ignore the state of those genitalia at the time of the alleged offence, simply because they were artificially created or were not the same at birth? (180)

In reaching this decision the judge made a distinction between Harris, a post-operative transsexual, and McGuiness who had not undergone sex assignment surgery, but nevertheless considered herself psychologically female. Mathews J continued (at 181):

> So far as the appellant McGuiness is concerned, it is urged that we should not only decline to follow *Corbett*, but that we should also treat biological factors as entirely secondary to psychological ones. In other words, where a person's gender identification differs from his or her biological sex, the former should in all cases prevail. It would follow that all transsexuals would be treated in law according to their sex of identification, regardless of

whether they had undertaken any medical treatment to make their bodies conform with that identification. Whilst I have the greatest of sympathy for Ms McGuiness and for others in her predicament, I could not subscribe to this approach. It goes far beyond anything which has so far been suggested by even the most progressive of reviewers. It would create enormous difficulties of proof, and would be vulnerable to abuse by people who were not true transsexuals at all.

In 1993, 190 males were proceeded against for an offence under s. 1 of the Street Offences Act 1959. In 1994 159 males were prosecuted for a female only offence. In the majority of cases upon conviction they were fined. The only conclusion to be drawn is that these 'males' are indeed pre and post operative transsexuals, for all intents and purposes these persons present as females and at the policing and prosecution stage are treated as such. Given this fact law in practice turns a blind eye to the ruling in *DPP* v *Bull* [1994] 4 All ER 411 which established that s. 1 of the Street Offences Act 1959 was applicable to females only.

Living on immoral earnings   Turning to the offences connected with male to female transsexuals engaged in prostitution, further conundrums are posed by the sex specificity of the law and the offences committed by those who live on the immoral earnings of prostitution. 'It is an offence for a woman for the purposes of gain to exercise control, direction or influence over a prostitute's movements in any way which shows she is aiding, abetting or compelling her prostitution' (Sexual Offences Act 1956, s. 31, formerly the Criminal Law Amendment Act 1912, s. 7(4)), and 'It is an offence for a man knowingly to live wholly or in part on the earnings of prostitution' (s. 30(1) Sexual Offences Act 1956, formerly the Vagrancy Act 1898, s. 1(1)(a)).

It was the case of *Tan and others* [1983] 1 WLR 361, following the judgment of Parker J, that was to extend the Ormrod dictum on sex beyond the immediate confines of the marriage question to determining sex for the question of criminal liability. In *Tan*, the appellant would subject a man to perverted sexual treatment and she used premises she leased from the appellant Greaves. Gloria Greaves had undergone sex reassignment surgery from male to female, and both Tan and Greaves were charged with the sex neutral offences of 'keeping a disorderly house' (s. 33, Sexual Offences Act 1956). Greaves was, in addition, charged and convicted of living on the earnings of a prostitute (i.e., *Tan*) (a male only offence). Section 30(1) of the Sexual Offences Act 1956, provides that it is an offence for a man to live knowingly wholly or in part off the earnings of prostitution (above). Greaves argued that as she was in fact female, having undergone sexual reassignment surgery, then she could not be charged with a 'male only' offence. (If the courts were to charge her in her post operative sex status they might have considered s. 31 of the Act which applies to women exercising control over prostitutes.) In addition, Brian Greaves, Gloria's 'husband', was also charged with living on the earnings of male prostitution (i.e., Gloria's) (Sexual Offences Act 1967, s. 7) a provision reserved for those living off homosexual prostitution.

Gloria Greaves appealed on the grounds that the premises used could not be classed as a disorderly house since sexual services were provided by one single prostitute, to one client at a time, and pertinent to this discussion both Gloria and Brian Greaves appealed on the basis that, as Gloria Greaves was in fact a woman, she could not be charged with a male offence, nor Brian Greaves with an offence of living on male prostitution. Parker J delivered the judgment of the court:

> In our judgment both common sense and the desirability of certainty and consistency demand that the decision in *Corbett* v *Corbett* should apply for the purpose not only of marriage but also for a charge under section 30 of the Sexual Offences Act 1956 or section 5 of the Sexual Offences Act 1967. The same test would apply also if a man indulged in buggery with another biological man. That *Corbett* v *Corbett* would apply in such a case was accepted on behalf of the appellant. It would, in our view, create an unacceptable situation if the law were such that a marriage between Gloria Greaves and another man was a nullity, on the ground that Gloria Greaves was a man; that buggery to which she consented with such other person was not an offence for the same reason; but that Gloria Greaves could live on the earnings of a female prostitute without offending against section 30 of the Act of 1956 because for that purpose he/she was not a man and that the like position would arise in the case of someone charged with living on the earnings as a male prostitute (369).

In the words of the court, 'Gloria Greaves was born a man and remained biologically a man albeit he had undergone both hormone and surgical treatment, consisting in what are called 'sex change operations', consisting essentially in the removal of the external male organs and the creation of an artificial vaginal pocket' (369).

The judgment of Parker J has been widely criticised (see Pace 1983, Kennedy 1973 and also the dissenting judgment of Martens J in *Cossey* (above) and Wilson J in *Harris* (above), in the court of first instance). In the UK the lack of *locus standi* in their new sexual status for transsexual prostitutes remains unrelenting. Although curiously it does seem to be the practice that where the transsexual prostitute is charged with an offence of soliciting and pleads guilty, the sexual status is not questioned and a conviction for the female only offence is recorded. It is only where a plea of not guilty is entered that the appositeness of the charge is subject to scrutiny. The case of *DPP* v *Bull* [1994] 4 All ER 411, involving a male prostitute was referred to the High Court as a case stated for their opinion. The court found that s. 1 of the Street Offences Act 1959 applied strictly to females (see the chapter entitled, Women's Work: Private Contracts, Public Harm for further discussion on this point). Nevertheless, it remains very tantalising that, notwithstanding the sex specific nature of loitering for the purposes of prostitution, so many males are being proceeded against for this offence.

The transsexual as victim of sex offences

There is, perhaps not surprisingly, very little case law throughout common law jurisdictions specifically addressing the transsexual victim of sexual offences. This suggests that courts have not had the occasion to consider this question or have been prevented from so doing by decisions made by prosecutors and police. Undoubtedly, it is the case that the transsexual victim of a sexual assault is more unlikely than any natal sex victim to report it. The troubles that lie ahead range from the belief that the police would do little about it and that a criminal prosecution would only lead to disclosure of the very fact of biological maleness or femaleness that the transsexual wishes to disavow. It is likely that such allegations made by male to female transsexuals of rape and attempted rape are dealt with by police and prosecutors as cases of indecent assault on a male or a female, or preferably as insulting behaviour under the Public Order Act 1986, s. 4 in view of the gender neutrality of the charge. The position is clear that where an offence of rape is perpetrated, until 1994 the *actus reus* required a male to penetrate a female's vagina. That definition has been extended to include penile penetration of the anus of either male or female. The issue of whether a rape can be committed on a person where that person's vagina is artificially constructed, as in the case of a male to female transsexual, raises a point of law yet to be decided in the interpretation of this section. It is likely, however, that given the spirit of the provision and the intention to move towards gender neutrality, the rape of a male to female transsexual would constitute rape for all legal purposes, since the only gender specific requirement is that the perpetrator is male; although, since an artificial vagina, *vagina manu facta*, is not specified, it is yet to be tested.

In *Cogley* [1989] VR 799, before the Supreme Court of Australia, this question was raised as a point of law, where the legal status of a post operative transsexual for the purpose of sexual victimisation and thereby the criminal liability of the perpetrator fell to be determined. Terresa Andrews, the victim, met the appellant Cogley at a nightclub, where they talked, had some drinks and kissed. He offered to take her home. She accepted his offer of a lift in his car and during the journey Cogley stopped the car and told Andrews that he wanted to make love to her. She replied that she didn't want to. Cogley punched her and told her he was going to rape her and that if she didn't take off her clothes he would kill her. The appellant punched her again, forcing her to remove all her clothes. Whilst escaping from the car she was dragged along and injured. Cogley claimed that he was not responsible, in essence denying that he was there at all. He was convicted of assault with intent to commit rape and detaining a person against their will. The court of first instance held the post operative male to female transsexual to be female and directed the jury accordingly. The appellant entered a plea of not guilty and was convicted. The trial judge published his ruling that a male to female transsexual was a woman for the purposes of the Crimes Act 1958, s. 2A. Directing the jury he said, 'Miss Andrews in law is a woman and for the purpose of assault with intent to rape ... she is a woman and must be treated by you as such' (803). On appeal against conviction and sentence the case for the appellant rested on a point of law *inter alia* whether the trial judge was correct in finding that the victim was female. The appellant's case rested on a strict application of the Ormrod dictum in *Corbett*. The Court of Appeal dismissed leave to appeal against conviction on the basis that there had been no miscarriage of justice and the jury had been properly directed. It was held that a finding of whether a transsexual male to female is a woman is a matter to be left to the jury and that in respect of the charge of assault with intent to commit rape, the criminal liability is derived from the assault and not from the sexual status of the victim/complainant (see Sharpe 1995).

SEX DISCRIMINATION IN EMPLOYMENT, PENSIONS AND WELFARE BENEFIT

Sex orders the entirety of our entitlement to employment benefits, to pensions and to social welfare. Changing one's sex means of necessity challenging the entire superstructure around which the entitlements of the nascent body are built. In the UK there are no specific rules of law in operation which offer employment protection to transsexuals on the basis of equality. The United Nations recognises the right to work and the right to be free from racial and sex discrimination (see United Nations Declaration on the Elimination of All Forms of Racial Discrimination, 1963, International Convention on the Elimination of All Forms of Racial Discrimination, 1966, Declaration on the Elimination of Discrimination against Women 1967 (see Ghandi, pp. 39, 42, 75)), although no express provision for transsexuals is made.

The relevant statutory provisions regarding employment protection are contained in the Employment Protection (Consolidation) Act 1978 and the Sex Discrimination Act 1975. In so far as the 1975 Act is concerned, discrimination against a transsexual can only be proven if a person of the opposite nascent sex would not be treated in the same way, so a male female transsexual would have to compare himself with the treatment of a male. The Employment Protection Act is equally problematic for the transsexual since s. 57(1)(b) allows the employer a defence of 'substantial reason'. This has been widely interpreted to include *inter alia* concerns of blackmail, adverse comments from customers etc.

In the past, UK post operative transsexuals have found that sex discrimination against them on matters such as retirement age and employment has been sanctioned as a result of their nascent sex. In *White v British Sugar Corporation* [1977] IRLR 121, an Industrial Tribunal heard a complaint under the Sex Discrimination Act 1975. Edwynn White applied for a post as an electrician's mate and was appointed. It became apparent, however, that Edwynn was biologically of the female sex. As a result of this discovery, White was dismissed. He made an application under the Sex Discrimination Act 1975 to an Industrial Tribunal on the grounds that the dismissal was effectively discriminating against him on the grounds that he was a woman. The Industrial Tribunal held that he was a woman and that it was not relevant that his name had been changed to a man's and that his unemployment benefit card and registration with the Department of Health and Social Security had been altered to that name. The Tribunal held that there had been no discrimination against him as a woman for three reasons. First, he had deceived the management in his application and at the original interview, with regard to his true sexual status. Secondly, the other men were justified in objecting to a woman sharing their locker room and toilets. Thirdly, and most importantly, the job entailed working on Sundays and under the Factories Act a woman could not work in a factory on Sundays without an exemption order from the Health and Safety Executive. The Tribunal decided that the job for which he had applied had a genuine occupation qualification for men as it involved Sunday working and as he was a woman the company had a valid defence to his claim under the Sex Discrimination Act (see Cohen 1978, p. 74, McMullan and Whittle 1994, p. 64, O'Donovan 1985, p. 71).

The case of *P* v *S and Cornwall County Council* (McMullan and Whittle 1994, p. 60), is instructive in respect of how a transsexual might be treated, if a pending sex change operation were to be disclosed in good faith to an employer. In *P* v *S*, a local authority employee of some seniority was made redundant when Cornwall County Council learned that he was going to have a sex change operation. The recommendation of the European Court of Justice's Advocate General was in favour of the applicant. This has just been ratified by the Court. The Equal Opportunities Commission is backing the case which should decide whether transsexuals are in fact covered by European Union legislation, especially the Equal Treatment Directive 76/207, which states in its first article that it brings into effect the principle of equal treatment for men and women as regards access to employment, including working conditions.

In other common law jurisdictions pre operative transsexuals who have been similarly open with their employers have experienced discrimination and victimisation in similar circumstances. In the celebrated US case of *Karen Frances Ulane* v *Eastern Airlines Inc* 581 F Supp 821 (1984); 35 Fair Empl Prac Cas (BNA) 1332, Karen Ulane was dismissed by her employer, Eastern Airlines, when she announced that she was to have a sex change operation. Eastern Airlines attempted to justify its conduct in contending that the sacking followed not transsexuality *per se* but the fact that Ulane was psychologically sick, taking female hormones, and was a threat to a co-ordinated crew, all of which were legitimate safety considerations. The threshold issue before the court was whether Title VII of the Civil Rights Act of 1964 US, Title 42 section 2000e-2 (a) which provides, 'It shall be an unlawful employment practice for an employer to fail or refuse to hire or to discharge any individual or otherwise to discriminate against any individual with respect to his compensation, terms, conditions or privileges of employment because of such individual's race, color, religion, sex, or national origin', applied to transsexuals. The specific question before the court was whether the term, '... because of the individual's sex', encompassed a person who is a transsexual. The defendant, Eastern Airlines, argued that since Ulane had not had surgical intervention when it dismissed her she was not a transsexual but a transvestite, and as such was not protected by statute. Her employers claimed to have sacked her because of, *inter alia*, the need for a co-ordinated crew. Grady J, finding in favour of the plaintiff asserted:

I find in summary that all of the reasons advanced by Eastern for the discharge of the plaintiff were pretextual and were not advanced in good faith. I further find that but for being a transsexual and but for having had the transsexual surgery, the sex reassignment surgery, and adopting the life style of a woman, the plaintiff would not have been discharged. I further find that the plaintiff was in almost every instance subjected to discriminatory and disparate treatment for conduct which was in almost every instance, if not every instance, far less serious than that of male alcoholics whose conduct was excused by Eastern (837).

(See Cotton 1986, for a discussion of this case.)

Transsexuality also emerged as a consideration in an action under the Equal Pay Act 1970. In *Collins* v *Wilkin Chapman* (unreported) (EAT 945/93, 14 March 1994, Lexis transcript), an appeal by Mrs Collins against a decision of an Industrial Tribunal held at Lincoln and later at Nottingham, it was decided that a claim brought by Mrs Collins against her former employees, a firm of solicitors, Wilkin Chapman, should be dismissed. The claims were of alleged sexual discrimination and victimisation contrary to the Sex Discrimination Act 1975 and of violation of Article 119 of the EC Treaty 1992 (equal pay for equal work). Mr Collins represented his wife on the issue of unfair dismissal and equal pay. Mrs Collins was employed by Wilkin Chapman as a word processor operator/secretary on 11 July 1989. On the 6 June 1991 she was dismissed without notice. She claimed unfair dismissal and failure to pay equal pay for equal work in breach of the Equal Pay Act 1970. She was not entitled to pursue her claim of unfair dismissal as she had not completed two years' service although the Tribunal commented that the decision to dismiss her was unjust. Mrs Collins had queried why her salary was less than that of a male secretary in the firm naming this person as her comparator, who it subsequently turned out was biologically a woman at birth, although neither Wilkin Chapman nor Mrs Collins's knew that person to be female. Mrs Collins's application was doomed to fail since there was no other nascent male employed as a secretary with whom she could compare her salary. The Industrial Tribunal could do little else than dismiss her claim if it was to apply the dictum in *Corbett*, albeit not expressly:

Under the Equal Pay Legislation, it is for the applicant to name a comparator. It must be, clearly since the allegation is over the person being paid less by reason of their sex, that the comparator is a person of different sex. The applicant named a person, who she understood was a male and was being employed as a male secretary. She identified that person (we do not, in public, identify that person for obvious reasons). As it turned out that person, although originally employed in the belief that the person was a man, was a woman. The fact that Wilkin Chapman were discriminating against her in paying her less and the male secretary more was a matter *de facto* although not *de jure*.

The Tribunal decided, notwithstanding the sex of the comparator, that it should not be struck out. Wilkin Chapman appealed to the Employment Appeal Tribunal (13 Feb 1993). The Employment Appeal Tribunal decided that it was arguable that the words 'or would treat a man' in s. 1(1)(a) of the Sex Discrimination Act 1975 'admit at least of an argument that you do not have to have an actual man for the section to apply'. Finally, it was held that a female to male transsexual regardless of the perception test, i.e., what she appeared to be, was in fact a female and therefore Mrs Collins's claim failed.

Nascent sex determination has also been the presiding consideration in retirement pension cases. In *R(P)* 1/80 the claimant, who was registered as a woman and had received medical and psychiatric treatment in relation to transsexuality and had also received sickness benefit as a woman, was refused a retirement pension until the age of 65 in accordance with the sex designation at birth. In *R(P)* 2/80 an appeal against the Tribunal was dismissed on similar grounds (see Reported Decisions of the Social Security Commissioner, Vol IX 671-677). The point is that discrimination against an employee on the basis of sexual orientation is not expressly outlawed in existing legislation and there is no mechanism of redress where this discrimination exists either for homosexuals or for transsexuals. Pension benefits as predicated on gender and marital status or gender and age have also had a bearing on transsexuals. The question of at what age a male to female transsexual qualifies for a pension arose in *Re: Secretary, Department of Social Security and HH* No Q90/118 AAT; No 6890 Administrative Appeals Tribunal, General Administrative Division (1991) 13 AAR 314. O'Connor J said:

Australian society has permitted sex reassignment surgery to take place. The law, in its turn, must acknowledge this fact and accept the medical decisions which have been made. It should also be borne in mind that such surgery is irreversible. A requirement that reassignment surgery be completed before the law recognises the reassigned sex of an individual protects the public against possible fraud and acknowledges that an irreversible medical decision has been made affirming the patient's psychological sex choice. The Social Security Act, primarily for historical reasons it would seem, does differentiate between men and women in some areas. One of those areas is the age pension. The Tribunal is satisfied that a decision that a post operative transsexual should be classified for the purposes of the Social Security Act as a person of the reassigned sex would not impose any significant burden on the Department of Social Security. Transsexuals who undergo sex reassignment surgery represent a very small percentage of the Australian population. The Tribunal is of the view that only those transsexuals who have undergone sex reassignment surgery should be classified for the purposes of the Social Security Act as their reassigned sex. This is a difficult area and the Department of Social Security will need to have (for ease of administration and to prevent fraud), workable and established criteria upon which to base its decisions. Post operative transsexuals should be required to furnish the Department with a certificate along the lines of that provided for in the South Australian Sexual Reassignment Act 1988. Under that legislation a person who has undergone reassignment surgery may apply to a magistrate for the issue of a sexual recognition certificate. For the purposes of South Australian law, a recognition certificate is conclusive evidence that the person to whom it refers has undergone reassignment surgery and is of the sex stated in the certificate. For the purposes of the Social Security Act post operative transsexuals should be required to furnish such a certificate provided by a recognised hospital in Australia which conducts a sex reassignment program. Transsexuals who undergo surgery outside Australia would still be required to obtain such a certificate from an Australian hospital. For the above reasons, the Tribunal affirms the decision under review.

Pension benefits available to spouses under social security legislation are also founded on a biological view of the institution of marriage rather than on the facts *in situ*. In *Secretary, Department of Social Security* v *SRA* No NG745 of 1992; Fed No 869/93 in the Federal Court of Australia, New South Wales District Registry on 13 February 1993 (unreported), Lexis, the court had to consider whether a male to female transsexual qualified for a 'wife's pension'. In this case an appeal was allowed against a decision of the Administrative Appeals Tribunal, affirming a decision of the Social Security Appeals Tribunal, that a pre operative male to female transsexual was qualified under s. 37(1)(a) of the Social Security Act 1947 to receive a wife's pension, as is the entitlement of a wife of an invalid pensioner. The appeal raised a question of law whether the Tribunal was correct to rule that a pre operative male to female transsexual was a woman for the purposes of the said legislation. The Tribunal gave prominence to the psychological sex of the transsexual and to the social and cultural identity of the person in deeming her to be a woman. The Tribunal did not consider themselves bound by the judgment in *Harris and McGuiness* (see above), distinguishing that case on the grounds that the area of social policy was distinctly different, with different objectives, from the criminal law, in that social policy is beneficial and criminal law is prescriptive. The Federal Court of Australia considered the appeal of the applicant, the Secretary of the Department of Social Security, against the decision of the Tribunal. As Lockhart J acceded, such a question involved fundamental judgments as to the sex of transsexuals. It was considered that the Tribunal had gone well beyond the accepted meaning and its judgment would create insuperable difficulties in the law, and the Federal Court concluded that the Tribunal had erred. The judgment of Lockhart J on the question of the legal status of the transsexual is (apart from Judge Martens' dissenting judgment in *Cossey*) perhaps the most erudite and finely argued judgment, if not the most comprehensive and incisive survey of case law and academic authority, on the point.

In respect of the status of pre operative persons the judge had this to say:

The principal difficulty which I have in this case is to pass beyond this point to the recognition of a pre operative transsexual as being a member of the adopted sex for the purposes of the law. I recognise the force of the argument in the case of a male-to-female transsexual, that she has doubtless lived most of her life in a position of ambiguity, wanting to be a female but entrapped in the body of a male, who later adopts the appearance of a woman, has hormonal treatment which may result in the enlargement of breasts, and adopts certain secondary sex characteristics. But such a person has not harmonized her anatomical sex and her social sex; they are not in conformity.

In Canada, similar considerations apply and in *The Queen* v *Owen* (1993) 110 DLR 4th 339, the claimant, a male to female pre operative transsexual who had lived as a female since 1951, was awarded a widowed spouse's allowance by a Social Security review committee. The Government brought an application for judicial review and in citing the ruling in *Corbett* (above), the Court set aside the decision of the review committee.

Throughout the common law jurisdictions it is clear that the transsexual has been denied rights and privileges enjoyed by other persons in their natal sex. This denial ranges from deprivation and discrimination to victimisation in all areas of social life. The response of the law has been to sanction their exclusion from civil rights, family life, employment rights and protection from sexual offences. The transsexual is responding in challenging this differential treatment by seeking recognition in their constructed sex and the rights incumbent upon that, by challenging the appositeness of domestic legislation in the European Court under the banner of Human Rights violations.

TRANSSEXUALS: THE RIGHT TO A POST OPERATIVE SEX — A HUMAN RIGHTS ISSUE

For the British, or indeed any, transsexual struggling to achieve recognition in the newly assigned post operative sex, the right to privacy and to alter the birth certificate in order to ensure legal congruity with the new sexual status, remains fundamentally necessary. The allegiance of British courts to the Ormrod dictum has left the UK transsexual in a greatly disadvantaged position compared with other common law countries, notably Australia. UK transsexuals have on several occasions taken their grievances to the European Court of Human Rights, invoking articles of the European Convention for the Protection of Human Rights and Fundamental Freedoms, notably Article 8(1) and (2) in respect of privacy (cited above) and Article 12 in respect of marriage (cited above).

Grievances regarding the denial of the right to marry and the right to alter the birth certificate have not been acceded to by the Court. However, there has been a change within the opinion of the court where these two questions now provoke some considerable disagreement and dissent. The position remains in 1995, as it did in 1980, that the court will not interfere with domestic legislation in respect of the paramountcy of heterosexual marriage and the ascription of sexual status being decided at birth and recorded for posterity. In the UK, change of name is permissible on documents including a passport, a driving licence, a car registration book, national insurance cards, tax codings and social security papers. Change of name is also entered on the electoral roll. In respect of the Register of Births, such registration is governed by the Births and Deaths

Registration Act 1953 which provides only for the correction of clerical errors. This is also the case in Belgium where on 8 February 1979 the Antwerp Court of First Instance granted Van Oosterwijck rectification of the birth certificate of a person who was externally of male sex at birth but had characteristics of both sexes (see below for a full discussion of the case). The criteria for sex registration are not laid down, but the practice of the Registrar General is to use exclusively the biological criteria, which include chromosomal, gonadal and genital sex. The sex classification of a person who undergoes sex change surgery and makes a request to change the sex status as recorded in the register, is not regarded as an error. These concessions are regarded as liberal compared with some other European countries which do not allow even this modicum of post operative identity (see *B* v *France* below).

To be a man

The position of the European Court of Human Rights with respect to the claims regarding the right to private life was expressed in *Oosterwijck* v *Belgium* (1981) 3 EHRR 557, 'In its case-law, the Commission has gradually evolved the opinion that private life embraces ... to a certain degree the right to establish and develop relationships with other human beings, especially in the emotional field, for the development and fulfilment of one's own personality.'. The function of the European Court of Human Rights is always to balance the various competing interests, unlike precedents which are applied in subsequent cases where facts are similar and the 'margin of appreciation' in determining where that balance might be struck differs from case to case. It cannot be determined with any certainty whether a judgment reached in respect of one individual case will be reached in another. What we have witnessed in recent years in the ECHR, is a gradual moving towards a more enlightened view respecting the transsexual's right to marry and a preparedness to alter the certificate of birth. However, whilst dissenting opinion grows stronger, their number has not been sufficient to form the view of the majority and where breaches of Articles 8 and 12 have been alleged, the Court continues to deny that states have been in breach.

   The central issue for transsexuals is to be able to alter the birth certificate. Few countries have been prepared to accede to such an application, Australia providing one of the exceptions, although alteration has been made in several countries where the individual is natally androgynous, has been reared as, or expresses a preference for one particular gender role rather than the other. The case of *Oosterwijck* v *Belgium* (Application No 7654/76), was brought before the Court by the Belgian Government on 22 June 1979 and by the European Commission of Human Rights on 16 July 1979. Mr Van Oosterwijck complained that the Belgian Government, through the Belgian courts, had refused to order the rectification of the birth certificate following his sex change surgery from female to male. Van Oosterwijck was born a girl and underwent sex change surgery between 1969 and 1974. He then attempted to have his birth certificate amended to accord with his newly assigned, post operative status. His application, placed before Brussels District Court, was rejected, a decision which was upheld by the Brussels Court of Appeal. In taking his case to the European Court of Human Rights, he addressed the Court on his own behalf, detailing the insuperable difficulties he had encountered, particularly in his last year at law school, *inter alia*, what name would appear on the certificate which he was to be awarded by the University of Brussels, Faculty of Law, and further when he entered the Bar, how was he to be referred to on the list. He was, as he expressed it, '. . . engaged in a struggle for my whole life'. Van Oosterwijck's case before the Court is both moving and instructive regarding the many difficulties that rain down on the transsexual because of the law's intransigence. '. . . I became aware of the existence of this problem when I was five. I appear before you today at the age of thirty-five. For exactly thirty years I have been fighting, and for what? Not to overturn case-law, but for the right to lead a normal life'. The ECHR found that compelling a post operative transsexual to carry documents relating to identity which stated the person's sex at birth was a violation of Article 8 of the Convention. The Commission also accepted that there had been a violation of Article 12 of the Convention since he was unable to marry on the basis of post operative sexual reassignment (see *Oosterwijck v Belgium* (1980) 3 EHRR 557). The court held by 13 votes to 4 that by reason of the failure to exhaust domestic remedies the court was unable to take cognisance of the merits of the case.

In *Rees v United Kingdom* (1987) 9 EHRR 56 (Application No 9532/81), the applicant was born biologically female and from a young age sought hormonal treatment which was eventually followed by sex change surgery from female to male. Once again, the issue before the European Court of Human Rights was whether, in denying a transsexual the opportunity to change the birth certificate following sex reassignment surgery, the domestic legislation was in breach of its obligations in respect of rights to privacy and family life. The Registrar General refused Rees's application to change the birth certificate or provide her with a new birth certificate. Mark Rees took his grievance to the European Court of Human Rights under Articles 8 and 12, on the grounds that the refusal of the Registrar General infringed his right to privacy as his sexual designation at birth could not be withheld from a third party and effectively prohibited him from marrying. In legal argument he contended that his case was indistinguishable from *Oosterwijck*. In the first stage of the proceedings the European Commission, in declaring admissible the complaints under Articles 8 and 12 in its Report of 12 December 1984, accepted Rees's argument as to a putative breach of Article 8, although rejecting his argument as to Article 12 (see (1985) 7 EHRR 429 the Commission's opinion) (see (1987) 9 EHRR 56 the European Court's judgment). The Court held by 12 votes to 3 that there had been no violation of Article 8 and, unanimously, that there had been no violation of Article 12. As to Article 8, the Court held that the mere refusal to alter a birth certificate could not be considered an interference with private life and that this was an area where States enjoyed a 'margin of appreciation', wherein a fair balance must be struck between the community and individual interest. As to Article 12, the Court held that the right to marry referred to a right between persons of the opposite biological sex and could not be said to have the effect of so restricting the right that its very essence was impaired. The

Court noted that, in the United Kingdom, no general decision had been adopted either by the legislature or by the courts as to the civil status of post operative transsexuals and also that transsexuals were free to change their first names and surnames. They could be issued with official documents bearing their chosen first names and surnames, 'This freedom gives them a considerable advantage in comparison with States where all official documents have to conform with the records held by the registry office' (see also para. 38-46, *X against the Federal Republic of Germany* (Application No 6699/74) Council of Europe, Strasbourg, 11 October 1978).

To be a woman

The same topics were considered in the case of *Cossey* v *United Kingdom* (1991) 13 EHRR 622. On this occasion a male to female transsexual complained that United Kingdom law would not allow her to obtain a birth certificate in her post operative sexually assigned status and as a consequence, she could not legally marry a man. Cossey alleged in her application breaches of Articles 8, 12 and 14 (above) of the European Convention on Human Rights. In 1985 her application was ruled admissible. When the application came for a *hearing* before the Commission, it expressed the opinion by ten votes to six that there had been a violation of Article 12 (right to marry), but not a violation of Article 8 (privacy and family life). The *opinion* of the Commission, however, had been more favourable. In its report of 9 May 1989, the Commission stated that it was unable to distinguish the present application from *Rees* in respect of Article 8, although regarding Article 12 the present case was distinguished on the factual basis that the applicant Cossey had a male partner who wished to marry her, and the Commission was of the opinion that the applicant, 'must therefore have the right to conclude a marriage recognised by the United Kingdom law with the man she has chosen to be her husband'. Dissenting opinion in respect of Article 8 was advanced by Messrs Ermacora, Frowein, Gozubuyuk, Rozakis, Schermers and Mrs Thune who focused on the principle of human dignity in the examination of this question. 'For us, Article 8, as protecting human dignity, requires that a person, after undergoing surgery for changing sex and being now socially accepted as a woman, be recognised legally in her new identity.'

The European Court of Human Rights did not follow the opinion of the Commission. Its judgment held by a slim majority of ten votes to eight, that there had been no violation of Article 8, and, by 14 votes to four, that there had been no violation of Article 12. The Court, having already decided this point in *Rees*, was prepared to re-examine it to ascertain whether a departure from the previous position in Rees was warranted. It concluded that this was not the case, on the basis of examination of scientific and societal changes, and was not of the opinion that the case was materially different from *Rees*, notwithstanding the opinion of those members of the Commission who dissented. With respect to Article 12 and the right to marry, the Court noted that the right to marry was not restricted in any way that might undermine its existence. The Court regarded the application of biological criteria in respect of the marriage question as a valid approach and although some States would recognise marriage between two men at birth, this was not a uniform practice and did not indicate the need to deviate from the traditional approach to the concept of marriage. With respect to Article 8 and the issue of an alteration to the birth certificate, the Court held that there was a need to balance the needs of the applicant against those of the community. It also held that sex change surgery did not amount to a complete change of sex and therefore an alteration to the Register would not be correct. 'The Court has been informed of no significant scientific developments that have occurred in the meantime; in particular, it remains the case — as was contested by the applicant — that gender reassignment surgery does not result in the acquisition of all the biological characteristics of the other sex.' Judges Bindschedler-Robert and Russo in their joint, partly dissenting opinion were particularly scathing, '... the United Kingdom has not taken all the appropriate steps to ensure ... that allowance is made for changes in certain persons' sexual identity ... it has therefore to this extent failed to respect the applicant's private life'. They continued arguing that whilst the 'wide margin of appreciation' was 'at a pinch' acceptable in the *Rees* case, this was no longer true today. Perhaps the most important judicial opinion to be delivered in these cases is the erudite dissent of Judge Martens in *Cossey*. They argued vociferously that although *Cossey* could not be distinguished from Rees, there were, notwithstanding, cogent reasons for departing from this earlier judgment. Judge Martens' line of argument focused on the interpretation of the right to human dignity and human freedom, where the refusal to recognise a transsexual in his post operative sex 'can only be qualified as cruel'. 'The BSD-system keeps treating post operative transsexuals for legal purposes as members of the sex which they have disowned psychically and physically as well as socially'. It is a system which holds them in lifelong dread of their sex being revealed, and a system which, if they conceal the truth, causes them under certain circumstances to face criminal charges. Judge Martens argued that States do not enjoy a margin of appreciation as a matter of right but as a matter of 'judicial self-restraint'. In the context of considering the question of whether the system of Biological Sex is Decisive (BSD) was compatible with the United Kingdom's obligation under Article 8, there was no room for a margin of appreciation. The European Parliament on 12 September 1989 (OJ C256/33 (9 October 1989)) and the Parliamentary Assembly of the Council of Europe (Recommendation 1117 (1989)) both adopted resolutions recommending the reclassification of the sex of a post operative transsexual and calling upon Member States 'to enact provisions on transsexuals' right to change sex by endocrinological, plastic surgery, and cosmetic treatment, on the procedure, and banning discrimination against them' (see the joint dissenting opinion of Judge Palm et al in *Cossey*).

The issue of the need for alteration to the birth certificate was at the basis of the application of *B v France, The Times*, 31 March 1992. This case was distinguished from *Rees* and *Cossey* since in France even minimal alteration to certain official documents was not permissible. The applicant was registered male at birth and in 1972 had sex change surgery from male to female. Since 1972, she had been living with a man whom she wished to marry. In 1978 she brought proceedings for the rectification of her birth certificate. In 1979 the Libourne Tribunal de Grande Instance refused her application, and her appeals were dismissed by the Bordeaux Court of Appeal in May 1985 and by the Court of Cassation in March 1987. On 6 September, the European Commission in its report expressed the opinion that there had been a violation of Article 8 of the Convention, but not of Article 3. Article 3 provides that no one shall be subjected to torture or to inhuman or degrading treatment or punishment. The Court held by 15 votes to six that there had indeed been a violation of Article 8. Although, the court conceded that attitudes to transsexuals had in fact changed there was not a sufficiently broad consensus to persuade the Court to reach a different conclusion from that reached in *Rees* and *Cossey*. The case was distinguished from *Rees* and *Cossey*, since the vital material difference is that the French system denies change of forename from one sex to the other for the purpose of official documents. This is not the case in the UK. The decision in *B v France* still leaves intact the fundamental question of a change to the birth certificate in those countries where change of name is permissible on certain official documents but not on a birth certificate which is regarded as a matter of historical record and not merely a document of contemporary fact. *B v France* called for rectification of the birth certificate where it is not regarded as a record of history, as in England, but where it can be updated through a person's lifetime and to that extent the claim of breach was recognised.

The European Court of Human Rights has not proved to be of assistance to applicants wishing to marry or to change their birth certificate outside the *B v France* case. The application of *X*, in *X, Y* and *Z* (above), again raises these two issues as two of the grounds of a broader grievance. Even given the changing climate of opinion, the Court is not likely to depart from its previous decisions in *Rees* and *Cossey*, although it may be persuaded that in the interests of the child, *Z*, it should accede to the parentage question. If this were to be the judgment of the Court it would leave the position of the Court in considerable confusion as between claims.

TRANSSEXUAL DIAGNOSIS: TRANSSEXUAL PROGNOSIS

Given the intransigence of legislation and public policy to provide official sanction to accompany the somatic changes of transsexuals, as of fundamental necessity (see the dissenting opinion of Judge Martens in *Cossey*), it is time to review the ethicality of current medical practice and nosology. The diagnosis of transsexualism, the identification of the cause of sexual dysphoria and the nature of subsequent treatment is rooted in competing etiologies. Gender dysphoria is explained for some by biological essentialism in the guise of an innate predisposition. For critics of this medical nosology and ontology, transsexualism is the product not of disease or biology but of social constructionism. The nature of medical intervention, whether by surgery or psychotherapy, and the legitimacy of the regime of treatment is a product of these competing theories. The transsexual describes his/her problem as a gender misalliance, speaking of a sense of profound discomfort and inappropriateness about one's natal anatomic sex, and a desire to be rid of those essential features of sex identity and to live as a member of the other sex. In addition to the transsexuals is a growing but not insignificant number of persons of the 'third sex' wishing to be rid of their secondary sex characteristics, breasts, genitalia and internal sex organs, uterus and ovaries and to live a life as a third sex. Many heterosexual men and women are also disconsonant with their body form and seek to change it. Many homosexual men and women are similarly disconsonant with their body form. Excepting the third sex, essential to all these sex categories is a desire to live within a gender category of masculinity or femininity and, within that, to conform to heterosexualism, and to conform to traditional orthodoxy on gender role. There are also transsexuals who wish to challenge this heterosexualist orthodoxy to live as 'homosexuals' or to challenge the heterosexualist orthodoxy, such is the rich variety of gender(s). The fact that the transsexual seeks ultimate salvation in conventional gender roles is a measure of the desire for ultimate acceptance rather than a measure of inner desire to conform. Rees writes (1995, p. 87), 'At a garage, I forgot to collect my petrol receipt. The attendant called out. "You've forgotten your receipt, mate!" "I'm sorry, my mind wasn't on my work." He laughed. "Got a piece of crumpet tucked away then?" I smiled to myself as I drove away. He'd treated me as a man. It was wonderful.'.

For those who adhere to the precept that biological dysfunction is the root cause of gender dysphoria, and for those who identify early childhood gender development as responsible, surgical and hormonal treatment is frequently held to be the transsexual's only salvation capable of correcting the misalliance. There is, however, little evidence to indicate that the transsexual is in fact biologically distinguishable from the heterosexual or homosexual more or less content with their body form. It is rarely the case that transsexualism can be traced to a chromosomal or hormonal abnormality. Although Stoller (1968) contends that transsexualism is indeed a problem of organic dysfunction, an 'organic disease', in 1975 he moves on to argue that transsexualism is a product of a miscreant relationship with the mother, its roots somewhere therefore in psychosexual development. For Benjamin (1971), 'The only question that should concern a physician worthy of his degree is, "What can we do to alleviate the suffering of the patient?" The primary means of alleviating the suffering is to alter the body by means of hormones and surgery.'. Constructions of transsexualism as a problem of the psyche produce other definitions and explanations but not necessarily other solutions. The American Psychiatric Association in 1980, defined transsexualism as a gender identity disorder, 'a persistent sense of discomfort and inappropriateness about one's anatomic sex and a persistent wish to be rid of one's genitals and to live as a member of the opposite sex' (DSM III 261–262). Although psychotherapy depends on treating the mental incongruity, Green (1992, p. 102), argues that no psychological or physiological explanation has proved satisfactory.

These competing etiological arguments were advanced in the application of *Oosterwijck* (above):

So far as the present case is concerned, it is not decisive to know whether this ailment should be attributed to a neuroendocrinian disfunction in the foetus, as would appear from an increasing number of recent studies, or whether the causes are rather of a psychological nature. Referring to the various studies cited or filed, the Commission argues in this connection with the Belgian Government that the causes of transsexualism, but not the existence of a transsexual syndrome, are the subject of scientific controversy, on which it is obviously incompetent to adopt a position (Report of the Commission, adopted on 1 March 1979).

Whether transsexualism is an organic, medical, mental health, psychiatric or social problem, prescribes the therapy model and determines the legitimacy and validity of a claim to provision of health care services. The issue of appropriate treatment is ever more central (see Lothstein 1982, p. 417). Studies offer no conclusive proof as to the efficacy of surgery one way or the other. Benjamin (1971) in a study of 73 men and 20 women found that 85 per cent of men and 95 per cent of women showed 'satisfactory' outcomes. Pauly (1965), in a research study of 121 transsexuals, concluded that those who had sexual reassignment surgery were ten times as likely to have a satisfactory outcome and has provided the authoritative support for surgical intervention. These studies and their alleged success can be contrasted with a study on 100 transsexuals, where 34 had undergone operations. These were carried out, from 1971 to 1977, at the Johns Hopkins Hospital in Baltimore where the medics found:

> Our study places the burden of proof on those who assert that sex-reassignment surgery accomplishes more in the way of an objective rehabilitation of the patient than does the simple passage of time or the patient's participation in a psychotherapeutic program with a skilled therapist. Physicians have to ask themselves is transsexual surgery medically necessary. To say that this type of surgery cures psychiatric disturbance is incorrect. We now have objective evidence that there is no real difference in the transsexual's adjustment to life in terms of jobs, educational attainment, marital adjustment and social stability. . . . The study shows that surgery serves as a palliative measure, relieving some of the patient's symptoms of discomfort, but not necessarily improving the individual's adjustment in life. It does not cure what is essentially a psychiatric disturbance, and surgery does not demonstrably rehabilitate the patient (cited in *Oosterwijck* (above)).

The critics of this rising tide of amputation and prosthetic reconstruction locate the root cause of gender dysphoria in the social construction of sex and gender. Illich argues in his seminal thesis, *Medical Nemesis* (1975), that the medical establishment has become a major threat to health and focuses on the expropriation of health from a personal challenge to a technical problem. Surgical intervention is, furthermore, replete with problems relating to consent, especially where the transsexual seeking sex change is psychiatrically a sick person who has usually tried to commit suicide. This is taken as a measure of his distress and the justification for the surgery where suicide attempts hold the surgeon to ransom. Indeed, even psychotherapists conclude that, faced with a suicidal patient, surgical intervention is at least life saving. 'Since the discovery of transsexualism, psychiatrists have expanded the uses of the "risk [i.e., threat] of suicide" — making it one of their criteria for granting transsexing as a life-saving procedure' (Szasz 1980, p. 89). Raymond (1981, p. xv), identifies the problem of socio-sexual constructionism thus

> Historically, individuals may have wished to change sex, but until medical science developed the specialties, which in turn created the demand for surgery, sex conversion did not exist. It is instructive that Johns Hopkins from the outset defined transsexualism as a medical problem and got the law to affirm its judgment. Thus, if sex-conversion surgery were challenged in the future, it could be defended as legitimate medical territory.

In recent years the concern to limit medical intervention and the right of health authorities to refuse surgery have been to the fore in litigation brought by transsexuals. This may suggest some resiling from what is now being increasingly recognised as a grossly invasive intervention. Surgery on demand gives rise to a plethora of considerations not least of all those relating to whether surgery really can cure the transsexual (see Schapira et al 1979). If gender dysphoria is a disease or illness, it follows that there must be a right to treatment to alleviate suffering and the legitimation of the medical terminology of transsexualism as an organic disease as against transsexualism as an expression of recalcitrant nonconformity.

In consideration of the economics of health care provision, debates about what is illness and what are the most appropriate forms of treatment are not medical questions *per se*, but questions which exist in a context of competing needs and limited resources. The transsexual is at the cutting edge of health care economics. The outcome is a reduction in the surgery programme which has led to massive litigation in the US around the issues of just how medically necessary is sex change, and to equal rights to securing in the US Medicaid and in the UK local health authority funding for transsexual surgery. In several States in the US, for example, treatment has been refused by the Department of Medical Assistance. Such medical policy has been overturned by the courts following the legitimation of surgery in *Doe v State of Minnesota, Department of Public Welfare, and Hennepin County Welfare Board*, 257 NW 2d 816 (1977) Minnesota Supreme Court. Here, an adult male transsexual appealed against the denial of medical benefit following the fact that a transsexual programme for sex conversion was terminated. The court acceded, 'Given the fact that the roots of transsexualism are generally implanted early in life, the concern of medical literature is that psychoanalysis is not a successful mode of treatment for the adult transsexual (see Benjamin 1971, p. 78; Stoller 1968, 1975, p. 249). The only medical procedure known to be successful in treating the problem of transsexualism is the radical sex conversion surgical procedure requested by Doe in the present case....' *Pinneke v Preisser* 623 F 2d 546 (1900) DC, declared that denying Medicaid benefits was contrary to provisions of Title XIX of the Social Security Act 1972, thus rendering the Iowa State plan void and, on this basis, violating the supremacy clause of the US Constitution.

It was followed by *Rush* v *TM Parham* 625 F 2d 1150 (1980), although with the qualification that, 'We do not read these cases as deciding the issue whether a state may define medical necessity to exclude experimental surgery'.

Medical opinion provides that a diagnosis of transsexualism is only appropriate if the discomfort has been continuous for two years and is not due to any other mental disorder such as schizophrenia. How to treat has also been the subject of much litigation. In *Jones* v *Flanningan and Vallabehiem* (1991) (unreported, US App Lexis 29605 transcript), the applicant alleged that doctors at the Menard Psychiatric Centre administered psychotropic drugs against his will, rather than performed surgery which he would have preferred. The court held that although a transsexual inmate is entitled to treatment he does not have the right 'to any particular type of treatment'. Willingness to endorse *Doe* has not extended to inmates where medical treatment has been regarded as unnecessary. The test for inmates is that there must be shown to be 'deliberate indifference to serious medical needs'; this was cited in *Meriwether* v *Faulkner* 821 F 2d 408, 411 (7th Cir 1987). (see *Supre* v *Ricketts*, 792 F 2d 958 (10th Cir 1986), *Lamb* v *Maschner*, 633 F Supp 351 (D Kansas 1986). In *Supre* the Federal Court refused to recognise the right to oestrogen treatment as a constitutional right but maintained that a transsexual was entitled 'to some kind of treatment'. In *Lamb*, a male sought transfer to a female prison, pre operative hormone treatment, a sex change operation, and protection from other inmates. The plaintiff's medical history, 'indicates that he is a nonconformist and receives an apparent delight in defying conventions, rules and regulations, [and] his motivation for the sex reassignment surgery is certainly in question . . . the self inflicted laceration to the scrotum is taken by the court to illustrate his desire to defy the norm.'. In *JD* v *Lackner* 80 Cal App 3d 90, 145 Cal Rptr 570 (1978), the court invalidated a state policy denying state medical benefits on the basis that such surgery is medically necessary for the treatment of transsexualism where the Director of Health had said that such treatment was only cosmetic. In his dissenting judgment Scott J expressed the nub of the problem both in the US and also in the UK, 'The issue is not whether the appellant is a true transsexual, but whether the state must finance transsexual surgery for a physically normal male'.

Whether to treat was considered in *Meriwether* v *Faulkner* 821 F 2d 408 (7th Cir 1987), where an inmate was denied medical treatment including chemical, psychiatric and other treatment in Indiana State Prison, Michigan City, having had, prior to incarceration, nine years of hormonal treatment for the condition, and surgery to construct breasts. Since 1983 she had been denied any treatment. She was told that 'as long as she was in the Department of Corrections she would never receive the medication [estrogen] and that he would make sure of this'. In response to this comment one wonders whether there is a challenge under the Eighth Amendment which prohibits cruel and unusual punishment: could oestrogen withdrawal be considered within this? Her claim was rejected and the district court found that her request for 'elective medication' was to maintain 'a physical appearance and life style in order to satisfy [her] psychological belief', concluding that there was not a 'serious' medical need. As Szasz (1980, p. 95) writes, '. . . one man's mutilation is another man's decoration, religious worship, or medical treatment', suggesting that the solution to the problem of gender dysphoria is a social construct.

Recent litigation in the US, particularly in respect of inmates, has been informed by the view that transsexuality is a preference, a deliberate deviance and yet another manifestation of the offender's truculence. The retreat from the medical nosology into the terrain of transsexuality as lifestyle has facilitated the denial of rights to any treatment at all and presumably further control and punishment. King (1987) notes with some relief that there has been no large scale promotion and hard selling of transsexualism in Britain, of the sort which has taken place in the United States and contributed to this spate of transsexual litigants. King found that the British medical profession dealing with the transsexual tended to regard patients not as ill, not suffering from a disease, but with problems. Even so, certain health authorities have recently spoken out against transsexual surgery as being too expensive. The question is, should we and how should we, treat transsexualism? The transsexual phenomenon remains as enigmatic as ever. Those who reject the 'disease' model and medicalisation of transsexualism and the urgency of the surgical solution, profess it to be a product of social constructionism. But, it is precisely because it is so accepted, so institutionalised that it is important to make the nature and process of acquisition of gender explicit and to treat this as problematic. For the transsexual wishes not only to take on the characteristics of the opposite sex, but to 'pass' as the opposite sex and considers that a reconstruction of the body is the only option. Raymond argues, '... a society that produces sex-role stereotyping functions as a primary cause of transsexualism' (1981, p. xviii, see Billings and Urban 1982). King (1987, p. 356) argues, 'the transsexual role is not, however, created out of nothing. The "real" disorders are effeminacy, homosexuality and transvestitism. Some who suffer from these disorders eagerly embrace the transsexual role because it removes the stigma from which they suffer by attributing their behaviour to a legitimate medical condition unamenable to psychotherapy'.

The irony is that Codes of Practice adopted by physicians, before sex change surgery is contemplated, depend upon the ability of the pre operative transsexuals to pass in their desired post operative gender role the subjective standard imposed by their therapists. Indeed, as passing in their given sex has failed them, it is the ability to conform and pass in the desired sex which provides the passport and gateway to surgical intervention. The transsexual merely exchanges one stereotype for another. Billings and Urban (1982, p. 275) note the subtle negotiation process between physician and patient:

Physician   'You said you always felt like a girl — what is that?'

Patient   [long pause] 'I don't know.'

Physician   'Sexual attraction? Played with girl's toys?'

Charing Cross's Gender Identity clinical management policy 1995, states:

The patient would need to demonstrate acceptance by society in this role and improved social and psychological functioning. For one year of this two year period the patient would need to demonstrate acceptance and integration in society by being financially independent in employment, or involved in full time education or employment.

Tully (1992, p. 202) details more revealingly the significance of 'passing', '... reassignment surgery is not likely to be granted to individuals who can only function at this intermediate level of gender expression'.

'Passing' is essential to the transsexual's validation of herself as an appropriate case for treatment and as a validation of the reconstructed gender as 'real'. Jan Morris's experience of being kissed by a London taxi driver would, to the emancipated woman, be regarded as sexual harassment. Jan Morris was instead thrilled at what she could achieve, she had passed, she had not been 'read' (Morris 1987, p. 142). Similarly, Tully reports on one of his interviewees, 'I went to a dance at work and the husband of a friend of mine danced with me. That was marvelous and convinced all the others that I was okay' (1992, p. 201). Tully explains, 'To pass as a member of the opposite sex to which one was biologically born is the central practical social task of transsexuals'. The continual reminder of their former state is distressing. Transsexuals who 'are read', or discovered, feel that having failed 'passing' is central to their being (see Garfinkel 1967, p. 137–164). As Tully (1992, p. 199), found in his research with transsexuals at the Gender Identity clinic, Charing Cross Hospital, London, 'If my female name is used, that is harsh, it's like crawling back into the rubbish bag.'.

There is a pressing need for coherent policy on the question of intervention and therapy when surgical intervention has fast become deemed the panacea of all gender ills. Whilst Australia has pioneered a radical approach to the legal position of the transsexual in rejecting *Corbett*, it does not axiomatically open its arms to surgical intervention. A standing committee of Federal and State Attorneys-General was established in 1979 to examine the question of the legal recognition of the post operative transsexual. In 1988, the South Australian legislature enacted the Sexual Reassignment Act 1988. The Act regulates the carrying out of sexual reassignment procedures (s. 6), and provides for the recognition in law of the reassigned sex of a person who has undergone a reassignment procedure (s. 8). The need for improving the standards of care and introducing some uniformity in treatment provision has been a growing concern (see Wilson 1984). These concerns were also raised in *Oosterwijck* (above). Whilst the European Parliament has called on member states of the European Community '... to enact provisions on transsexuals' right to change sex by endocrinological, plastic surgery and cosmetic surgery, on the procedure, and banning discrimination against them.'. At the same time there is concern that transsexual operations test the limits of the law (see Williams 1983, p. 589–91, Kennedy and Grubb 1994, p. 249–250). It could be argued that surgical intervention is not justified where amputation or removal involves healthy living tissue. Such cases raise the issue of consent and it is to be debated whether consent to such operations can negate the criminality of the surgeon, since not all are agreed that the operation is therapeutic, even if therapy defines their *mens rea*. There are no uniform approaches or standards of care in the UK and whilst doctors are bound by both consent and the law, as applied, there is no specific policy on the medical care of transsexuals. In Australia, in the case of *Re A (A Child)* (1993) FLC 191, the court considered whether the 14 year-old could consent to sex-change treatment. Doctors have a right to refuse treatment. Some undoubtedly will, on the basis that their refusal is reasonable, but on what grounds, moral, ethical, social, or legal? There are also issues raised around the informed consent of a sick man or woman. Unequivocally, surgery and amputation would not have progressed this far in the absence of policy or debate, were it not for the fact that transsexuals are regarded beyond the fringe, politically powerless minorities, less than worthy. It took much political persuasion to halt the all too automatic hysterectomies and lobotomies (Szasz, p. 95). Meanwhile, doctors face this dilemma, 'I must take responsibility for this because I thought his depression was due to his frustration as a transsexual. It is clear now that I made a misassessment of his personality for he is woefully inadequate and a chronically miserable person' (Tully 1992, p. 227). The dilemma for the courts is whether or not to validate the transsexual in the new sex in public and private and whether, now, to place some limits on the amputation programmes whilst a proper public debate is launched.

The nascent body in law is given supreme legal significance. Zones are accorded meaning and legal significance for sex and social status. Persons are controlled through the physical body which is a gateway and corridor to rights. Rights derive from a fundamental division of labour by sex. For example Posner's approach to the body is that of essentialism 'I see biology as explaining the drives and preferences that establish the perceived benefits of different sexual practices to different people (1992, p. 441). For Posner a transsexual cannot change his or her sexual identity and the biological imprint of sex in social organisation is sacrosanct, 'The sorting of all persons into male and female and the pairing of persons by opposite sex are fundamental elements of our construction or mediation of reality, and the violation of the pattern is felt as unnatural, transgressive'. For Ellis J, in *Attorney-General* v *Otahuhu* the law need not insist on entitlements based on some former physical state, but must address the state of the body as exists in the present time. Even in his judgment the law's search for reconstructed sex organs and public classification of outward appearances coincide. Whilst the edifice of according rights and duties and liability on the basis of nascent sex is eroding, the question remains how far, if transsexualism is a social construct, the product of a society's disapproval and disapprobation of those who refuse to align themselves with the gender demands predicated on anatomy, is the medical solution a sound one, even if politically expedient? Besides, transsexualism itself is a political question, a question of sexual politics, a challenge to the heterosexual patriarchal hegemony. But must the sculpture stop? Szasz (1980, p. 90) is unequivocal, 'Having first deceived the public by promoting transsexual surgery as therapy, sexologists now continue to deceive ... by opposing such surgery as insufficiently therapeutic. But transsexualism is not a disease; surgical operations creating fake males and fake females are not treatments ...'.

TWO

Gay prohibition, social engineering and heterosexual hegemonies regulating public and private rights

In the regulation of consenting sexual behaviour between men (and between women), the law performs the function both of prohibition through the criminalisation of homosexual intimacy, and the organisation of relationships in the public and the private sphere through legal engineering, especially in determining familial relationships (Cooper and Herman 1991). The agitation for reform of the law in this area has insisted on challenging the more overt manifestations of sexual inequality, particularly the application of the criminal law in its determination of the limits of gay sexual expression. The prohibition of homosexual 'sexuality' and the denial of equality to homosexuals in respect of family life, parenting, employment and access to services and resources, functions as a powerful mechanism of social control.

The law organises and controls heterosexuality and demands conformity, denying rights through regulating homosexuality in the spheres of public and private life.

Clearly, the legal construction of family life, which precludes homosexual parenting, is a key site of conflict in the contemporary struggle for gay rights. In this chapter four discrete areas of the legal organisation of homosexual relations are considered in an exploration of the legal stigmatisation of a minority group. First, consideration is given to the role played by criminal law as a vehicle of prohibition of gay sexual expression. Secondly, the role of law as a standard bearer of public policy and as a mechanism of social engineering of family relationships in family law, especially in the construction of parenthood, is explored. Thirdly, the role of law as an ideological state apparatus (Althusser 1971, p. 127) and vehicle of state control in determining the limits of public tolerance of homosexuality, is examined. Finally, there is a critique of the more recent and specific struggle by gay men towards the recognition of sado-masochism as a viable and legitimate form of expression of consensual gay 'sex' or homoeroticism.

HUMAN RIGHTS AND CIVIL LIBERTIES

The debate around homosexuality in recent years has been transformed from an exclusive concern with privacy and the criminalisation of sexually consenting behaviour, to an exploration of the wider ramifications of being gay for civil rights and freedoms. This includes discrimination against gay people in housing, employment, education and other public services as a direct consequence of their sexual preference or orientation (Sanders 1995; Clapham and Waaldijk 1993). In the field of employment, gay men and women experience security vetting procedures for all posts in the diplomatic service, the police special branch, UK atomic energy and for posts with firms with contracts involving classified material. The Security Commission recommended that homosexuality should not be treated as an absolute bar to positive vetting clearance which was first introduced in 1952 and revised as recently as 1990 to safeguard national security and counter terrorism (see Bailey, Harris and Jones 1991, p. 455). The absolute bar in the armed forces was recently the subject of challenge in *Ministry of Defence ex parte Smith and others* [1995] 4 All ER 427 (QBD), [1996] 1 All ER 257 (CA), when the four applicants, having been discharged from the Services under this policy, challenged the legality of the discharge, on the ground that the policy was irrational and breached the European Convention on Human Rights and the Equal Treatment Directive. All four applicants sought reinstatement and compensation. The grounds for the ban were moral, including the need for unit effectiveness, the fact that the services were *in loco parentis* and the conditions of communal living. In his judgment Simon Brown LJ said:

> The tide of history is against the ministry. Prejudices are breaking down; old barriers are being removed. It seems to me improbable, whatever this court may say, that the existing policy can survive for much longer. I doubt whether most of those present in court throughout the proceedings now believe otherwise. But the question arises: who should be determining the date of its demise? ... The real question becomes: is it reasonable for the Minister to take the view that allowing homosexuals into the Forces would imperil that interest? Is that, in short, a coherent view, right or wrong? I have already said enough to indicate my own opinion that it is a wrong view, a view that rests too firmly upon the supposition of prejudice in others and which insufficiently recognises the damage to human rights inflicted ... I for my part would refuse these applications albeit with hesitation and regret. I conclude that the decision upon the future of this policy must still properly rest with others notably the Government and Parliament (pp. 440, 447, 448).

On 3 November 1995 the ban on homosexuals serving in the armed forces was upheld by the Court of Appeal [1996] 1 All ER 257, see Wintemute 1995).

Lesbians and gay men have either been dismissed from employment because of sexual orientation or have found the atmosphere so intolerable that they have been forced out. In 1982, Susan Shell was suspended from her job with the London Borough of Barking as a residential social worker, later being dismissed by her employers for her sexual orientation (*Social Work Today*, vol.

13, no. 10, p. 19, 10.11.81). In 1977, Louise Boychuk was sacked from her job and lost her case at an Industrial Tribunal when the Tribunal ruled that 'an employer (was) entitled to set a standard within reasonable limits' (*Women's Report*, 1977, 5/2). (See *Smith* v *Gardner Merchant Ltd* (1996) EAT 13, Lexis.) In the UK, in Canada and in the US, whilst legislation is designed to counter discrimination in employment, housing and public services, and discrimination is prohibited on the grounds of a person's 'race, sex or marital status', nothing is said about sexual orientation. In the Council Directive 76/207/EEC, 'Council Directive on the implementation of the principle of equal treatment for men and women as regards access to employment, vocational training and promotion, and working conditions', the recitals refer to men and women. It has been argued that in the empowering provision (art. 235 of the Treaty), the word 'sex' can also apply to include orientation. Support for this construction is found in a recommendation from the Commission, 92/131/EEC, and in two decisions by international tribunals (see *Toonen* v *Australia*, in Sanders 1994, p. 4; 1996), although there is by no means agreement on this as the judgments of Simon Brown LJ and Curtis J in *Ministry of Defence ex parte Smith* in the High Court revealed. On 6 March 1996 the Sexual Orientation Discrimination Bill received its second reading in the House of Lords. It is designed to outlaw discrimination in employment (H.L. 6 March (1996) Col 385).

In North America similar problems of construction have arisen (see Posner 1992, p. 318, for a discussion of employment rights in America). In Canada, in *Board of Governors of the University of Saskatchewan, University of Saskatchewan, Kirkpatrick and Stinson* v *Saskatchewan Human Rights Commission* [1976] 3 WWR 385 9, W complained to the Saskatchewan Human Rights Commission after W, a sessional lecturer, was advised by the department head that he would not be allowed to go into public schools to supervise teaching practice because of W's admission to homosexual acts. In the construction of the word 'sex' in s. 3, Fair Employment Practice Act 1965 which provides, 'No employer shall refuse to employ or to continue to employ, or otherwise discriminate against, any person in regard to employment or any term or condition of employment because of his race, religion, religious creed, colour, sex, nationality, ancestry or place of origin', the court held that the word meant sex and not sexual orientation. In *Canada (A-G)* v *Mossop* (1993), 100 DLR 4th 658 (CSC), Mossop applied for bereavement leave as his male partner's father had died; his term of employment contained a bereavement provision which included father-in-law. The fundamental question for the Tribunal turned on the concept of biological and social families. It concluded that homosexual couples might constitute a social family (666), holding that a discriminatory practice had been committed. Marceau J, in the Federal Court of Appeal, rejected the idea of the social family, 'Even if we were to accept that two homosexual lovers can constitute 'sociologically speaking' a sort of family, it is certainly not one which is recognised by law as giving its members special rights and obligations.'. Strong dissent was expressed by Cory J and McLachlin J, arguing in favour of recognising the homosexual family as a social family (p. 723).

There have been some developments, however, and in Quebec in 1977 the law at State level prohibited discrimination on the basis of sexual orientation

(Sanders (1996), p. 69). In the US, eight States have now prohibited discrimination on the basis of sexual orientation (see Sanders 1994, p. 14). In Australia, discrimination against lesbian and gay people is prohibited, although in Queensland and Northern Territory certain jobs, namely those involved in working with children, are excepted (Sanders, 1994).

In the UK, where domestic laws have failed homosexuals, the European Court of Human Rights is the last resort for consideration and redress of grievances. Its key objective is to bring breaches of human rights to the attention of the international community, although cases before the Court have also raised questions of weaknesses or doubtful legal principles in legal systems. Issues relating to homosexual rights have been pursued both by victims of putative breaches and by those challenging statutory interpretation and the application of the common law to homosexuals as a class. The Court has considered cases from several countries including the UK where homosexual men have complained about the denial of their right to privacy under Article 8 of the Convention on Human Rights and Fundamental Freedoms 1950 (Sanders 1996).

There have been two major rulings against the UK's anti-gay laws on issues of sexual privacy and employment. In *Dudgeon* v *United Kingdom* (1982) 4 EHRR 149, the applicant complained that the prohibitions against homosexual conduct in Northern Ireland were a breach of his right to privacy, in abrogation of Article 8 and were unconstitutional. Until 1982, the law regulating homosexual behaviour in Northern Ireland remained bound by the Offences Against the Person Act 1861, ss. 61, 62, prohibiting homosexuality in private, and the Criminal Law Amendment Act 1885, s. 11, prohibiting gross indecency. Neither the Sexual Offences Act 1956, nor the Sexual Offences Act 1967, which permitted homosexual consensual sex over 21 in private, in England and Wales, had been extended to Northern Ireland. The applicant complained that the law in force in Northern Ireland rendered him liable to prosecution, and as such he lived in continual fear. The European Court found in his favour by 15 votes to 4, in respect of the contravention of Article 8 with regard to the existing law in relation to men over 21. As a result the British Government was required to revise the Northern Ireland legislation in accordance with the law in England and Wales. The case was the first case to raise the issue of homosexual and lesbian rights in international human rights law (see Van Dijk 1993, Kingston (1994)).

The Court does not have the jurisdiction to consider breaches of human rights Articles *in abstracto* where applicants fear that their conduct may be prosecuted sometime in the future. In *Norris* v *Ireland* (1991) 13 EHRR 186, in the absence of a specific threat of a prosecution for homosexual offences directed to a particular person, the applicant was not considered a victim for the purposes of Article 25(1) which provides, 'The Commission may receive petitions . . . from any person . . . claiming to be the victim of a violation by one of the High Contracting Parties of the rights set forth in [the] Convention . . .'. The Court noted that a state of desuetude existed (see also *Bowers* v *Hardwick* 478 US 186 (1986) (below)), 'Admittedly, it appears that there have been no prosecutions under the Irish legislation in question . . . except where minors were involved or the acts were committed in public or without consent', although the Court acceded that the Irish prohibition on homosexuality was illegal.

Ireland reformed its laws in 1993. This was followed by the ruling in *Modinos* v *Cyprus* (1993) 16 EHRR 485 and Cyprus reformed its laws in 1995. The Court has also provided a tribunal of last resort for homosexuals in the armed forces alleging breaches of human rights. In *App. No. 9237/81* v *United Kingdom* (1984) 6 EHRR 354, a UK soldier had been discharged from the army, following a series of convictions under the Army Act 1955, s. 66, relating to consensual homosexual sex with men under 21. The applicant complained of alleged breaches of Articles 8 and 12. The Commission distinguished *Dudgeon*, arguing instead that under Article 8 (2) the words 'for the prevention of disorder' and the 'protection of morals' under the Army Act, s. 66, could be considered justified and that the measures were not disproportionate in the need to prevent disorder in the armed forces, thereby legitimating the dual standard applying to gay men within and outside the armed forces. It was this same reasoning that influenced the High Court in its recent decision to uphold the ban on homosexuals in the armed forces.

Whilst the primary role of the European Court of Human Rights is in assisting victims of alleged breaches, it also functions in the capacity of reviewing the application and interpretation of statute and the common law. In respect of this function, a recent application, which has been ruled admissible, by several homosexual men who engaged in violent sexual practices (referred to as sado-masochism) to which they allegedly consented (App. Nos. 21627/93, 21826/93 and 21974/93, *Laskey, Jaggard* and *Brown* v *The United Kingdom*, discussed below), raises questions of interpretation of the common law. In this application the parties complained to the Commission that their prosecutions and convictions were a violation of Articles 7 and 8 of the Convention. Article 7 provides:

1. No one shall be held guilty of any criminal offence on account of any Act or omission which did not constitute a criminal offence under national or international law at the time when it was committed. Nor shall a heavier penalty be imposed than the one that was applicable at the time the criminal offence was committed.

Article 8 provides:

1. Everyone has the right to respect for his private and family life, his home and his correspondence. 2. There shall be no interference by a public authority with the exercise of this right except such as is in accordance with the law and is necessary in a democratic society in the interests of national security, public safety or the economic well-being of the country, for the prevention of disorder or crime, for the protection of health or morals, or for the protection of the rights and freedoms of others.

Invocation of Article 7 rested on their contention that their convictions for criminal assault were the result of an unforeseeable application of a principle in a field of criminal law regulating assault and not the result of any criminal liability under sexual offences legislation, which they contended was the only area of law which was of relevance. In breach of Article 8, the applicants argued that their prosecution and conviction was an interference of their right to privacy. The Government's case in reply was that regulation and interference with the applicant's conduct was necessary for the protection of morals *inter alia*, society's rejection of violent sado-masochism, the risks of serious injury and infection and the need to protect health; a concern with the possible adverse effect on the young was justified under Article 8(2). The Government relied on the 'very broad margin of appreciation' which is accorded to Contracting States in areas relating to morality and public policy.

Having considered the application, the Commission (the first stage of the application before the European Court of Human Rights) concluded that in respect of the submission under Article 7 the case did indeed raise serious issues of fact and law and held that where the law is developed by application and interpretation of the courts in a common law system, their law-making function must remain within reasonable limits. In respect of Article 8, the Commission noted that interference or restriction in the exercise of fundamental rights must be in 'accordance with law' or 'prescribed by law', this they contended depends on foreseeability. In consideration of the meaning of 'prescribed by law', the European Court of Human Rights set the standard of foreseeability to that of 'reasonable certainty', in *The Sunday Times* v *United Kingdom* (judgment, 26 April 1979) European Court of Human Rights, Series A, Judgments and Decisions, Vol. 30, p. 31, in which it was held:

> ... a norm cannot be regarded as a 'law' unless it is formulated with sufficient precision to enable the citizen to regulate his conduct: he must be able — if need be with appropriate advice — to foresee, to a degree that is reasonable in the circumstances, the consequences which a given action may entail. Those consequences need not be foreseeable with absolute certainty: experience shows this to be unattainable. Again, whilst certainty is highly desirable, it may bring in its train excessive rigidity and the law must be able to keep pace with changing circumstances. Accordingly, many laws are inevitably couched in terms which, to a greater or lesser extent, are vague and whose interpretation and application are questions of practice.

The Commission stated that it is compatible with Article 7(1), for the existing elements of an offence to be clarified or adapted to new circumstances. The Commission contended that the application of the Offences Against the Person Act 1861, ss. 47 or 20, to these offences must be regarded as having been 'reasonably foreseeable' to an applicant with appropriate legal advice. The Commission concluded that the applicants were not, as a result, convicted of conduct which did not constitute a criminal offence at the time when it was committed and thus ruled this part of their application inadmissible (Council of Europe, European Commission of Human Rights

Decision as to Admissibility, Nos. 21627, 21826, 21974/93). (As past case prognosis has indicated the opinion expressed on admissibility by the Commission may be controverted in whole by the Court itself upon final judgment.)

The European Commission recently considered the admissibility of a further application raising issues of sado-masochism and the criminal law, Application No. 22170/93 *V, W, X, Y* and *Z* v *The United Kingdom*. V was a founder of 'S-M Gays' in 1981, a social group for gays interested in sado-masochistic activities, and was in a stable relationship with two other gay men who engaged in sado-masochism, including the use of restraints, belts, straps and chewing *(sic)*. W was heterosexual and in a stable relationship with Z, they have two young sons and engage in sado-masochism including restraints and canes. X was also heterosexual and engaged in sexual activities which involved receiving minor injuries. Y was a lesbian and engaged in sado-masochism with her partner. The five applicants submitted that following the House of Lords ruling in *Brown* [1993] 2 WLR 556, their sado-masochistic activities rendered them subject to criminal sanction and this interference or threatened interference was contrary to Article 8 and to respect for their private lives. As in *Norris* above, the Commission took the view that since they had not been proceeded against and the existence of the law did not directly affect their private lives, then the applicants did not come within the definition of victim in Article 25(1). The Commission took the view that it should not entertain actions *actio popularis* nor claims *in abstracto* and found the application inadmissible. The problem of gay and lesbian rights is, however, more than a matter of the right to privacy or the right to freedom against discrimination in employment. Discrimination against persons, on the grounds of sexual orientation, is ubiquitous throughout the provision of public services and also in private and family life spanning the entire range of social experience for this minority group (Sanders 1996).

INTIMATE PROHIBITIONS — PRIVACY OR PUBLIC MORALITY

The most overt expression of the law's regulation of homosexuality is found in the criminal law which is concerned with governing sexual practices in both public and private. Resistance to this oppressive arm of the law has centred agitation around the right to privacy as a fundamental human right of gay minorities. The right to privacy has been the winning argument before the European Court of Human Rights and in more recent years the privacy principle has led to the relaxation and liberalisation of domestic law in lowering the age of homosexual consent. The degree and form of state interference has been shaped by two competing public policy interests. Following the classical liberal doctrine propounded by Professor Hart (1963), drawing on the philosophies of Bentham and Mill, the intervention of the criminal law is considered warranted only in the prevention of 'demonstrable harm'. Otherwise the intervention of the law thwarted freedom and the liberty of the individual.

This is to be contrasted with the rather more austere, utilitarian approach advocated by Lord Devlin, drawing on the approach of Stephen who argued that the promotion of morality was a thing of value and the function of legislating morality, '. . . is to protect public and accepted standards of morals from being grossly and openly violated' (cited in Edwards 1979, p. 110). The law has a symbolic and paternal function in the regulation of morals. Hart took issue with Devlin on this point arguing that the Devlin thesis that 'society has the right to take any step necessary for its preservation' is inadequate. Criminologist Schur (1965) argued that crimes without victims, of which homosexuality is an example, represent attempts to legislate morality for its own sake. In 1954, the Home Office set up a committee chaired by Sir John Wolfenden, whose function it was to examine the criminal law relating to homosexual offences and prostitution. The Report of the Committee on Homosexuality and Prostitution 1957, concluded that male homosexual relationships in private should no longer be criminal. 'We do not think that it is proper for the law to concern itself with what a man does in private unless it can be shown to be contrary to the public good that the law ought to intervene in its function as the guardian of that public good' (p. 21). But it made its ongoing condemnation of any public display of homosexual sexual conduct clear. '. . . we do not think it would be expedient at the present time to reduce in any way the penalties attaching to homosexual importuning. It is important that the limited modification of the law which we propose should not be interpreted as an indication that the law can be indifferent to other forms of homosexual behaviour or as a general licence to adult homosexuals to behave as they please' (p. 44) and in so doing upheld what Hart calls the moderate position adopted by Devlin and affirms the view that the function of the criminal law is 'to enforce a moral principle and nothing else' (Devlin (1959)). It was these two limbs of the law and morality debate that informed the presiding judgments of Lord Templeman in *Brown* [1994] 1 AC 212 and the dissenting judgments of Lords Slynn and Mustill.

By contrast in the United States, the privacy argument was firmly rejected and until 1961 every State had a sodomy law proscribing both anal and oral sex. In *Bowers* v *Hardwick* 478 US 186 (1986), the United States Supreme Court rejected the privacy argument and upheld as constitutional criminal law forbidding homosexuality in private in the State of Georgia. Michael Hardwick was arrested *in flagrante delicto*, engaged with another man in fellatio in his own bedroom, in his own home and behind closed doors. Police officers raided the bedroom after legally entering the premises with a view to serve a warrant for a drink related offence. Both men were arrested for violating the sodomy statutes which proscribe both oral and anal sex (although, as in *Norris*, Posner notes that the law in the US has similarly fallen into desuetude where no prosecutions have been recorded, 1992, p. 342). After several hours Hardwick and his companion were released without charge. But the policing of the private life of gay men in this arbitrary manner is oppressive and stifling and no doubt Hardwick had endured enough of this misery. In response he brought an unsuccessful suit before the Supreme Court to ascertain, under a privacy challenge, whether there was a fundamental right to engage in homosexual sodomy (478 US 191). The US Constitution XIV, 1 provides 'No State shall . . . deprive any person of life, liberty, or property, without due process of law . . .' (see Hamilton 1987–88, p. 301). The Court was divided in a five to four decision. In upholding State statute, the Court adopted the reasoning of the Devlin approach to law and morality *inter alia* that the function of the criminal law is to uphold a moral code. Burger CJ held, 'To hold that the act of homosexual sodomy is somehow protected as a fundamental right would be to cast aside millennia of moral teaching'. The question is, whose moral code is given prominence and which conducts are moral or immoral? Clearly, prohibitions on sexual conduct in private pose a fundamental threat to individual freedoms whether protected by the ninth amendment of the US Constitution or by Article 8 of the European Convention on Human Rights (see Johnson 1992, Hamilton 1987–88). By 1993, two States had achieved legislative freedom, namely Nevada and the District of Columbia. State appellate courts in Kentucky and Texas have recently invalidated sodomy laws following challenges to the constitutionality theories (see *Commonwealth of Kentucky* v *Wasson* 842 SW 2d 487 (1992), where Wasson invited an undercover police officer to go home with him, and *City of Dallas* v *England* 846 SW 2d 957 (1993)). In *Miller* v *State* 636 So 2d 391 (1994) in Mississippi, however, the court followed *Bowers* in convicting a man of fellatio, and in *State* v *Baxley* 633 So 2d 142 (1994) in Louisiana where an undercover police officer was importuned, the court rejected challenges to sodomy laws.

The criminal law, through common law and statute, has considered homosexuality as synonymous with what some men do to men, thereby regulating male homosexuality and largely ignoring female homosexuality. Indeed lesbianism has never been expressly regulated by the criminal law. It has been said that Queen Victoria was so scandalised when she saw the provisions of the Criminal Law Amendment Bill which alluded to female homosexuality that she struck the clause from the Bill (see Cohen 1978, p. 95, Pearsall 1969, p. 576). Parliament seemed insufficiently convinced or troubled by the thought of sexual conduct between women to legislate against it. In 1921, a clause in the Criminal Law Amendment Bill provided, 'Any act of gross indecency between female persons shall be a misdemeanour and shall be punishable in the same way as any act committed by male persons', although the proscribing clause was later dropped from the Bill. Lesbianism was an 'abnormality of the brain', a vice that would 'cause our race to decline' and produced insanity, so said Sir Ernest Wild. Lieutenant Moore Brabazon suggested three possible ways of dealing with lesbianism, the death penalty, locking such women up as lunatics or simply ignoring them (see Edwards 1981, p. 43). Since female sexual assertiveness in women in heterosexual relations was not recognised, it is not altogether surprising that homosexuality between women appeared unlikely, since the masculinist version of sex presumed that something had to be done to someone. The widely publicised Pemberton-Billing libel case, involved the actress, Maud Allen in a damages suit against Billing's newspaper, *The Vigilante*, whom, the paper had implied was a lesbian and a sadist with the words, 'lewd, unchaste and immoral woman', who was about to give private performances of an obscene and indecent nature, '... so designed as to foster and encourage obscene and unnatural practices among women ... addicted to obscene and unnatural practices' (see Kettle 1977, p. 65). Whatever else, lesbianism was recognised as casting a slur on the female character. Thus imputations of unchastity were construed to include lesbianism (see *Kerr* v *Kennedy* [1942] 1 All ER 412, and see Edwards 1981, pp. 43–45).

Lesbians were nevertheless subject to scrutiny, surveillance by police, and on occasion prosecution under the common law charged with breach of the peace for an overt display of lesbianism in public (see Crane 1982, p. 19). Lesbianism is recognised as an offence under the Army Act 1966, s. 66 (see Crane, pp. 185–7, *Ministry of Defence ex parte Smith and others* [1996] 1 All ER 257). Regulation of lesbian women is covert but nonetheless extremely intrusive. There is much evidence too, to support the view that as victims and offenders of crime, lesbians receive a differential treatment. For example, in 1992, at least 40 per cent of the 41 female inmates on death row in the US were lesbians (see Gessen 1993).

Male homosexuality

In regulating male homosexuality, the criminal law has focused on three concerns, buggery or sodomy, gross indecency (any form of sexual contact which is not anal intercourse) and solicitation for an immoral purpose. In addition to the criminal sanctions the common law has also been frequently applied where homosexual conduct may be considered unlikely to satisfy the test required for the offences of gross indecency, solicitation or buggery. Sexual expression between gay men ranging from buggery (anal intercourse with underage men in private) to any public display of homosexual intimacy, including kissing and fondling and including 'chatting up' is considered a crime. In England and Wales, the Criminal Justice and Public Order Act 1994, develops the law in two significant ways, whilst retaining the criminalisation of these activities. First, the law recognises non-consensual buggery as anal rape. Section 142(1) states that, 'It is an offence for a man to rape a woman or another man', and the basis of this offence is that it is without consent. Section 143 amends the current provisions prohibiting and regulating buggery and replicates the 1967 definition of 'private' whereby 'An act of buggery by one man with another shall not be treated as taking place in private if it takes place (a) when more than two persons take part or are present; or (b) in a lavatory to which the public have or are permitted to have access, whether on payment or otherwise'. The penalties for buggery and indecency between men, provided for in s. 144 have been revised to accord with the lowering of the age at which homosexual acts are lawful: s. 145(1) lowers the age of consent from 21 to 18 years. Until this latter amendment, legislation in England and Wales had been out of line with many European States where the ages of consent for heterosexuals, lesbians and gay men have been the same. There is still a total ban on homosexuality in Russia, and in Romania, Bosnia Herzegovina, Macedonia and Serbia (see Tatchell 1990, Helfer 1990).

The principal homosexual offence is that of buggery. The Sexual Offences Act 1956, s. 12 provides, 'It is an offence for a person to commit buggery with another person otherwise than in the circumstances described in subsection (1A) below ...'. These circumstances, inserted by the Criminal Justice and Public Order Act 1994, s. 143, are where the act is committed in private and the persons involved have attained the age of eighteen (Sexual Offences Act 1967, s. 1(1); amended by the 1994 Act, s. 143. Offences of consensual buggery are proceeded against by trial on indictment only: *Practice Direction* (1988) 86 Cr App R 142. Four penalties are available, amended in accordance with s. 144 of the Criminal Justice and Public Order Act 1994. First, where buggery occurs in private or public with a boy under the age of 16, or with an animal, the maximum penalty is a sentence of life imprisonment (s. 144(2)). Whilst buggery of a child might warrant the maxima, the penalty for buggery with an animal is most likely to be dealt with by way of a probation order as in *Higson* (1984) 6 Cr App R (S) 20, (where a wife returned home to find her husband trying to rape the dog!). Where the accused is over 21 and the other person under 18 years, a five year sentence applies, but otherwise the sentence is two years (s. 144(2)(a) this also applies to indecency between men s. 144(3)(a)). The same sentences apply to the offence of attempted buggery (s. 144(2)(b)). Where one or both parties are under eighteen, then the different sentencing policy will reflect this. The sentence of life imprisonment for non consensual anal intercourse, now classed as rape s. 142(1)(2), increases from the earlier ten year maximum reserved for anal rape perpetrated on those over 16 (see s. 37 1956 Act and s. 3 1967 Act), to reflect the gravity of the crime (see *Attorney-General's Reference No. 48 of 1994 (Robert Allan Jeffrey)* (1995) 16 Cr App R (S) 980. In *Richards* (unreported 9 June 1995), the 25 year old male defendant forced his 18 year old male victim to fellate him and then attempted to rape him. Lowry J in delivering the judgmentof the court sentenced him to life imprisonment (see Rumney and Morgan-Taylor (1996)). In cases where a male of 17 and a male of 16 engage in sexual intercourse the charge will be one of buggery and carries a sentence of two years. Arguably the legislation continues to put young adolescent males who are already vulnerable at a considerable risk of prosecution and imprisonment. Where the police are considering a charge of unlawful sexual intercourse with a 15 year old girl by a 17 year old male, the likely penalty will be a verbal warning or at most a caution. It is highly unlikely, however, that police and prosecution practice will lead to a similar treatment of adolescent homosexuals.

The definition of what is meant by 'private' has led to some considerable argument. The word 'private' was first defined by the 1967 Act, s. 1(2). The 1967 Act restricted the definition of 'private' to behind closed doors, extending the definition of 'non private' to include all public places even if no one other than the defendants are present at the time and where a third person may have access. Broadly speaking, this meant that only inside the bedroom and where there were only two parties present could it be said to be truly private, although this excluded the Merchant Navy and armed forces which operated their own finite logic and morality, claiming exclusivity behind a higher altruistic principle of the defence of the nation. This *de facto* definition applies to any homosexual act of indecency. In a sense the homosexual was allowed out of the closet to remain confined to the bedroom in all physically intimate encounters. Whether indecency of whatever kind takes place in private, or not, is a matter for the jury to decide and is a question of fact. The test generally applied is whether members of the public have access in fact and not whether their access is of right. Case law indicates that the interpretation of what is private is highly restrictive. In *Reakes* [1974] Crim LR 615, the Court of Appeal approved the direction of the trial judge to the jury as to privacy, 'You look at all the surrounding circumstances, the time of night, the nature of the place including such matters as lighting and you consider further the likelihood of a third person coming upon the scene'. Thus, the possibility, however negligible or unlikely, of a third person coming on the scene negates any claim to the indecency being committed in private. This strict definition has legitimated policing of gays in their nightclubs, pubs and bars, as well as on the streets and in their homes and outside public lavatories. One example of the extent of the incursion into gay rights and freedoms is provided where police raided a private birthday party in October 1982 in Acton, London, on the grounds that since sexual activity was taking place between males in the bedrooms and that more than two people were present in the house, offences of buggery, gross indecency and keeping a disorderly house were being committed. Thirty seven guests were arrested, although the case was subsequently dropped (Tatchell 1990, p. 29). Where consensual sex is occurring in private, the law's intervention is justified by the utilitarian approach to morals *inter alia*, that it is the law's business to convey a message that sex between consenting couples, where one party is below eighteen years, is not to be tolerated and is a matter for state intervention, public policy and state paternalism.

The governing of homosexual behaviour in 'public' is grounded in the provisions covering gross indecency (the second homosexual offence) and is derived from the moral imperative of protection of public morals and public interest. Arguably, where homosexual conduct occurs in public, like heterosexual conduct, it is no longer a privacy question but a legitimate matter for public policy. The problem arises in the discrimination between gay expression in public and heterosexual expression. Understandably the standard of sexual intimacy required is lower and broader in its definition. Section 13 of the Sexual Offences Act 1956 provides, 'It is an offence for two men to commit an act of gross indecency, whether in public or private'. Gross indecency embraces any form of homosexual intimacy, kissing, cuddling, fondling in public, including indecent exhibitions one to another in a garden shed with the door locked and police looking through a window. The penalty for such conduct was raised from two to five years where one of the parties involved is under 21 (Criminal Justice and Public Order Act 1994, s. 144(3)(a)). In *Hunt and Badsey* (1950) 34 Cr App R 135, where two men were discovered in a shed 'making grossly indecent exhibitions to each other', in interpreting the Criminal Law Amendment Act 1885, s. 11, the Lord Chief Justice held that the offence had been committed where, although there was no physical contact between them, 'they were making filthy exhibitions the one to the other'. Lord Justice Scarman in *Preece and Howells* (1976) 63 Cr App R 28, in interpretation of the same section, upheld a conviction for gross indecency affirming *Hunt and Badsey*, that whilst two men must be 'acting in concert', it is not necessary for there to be any contact between them. Following the 1967 Act gross indecency is triable either way before a jury in the Crown Court or before magistrates. The 1967 Act was widely held to be a liberalising statute in that it permitted consensual acts in private for those 21 years and over, yet in its policing of the realm of the 'private' it was as punitive as ever. Indeed, since 1967, 'The recorded incidence of indecency between males has doubled, the number of persons prosecuted has trebled and the number of persons convicted has almost quadrupled' (Walmsley and White 1979, p. 39). Walmsley and White explain this increase thus:

> ... the most likely hypothesis is that the Act itself is the source of the increases in the statistics, and for two reasons. First, the Wolfenden report (1957) resulted in the law prohibiting all homosexual acts between males being called into question, the 1967 Act reaffirmed the unlawfulness of homosexual acts in public and thus provided the police with a basis on which action could be more confidently taken against those involved in such behaviour. Second, the 1967 Act introduced summary trial for the offence of indecency between males, thus making it easier to bring prosecutions (Walmsley and White 1979, pp. 41–42).

Prosecutions for gross indecency since 1967 have been transformed into an offence whose complainants are largely, if not always, police officers. This is the result of specifically targeted operational policies which have led to the growth of specialist police squads, vice squads and routine surveillance to police the 'grossers' (men under suspicion of committing offences of gross indecency) in well-known cruising areas outside and in gay clubs, male public lavatories. Well known meeting places for gay men, such as Hampstead Heath and Tooting Common, are all targeted in police operations. The approach of police forces to the policing of this problem has depended largely on operational force policy rather than on a reflexive response to the 'cottaging' or 'tearoom' problem. It seems that police surveillance of gays has historically targeted gay men on the streets. Statistics submitted by police to Sir John Wolfenden's committee of inquiry, in 1954 found that of 480 men convicted of offences in the years 1953–1956, 121 offences (25 per cent) were committed in 'public places' including parks and toilets. Gallo, Mayson, Meisinger, Robin, Stabile and Wynne (1966, p. 864)), in a study in the US in 1966, found that of 493 charges of felony for homosexuality, 56 per cent were preferred against persons arrested in lavatories. Walmsley and White (1979, p. 33) similarly found that in most of the cases proceeded with, the conduct took place in public lavatories or in open spaces. The scale of prosecutions is an artefact of police policy and commitment to surveillance and detection of the problem (see Table 1).

Table 1: Variations in notifiable offences for indecency between males by police force area

Area	1993	1983
England and Wales	671	1,362
Avon/Somerset	6	41
Bedford	3	4
Cambs.	6	8
Cheshire	1	31
Cleveland	1	0
Cumbria	1	1
Derby.	5	16
Devon/Corn.	18	57
Dorset	16	7
Durham	5	4
Essex	14	13
Gloucs.	3	10
Greater Mancs.	30	60
Hants.	68	41
Herts.	6	6
Humb.	5	10
Kent	17	12
Lancs.	13	16
Leics.	3	10
Lincs.	3	5
City of Lon.	2	20
Mersey.	22	19
Met. Police	126	268
Norfolk	9	11
N'Hants.	9	3
N'humbria	9	21
N. Yorks.	7	8

Area	1993	1983
Notts.	5	7
Sth. Yorks.	9	16
Staffs.	28	36
Suffolk	9	6
Surrey	5	15
Sussex	35	49
Thames V.	12	317
Warwicks.	3	0
West Merc.	8	21
W. Mids.	86	73
W. Yorks.	31	59
Wiltshire	8	9
Dyfed	4	11
Gwent	0	19
N. Wales	8	11
S. Wales	12	11

Source: Criminal Statistics Supplementary Tables Vol 3

Laud Humphreys (1970) in the ethnographic classic, *Tearoom Trade* on 'cottaging' in the US, dispels the police construction of importuning as importunate, revealing it instead to be a silent ritual consisting of reciprocal symbols where speech is avoided for fear of incrimination and silence satisfies the demand for privacy. Sentencing practice in cases of gross indecency where both parties are over 21 years has followed *Morgan* and *Dockerty* [1979] Crim LR 60, in the imposition of a fine. The Criminal Justice and Public Order Act 1994, s. 144(3)(a) provides for a sentence of five years where one man is over 21 and the other under 18, otherwise the sentence is two years.

The third homosexual 'crime' is that of 'solicitation for an immoral purpose'. This can amount at one end of the spectrum to gay men approaching non-gay men in the street and causing an affront and nuisance, in the same way that a non-prostitute is importuned by a kerb crawler for the purpose of prostitution. For gay men, solicitation, 'cruising', or 'chatting up', is a way of contacting other similarly minded men for friendship in the way in which heterosexual men have chatted up women on the street with impunity! Within the rigours of the law such behaviour by homosexuals amounts to solicitation for an immoral purpose. Section 32 of the 1956 Act provides, 'It is an offence for a man

persistently to solicit or importune in a public place for immoral purposes.'.
Statutory interpretation has construed solicitation to amount to a smile, wink
or gesture. In *Horton* v *Mead* [1913] 1 KB 154, the pursing of lips and wiggling
of the body was deemed sufficient. In rather more contemporary expression
and idiom, in *Dale* v *Smith* [1967] 1 WLR 700, the use of the word 'Hello' was
held to be importuning and satisfied the test of 'persistently' where on the
previous day the defendant had used the same word to another youth. The
maximum sentence for an offence of solicitation is two years' imprisonment. By
comparison the heterosexual solicitation of female prostitutes by male punters
is sanctioned by means of a fine and the solicitation of a non-prostitute is
merely a public order offence of insulting behaviour if anything at all. The
offence is committed regardless of the age of the person concerned and thus,
arguably, creates an anomaly in that it is an offence for gay men to meet each
other for the purpose of behaviour which if committed at all and in private,
between persons of 18 years and over, is legal. The regulation of homosexual
intimacy in the public sphere has been furthered by the use of the common law
offence of 'outraging public decency' where, for example, there has been a
display of affection in public which, if judged by contemporary standards,
might not satisfy the test required for an offence of gross indecency. *Masterson*
and *Another* v *Holden* [1986] 1 WLR 1017, has given further credence to the
puritanical anti-gay backlash. The defendants were standing by a bus stop
kissing and cuddling in Oxford Street, Central London, at 2 a.m. when two
girls and their male partners walked past. One of the girls voiced surprise, the
young men then walked back to the defendants and one of them shouted
indignantly, 'You filthy sods. How dare you in front of our girls?' The men were
cautioned by police officers who were in the vicinity and Masterson replied 'We
can cuddle, can't we? What's up with you?' (p. 1019). The defendants were
charged under the Metropolitan Police Act 1839, s. 54(13) with insulting
behaviour. The justices formed the opinion that the defendants' behaviour was
insulting. The defendants appealed on the grounds that their behaviour was
not insulting. The court deemed it to be irrelevant that they did not know
anyone was present in the vicinity. The fact that the conduct was insulting and
might have caused a breach of the peace was sufficient.

There is, in addition, some evidence of a growing use of s. 4 of the Public
Order Act 1986. 'A person is guilty of an offence if he (a) uses towards another
person threatening, abusive or insulting words or behaviour', as in the case
against two men who were kissing in a public street and such behaviour was
likely to cause 'public alarm or distress' (Tatchell 1990, p. 30). A television
documentary, *Gay Murders*, indicated that approximately 2,000 men were
prosecuted for public order offences and under local bye laws for offences
relating to homosexual intimacy. Whilst from 1967 (where relations over 21
were lawful) to 1994 (where the lowering of consent to 18 years gives rise to a
veneer of decriminalisation), the policing of gay communities on the streets has
been as vociferous as ever, while the definition of private contracts and police
powers to regulate homosexuals expands. Michael Howard, the Secretary of
State for the Home Department, announced in his conference speech in 1995
that he would be introducing plans to ensure a life sentence for the second time

sex offender. The proposal will form part of a White Paper on Sentencing issues to be published in 1996. How far this proposal, if effected, will affect gay men is as yet unknown.

PROSCRIBING HOMOSEXUAL PARENTING

The second site of conflict and one of human rights in respect of family life, emerges out of the right of homosexuals to family life, especially to parenting. Marriage in England and Wales is quintessentially heterosexual (*Hyde* v *Hyde* 1886 LR 1 P&D 130) 'the voluntary union for life of one man and one woman to the exclusion of all others' (per Lord Penzance). Families are essentially heterosexual. The law shapes and moulds what is regarded as the legal family, and whilst there may be all manner of other groups of people living together as a 'family unit', such units are not regarded as families for legal purposes. Research evidence shows that many 'families' are indeed homosexual. The hegemony of the biological heterosexual legal family is being challenged in several jurisdictions and the notion that homosexuality is a pretended family relationship is being challenged in many forums including custody decisions.

The *de facto* reality of the non-traditional social family is challenging the omnipotence of the biological family. In England and Wales the proportion of people living in a traditional married heterosexual family makes up 42 per cent of the total population (Social Trends 1995). In the US, it is estimated that there are between one and five million lesbian mothers and between one and three million gay fathers. Six to fourteen million children have a lesbian or gay parent (Singer and Deschamps 1994, p. 36). The law, in various ways, ensures the reproduction of the desired family unit by upholding rights of heterosexual parents but only where these parents conform to traditional role models and conduct. The idealised notion that rights are conferred equally on all citizens, is exposed as a myth when the rights of the homosexual parent regarding access to their children is under consideration. The difficulties and obstacles that have beset the lesbian mother or gay father are replete throughout all jurisdictions (Sanders 1994, 1996). In Britain, North America and Australia, the courts have regarded homosexuality as detrimental to 'the best interests of the child' and instrumental in 'scarring children for life'. Upon matrimonial dispute and breakdown, custody has been awarded to the heterosexual parent unless that parent is deemed 'unfit'. The homosexual parent ipso facto fails the 'fitness test' and where the mother is the homosexual parent the maternal preference principle is subordinated to the hegemony of the heterosexual imperative. Such discourses emphasise the damage to the child of a parent's homosexuality and persist even where court welfare reports and those of the *guardian ad litem* indicate a warm and affectionate relationship between the homosexual mother and her child and even where the child expresses a wish to remain with the homosexual parent. The Children Act 1989, s. 1 in England and Wales places the welfare of the child as paramount; it also provides the child with a voice, since the court must take into account the needs and wishes of the child in accordance with s. 1(3)(a). But it is rarely the case that this voice can be articulated or can be heard, since, where the view of the court conflicts with the child's wishes, the court overrides this voice by application of the 'welfare principle' or by deeming the child not sufficiently competent. Courts endorse the denial of lesbian and gay men to custody and access rights on the basis of public policy and a family law that is inherently heterosexualist. As it is the mother in all jurisdictions who is the more likely to have custody of the children, it is the lesbian mother who has been under closest scrutiny and whilst lesbian women have escaped the clutches of the criminal law (see Wolfenden p. 38, para. 103), their sexual orientation has been subject to rigorous examination and 'policing' within the arena of family law (see Polikoff 1989-90, Arnup 1989, Leonard 1994, Gavigan 1993). Lesbianism has been considered as axiomatically antipathetical to the interests of the child and incongruous with the construction of motherhood (see Brophy 1985, Sheppard 1992, Arnup 1989, Cox 1994).

In an unreported case (see *Guardian*, 7 August 1975), a lesbian mother was told that there was no point in contesting custody so she applied for access. The husband went back to court and tried to deny her access. The judge agreed that there was considerable ground for concern. Eventually the mother was allowed to preserve access only after signing a formal undertaking that she would not sleep with her partner while her son was staying, would hide all literature on the subject, and would never ever mention the matter nor discuss it in her son's presence. In a further unreported case (see *Spare Rib*, 22 August 1976), a mother lost custody when the judge placed great emphasis on a psychiatrist's report which read:

> The mother practises statistically abnormal sexual acts which can be looked upon as a deviation from the normal and is frankly perverted. It will be difficult to imagine that this young boy could go through his adolescent period of development without feeling shame and embarrassment at having a mother who has elected to engage in sexual practices which are statistically abnormal.

In a further unreported case (see Crane 1982, p. 130), the court 'dwelt on the minutiae of who was in which bedroom, whether or not the women slept in the same bed — and whether the ex-husband had found a depression on the second pillow that indicated his wife's promiscuity and that the other woman had been in the house.'. In *W* v *W* (1976) (unreported Court of Appeal 3, 4 November 1976), where a lesbian mother was awarded custody of her twin daughters aged 11, Ormrod LJ stated, 'the case turned on practical day to day grounds . . . and I hope no one will regard this judgment as containing any pronouncements for or against homosexual activities.'. Sir John Pennycuick made it clear that the children would have been removed from the mother 'if any acceptable or practical alternative had been available' (see Rights of Women, Lesbian Custody Group 1986, p. 110).

Homosexual fathers have not fared any better. In *Re D (An Infant) (Adoption: Parent's Consent)* [1977] AC 602, the marriage broke down and the mother was awarded custody, with reasonable access to the father who was a homosexual. The mother remarried and the new family wished to adopt the children, the natural father refusing to give his consent. The court held that his refusal was unreasonable and dispensed with the case (s. 5(1)(b), Adoption Act 1958). He applied to the Court of Appeal and the Appeal Court held that his refusal was not unreasonable (Stephenson LJ). The House of Lords, in overruling the Court of Appeal, restored the order of the county court judge, who had said that the correct approach of such a father should have been, 'I must protect my boy even if it means parting from him forever' (p. 624). The judge also said, 'The father has nothing to offer his son at any time in the future' (p. 624). Wilberforce LJ, in delivering the judgment of the House of Lords, said:

> ... there is nothing in the present decision which would warrant or support a general principle of dispensing with a parent's consent on the ground of homosexual conduct alone. . . . Whatever new attitudes Parliament, or public tolerance, may have chosen to take as regards the behaviour of consenting adults over 21 *inter se*, these should not entitle the courts to relax, in any degree, the vigilance and severity with which they should regard the risk of children at critical ages, being exposed or introduced to ways of life which, as this case illustrates, may lead to severance from normal society, to psychological stresses and unhappiness and possibly even to physical experiences which may scar them for life. I think the reasonable parent in the circumstances here shown would inevitably want to protect his boy from these dangers . . . (pp. 628–9)

In *S* v *S (Custody of Children)* [1980] 1 FLR 143, a lesbian mother lost the custody of her seven and a half year old daughter and her six year old son. On appeal the Court reiterated the view of Lord Wilberforce in *Re D* (above). This judgment was made notwithstanding that the welfare report on both of the children had stated that the personality and identity of both children were well established, that the children expressed a wish to be with their mother and she could provide better material care for them. In addition, the expert witness acting for the mother said that there was no danger to the children, although the witness for the father was of the view that there would be embarrassment and hurt resulting from the local knowledge of the mother's lesbianism. Similarly, in *Eveson* v *Eveson* (Court of Appeal (unreported) (Civil Division) 27 November 1980 Lexis, Enggen), where the mother appealed against an order of the court awarding interim custody to the father, the Court of Appeal upheld the order. Dame Elizabeth Lane said, 'I desire to say this: there is no rule or principle that a lesbian mother or homosexual father cannot be granted custody of a child', but she upheld the judgment of the Recorder who had said, 'My inclination is to decide the case not on personalities but rather that the child is getting on well where it is and not to expose it to risks of putting it with the mother.'.

In the very rare cases where the lesbian parent has been granted custody, this decision is made in cases where the father is totally unsuitable. In the case of *Re P (A Minor) (Custody)* [1983] 4 FLR 401, where the mother was a lesbian, and was living in a lesbian household, Watkins LJ held:

> I must confess to having had, ever since I first read the papers in this troublesome case, a considerable unease about the decision which placed a

child, who is now our concern, in the custody of the mother. I accept that it is not right to say that a child should in no circumstances live with a mother who is carrying on a lesbian relationship with a woman who is also living with her, but I venture to suggest that it can only be countenanced by the court when it is driven to the conclusion that there is in the interests of the child no other acceptable alternative form of custody. There is, in the weighing of the scales here for this child, on the one side living with the mother and on the other a care order . . . It would be wholly wrong to substitute any views that I may have about such matters as this . . . (pp. 405–6)

The court granted custody to the mother following allegations about the father by the child which, if it were true, would disqualify him. The mother was granted custody to be under the supervision of the local authority.

These same attitudes have been reflected in applications for access. In G v D (1983) ((unreported) Court of Appeal 16 February), an appeal was brought by a father against a mother having custody of two daughters. On appeal it was stated that the daughters did not wish to live with their father and new stepmother. The Court said, 'That being so, the Court has to give very careful consideration indeed to whether it is wise, particularly in such an abnormal situation as this, to force the children into a way of life that they did not like, although the judge said that this did not mean that cases ought to be decided on the views of young children'. Ormrod LJ stated, 'The mere fact of this homosexual way of life on the part of the mother is not, in itself, a reason for refusing to give her the control of her children, although of course it is a factor that one has to take into account and think about very hard. Experience shows, just as in this case . . . that homosexual relationships do tend to be even more unstable than heterosexual relationships are . . .' (Rights of Women 1986, p. 120).

This same aversion to homosexual parenting is evident from an examination of North American case law. In 11 States in the US, courts have ruled that gay men and woman are unfit to receive custody of their children and in 17 States courts have ruled that sexual orientation can be a factor if a connection can be made between the parents' sexual orientation and an adverse impact on the child (see Polikoff). Although homosexuality *per se* is not an automatic bar it is seen as a major impediment. In Canada, in K v K (1976) 23 RFL 58, 64, the court held, 'One must guard against magnifying the issue of homosexuality as it applies to the capacity for performing the duties of a parent'. In Case v Case (1975) 18 RFL 132, Macpherson J said, 'It seems to me that homosexuality on the part of the parent is a factor to be considered along with all the other evidence in the case. It should not be considered a bar in itself to a parent's right to custody . . . but . . . her way of life is irregular . . . I greatly fear that if these children are raised by the mother they will be too much in contact with people of abnormal tastes and proclivities.' (pp. 136, 138). In Bezaire v Bezaire (1981) 20 RFL (2d) 358, Arnup J, in the Court of Appeal, said, 'In my view homosexuality, either as a tendency, a proclivity, or a practised way of life, is not in itself alone a ground for refusing custody to the parent with respect to whom such evidence is given. The question is and always must be what effect upon the welfare of the children that aspect of the parent's make-up and life-style has.'. The dissenting judgment of Wilson JA is informative, 'I would like to add as an addendum to these reasons that in my view homosexuality is a neutral and not a negative factor as far as parenting skills are concerned.'.

The courts in Canada in recent years, whilst moving towards an acceptance of lesbian motherhood, have stipulated that a condition of custody or access is conventional and not militant lesbianism (see *Barkley* v *Barkley* (1980) 28 QR 3d 141; Gross 1986; Arnup 1989). In the United States the selfsame attitudes to gays are apparent. In *Constant A* v *Paul* 496 A 2d 1 (1985) a Pennsylvania court deprived a mother of custody, 'We conclude that the natural mother's lesbian relationship shows her moral deficiency ... To reverse ... (decision of lower court) will require the children to accept their mother's role, and to some extent, to proselytize the children by indicating that because of the role model now found acceptable, it is a suitable life style for the children ...' (pp. 3, 8). In *Chicoine* v *Chicoine* 479 N W 2d 891 (1992), a South Dakota judge held, '... to give her rights of reasonable visitation so that she can teach them to be homosexuals, would be the zenith of poor judgment for the judiciary of this state'. In *Blew* v *Verta* 617 A 2d 31 (1992), a Pennsylvania court displayed a much more enlightened view in citing *Fatemi* v *Fatemi* 489 A 2d 798, 801 (1985) and vacated the lower court's order restricting the mother's custody. 'Courts ought not to impose restrictions which unnecessarily shield children from the true nature of their parents unless it can be shown that some detrimental impact will flow from the specific behaviour of the parent. The process of children's maturation requires that they view and evaluate their parents in the bright light of reality. Children who learn their parent's weaknesses and strengths may be able better to shape lifelong relationships with them.'

By 1990, in England and Wales the notion of the lesbian mother as 'unfit' was finally laid to rest, although the courts continue to prefer heterosexual parenting notwithstanding the wishes of the child. In *C* v *C (A Minor) (Custody: Appeal)* [1991] 1 FLR 223, *C* v *C (No. 2)* [1992] 1 FCR 206, the Court of Appeal, whilst affirming that a lesbian relationship does not render a mother unfit, nevertheless considered applying the welfare principle, that the upbringing most conducive to the child's welfare was that which came closest to the ideal norm, i.e., heterosexuality and set an order aside which had granted custody to the mother, in favour of a joint custody order (p. 229), with the proviso that the father's application for care and control be reheard. In *Walker* v *Walker* (1980) Court of Appeal (Civil Division) No. 79 D 519 (unreported) *Lexis*, where the father had an interest in homosexuality and the mother had a lesbian relationship and was living with her partner, the child was allowed to remain with the father on the basis that he had lived with the father for a period of three years. In *B* v *B (Custody of Children)* [1991] FCR 1, the court granted custody to the mother notwithstanding her sexual orientation, on the basis that the child's age demanded that it be with the mother.

It remains clear that at the site of family law and in custody and access arrangements (known as residence and contact under the Children Act 1989 in the UK), and in other jurisdictions, notwithstanding the changing nature of the social family, the homosexual family exists as an anathema, to be sanctioned only as a last resort and in preference to a care option (see Graycar and Morgan 1992, p. 251). There are some, however, who are rejecting the imposition of heterosexual hegemony, believing that the best interest of the child is served by working on the de facto family. These matters are being considered in respect of homosexual families and transsexual families and in the latter regard the European Commission has recently made some important statements with regard to rights of social families to family life (see the chapter entitled, Transsexuals: In Legal Exile and the application and Commission opinion in *X, Y* and *Z*).

IDEOLOGICAL CONTROL: PROPOSITION 6 (CALIFORNIA), AMENDMENT 2 (COLORADO), SECTION 28 (UK)

The law has also functioned as a mechanism of ideological control in the promulgation of certain attitudes and in the determination and sanction of the degree of tolerance of homosexuality both in the UK and in North America. Essential to the reproduction of the State and its institutions, is the production and reproduction of ideology central to the maintenance of these institutions (Althusser 1971). The recent limitations placed on 'promotion' of homosexuality serve to reproduce the ideological conditions necessary to maintain intolerance of homosexuality and promulgation of heterosexual supremacy. The increasing openness of homosexuality in the 1980s which was perceived as a political challenge to traditional family values, resulted in an anti-homosexual backlash, attempting to regulate not only freedom of expression but freedom of thought, emerging largely out of a fear that homosexuality would corrupt young people if it was not made abundantly clear that it was unacceptable behaviour and not merely an 'alternative lifestyle'. In North America, Proposition 6, introduced in California, outlawed the employment of homosexuals in schools where homosexuals were considered 'unfit for service'. A District School Board would be required to dismiss or refuse to hire, any person who has engaged in homosexual activity or conduct if the Board believes such activity renders the person unfit for service (see Carter 1992, p. 217). In addition, in the US, Amendment 2 in Colorado in 1992, prohibits enactment of laws that protect homosexual men and women from discrimination. (See Sanders 1996 for a similar experience of suppression under Finnish law.)

Section 28 of the Local Government Act 1988 added s. 2A to the Local Government Act 1986. Section 2A outlaws the 'positive promotion' of homosexuality:

(1)   A local authority shall not (a) intentionally promote homosexuality or publish material with the intention of promoting homosexuality; (b) promote the teaching in any maintained school of the acceptability of homosexuality as a pretended family relationship.

Here the law regulates both speech and thought and action and was a development welcomed by many homophobes. 'The strident boasting

arrogance of the homosexual community seems to have quietened down a bit'
said David Wilshire in the *Guardian*, 11 October 1989 (cited in Kaufman and
Lincoln 1991, p. 1, Thomas and Costigan 1990). 'Those bunch of queers that
legalise filth in homosexuality have a lot to answer for and I hope they are proud
of what they have done. . . . It is disgusting and diabolical. As a cure I would put
90 per cent of queers in the ruddy gas chamber. I would shoot them all. Are we
going to keep letting these queers trade their filth up and down the country? We
must find a way of stopping these gays going round.'. This was said by the
Leader of South Staffordshire Council (cited in Kaufman and Lincoln 1991,
p. 4). Section 28 is a blatant form of censorship, intellectual and moral thought
control. It was met with some considerable confusion by local authorities; some
used it against gay activities, others tolerated it, either way local authorities are
obliged to apply it. If the local authority engages in something which is
proscribed by the section, the most likely form of action would be judicial
review where a council's decision may be regarded to be in breach of the
section.

The interpretation of the section turns on the meaning of 'intentionally' and
'homosexuality'. The difficulty is with the proof of intention. As Thomas and
Costigan show (1990, p. 11), there is high legal authority for suggesting that to
make something easier is not necessarily intentionally to promote or encourage
that thing (*Gillick* v *West Norfolk and Wisbech Area Health Authority* [1986] AC
112, see McK. Norrie). The government of the day emphasised that it would
only, 'apply to authorities who set out deliberately to promote homosexuality'
(Home Office Circular 12/88). Similarly the Department of Environment
Circular stated, 'So long as they (local authorities) are not setting out to
promote homosexuality, they may, for example, include in their public libraries
books and periodicals about homosexuality, and fund theatre and other arts
events which may include homosexual themes.'. This view was supported by a
letter from the Arts Minister, Richard Luce to Councillor R Hoyles, Chair of
the Arts, Recreation and Tourism Committee of the Association of Metropolitan Authorities. Luce wrote:

> If, for example, an authority clearly has a policy of seeking to bring the work
> of all sorts of artists and playwrights before the public, and from time to time
> put on exhibitions or plays for this purpose, the fact that the artists concerned
> include some who were homosexual would not put the local authority at risk
> under the section. The local authority's intention would clearly be the
> promotion of art rather than the promotion of homosexuality (Colvin and
> Hawksley 1989, p. 21).

The section has led, through creating a climate of uncertainty of legal action,
to councils erring on the side of caution and at the same time has served to
legitimise opposition to gay activities on the grounds that rendering any
support might lead to legal action. It has also led to creating a climate of fear
among local authorities about funding any activities relating to homosexuality,
although, at the same time, under the equal opportunities obligations,
authorities are under a duty to provide facilities and services, including

funding, to meet the needs of all those for whom they have a responsibility. Under equal opportunities policies the obligations of local councils are clear, namely that all sections of the population have equal access to jobs and resources and that a person's sexuality is not a matter to be taken into account when determining recruitment, promotion, training or welfare resources. That responsibility is owed to homosexuals and transsexuals as it is to every other group in the community.

Following the implementation of the 1988 Act, many councils have taken decisions to withdraw funding and support from a range of services and facilities. It is less easy to see how far this fear of legal action may well have influenced at the outset a decision not to fund a particular application for resources. In May 1988, East Sussex County Council banned the distribution of a National Youth Bureau directory on the grounds that it infringed s. 28: in its listing *inter alia* gay and lesbian organisations were included. On 23 September 1988, a production of '*Trapped in Time*', due to be performed in a secondary school was cancelled by the head teacher, who said he might be in breach of s. 28, since the play included a scene of a man coming out (i.e., declaring his homosexuality). Student unions have been subject to restrictions, and in January 1988, the Director of the City of Leeds College of Music banned the students' Gay and Lesbian Society from meeting on college premises (Colvin and Hawksley, pp. 5–6). Thomas and Costigan (1990), in a study of local councils' responses to s. 28, noted that specific threats of legal proceedings were made against several councils. A threat of legal proceedings was made against Waltham Forest Council following its practice in recruitment of gay people as foster parents. On 2 August 1990, a resolution was passed to formalise this policy stating that it is 'not intended to recruit and assess lesbians and gay men in preference to any other group of potential carers in the community'. More recently the Leisure Services Department of Ipswich Council cancelled a poetry reading evening when it was realised that the lesbian poet, Storme Webber would be reciting some of her work (*Pink Paper*, 2.2.92).

It is difficult to see from all this where equality of opportunity ends and intentional promotion of homosexuality begins. The presence of s. 28 on the statute book stands in contradistinction to efforts of some local councils to promote equality of opportunity for all groups including gays and the disabled. Many councils, so far as interpretation of the Equal Opportunities Act and their obligations under it are concerned, are interpreting 'sex' to include 'sexual orientation' and attempting to ensure that there is no victimisation of gays and lesbians. As Thomas and Costigan point out (1990, p. 31), the 'vague construction of section 28 leads to uncertainty about what the legislation renders unlawful.'. The ideological control of expression and thought has been furthered by the use of indecency and obscenity legislation to control the sale of books which address and cater for a particular sexual orientation. The standard of control for homosexual literature is more stringent than that for heterosexual books and magazines. Gay bookshops are particular targets both in the UK and in North America of this kind of ideological control (see Kendall 1993, Moon 1993), and it is this kind of policing which leads those who are opposed to censorship to argue that pornography legislation exerts pressure on gays in particular. The experience of one gay bookshop in London lends itself to the conclusion that any further controls on pornography will impact more determindly on the gay community. HM Customs and Excise confiscated several consignments of books destined for the bookshop, 'Gay's the Word', in Bloomsbury, London. The Customs operation involved the confiscation of many titles including books on herbs and spices as well as books on sex. After several years it was acceded that, with the exception of a few titles, the majority confiscated could be legally purchased in this country. Customs proceeded with the handful of titles against the bookshop which challenged Customs and Excise in an action before the High Court. The legal wrangle and Customs surveillance of 'Gay's the Word' began in 1984 and was not resolved until five years later; *Bow Street Magistrates' Court, ex parte Noncyp* [1988] 3 WLR 827 (see Edwards 1986, p. 44–45; discussed in further detail in the chapters entitled, Freedom from Pornography in an Age of Sexual Liberalism, and Women's Work: Private Contracts, Public Harm). Similarly, the problem of conservative interests co-opting pornography reform is ever apparent. In *Glad Day Bookshop Inc.* v *Deputy Minister of National Revenue (Customs and Excise)* (1992) 90 DLR (4th) 527, obscenity legislation was used to suppress gay sexual expression.

HOMOSEXUAL CONTUSIONS

Discrimination against the homosexual community and their lack of civil equality has extended to the differential treatment of gay victims of violence. Violence against gays has been construed as something which they bring upon themselves by refusing to give up their deviant lifestyle. Blaming the gay victim for his or her own demise is intrinsic to analyses of their own victimisation. Whilst violence against gay men in prison was recognised (Sagarin 1976; Anderson 1982), there has been little, if any, recognition of violence against gay men in everyday life (see Mezey 1994 and King 1992), the result of the gendered definition of rape in many jurisdictions, and the presumption that rape of men by men is consensual (Groth and Burgess 1980). Gay men and women along with ethnic minorities are victims of hate violence. They are kept in fear of attack by strangers because of the considerable hostility against gays and the legitimation by some of 'queer bashing'. This is one of the most hidden of crimes and most underreported. Many gay men have heterosexual families and in any event want to keep even their victimisation hidden lest it lead to further victimisation.

Some States in the US have responded by enacting hate crime legislation which includes crimes based on sexual orientation, e.g., Hate Crime Statistics Act 1993. Whilst violence by strangers against the gay community has been a site of political focus for gay men and women, any examination or recognition of violence within gay relationships has been largely out of bounds, guided by a monoistic construction of gay relationships as being of necessity celebratory. Thus, it is only in recent years that domestic violence in gay relationships has been recognised (see Bricker 1993, Island and Letellier 1991, West 1992, Kennedy 1992, p. 94, Hunter 1992–3).

One of the most interesting recent battles in respect of homosexual liberties and freedoms has centred on a recent legal suit and the issues it raises, *inter alia*, the right to consent to sado-masochistic sexual practices in private without legal interference. This conduct, it would seem, is considered an unalienable right by what appears to be the entirety of the gay lobby and civil liberties groups, sexual liberals and academics, all of whom have regarded the police investigation and subsequent prosecutions of a group of men involved in such practices as yet another expression of the incursion of the criminal law into the private lives of homosexual men (see Tatchell 1992, p. 238, Thompson 1994a). The error, lack of judgment and vacuity in their analysis mirrors the same lack of self-scrutiny and criticism that characterises the absolutist stance of gay men on the inexorable freedom, implicit in gay pornography (see the chapter entitled, Freedom from Pornography in an Age of Sexual Liberation). There is regrettably a fundamental blind spot which results in any expression of homosexuality being regarded *ipso facto* as an expression of freedom and liberty, and any attempt to explore other analyses, especially those which legitimise restriction or regulation, are regarded as implacably homophobic (see Sherman 1995).

This absolutist position leaves the gay political debate around such issues as homoerotica, and the need to extend the law in the protection of gay men from each other, intellectually lost and barren. It is perhaps not surprising that a hounded and vilified group throughout history regards any internal criticism of gay conduct as heresy, although there are some voices of self-scrutiny in this hopeless wilderness (see Kendall 1993, Stoltenberg 1991a and b, Jeffreys 1994). Stoltenberg (1991b, p. 252) writes perceptively:

> The patterns of subordination that go on between men help resolve internalized homophobia, momentarily, while you're having sex. Power-game, dominance-and-subordination sex works because it lets someone 'be the man there'; in fact it can let two males be the man if they're courteous about it, if they follow the rules. The trouble is, this kind of sexuality can escalate; and often as not it must, completely crossing the line of what is physically and emotionally safe for one partner or the other. Thoroughgoing subordination in sex is not victimless; there *must* be victims, and there are — nobody really knows how many. Coroners know when someone gets killed from something that looks a lot like extreme S/M; there are boys who have been molested, gay men who have been battered and raped in *sexual relationships*.

In *Billia* [1996] 1 Cr App R (S) 39, a sentence of nine years was reduced to five where death was caused by asphyxiation during a sexual act. The deceased was found with a tie tied around his neck following a homosexual encounter. The pathologist for the Crown accepted that he could not exclude the possibility that death had occurred as a result of a sexual act that had gone wrong.

Within this debate on sado-masochism there is also a powerful lesbian and feminist sexual liberal lobby arguing for the realisation of sado-masochism as freedom. McClintock (1992, p. 87) argues, 'To argue that in consensual S/M the 'dominant' has power, and the slave has not, is to read theatre for reality; is to play the world forward.'. Sherman (1995, p. 701) presents an equally noxious argument when he contends that sado-masochism is not about domination and submission but is instead about trust and about the intimacy and exhilaration that 'flow from putting your body at the disposal of your lover'. Sherman continues in the same vein, 'sado-masochism has saved relationships; it is arousal, it is theatre it is magic'. Sherman's argument is fundamentally flawed when he argues that gay S/M is different and equal, 'Any pain experienced in an S/M encounter arises as part of a ritual established through negotiation, and the pain is consensual where, as in a gay male relationship, the negotiation involves persons of equal sexual bargaining power.'. This is the fundamental blind spot that affects much of gay critique, *inter alia* the belief that there is an arena which stems from the homosexual experience, men encountering men, women encountering women, that is free from patriarchy and its master/slave power and inequality resonances. Cain's (1989–90) critique of MacKinnon is born of the same conviction. Cain argues that homosexual relationships are stripped bare of inequality, free in some sublime state of being, simply because of the matching of anatomical identities. Cain cites lesbian, Mary Dunlap's response to MacKinnon's claim of women's subordination. Cain states of lesbian women:

When we leave the male-dominated public sphere, we come home to a woman-identified private sphere. That does not mean that the patriarchy as an institution does not exist for us or that the patriarchy does not exist during the time we experience freedom from male domination. It means simply that we experience freedom from male domination. It means simply that we experience significant periods of nonsubordination, during which we, as women, are free to develop a sense of self that is our own and not a mere construct of the patriarchy (p. 212).

The belief in their own self determination and equality in the private is compelling but wishful. Extended into the analysis of sado-masochism it is a dangerous ideology which may be fatal.

Gay men and gay women have the right to the same protection from themselves and from one another as heterosexual men and women. This same standard has to be a fundamental demand of gay groups in their march for equality. Yet, restrictions on sado-masochism have been rejected as yet another expression of homophobia. The issues arising out of *Brown* [1993] 2 All ER 75, the sado-masochistic *cause célèbre*, have wide ramifications. The central imperative rests not merely with the evolution of valid and appropriate legal principles, in respect of consent, but with the need to ensure the recognition and protection of powerless, coerced victims. This concern was one which the Law Commission in its Consultation Paper on *Consent and Offences Against the Person* (1994) No. 134, and *Consent in the Criminal Law* (1995) No. 139, from herein referred to as *Consent (No. 1)* and *Consent (No. 2)* considered paramount (see Ormerod 1994, p. 928), although Leonard Leigh (1976, p. 142) had recognised, somewhat prophetically, the urgency of this endeavour rather earlier, '... one must in some measure meet an obvious need for safeguards for the victim.' The main criticism of the House of Lords ruling in *Brown*, is that the use of the criminal law is an inappropriate tool to deal with sado-masochism between consenting adults (see Thompson 1994a, p. 3). The use of the rule of law is formidably opposed, although in a somewhat feeble analysis, Thompson writes '... as they were gay, the defendants' acts were technically illegal under the 1967 Sexual Offences Act, which forbids gay men from having sex if a third party is present.'. This for Thompson (1994a) was the only strictly legal basis for legitimate intervention.

On the facts, the defendants had taken part in a series of violent acts which were filmed, including the insertion of fish hooks through the penis, beatings with carpet grippers, a scrotum being nailed to a board, and penises being skinned. The police discovered these videotapes during the course of another investigation and upon viewing the incident where a man's penis was being skinned, came to an understandable conclusion that a murder investigation would not be inappropriate. The investigation subsequently led to the arrest of over 40 men and 16 men were finally charged and found guilty. The police operation involved the prosecution of the defendants for an array of offences under the Offences against the Person Act 1861, including s. 47 assault and s. 20 grievous bodily harm. As a result terms of imprisonment of up to four years followed, although the length of sentence was reduced on appeal. According to the general rule governing assault, no offence is committed if harm, 'of a minor and limited kind' is inflicted with the consent of the victim (see also clause 6(1) of the Criminal Law Bill, that forms part of Law Com 218). When the injury amounts to maiming or ending life, consent is no defence (see Hawkins, *Pleas of the Crown 1*, chapter 44. See also Archbold 1994, vol. 2, para. 19.182, Blackstone's *Criminal Practice* B.2.7, 1996). The issue in *Brown* was whether in fact the harm inflicted was of a minor and limited kind and therefore beyond the law's reach, or whether it was harm of a more serious kind and thereby firmly within its grasp.

The general rule, so called, has developed in accordance with previous case law deemed by some judges to be authority, albeit that the cases deal with very different facts. Moran (1995, p. 228) rightly points out:

> Throughout the Court of Appeal and the House of Lords, judicial practice represents itself as a tireless search for authentic sources of law which demands the expenditure of extravagant amounts of time and effort. Lavish attention is paid to these authentic sources in order to expose the reason that will not only control but dictate specific outcomes, producing a predetermined order.

In *Coney* (1882) 8 QB 534, 11 judges were of the opinion that prize fighting was illegal, and so spectators were liable for aiding and abetting assault (Archbold 1994, vol. 2, para. 19.182). In *Donovan* [1934] 2 KB 498, it was considered whether, in the course of sexual gratification, a man who caned a woman who gave her consent was exempt from the general rule. Swift J, in delivering judgment, said that consent was immaterial and convicted. In *Attorney-*

General's Reference (No. 6 of 1980) (1981) 73 Cr App R 66, the question was whether two men engaged in a fight by mutual consent negated their criminal liability for assault. Lord Lane held in the negative, it was, he said, '. . . not in the public interest that people should try to cause or should cause each other actual bodily harm for no good reason.'.

In response to *Brown*, the Law Commission in Consultation Paper No. 134 on *Consent and Offences Against the Person* queried whether the general rule should be retained in its present form, or whether the limit should be placed at a level somewhat higher than that drawn in *Brown*, extending consent to assaults higher than assault occasioning actual bodily harm, but not as high as serious injury (*Consent No. 1*, para. 22.1, p. 48), and further proposed for consideration that whether the conduct constitutes injury or serious injury might be more properly a matter for jury determination (see Criminal Law Bill, which forms part of Law Commission 218). In arriving at this proposal the Law Commission (*Consent No. 1*) relied on *Miller* [1954] 2 QB 282, since this case suggested that assault occasioning actual bodily harm may connote a fairly low level of interference, potentially bringing many within the arm of the law. *Consent (No. 2)* proposes (at para. 4.16, p. 36) '. . . the consensual infliction of injury that falls short of serious disabling injury should in general be lawful even if intentional, it follows *a firtiori* that in our view it should also be lawful to inflict such injury *unintentionally* through an act consented to by the victim. In practice, however, the level of violence required before a charge of s. 47 assault is brought by police and proceeded with by the Crown Prosecution Service (CPS), relies not on the ephemeral, legal *prima facie* test of ingredients alone, but on the weight of the probative evidence and the likelihood of conviction. The practical realities of police charges and charge reduction by the CPS tend to demolish the argument that the level of consent to assault is pitched at a level that is too low as was suggested in *Miller*. As I have indicated in the chapter entitled, All in the Name of Privacy — Domestic Violence, it is the case that the CPS regularly reduce charges of assault occasioning actual bodily harm to charges of assault and battery under the Criminal Justice Act 1988, s. 39, in order that they can be dealt with quicker and cheaper at a summary hearing and so that a less serious charge might induce the defendant to plead guilty. The reference to *Miller* merely allowed the Law Commission (*Consent No. 1*) the leeway it needed to continue with its theme that s. 47 assault is not the appropriate boundary line for liability where consent is a material factor. In *Consent (No. 2)* the level is raised to a 'seriously disabling injury'. In my view this demarcation is too high where the injury was intended, albeit consent was given. Suggesting an alternative scheme, the Commission said, '. . . in addition to the question of whether the victim has consented to the relevant acts or risk of injury, other circumstances should be considered that might render consent ineffective in law' (para. 25.5). These other circumstances include where consent is induced by means of fraud or misrepresentation (para. 26.1); and mistake (para. 27.1). The most pertinent considerations are: threats and duress (para. 28.1); immaturity of the victim (para. 30.3), or inequality in power. Threats in this context also include threats which prevent compliance or resistance and such threats may be directed at the victim or at another person.

The Law Commission provides examples of inducements which may ensure compliance or *de facto* consent, where, for example, the victim may receive other benefits in the work sphere (citing the case of *McCoy* 217 (1953) 2 SA 4). Leng (1994, p. 483) also considers this aspect in some depth arguing that it places on the prosecution the task of proving beyond doubt that consent which appears freely given was obtained by the exercise of authority. The Law Commission rightly recognises some of the existing limitations (para. 25.3). In consideration of power, the Law Commission asserted (paras. 29.3, 29.4), 'We are minded to think, though we invite comment, that the defendant should not be allowed to rely on the consent of another obtained by his own misuse of power' and 'Consent given by minors, or other vulnerable groups, nonetheless raises difficult questions of policy.'.

Neither the Law Commission (*Consent*) nor the House of Lords considered fully this difficult question of public policy. The need to protect the consenting victim is overwhelming. The Law Commission takes the view that, '. . . it is only safe to allow very modest interference.' Commentators writing on the *Brown* judgment similarly treat consent as absolute and non-problematic (see Thompson 1994a, Moran 1995). Yet it is precisely at this point that the law should maximise its interference in view of the likelihood that consent cannot *ipso facto* be assumed to have been freely given and that assent, where there is inequality in power relationships, is no consent at all.

Counsel for the defence in *Brown* contended that no permanent harm was done, in an effort to bring the conduct within the ambit of the general rule, below the level of criminal liability. The second strategy was to argue that sado-masochistic acts should form a special category falling outside the general rule. In pursuit of this endeavour the defence attempted unsuccessfully to persuade the court that the injuries inflicted were 'trifling and minor'. The interpretation of the fact that the appellants did not seek medical attention, claimed the defence, was that the only possible conclusion was that medical attention was simply not required. That no medical assistance was sought, however, seems hardly surprising. How would the appellants have explained the nature of their wounds to their general practitioner? The Hippocratic oath notwithstanding, a consultation on such grounds might well have resulted in a psychiatric referral by the general practitioner, and in embarrassment as the complexities of their sexually deviant activities unfolded. It is worth noting that victims of domestic violence rarely seek medical assistance, although no one but a fool would draw the conclusion that this in any way is evidence of them not requiring such assistance and assaults being trifling and minor.

Luckily for the appellants, none suffered from septicaemia or infection (unlike the victim in *Slingsby* [1995] Crim LR 570, discussed in detail in the Chapters entitled, Sex Crime, and The Gender Politics of Homicide). The majority opinion in *Brown* [1993] 2 All ER 75 deemed minor injury to be the appropriate standard of legal intervention informed by a consideration of physical and moral injury or harm (on this point see Williams 1962, Feinberg 1986). Lord Templeman adopted a Devlinesque approach to legal intervention, asserting that society is right to protect 'moral values', concluding and arguing in the same vein as Lord Devlin who said that, 'the suppression of vice is as much the law's business as the suppression of subversive activities', arguing that consent becomes negated by the level of harm inflicted and that sado-masochistic consensual activity was not for the general good and thus there was no sense in extending the special category to include such activities. Lord Templeman referred to these activities as 'increasing barbarity', activities that 'will get out of hand' and a 'cult of violence'. 'I am not prepared to invent a defence of consent for sado-masochistic encounters which breed and glorify cruelty . . .' (p. 83)

The moral paternalism of Lord Templeman's judgment is apparent, under-pinning it, some would argue, is a homophobia. Certainly the rehearsal of the law proscribing homosexual offences seemed unnecessary, indicating that the matter was approached first as a 'homosexual' problem. Setting the reasoning aside, the judgment is a correct one, although, as I will go on to argue, for reasons not adequately considered by the House of Lords. Society has a duty through the courts to protect its members from this kind of behaviour.

In contrast, Lord Slynn (dissenting) was of the opinion that the limits to which the general rule should apply are set somewhere between really serious injury and less serious assault and not at the level of assault or minor harm. Neither Lord Slynn nor Lord Mustill (dissenting) accepted that the common law in *Coney, Donovan* or *Attorney-General's Reference (No. 6 of 1980)* was conclusive as to the formulation of the general rule and on this point their concern is conceded. Lord Slynn, influenced by Professor Hart's (1963) approach to the question of legal intervention in moral concerns and preferring the JS Mill formulation that revulsion or dislike of behaviour was not the focus or function of legal intervention, argued that the law could only be justified to prevent demonstrable physical harm. Dissenting from the judgment in *Attorney-General's Reference (No. 6 of 1980)* Lord Slynn said that where consent was concerned, the level of harm should be raised before consent was negated as a defence.

Most significantly, Lord Slynn defined the conduct in *Brown* as essentially 'sexual', whereas Lord Templeman recognised the activity thus, 'In my opinion sado-masochism is not only concerned with sex. Sado-masochism is also concerned with violence' (p. 82). Lord Slynn, whilst acknowledging the public revulsion proceeded in his reasoning to argue that as sexual conduct between consenting adults was a matter of morality and even indeed immorality, it was quintessentially a private affair and no business of the criminal law. Lord Mustill shared a similar view, 'My Lords, this is a case about the criminal law of violence. In my opinion it should be a case about the criminal law of private sexual relations.'. He went on to say, 'What I do say is that these are questions of private morality; that the standards by which they fall to be judged are not those of the criminal law . . .'. (pp. 101, 115–116)

On the centrality of the issue of consent the judgments were lamentably lacking. Lord Templeman did, however, acknowledge that the law must ensure that another person's will must not be overborne, recognising that consent is by no means implacable. 'Sado-masochistic participants have no way of foretell-ing the degree of bodily harm which will result from their activities.' (p. 82) By contrast, Lord Slynn (dissenting) missed the mark entirely, when he said, 'In the present cases there is no doubt that there was consent; indeed there was more than mere consent.... All the accused were old enough to know what they were doing.' (p. 122) Academic debate and analysis has been similarly impervious to the problematic nature of consent. Leng (1994, p. 483), for example, in responding to the Law Commission's proposal on threats to enforce compliance, is concerned that, '... it carries the risk of penalising truly consensual violence' (as in *Brown*) where threats were 'part of the "fantasy and role-play"'. Bibbings and Alldridge (1993, p. 360) similarly take for granted the central question of consent. The dissenting speeches of Lord Slynn and Lord Mustill were hailed by gay rights and civil liberties lobbies and sexual liberals as the lighthouse of liberalism in a sea of puritanism and homophobia.

My support for the House of Lords ruling derives from, and rests upon a very different discourse and consciousness altogether. It is informed by an understanding of sexual violence as primarily a question of violence and inexorably dependent on structural inequality within relationships. In the arena of sado-masochism the level of violence is indeterminate, where the aggressor and the victim are bound in a potent dyad, where the aggressor and the victim push each other further into a downward spiral of violence. Part of the cult of sexual violence demands the endurance of physical pain, where peer group pressure is overwhelming and any admission of duress, entrapment or retreat, is regarded as betrayal and heresy. In respect of homosexual sado-masochism, withstanding violence inflicted by the perpetrator is a mark of sexual bravado, often involving the wearing of insignia to indicate the extent of sexual practice and for identification by other like minded persons. For the *Brown* cult, testing the ultimate boundaries of human endurance and physical limits was arguably part of the enterprise, the very *cri de coeur* of the perpetrators.

Where the victim gives his consent or assent there is always the problem of unintended consequences where violence may well extend far beyond that envisaged by any of the participants. As Leigh (1976, p. 141), recognised, '... it does not follow that the only harm which occurs will be the harm which is consented to in advance.'. Lord Mustill found instead, '... the appellants' behaviour which, however worthy of censure, involved no animosity, no aggression, no personal rancour on the part of the person inflicting the hurt towards the recipient and no protest by the recipient.' (pp. 102, 115). We cannot be sure of this, however, because we cannot know the various traits of the sadistic personality, whether sadistic acts involve rage, or how far rage is a part of passion. We do not know with any certainty that the recipients did not make any protest. In their defence, Bibbings and Alldridge (1993) would have us believe that the victims were able to control the exact amount of pain the perpetrator exacted, which seems an extraordinary assumption where a desire for pain is supposedly the credo of masochism. The 'passive' participants in *Brown* were often drugged with amyl nitrate, overborne by group and peer pressure exacted by the presence of the several onlookers.

In response to this limited reasoning and analysis three focal points of concern arise. First, it cannot be the case that conduct which occurs in private becomes *ipso facto* not the law's business. Invoking the privacy shield cannot negate liability where violence of the level of assault occasioning actual bodily harm is inflicted. Turning to the question of whether the cited cases provide authority or not, the House of Lords was still free to develop its more creative role and reject the authority of the so-called authorities through distinguishing those earlier cases and then putting forward sounder public policy proposals. Secondly, in discerning whether the behaviour is sexual or violent, the individual circumstances, desire for pain and infliction of it, cannot transform conduct, which is principally an act of violence by the perpetrator, into an act of sexual preference merely to encompass a minority construction. In developing the private morality perspective, it was the sexual component of the conduct which became the dominant issue for both Lords Slynn and Mustill, around which their thinking was focused; the violence subsequently became a secondary characteristic. If the thinking had started out from a position that the conduct was primarily violent, albeit for the purpose of sexual gratification, then crying the 'privacy shield' becomes irrelevant, as does the motive, secret or otherwise. For Lord Slynn, in prioritising the sexual motive as the determining factor in the construction of consent and defining the conduct firstly as sexual, he could then move on to his conclusion that, as a matter of sexual morality, it was not the law's business, thereby conferring a privacy privilege upon violent conduct.

In further examination of the complexity of the question of whether consent exculpates the aggressor, it is necessary to draw on other areas of sexually intimate conduct where a power differential between aggressor and victim is a component, with a view to shedding light on additional concerns which seem to have been overlooked by the House of Lords, the ensuing academic debate and the gay rights lobby. An understanding of consent in both lay and legal context is culturally and historically bound, it cannot be stripped of the context in which it arises. A comparison may be made with the 1960s when the social and legal understanding of the rape victim was informed by the belief that she desired to be raped, she was responsible for the rapist's actions and that 'no' meant 'yes' and so on. In the 1990s the understanding of rape has dramatically changed with a heightened political consciousness and the status of women which make previous myths intolerable. Women do not desire rape, a man is responsible for his own actions and 'no' means just that. In the abstract sense only the truly equal can consent. Consent implies an agreement and yet, where there appears to be consent, that agreement is often between unequals. How does structural inequality affect the nature of consent, how does it dilute the authority of consent and at what point can it render consent negated? All these questions are imponderables. They are not amenable to legal rules but they are nevertheless part of the circumstances of each individual case and important considerations in the formulation of policy. What appears at first hand to be a case of consent may instead involve assent on the part of one of the parties; compliance may be obtained as the result of duress, through fear, psychological entrapment, economic or social dependency and so on. Acquiescence is not the same as consent (*Consent No. 1*, p. 83) nor does non-consent have to be expressly stated for there to be consent.

In situations where compliance is obtained through duress, the victim may expressly consent or may expressly withdraw consent, either way they may have many reasons for continuing with the deception of consent. These complexities may not be ones with which the law can deal, but to assume that a person has consented to violence because the perpetrator says so and because the victim does not expressly withdraw consent, does not mean that the several possibilities of duress both at the point of consent to the action and thereafter can be overlooked. The Law Commission (*Consent No. 1*) recognised that consent may not always be full and freely given yet outlined a very limited set of circumstances when consent might be regarded as problematic. The Law Commission (*Consent No. 1*) argued that it seems unlikely that in the type of case with which we are concerned misunderstandings would arise as to whether or not the victim has consented to be injured (although the *Billia* case raises just these doubts). In the context of sado-masochism, the aggressor perpetrates violence intentionally against the victim. Where the victim does not consent to such violence the full weight of the criminal law and criminal sanctions apply. In *Clayton* (1994) 15 Cr App R (S) 247, 12 years' imprisonment was reduced to 10 for causing grievous bodily harm with intent. Here, the appellant attacked another man, pinching his penis with pliers, attacking his testicles with a hammer, beating him on the back and buttocks with a walking stick and forcing a broom handle into his anus and scoring marks down his back with a knife. The victim was a homosexual, the attack was committed in the presence of another. The victim screamed and begged his aggressor to stop. The violence inflicted against the victim parallels the degree of violence expended in *Brown*. The judge in *Clayton* remarked, 'This is one of the most appalling cases of grievous bodily harm with intent that I have ever heard. The injuries, mercifully, were not so serious but the sadistic and systematic torture of this victim, a man of 60, described by you as pathetic, was vicious, cruel and degrading.' (p. 249).

Yet, where the victim apparently consents in a sado-masochistic context it is being argued that the aggressor should escape from the consequences of his acts if the violence is not 'serious' or 'seriously disabling'. It is assumed that in sado-masochistic encounters the victim desires the infliction of pain and so inner desire results in the recipient forfeiting the right to protection from harm. Protection from harm is not a socially propitious gift, but it appears it must be earned. And once the victim consents, this consent, however tenuous, exonerates and exculpates the sadist, dilutes his *mens rea* and removes the violent act out of the violent domain. Even though the status of consent within the intimate relationship is suspect, this is overlooked. Whilst sado-masochism has preoccupied psychoanalysis, there has not been agreement on its understanding. For Freud, a sadist was always a masochist. Krafft-Ebing regarded aspects of sado-masochism as sexual deviation (1901, p. 129). More recently, Anthony Storr has commented, 'Both sadists and masochists begin by treating the partner as being unusually powerful. For someone who has to be forced into submission is almost as strong as someone to whom one has to yield ... in neither case is there a sense of equality or of willing co-operation.' (1964, p. 43–44). At the heart of the sado-masochistic relationship is an inherent power differential. Consent of the victim is regarded as his choice rather than the aggressor defining the needs and aspirations and limits of the victim in the light

of the aggressor's desires. For the sadist power is his credo, his *raison d'être*.
For the victim, the desire to please, to be accepted, to be loved, to be valued,
is ever present. Even where the victim gives consent fully and freely,
injuries amounting to assault cannot be sanctioned: sado-masochism is not a
sufficiently good reason. As Lord Lowry rightly asserted in *Brown* at p. 99, '...
the satisfying of sado-masochistic libido does not come within the category
of good reason nor can the injuries be described as merely transient or trifling'.
Leigh (1976, p. 141) expresses his concern thus, 'If sado-masochistic activities
are to be non criminal we must recognise that the law explicitly sanctions
situations in which acts of violence occur.' The Law Commission in *Consent
(No. 2)* clearly misunderstands the power of one party over another, '...
a person who gives in to a threat (other than one of force) is not literally
compelled to submit; he or she could refuse' (para. 6.45, p. 70).

In support of my theories, I draw on prostitution as yet another relationship
which is saturated with power and inequality. Power is shown in the nature of
consent in prostitute-pimp encounters, where the prostitute often operates
under continuing duress and where any consent must be seen in the specific
context in which it is given. An understanding of the entrapment and duress in
this relationship again sheds further understanding on the illusory nature of
consent and the paramount need to be aware of the exercise of authority in such
intimate relationships, and relationships of non-intimates which are still
characterised by power and control. In *Parker* (1985) 6 Cr App R (S) 444, the
appellant was found guilty of living on immoral earnings and aiding and
abetting buggery and bestiality. He was able to keep his victim compliant and
apparently consenting by threatening to expose her prostitution to the Social
Services. She complied and 'consented' to his demands, meeting them all,
fearing that exposure might result in her children being taken into the care of
the local authority. He advertised her services in a contact magazine, forced her
to have intercourse with a dog and sold these pictures to publishers of
pornographic magazines. Power may also be seen in prostitute-client encounters, where violence is frequently perpetrated against the client by the prostitute
or against the prostitute by the client (see Edwards 1993a, pp. 89, 92–4,
99–100, McLeod 1992, pp. 70–71). This element of violence was recognised
by the Criminal Law Revision Committee (Seventeenth Report):

> According to police evidence heard by the Policy Advisory Committee the
> nuisance to the public involved men being seen leaving the premises showing
> obvious signs of injury or distress, behaving indecently, vomiting in the
> vicinity and depositing offensive litter (such as soiled and bloodstained
> linen), in nearby litter bins. The Policy Advisory Committee heard details of
> a number of cases which make it plain that the men who visit such places do
> so with the deliberate purpose of subjecting themselves to torture, pain and
> humiliation (p. 16, para. 3.8).

Our understanding of domestic violence educates us in recognising the
errors of the all too ready acceptance of consent. Two questions arise from this
understanding. First, why do women stay on with men who beat them?

Secondly, how has the law responded? Until recently there has been a tendency to view women who stay on in situations of violence as in some way consenting to what is happening to them. As Edwards (1989a) found, some of the literature actually suggests that women are masochistic and enjoy the violence. Erin Pizzey in her controversial book, *Prone to Violence* (1982), proposed that women were chemically addicted to violence. In *Owen* [1972] Crim LR 324, Roskill LJ asserted that a woman who had failed to leave a violent marriage had willingly exposed herself to violence and was partly to blame. Women in these situations may well do nothing but that does not mean they consent to acts of violence.

The response of the law to women in violent relationships has been to make the woman responsible for the man's behaviour by requiring her to prosecute him, making the matter *Mrs Smith* v *Mr Smith* rather than *The State* v *Mr Smith*. The law has totally misunderstood the illusory nature of choice in this context and has placed the decision to give evidence in the woman's hands, wherein the wife was not a compellable witness until 1984, (see *Hoskyn* [1978] 2 All ER 136), where privacy arguments justified the House of Lords decision their decision to overrule common law. Lord Edmund-Davies (dissenting), contended that the only right course and public policy consideration where violence was concerned, lay with the protection of the victim. The Court of Appeal had similarly considered that they were bound by *Lapworth* [1931] which held that a wife was a compellable witness. The House of Lords took a different view: that *Lapworth* was wrongly decided and must be overruled. Lord Edmund-Davies took the view that there were no binding precedents and no authorities directly on the point, and that judges in *Hoskyn* were free to make law. He also argued that *Lapworth* was indeed good law and was not irreconcilable with *Leach* [1912]. In the domestic violence situation women rarely give evidence when not compelled to do so because of continuing duress (see Edwards 1989a, 1989b); in such circumstances continuing duress may compel the victim to say that she was a willing participant (see Leng 1994, p. 483).

Both the House of Lords in *Brown* and the Law Commission considered the rule in rape, i.e., that consent vitiated liability, the legal rules respecting the defendant's belief (*DPP* v *Morgan* [1975] 2 All ER 347), and the rule in respect of recklessness, in relation to whether or not a woman can be said to have consented. The problem of when consent is true consent is all too apparent in rape. Indeed, the courts have had great difficulty in interpreting the meaning of acts of violence in this context. Violence, characteristically in the common law, has been regarded as vitiating consent to rape. However, in the common law the degree of violence had to be extreme and had to be against the private parts, as minor assault was regarded as part of sexual enjoyment. Since 1976, the degree of violence required to vitiate the defence of consent has been probably at the level of assault. In two cases heard in different courts at Birmingham Crown Court during one sample week of court research, the evidence of violence was regarded as evidence not of rape but of sexual passion. A cut to the lip was, alleged the victim, evidence of violence perpetrated against her. The defence claimed that this was the man's response to the woman's demand,

'Hit me, hit me, I'm kinky'. The parallel here with the co-defendants in *Morgan* is memorable. They too claimed that the husband had told them to ignore his wife's struggle and protestation, for she was a woman who was 'kinky', and liked the additional thrill of violence (see the chapter entitled, Sex Crime for further discussion).

We can also draw on what is known about pornography to assist in understanding *Brown*. 'Flagellation is the hall mark of British pornography', writes barrister Geoffrey Robertson (1979, p. 296). Two issues arise here: first how people in pornography become involved and are kept there and, secondly, what happens in the pornography and what is the central message? At the heart of pornography is violence. Much of pornography involves the staple diet of violence, from minor assaults, to assault, to grievous bodily harm and also to murder. It is worthy of note that when the police came upon the tapes in *Brown*, in the course of an investigation into child pornography, they set up a murder inquiry after viewing the infliction of the injuries. It was reasonable to suppose that, after viewing particularly the scenes of a man skinning another's penis, the victim may have been disposed with off film.

Consent in intimate relationships is illusory. The need to protect the genuine victim from harm is overwhelming. The vulnerability and the power at the heart of relationships must be considered before it is assumed that consent is implacable and is freely given and full, if the victim says so. The divide between what is considered public and what is considered private is irrelevant and, already, it is clear that many women and children have experienced violence in the home because of the law's visceral reluctance to intervene in the private sphere. Such conflict of public policy arose in *Davis v Johnson* [1978] 1 All ER 1132, which juxtaposed the public policy of protecting women from aggressive partners against the man's proprietary interest. The invocation of Article 8 and the right to privacy by Brown et al is a red herring and absurd. It may not be possible to lay down hard and fast rules as to when consent is full and free and when it is not. At the same time the court cannot adopt a paternalistic approach and take upon itself the task of determining this matter. But in its deliberations a fuller consideration of consent in relationships is required.

Finally, supposing that in *Brown* the victims truly consented, as the sexual liberals would have us believe, what then? How do we deal with that, through moral paternalism or moral nihilism? The answer is as argued earlier; the recognition that such men or women are in urgent need of psychiatric treatment. Perhaps, in sentencing, the courts might have made a probation order with a condition of treatment. If we believe that behaviour of that kind is just another manifestation of sexual appetite, 'vigorous sexual activity', then the law provides the authorisation and legitimation of sadism, of brutality, of physical domination — a proverbial 'sadists' charter', for the infliction of cruelty, a positive boon to the sadist and a betrayal, by those who think themselves *avant garde*, liberals, of the need to recognise the harmful and dangerous aspects of the human psyche and spirit which desire to harm others, and for some, occasionally, to be harmed themselves.

At the end, however, there is the insuperable dilemma of whether the victim should also be criminalised. Victims have been frequently blamed. Judge

Betrand Richards said of a rape victim, 'You are guilty of a great deal of contributory negligence' (see Edwards 1982), putting the victim on an equal footing in so far as the liability and sanctions are concerned. It seems that in cases where full and free consent of the victim is suspect, it is not right to punish the victim for receiving, or aiding and abetting the violence. The sexual liberals' response to *Brown* is a betrayal of homosexuality, exposing homosexuals both to inequality and to a lack of the protection that we would otherwise demand for heterosexuals. For Moran (1995, p. 246) *Brown* symbolises the law's violence. 'The meeting between law and sado-masochism not only demands that we acknowledge the violence of the law, but that we recognize its particular qualities. As such, it is important to recognize that law's violence is concerned with coercion, terror, fear, domination, hostility, subordination, silence and inequality.'. Surely it is the very inequality of law which means that violence against gay men by gay men can be made invisible or else denied and reconstructed as celebratory sex. The *Brown* judgment ensures that gay men have a right to protection in a world where the drawing of boundaries of legitimate and illegitimate conduct and the regulation of homosexual conduct is not of necessity homophobic.

THREE

Freedom from pornography in an age of sexual liberalism

It has been a major consideration of the critique of law by contemporary feminists to transform law in a way which embraces women's experiences and is more consonant with their lives. A major consideration of engaging with pornography and pornography law is to deconstruct and reconstruct pornography from the viewpoint of anti-sexism and anti-racism. Sexual liberals and feminists are locked in a battle over what is to be done, if anything, about pornography. For sexual liberals pornography is freedom, for feminists pornography is a fundamental attack on both the anti-racist and anti-sexist movement. MacKinnon explains 'liberals ... discovered that they liked speech — i.e., women being used — a great deal more than they liked sex equality' (1990, p. 9). Sexual liberals in turn consider feminism a threat to liberation (see Sherman 1995, p. 691, Thompson 1994b). Greenberg and Tobiason (1993), critique the MacKinnon and Dworkin feminism as legal puritanism and certainly many argue that an unholy alliance has been forged between the moral right and feminism (Downs 1989, p. 124).

In exploration of these dichotomies (see Eckersley 1987, Smart 1989), this discussion proceeds, first, with an examination of the competing meanings of pornography and the consequences that each meaning has for legal intervention. Secondly, the intellectual basis and justification for the laws governing obscenity in the UK, particularly the Obscene Publications Act 1959 and the Protection of Children Act 1978, their operation, including policing and prosecuting practices, is considered. Thirdly, this exploration concludes with an evaluation of the efforts in North America to reconstruct and reconstitute obscenity as a problem of harm and as an issue of sex equality, removing it from the ambit of the criminal law, placing it instead within the domain of civil and human rights.

COUNTERVAILING DEFINITIONS OF PORNOGRAPHY

The sex in pornography

For sexual liberals, pornographers, producers and consumers of pornography, it is about sex. 'Pornography' is a generic term describing a wide range of conduct which is committed to record, on film, on computer disk, in the written word and on the internet. It describes a range of conduct from explicit sexual intercourse, to coprophilia, including intercourse with animals, bondage, beatings, fisting, torture, rape and murder. To feminists, the term misleads, 'pornography' functioning as a prefix, a headnote, a sub-text, constructing expectation and levelling all that is subsumed within it, as of the same ontology. The question is, what, if anything, do torture and bondage and explicit sexual intercourse share in common, that the term 'pornography' can be used to explain it all? The answer may be that all this 'pornography' has the potential to arouse a physiological response in a male audience. Pornography thus describes the reaction to it, the response, but only the response of those who are sexually aroused by its content. Sexual liberals focus on the arousal aspect. Sexual liberalism, for the purposes of this discussion, derives its definition from Leidholdt (1990, p. ix), 'Sexual liberalism: a set of political beliefs and practices rooted in the assumption that sexual expression is inherently liberating and must be permitted to flourish unchecked, even where it entails the exploitation or brutalisation of others'.

'Pornography' is defended by its producers and distributors and by all those who profit from it, by its consumers and by sexual liberals and civil libertarians, who are in the main absolutists in opposition to censorship, to be exclusively a matter of sex, of the erotic. Curiously, civil libertarians and the left, think it is something to do with freedom from totalitarianism. MacKinnon (1982, p. 531) identifies the way in which the parameters of the debate have been so cleverly articulated, 'Pornography has been considered a question of freedom to speak and depict the erotic, as against the obscene or violent'.

Even where 'pornography' contains violence, humiliation, and subjection, it is frequently defined as sexual, and the inequality, harm and exploitation is masked and negated as 'real harm' by the woman's apparent compliance, or her deserts. Yet, this compliance is induced by fear and duress. Within this configuration of what is essentially inequality and violence as sexual, gay pornography, like heterosexual pornography, takes on the same predictable stylisations. It, too, is inexorably genderised. The dominator, the one who is doing, is cast in the role of the male gender; the victim, or the one who is being done to, is dramatised in the role of female. Gay pornography is the realisation of a metaphor, the 'one under becomes the woman'. Gay pornography, in whatever form, from anal intercourse, to anal rape, to beatings and fistings, is generally mistakenly regarded as a valid expression of homosexuality, the defence of which is quintessential to homosexual liberation. This recalcitrant defence of 'anything gay' led to an homogenised and implacable response from the gay community in their opposition to the House of Lords judgment in *Brown* [1993] 2 All ER 75 (discussed at length in the chapter entitled, Gay prohibition, social engineering and rights). The presiding judgment is regarded by sexual liberals, the gay lobby and some feminists as yet another expression of a homophobic judiciary intent on the suppression of gay sexuality. Sherman (1995, p. 691), adds his voice to the gay liberal lobby, unstinting in its defence of gay pornography, attacking feminism which he perceives as a threat emphasising 'the uniqueness of their experience'. The argument of the gay pro pornography lobby seems to be assured of absolute reciprocity in homosexual relationships (Sherman 1995), which is not taken for granted in heterosexual relations. The *naïveté* of this position allows gay supporters to deny some very real inequalities.

Stoltenberg (1991b, p. 250), in challenging the claim made by many (see Stychin 1992), that gay pornography is truly equal, explains the inequality, '. . . men who have sex with men are believed to be treated like a woman in sex'. The metaphor at the heart of gay male porn is described by Kendall thus, 'It tells gay men either to retain their degraded status as 'female' or become the real men they should have been all along' (1993, p. 29). MacKinnon (1989, p. 114), explains what lies at the heart of this sex division, '. . . [m]ale is a social and political concept, not a biological attribute, having nothing whatever to do with inherency, preexistence, nature, essence inevitability, or body as such'. In defence of gay male pornography, gay men are adamant that their pornography is different, it is about gay sexuality as a discrete entity and it contributes to the affirmation and celebration of male homosexuality. Tucker (1991, p. 263) opposes radical feminism which in his view, 'has directed so much of our activism, and has dominated so much of our discourse on sexuality'. And, at the heart of the meaning of transvestite porn is a similar genderisation, '. . . the hermaphroditic/transsexual body is adorned as "woman" through erotic accoutrements . . .' (Kaite 1988, p. 152).

Lesbian pornography is similarly couched as a celebration of lesbian sexuality. Lesbian pornography, it is argued, is free from gender inequality, from concepts of power domination, because its actors are women. Raymond (1992, p. 166), explores the recent trend within what she calls lesbian 'lifestyle', distinguishing this from lesbian politics. Raymond vehemently opposes the argument that female to female sexuality must be 'freed up' to take on the forms of male power, rejecting the argument that female to female sexuality must take on sado-masochism etc. Raymond (1992, p. 175), argues that there are those, '. . . who think that the objectification, subordination and violation of women is acceptable just as long as you call it lesbian erotica or lesbian sado-masochism . . .'. Any examination of lesbian pornography exposes this argument of true equality as mythology. The morphology of images in this pornography, as in any other, are similarly about violence, domination, and inequality. Jeffreys (1994) argues that pornography and sado-masochism are hostile to lesbianism and feminism and calls it heresy. Whether straight or gay, Kappeler's response (1986, p. 3), like MacKinnon's (already cited in the context of heterosexual pornography), is that it is the structure of representation that must be taken into account. The dangers of sexual liberalism are all too apparent. Sexual liberalism endangers feminism, human rights and sexual and racial equality. In the dissenting judgment in *Brown* it was the sexual liberalism of Slynn LJ and Mustill LJ, which defined the sado-masochistic practices of a group of men, by interpreting such conduct within the realm of the sexual instead of in the realm of the violent (see the chapter entitled, Gay prohibition, social engineering and rights).

Pornography as violence

The contemporary feminist critique of pornography challenges sexual liberalism and formulates pornography as inequality, objectification and as violence. Feminists instead focus on the meaning and content, and suggest that the exploitation and subordination of the woman within the pornography and the concept of womanhood, whether being subjected to sexual intercourse, or being beaten and tortured, where the archetypal scenario depicted in pornography, whether explicit sex or violence, depends quintessentially on the 'powerlessness' of the victim/recipient, is the common element. For feminists the ontology and morphology of pornography is what is significant. MacKinnon (1984, p. 343) writes, 'In pornography, the violence is the sex'. As Leidholdt (1990, p. xi), points out, 'For feminists, the issue was not morals, taste, or aesthetics but the attitudes about women that pornography inculcated, the acts of sexual brutality engendered by those attitudes, and the exploitation of real women in the manufacture of pornographic materials.'. As Kappeler suggests (1986, p. 105), 'The fundamental structure of the transitive plot, which assigns her object status, remains the same. It is a paradigm of domination, or coercion and of the degradation of the Other to object status.'. Berger (1987, pp. 45–46) explores this element of 'object status' further:

> According to usage and conventions which are at last being questioned but have by no means been overcome, the social presence of a woman is different in kind from that of a man. A man's presence is dependent upon the promise of power which he embodies. If the promise is large and credible his presence is striking. If it is small or incredible, he is found to have little presence. The promised power may be moral, physical, temperamental, economic, social, sexual — but its object is always exterior to the man. A man's presence suggests what he is capable of doing to you or for you. His presence may be fabricated, in the sense that he pretends to be capable of what he is not. But the pretence is always towards a power which he exercises on others. By contrast, a woman's presence expresses her own attitude to herself, and defines what can and cannot be done to her. . . . To be born a woman has been to be born, within an allotted and confined space, into the keeping of men.

It is not merely the objectification of women in pornography but the violence in pornography that constitutes the main objection. It is for the latter reason especially, that the generic application of the label 'pornography' must be challenged. The power of the word, of the name that is given to rape and torture, to acts of humiliation, defines the material as sex, the name 'pornography' functions to persuade its audience that the text is really about something else. In prefixing the text as 'pornography,' above all, what is seen, read or heard is regarded primarily as 'sexual' because of men's physiological response or reaction to it. Thus, the very act of naming is political, in that it has very specific consequences for the understanding and authorisation of the text. My objection to the label 'pornography' is that it has been used by sexual liberals, pornographers and consumers to define abuse, degradation and torture as a matter of sex and therein legitimate. In the same way the use and re-use of the term 'ethnic cleansing' has described the genocide of the Bosnian people, and made murder legitimate. Again, the use of the term 'housecleaning' denoting the 'round up' of Jews for ultimate genocide by the Nazis (Shirer 1968, p. 794) apparently bestowed legitimacy on that act. Applying the term 'pornography' to visual statements about the degradation and abuse of women and children, conceals the reality of the message and meaning contained in those statements, eclipsing the inequality and violence inherent in the text itself. By signifying and encoding the text with sexual meaning, through labelling, the violence or perversion within its content is legitimated as part of the domain of the 'sexual'. It is not the language of its victims, and it is men from the first to the last who have defined violence against women as 'pornography' in defence of their own interests. Pornography's claim to sex, to equality and to freedom, is emphatically challenged and refuted. The power of 'naming', the authority of the definition, is a theme raised in several of the chapters in this book. It is no less significant here. This power enables men and the most powerful of men, to define male experience as standard 'human' experience and all legal definitions that flow from this are similarly presented as standard legal subjects. Their experience is authorised as the standard, whilst the experience of women and children is invalid, without authority (see Dworkin 1989, p. 17). Within this, men are duped into the pursuit of real masculinity and its validation, through the consumption, celebration and staunch defence of pornography (see Stoltenberg 1990, 1991a, p. 60).

Pornography depends for its effect on a narrative of violence and inequality. Whilst some 'pornography' is arguably erotica (see Steinem 1980, p. 35), the same word is employed to describe the knifing of a woman, the disembowelling of a woman, and the rape of a child. Pornography, formulates Dworkin (1989, p. xxvii), is, '... the orchestrated destruction of women's bodies and souls; rape, battery, incest and prostitution animate it; dehumanization and sadism characterize it; it is a war on women, serial assaults on dignity, identity, and human worth; it is tyranny.'. In her evidence to the *Attorney-General's Commission on Pornography* (1986, pp. 769–72), Dworkin had this to say about the nature and content of pornography:

> ... in this country where I live, every year millions of pictures are being made of women with our legs spread. We are called pussy, our genitals are tied up, they are pasted.... In this country where I live as a citizen, women are penetrated as animals and objects for public entertainment, women are urinated on and defecated on ... there is amputee pornography, a trade in women who have been maimed in that way, as if that is a sexual fetish for men. In this country where I live, there is a trade in racism as a form of sexual

pleasure ... Black skin is presented as if it is a female genital, and all the violence and all the abuse and the humiliation that is in general directed against the female genitals is directed against the black skin of women. (pp. 769–72)

For some in the liberal nineties it is a matter of freedom. The gratuitous violence in *American Psycho* by Bret Ellis (1991) is of the same genre, 'Scream honey', I urge, 'keep screaming. No one cares, no one will help you . . . and with the same pair of scissors I cut her tongue out . . .'. This book which details the sexual torture of women, 'soared to the Best Sellers' list, made a few wealthy men a little wealthier, and has finally triggered a national boycott of Knopf, inc., by people who are saddened and angered by the rising visibility and respectability of real and simulated sexual sadism' (see Brannon 1993, p. 239–240).

This word 'pornography' is also used to describe violence against children, the rape and buggery of children, masturbating over children, abusing children in so many ways, all of which by definition and without argument involve power, inequality and exploitation and the committing of real crimes on children to film. Why is it called child pornography? The dealers merely regard it as another commodity. The attitude of Catherine Wilson, a child pornography dealer, was that, 'She compared it to toothpaste. She said child pornography to her was just like toothpaste in that people wanted it, so people would find a way to get it. As far as she was concerned she was simply distributing something that people wanted, just as they wanted toothpaste.' (Tate 1990, p. 83.) The relaunched 1991 Arrow edition, an imprint of Random Century Group, of an otherwise obscure text by de Sade, *Juliette*, suggests that this publisher of 'books' applied the same demand and supply rationale as Catherine Wilson. *Juliette* details child torture and murder, as almost each page is filled with lurid descriptive passages of interminable violence and cruelty, '. . . I humbly submit that another serving of omelette be eaten off this engaging little thing's face, that we so manage our silverware as to pluck out her eyes, that she be impaled in the center of the table, for a decoration. All these proposals are put into howling effect; we four swill and eat ourselves giddy while watching the divine spectacle of that charming little girl writhing and slowly expiring in hideous pain' (de Sade 1991, p. 740). Whilst Krafft-Ebing (1901), writing at the beginning of the twentieth century, defined such individuals who celebrated and enjoyed child pornography as sexual psychopaths, it seems that the sexual liberals of the 1990s defend such works as a celebration of freedom.

Prescribing racial and sexual hatred

Pornography is also a powerful medium of communication, propaganda and aculturisation, defining and legitimating the subjection of women and children to men, institutionalising male supremacy, eroticising male domination. In the communication of sexual and violent scenarios, the subordination and insult of all women and children is legitimated and masculinity is equated with sexual violence. Helen Longino (1980, p. 40) defines pornography as, '. . . verbal or pictorial material; which represents or describes sexual behaviour that is degrading and abusive to one or more of the participants in such a way as to endorse the degradation.'. Dworkin (1985, p. 15) explains, 'In the subordination of women, inequality itself is sexualised: made into the experience of sexual pleasure, essential to sexual desire'. Pornography provides a powerful script of an undesirable sexual socialisation, channelling male sexual arousal not around love, passion, nurturing, protecting, but through conflating sexual arousal and stimulation and orgasm with the subordination of women, starting with submission at one end of the continuum to violence at the other. The woman or child in the pornography is presented as compliant, a willing participant, or if unwilling then deserving of what is done to them, thereby diminishing men's responsibility, and the overt *mens rea* for any of the harm inflicted, providing men with a vocabulary of excuses and justifications which render their action legitimate through her assent. This is the message pornography communicates. Dworkin (1985, p. 9) says, 'The insult pornography offers, invariably, to sex is accomplished in the active subordination of women: the creation of a sexual dynamic in which the putting-down of women, the suppression of women, and ultimately the brutalization of women, is what sex is taken to be.'. The untruth contained within the message pornography communicates is as much an untruth as Freud's (1974, p. 116), conclusion that women are narcissistic, masochistic and passive. Jacques Lacan (1994, p. 149) by reversing the Freudian theory that unconsciousness precedes language, advocated instead the proposition that language precedes the unconscious, and that meaning is a product of differences between signs. Adapting this Lacanian formulation as a method for understanding the construction of pornography, then, at least in part, pornography precedes sexual relations, communicating largely to men a particular meaning for 'sexual relations' underpinned by the conflation of sex and violence and pleasure. These scenarios form part of the socially structured and contoured fantasy world which for some men is demanded in reality. As Lacan suggests (1994, p. 20),

> Before any experience, before any individual deduction, even before those collective experiences that may be related only to social needs are inscribed in it, something organizes this field, inscribes its initial lines of force ... Before strictly human beings are established, certain relations have already been determined. They are taken from whatever nature may offer as supports, supports that are arranged in themes of opposition. Nature provides — I must use the word — signifiers, and these signifiers organize human relations in a creative way, providing them with structures and shaping them.

'The symbolic is an order that exists prior to the individual subject. It is an order into which that subject must be inserted if he or she is to be able to speak and desire.' (Lacan, (1994) p. xxv.) Applying Lacanian insights to the problem of pornography, pornography is a metaphor for the enslavement, entrapment and captivity of women and children (Dworkin 1989, p. xxvii) and the sexual arousal which pornography promises its consumer is clearly culturally orchestrated and socially constructed.

The metaphor of inequality and power in pornography relies not only on sexist, but racist stereotypes implicit in pornography's narrative. Both hetero-sexual and homosexual pornography relies upon racism. The message is constant and unremitting. Black men are depicted as savage, sexually voracious and hypersexual. Black women and Asian women are portrayed as worthless and dispensable. Hernton (1970, p. 12), writes, '. . . coloured men and women become the objects onto which all kinds of sexual derangements of the culture, as well as those of individual whites, are projected.'. Franz Fanon's white psychiatric patients allegorise the white man's fear and envy of black men, 'One is no longer aware of the Negro, but only of a penis: the Negro is eclipsed. He is turned into a penis. He is a penis' (Hernton 1970, p. 120). In this same way black men are allegorised within pornography, eroticised as objects of our gaze, their hypersexuality is one which many black men, in internalising the stereotype, do not want to give up. Robert Mapplethorpe's controversial photographs of black male nudes, with their beautiful, sinewy, sensual bodies with penises of exaggerated size, serve to reinforce the power of that stereotype and the truth of black nubility (see Mercer 1991, p. 169). As Mercer and Julien (1988, p. 152) explain, 'The fetishistic figuration of the black male subject in Mapplethorpe's photography underscores the cultural politics of *ambivalence* which concerns the strange, uncharted and unknown landscape of the "political unconscious" of the West in which black bodies function as signs of radical otherness'. Stoltenberg (1991b, p. 260), recognises the racism and inequality underscoring the pretentiously erotic. 'There also exists a mass of pornography that targets gay men for homophobic violence because it contemptuously presents them as faggots, and a mass of pornography that targets black men for racist violence because it presents them as rapists.' The Mapplethorpe exhibition resulted in considerable controversy over arts fund-ing since the Mapplethorpe exhibition had been partly funded by the National Endowment for the Arts. Senator Jesse Helms proposed the drafting of new restrictions for such funding on the basis of harm, restricting 'material which denigrates, debases, or reviles a person, group, or class of citizens on the basis of race, creed, sex handicap, age or national origin.' (135 Congress Record 58806, daily ed., 26 July 1989). The Helms proposal was later dropped in favour of a return to the principle of a literary and artistic merit test (see Garvey 1993).

The recent prosecution in the UK of the publication *Black Masters White Slaves* under the Obscene Publications Act 1959, serves as an example of the prevalence of racist imagery in pornography. Pandering to the racist sexual stereotype, the black man in this magazine is presented as the dominator, eager to bugger the white man, and to commit any kind of sexual practice on the white male slaves. Black men are portrayed as the sexual masters, rampant, uncontrollable and sexually voracious. But it is not solely the allegorisation of the black man as sexually voracious, threatening, rampant, and uncontrolled that is the only problem within racist pornography. Fung (1991, p. 145), rather differently explores how gay pornography constructs orientals especially East and Southeast Asian peoples. Drawing on Rushton's (1982) work, Fung explores how both European explorers and missionaries identified the sexuality of certain races, where Asians are considered to have an undisciplined and dangerous libido as 'worthy' recipients of violence, where anal sex is about punishment power and domination. Fanon's discovery in psychiatry is immortalised in the allegory of pornography in which the black man is imprisoned.

Within heterosexual pornography the black man's sexuality is a threat to the inalienable sexual proprietorial right of the white man over white and black women. But the repercussions of this imagery have had direct consequences for broader civil liberties of black people and other races. The white man's fear of the black man's sexuality personified in penis size, has led directly to the legal restraints placed on the black man, throughout the world, such that laws have prohibited his sexual access to white women across the world sanctioning vilification against him.

Laws have sanctioned death penalties for black men who rape white women (US). In Papua, in 1926, the White Woman's Protection Ordinance Act sanctioned the death penalty for the attempted rape of a white woman (see Inglis 1975). And in 1912 a Saskatchewan law barred white women from employment in Chinese owned businesses (Fung 1991, p. 147). Atoki (1995) examines the racism implicit in the Crewe Circular operating from 1909 to 1934 which regulated sexual conduct of colonial officers with the natives. More recently this issue was politicised when William Horton, a black prisoner, whilst on weekend leave, raped a white woman which fuelled emotions that Dukakis the (US) Democratic candidate had gone soft on crime (Forna 1992, p. 103). We might also question why, whilst 74 per cent, 12 per cent and 14 per cent of the American population are Whites, Blacks and Hispanics respectively, of all those serving prison sentences 55.51 per cent White 38.02 per cent of those executed were Black, and 6.46 per cent Hispanic. As ever blacks are disproportionately represented in prison and in the number executed (*The Guardian*, 8 April 1995).

In heterosexual pornography, Black and Asian women are especially despised and violated and always deserve what is being perpetrated against them, because they are regarded as worthless (Gardner 1980, p. 105, Forna 1992, p. 102). Alice Walker powerfully encompasses the meaning of black women's bodies for abuse and pornography. 'For centuries the black woman has served as the primary pornography 'outlet' for white men in Europe and America. We need only think of the black women used as breeders, raped for the pleasure and profit of their owners.' (Walker A 1981, p. 42). Gilman explores the fetishistic obsession with Sarah Bartmann and how black women in slavery were used as sexual objects (see Gilman 1985 cited in Collins 1993, p. 99). 'It is no accident that racist biology, religious justifications for slavery and women's subordination, and other explanations for nineteenth-century racism and sexism arose during a period of profound political and economic change. There is a need for an Afrocentric analysis of the relationship of race to pornography.' The final step of sex and race hatred and vilification is expressed by the psychologist Gordon Allport (1954) who in identifying five stages of prejudice from prejudicial attitudes, avoidance, discrimination, attack and extermination asserts, 'It was Hitler's antilocution that led Germans to avoid their Jewish neighbours and erstwhile friends. This preparation made it easier to enact the Nuremburg laws of discrimination which, in turn, made the subsequent burning of synagogues and street attacks on Jews seem natural. The final step in the macabre progression was the ovens at Auschwitz'.

HARM IN PORNOGRAPHY

Pornography is not only a question of violence but also a question of harm. The consumption of pornography is harmful, the acts perpetrated on the victims within the pornography are harmful, the acts committed by those who ingest and reproduce the narrative in real life are harmful, as are the effects of the ubiquity of pornography on women's fear of sex crime, public safety and security. Recognition of the harm of pornography has been developed in the law of North America especially. There is a recent concern too that an over deterministic interpretation of harm may result in sex offenders claiming pornography as a legitimate defence of diminished responsibility (see Strossen 1993, Hunter 1992). The exposure to pornography as mitigation, has thus far failed in reducing sentence. In *Schiro* v *Clark* 963 F 2d 962, 971–73 (1992), counsel pleaded at trial that the defendant's capacity to appreciate the criminality of his conduct was substantially impaired as a result of mental disease or defect. He argued that the sexual sadist's extensive viewing of rape, pornography and snuff films rendered him unable to distinguish right from wrong. Rosen J rejected the argument, 'The result would be to tell Indiana that it can never ban pornography nor hold criminally responsible persons who are encouraged to commit violent acts because of pornography.' (p. 973).

Defenders of pornography, consumers, producers and sexual liberals, demand empirical proof (see Delgado and Stefanic 1992), of the alleged harm before considering the harm thesis. What then is the evidence of the 'demonstrable harm'? First, there is the generalised harm which is perpetrated on all women and children by the ubiquitous presence of pornography in our communities affecting our feeling of safety. That harm is demonstrated in and by the vile statements which pornography makes of primarily women and children but also of men within gay pornography. Secondly, harm is also done to women whose sense of security, safety, peace, well-being, comfort, dignity and worth is utterly demolished by the ubiquity of pornography. The consequence of the infiltration of pornography is to engender a feeling of despair, hopelessness and funereality. Thirdly, there is ample evidence of the harm demonstrated in the link between violent and pornographic films and material, and real violence committed by adults on women and children.

For some protagonists, zealous in rebuttal, the difficulty with measuring a direct monocausal relationship between pornography and crime means for them that it is impossible to talk of such a link. The *Attorney-General's Commission* (1986, p. 326) reached the conclusion, 'Substantial exposure to sexually violent materials as described here bears a causal relationship to anti-social acts of sexual violence and, for some sub-groups, possibly to unlawful acts of sexual violence.'. Opponents of legislative intervention have argued that there is no proof that pornography causes violence and therefore spend their energies attacking the epistemology and methodology of causation arguments. D'Amato (1990), one of the staunchest critics of the *Attorney-General's Commission Report*, D'Amato argues (p. 602) that the Commission's finding of causation amounts to correlation. 'In the first place, even if there is a correlation between viewing pornography and committing anti-social acts, there is also a correlation between viewing pornography and not committing anti-social acts.' In D'Amato's view (p. 604) the presentation of the Commission's findings has been political. 'Showing "causation" is vastly more important to those who would restrict freedom of expression than showing mere "correlation". Similarly, showing "probabilistic causation" is much stronger than showing "probabilistic correlation".' This might be so, but it does not weaken the proposition that if there is a correlation, between sexual violence and pornography, heed should be taken since it does not make the outcome any less real, specific or harmful.

In the UK some have argued that there is a correlation. In the UK there are the critics, like Cumberbatch, who, whilst perhaps not as strident in their criticism of the causality thesis, have talked about 'a measure of uncertainty' (Cumberbatch 1993). The *Attorney-General's Commission Report* (1986, p. 303), stated:

We refuse to truncate our consideration of the question of harm by defining harms in terms of possible government regulation. And we certainly reject the view that the only noticeable harm is one that causes physical or financial harm to identifiable individuals. An environment, physical, cultural, moral, or aesthetic, can be harmed, and so can a community, organization, or group be harmed independent of its identifiable harms to members of that community.... Issues of human dignity and human decency, no less real for their lack of scientific measurability, are for many of us central to our thinking about the question of harm. (See Bruce 1987.)

Simply, are we seeking an answer to the wrong question? 'Positivistic causality-linear, exclusive, unidirectional, has become the implicit standard of the validity of connection between pornography and harm' (MacKinnon 1985, p. 52). (It is to be noted that in other fields of human behaviour, in advertising for example, a causation between sales and advertising is assumed. In education we generally believe that education, its content and form, has an effect on development in its broadest sense. It is also to be noted that we are not resistant to supporting a hypothesis proposing that there is a relationship between the family and crime etc. Indeed, it is widely accepted in a wide range of circumstances that there is a causation, or at the very least a correlation, between a and b in the absence of empirical proof. Interestingly in the area of pornography there is a steadfast resistance to applying this kind of reasoning and to entertain the belief that pornography causes harm, in the absence of quantitative empirical proof).

Recognising the harm

North American and UK courts, whilst wary of lending support to the causation argument, have, in obscenity trials as well as in trials of sexual offences, acceded to the correlation hypothesis. In *Miller* v *California* 37 L Ed 2d 419 (1973), it was held that in determining whether something was obscene or not the court had the right to assume that there was a causal connection between pornography and crime or other anti social behaviour. In *Paris Adult Theatre I et al* v *Slaton* 37 L Ed 2d 446 (1973), the court said that, 'Even though there is no conclusive proof of a connection between antisocial behaviour and obscene material, a state legislature may reasonably determine that such a connection does or might exist, and may legitimately act on such a conclusion to protect the social interest in order and morality.' (p. 449). Burger CJ, in delivering the opinion of the court, said:

> ... it is argued, there are no scientific data which conclusively demonstrate that exposure to obscene material adversely affects men and women or their society. It is urged on behalf of the petitioners that, absent such a demonstration, any kind of state regulation is 'impermissible'. We reject this argument. ... Although there is no conclusive proof of a connection between antisocial behaviour and obscene material, the legislature of Georgia could quite reasonably determine that such a connection does or might exist. ... If we accept the unprovable assumption that a complete education requires certain books ... and the well nigh universal belief that good books, plays, and art lift the spirit, improve the mind, enrich the human personality, and develop character, can we say that a state legislature may not act on the corollary assumption that commerce in obscene books, or public exhibitions focused on obscene conduct, have a tendency to exert a corrupting and debasing impact leading to antisocial behaviour? ... The sum of experience, including that of the past two decades, affords an ample basis for legislatures to conclude that a sensitive, key relationship of human existence, central to family life, community welfare, and the development of human personality, can be debased and distorted by crass commercial exploitation of sex. Nothing in the Constitution prohibits a State from reaching such a conclusion and acting on it legislatively simply because there is no conclusive evidence in empirical data.

In *Brandenburg* v *Ohio* 23 LEd 2d 430 (1969), however, where a leader of the Ku Klux Klan spoke at a rally, at which he said, 'Bury the niggers', and 'send Jews back to Israel', the court held that to regulate free speech, speech must go beyond the standard of mere advocacy and must amount to incitement to imminent lawless action. Indeed, the point raised by the Canadian Supreme Court in *Butler* 89 DLR (4th) 449 (1992), was whether Parliament was '... entitled to have a "reasoned apprehension of harm" resulting from the desensitization of individuals exposed to materials which depict violence, cruelty, and dehumanization in sexual relations' (p. 458).

The harm of pornography is not only in what it means, but what is done to those in the making of the pornography, and the use to which the pornography is put as if it were a sexual script for committing the crime itself. In sex offences committed against young children, often the taking of photographs of the sexual abuse and the use of pornography are linked with the perpetrating of the crime. As the police say of the link, 'What they [police and social workers] don't always realise is the evidential importance of child pornography. They look on it as evidence of another, quite separate crime without understanding that very often the pictures will have been taken by the abuser himself, and could be the best way of getting him convicted' (cited in Tate 1990, p. 249). In *Gale* (unreported 1987) (cited in *Wright* (1990) 90 Cr App R 325, 331) a stepfather had taken indecent photographs of his stepdaughter and had written porno-graphic fantasies about the sexual initiation of a girl by her father, claiming that the photographs were for artistic purposes. In *Attorney-General's Reference No. 1 of 1990 (John Cameron Atkinson)* (1990) 12 Cr App R (S) 245, the offender pleaded guilty to three counts of indecent assault on a male and one of taking an indecent photograph of a child. He had encouraged a boy of seven years in indecent acts in which, although not amounting to buggery, the boy was induced to remove his clothes and photographs were taken. In *Thompson* (unreported 1992) the defendant was charged with several counts of indecent assault on young males in residential care and of taking indecent photographs of them. In *Stevenson* (1992) 14 Cr App R (S) 22, the appellant was convicted of two offences of rape, five of indecent assault and one of taking indecent photographs. He had obtained employment as a nanny to small children through answering advertisements in *The Lady*. He had over a period of time assaulted young children from three to seven years and taken photographs with a sophisticated camera of the victims and himself committing the assault and rape. In a further case involving an eminent paediatrician (cited in Tate 1990, p. 257), the defendant was found guilty of procuring and distributing child pornography. When police searched the premises they found pictures of children in sexual acts, and pictures of men having sexual intercourse with very young girls, and indecent photographs concentrating on the genitalia. His barrister said the defendant had become 'hooked on child pornography'. He had commissioned others to photograph children and to one photographer he said, 'Very nice, but not quite enough crotch. Nice, but I think this would be ideal if she was dressed in the school girl costume and if she placed her hands beneath her thighs as if to help hold them apart' (see Tate 1990, p. 260). Sentencing him McCowan J said, 'This is a trade disgusting in itself, but the court also has to bear in mind that anyone playing a part in it is contributing to the corruption of children, and may well be causing adults to commit serious offences against children.'. Lord Lane, in reducing the sentence to six months, obviously did not share the view of the lower court. He said:

> The circumstances of the case are truly extraordinary in the literal meaning of that term, because the appellant is a man of the highest reputation in the medical world as a consultant paediatrician. One only has to glance at the great bundle of testimonials which are before the Court to realise that the

reputation has been hard won; a reputation enjoyed not only among the students and perhaps more importantly amongst the members of the public who may have been lucky enough to have his skills applied to their children.... An investigation carried out by the police ... revealed that in his professional office was contained a large quantity of pornographic indecent photographs of young girls. It emerged that for reasons which it is hard to gauge this man over the years had amassed a huge and minutely documented and indexed collection of this type of photograph. The possession needs no further explanation. The distribution was on a very limited scale. It is not inappropriate, perhaps, in view of the puerility of this type of behaviour, to compare it rather to a schoolboy collecting cigarette cards in olden times, because the duplicates were handed on to other adults — three or four of them only — who were likewise minded to indulge in this sort of puerility. (See Tate 1990, p. 261)

One of the investigating officers said, 'We couldn't believe it, we just couldn't believe it. He had been buying and dealing for years. He had refused to talk about his contacts here or abroad. He had to be rated a risk, a dangerous man. Yet the Lord Chief Justice of England opened the gate and waved him goodbye. It was an absolutely appalling decision.' (Tate, p. 261). In *Holloway* (1982) 4 Cr App R (S) 128, 131, in dismissing an appeal against a six month sentence of imprisonment for an offence under the Obscene Publications Act, Lawton LJ said:

In the course of our judicial experience we have dealt with cases of sexual offenders who have undoubtedly been incited to engage in criminal activity and criminal conduct by pornographic material ... pornography, and particularly the type known as 'hard porn', in our experience ... has a corrupting influence. Those of us who have had to deal with matrimonial cases in the Family Division ... know that sometimes, matrimonial troubles are started by husbands who have been reading or seeing this kind of material and try to introduce in the matrimonial bed what they have read or seen. There is an evil in this kind of pornography. It is an evil which in our opinion has to be stopped.

US case law similarly reflects the influence the correlation argument has had on legal argument and opinion in trials of sex offenders. In *Hoggard* v *State* Ark, 640 SW 2d 102 (1982), Cert. denied, 460 US 1022 (1983), the appellant was convicted of the rape of a six year old boy. The victim alleged that on visits to the appellant's apartment he had been shown pictures of homosexual acts and asked to do likewise. The child alleged fondling and also said that the appellant had put the child's penis into his mouth. On appeal the appellant's case was that evidence of possession of pornographic material was wrongly admitted. The court held:

We readily agree that the material was prejudicial It could hardly be otherwise. But the argument that its probative value was lacking fades under scrutiny. This pornography and the offences being tried had a clear correlation: the pornography depicted deviate sexual acts by young males and the crime charged was deviate sexual acts of a forty two year old man and a six year old boy. More importantly, the pornography was used as the instrument by which the crime itself was solicited — the child was encouraged to look at the pictures and then encouraged to engage in it. The value of the evidence as proof of the crime is obvious. (Cited in Mackinnon 1985, p. 46.)

In *State* v *Herberg* Minn, 324 NW 2d 346 (1982), (see Mackinnon 1985, p. 50), where the appellant had tortured his 14 year old female victim (including cutting her vagina and fingers, gagging, rape, choking, forcing her to ingest excrement and urine), books of sadism and torture were found in his possession. The Minnesota Supreme Court said, 'It appears that in committing these various acts, (*sic*) defendant was giving life to some stories he had read in various pornographic books. These books, which were seized from the defendant following his arrest, bear titles such as *Violent Stories of Kinky Humiliation, Violent Stories of Dominance and Submission, Bizarre Sex Crimes: Shamed Victims,* and *Watersports Fetish: Enemas and Golden Showers.*' Further in *Memoirs* v *Massachusetts* 16 L Ed 2d 1 (1967), Douglas J, concurring, said, 'We agree that the mere possession of pornographic or sexually oriented literature does not show an intention or propensity to violate the law ... However, where there is evidence of the use of such pictures in connection with the perpetration of the crime charged, then in our opinion such pictures become relevant and are admissible.'. The court also stated, 'Some rapes are performed by men with paperback books in their pockets'. In *Qualle* v *State* Alaska App, 652 P 2d 481, 483, (1982), various acts were performed on a child while photographs were taken. In this case the father tried to sell sexually explicit films of his own daughter. In *State* v *Natzke* 544, P 2d 1121, 1123 (1976) where the appellant used pornography to persuade his own daughter that raping her was normal and 'everybody does it', the court acceded '... judges cannot gear the literary diet of an entire nation to whatever tepid stuff is incapable of triggering the most demented mind'.

WHAT SHOULD LAW DO?

It might be asked, but what has all this got to do with law? Or, what can the law do, if anything, about all this? If it is to be argued that the law has some role to play in the regulation of pornography, we must be clear about the law's object of regulation and about the most appropriate object for regulation. These matters can only be clarified if we know what is happening in the pornography in order that a legal strategy can be argued and sustained. So, is all pornography exploitative and harmful, or is pornography, as the sexual liberals would prefer, about sex? Or is there a discrete domain within pornography that is truly erotic, non-violent, based on equality, that must be identified and separated from the harmful before arguments for prohibition can be proceeded with?

Whether pornography is defined as sex or violence, as a metaphor for inequality, as inequality, as harm or a basis for harm, determines the configuration of the legal regulation. Is the text to be protected as an expression of sexual freedom, or is the text to be regulated as a promulgation of violence and inequality? If the answer is that the text is primarily sexual then the debate becomes a matter of privacy, choice and individual freedom. Pornography is defended in the US by traditional liberal legal theorists (see the dissenting judgments of Marshall J, Stewart and Brennan JJ, in *Paris* (1973) above, p. 467 and *Miller* (1973) above, p. 444 who base their arguments on the classic liberal thesis embraced in American jurisprudence in the philosophy of Holmes J, and espoused in *Abrams* v *United States* 250 US 616, 630 (1919), where the 'free market place' is the constitutional foundation of free speech. In England and Wales, in consideration of how far the law should regulate inalienable rights, this question was taken up by Professor Hart and Lord Devlin in 1960s. Lord Devlin argued for regulation when intolerance, indignation or disgust flowed from the expression of any material or conduct. His argument was informed, by the same premise that underpinned the deliberations of the Wolfenden Committee's *Report on Homosexuality and Prostitution* (1957), in consideration of homosexual behaviour between consenting adults in private, that it should no longer be a criminal offence, on the ground that such offences were within 'a realm of private morality and immorality which is, in brief and crude terms, not the law's business' (1957, p. 24). Professor Hart argued that suppression could only be justified in the presence of evident harms. Liberal moralists are not concerned with the inherent nature or content of the material but are more concerned with the harm flowing from its suppression. They argue that pornography is exclusively about private morality and not public harm, and so is not the law's business. They are concerned with the balance of what they regard as competing harms, as if we were in some way on a level playing field.

The spirit of this staunch defence of freedom is contained within the First Amendment of the US Constitution. Yet, the First Amendment does not protect pornography, because following *Roth* v *United States* 354 US 476; 1 L Ed 2d 1498 (1957), pornography is not held to be within the area of constitutionally protected speech and hence the obscenity statutes were held not to violate the free speech guarantees of the First or Fourteenth Amendment. In *Roth* the defendant's conviction was affirmed, and an appeal was made to the US Supreme Court to consider whether the statute was unconstitutional and violated the First Amendment guarantees to speech. The court considered, 'whether obscenity is utterance within the area of protected speech', concluding that obscenity was not protected speech, and that the First Amendment was not intended to protect every utterance. Yet there is a conflict of interests between freedom of men to consume what they will in the name of choice and of privacy, and the freedom contained in the concept of equality which proceeds from the right of the powerless to protection from hatred and ridicule. On a number of levels and from several perspectives it is not simply a question of limiting the harm but also of being engaged in the positive promotion of good. This principle is found in Rawls, *A Theory of Justice* (1971). Such a theory provides the ideological foundation for the concept of equality given legal form in equality legislation. The basis of equality legislation seems twofold, to promote the rights of all individuals as a common good and to protect groups from the denial of equal treatment and the harms that flow from this. Yet, before the legislators are prepared to draft laws that intervene and interfere with absolute freedom, proof of harm is demanded. The debate over what is harm and whether it can be quantified or empirically measured, has provided a site of conflict for civil libertarians and feminists. Liberal feminists against censorship and the gay lobby subscribe to the classic liberal thesis. The dissenting judgment of Brennan J, in *Roth* resonates with a similar liberal argument.

Mahoney, a contemporary feminist critic, suggests that both these positions can be traced to a male defined concept of justice and individual rights, since each standpoint focuses on the rights of the individual whilst applying different standards to determine when the State is justified in infringing those rights (1984, p. 41). The principle expounded in the work of John Stuart Mill (1859, p. 13) that, 'the only purpose for which power can be rightfully exercised over any member of a civilised community, against his will, is to prevent harm to others . . .', has provided the philosophical rationale for legal intervention. The late Lord Devlin (1959), adopting the Millean thesis, argued that the law should intervene only when there was 'demonstrable harm'. The harm pornography does is specific, it is both physical, and it is ideological in the sense that it promotes the vilification of the powerless, primarily women and children.

Engaging with the law

How far the law should be employed in the regulation or prohibition of pornography, is a question which is a site of conflict between and within feminists and civil libertarians. Four responses to the problematic of legal intervention are identified. First, there are the feminist sceptics who are opposed to legal intervention on the basis that little, if anything, can be achieved. The law is masculinist and immutable and women's entry into the law, by placing a greater importance on female qualities, female experience or viewpoint, cannot bring about the holistic reconstruction that is required. Smart (1989), argues that feminists should avoid the 'siren call of the law'. Law is seen 'as maintaining male domination', 'a powerful conduit for the reproduction and transmission of the dominant ideology', 'a paradigm of maleness', and is 'a particularly potent source and badge of legitimacy, and site, and cloak of force' (MacKinnon 1989, p. 238, Anleu 1992, p. 423, Jackson 1992, p. 298, Lacey 1993). Accepting all these apparently insurmountable problems as both real and substantive, this position leads to a pragmatic surrender, it is unsatisfactory and nihilistic, resonating with the same objections as the responses of left idealists to the crime problem. Retreating from the law has been regarded as *de rigueur*. Secondly, there are those who are opposed to legal intervention on the basis that the same representations of women and children in pornography also exist outside pornography in popular culture, art, advertising and the media. Coward (1982, p. 19), is against such a prohibition on the ground that legislation would only be capable of addressing the extremes of representation: the iconography of women begins with female sexual pleasure through submission, ultimate passivity and death. Of course, Coward is right, but again without making practical interventions in and continuing to agitate around the site of law, the law is left untrammelled by the feminist critique to the vestiges of those who have owned it and continue uninterrupted to interpret and define it. Thirdly, anti-interventionists like, Feminists against Censorship (UK) and Feminist Anti Censorship Task Force (FACT) (US) (see Raymond 1992, MacKinnon 1990, p. 9 for a critique), the 'sexual liberals' so-called, are opposed to legal intervention, because in their view pornography is not offensive to women, nor is it threatening: in contradistinction, it is the bastion of their equality and freedom. Indeed it was FACT in the US who filed an *amicus curiae* brief in *American Booksellers* v *Hudnut* 771 F 2d 323, 327 (7th Cir 1985), against the Dworkin/MacKinnon ordinance, declaring it to be unconstitutional on gender equality grounds (see MacKinnon 1990, p. 11). Nan Hunter and Sylvia Law were joined, amongst others, by Betty Friedan, Kate Millett, Adrienne Rich and Susan Schecter. Feminists Against Censorship's objection to censorship is that it is antithetical to women (see Strossen 1993, Segal and McIntosh 1992, Rodgerson and Wilson 1991, Assister and Avedon 1993). Fourthly, there are the anti-pornography campaigners who, whilst opposed to the use of the criminal law in regulating pornography around obscenity and morality, are concerned to reconstitute the debate around sexual violence, harm and inequality legislation (see Dworkin 1989, MacKinnon 1985, 1994, Itzin 1992, Edwards 1991a, 1992a, McMurtrie 1996).

OBSCENITY LAWS: MORALITY ISSUES

In England and Wales, current legislative provisions regulating obscenity are formulated on the notion that pornography is a morality issue . Sexual liberals have regarded pornography laws as an abrogation of freedom, whilst feminists have acceded that pornography laws are ineffective and focus on the wrong object of concern, i.e., that of prurience and lewdness rather than harm. For a conviction under this legislation, the material on trial must be deemed likely to 'deprave and corrupt'. Some jurisdictions remain focally within this 'deprave and corrupt' definition of obscenity, e.g., the UK and the US, whilst Canada and Australia, through statutory interpretation or statute respectively, have reconstituted this test to embrace harm. The standard for obscenity in the US depends upon community standards. The US Supreme Court decision in *Roth* v *United States* (1957) (above), held that the test for obscenity is, '... whether to the average person, *applying contemporary community standards*, the dominant theme of the material taken as a whole appeals to prurient interest' (emphasis supplied), and adopting this test Brennan J affirmed the judgment. In Canada, an Act to amend the Criminal Code, SC 1959, c. 41. s. 11, provides a definition of obscenity whose emphasis encompasses harm. 'Any publication, a dominant characteristic of which in *undue exploitation of sex*, or of sex and any one or more of the following subjects, namely, crime, horror, cruelty and violence, shall be deemed to be obscene' (emphasis supplied). In 1962, in *R* v *Brodie* [1962] 32

DLR (2d) 507, the lynchpin of the legislation was 'undue exploitation of sex', where the court interpreted s. 3(2) of the Obscene and Indecent Publications Act 1901–1955 NSW, '... any publication or advertisement shall be deemed to be obscene if it unduly emphasizes matters of sex, crimes of violence, gross cruelty or horror'. But it was left to the judge to decide whether there was any 'undue exploitation'. Ritchie J asserted, '"undue exploitation" as employed in s. 150 (8) means undue having regard to the existing standards of decency in the community ...'. The principal feminist objections to *Roth* are directed at the construction of obscenity as something in the mind, rather than as a matter which can exert a negative influence in real life. The trial judge instructed the jury, 'The words "obscene, lewd, and lascivious" as used in the law, signify that form of immorality which has relation to sexual impurity and has a tendency to excite lustful thoughts'. The dissenting judgments of Douglas and Black were based on a selfsame construction of obscenity: '... that punishment is inflicted for thoughts provoked, not for overt acts nor anti-social conduct', in their view 'drastically curtailed First Amendment rights'. It is this misapprehension of what presents as the problem of obscenity that is at the basis of the feminist agenda and dialogue.

Australian courts, whilst not abandoning the 'deprave and corrupt' formula, also consider whether the material, 'by reason of the extent to which and the manner in which it deals with sexual matters, transgress[es] the generally accepted bounds of decency'; *Crowe* v *Graham* (1968) 121 CLR 375, 395 (1969–70). Many States have enacted statutory offences: for example the Police Offences Act 1958 (Vic), s. 164(1) makes it an offence to publish an obscene article, '... tending to deprave and corrupt persons whose minds are open to immoral influences; and (b) unduly emphasising matters of sex, crimes of violence, gross cruelty and horror.'.

Current legislation regulating pornographic material in the UK straddles several statutes. First, the Obscene Publications Act(s) 1959 and 1964 regulate the publication and distribution of obscene material, where a conviction depends upon the capacity of the material or article to 'deprave and corrupt,' a decision arrived at through the application of the subjective test. Secondly, the Customs Consolidation Act 1876, s. 42 and the Customs and Excise and Management Act 1979, s. 50(1)(b) empowers Customs and Excise to take action against importation. Until 1986 and the ruling in *Conegate Ltd* v *HM Customs and Excise* [1986] 1 CMLR 739, operated with a wider definition than that of 'indecent and obscene', again based on a subjective test. Following *Conegate*, in conformity with EC Treaty Article 36, it is no longer possible to apply a lower standard of indecency to imported goods, at variance with existing domestic standards of obscenity. Thirdly, the Post Office Act 1953, s. 11 regulates the sending of obscene material through the post: the standard is contained in the wider definition of 'indecent and/or obscene'. This creates a lower standard of obscenity; see *Stamford* [1972] 2 QB 391, *Kosmos* [1975] Crim LR 345, *Stanley* [1965] 2 QB 327. The test is objective, based on the potential of the material to 'offend against standards of propriety'. In addition, the Unsolicited Goods and Services Act 1971, s. 4 makes it an offence to send unsolicited mail through the post which depicts human sexual techniques.

Fourthly, obscenity offences relating to indecent photographs of children employ instead a test of 'indecency', as in the Protection of Children Act 1978, the Criminal Justice Act 1988, s. 160 and the relevant amendments contained within the Criminal Justice and Public Order Act 1994 (see Edwards 1995, Manchester 1995a).

Policing, publishing and distribution

The police, and especially the Obscene Publications Branch of the Metropolitan Police in London, are required to police the publishing and distribution of adult and child pornography and the possession of child pornography. While police forces outside London rely on their own specialist pornography squads, as in Greater Manchester and the West Midlands, or else tackle pornography as part of routine duties, operations often rely on close liaison with Customs and Excise in respect of importation offences. The British Government in recent months has claimed to strengthen the law in respect of pornography and child pornography. However, given the development of computer technology, any 'strengthening' of the law more accurately reflects the continual revisions which are required in order that law keeps pace with the latest methods in data transmission and communication. Police acting on information, or following a 'test purchase', apply to the court for the purposes of obtaining a warrant. Where a prosecution under the Obscene Publications Act is likely, powers under s. 3 provide for the authorisation of a warrant to search and seize, and similar powers are provided in s. 4 of the Protection of Children Act 1978. Section 5 provides for powers of forfeiture. In reaching a decision to grant such a warrant, magistrates must consider whether there are reasonable grounds for suspecting that articles are obscene. The test under the Protection of Children Act is whether indecent photographs (s. 4(2)) of children are more likely than not to be discovered. Under s. 3(3) of the Obscene Publications Act, which is a quasi-civil power, a magistrate may issue a warrant to search and seize, if he thinks the material is *prima facie* obscene. A warrant under s. 3 permits search and seizure of 'obscene' material and not sexually explicit material which is not obscene; *Darbo* v *DPP, The Times*, 11 July 1991. The Criminal Justice Act 1977, s. 25 provides that a warrant under s. 3 may not be issued except on information laid by or on behalf of the DPP or by a constable. These provisions followed the successful private forfeiture of the book *Last Exit to Brooklyn* by Hubert Selby; *Calder and Boyars Ltd.* [1968] 3 WLR 974.

Confiscated material is viewed by police who may recommend prosecution under s. 2 of the Obscene Publications Act to the Crown Prosecution Service, although a prosecution is a matter wholly for the CPS. A 'representative' sample of material is submitted, following *Crown Court at Snaresbrook* [1984] 79 Cr App R 184–190 (see Stone 1984). In this case, police selected sample items to be put forward as prosecution exhibits in each class. The appellant could, if he disagreed with this procedure, put forward two samples of his own. Challenges are rarely made against the police sample. Owing to the increasing difficulties of bringing successful prosecutions under s. 2 of the Obscene Publications Act, forfeiture proceedings are preferred.

Table 2: Items seized under s. 3 of the Obscene Publications Act 1959, by the Metropolitan Police

Year	Warrants executed	Items seized
1985	52	286,511
1986	46	560,047
1987	90	813,243
1988	101	655,119
1989	166	356,478
1990	142	120,821
1991	116	34,726
1992	90	39,697
1993	78	24,156

Source: *Hansard 5 March 1993 (1985–1990) and Metropolitan Police Obscene Publications Department (1991–1993)*

Importation and posting

The importation of pornography is regulated by the Customs and Excise Management Act 1979. Section 50(1)(b) makes it an offence improperly to import prohibited goods. The offence is triable either way. The procedure for stop and search of travellers must be based on reasonable suspicion and prosecutions follow under s. 170(1)(b) where the evidential requirement depends on, 'knowingly concerned in concealing goods with intent to avoid prohibition on importation'. The compound penalty is used in place of court proceedings where the penalty is £30 per video or seizure, and the person has one month to appeal. Until 1986 and the ruling of the European Court of Justice in *Conegate Ltd* v *Customs and Excise Commissioners*, British customs officers could apply the broader test of indecency to imported materials. *Conegate* revealed an anomaly between the test to be applied to imported goods from EC countries and those from non-EC countries imported direct or through EC countries. Customs and Excise took a policy decision to apply the *Conegate* ruling across the board to all imported material whatever the country of origin (see Robertson 1991, p. 205 and see *Henn* and *Darby* below).

Bow Street Metropolitan Stipendiary Magistrate, ex parte Noncyp Ltd [1989] 3 WLR 467, [1989] 1 CMLR 634, referred to in the chapter entitled, Gay Prohibition, Social Engineering and Rights, indicates that even given the *Conegate* ruling, the courts have not strictly adhered to its message where publications are concerned, thereby facilitating a distinction between types of goods. The case of *Noncyp* involved the importation of books. The Divisional Court held that there was no discrimination against importations under Article 36(2) EC and the public morality principle could be applied where a different standard was applied to the importation of homosexual books. Customs and Excise brought condemnation proceedings under the Customs and Excise Management Act 1979, s. 139. Noncyp responded, wanting to call a s. 4 public good defence, and sought judicial review of the magistrates' refusal on the ground that if publication of the books did not constitute an offence under the Obscene Publications 1959, then the prohibition of the importation contravened Article 30 EC and was not permitted under Article 36. The Divisional Court held that the prohibition on the importation of obscene articles imposed by s. 42 of the Customs Consolidation Act 1876 was permitted by Article 36 EC in so far as it related to articles in which there was no lawful trade in the United Kingdom. Imported articles which were obscene within the meaning of s. 1 of the 1959 Act were therefore liable to be forfeited under the 1979 Act if they were also obscene within the meaning of the 1876 Act. Of course what this meant was that Customs still preserved a dual system which took on a new guise in practice. If there was no public good defence in respect of importation, no challenge could be made to Customs' decision making and a lower standard of obscenity could be applied than the standard which would otherwise be applied.

Table 3: Customs and Excise seizures

Years	Commercial	Private	Preventive	Postal	Total
1989–90	7	436	2,380	4,067	6,890
1990–91	26	452	2,516	4,438	7,432
1992–93	18	133	2,784	4,311	7,246
		paedophile*			
1993–94	44	71	1,687	3,370	5,172

Source: Figures supplied to author by HM Customs and Excise, London
* Indicates a new system of classification from 1993–4.

Table 4: Customs and Excise prosecutions

Years	Prosecutions	Imprisoned
1989–90	98	11
1990–91	88	4
1992–93	48	1
1993–94	32	4

Source: Figures supplied to author by HM Customs and Excise, London

Table 5: Customs and Excise seizures by type

Year	Books	Magazines	Films	Videos	Other	Total
1989–90	696	18,677	583	7,399	4,983	32,338
1990–91	902	14,203	543	9,253	14,099	39,000
1992–93	690	8,417	49	9,727	25,884	44,767
1993–94	414	18,205	99	9,201	9,095	37,014

Source: Figures supplied to author by HM Customs and Excise, London

The Customs and Excise Management Act 1979 allows Customs and Excise to conduct their own prosecutions (see Tables 3, 4 and 5). Where there is paedophilic material this is followed by an investigation which results in a search and interviewing. This may result in a prosecution and/or a joint police operation. The sentencing powers of Customs and Excise are more onerous than those available under criminal law. For example, a conviction for publication of child pornography carries with it a penalty of three years, whilst the penalty for possession under the Criminal Justice Act 1988, s. 160, now amended by s. 86, Criminal Justice and Public Order Act 1994, is six months. The penalty available on indictment for importation under the Customs and Excise Management Act 1979, s. 50(1)(b) is a fine of any amount, or imprisonment for a term not exceeding seven years, or both. On summary conviction the penalty is a fine three times that of the value of the goods, or a term of imprisonment not exceeding six months, but for the importation of paedophilic material, the penalty can be up to seven years' imprisonment. An amendment to this provision will redefine obscene and indecent articles to ensure that both articles and goods include electronic signals made into pictures within the scope of import prohibition. The burden of proof under, s. 170(1) Customs and Excise Management Act 1979 is that the accused knowingly performed certain acts with intent to defraud or to evade a relevant prohibition or restriction. In *Stamford* [1972] 2 QB 391, the defendant was charged with sending postal packets containing copies of homosexual material. The defendant was refused leave to call evidence on the effect of the material on the recipients. This was a matter for the jury; the test to be applied was the 'technologised standards of propriety' and the character of the addressee was immaterial. In *Anderson* [1972] 1 QB 304, one of the counts related to sending articles through the post. The article in question was *Oz No. 28, School Kids Issue* which included drawings of cunnilingus, fellatio and sado-masochism. Lord Widgery CJ said, 'So far as the Post Office count is concerned there is no doubt in our judgment but that obscene in its context as an alternative to indecent has its ordinary or as it is sometimes called dictionary meaning' (p. 311).

Prosecuting pornography

Given the insuperable definitional problems arising from the meaning of deprave and corrupt, very little pornographic material is subject to prosecution, nothwithstanding the enormous expansion of the pornography market in recent years. Whilst the law is ambiguous as to the object of concern, feminists remain concerned that rather than put up a test case for prosecution, prosecutors would rather do nothing than risk an acquittal. Where a moving film is concerned, a prosecution requires the consent of the Director of Public Prosecutions (DPP), in accordance with s. 2(3A) of the Obscene Publications Act 1959. This prosecution policy derives authority from the Criminal Law Act 1977, s. 53. Where the prosecution of persons for child pornography is concerned, a certificate from the DPP is required before issuing proceedings (s. 1(3)). It is then *de jure* a matter for police to investigate and put the matter up to the CPS in the usual way. Yet, in all other cases involving pornography, *de facto*, police consult with the CPS prior to any investigation. As this is not required by law, it is a practice which challenges the very basis of the statute which deems obscenity exclusively a jury question. The argument in support of this practice is that its purpose is to ensure uniformity in prosecutorial approaches in all parts of the country. What makes pornography prosecution practice distinctive, is that in other criminal cases the police initiate proceedings and prosecutors enter the arena later. In all other cases decisions made against prosecution are recorded as cases 'discontinued', whilst pornography cases that do not proceed on advice from prosecutors are not officially recorded and therefore the exercise of discretion in this arena is not open for public scrutiny, comment or debate.

Conflict between police and prosecutors over the different evidential tests applied, has been made particularly transparent in the case of de Sade's *Juliette*, and Bret Ellis's *American Psycho*, and more recently, although a matter less well publicised, in the *Shakespeare* case (reported in the Home Affairs Committee report on *Computer Pornography* 1994, p. 2, para. 7). The Crown Prosecution Service, in consideration of a prosecution, applies the test of whether there is a 'realistic prospect of conviction'. Since the test of obscenity is subjective, based on the potential of the material to deprave and corrupt, what this jury or that may decide, is totally unknowable. Arguably, in pornography cases, the degree of uncertainty as to outcome is more precarious than in other criminal prosecutions where evidence depends on proof of *actus reus*, and *mens rea*. Once the first hurdle of the realistic prospect of conviction has been crossed, the second consideration is whether a prosecution is in the public interest. Decisions not to prosecute continue to fuel concern over the ineffectiveness of obscenity laws, and over a prosecution service whose current practice appears to be evidence of running only with the winners. Figures for males proceeded against in 1994 in the Crown Court and in the magistrates' courts are presented in Table 6, indicating a decline over 1984 when there were 583 males proceeded against (see Table 8).

Table 6: Male defendants tried for obscenity offences

Year	Magistrates' courts			Crown Court		
	proceeded against	withdrawn *	found guilty	for trial	found guilty	acquitted
1990	212	56	98	67	57	10
1991	394	149	156	103	88	15
1992	259	57	145	101	69	28
1993	330	58	187	68	54	13
1994	346	45	219	100	69	28

Source: Criminal Statistics Supplementary Tables Vols. 1 and 2
* *Withdrawn includes: proceedings discontinued in accordance with s. 6, Magistrates' Courts Act 1980, charge withdrawn, charge dismissed.*

Rather than risk an acquittal in 1991, the CPS decided against prosecution of the publishers of de Sade's *Juliette*. The book details the torture and killing of hundreds of children, events which the author clearly celebrated. Moyra Bremner, who has conducted a content analysis of the book, found details of the torture and murder of over 2,000 victims under sixteen. This is the style of de Sade's writing:

> ... he secures her hands upon a butcher's block, embuggers her, and I cleave off her hands while he is operating: the blood is staunched, the stumps bandaged, immediately fucking uninterruptedly, the barbarian orders his victim to open her mouth and stick forth her tongue; I seize it with tongs, I sever it at the root; I gouge out the remaining eye — Noirceuil discharges — 'Good', says he, withdrawing and dressing the girl in a shift of sackcloth, 'We are now assured that she shall not write, that she shall be blind ..., that she shall never a word to any soul that lives' (p. 1183–1184) the victim is 14 years old. [De Sade claims] ... the more horror one enwraps pleasure in, the more charming pleasure becomes.

A decision against a prosecution was taken by the CPS in respect of the book *American Psycho*. This was Case 7 in my research sample and private correspondence from the CPS to me, dated 6 March 1992 read, 'I am of the opinion that there is insufficient evidence to provide a realistic prospect of conviction, taking into consideration any defence which may be raised'. In both these cases, the decision not to prosecute was taken having considered the possibility of a public good, s. 4, defence being invoked. Certainly there are many respected writers who consider that de Sade has made an important contribution and by association have made de Sade respectable. Angela Carter in *The Sadeian Woman* (1979, p. 27), writes, 'One of Sade's singularities is that he offers an absolutely sexualised view of the world, a sexualisation that permits everything, much as his atheism does and, since he is not a religious man but a political man, he treats the facts of female sexuality not as a moral dilemma but as a political reality.'. Norman Mailer (1991) writing on Ellis says, 'He has forced us to look at intolerable material, and so few novels try for that much anymore.'. In another case referred to the CPS, a prosecution was declined since in the CPS's opinion the material, even though 'obscene', was 'not strong enough' (Case 2 in my research sample). The recent prosecution demise may be the product of a disinclination on the part of the CPS to proceed, either by discontinuing cases, or by encouraging police to consult them prior to charging, thereby influencing police practice at the onset.

There is arguably a conflict between the police investigator's application of the *prima facie* test, and the prosecutor's preference for considering instead whether there is a 'realistic prospect of conviction'. The result is that the only material put up for trial is that which the CPS divines is likely to result in a conviction. Negotiating the prosecution of pornography in this 'shadow of the law' (see Mnookin and Kornhauser (1979, p. 950), ensures that the police pragmatist puts up for CPS consideration only those cases which he thinks prosecutors are likely to consider merit the instigation of proceedings. It is here, especially in the arena of the extra-legal adjudication on 'obscenity', that such an 'estop' amounts to a usurpation of the jury function, where the CPS becomes the self-appointed gatekeeper of the prosecutorial process. In the arena of computer pornography since 1 January 1991, '... the CPS Areas have dealt with 11 cases of computer pornography, in four of which no prosecution was advised. In three of those cases, the reason given for non-prosecution was insufficiency of evidence' Home Affairs Committee *Report on Computer Pornography*, 1994, p. 2), reflecting the disinclination of the CPS to prosecute in threshold cases. One of the justifications against prosecution of 'threshold' cases is the effect of an acquittal on the symbolic authority of the law itself and on the notoriety of the said publication in escalating sales. Following the *Lady Chatterley* trial the book sold over one million copies. But there is also the view that publicity following an obscenity acquittal would have the effect of galvanising a movement for change in the law as a result of wholesale recognition and realisation of its impotency to deal with the legislative purpose. Consider Lawton LJ who in *Waterfield* [1975] 2 All ER 40, in a case involving the importation of indecent material said (at, p. 44):

If the public learns through the press what kind of films some jurors are adjudging not to be indecent, it may say 'enough is enough'; but if it does not know, persons with a taste for pornography may suggest and convince some that obscurantist prosecuting authorities are trying to impose a form of film censorship which might have satisfied standards of sexual behaviour which have long been abandoned: a slide into public licentiousness may result.

The result is that obscenity and indecency are concepts constructed extra-judicially, outside the courts, neither by judges nor by jurors, but by those producing the pornography on the margins of prosecution (near porn), assisted by the growing ubiquity of 'near porn' in the popular press which lends further legitimacy to pornography and brings pornography into the mainstream popular culture.

Pleading

Contrary to popular belief, legal argument about what is pornographic and obscene takes place outside the courtroom between the Crown Prosecution Service and the police. Contrary to popular belief it is pornographers and not the jury or the magistrate who determine the 'threshold' of legal pornography. In the absence of any Crown Prosecution Service policy commitment to prosecute 'threshold' cases, i.e., pursuing only of cases where conviction is certain, pornographers *de facto* determine the boundary of legitimate porn. Not guilty pleas fall into one of two categories. The first category comprises cases where material is, or may be, on the threshold of illegitimacy. Such cases are likely to be dropped since the likelihood of an acquittal is strong. The second category comprises material where the chances of conviction are reasonable, if not high. Such cases proceed as 'not guilty' pleas where the defendant is likely to change the plea to one of 'guilty' immediately before trial (see Table 7). Uncertainty in the law provides a positive boon to the pornographer, who takes advantage of the uncertainty and pleads 'not guilty', 'giving it a run' so to speak.

Table 7: Convictions for possession of obscene material

Found Guilty	OPA		POCA		IDA	
Year	Mags	Crown	Mags	Crown	Mags	Crown
1990						
m	68	41	16	15	14	1
f	5	2	3	1	2	
o				2		
1991						
m	136	70	16	18	4	
f	5	5	3	2		
o	1	1				
1992						
m	122	45	17	22	5	2
f	1	3	2	3	1	
o	1					
1993						
m	167	35	17	19	3	
f	6	1		1		
o						

Source: Information supplied by kind permission of the Home Office, London

m = males,   f = females,   o = others
OPA = Obscene Publications Act 1959
POCA = Protection of Children Act 1978
IDA = Indecent Displays (Control) Act 1981

Table 8: Defendants prosecuted at magistrates' courts and found guilty

	1981	1982	1983	1984	1985	1986	1987	1988	1989	1990
Total for trial	347	282	491	583	275	129	121	158	125	174
Total guilty	211	234	370	429	226	126	93	130	96	116
Total sentenced	208	235	370	429	225	129	93	130	96	118
Abs disc.			2		1			3		
Cond. disc.	10	9	9	13	11	3	4	8	1	5
Fine	136	128	248	291	130	80	63	77	53	57
Prob. ord.			1		3	1		3	2	1
CSO	2	1	3	3	4	1	4	1	1	4
Prison										
Fully susp.	39	39	60	77	50	20	10	17	17	30
Imm cust.	21	56	50	42	25	15	10	18	19	19
Otherwise dealt with				3	1	9		3	3	2

Source: Hansard 13 July 1992, Vol 211, cols. 495–96

R v PORNOGRAPHY LAW

The criminal law is totally ineffective as a vehicle for the regulation of pornographic material. The major problems lie not only with the statutory definition but with the reluctance of judges to interpret statute and direct juries accordingly and the reliance on past case law which is anachronistic. In accordance with the Obscene Publications Act 1959, s. 1(1):

> ... an article shall be deemed to be obscene if its effect or (where the article comprises two or more distinct items) the effect of any one of its items is, if taken as a whole, such as to tend to deprave and corrupt persons who are likely, having regard to all the relevant circumstances, to read, see or hear the matter contained or embodied in it.

By the Criminal Law Act 1977, s. 53, cinematographic exhibitions were brought into the ambit of the 1959 and 1964 Obscene Publications Acts and the Broadcasting Act 1990, s. 162 extended those provisions to television broadcasting. The offence is that of publication of an obscene 'article'. The legislation is virtually unworkable given the ambiguity of the meaning of 'deprave and corrupt'. Additional problems have arisen because the definition of what constitutes an article has not been without uncertainty.

Statutory interpretation

The drafters of the 1959 Act envisaged that an obscene article might encompass the written word, a film, a book, a work of art, or a sculpture.

Section 1(2) provides: 'a person shall be deemed to have an article for publication for gain if with a view to such publication he has the article in his ownership, possession or control.'. '"Article" means any description of article containing or embodying matter to be read or looked at or both, any sound record, and any film or other record of a picture or pictures.' (s. 1(2)). In 1959, it could not have been envisaged that obscene articles could be created using computer technology and electronic signals. It has been necessary, therefore, to expand the definition of 'article' beyond that expressly provided for in the statute, so as to include videos within the definition (*Attorney-General's Reference (No. 5 of 1980)* [1981] 1 WLR 88), and also pornographic images produced by computer, i.e., computer disk or any other means of storage of information technologies (see *Dash* (1993) 15 Cr App R(S) 76). At the time of writing, possession of adult pornography on computer and downloading it is not an offence. The Crown Prosecution Service in evidence to the Home Affairs Committee on *Computer Pornography* (February 1994, para. 20, p. ix) said, '. . . we take the view that a computer disk is an article'. The opinion of the CPS notwithstanding, since the question of whether a computer disk is an 'article' for the purpose of the Act is a question which has never been tested by the courts, as defendants charged under the Act have pleaded guilty. The Home Affairs Committee recommends that s. 1(2) is amended to include the words, '. . . any items which store data for immediate or future retrieval' (para. 21, p. x). In respect of s. 1(3) the Home Affairs Committee suggested (at para. 23, p. x) an amendment to that part of the Act which deals with 'publishing':

> . . . in the case of an article containing or embodying matter to be looked at or a record, shows, plays or projects it to another, or, in the case of an article which stores data for immediate or future retrieval, transfers some or all of the information held on it to another article which stores data for immediate or future retrieval.

By 1994, these points were considered and a conviction was secured against Trevor Sharples following the making of indecent photographs of children using computer technology and storing the images on disk. Havering magistrates ruled that images of child pornography on computer disk were photographs and therefore came within the Obscene Publications Act and Protection of Children Act. The defendant accessed bulletin boards and downloaded (*Daily Mail*, 26 March 1994. The first case in which the OPA was applied to computer disks was in April 1992, see *The Guardian*, 25 April, 1992, p. 3.) There are, however, particular problems with how far the transmission of material can be regarded as a publication (see Manchester 1995b, p. 549).

For a successful conviction for publishing an obscene article under s. 2 of the 1959 Act, the article must fall within the definition of obscene as provided in s. 1(1):

> . . . an article shall be deemed to be obscene if its effect or (where the article comprises two or more distinct items) the effect of any one of its items is, if

taken as a whole, such as to tend to 'deprave and corrupt' persons who are likely having regard to all relevant circumstances, to read, see or hear the matter contained or embodied in it.

'Likely' readers or viewers lies at the heart of the test, not merely 'possible' readers or viewers (see *O'Sullivan* (1995) 1 Cr App R 455 (Blackstone's 1996 B19.26), where the ruling in *Calder and Boyars Ltd* [1968] 3 WLR 974 was considered, in respect of the interpretation of 'significant proportion' where a negligible number was in fact involved, although the court took the view that the absence of any direction on the number of persons did not amount to a misdirection).

This 'deprave and corrupt' test presents an obstacle to successful prosecutions. In dealing with both child pornography and violent pornography and with sexually explicit and arguably erotic materials, the particular and specific problems and harms of child pornography and violent pornography are assessed by and through this chameleon framework. MacKinnon writes:

> British obscenity law has centred its solicitude on the mind of the consumer, specifically on whether the materials have a tendency to 'deprave and corrupt' his morals. While one might well worry about what pornography does to those who use it, this test makes invisible those who are violated in making the materials, as well as those who are injured and subordinated by consumers acting on them. A substantive equality approach would make those harms visible (1994, p. xi).

Offences under this Act are triable either way. The maximum penalty on indictment is three years' imprisonment, a fine, or both and summarily six months' imprisonment, a fine not exceeding the statutory maximum, or both. In 1992, 209 and 76 defendants were proceeded against under the Obscene Publications Act in the magistrates' courts and Crown Court respectively (figures provided by Home Office for author).

The 'deprave and corrupt' formula is derived from the common law in a judgment of Cockburn CJ in *Hicklin* [1868] LR 3 QB 360, 371, concerning the publication, *The Confessional Unmasked*, which was held to be obscene: '... I think the test of obscenity is this, whether the tendency of the matter charged as obscenity is to deprave and corrupt those whose minds are open to such immoral influences, and in whose hands a publication of this sort may fall.'. Under the Obscene Publications Act, although still undefined, the test became transformed from a matter which could largely be assumed if the material was deemed to be obscene, to one which could only be decided on by the effect of the material alone. The phrase 'deprave and corrupt', defined neither in statute nor in the case law, has created enormous difficulties of interpretation. In *Penguin Books Ltd* [1961] Crim LR 176–180 (see Clark 1961a, b), applying a literal interpretation, Byrne J told the jury, '... to deprave means to make morally bad, to pervert, to debase, or corrupt morally. The words "to corrupt" mean to render morally unsound or rotten, to destroy the moral purity or chastity of, to pervert or ruin a good quality, to debase, to defile' (the *Lady*

Chatterley's Lover case Transcript 1961). Rogers J in *Calder and Boyars Ltd* [1968] 3 WLR 974, (the *Last Exit to Brooklyn* case) said, 'Those other vital words "tend to deprave and corrupt" really mean just what they say. You have heard several efforts to define them. "Tend" obviously means "have a tendency to" or "be inclined to". "Deprave" is defined in some dictionaries, as you have heard, as "to make morally bad; to pervert or corrupt morally . . ."' (p. 983). The Appeal Court in *Calder and Boyars* found no fault with this direction, although it allowed the appeal on other matters which related to the absence of a proper direction respecting the public good defence under s. 4. Lord Wilberforce in *Director of Public Prosecutions* v *Whyte and another* [1972] 3 All ER 12, where a husband and wife ran a bookshop and were charged with selling obscene articles for gain, found the phrase somewhat opaque and incapable of precise definition. Detailing the way in which the courts have dealt with the term, he said:

> What they have said is, first, that no definition of 'deprave and corrupt' can be provided (*R* v *Calder and Boyars Ltd*), though the words are meant to be strong and emphatic (see *Knuller (Publishing, Printing and Promotions) Ltd* v *Director of Public Prosecutions* per Lord Reid and Lord Simon of Glaisdale); secondly, that judges or juries must decide for or against a tendency to deprave and corrupt as a question of fact and must do so without expert, i.e., psychological or sociological or medical, advice (*R* v *Anderson*) (p. 19).

These cases are pretty useless in assisting the courts today in the task of statutory interpretation.

The effect of the material

In arriving at a decision on whether or not the article(s) in question are obscene the court must take into consideration factors which provide the context in which the articles 'on trial' are to be judged. The article must be taken as a whole, it must be considered in its context including the effect on the 'likely audience'. But what effects are the courts looking for; what effects are considered material? Judges in addressing this question have construed statute to include procurement of sexual fantasy, sexual arousal, the capacity to lead morally astray and criminal conduct. By contrast, physical illness, shock, distress and trauma, sleeplessness, and depression, that is effects of demonstrable harm to the person viewing the material and harm to society as a consequence, have been deemed immaterial, as they are indicative of aversion harm and not of a tendency to deprave which is the acid test. Let us consider what 'effects' the courts have had in mind and whom they have in mind as capable of being so affected. Lord Wilberforce, whilst he queried in *Whyte* (above) whether the effect might include imitative behaviour of a criminal kind, preferred the effect on the mind as of central relevance and the primary target. 'It is criminal conduct, general or sexual, that is feared (and we may note that the articles here treated of sadistic and violent behaviour) or departure from some code of morality, sexual or otherwise, and if so whose code, or from accepted or other beliefs, or the arousing of erotic desires "normal" or "abnormal", or as the justices have said "fantasies in the mind" ', concluding, '... influence on the mind is not merely within the law but is its primary target' (pp. 18, 19, 20). Lord Cross in *Whyte*, considered this point further, 'It is, I think, reasonable to suppose ... that the production of such fantasies would in some cases be accompanied or followed by masturbation' (p. 25).

In *Knuller (Publishing, Printing and Promotions) Ltd and others* v *Director of Public Prosecutions* [1972] 2 All ER 898, the House of Lords held that the word 'corrupt' was to 'lead morally astray'. Lord Simon said, 'Corrupt is a strong word. The Book of Common Prayer, following the Gospel, has "where rust and moth doth corrupt". The words "corrupt public morals" suggest conduct which a jury might find to be destructive to the very fabric of society'. Judges have not held the meaning of 'deprave and corrupt' to imply that the effect is one of imitative behaviour, although Rogers J in *Calder and Boyars*, did say that 'the essence is moral corruption' (p. 978). In *O'Sullivan* (1995) 1 Cr App R 455 (affirmed on appeal) it was said:

> It is not necessary for the prosecution to prove that anybody was depraved and corrupted by reading or seeing the article which is the subject of the charge. The expression 'deprave and corrupt' is directed to the effect of the mind, to those who might be exposed to the material. . . . The fact that the article in question is sold in premises frequented only by persons who are already depraved and who go there for the purpose of feeding their depravity, is not in itself sufficient to negative obscenity. . . . In having regard to all the relevant circumstances, it may or may not be your experience, and this is entirely a matter for you, that reading and viewing pornographic magazines and video recordings is not necessarily confined to the purchasers of these articles. They may be shown to others as a stimulus and spur to inducing a particular frame of mind, or inviting them to adopt a course of conduct similar to that kind illustrated by the material (p. 464).

Absolutely relative: the effect on whom

In assessing whether the material is obscene, the jury must consider the effect on the 'likely audience'. The test of obscenity is both relative and subjective. On the relative conception of obscenity, Lord Wilberforce in *Whyte* had this to say, 'Both the policy and the language of the Act have been plentifully criticised: the former we cannot question, and with the latter we must do our best. One thing at least is clear from this verbiage, that the Act has adopted a relative conception of obscenity. An article cannot be considered as obscene in itself: it can only be so in relation to its likely readers.' (p. 17). Kenneth Jones J in *Attorney-General's Reference (No. 2 of 1975)* [1976] 2 All ER 753, 757 (the *Last Tango in Paris* case), reiterated this principle of relative obscenity, 'There is no absolute test of obscenity. It can only be obscene, or deemed to be obscene, in relation to likely viewers of it'. Lord Pearson in *Whyte* disagreed, the meaning of 'obscene' was neither relative nor subjective, the obscene can be discerned by something inherent and by the purpose or intention of the material in question. 'The question whether an article is obscene depends not only on its inherent character but also on what is being or is to be done with it.'

The absence of any effect at all on those already depraved was a legal point persuasively argued in *Whyte*. The fact that young people were excluded from the sex bookshop in question was taken to mean that those entering the bookshop were already beyond being depraved and corrupted and therefore no effect on the likely audience could properly be adduced. The prosecution appealed to the House of Lords. Lord Wilberforce alluded to the obvious absurdity of this position. The Act, he said, '... could never have been intended to except from the legislative protection a large body of citizens merely because, in different degrees, they had previously been exposed, or exposed themselves, to the "obscene material"'. (p. 19). In assessing the likely effect 'on whom', the court has considered 'the target audience'. Clearly, in the case of material for sale in an adult bookshop prohibiting persons under 18, the likely audience cannot include under 18s and so the courts are not considering the effect on this age group of the material before them. Accessibility and availability of the material become, at least theoretically, key issues in this assessment of the target audience. Lord Wilberforce in *Whyte* took the view, 'In the case of a general shop, open to all and sundry, and offering all types of books, common sense suggests the conclusion that likely readers are a proportion of all such persons as normally resort to such shops ...' (p. 18). Consideration of accessibility and availability are also influenced by the price of the material, following the interpretation of 'all relevant circumstances' as per Byrne J in *Penguin Books*. When referring to the book *Lady Chatterley's Lover*, he said, '... 3/6d you might think would be putting this book within the grasp of a vast mass of the population', and therefore arguably within the definition of 'primary audience'. (Transcript).

However, it is to be noted that in practice this consideration has been lamely applied both in arriving at a decision of obscene and in the restriction of sale. Consider for example, the availability of 'soft pornography' to the eight year old child. Many high street newsagents display this material traditionally on the top shelf, although there is still nothing in law requiring them to do so. Soft porn magazines are stocked in such quantities today that they take up two shelves and in the smaller newsagent these top two shelves may well be at shoulder height of the eight year old. In this case children are very much drawn into the pool of the 'likely audience'. A strict application of this should make such magazines a suitable case for prosecution. Similarly, in a family bookstore, such as Dillons, it is to be expected that the family and, by definition, children are the target audience, situated as this chain store is in the high street shopping malls. And yet this bookshop stocked copies of *Juliette* and *American Psycho* at a child's shoulder height. In rebutting the proposition that young children are indeed the likely audience, it cannot be realistically claimed that they are unlikely to be able to afford to purchase these books at £10.95 and £8.95 respectively.

Obscenity in the public good

Denial of public good defence   The Obscene Publications Act 1959, s. 1, provides the author or maker of pornography with a defence, entitling the maker to adduce evidence that the article, once found obscene, is worthy of artistic, scientific or literary merit. 'A person shall not be convicted of an offence against section two of the Act, and an order for forfeiture shall not be made under the foregoing section, if it is proved that publication of the article in question is justified as being for the public good on the ground that it is in the interests of science, literature, art or learning, or of other objects of general concern.' Here, and only here, the opinion of experts may be canvassed to affirm or negate this public good claim. It cost the Crown £1,131.17s.3d. to bring the test case, *Penguin Books Ltd*, which involved much expert opinion on the literary merit. Byrne J (cited in Robertson 1979, p. 41), in the *Lady Chatterley* trial in his summing-up said, 'You must consider the book as a whole. The mere fact you are shocked and disgusted, the mere fact you hate the sight of the book does not solve the question.' The jury returned a 'not guilty' verdict. Section 4 might have ostensibly been an important provision, the purpose of which is to defend and protect works of literature where sexual explicitness is quintessential to the narrative, as in *Lady Chatterley*. There are few if any cases today where a public good defence is invoked, since such potential defences are diverted away from prosecution by the CPS making a decision against a prosecution (see de Sade's *Juliette* and Bret Ellis's *American Psycho*). In *Gibson and Sylveire* [1990] Crim LR 738, [1990] 91 Cr App R 341, where Sylveire made human foetuses into droplet earrings and Gibson put them on display in a private art gallery, as exhibit No. 9 'Human Earrings', a s. 4 defence was indicated. The defendants were charged instead with a common law offence of 'outraging public decency'. They appealed against conviction on the grounds that they had been denied a prosecution under the OPA and the defence that the work was in the public good. In trials of obscenity it has been a rule that the effect is a matter for the jury to consider. In *DPP* v *ABC Chewing Gum Ltd* [1968] 1 QB 159, an exception was made to this rule where in the cases of bubble gum battle cards, Lord Parker held that it was, 'perfectly proper to call a psychiatrist to say what the effect on the minds of children of different groups would be.' (p. 164). It was reiterated in *Anderson* [1972] 1 QB 304,that a defence must go to the public good and not to whether it is obscene since '... whether the article is obscene or not is a question exclusively in the hands of the jury ...' (p. 313). In *Noncyp* (above), Customs and Excise were able to evade a public good defence in cases of importation of pornographic books.

Porn as therapy   Those invoking the public good defence have used the *ejusdem generis* rule to advantage. Defenders of pornography frequently argue that the material has a social value in preventing excesses of behaviour and in providing a sexual outlet for men. In the *Ben's Books* trial, unreported, the defence put forward the argument that pornography was for the public good because it had a therapeutic value.

Counsel for defence   'This is a picture of a female in chains, tied up, and a naked man pointing a sword at the woman's genitals.'

Dr Richards 'This is for the public good because it produces a masturbatory situation. I would certainly prescribe it for a patient.'

Counsel 'Picture of a naked man with a cat of ninetails striking a woman on her genitals.'

Dr Richards 'This can stimulate a man. It has great therapeutic value.'

Counsel 'Girl, with distress in her face, arms manacled, and has cuts, she is tied up. A man with a bayonet is inflicting cuts.'

Dr Richards 'I have known patients who could benefit by masturbating on this.' (See Whitehouse 1993, p. 128.)

In *Staniforth* and *Jordan* [1976] 2 All ER 714; *DPP* v *Jordan* [1977] AC 699, the appellant was an owner of a newsagent's shop which contained 'hate pornography'. The defence sought to rely on s. 4, admitting evidence of the medically therapeutic value of obscene materials. The case of *Jordan* was referred to the House of Lords on a point of law of general public importance, '... whether on the true construction of section 4 of the Obscene Publications Act 1959 expert evidence is admissible in support of the defence under that section to the effect that pornographic material is psychologically beneficial to persons with certain sexual tendencies in that it relieves their sexual tensions and may divert them from anti-social activity.'. The House of Lords held that to argue that such material was 'medically therapeutic' (p. 712) was no defence. Lord Wilberforce said, 'In interpreting section 4 (1) the ejusdem generis rule should be applied ... In intellectual and artistic matters there is an objective code of merit. There are established values ... [on] which experts can express an opinion. They are matters of the mind and of sensibility. That category is far removed from mental and medical treatment.' (pp. 713, 719).

It has been argued that the capacity to deprave and corrupt becomes negated when the material depicted is so evil and revolting (an argument extended in discussions of *Juliette* to which I will return later). Shock and disgust has been deemed both highly relevant and irrelevant. On the one hand shock and disgust has been held not to solve the deprave and corrupt question; see Byrne J in *Penguin Books* (above) and Stable J in the trial of Stanley Kaufman's *The Philanderer*, i.e., *Martin Secker Warburg Ltd and others* [1954] 1 WLR 1139. At the same time the shockability of the material has been crucial to rebutting any argument that the material is likely to deprave and corrupt. In *Calder and Boyars* (above), the book, depicting homosexuality, drug-taking and brutal violence, was said not to incite others but rather to act as a deterrent. Salmon LJ, echoing the sentiment of the defence, said, '... the only effect that it would produce on any but a minute lunatic fringe of readers would be horror, revulsion and pity ...'.

This argument was extended by the defence in the *Oz Magazine* trial, *Anderson* [1972] 1 QB 304, [1971] 3 All ER 1152, where Lord Widgery CJ, commenting on the status of the aversion argument, held: '... in this court counsel argued, and this court held rightly argued, that the failure of the learned judge to put what one might call the aversion argument was fatal to the retention of the conviction.' (p. 1160). The failure of the trial judge to put this aversion 'defence' before the jury in summing-up was the major ground for quashing the conviction. It seems that the aversion theory has often been put forward as a 'defence' under s. 1 and in addition has been extended as a reason for not prosecuting. Considering the latter point, the aversion theory was extended by the Attorney-General to the House of Commons in explaining his decision not to prosecute Norman Mailer's *The Naked and the Dead*. Again this was one of the considerations the DPP took into account when deciding not to prosecute the publishers of *Juliette* and *American Psycho*, '. . . in the light of the defences that may be raised.' (private correspondence dated 6 March 1992). The aversion test has been described by Lord Denning as a 'piece of sophistry'; see *Commissioner of Police of the Metropolis, ex parte Blackburn and Another (No. 3)* [1973] 2 WLR 43, 48 where '. . . the test of obscenity is too restrictive, or it has been interpreted too narrowly'. Of the aversion argument, 'It is so plausible that the courts have held that, when raised by the defence, it must be put to the jury. If it is not put the conviction may be quashed.'.

The pornography industry's sales stand as a testimony to the fact that the aversion theory is indeed a piece of sophistry. It fails in my view because, whilst the average reader or reasonable man may be the test for deciding whether something is obscene, it is erroneous to apply this same test to determine whether or not the average reader will be averse to the content of a book, film or video. There are plenty of non-average, non-reasonable persons for whom much of this material is bought for pleasure rather than mere idle curiosity, and who are certainly not aversed. Moreover, it is precisely the non-average, non-reasonable man who is fast becoming the average norm. Geoffrey Robertson (1979, p. 53) in reference to *Mishkin v New York* 16 L Ed 2d 56 (1966), shows how the US Supreme Court pointed to the inherent fallacy of this argument; see Brennan J, 'Where the material is designed for and purely disseminated to a clearly-defined sexual group, rather than the public at large, the prurient-appeal requirement of the *Roth* test is satisfied if the dominant theme of the material taken as a whole appeals to the prurient interest in sex of members of that group.'.

The trouble with the Obscene Publications Act is that it is drafted with the object of regulating matters of morality, sexuality, prurient and lascivious conduct and not with the object of regulating the kind of graphic descriptions of extreme violence and torture detailed earlier. The 'deprave and corrupt' test was one which it was envisaged, would be capable of drawing a distinction between works of literary merit and works of smut, a distinction articulated by Stable J, when summing-up in *Secker Warburg* [1954] 1143:

I do not suppose there is a decent man or woman in this court who does not whole-heartedly believe that pornography, the filthy bawdy muck that is just filth for filth's sake, ought to be stamped out and suppressed. But in our desire for a healthy society, if we drive the criminal law too far, further than it ought to go, is there not a risk that there will be a revolt, a demand for change in the law, and that the pendulum may swing too far the other way and allow to creep in things that at the moment we can exclude and keep out?

Yet, the test of obscenity is assessed not on the intrinsic nature of the material (so as to avoid drawing lines which are considered by some impossible to draw), but on the subjective assessment of the likely effect of such material on a particular audience (the subjective test). Currently, the written word which, in the case of *Juliette*, involves the dismemberment of women, hideous torture of children whose orifices and bodies become the receptacle of ejaculation and where details of pouring acid into a child's vagina while she is watched 'slowly expiring in hideous pain', and men are discharging in entrails, is detailed and repeated *ad infinitum*. *American Psycho* similarly glorifies and luxuriates in the killing of women where heads are sawn off and tongues cut out whilst masturbated over in revelry. What possible defence is there to raise? And if there is such a defence, then the law has facilitated one and the law promotes the intrinsic harm contained within these books. What these decisions raise is first the question of what, indeed if anything, in the written word, would be considered prosecutable. Secondly, they highlight a major lacuna in current legislation respecting the protection of children: whilst the possession of an indecent photograph of a child is a criminal offence, it is apparent that any act of murder, torture or sexual crime recorded and detailed in the written word is no offence at all (Edwards 1992a).

PROTECTION OF CHILDREN: PUBLIC HARM

When child pornography is considered it is much more difficult to sustain the arguments of freedom, choice and privacy and much more difficult to ignore the harm. The public policy concern and legal emphasis moves from protecting the rights of the consumer to a concern with the rights of the child within the pornography and the right of all children to security and protection etc. This endeavour is reflected throughout several jurisdictions at the level of statute although not all jurisdictions provide expressly for harm within statute. In the US the Child Protection Act 1984, s. 2 states, 'The Congress finds that (1) child pornography has developed into a highly organized, multi-million dollar industry which operates on a nationwide scale; (2) thousands of children including large numbers of runaway and homeless youth are exploited in the production and distribution of pornographic materials; and (3) the use of children as subjects of pornographic materials is harmful to the physiological, emotional, and mental health of the individual child and to society.'. Some States, in addition, have criminalised possession of child pornography, and attempts to challenge this on the basis of the First Amendment rights have been rejected. In *Osborne* v *Ohio* 110 S Ct 1691; 110 L Ed 2d 285 (1990), the defendant was charged with violating a State statute protecting a minor. Osborne's contention was that the First Amendment prohibited the State from proscribing the private possession of child pornography. This was an argument which the court rejected, Brennan J, Marshall J and Steven J dissenting on the grounds that the statute, as construed by Ohio's Supreme Court, was fatally overbroad and vague.

In *New York* v *Ferber* 73 L Ed 2d 1113 (1982), the court upheld a New York statute prohibiting the use of children in 'sexual performances' on the grounds of (1) the special state interest in protecting minors, (2) the recognised relationship between the production and distribution of child pornography and child sexual abuse. Paul Ferber was arrested for selling two homosexual child pornography films depicting boys masturbating, to police officers acting undercover. His appeal was allowed on the grounds that the sale or distribution of such material could not be prohibited unless it was legally obscene. The US Supreme Court in a ruling by White J overruled the appeal ruling and reinstated the New York State Law, 'The prevention of sexual exploitation and abuse of children constitutes a government objective of surpassing importance. It has been found that sexually exploited children are unable to develop healthy, affectionate relationships in later life, have sexual dysfunctions and have a tendency to become sexual abusers as adults.' Child pornography, said the Supreme Court, was outside the protection of the First Amendment and the Court recognised that it was necessary to safeguard the psychological and physical well being of a minor and that the distribution of photographs depicting sexual activity by juveniles was intrinsically related to the sexual abuse of children.

The Protection of Children Act 1978

In England and Wales, as in the US, there is a significant shift in the attitude to pornography where minors are concerned. The matter is no longer a morals issue but a question of harm. The test is no longer concerned with the effect of the material but the nature of the material itself. The Protection of Children Act 1978, regulates the taking, distribution and showing of 'indecent photographs'. Section 7 provides:

(2)   References to an indecent photograph include an indecent film, a copy of an indecent photograph or film, and an indecent photograph comprised in a film.   (3)   Photographs (including those comprised in a film) shall, if they show children and are indecent, be treated for all purposes of this Act as indecent photographs of children.   (4)   References to a photograph include the negative as well as the positive version.   (5)   'Film' includes any form of video-recording.

Section 1(1) provides:

It is an offence for a person (a) to take, or permit to be taken, any indecent photograph of a child (meaning in this Act a person under the age of 16); or (b) to distribute or show such indecent photographs; or (c) to have in his possession such indecent photographs, with a view to their being distributed or shown by himself or others; or (d) to publish or cause to be published any advertisement likely to be understood as conveying that the advertiser distributes or shows such indecent photographs, or intends to do so.

Section 2(3) provides, 'In proceedings under this Act a person is to be taken as having been a child at any material time if it appears from the evidence as a whole that he was then under the age of 16.'. The Act prevents the exploitation of children by making indecent photographs of them illegal; and penalises the distribution, showing and advertisement of such indecent photographs (s. 1(1)(a)–(d); amended by s. 160(1) of the Criminal Justice Act 1988, to make possession of an indecent photograph an offence (see Edwards 1995).

More recently, convictions have been secured against those possessing indecent photographs of children which have been stored on computer disk or tape. In *Jones* (1994) unreported 31 October, photographs were discovered on the defendant's computer at his place of work. He had used his computer to access various bulletin boards abroad. He pleaded guilty and was fined £100 on each count. So, what is the protection of children worth if the penalty compares with a minor road traffic offence? The maximum penalty for an offence under the Protection of Children Act is three years' imprisonment on indictment and on summary conviction six months' imprisonment and/or a fine. The maximum penalty for an offence under the Criminal Justice Act 1988, s. 160 is a fine, yet, I have not been able to find any cases brought under this section. In 1992, there were 41 and 23 prosecutions under the Protection of Children Act in the magistrates' courts and Crown Court respectively. As with obscenity, prosecutions have also declined over the years.

The primary purpose of the Act is to address the problem of child pornography which might otherwise not be considered likely to satisfy the 'deprave and corrupt' test of obscenity under the Obscene Publications Act, but nevertheless requires regulation. The problem was elucidated by Bridge LJ in respect of the publication of a book, *Boys are Boys Again*, containing 122 photographs of naked boys, in *Commissioners of Customs & Excise* v *Sun and Health Ltd* [1973], where he accepted that the publication was not obscene but was not innocent either. 'It is a series of photographs the great majority of which the male genitalia, sometimes in close up, are the focal point of the pictures ... they aim to be interesting pictures of boys' penises' (cited in Robertson 1979, p. 304). In deciding the matter juries must be satisfied of the 'indecency' of the photograph in order to sustain a conviction, and a finding of indecency is arrived at via an assessment of the photograph itself. It is for the prosecution to prove that the photograph is 'indecent'. This is to be decided by a jury on the basis not of the 'effect' of the material, as is the test of obscenity, but whether or not they consider the photograph itself 'indecent'. Once indecency has been determined, the exploitation of the child in the photograph is axiomatic. In deciding upon whether a photograph is indecent, the jury may take into account the age of the child (*Owen* [1988] 1 WLR 134). The Court of Appeal did not comment on the centrepiece of the prosecution argument, *inter alia* that the jury are entitled to have regard to all the circumstances:

> In our view, though we do not purport to lay down any particular construction of that subsection, it would be apt to prohibit a photograph of, let us say, a highly indecent act being carried on by adults in which children appeared, albeit the children themselves were not photographed in an

indecent manner. Their presence in a photograph which was indecent would fall within the ambit of subsection (3) (p. 138).

In *Graham-Kerr* [1988] 1 WLR 1098, where the defendant, a qualified swimming instructor, had taken a photograph of a naked seven year old male child at the swimming pool, the Court of Appeal rejected the suggestion that the correct approach was to look at 'all the circumstances' including the motive of the defendant, where the appellant had said that he derived sexual gratification from taking or looking at such photographs. The Court of Appeal rejected the approach of the trial judge at first instance who, in following *Court* [1988] 2 WLR 1071, where evidence of secret motive of a buttock fetish was admissible, ruled that the circumstances in which the photographs were taken was relevant and admissible and that the prosecution were entitled to adduce evidence of motive. The Court of Appeal in contradistinction asserted:

> The question, as it seems to us, is whether the photograph itself is indecent. Photographs, after all, may last a large number of years, pass from hand to hand and so on. In our view it is not possible to relate the question of whether or not a photograph is indecent with the original motivation of the person who took it. It may be that the original motivation was perfectly innocent subjectively regarded; but if the photograph is one which right-thinking people would regard as indecent, the motivation of the original taker, in our view, cannot be a relevant matter (p. 104).

The Court quashed the conviction on the basis that there was nothing inherently indecent in a nude photograph of a seven year old boy. However, the Court of Appeal went on to say that secret motive could be relevant and admissible in rebutting a defence under s. 1 (4) that the photographs were taken accidentally.

Where the indecent photograph or film is of sufficient 'seriousness' and likely to approximate to the test of 'obscenity', prosecutors have proceeded under the Obscene Publications Act. Police officers, however, are particularly anxious that child pornography, however serious, is prosecuted under the Protection of Children Act in order to enable a distinction to be drawn between the adult and the child pornographer. As Iain Donaldson, a former Head of the Obscene Publications Branch of the Metropolitan Police (now renamed the Paedophilia Unit), said, 'Part of the control we can put on paedophiles — and I say control because there is no cure — is publicity. That's why it's crucial to have a case recorded as one involving offences against children, not just general obscenity. The embarrassment and shame involved for the paedophile can help control his illness.' (quoted in Tate 1990, p. 234).

Protecting children: legal lacunae

The Protection of Children Act is restrictive in its application. First, its application is limited to a consideration of photographs. This means that the written word does not come within its ambit. Given the invincibility of the Obscene Publications Act and the reluctance to prosecute the publishers of

Juliette for what in essence was the description of and script for assault, torture and murder of children for sexual pleasure, one wonders if the Protection of Children Act had included the written work within its scope whether a prosecution would have followed. This lacuna has inspired pornographers to exploit the market of the written word. Secondly, in focusing on the content of the material itself and disavowing the relevance of secret motive, and other circumstances of relevance, child pornographers who film children in apparently innocent situations, where they are undressed, such as bathing, on the beach, swimming, etc. will evade prosecution (see *Graham-Kerr* (above). Indeed, this scenario presents an ongoing problem for police where, for example, a man in the course of his work has regular contact with children, e.g., as a Scout leader or as a teacher, and at the same time collects what he describes as naturist pictures of young children, but although the police may have other information on him, he will not be subject to prosecution unless the photographs are likely to be considered indecent by a jury. The indecency must be found in the pictures themselves, it is not to be derived from anything else that may be known about the man. The '*Graham-Kerr* effect' has resulted in the prosecution only of cases where the indecency is very clear and inherent in the photograph whilst the surrounding circumstances, however hugely circumstantial, are treated as irrelevant.

Until the amendments to the Protection of Children Act 1978 by the Criminal Justice and Public Order Act 1994 (the relevant sections came into force in February 1995), child pornographers were compiling indecent pseudo-photographs of children, without fear of prosecution. Section 84(3) adds a new subsection (7) to s. 7 of the 1978 Act: 'Pseudo-photograph' means 'an image, whether made by computer-graphics or otherwise howsoever, which appears to be a photograph'. Section 84(2)(a)(i) amends the Protection of Children Act 1978, s. 1(1)(a) by inserting after the word 'taken' the words 'or to make', thereby including the compilation of a photograph. Section 84(2)(a)(ii), inserts the words 'or pseudo-photograph' in s. 1(1)(a) of the 1978 Act and thus extends the word 'photograph' to allow for the prosecution of persons who compile and make indecent pseudo-photographs. Section 84(3) provides for modern computer technology by inserting words into s. 7(4) of the Protection of Children Act which allow for the regulation of 'data stored on a computer disc [sic] or by other electronic means which is capable of conversion into a photograph.'. 'Child', subject to subsection 8, means a person under 16 (s. 84(3) inserting subsection (6) into s. 7 of the 1978 Act), and new subsection (8) to s. 7 provides for liability, 'where the predominant impression conveyed is that the person shown is a child notwithstanding that some of the physical characteristics shown are those of an adult.'. However, it would appear that computer generated images, for example, those images in cartoon form, will not be embraced within the meaning of pseudo-photograph and so are arguably outside the Act (although may well fall within the revision to the Video Recordings Act 1984 which also covers computer games).

For the purposes of the Protection of Children Act, 'a photograph' includes a positive or a negative (s. 7 (4)) (see *Owen* [1988] 1 WLR 134). The ability to create indecent composite images or indecent pseudo-photographs of children using a computer paint package has meant that the pornographer can devise any image he wishes. In recent years advances in computer technology have enabled the creation of child pornography without actually involving any particular child. Computer software enables the compilation and production of child pornography by combining manipulated photographs of adult women and children, which involves transposing a young child's face onto the naked body of a woman assuming an indecent or obscene pose prior to the Criminal Justice and Public Order Act 1994 amendments discussed above'. Where such pseudo-photographs have become known to police, the Crown Prosecution Service has declined to prosecute the makers, distributors, or possessors of such images, on the basis that, '. . . there is considerable doubt whether a manipulated photograph is an indecent photograph of a child' for the purposes of s. 7(4), Protection of Children Act. In oral evidence to the Home Affairs Committee, *Computer Pornography*, the CPS with reference to a specific case said, '. . . we were unable to prosecute because it related to manipulated photographs' (page vii, para. 11, fn 15; page 22, para. 17). It remains a moot point whether in interpreting the Protection of Children Act 1978, s. 7(4), if the Crown Prosecution Service had given the court the opportunity to construe the statute, judges might have avoided this obvious absurdity and, in looking to the intention of the Act, construed the term 'photograph' to include 'pseudo-photograph' irrespective of the method of production. Yet again, this incident provides further evidence regarding the powers of the CPS in obscenity to dictate which cases are to proceed to prosecution cases, on the basis of their interpretation of statute and not that of judges. An indecent pseudo-photograph of an adult or a child would, however, be embraced by the wider ambit of the meaning of 'article' within the Obscene Publications Act. However, it is not necessarily the case that such pseudo-photographs would satisfy the rather different test of obscenity. As a consequence vast quantities of indecent pseudo-photographs evaded prosecution until the 1994 Act amendments.

Punishment: deterrence and existing penalties

Existing penalties are derisory. However extreme, violent or exploitative the material, the maximum penalty under the Obscene Publications Act is three years' imprisonment for a conviction on indictment and under the Protection of Children Act three years for a conviction on indictment. Part of the problem is that judges very often fail to understand the seriousness of the problem, as is illustrated already in Lord Lane's treatment of a paediatrician child pornographer. The imposition of fines as a penalty is largely ineffective as Lawton LJ in *Holloway* (1982) (above) acceded. 'Experience has shown . . . that fining these pornographers does not discourage them. Fines merely become an expense of the trade and are passed on to purchasers of the pornographic matter, so that prices go up and sales go on . . .' (p. 131).

Beyond control: gaping holes in the net

The advent of new technologies for the production and distribution of child and adult pornography means that current legislation is limited in its application and pornography in computerised form, is beyond control. Developments in new technologies, including computer bulletin boards which are accessed by modem, the abuse of data base facilities where educational CD-Rom disks have been corrupted via electronic mail, and computer clubs allowing for receipt of material from outside the UK are creating a more accessible and less detectable child and adult pornography market. New technologies allow anyone to produce child and adult pornography with a home computer, desk top publishing and a scanner and printer. Pseudo-images of child pornography are being compiled by paedophiles and passed around by the Internet. It is illegal but is difficult to 'police'. The problem of the recently emergent computer pornography is summarised by the Home Affairs Committee thus, 'Unlike magazines, photographs or video cassettes, pornographic images held on computer are easily copied without expensive or bulky equipment. The quality of the image, since it is in digital form, does not deteriorate during reproduction, no matter how many times copies are made. Furthermore, computer pornography can easily be passed on, either on small and anonymous disks, or over telephone lines, not just within the United Kingdom but also between countries and between continents.' (See Manchester 1995b.) Whilst there are measures, legal and policy, to censor the Internet, it is possible to get to other 'gateways' that are not patrolled. In the UK there have been several recent successful prosecutions for downloading material from the Internat. Christopher Sharpe pleaded guilty to two counts of possession of indecent images of children and was fined £9,000. Martin Crumpton was jailed for three months for possession of indecent photographs of children (*The Independent*, 5 January 1996).

In the US, government attempts to introduce new legislation designed to prohibit the transmission of indecent material are contained within the Telecommunications Act 1996). The anti-pornographers have supported these new measures but they have been opposed by sexual liberals including the American Civil Liberties Union (ACLU) who have filed a suit to challenge the indecency provisions of the Act on the grounds that it breaches the First Amendment fearing that it will be used to prohibit materials on abortion, sex education, art etc. And so regulation of the Internet now becomes the academic battleground for protection from harm versus freedom of speech. Ira Glasser of ACLU said the proposed measures 'place the free speech and privacy rights of all Internet users in permanent jeopardy'. In the UK, arguments of free speech and privacy are used to defend users and provides. (See Byassee 1995, Wright 1995.) The law remains unclear both in the US and in the UK as to whether providers of the service are liable for what users may access and the issue is yet to be tested in law. It would seem that the providers of the service are not liable for what its users may upload or download since they have no knowledge of what material is being carried.

Current restrictions placed on telecommunication in the UK under the Broadcasting Act 1990, which is supposed to abide by the standards of the Obscene Publications Act 1959, are currently being circumvented. Satellite broadcasting is now trying to get around the British censors by showing explicit sexual and anal intercourse and other acts said to be of a sexual nature by providing, in their view, the necessary censorship. Users who have not subscribed to this material because they wish to exercise freedom of choice will find that it is being thrust upon them by aggressive advertising which provides fifteen minute 'tasters' of the nightly intercourse movies by blotting out with a black dot the point of entry into the anus or vagina. This has allowed satellite channels to send obscenity and highly offensive material into homes where users have, by not subscribing to these channels, considered their home to be pornography free, and their children protected. Advertisers are determined to push their product: they impose upon those who do not seek it. One minute the unsuspecting users may be watching a chosen programme, the next minute pornography advertising is invading their living room.

The government has banned the sale of decoder cards and any advertising of TV Erotica in Britain but has done nothing to outlaw Rendezvous, the French channel. The government in the UK has set up an Inter-Departmental Committee to review the Obscene Publications Act 1959. It is to be hoped that they will take this problem on board.

Currently, the government is considering the introduction of the V chip to allow parents to exercise parental responsibility and determine the amount of violence and sex their children are watching. The government should take responsibility and not pass the buck onto parents. It has already been demonstrated in a society where women and children are abused in their own homes that parental responsibility cannot be exercised by abused mothers. Any support for this V chip proposal would mean that hard core pornography would be legitimated and governments would degenerate into nihilism.

There is no freedom of choice in the pornography state. The decision to say 'yes' to pornography has been taken. Pornography will be available as a matter of course, the only choice will be to resist: a *de facto* choice imposed against our will. Our choice will be to fight it in the sexual liberal pornography state.

FEMINISM: REFORMULATING PORNOGRAPHY LAW FROM DEPRAVITY TO HARM

North America

The response of feminism to the masculinist framing of pornography as a morality question, a question of personal choice, freedom and privacy, a question of fantasy (see dissenting judgments of Douglas J and Black J in *Roth* above), has been to construct pornography around the recognition of harm to women and children and devise new legislation to meet this standard. Attempts at law reform in jurisdictions other than the UK have been informed by the construction of pornography as harm and pornography as inequality (Dworkin 1989, MacKinnon 1985 *supra*). Article 6 of the *UN Convention on the Elimination of all Forms of Discrimination Against Women* states that: 'State parties shall take all appropriate measures, including legislation, to suppress all forms of traffic in women and exploitation of prostitution of women.'. The feminist analysis of pornography has been influential and has shifted the emphasis away from morality and obscenity reconstituting pornography as an issue of women's human rights. In Canada, and in the United States and in Australia, pornography is a specific form of sex discrimination and has been reconstructed around the question of rights. In Canada, Mahoney (1984) argues, 'Pornographic expression which causes harm to the social status and concrete interests of women negates and limits their equality rights, which ss. 15 and 28 affirm as fundamental values of Canadian society.' (See Mahoney 1992). In *Saskatchewan Human Rights Commission v Engineering Students Society* 5 CHRR 2074 (Sask. Human Rights Code Bd. of Inquiry 1984), it was held that the students' magazine had breached s. 14 of the Saskatchewan Human Rights Code because it interfered with women's rights to enjoy education, employment and security of the person, by being belittled and ridiculed, reconstructing pornography instead as 'the graphic sexually explicit subordination of women ... in words or pictures' (Indianapolis Ordinance sec 2 16–3 (v)).

Mackinnon argues,

> The fact that pornography, in a feminist view, furthers the idea of the sexual inferiority of women, does not make the pornography itself a political idea. That one can express the idea a practice embodies does not make that practice into an idea. Pornography is not an idea any more than segregation is an idea, although both institutionalise the idea of the inferiority of one group to another (1989, p. 121).

In the US in 1983, Andrea Dworkin and Catherine MacKinnon drafted an amendment to the Human Rights ordinance of the City of Minneapolis (see Spaulding 1989–90). Their objective was to deal with pornography under city civil rights legislation as discrimination against women. The ordinance did not regulate pornography, instead it recognised the harm and provided redress for those who had been harmed. Pornography was defined under the amendment as:

> ... the graphic sexually explicit subordination of women through pictures and/or words that also includes one of the following: (i) women are presented dehumanized as sexual objects, things, or commodities; or (ii) women are presented as sexual objects who enjoy pain or humiliation; or (iii) women are presented as sexual objects who experience sexual pleasure in being raped; or (iv) women are presented as sexual objects tied up or cut up or mutilated or bruised or physically hurt; or (v) women are presented in postures of submission, servility or display; or (vi) women's body parts — including but not limited to vaginas, breasts, and buttocks — are exhibited, such that women are reduced to those parts; or (vii) women are presented as whores by nature; or (viii) women are presented being penetrated by objects or animals; or (ix) women are presented in scenarios of degradation, injury, torture, shown as filthy or inferior, bleeding, bruised or hurt in a context that makes these conditions sexual. (MacKinnon 1985.)

The amendment provided four causes of action. First, anyone coerced into pornography could seek damages in tort and injunctive relief prohibiting the distribution of the photographs or films (see a discussion of such actions in Kirby 1994). Secondly, any person could sue for violation of a right not to have pornography forced upon him in 'any place of employment, in education, in a home, or in a public place'. Thirdly, a person could seek damages for injury directly caused by the pornography (see Cohen 1994, Pacillo 1994, Winkelman 1993). Finally, women could bring an action against anyone trafficking in pornography. The fact that few persons might take advantage of the ordinance and sue was less material than the fact that the ordinance reshaped the public perception of pornography. The Minneapolis City Council passed the ordinance in 1983 but it was vetoed by the Mayor; passed again by another city council and vetoed again by the same Mayor in 1984 on the basis that it was unconstitutional. A modified version of the ordinance was drafted in Indianapolis in 1984, this time the redrafting targeted only violent pornography, it too, was held unconstitutional (see *American Booksellers Association* v *Hudnut* 771 F 2d 323 (1986). The ordinance was taken up more broadly, but in 1988 in Bellingham, Washington, the city was sued by the ACLU (American Civil Liberties Union) in the Federal Court and the ordinance was found to be unconstitutional (see Dworkin 1989, p. xxxi).

There have also been developments in the law of tort in the US focusing on the harm done to those in the making of pornography (see *Ferber* 458 (US) 747 1982). Civil action for defamation has been utilised. In *Thoreson (Anneka Di Lorenzo)* 611 NE 2d 298 (1993), the plaintiff brought an action for damages against the defendants, Penthouse International. The cause of action was for sexual harassment by Bob Guccione who, it was found, utilised his employment relationship with her to coerce her to participate in sexual encounters to further Guccione's business interests. The plaintiff sought punitive and compensatory damages. The court held: '. . . the defendants used the plaintiff in furtherance of their business as if she were property owned by them. Although the plaintiff's employment enabled the defendants indirectly to profit from her physical appearance and acting abilities, it did not render her a commodity to be leased, sold, traded or exploited because of her womanhood.'. Thoreson was awarded four million dollars in punitive damages. In *Robinson* v *Jacksonville Shipyards* 760 F Supp 1486, US Dist (1991), the plaintiff brought an action in respect of offensive material in the work environment. The court ordered that the defendants cease and desist from the maintenance of a work environment that was hostile to women because of their sex. The plaintiff was granted the injunction sought and awarded nominal damages of one dollar.

In Canada, attempts to introduce anti-porn legislation have applied, as the appropriate test, the community standard of tolerance, and more recently have focused on the harms of pornography, representing a break with the moralism preceding it (see Attorney-General (Canada) 1985. *Report of the Special Committee on Pornography and Prostitution in Canada*, Vols. I and II. Canadian Government Publishing Centre). Feminist perceptions of pornography were instrumental in shaping decision making. In 1992, the Supreme Court of Canada was asked to interpret the constitutional validity of these provisions. In *Butler* 89 DLR 4th 449 the Supreme Court, in affirming the decision of the lower court in its statutory interpretation of the Criminal Code, s. 163(8) which stated that: 'any publication a dominant characteristic of which is the undue exploitation of sex, or of sex and any one or more of the following subjects, namely, crime, horror, cruelty and violence shall be deemed obscene', recognised that not all speech is equal, if some is the source of inequality itself. Thus pornography for the first time became reconstructed in the arena of equality and not in the area of prurient interest, public or sexual morality. The Court explained:

> ... degrading or dehumanizing materials place women (and sometimes men) in positions of subordination, servile submission or humiliation. They run against the principles of equality and dignity of all human beings ... [T]here is a substantial body of opinion that holds that the portrayal of persons being subjected to degrading or dehumanizing sexual treatment results in harm, particularly to women and therefore to society as a whole. (p. 479).

The test for deciding whether exploitation was undue is vested in the vicarious construct of 'community standards', 'respect for all members of society, and non-violence and equality in their relations with each other'. *Butler* represents an epistemological break in the conceptualisation of pornography (see Moon 1993, Mahoney 1992). The interpretation of *Butler* has led to some difficulties given that three tiers or categories of material are created: (1) explicit sex with violence, (2) explicit sex that is degrading and dehumanising, (3) explicit sex *per se* (per Sopinska J) (p. 471). *Butler* is not all that its judgment promised, since where explicit sex is under consideration, proof of social harm must be established (see McMurtrie 1996). The question of what is regarded as 'proof' of harm brings the debate full circle to the very problems raised at the beginning of this chapter.

Butler has been criticised by the gay lobby (see Sherman 1995, p. 690, Kendall 1993), who argue that feminism's reconstitution of pornography as gendered is detrimental to gay freedom. Sherman reports on the impact of Mahoney's approach. Mahoney said of the Legal Education and Action Fund Strategy, 'How did we do it? We showed them the porn — and among the seized videos were some horrifyingly violent and degrading gay movies. We made the point that the abused men in these films were being treated like women — and the judges got it' (Sherman, p. 690). Defining 'undue exploitation of sex' is problematic. It would appear that sex coupled with violence will satisfy this test, so will degrading or dehumanising sex, and explicit sex which includes children in its production. The problematic nature of the term 'degrading and dehumanising' is illustrated in the case of *R* v *Towne Cinema Theatres Ltd* (1985) 18 CCC 3d 193, 18 DLR (4th) 1, where what is defined as obscenity depends upon what is considered as acceptable to the community not merely, '... one's own ideas of what is tolerable'. The test in *Butler* is somewhat differently framed. The purpose of the provision is to prevent harm; it is not simply an attempt to vindicate conventional morality. Harm is defined by Sopinska J as something that '... predisposes persons to act in an anti-social manner as, for example, the physical or mental mistreatment of women by men' (p. 485). In defining the scope of the prohibition Sopinska

J uses language like harm, moral corruption, degradation, dehumanization. *Butler* may be acclaimed by feminists as moving the construction of pornography onward in the march towards the recognition of the harm it does to women and children, but it must also be acceded that the conservatism which drives this decision does not advance the cause. Criticism of *Butler* springs inevitably from the sexual liberals, but also from those who argue that its implications are censorial (see Cameron 1992, Moon 1993). For Moon, *Butler* merely gives a feminist gloss to a conservative enactment.

UK harm and certification

UK legislation continues to be predicated on morality. The Criminal Justice and Public Order Act 1994, makes some minor amendments to existing provisions but for the purpose of pornography makes no changes whatsoever to the existing ontological formulation of obscenity as a matter of morality. Police powers are extended by making offences under both the Protection of Children Act 1978 and the Obscene Publications Act 1959 serious arrestable offences (see s. 85 of the 1994 Act which amends s. 24(2), Police and Criminal Evidence Act 1984). Police officers can arrest without warrant which means that those arrested are denied the opportunity they had hitherto to contact other pornographers to warn them so that they could evade detection and prosecution.

The basis of the existing tests of obscenity and indecency remains intact, the test being the potential material has to deprave and corrupt. The recognition of harm is, however, for the first time given statutory authentication in respect of film certification and this represents a radical development in the construction of obscenity for this purpose. In this regard the construction of harm is broad and multifaceted. Harm to the viewer or consumer is recognised as resulting from the viewing of, amongst other subjects, violence and pornography. Harm is also recognised if certain albeit unspecified 'behaviour' arises from this viewing to society following as a result of viewing violent and pornographic films. The Criminal Justice and Public Order Act obliges the British Board of Film Classification (hereafter BBFC) to have 'special regard ... to any harm that may be caused to potential viewers, or through their behaviour, to society ...' (s. 89(2), potential viewers includes a child or a young person), and a list of new considerations is to be added to the existent scheme in s. 2(2) of the Video Recordings Act 1984 (s. 2(2), Video Recordings Act 1984 lists (i) human sexual activity; (ii) gross acts of violence; and (iii) human genital organs, urinary and excretory functions). Section 89 of the 1994 Act amends s. 2 of the Video Recordings Act 1984 to include further considerations in the classification of videos based on issues relating to the depiction of violence and criminal activity. In s. 2(2) a new paragraph to be inserted requires consideration of '(d) techniques likely to be useful in the commission of offences;' and after subs. 2 there is to be inserted the following: '(3) A video work is not an exempted work for those purposes if, to any significant extent, it depicts criminal activity which is likely to any significant extent to stimulate or encourage the commission of offences.'. Section 90 of the 1994 Act amends s. 4 of the Video Recordings Act and introduces the novel concept of 'harm'. The new s. 4A(1) provides:

The designated authority shall, in making any determination as to the suitability of a video work, have special regard (among the other relevant factors) to any harm that may be caused to potential viewers or, through their behaviour, to society by the manner in which the work deals with — (a) criminal behaviour; (b) illegal drugs; (c) violent behaviour or incidents; (d) horrific behaviour or incidents; or (e) human sexual activity.

(New section 4B allows for the retrospective review of works already classified as suitable, allowing for the re-issue of a different classification certificate or cancellation of any certificate.) Section 88 provides for an increase in maximum penalties where unclassified videos are supplied or are in possession for supply. This increase in penalties provides for the maximum penalty of up to two years' imprisonment and/or a fine not exceeding £20,000 for supply of unclassified videos on indictment.

The background to these new harm amendments and this new direction emerges from the opinion of psychologists in early 1994, who held that psychological harm was caused to children by viewing video violence. MP David Alton's original amendment (the new Clause 42 at the Report Stage in the House of Commons of the Criminal Justice and Public Order Bill (Hansard 12 April 1994) addressed this concern. The amendment, if carried, would have placed restrictions on the distribution and showing of videos likely to cause 'psychological harm' to children and/or likely to provide an 'inappropriate role model for children'. (Before clause 83 in s. 7(2) of the Video Recordings Act 1983/4 a New Clause 42 would have been inserted to amend the Video Recordings Act 1984 classification relating to certificates, to read: Supply and viewing of videos likely to harm children where the following words shall be inserted '(d) a statement that, either because it presents an inappropriate model for children, or because it is likely to cause psychological harm to a child, no video recording containing that work is to be supplied for private use, or viewed in any place to which children under the age of 18 are admitted.'). David Alton, in developing the harm argument, went further, referring to video nasties as a form of child abuse. His proposals were thought too draconian and unworkable and the amendment was subsequently withdrawn. The argument that children are at risk from video violence and pornography from then on was a matter recognised, and of concern. The Home Affairs Committee, in examining the effect of computer pornography, focused on 'the threat to the innocence and decency of our children posed by computer pornography' (page xv, para. 42), in investigating links between video violence and crime. Their report, Home Affairs Committee Fourth Report *Video Violence and Young Offenders* 1994, concluded that there is some evidence to support the common sense view that videos do have some corrupting influence on the young (page xi, para. 27).

The harm provisions in the Criminal Justice and Public Order Act 1994, amending the Video Recordings Act 1984, although somewhat modified from their original form, are already creating insuperable difficulties of interpretation. The concept of harm rests on the presumption that violent sexually explicit videos have the potential to harm young people in two ways, first harm can be done to young people by exposure to the material and secondly by their subsequent behaviour in society. The tepid application of these provisions has cast further doubt on their ability to curb harmful material: the film *Natural Born Killers* was granted a certificate despite the initial delay. In *Kent County Council* v *Multi Media Marketing (Canterbury) Ltd and Another, The Times,* 9 May 1995, in an appeal by the prosecution , it was ruled that human sexual activity for the purpose of s. 2(2) of the Video Recordings Act 1984 could be said to be designed to stimulate or encourage such activity even though it could not be regarded as hard core pornography or as offensive, in respect of erotic computer entertainment. The court held, overruling the justices, that provided the sequence was long enough to show continuing movement it could be properly be described as a moving picture. But, already it is clear that the new provisions are having little bite.

As I argued at the outset, what we define pornography to be, e.g., sex, violence or inequality, what we define as the object of concern, e.g., depravity, sexual morality or harm, has consequences for the framing of any attempts at legislative regulation. These very questions are currently being debated in Europe, following the ruling by the European Commission of Human Rights declaring admissible the application of *Laskey, Jaggard and Brown* against the decision of the House of Lords (discussed in detail in the chapter entitled, Gay Prohibition Social Engineering and Rights). As Kendall (1993) suggests, harm based research has thus far restricted its gaze to heterosexual pornography. Europe including the UK has yet to consider these questions, as the regulation of pornography is fast becoming obsolete and pornography is imposed upon us as 'post popular culture'. Itzin writes, 'pornography plays an important part in contributing to sexual violence against women and to sex discrimination and sexual inequality' (1992, p. 1). Her work and that of a group called *Campaign Against Pornography and Censorship* represents one of the driving forces in the UK behind efforts to reconstruct obscenity around the issues of sexual inequality using the Race Relations Act as a model. Already, however, since much pornography depends on using black and Asian men and women and relies on racist imagery, in theory the current anti-racist legislation in the civil arena should provide immediate redress. The Public Order Act 1986, s. 19, provides, '(1) A person who publishes or distributes written material which is threatening, abusive or insulting is guilty of an offence if— (a) he intends thereby to stir up racial hatred, or (b) having regard to all the circumstances racial hatred is likely to be stirred up thereby' (see Blackstone's 1996 B11.135–B11.145). Under s. 23(1):

A person who has in his possession written material which is threatening, abusive or insulting, or a recording of visual images or sounds which are threatening, abusive or insulting, with a view to — (a) in the case of written material, its being displayed, published, distributed, or included in a programme service, whether by himself or another, or (b) in the case of a recording, its being distributed, shown, played, or included in a programme service, whether by himself or another, is guilty of an offence if he intends racial hatred to be stirred up thereby or, having regard to all the circumstan-ces, racial hatred is likely to be stirred up thereby.

The application of the provisions is immediately limited by the need to prove intent: s. 19(1)(a) (see Blackstone's 1996 B11.123). In a society which has assimilated as normal so much racist stereotyping (see Guillaumin 1995), it is difficult if not impossible to prove that anything racist was intended. The reality of the Act falls well short of its promise and this is reflected in the infinitesimal number of prosecutions under the Act and the impossibility of securing more than one or two convictions yearly. There were 62 prosecutions in 1992 and 71 in 1993 resulting in four convictions in 1992 and four convictions in 1993 (figures supplied by the Home Office Statistical Department).

However, in theory, any pornography which comes within this definition should be amenable to prosecution. The legislation has not yet been tested as to its appropriateness in dealing with pornography which whilst failing the 'deprave and corrupt' test under obscenity legislation might succeed under racial equality legislation. No doubt defence counsel would eagerly argue that since white, indigenous women are depicted daily in the same manner, racist inequality in the self same depiction of black women was thereby negated. So far the battle for recognition of pornography as a question of violence and harm not sex, and inequality not freedom, has only just begun.

Dworkin's civil measures have had arguably little measurable success (Cohen 1994, Pacillo 1994, Winkelman 1993, Whitaker 1993, Kirby 1994), having been struck down in most States as un-constitutional but reshaping and redefining the debate in a way which equates with women's perceptions and definitions is important in the process of social constructionism and legal deconstructionism. Eckersley is sceptical (1987, p. 175) 'Given feminism's minority position in the pornography debate and in society in general, any attempt to graft a specifically feminist reform onto existing practices and institutions of the state would result in the "engulfment" of the feminist objection by transferring bodies over feminism has little control the power to determine what are and what are not acceptable representations of women'.

Whilst those who oppose engaging with the law on the basis that law will strengthen the arm of the moral right and the anti-sex brigade, a point well made and evinced in the Government's several assaults on explicit sex (Eckersley 1987, Smart 1989, p. 116, Strossen 1993). The alternative of leaving this area unregulated to find a community level or dependant on parental responsibility is putting pornographers, producers and consumers before the women and children degraded, abused and insulted in, and by, the material and in doing so, assisting and facilitating the birth and growth of the pornographic state.

FOUR

Women's work: private contracts, public harm

Constituting prostitution as a question of morality, of 'sex', and as a question of freedom are countervailing approaches which have had an impact in shaping the law in various ways. The law is a reflection of dominant discourses about prostitution and its instrinsic meaning. It is variously constituted as sex and as a contract. Both constructions disqualify alternative discourses. In recent years the emergence of sexual liberalism seeks to redefine prostitution as a question of sexual freedom and at the end of that continuum a performance art (see the celebration of Annie Sprinkle's pornography as art (see Williams 1993, p. 117)). Current legal efforts, in England and Wales, reflect particular interpretive frameworks and the effect of different conceptualisations of prostitution in organising the legal form. More recently challenges to the liberal arguments currently formulated in the direction of decriminalisation are being debated in the UK, US and in Europe and have reconstructed prostitution around the construct of 'rights'. Whilst in opposition to the professionalisation of prostitution, feminist lobbies identify prostitution as yet another form of enslavement and a miserable choice which patriarchy provides for women (see Dessaur 1979).

COMPETING IDEOLOGIES INFORMING PROHIBITION

Two dimensions of analyses have informed and underpinned the conventional legal orthodoxy on prostitution. The first response is an embodiment of the view that prostitution is inherently immoral and women's involvement in it debasing. Secondly, and not altogether separate, prostitution is constituted exclusively as a private contract. Essential to this contract approach is the differential construction of the sexes which underpins it, such that men's use of prostitution conforms to an accepted sexual need, whilst women in addressing this male need are regarded as worthless. The Wolfenden Committee of 1957, retreated somewhat from this moral crusade stating that prostitution was not the law's business. Yet, it is the morality facet which continues to inform statute where it is an offence for a woman to solicit or loiter for an 'immoral purpose'. Just as the private/public divide in law has been instrumental in the organisation and legal institutionalisation of women's position and relationship to society and to institutions of work and the family (see O'Donovan 1985, Pateman 1989), this dichotomy also informs the legal construction and organisation of prostitution. The relevance of contract theory to the interpretation of prostitution as essentially a private agreement is all too apparent where it has been considered reducible to a private contract of sale of a service between prostitute and client. 'Like other forms of capitalist enterprise, prostitution is seen as a private enterprise, and the contract between client and prostitute is seen as a private arrangement between a buyer and a seller' (Pateman 1989, p. 189). The contractarian formulation of prostitution has been adopted by some feminists in their pursuit of the promotion of prostitution as a profession, with the attendant recognition of trade union rights and employment protection (see Pateman, p. 191, Schwarzenbach 1990–91).

The legal and social significance of constituting prostitution as a wholly private contract is twofold. First, it serves to depoliticise prostitution, veiling and concealing its inherent inequality and sexual exploitation. Secondly it precludes an analysis of prostitution within the broader context of harm and exploitation, orchestrating the debate around consensual sex (Barry 1984, 1995, Dworkin 1989). Challenges to both arguments that prostitution is immoral and is a private contract voice a very different concern, *inter alia*, the failure to recognise the institutionalisation and commercialisation of prostitution on both a national and an international scale. Barry contends that the industrialisation of prostitution and the selling of women in its several guises and forms makes prostitution irreducible to a private contract situated as it is in the public domain controlled by interests outside the mere contractor/ contractee. Within this formulation prostitution is an institution of exploitation, of which street prostitution is one of its more visible expressions (see Barry 1995). Within this critique prostitution is not about sex, although it is about what sex and power have become for men.

The objections to the social and legal recognition of prostitution as a sexual service are threefold. First, such a definitional assignment supports men's unconditional access to women's bodies in various ways, and is an inherently masculinist construct defined through the experience of men and serving their interests. In this respect prostitution has been regarded by some contemporary feminists as antithetical to women, reinforcing women's sexual objectification, symbolising the general sexual degradation and loss of dignity of women as a class. Secondly, constructions of prostitution as immoral or as a contract fail to recognise the wider interconnections between prostitution, male power, coercion and control, through domestic violence, to pornography and organised crime, where women's involvement is not solely a matter of economics but the product of duress, coercion, entrapment and threats. This then is the reality of the 'choice' for women in prostitution and this is the extent of their freedom (see the case of Linda Marchiano in MacKinnon 1994, p. 83, n2).

Women are coerced into both prostitution and pornography. Notwithstanding *de facto* evidence of duress, courts are reluctant to regard evidence of duress for the purpose of a legal defence (see *United States* v *Gant* 487 F 2d 30 (1973), *Woodby* v *Immigration and Naturalisation Service* 370 F 2d 989(1965). There is considerable evidence that women's place in prostitution is the product of subtle forms of covert control as well as overt physical violence by pimps and managers. In *Parker* (1984) 6 Cr App R (S) 444, the defendant pleaded guilty to one count of living on immoral earnings and to aiding and abetting buggery and bestiality. He was able to keep the woman under his control by threatening to expose her prostitution to the Social Services; the woman complied with his demands fearing that her children would be removed from her care. The woman ran away on three occasions but in each case the defendant found her and forcibly brought her back. He advertised her services in a contact magazine and forced her to have intercourse with a dog, pictures he then sold to pornographic publishers. Women's vulnerability to male violence (Ohse 1984, p. 34, Jaget 1980, p. 124, Roberts 1986, p. 81, Edwards 1993a) has resulted in death at men's hands (Edwards 1991a), assault, rape and buggery, from those who seek to control and profit from women's bodies and from those who buy their 'sexual services' (see *Wilmot* (1989) 89 Cr App R 341). In *Attorney-General's Reference No. 12 of 1992 (Tahir Mahmood Khaliq)* (1993) 14 Cr App R (S) 233) where a prostitute was raped at knifepoint, a two year sentence was increased to three years. In *Wilmot* (1989) a sentence of ten years was varied from 14 in the case of a man who raped and robbed six women, five of whom were prostitutes. He violently attacked them, head butted them, used a knife against them and terrorised them. Evidence, however, on this point is overwhelming that prostitute women are the most vulnerable to physical and sexual assault and the most vulnerable to lack of legal protection (see also Edwards 1993a, b, Barnard 1993). Some women in prostitution break free to find that self-defence is no defence. Mary Bernard killed her brutal husband who forced her into prostitution in 1982 and had her plea of manslaughter accepted by the court (Edwards 1985, p. 201). *Emma Humphreys* (1995) NLJ 1032, served ten years of a sentence for murder until the Court of Appeal quashed the murder conviction, substituting one of manslaughter. She had killed her brutal partner after years of his violence against her and his coercion of her into prostitution (for further discussion, see the chapter entitled Gender Politics of Homicide).

The third objection to the contractual argument is that such an individualised perception of prostitution negates any recognition of the international scale of prostitution and its connection with other forms of abuse of women and children. At this level women are sold to business associates. In 1989 Bob Guccione was ordered to pay out a sum of substantial damages in *Marjorie Lee Thoreson a/k/a Anneka Di Lorenzo* v *Penthouse International Ltd and Robert C. Guccione* 81 NY 2d 835; 611 NE 2d 298; 1993, 595 NYS 2d 397, to Thoreson whom he had forcibly hired out for sex to his business colleagues (see chapter entitled Freedom from Pornography in an Age of Sexual Liberalism). Children are the biggest 'cash crop' of 'sex tourism'. British tabloids advertise trips to the Far East. Travel companies convey men and paedophiles for the purpose of sexual abuse of women and children, sanitised in the term 'sex tourism' (Ohse 1984, p. 10, Matsui 1984). The military talk of 'rest and recreation' which means abuse of women and children in prostitution at military bases across the world, purified as entertainment and relaxation (see Barry 1995, p. 123). In poor countries and in the West in times of high unemployment the prostitution of women and young girls is legitimated as a viable alternative to poverty.

It is no longer appropriate or possible to consider prostitution in isolation from the institutions which support it, nor is it possible to limit an analysis to the domestic context alone. The support of prostitution by the West in various ways makes Western governments accountable. The experience of military prostitution serves as an example of how Western imperialism shields and legitimates the use of women and young girls by military personnel in third world countries. Javate De Dios (1991), sees no sexual contract here but a specific form of sexual violence and exploitation manifested against Filipino women through sex tourism, military prostitution, migration, the trade in mail order brides and in pornography. She argues that it is 46 years of American colonisation and the continuation of US military bases in the Philippines that has served to legitimate and authorise this exploitation. Barry found the American presence not only legitimated and regulated prostitution but the conduct of all women. In 1972, women working as prostitutes were openly welcomed onto US bases in Vietnam, where they were known as 'local national guests'. At Longbinh, near Saigon it was reported that soldiers could take onto the base as a 'local national guest' any of the 50 or 60 girls who waited outside the base (Barry 1984, p. 72). A recent report on *Women Entertainers in Angeles and Olongapo in the Philippines* (Miralao, Carlos and Santos 1990), concluded, '... underlying the bases' flesh trade are the exaggerated notions of manliness embedded in military thinking which encourage the control and use of women ... whether as wives, reserve labor or as prostitutes to serve military objectives and the needs of men in uniform'. Under Filipino law, Art. 202, Penal Code, prostitution is a crime against public morals, and prostitutes defined as 'women who for profit or money habitually indulge in sexual intercourse or lascivious conduct', although women are permitted to register as entertainers 'casa girls' or as 'bar workers' both of which provide a veiled form of prostitution and allow the Philippine Government to turn a 'blind eye' to the saturation of prostitution in their midst, focusing instead on the financial benefits of tourism in boosting the gross national product. The Department of Labour colludes, institutional-ising and by condonation classifying these women as professionals. De Dios found that about two million navy and marine personnel pass through Olongapo City spending US $66 million in 'rest and recreation' annually. Until recently the clientele of Angeles City was ensured by the steady stream of American servicemen from the Clark Air Base, and in Olongapo City the clientele, until 1992, was drawn almost exclusively from the American servicemen of Subic's Naval Base, creating a large scale demand for cheap sex. After the Iraq war, thousands of American soldiers docked both at Pattaya in Thailand and at the Subic base in the Philippines The *Philippine Standard* (25 March 1991) reported exuberantly, 'Thousands of American marines and sailors turned Desert Storm into a Philippino Fiesta on Sunday night, crowding into bars and nightclubs in a wild celebration of the Gulf War.' These cities or bases come to symbolise not sex as a contract nor sex as freedom and choice, and have become the essence of dehumanisation and debasement of thousands of women and children. The *Philippine Daily Inquirer* (March 1991) reported a very different side of that celebration, detailing a story of Rosario Baluyot, 12 years of age, who died near the Subic base. Baluyot was a street child who died of blood poisoning caused by an infection from part of a vibrator that was left inside her vagina. Heinrich Stefan Ritter, an Austrian national, was found guilty by a lower court of her rape and murder. But the Supreme Court on 5 March reversed the court's sentence of life imprisonment on grounds of reasonable doubt, although it said it was not ruling that Ritter was innocent or blameless. Associate Justice Hugo Guttierez of the Supreme Court said, 'In spite of his flat denials, we are convinced that (Ritter) comes to this country . . . in order to satisfy the urgings of a sick mind'. In making an order for deportation the Supreme Court also ordered that a sum of compensation be paid to the dead girl's family of 30,000 pesos (US$1,070) (*The Reuter Library Report* 22 March 1991 Lexis) (see Barry 1995, p. 127, O'Grady, *ECPAT, To End Child Prostitution in Asian Tourism*). In 1995, Bengt Bolin, a retired civil servant from Sweden, was arrested in the beach resort of Pattaya and convicted of sexually assaulting a 13 year old boy. He fled back to Sweden whilst on bail awaiting trial. A Swedish court in June 1995 secured a conviction and sent him to prison for three months (*The Independent*, 13 July 1995). At the time of writing two British men are facing charges of trafficking children for sex in Olongapo and in Angeles (*The Times*, 9 August 1995).

'Sex tourism' is further sanitised and sanctioned and made marketable where prostituted women and children are given the title of 'hospitality workers' (Aguilar 1989, p. 5 cited in De Dios 1991). The five top travel markets cited by the Department of Tourism for 1990 are USA, Japan, Hong Kong, Australia and Taiwan. Lord Hylton, reading a Bill for the second time on 15 March 1995, said of UK tourism:

> There are estimated to be between 60,000 and 100,000 child prostitutes in the Philippines serving both the local population and many expatriates and tourists from Europe and America. . . . In Sri Lanka, estimates of child prostitutes vary between 15,000 and 30,000. The United Kingdom is the second largest source of European visitors. The lowest estimate in Thailand for child prostitutes is 40,000 and the highest figure is 200,000. There the UK ranks third among sources of European tourism (Hansard 15 March 1995, p. 892).

In 1980, the then Deputy Prime Minister of Thailand, in validation of the tourist industry, spoke at a national conference of provincial governors and urged them to boost tourist numbers by encouraging 'certain entertainments, which some of you may find disgusting and embarrassing because they are related to sexual pleasure' (*Hansard* 10 March 1993, p. 1081, see Hodgson 1995).

Recent attention in the UK has focused on the involvement of UK nationals in the sexual abuse of women and children under the guise of 'sex tourism'.

This has led to recent moves by the British Government to explore the possibility of legislation which will enable the prosecution of men who commit illegal acts abroad to be undertaken here on their return.

Such prosecutions are already being brought by other States against their offending nationals including Australia, France, Germany, Norway and Sweden. In Australia, the Crimes (Child Sex Tourism) Amendment Act 1994 allows for the prosecution of persons for engaging in proscribed sexual offences committed against overseas children under the age of 16. Lord Hylton's Sexual Offences (Amendment) Bill [HL] 15 March 1995 (*Hansard* 15 March 1995, p. 891), would have allowed the adult participants in under age sex to be tried on their return home and would have allowed for the prosecution of tour operators, i.e., those whom the Bill referred to as 'aiding, abetting, counselling or procuring'. On 2 February 1996, the Sexual Offences (Conspiracy and Incitment) Bill received its second reading. It proposes to allow for the prosecution of anyone who conspires or incites certain sexual acts outside the UK, including the rape of a girl under 16 and indecent assault. The aim is to target sex tour operators. The Sexual Offences Act 1956, s. 23(1) provides, 'It is an offence for a person to procure a girl under the age of 21 to have unlawful sexual intercourse with a third person in any part of the world'. Following *Johnson* [1964] 2 QB 404, the procuring was restricted to England and Wales. Yet, since the term 'any part of the world' has not been subject to statutory construction it remains to be seen whether this section might permit prosecutions to be brought in respect of sex tourism offences. Other governments have embarked on similar measures. In 1987 Siriporn Skrobanek from Thailand together with the Norwegian Women's front faced a legal suit brought by a sex tourism agency against a feminist organisation. The court acceded, 'Generally one must see prostitution as a form of exploitation of women, as oppression of women. When this oppression of women takes place in the Third World and is maintained by mass tourism from Western industrialised countries, an element of racial discrimination is undoubtedly added to the sexism' (see Barry 1995, p. 151–153). Under the terms of the Criminal Justice (International Co-operation) Act 1990, states are able to provide mutual legal assistance for foreign authorities investigating crimes involving British Nationals.

Most analyses of prostitution divorce the exploitation of third world women and children from consideration, contending that this is the unacceptable face of prostitution but is an anomaly to the otherwise equality of prostitute and client encounters observable on the streets of London, New York and capitals in European countries. It is thus that analyses of prostitution in Europe, US and the UK are able to reduce prostitution to a sexual contract where the concerns are not with potential exploitation and abuse, but with its visibility, prurience and offensiveness. There are also persuasive arguments that prostitution can be sanitised and the *raison d'être* for many is the maintenance of prostitution through empowering prostitute women, by improving the lives of prostitutes and the degree of control they exercise. This is the reality of prostitution and this is the reality of what some prefer to regard as a private matter, a matter of choice and freedom for the woman within it. This is the reality of what is called a 'sexual service'.

DOMESTIC LEGAL REGULATION

State efforts to control domestic prostitution in the West, the UK and North America, have been informed largely by the view that prostitution is sexually amoral, risky, private and prurient. It has been moral legislation based on the concept of 'moral harm' which has legitimated state intervention from prohibition to regulation. Occurring solely in the private domain, it is only coercive (pimping) or management and the more visible public spectacle of street solicitation that have been subject to regulation. The feminists' concerns have been largely sidestepped, having little impact on legal thinking or argument in the regulation of prostitution and allied offences, with the exception of feminists' efforts in the nineteenth century around the repeal of the Contagious Diseases Acts 1864,1866,1869, spearheaded by Josephine Butler.

In Europe, where state regulation is favoured and prostitution is legal, the efforts have been less concerned with a moral crusade and more eager to 'Remove the worst outgrowths. Make it clean, see to it the women have obligatory checkups, set up brothels, and impose governmental control' (Hoigard and Finstad 1992, p. 176, Finstad and Hoigard 1993). Germany and the Netherlands (Golding 1992, Edwards 1993a), provide examples where prostitution is legal and regulated by the State via a system of local zoning and State regulated brothels. Here, prostitution is regarded as a matter of sex, choice and freedom, and it is out of the bounds of Europe that the move towards recognition of prostitution as a right emerges. Women working in the brothels must register and undergo periodic medical examination (see Attorney-General of Canada, Committee on *Pornography and Prostitution*, 1987, Vol. 2, p. 417). In Amsterdam, streetwalking is illegal and prostitution legalised in state licensed brothels. Both Germany and Holland are of the view that this is the way ahead to deal with the demand for sexual services; it is regarded as a structural necessity. Drawing on the functionalist arguments of prostitution especially the work of Kingsley Davis (1937, in Dinitz et al 1969) in this climate, the brothel, 'becomes the ultimate confirmation of prostitution as a natural necessity' (Hoigard and Finstad 1992, p. 178). They argue however that 'there is a big difference between decriminalizing the prostitute and legalizing the purchase and sale of sexual services' (Finstad and Hoigard 1993, p. 220). Given this ideology, prostitution as an activity or contract has no special meaning or significance, and there follow attempts to improve the conditions for prostitute women workers which are premised on the contractarian argument that prostitution is like any other form of wage labour and the State has no business as moral entrepreneur. Yet, as I will argue in the conclusion, whereas alienation is an anathema to the wage labourer, alienation is essential to the psychological survival of the prostitute. In this construction, 'Contract theory thus appears to offer a convincing reply to well-known criticisms of and objections to prostitution. For example, for contractarians, the objection that the prostitute is harmed or degraded by her trade misunderstands the nature of what is traded. The body and the self of the prostitute are not offered on the market; she can contract out use of her services without detriment to herself. . . . Contractarians even proclaim that "people have a human right to engage in commercial sex"' (Pateman 1989, p. 191).

Controlling women *(impossible!)*

Prostitution itself has never been a criminal offence. The law in England and Wales like other common law jurisdictions has focused on activities which offend against the moral code of 'public order and decency', and exploitation and control, thus those who 'live on the earnings of prostitution' and those who 'exercise control over prostitute(s)'. The muscle of the arm of law has exerted its strength on all women in prostitution and especially the female street walker. Prostitutes working from agencies, male clients and male pimps are subject to a lesser surveillance. This differential *de jure* emphasis finds further expression in the disparate application and enforcement of law. Consider, for example, that in 1993, 7,912 females were prosecuted for loitering and soliciting (see Table 9) compared with the prosecution of 857 males for the offence of kerb crawling (men soliciting women for the purpose of prostitution) (see Table 10). In practical terms if this reflects the reality of numbers on the streets, every 11 prostitutes would be fighting for every one punter. As the Metropolitan police accede, 'In the overwhelming majority of cases, the man will only solicit one prostitute to make his sought-for contact' (Metropolitan Police 1994, submission, p. 4). Increasingly, street prostitutes have resorted to other ways of meeting clients beyond the law's immediate surveillance via the less visible client prostitute encounters in saunas and massage parlours, clip joints, bars, clubs and escort agencies, and women who might never have worked the streets are turning to the invisible face of prostitution. The number of women working in 'off street' prostitution is largely unknown and by comparison with the street prostitute such women are rarely the subject of prosecution.

Table 9: Prosecutions for loitering and soliciting (Street Offences Act 1959) and kerb crawling (Sexual Offences Act 1985))

Year		Loitering	Kerb crawling
1986			
	f	9,402	1
	m	2	220
1987			
	f	8,486	6
	m	3	354
1988			
	f	9,196	9
	m	2	622
1989			
	f	10,490	18
	m	0	1,047
1990			
	f	10,470	18
	m	179	1,470
1991			
	f	10,175	9
	m	99	1,406
1992			
	f	9,459	4
	m	147	1,089
1993			
	f	7,912	12
	m	195	857
1994			
	f	7,039	8
	m	159	1,185

Source: Criminal Statistics England and Wales Supplementary Tables Vol. 1

The legal regulation of prostitution is directed at regulating and controlling what women do. The construction of prostitution as a 'female only' offence is enshrined within the common law. In more recent times the sex-specificity of the law's intention is made transparent in the provisions of the Vagrancy Act 1824, s. 3, where powers to penalise a common prostitute for engaging in a 'riotous and indecent manner' were used by police to keep surveillance over, charge and prosecute women on the streets (Edwards 1981, p. 56-57, Walkowitz 1977, p. 72). Section 3 was repealed in 1989, see Rook and Ward 1990, p. 230.) These powers were later extended by the Metropolitan Police Act 1839, which applied to Londoners, and the Town Police Clauses Act 1847, s. 28, 'Every common prostitute or nightwalker loitering and importuning passengers for the purposes of prostitution', which extended these powers to police forces in cities and towns outside the capital. In interpreting the Criminal Law Amendment Act 1885, s. 2(2), 'the ruling in de Munck [1918] 1 KB 635, established that sexual activity which is sold, 'commonly in lewdness for payment', is exclusively restricted to females. This sex-specificity was re-enunciated in Webb [1964] 1 QB 357. Law's sexual inequality is institutionalised by and through the common law's definition of a prostitute as female, whilst ignoring de jure and de facto the involvement of men, unless the coercion exercised is considered gross.

Street solicitation of males by males, in contrast, has been restricted to homosexual solicitation, men de jure have not been regarded as part of the prostitute problem albeit de facto they clearly are. The Sexual Offences Act 1967, s. 32, makes it an '... offence for a man persistently to solicit or importune in a public place for immoral purposes'. Here, the essence of the 'immoral purpose' has been taken to imply homosexuality (see Selvey v DPP [1990] AC 304), and not the offering of sexual services by heterosexual women to men. The sex-specific judicial construction was recently unsuccessfully challenged in the case of DPP v Bull [1994] 4 All ER 411. An application by the Director of Public Prosecutions by way of case stated against a decision of Wells Street magistrates, that s. 1(1) of the Street Offences Act 1959 was limited to the activities of female prostitutes and excluded from its scope the similar activities of males, was dismissed by Mann LJ and Laws J. In their deliberations, following the ruling in Pepper v Hart [1993] 1 All ER 42, i.e., that the intention of Parliament could be considered with reference to other official sources, Mann LJ and Laws J considered the recommendations of the Departmental Committee on Homosexual Offences and Prostitution (1957) on the matter of sex-specificity, concluding that, 'It is plain that the "mischief" that the Act was intended to remedy was a mischief created by women'. In other jurisdictions statutory interpretation has led to the extension of the legislative provisions to regulate the activities of both sexes. In Australia, in deciding the same question, in Poiner v Hanns ex p Poiner (1986) 22 A Crim R 370, 373, magistrates having already ruled that the offence of prostitution was restricted to women only, Demack J held that the term 'prostitution' might apply to the activities of both males and females and to both heterosexual and homosexual activities, as the essence of the activity was sexual gratification.

What activities? Flagellation, bondage or straight sex?

What activities amount to prostitution have never been defined in statute, although the common law has embraced a wide interpretation. In *de Munck* [1918] 1 KB 635, it was held on appeal by Darling J:

> The Court is of the opinion that the term 'common prostitute' in the statute is not limited so as to mean only one who permits acts of lewdness with all and sundry, or with such as hire her, when such acts are in the nature of ordinary sexual connection. We are of the opinion that prostitution is proved if it be shown that a woman offers her body commonly for lewdness for payment in return. (pp. 637–8)

This has led to a wide interpretation not restricted to sexual intercourse nor to whether the woman permits lewd acts to be done to her or submits or inflicts lewd acts on others. Reaffirming this opinion, the Court in *Webb* [1964] 1 QB 357, took the view that it matters not whether she plays the active or the passive role, in a case where the activity paid for amounted to the masturbation of male clients. In the words of the court, it matters not, '. . . whether she whips the man or the man whips her'. Prostitution seems dependent on lewdness and lewdness dependent on sexual motive, desire and arousal of the one paying for the service. In this sense a man who believes that he should be punished, seeks chastisement and pays for it, and derives absolutely no sexual pleasure from this experience may not come within the definition of 'prostitution'.

Much prostitution involves the provision of such chastisement, bondage and allied services (see Edwards 1993a). As researchers on prostitution have found, masochistic services without a whiff of conventional sexual intimacy, kissing, fondling, or even sexual intercourse are much in demand. As one prostitute remarked, 'There are those who are just happy grovelling around begging for mercy' (Perkins and Bennett 1985, p. 128, cited in McClintock 1993, p. 93).

Edwards (1993a, p. 99), in a study of ethnographies of prostitutes, found that clients' demand for these services was not uncommon, ranging from the masochistic client who wanted the prostitute to inflict violence to those men wanting to inflict violence. 'Some are weirdos and some are kinky. You know they like to be spanked and they dress up in stockings and suspenders . . .' Jaget notes (1980, p. 105), 'The masochistic clientele is something of a special breed, generally they're men who are cultured, who've got money and who've got some pretty incredible vices. They want us to hit them, stub cigarettes on their chest, stick pins through their penis, drag them round the room . . .'. Krafft-Ebing in his classic *Psychopathia Sexualis* provides detail on the masochistic client, 'At last I overcame the last vestige of my shyness, and one day to realize my dreams, had myself whipped, trod upon etc., by a prostitute' (1901, p. 121).

Case law has not been without such encounters. In *Donovan* [1934] 2 KB 498, the appellant was charged with caning a girl of 17 for the purpose of sexual gratification. He said she consented. The prosecution case was that she went with him to a garage in Morden, out of fear. The defence appealed on the grounds that the judge had misdirected the jury on the basis of consent. The Court of Appeal quashed the conviction as it said that it could not substitute its decision for that of a jury! (Although it does substitute its decision when it pleases!) In *Tan and others* [1983] 1 WLR 361, the appellants were charged amongst others with keeping a disorderly house defined as such because of the extraordinary sado-masochistic paraphernalia. In the trial of Cynthia Payne in 1987 on charges of exercising control over prostitutes (Sexual Offences Act 1956, s. 31) of which she was acquitted, the details of her luncheon vouchers parties were disclosed which included sex shops, sex, to spanking and almost every kind of 'sexual service' (Walker and Daly 1987).

The loathing of prostitute women derives from a sense of disgust about what perverse activities they are prepared to provide. As prostitutes make clear, the more the activity can be distanced from traditional intimacy, fondling, kissing, caressing, the more they can retain a sense of self (Edwards 1993a, Giobbe 1990, p. 68). The mere offer of the service without an intention to honour the offer also amounts to prostitution. In *McFarlane* [1994] 2 All ER 283, (1994) 99 Cr App R 8, in dismissing an appeal brought by a man convicted of 'living off immoral earnings', the Court deliberated once again on the question of what activities amounted to 'prostitution' and more specifically whether a 'clipper' was in fact a 'hooker'. The appellant claimed that he was wrongly convicted since he was living on the earnings of a 'clipper' and not off the earnings of a 'prostitute'. Legal argument on his behalf sought to draw a distinction between a 'clipper' and a 'prostitute'. A prostitute, it was argued, offered services, accepted payment and provided those services, whilst a 'clipper' offered sexual services for reward, then accepted payment in advance but with no intention of providing those services. Miss Joseph, the clipper in question, had explained to the court, 'Yes, I do offer sexual services, but I do not mean to make that offer good' (p. 10). The issue on appeal was whether as a matter of law the trial judge was correct to direct the jury that a woman who offered sexual services in receipt for payment and failed to provide those services, was in fact engaged in 'prostitution', within the meaning of the Sexual Offences Act 1956, s. 30, since a woman becomes a prostitute at the point of making the offer. The Lord Chief Justice, Lord Taylor, in delivering the judgment of the Court upholding the conviction of 'living on immoral earnings', ruled that '... the distinction between 'clipper' and 'hooker' is immaterial. The contract was illegal *ab initio* as it was a contract respecting illegal activity.'.

'On street' prostitution

While prostitution of itself is not an offence, ways of pursuing it are. The law has focused principally on the public prelude to the offer of 'sexual services' for payment, either in the guise of 'loitering and soliciting' by the seller, or more recently the solicitation by men of women for the purpose of consuming 'sex', focusing on the sale rather than on the purchase side of the transaction. The sale, or offer of sale, of sex has been the law's preoccupation and the control of the streets as the marketplace for negotiation and transaction. In recent years street prostitution has been referred to as part of the public order problem, although it is doubtful that public order in the conventional usage of the term is ever involved; the use of the term is intended to elevate public and police awareness of the importance of the problem. Solicitation by women, more commonly described as 'streetwalking', is provided by the Street Offences Act 1959, s. 1(1) where, 'It shall be an offence for a common prostitute to loiter or solicit in a street or public place for the purpose of prostitution'. Following the recommendations of the Report of the Committee on Homosexuality and Prostitution, the Wolfenden Committee (1957), a cautioning system already in operation in Glasgow and Edinburgh, was introduced nationally, where police were empowered to caution women whom they considered to be soliciting on the first and second occasion, and on the third occasion of solicitation, women were then charged and proceeded against. This method of surveillance of first time prostitutes was devised to ensure that women had an early opportunity of redeeming themselves before being stigmatised in court as a 'common prostitute'. Once a woman had been convicted of an offence of 'loitering and soliciting' the cautioning system became redundant and obsolete. Women with one or more previous conviction(s) find themselves under continual police scrutiny and their mere presence on the streets often leads to further arrest and prosecution. (For a discussion of policing, see Edwards and Armstrong 1988, Edwards 1991b, c, 1993b, Benson and Matthews 1995).

Prosecuting prostitutes or vulnerable young girls The prosecution of the seller of sexual services and her treatment in court provides an extraordinary example of male bias in law which reveals a willingness to breach the cornerstone of criminal justice. Women charged with 'loitering and soliciting' find that the charge against them contains unique wording, 'Miss X, you being a common prostitute, did loiter and solicit in Oxford Street on January 1st 1995 for the purposes of prostitution'. It is at this point that the defendant is asked, 'What do you plead?'. In a criminal justice system founded on the maxim of 'innocent until proven guilty beyond reasonable doubt', it is anomalous that it is the offence of loitering and soliciting which remains as the only offence where an antecedent presumption of guilt is all too readily presumed as the defendant's antecedent history is made public. This blatant abuse of process is clearly flouting the principles of contemporary statute (see the Criminal Justice Act 1991, s. 29(1) repealed by the Criminal Justice Act 1993, s. 66(6)). Case law prior to 1991 has held that a poor criminal record should not be regarded as an aggravating factor relevant to offence seriousness in sentencing and certainly not a factor relevant to guilt in the instant case, as any previous convictions are withheld from the jury. Given the anomalous situation it is not surprising that the percentage rate of guilty pleas for this offence is higher than for any other offence (see Edwards 1984, p. 71). Several unsuccessful efforts have been made to amend this overtly discriminatory aspect of the legislation. Lord Chorley introduced two Bills, one in 1967 and one in 1969, in an effort to amend the use of the term 'common prostitute'. In 1990 a further Bill was introduced to no avail.

Over the past decade the involvement in prostitution of young women under 17 years of age especially has been increasing (Edwards 1991b). In 1989, 29 per cent of prostitute women proceeded against were under 21 years of age. It is significant too that in a local case study of prostitution in Wolverhampton (see Edwards 1991b), there was an increase of 24 per cent to 42 per cent of women arrested for prostitution under 21 in the period 1986 to 1991. Young women under 17 were being referred to the juvenile bureau at the rate of three a week (Edwards 1991b). There is, and always has been, considerable ambiguity about the punishment or protection of young girls. The female adolescent who had had sex at thirteen was regarded as a 'problem', 'beyond control' and a fit subject for local authority care.

The legal system, far from protecting young girls, reveals that young girls who have had sex are treated as worthless or less worthy of protection than those who have not. The public policy concerns of the prostitution of young women and teenage girls have been reflected in two recent decisions of the Court of Appeal suggesting that child protection principles become hollow rhetoric and hyperbole where children in prostitution are seen as contributing to their own demise. Child protection lies at the heart of the Children Act 1989, s. 1(1) and at a wider level is promoted in and by the UN Convention on the Rights of the Child 1989. Article 34(a), ratified by the UK in 1991, provides that all appropriate national, bilateral, and multilateral measures State Parties shall in particular take to prevent: '(a) the inducement or coercion of a child to engage in any unlawful sexual activity; (b) the exploitative use of children in prostitution or other unlawful sexual practices; (c) the exploitative use of children in pornographic performances and materials' (Ghandi 1995, p. 111).

The principles of the Children Act 1989 are directed at safeguarding the interests and promoting the welfare of the child.

It is apparent that at the level of policing and in the courts there is some conflict regarding the correct approach to juvenile prostitution. Some police are treating under age females who sell 'sex' as prostitutes, whilst some forces are treating such adolescents as vulnerable young girls. Judicial utterances add to this conflict and inconsistency in approach where some judges reinforce the belief that whether child or adult, females are responsible for their own demise. In the case of *Pickup* (1993) 14 Cr App R (S) 271, a man of 34 years was charged with indecent assault upon a 14 year old girl. She claimed that he had inserted his fingers and also his penis into her vagina. In his defence, he claimed that he had only inserted his finger into her vagina to which she consented in exchange for money. The trial judge said 'It is clear beyond peradventure that she came to your home expecting to be paid for giving you sexual favours. Indeed, she was paid. For payment you were able to masturbate her.'. The Court reduced his sentence on appeal to nine months. It is this very factor of evidence of prostitution which renders such women and girls less worthy of protection. When young girls are victims of sexual assault, evidence of past sexual conduct including prostitution is often considered to go to the issue of consent (see *SMS* [1992] Crim LR 310, cited in the chapter entitled Sex Crime). In *James* (1994) 15 Cr App R (S) 100, where a man in his fifties was convicted of indecent assault, a sentence of 18 months was upheld and a rather different approach taken by the Court. He had fondled girls of 12 and oral sex was performed for £20. The law report stated that three girls had been working as prostitutes. The Court of Appeal upheld the sentence of the Crown Court whose presiding judge said, 'I accept . . . that these girls were already corrupted when you became involved with them. They were already prostitutes, their own statements make that clear. I accept also that you were not responsible for that condition ... Nevertheless, you corrupted them further. It has, in my judgment, to be made clear that child prostitution is vicious and evil, and in my judgment any man who engages in it, whatever his background and circumstances, and albeit that the girls are already corrupt, already prostitutes, must go to prison. In my judgment society will be affronted by any other penalty.'

In 1995, The Children's Society report on child prostitution, *The Game is Up* by Lee and O'Brien, focused attention on what it considers inappropriate responses to some of the most vulnerable children. The report expresses the ambivalence thus:

> When it is accepted that there is a high correlation between child sexual abuse and entry into prostitution the young people involved are regarded as victims worthy of help and protection. On the other hand, when a young person steals from a client or is apparently making a choice to engage in prostitution, he or she may be viewed as the guilty party in need of legal control and moral sanctions.

This ambivalence is further reflected in sentencing approaches to rape of young children and incest (see *Billam* [1986] 1 All ER 985 guidelines, *Attorney-General's Reference (No. 1 of 1989)* [1989] 3 All ER 571, on incest).

'Off street' prostitution, brothels and escort agencies

In response to the increased police presence on the streets to cope with prostitution, and to the law regulating street walking in the post 1959 period, women have moved into other forums for meeting clients and have depended on advertising for this 'trade'. The increasing overlap of off street activities with the glamour and pornography industry further reflects the institutionalisation of prostitute activities as a 'professional' or 'sexual' service.

In *Shaw* v *DPP* (1961) 45 Cr App R 113, 114, a brochure advertising prostitutes' services was declared indecent and obscene and a corruption of public morals. In recent years, as the Indecent Displays Act 1981 proves to be increasingly ineffective with its unsurmountable 'indecency' test, prostitute women advertise more freely in local newspapers and by way of the 'call card' in telephone booths. Feminists on both the right and the left are demanding a safe environment, and a provision of public services free from such advertising and the need to reclaim the streets from this pollution of the environment (Fairweather 1982). In *Howard* (1991) 94 Cr App R 89 the appellant was charged with living on immoral earnings: he produced cards and adhesive stickers to be used by prostitutes to advertise their services. On appeal his conviction was upheld but the original sentence of thirty months was reduced to three months.

The law has been eager to regulate the excesses of the control and coercion of prostitute women by pimps by imposing heavy sentences for those who financially profit from managing brothels (Sexual Offences Act 1956, s. 33), escort agencies, massage parlours etc. Women exercising control over prostitutes for the purposes of gain have been prosecuted under the Sexual Offences Act 1956, s. 31. In 1975, Janie Jones received a phenomenal seven year prison sentence for 'exercising control'. The prosecution alleged that Jones intimidated women in her control and that their involvement had been obtained by false pretences. It was under this section of the Act that Cynthia Payne was prosecuted on more than one occasion and convicted following an early morning raid on her 'sorority house' (*Payne* [1980] Crim LR 595). It was the constant apprehension of further brushes with the law that resulted in her devising the luncheon voucher scheme where she opened her house to parties of carefully invited guests who paid for sex and other services. This led to a further prosecution in 1987 (see Walker and Daly 1987).

Table 10: Proceedings for procuration and brothel keeping

Year		Procuration	Brothel keeping
1986			
	m	319	22
	f	16	91
1987			
	m	387	34
	f	18	80
1988			
	m	507	49
	f	20	117
1989			
	m	532	32
	f	30	123
1990			
	m	482	36
	f	23	150
1991			
	m	346	25
	f	23	107
1992			
	m	177	36
	f	31	124
1993			
	m	124	26
	f	10	70
1994			
	m	130	19
	f	21	85

Source: Criminal Statistics Supplementary Table Vol. 1 for the years 1986–1994

Notwithstanding legal efforts to penalise these 'allied' offences, prosecutions for procuration and brothel keeping are few in comparison with annual prosecutions for streetwalking see Table 10. The figures indicate a decline in prosecution for all vice offences over the past few years. Women who work alone from flats and apartments circumvent the legislation, since a definition of a brothel requires two or more women to be working as prostitutes. In *Tan* (above), although a single prostitute and a single client were involved, the conviction for keeping a disorderly house was upheld. The Court of Appeal certified under s. 33(2) that a point of law of general public importance was involved in the decision, namely, 'Can premises be a disorderly house notwithstanding that every sexual act that takes place therein is between a single prostitute and a single customer unobserved by any other person?'. The Appeals Committee of the House of Lords dismissed the petition for appeal. Where one woman works as a secretary booking in telephone calls for appointments, she cannot be prosecuted for 'living on immoral earnings' as this is a male only offence. Although 'exercising control' (s. 31) applies to women, it cannot be said that such a woman in any way exercises control. It may, however, be possible to prosecute such an establishment under the disorderly house provision of s. 36. This requires evidence that the house is contrary to good order, an outrage of public decency or tends to corrupt or deprave (see *Quinn and Bloom* [1962] 2 QB 245).

Crackdown on Pimping UK law recognises the presence of coercion in prostitution but only where there is financial gain and control. The Sexual Offences Act 1956, s. 22(1), provides for the prosecution of the male procurer; s. 30(1) the prosecution of the pimp who lives on the earnings of prostitution; and s. 31 the prosecution of women who exercise control over prostitute women. The court in *Broadfoot* [1976] 3 All ER 753, in dismissing an appeal against a conviction for procuring women to become prostitutes in massage parlours, ruled that procuration, 'applies to any activity which brings about the course of conduct of prostitution which the girl would not have engaged in of her own volition'. Living on the earnings of prostitution in s. 30(1) by contrast provides, 'It is an offence for a man knowingly to live wholly or in part on the earnings of prostitution'. However, proving the evidential element of 'knowingly' living on the earnings of prostitution has been shown to be a difficult hurdle to cross, since the most common line of defence is that he did not know that the woman in question was a prostitute. In interpreting this section, the courts have sought to draw a distinction, when sentencing the offender, between the passive and coercive ponce. In *Farrugia Borg, Agius, and Gauchi* (1979) 69 Cr App R 108, where the men did not exercise control but operated a mini cab service to drive prostitutes to clients, the court considered this 'living on immoral earnings' and sentenced them to twelve months (see *Dixon and Dixon* (1995) 16 Cr App R (S) 779). In *Hassan El-Ghazzar* 1986 8 Cr App R (S) 182, where the defendant operated an escort agency, a sentence of two years' imprisonment was upheld. The reality for many women is that this section unfairly penalises male members of their family, sons, brothers and anyone who might be living with them in a household, or considered in some way to receive money from them. The object of the law was the control of the coercive ponce (Report of the Committee on Homosexuality and Prostitution 1957 (Wolfenden)).

The Sexual Offences Act 1967, s. 5, also penalises a man or woman for living on the earnings of the prostitution of another man, and so for the purposes of 'living on immoral earnings', male prostitution is recognised in the law. In *Puckerin* (1990) 12 Cr App R (S) 602, the appellant lived on the immoral earnings of male prostitution. The appellant's sentence of two years was reduced to nine months; he was seen to approach young men at London railway stations and introduce them to clients but there was no evidence of coercion.

Policing the purchasers   It is anomalous, given that prostitution has been legally formulated as essentially a private contract, that the conduct of the receiver/consumer has not been similarly subject to regulation. Despite decades of agitation and mounting pressure for regulation, the punter or purchaser has been subject to prosecution in only very recent years, and even then the focus has been on the visibility of his conduct, emphasising once again the law's preoccupation with the public nuisance and visibility of the negotiation of the contract (see Street Offences Report 1929, Wolfenden Committee, *Report on Homosexuality and Prostitution* 1957). Solicitation of young women under 16 is provided for by the Sexual Offences Act 1956, s. 32. In *Crook* v *Edmondson* [1966] 2 QB 81, in a case stated for the consideration of the High Court, where a man who solicited young women was prosecuted under the Sexual Offences Act 1956, s. 32, the Court, in testing the application of the section, held that a man soliciting women for the purpose of prostitution was not an 'immoral' purpose. Thus it would appear to be the case that if women are soliciting this is considered to be for an 'immoral' purpose, but if men are soliciting women for the same purpose this is not considered immoral.

The law clearly demonstrates its differential treatment of men and women in the interpretation of statute and its predilection to turn its attention away from the activity which is the object of legislation, to the person doing it, and the emphasis is concerned to regulate the sale aspect of the operation. In *Dodd* (1978) 66 Cr App R 87, the words, '. . . come here I want to screw you', spoken to two 14 year old girls was behaviour deemed unlawful under the Sexual Offences Act 1956, s. 6(1), and considered 'immoral' since the girls so propositioned and insulted were under the age of consent. The result has been that men have been free to solicit/importune all women of 16 and over with impunity, threatening the sense of security and safety of women. There have been other efforts to penalise the kerb crawler outside s. 32. In the early 1980s several kerb crawlers were prosecuted under the Justices of the Peace Act 1361 and in *Hughes* v *Holley* [1987] Crim LR 253, the defendant was bound over to be of good behaviour, the court having concluded that his behaviour was 'offensive and contrary to standards of decency' (*contra bonos mores*). His appeal against the decision of the magistrates was dismissed. The use of other legal measures to penalise the kerb crawler received a mixed reception. Those who supported legal measures to control kerb crawling comprised moral crusaders, feminists wanting safer streets for all women, and left lobbyists wanting to improve the quality of life in run down neighbourhoods and remove the detritus; all regarded the intervention of the law as a positive step. It seemed that at last all women, including non-prostitute women, who used the streets to move to and from work, to the supermarket, to places of entertainment in the course of their everyday lives, would now have some measure of protection from harassment by men and their fear of crime be reduced (see the chapter entitled Sex Crime). At the same time feminists and those on the left opposed proposals to criminalise kerb crawling on the basis that this would legitimate the increased surveillance of marginalised men, especially men from the black community. The second objection was that the surveillance of both potential male kerb crawlers, and potential prostitute women would increase the vulnerability of women, who would be forced into making snap judgments about potential punters without having sufficient time to weigh up whether they were 'normal' men. The Sexual Offences Act 1985, s. 1, penalised men who solicited women for the purposes of prostitution.

Section 1 (1)

A man commits an offence if he solicits a woman (or different women) for the purpose of prostitution—

(a) from a motor vehicle while it is in a street or public place; or
(b) in a street or public place while in the immediate vicinity of a motor vehicle that he has just got out of or off, persistently or, subject to section 5(6) below, in such a manner or in such circumstances as to be likely to cause annoyance to the woman (or any of the women) solicited, or nuisance to other persons in the neighbourhood.

It fell short of its promise and dropped the controversial clause that would have extended 'protection' against such harassment to non-prostitute women. It was doomed from the start. The evidential proof required depends on the 'persistence' of the solicitation, or else solicitation in such a manner as to be 'likely to cause annoyance' to the woman or a nuisance to other persons in the neighbourhood. The Home Office introduced Circular 14/1985 offering guidance pursuant to the Act on the use of a caution rather than prosecution as an alternative in exceptional circumstances, suggesting the hesitancy which the legislation had created. The Act soon proved to be unworkable (Edwards 1987a). Police found the evidence required to satisfy the standard of proof of persistence, insurmountable. By comparison the evidential requirement for solicitation by women under the Street Offences Act 1959, s. 1, was much lower, one instance of solicitation was sufficient. This is a prime example of gender politics inflicting differential treatment even at the point of the weight and cogency of the evidence required.

These insuperable evidential difficulties prompted the introduction of a private member's Bill on 11 May 1990, although to no avail, with the precise aim of removing the 'persistent' requirement from the Act. Alongside the inherent evidential obstacles to effective prosecution was the unwillingness of police to prosecute men whose only error in their view was to consort with a prostitute. Police forces preferred to use other methods of deterring prostitution and considered the exposure of men to prosecution and attendant publicity overly punitive, developing instead their own local methods of dealing with the problem ranging from informal warnings to cautions and thus only a few selected cases resulted in a full blown prosecution. Some police officers saw themselves as moral vanguards of family values offering advice to kerb crawlers, and sending letters to the addresses of the registered owners of cars who were seen kerb crawling 'What would the wife say, think about the kiddies' said one officer interviewed by the author. Kate Millet in a footnote in *The Prostitution Papers* (1973, p. 87), found a similar underenforcement of the law relating to kerb crawling in the United States. 'The recent New York statute which declares the male client guilty too, in an act of female prostitution, is simply not enforced . . .'

Benson and Matthews (1995) found in their Vice Squad Survey wide variations in police response as between forces. Of men who faced prosecution in the early days of the legislation, one of the more notorious prosecutions was that against Colin Hart Leverton QC in 1986 (a conviction overturned on appeal). And in 1991, police in King's Cross, London warned the former Director of Public Prosecutions, Allan Green. The attendant high profile publicity led to his resignation (Edwards 1991c). In 1989, with the Court of Appeal decision in *Paul* v *DPP* (1990) 90 Cr App R 173, a conviction for kerb crawling was upheld in the High Court where the evidence tendered was that his behaviour was 'likely to cause a nuisance'. Although no one particular person was in the vicinity at the time, the magistrates took into account their local knowledge of the area, the fact that the area was residential and decided on this basis that it was reasonable to draw the assumption that the behaviour was 'likely to cause a nuisance'. Woolf LJ said:

> The offence created by the Sexual Offences Act 1985, s. 1, deals with conduct which was notoriously known to be able to cause nuisance in residential areas. The procession of cars stopping to solicit women for the purposes of prostitution can be highly offensive conduct in a residential area. In my view it is the clear intent of the section that where conduct of that sort takes place, which is likely to cause grave offence in the locality, the offence should be regarded as being established. (p. 177).

The ruling in *Paul* meant that prosecutions were thereon sanctioned under the nuisance aspect of the Act (see Table 12) thus contributing to the increase in prosecutions from 220 in 1986, to 1,047 in 1989, and 1,470 in 1990, although it is curious that 1993 prosecutions have fallen dramatically to 857 (Table 9). It is to be noted that the author's researches in a study of prostitution in Wolverhampton, *Prostitution Whose Problem* (1991b), found that the nuisance to workers on an industrial estate was a real problem. When staff turned up for work their first job would be to sweep up condoms and related detritus from the entrances of their premises.

Table 11: Males proceeded against for kerb crawling 1993 under s. 1 (persistence) Sexual Offences Act 1985

1985 section 1	Total proc. against	Total found guilty
Bedfordshire	56	52
Cleveland	1	
Dorset	50	48
Essex	1	1
Greater Mancs.	82	72
Hampshire	8	4
Humberside	3	3
Lancashire	6	5
Leicestershire	5	5
Merseyside	17	14
Metropolitan Police	198	154
Norfolk	42	40
Northumbria	1	1
Nottinghamshire	72	52
South Yorkshire	2	1
Staffordshire	18	14
Suffolk	4	4
West Midlands	184	150
West Yorkshire	16	12
South Wales	6	4
England	766	632
Wales	6	4
England and Wales	772	636

Source: Home Office Statistical Department

Table 12: Males proceeded against under section 1 for kerb crawling (nuisance) Sexual Offences Act 1985 in 1993

1985 Act, section 1	Total proc. against	Total found guilty
Bedfordshire	5	4
Cheshire	1	1
Dorset	2	1
Essex	1	1
Greater Mancs.	6	6
Merseyside	4	1
Metropolitan Police	38	25
Nottinghamshire	1	0
West Midlands	7	7
West Yorkshire	1	0
South Wales	1	1
England	67	47
Wales	1	1
England and Wales	68	48

Source: Provided by the Home Office Statistical Department

The standard required by the Crown Prosecution Service also provides a further obstacle particularly since where the offence is not serious and the penalty nominal, the police are encouraged to consider whether the public interest would be better served by some other means of disposal. Such policies against prosecution impact on police at the outset: many officers policing vice with ambiguous legislation prefer to use other methods such as cautioning. Recent research by Benson and Matthews (1995, p. 32) found that vice squads regarded the legislation as difficult to implement. It is not only the kerb crawler, but also the cruiser, that is the man who drives round red light areas watching street prostitutes and sometimes stopping his car and in a public place behaving indecently, by masturbating for example, who also creates a nuisance (see Edwards 1993 a, b for a discussion of punters). In *Darroch* v *DPP* (*The Times*, 11 May 1990; (1990) 91 Cr App R 378), it was held that the act of driving round and round a red light district did not constitute solicitation. This has left the cruiser immune from prosecution (see the chapter entitled Sex Crime for further discussion of voyeurism). It means that so long as the man does not speak to a prostitute he cannot be deemed a kerb crawler, nor can he, by extension, be prosecuted under the nuisance limb of the Act. Cruisers may be a nuisance *de facto* but are not creating a nuisance or soliciting *de jure*. Notwithstanding the ineffectiveness of this legislation, it has resulted in more women turning from streetwalking to escort agency work, a drift which will increase as some police forces are turning to video surveillance techniques to provide the much needed evidential proof (*The Times*, 30 September 1995).

RIGHTS DISCOURSE AND PROSTITUTION

The debate on prostitution in more recent years has been reconstructed and reshaped. The politics of prostitution has been waged by a plurality of interested factions taking on a new guise, breaking with the conventional orthodoxy of competing claims of prostitution as immoral and prostitution as a private contract. Right wing moralists have been resolutely determined that prostitution must be more stringently regulated, calling for more law and punitive sanctions, more policing and more prosecution. Civil libertarians and those on the 'left' broadly share the concern that prostitution laws are oppressive, penalise women and working class women in particular. But it is within the site of rights that new discourses and interpretative frameworks have emerged, promising to shape the face of legal regulation.

Some on the left include feminists who argue that prostitution is essentially about sexual choice, that there is a free market and women should be free to sell sexual services unhampered, just like any other commodity, goods or service (Baldwin 1992, Freeman 1989–90). Such protagonists seek to decriminalise prostitution and draw a distinction between free prostitution and forced prostitution with only the latter to be controlled and regulated, arguing that 'sound prostitution' is possible. Nickie Roberts (1986, p. 16), a former stripper, in writing on the 'industry' in Britain asserts:

> Feminist anti-porn campaigners or the Mary Whitehouse brigade: it makes no difference to us. Both factions clamour for more repression and censorship at the hands of the state; both divert attention from the real issue of women's poverty in this society; and both are responsible for the increased hounding and vilification of women who work in the sex industry.

Other, left feminists (Giobbe 1990, Barry 1984, 1995, Finstad and Hoigard 1993, Hoigard and Finstad 1992) are of the view that prostitution is exploitative and involves overt and covert abuse and the way forward is to wage a war on the institutions which support prostitution and eliminate them. Part of this 'war' demands a degree of criminalisation, even if, regrettably, some women are penalised and some aspects of the law are unjust. It is the contention of Women Hurt in Systems of Prostitution Engaged in Revolt (WHISPER): 'We believe that the function of the institution of prostitution is to allow males unconditional sexual access to women and children limited solely by their ability to pay for this privilege.'.

Right to prostitute: a human right

For the pro-prostitution lobby prostitution is a matter of sex, sexual liberation and of freedom (see Pheterson 1989), it is about providing a sexual service and, since prostitution is a contract freely entered into, then arguments of exploitation and coercion are vigorously rebutted. This conceptualisation of prostitution is one which has found favour amongst liberals, prostitutes and those who own and control the sex industry. It is a view which will ensure the perpetuation of prostitution and its corollaries. This contractarian position seeks to improve the working conditions of prostitutes and their general social status in society by officially sanctioning prostitution as legitimate business. The politics are naïve and confused *laissez-faire* to the point of absurdity: the sexual contract is inherently masculinist. Laws formulated around the recognition of man's inexorable needs for women's sexual services ratify and condone the social construction of male sexuality as uncontrollable, insatiable and inevitable and cater for this by trading inexorably on the poverty and economic marginalisation of women. Such laws also ratify women's unlimited availability for men. As Pateman argues, 'The feminist argument that prostitutes are workers in exactly the same sense as other wage labourers, and the contractarian defence of prostitution, both depend on the assumption that women are "individuals", with full ownership of the property of their persons' (1989, p. 209). 'Contract is conventionally believed to have defeated the old patriarchal order, but, in eliminating the final remnants of the old world of status, contract may yet usher in a new form of patriarchal right' (Pateman, 218).

In 1973, the organisation *COYOTE* was founded in the US and in 1985 was affiliated to the International Committee for Prostitutes' Rights formed in Amsterdam (Pheterson 1989, Miller, Romenesko, and Wondolkowski 1993, p. 323). The basic principles of the alliance are that prostitute women have basic rights to occupational choice, to sexual self-determination, and to work as prostitute women (*sic*). Their struggle is towards the freeing of prostitution from state control and the recognition of prostitution as a legitimate form of work in exactly the same way as any other form of wage labour is recognised. Denial of self-determination for prostitutes and the right to work as a prostitute is their central grievance . The pro-prostitution lobby wishes to press national governments, the UN Working Group of Contemporary Forms of Slavery, the Council of Europe and the European Parliament for a new convention, the Convention for the Suppression in Traffic in Persons, and also into recognising the right to self-determination of prostitute women. It also seeks to differentiate between prostitution as chosen work and forced prostitution and uses the human rights language and rhetoric to achieve this purpose. 'It follows from the right of self-determination, which is enjoyed by an independent adult man or woman on whom no unlawful influence has been brought to bear, that he or she is at liberty to decide to act as a prostitute and allow another person to profit from his or her earnings' (UN E/1990/13 p. 7). The Dutch Government has not ratified the 1949 Convention on Prostitution, on the basis, as the Dutch Government sees it, that where prostitution is freely chosen, prostitute women should have the right to self-determination. Similarly, the Turkish Government takes the view that prostitution is legitimate work and should only be controlled in order to prevent the spread of venereal diseases. The Dutch Government supports the move towards legalisation through state control which will lead to prostitution being ultimately recognised as just another form of paid work (see Van Der Poel 1995). Whilst the Netherlands, in common with other European countries, quite rightly wish to outlaw the traffic in women as domestic workers, cultural entertainers and mail order brides, they seek to draw a distinction between these forms as forced prostitution and the prostitution of women on the streets of Sussex Gardens or Amsterdam as free prostitution. It is not a distinction easily drawn and the legislation in the Netherlands in particular and this dimorphic approach suggest ambivalence.

Whilst pressing for reforms to enhance the social, political and work status of prostitutes, the Dutch Government has taken a strong line on what they consider the traffic in women, pimping and control of prostitutes. The prosecution of a Dutch trafficker, Jan Schoemann, following the trafficking in Lisa Mamac who was sold to a sex farm in Holland, stands as an example of this commitment. Yet it is now clear, given the free movement of workers in Europe, that traffickers are shifting their attention from the Third World to Eastern Europe, trafficking women from Manila, Bangkok, Bogota and Santo Domingo as well as prostitutes from Warsaw and Prague. 'Eastern European women don't need a visa for the Netherlands, and a bus ticket from Prague is much cheaper than a flight ticket from Bogota,' de Winter, a Dutch police squad officer, explains. The number of women sold to the Netherlands as prostitutes runs into the thousands, according to a recent report commissioned by the Dutch foreign ministry. Last year, a conference of South-East Asian women's organizations estimated that 30 million women had been trafficked worldwide since the mid-1970s. Lisa Mamac of the Philippines, was promised a job as a hotel receptionist, but ended up as a prostitute in a Dutch sex farm. She was bought out of the farm by a friend, and in 1987 lodged a complaint against the Filipino public prosecutor who had offered her the job. In 1989, her case went to the Supreme Court in Manila supported by funds raised in the Netherlands. She lost the case. Korvinus, a Dutch Foreign Ministry consultant, explains why 'the testimony of the public prosecutor was deemed more reliable than that of a mere prostitute'. Korvinus's report to the Dutch foreign ministry recommends that the definition of trafficking in human beings be broadened to include not only those forced into prostitution, but also the trade in brides and servant girls as well as the exploitation of illegal migrants (see *Inter Press Service*, 12 June 1992, Nexis).

Those wishing to press ahead with what they see as the emancipation of prostitute women are adopting the language of human rights to further their cause. It is curious that Article 1 of the Universal Declaration of Human Rights, 1948 which asserts, 'All human beings are born free and equal in dignity and rights', turns on its head the concept of self-determination and freedom by arguing for the self-determination of a dis-empowered group to enjoy other unalienable rights which further their sexual enslavement whilst sanitising it. Article 4 of that Declaration states, '... no one shall be held in slavery or servitude', and Article 5, 'no one shall be subjected to torture, or to cruel, inhuman or degrading treatment'. To propose that prostitute women should also have the right to self-determination which facilitates further prostitution, seems on the contrary to be an abrogation of self determination, dignity and respect. The way in which this argument is construed depends on how one sees prostitution; it is without doubt confusing and ambivalent. If self-determination for prostitute women allows them to prostitute (which is the argument advanced by the Netherlands), such a position facilitates the perpetuation of a condition which involves the sale of a woman's body and results in the objectification and dehumanization of the seller or prostitute, a depressed condition which cannot be altered or improved simply because prostitute women are allowed to prostitute. (In the context of class and revolution, Marx predicted the embourgeoisement of the proletariat, the increasing apparent improvement of their condition generating a state of false consciousness.) For Plato, in the happy slave analogy, the tautology is clear, if slaves are given rights to their own enslavement, does that alter the fundamental existence of their slavery? At the heart of this issue of self-determination for the 'free' prostitute is the right to work and to be taxed.

Van Der Poel (1995), charts the development of the prostitute as emancipation in the Netherlands and the support for prostitution as merely another 'official occupation' and how the movement promotes the belief that a dignified existence is possible via the path of self-determination (Dessaur 1979 in Van Der Poel 1995). Van Der Poel cites Buijs (1987, p. 94) who recognises that the distinction between forced and free prostitution is mythical:

There is a fluid transition because many non-traded prostitutes have little freedom of movement and are forced to pay sums of money to pimps, protectors, and managers. The freedom of most of the 'free' prostitutes is only relative. There are only a few who can work according to their own conditions and under acceptable circumstances. The vast majority of the world of prostitution is controlled by men (and a few women) who seek to profit in a variety of ways from the women's work. Accordingly, the organisation of prostitution and the organisation of the trade in human beings partially overlap.

The situation in Holland is to become even more lenient as s. 250b of the Penal Code is to be amended to make the brothel prohibition more lenient, each municipality being free to formulate its own policy. Street prostitution is illegal and the only women working the streets are largely drug addicts and those who are HIV positive who would not be welcomed following health checks in the regulated brothels.

Both these issues of emancipation and equality of treatment with all other workers in market capitalism were raised by the UK case of Lindi St Clair (*Aken*) in her struggles with the inspector of taxes. Here the issue raised was whether prostitution is lawful and therefore subject to taxation as any other activity. In Europe, many prostitute women are seeking to have their activities validated by being taxed as any other profession. The courts in England have considered this matter too, albeit not at the instigation of the would-be taxpayer but at the instigation of the Inland Revenue, in *Inland Revenue Commissioners* v *Aken* [1990] 1 WLR 1374. Aken had practised as a prostitute for many years. The Inland Revenue became aware of her activities and undeclared income following a television programme about her. The inspector raised assessments under Schedule D (Case 1) for the year 1973–74 on income described as 'professional fees' and for the years 1974–75 to 1980-81 on income described as 'profits of prostitution'. Aken gave notice of appeal against the assessments, but subsequently reached a written agreement in 1981 with the Inland Revenue as to the amount due. She did not, however, pay the agreed sum. The Inland Revenue issued proceedings against her to recover the tax owed, and sought summary judgment under RSC Order 14. But in the ensuing proceedings, the Court refused to enter the judgment for the Inland Revenue, giving the taxpayer leave to defend. The Inland Revenue appealed on the basis that the matter of whether tax should be paid had already been determined in law and the agreement was binding as prostitution was considered a trade under the Income and Corporation Taxes Act 1970, s. 109. Aken appealed and the appeal was dismissed on the grounds that prostitution was a trade under s. 109 of the Act, and that it was not open to a taxpayer in collection proceedings to raise by way of defence any issue as to the validity of the assessments, the agreements being binding on her.

As a result of tax assessment Lindi St Clair got involved with a further legal wrangle over efforts to register as a registered company. In *Register of Companies ex parte Attorney-General* [1991] BCLC 476, the court quashed a decision to register Lindi St Claires' (Personal Services) Ltd as a registered company. The Attorney-General applied to quash the incorporation and registration by the Registrar of Companies on 18 December 1979, under the provisions of the Companies Act 1948 to 1976. The grounds of the application were that in certifying the incorporation of the company and in registering the same, the Registrar of Companies acted *ultra vires* or misdirected himself or otherwise as the object of the company was to carry on the business of prostitution, which was unlawful. The applicant said, when she was granted leave for judicial review, 'I would like to say that prostitution is not at all unlawful, as you have stated, and I feel it is most unfair of you to take this view, especially when I am paying income tax on my earnings from prostitution to the Inland Revenue'. Ackner LJ ruled, 'It is well settled that a contract which is made upon a sexually immoral consideration or for a sexually immoral purpose is against public policy and is illegal and unenforceable. The fact that it does not involve or may not involve the commission of a criminal offence in no way prevents the contract being illegal, being against public policy and therefore being unenforceable.'

The British Government then is not prepared to condone prostitution as a form of work for the purpose of registration, although it is not unhappy to require women who prostitute to pay tax.

Violating human rights

For the protagonists of the view that prostitution is a human rights violation, such an interpretation is underpinned by the conceptualisation that prostitution is the institution upon which the sexual exploitation of women and children is built and which reduces women to a sexual commodity to be bought and sold and abused. There is a need to move away from the moral basis of prostitution legislation and to reframe future legislation along the basis of exploitation and harm. Any distinction between forced and free prostitution is artificial and specious. Whilst this is not generally considered a persuasive argument where adult women are concerned, it is especially in the arena of juvenile prostitution and the prostitution of children that harm, abuse and coercion are all recognised as integral features.

It is part of a wider systematic abuse, namely the commoditisation and objectification of women as a 'sex class' and is sustained by, and in, several forms, *inter alia* pornography. Prostitution is part of a wider violence against women, perpetrated against women in peace and in plenty, in war and in poverty. This wider violence against women claims wife beating, bride burning, rape, incest, pornography, genital mutilation, and rape as torture, amongst its several forms. For MacKinnon, it is precisely sexual objectification which is the central process within the dynamic of gender inequality (MacKinnon 1982, in Bort (ed) 1993, p. 201). For Dworkin (1989, p. 203), 'The sexual colonisation of women's bodies is a material reality ... the institutions of control include law, marriages, prostitution, pornography ... and for Pateman part of this colonisation depends upon presenting prostitution exclusively as a private contract. She writes, 'Like other forms of capitalist enterprise, prostitution is seen as private enterprise, and the contract between client and prostitute is seen as a private arrangement between a buyer and a seller' (1989, p. 187).

There is nothing new in the formulation that prostitution is a form of violence against women. Engels in *The Origin of the Family Private Property and the State* (reprinted 1986), characterised prostitution as a form of sexual slavery. Alexandra Kollontai (1978) in *Sexual Relations and the Class Struggle*, regarded prostitution as the heart of the problem. Speaking to women she urged them to, 'Make yourselves free from the enslavement of man'. Indeed, central to the struggle for socialism is the necessity of women's freedom and equality and freedom from male exploitation and control. Capitalism and the growth and proliferation of the capitalist 'sex industry', even in the liberal democracies of Europe, has grown to obscure the fundamental exploitation that persists as a visceral part of the institution of prostitution. There is the growing recognition that prostitution is exploitative but such a perspective is difficult to sustain when those who own one of the biggest capitalist enterprises, the media, benefit from the trade in pornography and prostitution, seeking to suppress the argument of exploitation and to promote the issue of sexual freedom and choice. Prostitution is part of the new free market enterprise. As Kathleen Barry argues, prostitution is a part of the 'cultural climate of sadism'. This appreciation was influential in guiding the deliberations of the Attorney-General's Committee on *Pornography* (1986), when it conceded the arguments of WHISPER *inter alia*, '... prostitution is the foundation upon which pornography is built' (1986, p. 1058).

Part of the struggle of some feminists (Barry 1995, Dworkin 1989, Giobbe 1990, MacKinnon 1985), to deconstruct and reconstruct prostitution as within the domain of the violent and not within the domain of the sexual, has involved resisting efforts to legitimate prostitution. One of the more visible forms of legitimation has been through state legalisation. Evelina Giobbe of *WHISPER* argues, 'Dismantling the institution of prostitution is the most formidable task facing contemporary feminism' (Giobbe 1990, p. 80), in emphasising the systematic organisation of prostitution which is at the heart of the problem, instead of reducing prostitution to individual prostitute-client encounters abstracted from the societal power structures of which it is a part. *The Coalition Against Trafficking in Women*, a non-governmental (human rights) organisation, together with other abolitionist societies including the *International Abolitionist Federation*, is one of several organisations against the systematic organised abuse which is the heartbeat of prostitution. Prostitution involves the historical, cross-cultural exploitation, control and coercion of women and children. Legal strategies designed to regulate it focus on sanitising the 'sex' of prostitution, and its visibility and have been content to remove the public face of prostitution from the streets, as the key obligation. Both factions are using the language of rights.

The distinction between forced and free prostitution is artificial. Giobbe (1991, p. 67) writes:

> This mythology, which hides the abusive nature of prostitution, is illustrated by the ideology of the sexual liberals which erroneously claims that prostitution is a career choice; that prostitution epitomizes women's sexual liberation; that prostitutes set the sexual and economic conditions of their interactions with customers; that pimp/prostitute relationships are mutually beneficial social or business arrangements that women enter into freely; and that being a prostitute or a pimp is an acceptable, traditional occupation in communities of color.

Prostitution is considered a violation of human rights and the *Coalition Against Trafficking in Women* draws on the United Nations conventions to strengthen its case. The 1949 Convention of 2 December, entitled *Convention for the Suppression of the Traffic in Persons and of the Exploitation of the Prostitution of Others* contains in its preamble, the following statement, '. . . prostitution and the accompanying evil of the traffic in persons for the purpose of prostitution are incompatible with the dignity and worth of the human person and endanger the welfare of the individual, the family and the community' (Ghandhi 1995, p. 25). Article 1(1) defines a trafficker as someone who 'Procures, entices or leads away, for purposes of prostitution, another person, even with the consent of that person;'. Article 1(2) defines a trafficker as someone who 'Exploits the prostitution of another person, even with the consent of that person.' Article 2(1) agrees to punish any person who, 'Keeps or manages, or knowingly finances or takes part in the financing of a brothel;', and Article 2(2), any person who, 'Knowingly lets or rents a building or other place or any part thereof for the purpose of the prostitution of others' (UN 1988, p. 182). There are two other provisions which have a bearing on this question. *The United Nations Declaration on the Elimination of all forms of Racial Discrimination* (1963),

(Ghandhi, p. 39), and *The Convention on the Elimination of all forms of Discrimination Against Women* (CEDAW, 1979), (Ghandi 1995, p. 82), both address the violation of human rights and condemn sexual and racial discrimination in all its forms. CEDAW, Article 6 provides, 'State Parties shall take all appropriate measures, including legislation, to suppress all forms of traffic in women and exploitation of prostitution of women' (Ghandi 1995, p. 84).

On 11 February 1981 the European Community passed a resolution on the position of women in the EEC. Article 55 asks the Commission to conduct a systematic inquiry into the purpose of prostitution and to carry out a study of the ways of harnessing suppression of such activities within and between the member States (*Women of Europe*, Brussels 1981, OJ C59 p. 89). Prostitution in itself violates women's human rights because prostitution is a violation of Articles 1, 4, 5 and 6 respectively of the Universal Declaration of Human Rights (1948) where Article 4 provides, 'No one shall be held in slavery or servitude' and Article 5, 'No one shall be subjected to torture, or to cruel, inhuman or degrading treatment . . .' and Article 6, 'Everyone has the right to recognition everywhere as a person before the law' (Ghandi 1995, p. 22).

The *Coalition Against Trafficking in Women* wishes to take the 1949 Convention further and make some important amendments, with *UNESCO* wishing to see a redrafting of the Convention which takes sexual exploitation as its starting point. Sexual exploitation has been missing from Conventions since 1949 and is also absent from CEDAW. *The Coalition Against Trafficking in Women* drew up the draft Convention Against Sexual Exploitation, entitled *Elements of a New Convention* (Barry 1995, p. 323, 304). Its guiding premise was, 'it is a fundamental human right to be free from sexual exploitation in all its forms' (see *The Penn State Report*, International Meeting of Experts on Sexual Exploitation, Violence, and Prostitution, 1991). That report defined sexual exploitation as a:

> practice by which person(s) achieve sexual gratification or financial gain or advancement through the abuse of a person's sexuality by abrogating that person's human right to dignity, equality, autonomy, and physical and mental well-being (Barry 1995, p. 305).

The purpose of the draft Convention was also to provide mechanisms and structures which would outlaw the positive promotion of sexual exploitation, and to challenge the perpetuation of images of women and children which define them as less than human and which facilitate the hatred of these groups. Part of this endeavour was to provide positive programs in education, work and other economic and supportive structures which would diminish the necessity for prostitution. Prostitution was considered to be a form of discrimination embracing racism and sexism, the existence of systems of prostitution served to condone and legitimate discriminatory practices against women at all levels of society. The *Coalition* called for all States to depenalise illegal activities of prostitutes whilst at the same time strengthening those measures which seek to control the client, the procurer and the pimp as defined in Articles 1 and 2 of the 1949 Convention. The *Coalition's* overriding concern and objection to the 1949 Convention was that it sought to draw a distinction between free prostitution and forced prostitution, regulating only the worst excesses of the latter. This formulation precluded the recognition of prostitution in all its forms as abuse and victimisation. The solution is with government responsibility to provide viable alternatives to prostitution (Finstad and Hoigard 1993). This is a continuing struggle against exploitation which must continue so long as prostitution is likely to be further condoned and legitimated.

Both viewpoints recognise the discriminatory practices against women who are engaged in prostitution on the basis of this prostitution. Covert legal regulation has meant that prostitute women have not received the same access to services or resources or legal treatment as victims especially of sex offenders (see Chambers and Millar 1983, 1986) compared with non-prostitute women in respect of rights, liberties, and freedoms, in housing, education, health care, and issues relating to the custody of and access to children. Prostitute women have suffered in various ways (see *Re Y (minors)* 1990 Fam Law 223, *Re S (Minors)* 6 April 1989, unreported; see Edwards 1989a) and even in the exercise of discretion for suitability for a place on an *in vitro* fertilisation programme.

SEX TRADE IN EUROPE

In *H P Bulmer Ltd* v *J Bollinger SA* [1974] 2 All ER 1226, Lord Denning, speaking on the impact of the EC Treaty said:

> The Treaty does not touch any of the matters which concern solely the mainland of England and the people in it. These are still governed by English Law. They are not affected by the Treaty. But when we come to matters with a European element, the Treaty is like an incoming tide, it flows into the estuaries and up the rivers. It cannot be held back.

How far, and for how long, will UK domestic laws and policy be able to hold back the incoming tide of Europe's 'sex' market? European Community law has already pronounced upon certain issues pertaining to the 'sex industry' and EC law is governed by regulations protecting free movement of goods and services between member states and the free movement of workers. Whilst most of the provisions in the EC Treaty are concerned with creating and enforcing obligations of an economic character, Article 36 allows States to derogate on the grounds of public policy, public health or national security. Article 36 provides:

> The provisions of Articles 30 to 34 shall not preclude prohibitions or restrictions on imports, exports or goods in transit justified on grounds of public morality, public policy or public security; the protection of health and life of humans, animals or plants; the protection of national treasures possessing artistic, historic or archaeological value; or the protection of industrial and commercial property. Such prohibitions or restrictions shall

not, however, constitute a means of arbitrary discrimination or a disguised restriction on trade between member States.

It may become increasingly difficult to invoke public policy as the grounds of derogation, if public policy in Europe marches in an opposite direction. Already in the name of freedom of movement of goods and services, European Community law and the trade in sex have begun to make an impact. In *Conegate Ltd v HM Customs and Excise* [1987] QB 254, [1986] 1 CMLR 739, it was held that following EC Treaty, Article 36, goods lawfully made or sold in the UK can also be imported provided they are of EC origin, where the customs haul consisted of inflatable sex dolls imported from Germany destined for British sex shops. The *Conegate* ruling has had implications for the importation of other similar pornographic materials into Britain and established that the standard to be applied in considering prosecutions for breach of importation regulations was to conform to the standard required for goods manufactured and sold in the UK (see the chapter entitled Freedom from Pornography in an Age of Sexual Liberalism and the case of *Noncyp*).

A vital mainstay in the sale of sex artefacts are the licensed sex shops. In respect of this matter the European Court of Justice deemed that it had no control in deciding whether sex shops should be established and could not override domestic discretion contained in the Local Government Act 1982 (see *Sheptonhurst Ltd v Newham Borough Council* [1991] 3 CMLR 463; *Quietlynn Ltd v Southend Borough Council* [1990] 3 CMLR 921; *Portsmouth City Council v Brian James Richards and Quietlynn* [1989] 1 CMLR 673). Sex is further traded in the transmission of soft porn satellite television stations. European regulations are again decisive. To date, the satellite channel *Red Hot Dutch*, has been prohibited through proscribing the encoders necessary to its reception. This has only been achieved through the public policy commitment to child protection in accordance with Article 22 of the EC Directive on Broadcasting which ratified the granting of an injunction in April 1993 (*Secretary of State for National Heritage, ex parte Continental Television BV,* Queen's Bench Division CO/837/93, 23 April 1993, Lexis, Enggen, where an appeal by Continental Television against the refusal of the Divisional Court to grant an interlocutory injunction against the Secretary of State for National Heritage was dismissed, thereby preventing the sale of the equipment necessary for reception of the satellite station transmitting Red Hot Dutch. Article 22 of the EC Directive on Broadcasting 89/552/EEC provides that:

Member States shall take appropriate measures to ensure that television broadcasts by broadcasters under their jurisdiction do not include programmes which might seriously impair the physical, mental, or moral development of minors, in particular those that involve pornography or gratuitous violence. The provision shall extend to other programmes which are likely to impair the physical, mental or moral development of minors, except where it is ensured, by selecting the time of the broadcast or by any technical measure, that minors in the area of transmission will not normally hear or see such broadcasts.

The primary responsibility for ensuring compliance with this requirement rests on the member State in whose jurisdiction the broadcaster is situated (see also Coleman and McMurtrie 1993).

Freedom of movement of persons, the movement of workers and the rights of residence and of establishment, may also have implications for those working in the 'sex industry'. The question arises, now that passport restrictions have been removed, whether such provisions will encourage European prostitutes to seek work in the UK 'sex industry'. We know already that it has led to the clandestine traffic in women within Europe. The judgments in the *Adoui* and *Roux* cases are instructive since they indicate that, in respect of the regulation of free movement of prostitutes for the purposes of work, existing law would not put the UK in breach of its community obligations under EC law, on the grounds of 'public policy'. *Rezguia Adoui and Dominique Cornuaille v Belgian State* [1982] 3 CMLR 631 raises the question of residence and expulsion of women suspected of prostitution. Two French women were expelled from Belgium on the grounds of 'public policy', following their suspected prostitution, although prostitution was not unlawful in Belgium. Miss Adoui applied for a residence permit, which was refused on the grounds that her personal conduct was not approved of as she worked in a bar with waitresses suspected of prostitution. She left Belgium and returned one month later summonsing the Belgian State to grant interlocutory relief that she had been the victim of unlawful acts. Miss Cornuaille similarly applied for residence, she too was suspected of prostitution. Her presence was said to be detrimental to 'public policy'. The Court held, '. . . the public policy provisions in Articles 48 and 56 EC do not permit a member State to expel a national of another member State (or refuse him access) on the grounds of personal conduct, if such conduct on the part of the local nationals does not give rise to repressive measures or other genuine and effective measures intended to combat such conduct' (see *Bouchereau* [1977] 2 CMLR 800). The Court interpreted Articles 48 and 56 of the EC Treaty and Articles 6 and 9 of Directive 64/221, ruling that: (1) a member State may not, by virtue of the reservation relating to public policy contained in Articles 48 and 56 of the Treaty, expel a national of another member State from its territory or refuse him access to its territory by reason of conduct which, when attributable to the former State's own nationals, does not give rise to repressive measures or other genuine and effective measures intended to combat such conduct; (2) circumstances not related to the specific case may not be relied upon.

The court deemed the action of Belgium unlawful. These cases raise the question of the limits within which member States may adopt individual measures deporting or expelling nationals of other member States who enjoy the benefit of the freedom of movement for workers or the right of establishment. In respect of public policy, national authorities have been allowed some discretion but it is not to be applied in an arbitrary manner.

In *Roux v The State (Belgium)* (Case C-363/89) [1993] 1 CMLR 3, the issue for consideration was whether a member State may not require affiliation to one of its social security schemes as proof that a Community national enjoys freedom of movement under Articles 48, 52 and 59 EC. Here, a French '*fille de joie*' who had been a street prostitute in Belgium since her arrival in 1988, applied for a residence permit giving her profession as a self-employed waitress. When the authorities discovered the real nature of her work they refused to grant her a work permit, justifying their decision on the grounds that her work, 'was not in conformity with the social legislation in force'. Under Council Directive 64/221 on the co-ordination of special measures concerning the movement and residence of foreign nationals, States can derogate if grounds are justified on grounds of public policy, public security or public health. In a reference from Belgium by the Tribunal de Première Instance (Court of First Instance), Liège, under Article 177 EC, the European Court of Justice ruled that under the Treaty of Rome citizens of one country have the right to live in another country, the only condition being that they are pursuing an economic activity, within the meaning of Articles 48, 52 or 59 EC: non-conformity with state social legislation is not a reason for denying right of residence. In the case of an employed person the conditions to be satisfied by a Community citizen are twofold: he must be in possession of a passport or identity card on entry into the territory of another member State and must produce an employer's certificate (Article 4 of Directive 68/360). A self-employed person, in addition to being in possession of one of the above-mentioned identity documents, must prove — by any appropriate means — that he is carrying on an activity as a self-employed person (Article 6 of Directive 73/148 (p. 9)). The Court held that the documents submitted by Roux satisfied the requirements for the grant of the residence permit and in February 1991, the Court handed down a judgment in her favour (see *Observer*, 10 February 1991).

The cases of *Bouchereau* and *Roux* relate to rights of all workers, including women working in the sex industry, signalling that public policy is insufficient for their exclusion. Whilst our domestic 'public policy' may allow derogation from Community obligations, given that the approach to prostitution in most European countries is very different from our own in that prostitution is tolerated as a form of work, even if we may not be required to bring domestic legislation into harmony with Europe there may be other pressures exerted for harmonisation. This will depend on how the phenomenon of prostitution is defined and articulated in the years ahead, whether as 'forced' or 'free', or a matter of private contract or institutionalised exploitation, whether an abrogation of women's human rights and equality or as a fundamental aspect of the right to self-determination. It is clear that prostitution is regarded as a legitimate dimension of a legitimate industry, the 'sex industry'. Derogation on public health grounds and arguments that prostitutes are a health risk may be used (see Kinnell 1989 for a discussion of prostitution and AIDS).

There are mighty forces which seek to promote the idea that prostitution is sexual freedom and that those who engage in prostitution do so from personal choice. Those who argue against that will find their voice eclipsed by the mega power of the pornography industry which continues to sell the lie that prostitution is sex and is a matter of choice. The only people who are free are those perpetuating this fiction, the commercial pimps who print and communicate the lie that prostitution is freedom and the nation States who benefit from the taxes and fines imposed on these women. Dismantling prostitution is about dismantling a system of exploitation. The *Coalition* and *WHISPER* accept that decriminalisation of female prostitution is an interim solution, with support mechanisms to assist women in disentangling themselves from prostitution. As Miller et al (1993) note, '... the structural and cultural supports for the system of dramatic racial, gender, and class inequality that remains mean that the system that draws women into prostitution and the interpersonal dynamics and abuse that make women vulnerable to recruitment' persist.

The framing of prostitution laws in years to come will depend upon whether the laws will focus on the experience of women and the need to protect them or whether prostitution is a matter of choice or freedom.

FIVE

All in the name of privacy — domestic violence

Domestic violence until the 1970s was regarded as a rare phenomenon. Criminal law was rarely, if ever, invoked to prosecute aggressors, and until the 1970s injunctive relief in civil law was available only in cases where the court was already considering a matrimonial order or else in accordance with injunctive relief or remedies in tort (see Scherer 1992). A far wider range of remedies is now available. But stereotypical attitudes and expectations of women and men persist, these inform the law and militate against the justice and protection victims receive. The law, whilst it makes claims to offer remedies and protection to victims, is replete with obstacles and difficulties for the applicant or complainant seeking safety and protection. Whilst it is of course acceded that the law is only one of several ways in which male violence against women can be addressed, its importance remains as a powerful symbolic statement and barometer of a society's unwillingness to tolerate such violence or indeed its indifference to such conduct. For both these reasons, reform of the law, more effective application and implementation of existing law, together with the exposure of the ubiquity of such violence has been a major task of contemporary feminism.

The conventional stereotype of the nature of domestic violence is one of minor petty altercation culminating in a shove or a slap, or at the extremes — a punch. So long as these expressions of violence remain the considered form, the seriousness of domestic violence continues to be shrouded and underestimated. Domestic violence perpetrated by partners is manifested in a myriad of forms of abuse. Slapping, punching, kicking, mental cruelty, humiliation, domination and keeping a woman in a continual state of subjection and fear, are just some of the ways in which men enforce their will. Many commentators have argued that such expressions of violence and cruelty are merely symptoms of 'family disequilibrium' (see Jackson and Rushton 1982), essentially isolated events without history in an otherwise happy and normal family. Rather than acknowledge the seriousness and habituation of this form of male violence, thereby shattering the hermeneutically sound construct of the idealised family and the view of patriarchy which sustains it with its proclamation of chivalry and male protectiveness, such mythologies have orchestrated a fantastic duplicity denying the seriousness, frequency and pervasiveness of violence. By exonerating the offender, pathologising the victim and particularising and problematising those families in which violence occurs, the belief in the universality of the 'happy family' survives and endures. Essential to this myth is the projection of domestic violence not only as a trivial episode, but also as a rare and exceptional phenomenon, exclusive to poor, socially deprived and 'problem families'. Domestic violence is all too frequently exonerated by locating external factors such as alcoholism or unemployment as the root cause. Frequently, however, domestic violence is explained as a reaction, a justifiable response to the provocation of women, who, within this explanatory model, are considered ultimately responsible for their own demise.

Research evidence controverting these several myths shows that domestic violence is by no means a rare or an isolated event in an otherwise happy family (Straus and Gelles 1986). Dobash and Dobash in their seminal work, *Violence Against Wives* (1980), argue that whilst it is true that domestic violence occurs with frequency in working class families, it is by no means a phenomenon peculiar to them. In this respect consider, for example, the case of Joel Steinberg, a middle class criminal defence lawyer who killed his adopted daughter Lisa Nussbaum and brutalised his wife Hedda. Hedda's face and body were deformed from his continuous assaults upon her. She was described by prosecution lawyers as passively standing by as her daughter Lisa was beaten and eventually murdered by Steinberg, although this passive inertia was recognised by those working in the field of domestic violence as the product of her own fear of him (see *People* v *Steinberg* 79 NY 2d 675 (1992), Dworkin 1989, Brownmiller 1989, Dobash and Dobash 1992, p. 5). Such apparently 'passive partners' to child abuse have been misunderstood. Mothers are also in fear of the abuser and very rarely in fact or in law is it recognised that women's failure to act is the result of fear and duress. As Davidson (1995 p. 364) points out in her research, fathers are never charged with failure to protect when the child abuser is the mother. OJ Simpson, television presenter, and actor was tried and acquitted for the murder of his wife and a her male companion. Evidence during the trial established his continual violence against her during the years of their marriage. Sandra Horley of the battered women's charity, *Refuge*, in London, has counselled, 'wives of vicars, doctors and lawyers' whom she found to be just as much at risk from assault as women from poor neighbourhoods (Horley 1988, p. 14). Lenore Walker, executive director of the Domestic Violence Institute, Denver, Colorado, a clinical psychologist who has given expert evidence in trials of battered women who kill, has counselled women from every professional group (Walker 1984). Similarly, the belief that women who experience domestic violence are always inadequate or deprived or passive is also controverted. Hedda Nussbaum, who reportedly suffered ten black eyes and a ruptured spleen, was during her relationship with Steinberg a successful children's book editor with the publishing company, Random House (see Dworkin 1993, p. 237). In her public life she was a successful professional woman, in her private life she was both a prisoner and a victim.

Although domestic violence is indeed frequently committed by men who are drunk, men who physically and mentally abuse their partners are frequently sober. The 'I only beat my wife when I am drunk' myth serves to exonerate and mitigate men's responsibility for violence. The alcohol/violence theory serves to orchestrate the etiological debate around extraneous factors acting upon the aggressor, rather than focusing on the man, his motivation and his responsibility. Given that contemporary criminologist Box (1987), in an attempt to understand crime causation, focuses on unemployment and recession it is not altogether surprising that theorists, seeking an understanding of why men batter their partners, consider the role played by economic and status factors such as unemployment. Such analyses are limited since they preclude consideration of domestic violence within the family and the inequality within power relations which is the primary cause giving rise to its expression.

The idea that women are responsible for male violence is perhaps the most impenetrable of all myths. 'Blaming the victim' is so much a part of the construction of domestic violence that to suggest that there is any other version verges on heresy. At the end of the day the durability of this myth allows male violence to continue unchallenged so that even in the more extreme cases women can be blamed for provoking or tolerating violence. Challenges to such duplicity provide an alternative version of probity where men are deemed responsible for what they do and women who stay with violent men are understood to stay because of housing needs, shelter, children's needs and economic dependency. Yet it is the resilience of these mendacious constructs on domestic violence that have facilitated the inadequacy of public and community support, the trivialisation of the extent of violence by society and the legal process. In turn, decisions made by practitioners in the criminal process support these myths, judges frequently rely on them in their judgments and in decisions to reduce sentence with the result that mendacity on domestic violence is institutionalised in a legally reified form, reproduced by police, by counsel and by the judiciary. This chapter explores how the conventional misunderstanding about domestic violence, its pathogenesis, ontology and morphology, its victims and its offenders, inform and shape the nature and content of law *de jure*, its interpretation and its application *de facto*.

MANIFESTATIONS OF DOMESTIC VIOLENCE

Domestic violence is the systematic, ahistorical, acultural manifestation of male power. It is as immutable and enduring as patriarchy which supports and sustains it. Male violence against women is an expression of the will to power, of supremacy and domination by brute force. The pathogenesis or morphology of domestic violence develops from common assault to grievous bodily harm and on occasion escalating to murder. Domestic violence characteristically includes acts of physical and mental cruelty progressing from a slap or shove, to a punch or kick, and to the more extreme manifestations of violence, in suffocation, strangulation, attempted murder and murder. The prefix 'domestic' serves to neutralise the full horror, viciousness and habituation of the

violence, concealing the imprisonment of its sufferers, neutralising the seriousness and the dangerousness of the aggressor, thereby rendering its victims a
different and lesser standard of response from the justice system and ultimately
a lesser standard of protection.

Physical violence: brute force

Women are at the receiving end of many forms of abuse, where the aggressors
seek to rationalise and justify, exonerate and excuse the use of brute force by
offering drink, her refusal of his sexual demands, her questioning of his fidelity,
her ending the relationship, as plausible and worthy explanations. Male
violence is the trajectory of unrestrained power where men seek control over
women to possess and repossess them, and where male rights are a matter of
ownership. Homicide is the disastrous demise domestic assaults may run
(Edwards 1985, 1987b) where victims are repeatedly beaten, abused and
finally murdered. On 9 August 1989, Lawrence Lucien was convicted of
manslaughter and sentenced to four and a half years' imprisonment. Following
an argument about his wife's friend, Joe Murray, he stabbed his wife in
the stomach. At the trial, Lucien entered a plea of provocation. Yet, police
records showed that he had been assaulting his wife for eight years, and
that police had refused to grant him bail when he had assaulted her earlier
in that same year. The magistrates took a different view, granting him bail
and he returned to the marital home and killed his wife (*Islington Gazette*, 10
August 1989, and author's examination of police records). Researchers
are agreed that homicide '... is rarely a sudden explosion in a blissful
marriage' (Chimbos 1978, p. 67). Homicide statistics reveal a high proportion
of such killings in many jurisdictions. Criminal statistics for England and Wales
reveal a remarkably high level of spousal homicide expressed as a proportion of
all homicides, when compared with other jurisdictions notably the US. In
1991, of a total of 631 homicides, 107 were female spouse victims and 14 male
spouse victims, constituting 17 and 2 per cent respectively of total homicides.
In 1992, of 594 homicides, 90 were female spouse victims (15 per cent)
compared with 20 male spouse victims (3 per cent). For 1993, of 606
homicides, 78 (13 per cent) were female spouses and 15 (2 per cent) male
spouses. Homicide statistics for England and Wales for the period 1972–1982
revealed that between 21 per cent and 29 per cent of all victims have been
acquainted as spouse, cohabitee or former spouse or cohabitee or lover (see
Edwards 1987b). This figure is still an underestimate of the totality of partner
homicides since the spousal category excludes homicides of girlfriends by
boyfriends.
    By contrast, whilst the homicide rate in the US is far higher per 100,000
population at 9.4 compared with England and Wales at 1.02, the proportion of
spousal homicides perpetrated against female spouses expressed as a percentage of all homicide, constitutes only 6.5 per cent. The relationship of victim to
offender is denoted thus, husband 2.1 per cent, wife 4.3 per cent, boyfriend 1.3
per cent, girlfriend 2.2 per cent, of all 20,045 homicides in 1990 (*Sourcebook of
Criminal Justice Statistics*, 1991, Table 3.140). In 1992 of 22,540 homicides,

husbands were killed in 1.7 per cent of cases, boyfriend is 1 per cent, wives constituted 4 per cent and girlfriends 2.3 per cent (US Department of Justice, Sourcebook of Criminal Justice Statistics 1993, Table 3.125). The Canadian profile is more comparable with England and Wales, where figures for 1991 show that 85 men killed their spouses and 25 women killed their husbands (Fine 1992). This constituted 14.17 per cent and 4.17 per cent of all homicides respectively. Daly and Wilson (1988, p. 219), found that among legally married cohabiting spouses in 1974–83 a man was almost four times as likely to kill his wife as to be killed by her (404 cases as against 107), and among estranged couples he was more than nine times as likely to kill her as she him (119 cases as against 13), (see the chapter entitled, The Gender Politics of Homicide for a more detailed discussion of these figures).

Men's violence against women is frequently sadistic, devoid of any rhyme or reason. MacLean, Jones and Young, (1986, p. 172), authors of the Islington Crime Survey found, 'In the cases where other forms of violence were reported, the interviewers recorded such things as strangulation, cigarette burns, punched and bitten, stabbed in the face with a cigarette, spat at, hair pulled and head butted'. The violence which is described as 'domestic' frequently results in endangering life. In *Cenci* (1989) 11 Cr App R (S) 199, a female cohabitee, in an attempt to escape further violence from her boyfriend, smashed a window with an iron in order to escape and fell to her death. He was convicted of manslaughter and a ten year sentence of imprisonment was reduced to five years (see the chapter entitled, The Gender Politics of Homicide for further detail).

Many women survive potentially murderous attacks sometimes motivated by nothing at all, at other times by a suspicion devoid of foundation, at other times, jealousy. In *Davies* (1986) 8 Cr App R (S) 97, a husband struck a wife on the back of the head with a hammer and rendered two further blows to the face fracturing the bridge of her nose and the upper part of the bony cavity of the eye. He also fractured the jaw bone and the eyeball had to be removed. The court conceded, 'Indeed she was lucky to have survived', sentencing him to seven years' imprisonment. In *Di Palma* (1989) 11 Cr App R (S) 329, the victim was attacked by her boyfriend with a hammer causing an extensive compound, depressed comminuted fracture of the skull, and the destruction of an eye which had to be removed leaving her permanently disfigured and disabled. The boyfriend had attacked her in jealousy of her former husband, although there was no evidence of her resuming any relationship with him. In *Dunning* (1987) 9 Cr App R (S) 81, a man attacked his estranged wife with an axe whereby she suffered a fractured skull, deep lacerations to the scalp and partial amputation of two fingers. The judge explained his conduct thus, '...these factors (the ex-wife's relationship with another man) no doubt led you to behave in a way which you normally would never have done', imposing a seven year sentence. In *Giboin* (1980) 2 Cr App R (S) 99, a husband had stabbed his wife after she had told him that she had become emotionally involved with another woman. He had been previously convicted for stabbing a former girlfriend who had formed an association with another man.

Attacks by male partners with petrol and inflammable liquids are further ways in which men terrorise women and attempt to control and possess or punish them. In *Casseeram* (1992) 13 Cr App R (S) 384, following other previous incidents of violence which were explained as a manifestation not of his repeated violence towards her but as the expression of a deteriorating marriage, the husband attempted to strangle his wife, poured petrol over her and set her alight resulting in 17 per cent burns to her body. In *Bedford* (1993) 14 Cr App R (S) 336–337, the wife was doused with petrol and ignited when she refused to sleep with the appellant. She said she would sleep on the settee. The appellant left the room and returned with a container of petrol he kept in the car. He set her alight and when she tried to leave the burning room he held the door shut against her. She sustained 40 per cent burns. When arrested he said to police, 'You know what it's like, you know what women are like. I just snapped.'. In an application to the Criminal Injuries Compensation Board by a wife victim of 'domestic violence', where turpentine was poured over her head and body and she was set alight resulting in extensive injuries including burns to the head, neck, arms, hands, back and chest, covering forty two per cent of her body, and respiratory burns from inhaling the fumes, the Board made an award of £162,000 (NLJ 12 February 1993, p. 204).

A common method of assault on women is attempted strangulation and asphyxiation, men frequently explain this behaviour by reference to a woman's nagging and her infidelity. In *Dearn* (1990) 12 Cr App R (S) 527, the husband admitted tying a piece of electric flex around his wife's neck. Medical evidence estimated that the flex must have been held for at least five minutes causing irreparable brain damage. The husband explained that she had been, '. . . nagging him all that day' and he had tried to shut her up by using the flexible cord of the vacuum cleaner cable. A sentence of fifteen years was reduced to twelve years. Women are at risk of assault at the point of ending relationships. In *Attorney-General's Reference No. 13 1990 (Trevor Bailey)* (1990) 12 Cr App R (S) 578, a husband slashed his former wife's face when she said that she did not want to go back and live with him. He spoke of love, '. . . she didn't want to make it up. I still love her. I took the knife from home to cut her face.'.

The perpetration of violence against women can also result in child destruction as when pregnant women are kicked by violent partners. In *Virgo* (1988) 10 Cr App Rep (S) 427, the appellant committed grievous bodily harm against his girlfriend. He forced her to remove her clothes, piled snow upon her naked stomach, pushed snow into her vagina and repeatedly punching her in the stomach said he was going to kill her and the baby. When she tried to run away he caught up with her and threw her to the ground kicking her in the stomach causing inter-cranial haemorrhage and death to their unborn child (see *The Times*, 18 September 1995 for a further case on this point).

In terrorem

Threats of violence and threats to kill are the most typical ways in which men keep women in subjugation and fear, i.e., *in terrorem* (see Hanmer and

Saunders 1984, Binney, Harkell and Nixon 1981). Yet, where such threats have been alleged by victims, the police have been reluctant to investigate, and when charges have been preferred in the absence of physical corroboration, such threats are regarded as hyperbole. Neither the police, nor the courts, have understood the fear and terror experienced by victims, nor have they acceded that victims are in imminent danger. Indeed, the judicial attitude revealed in the case which follows allegorises how society, the police and the courts have constructed male threats of violence as 'drama' and not as a promise of future conduct. In *Munroe* (1987) 9 Cr App R (S) 408, where there was a history of violence and on two occasions the appellant had threatened to kill the woman, the Appeal Court reduced a custodial sentence of three years to two, asserting, 'On the first occasion he made verbal threats when he met her in the street with the children . . . on the second occasion he went to her home . . . broke the glass in the front door . . .'. The Court held:

These were threats to kill. The complainant would have been fearful. She would have believed that he meant what he said. But, in truth, when one examines his actions there appears to be nothing to suggest that these were more than words in his mind as he spoke them and that there was no fear of his contemplating anything more than this sort of abuse.

Yet the words of aggression were, 'Don't walk away from me . . . when are we going to live together? I will never leave you alone, you know you can't get away from me . . . wherever you are I will find you . . . I will have you all . . . I will kill you all.'. In *O'Callaghan* (1987) 9 Cr App R (S) 187, where the offender had perpetrated considerable violence on his victim, the threats to kill were on this occasion taken not as drama, but as an indication of future conduct. Again, the wounding of male prowess and hubris following on from her association with another man resulted in the threats, 'You're dead, I'll get you and I'll get your boyfriend, you're nothing but a fucking slag, I'm going to cut your throat.'. The judge in passing sentence said he was not wholly convinced that the appellant would have committed the offence of cutting Miss Evans's throat, but he thought the appellant intended to give her a nasty fright. 'In our judgment that was an accurate reading of the situation'. In *Coleman* (1994) 15 Cr App R (S) 713, the appellant had threatened his girlfriend, 'When I find you I will burn you to fucking bits'. Sentence was reduced on appeal to thirty months, the judge acceding that 'the complainant was not entirely free of some kind of blame'. Clearly, judges engage in the imprecise art of divining what a man may or may not do on the basis of their own subjective hunches and sophistry, and on the degree to which they consider that women should be blamed for provoking their own demise. Finally, where girlfriends, partners and wives escape from violent men they find that their refuge is shortlived, they are stalked, often kidnapped, imprisoned, and made to return. In *Butterworth* (1993) 14 Cr App R (S) 674, the appellant kidnapped a former girlfriend threatening her with an imitation hand gun. He got into the passenger side of her car and held an automatic Libera Vendita 8 mm pistol to her head saying, 'Let's play a little game'.

In very recent years there has been some indication that threats to kill are being taken more seriously, reflected in the marked increase in notifiable (recorded) offences for 'threat to kill and threat of conspiracy to murder'. In 1986, there were 1340 notifiable offences recorded. In 1987, this rose to 1785, in 1988 to 2730, in 1989 to 3579, in 1990 to 4162, in 1991 to 4712, in 1992 to 5487, and in 1993 to 5638 and in 1994 to 6846 (*Criminal Statistics* Table 2.15, p. 52, 1994). The increase in this offence since 1986 reflects an increase of over 400 per cent. Statistics on domestic violence show a substantial increase in recent years, this is largely the result of changes in police recording practices and particularly as a result of the Metropolitan Police Force Order of 1987. The *modus operandi* in such cases is strikingly similar in the jurisdictions already referred to. The principal method of killing female spouses in England and Wales has been strangulation and asphyxi-ation, present in over one third of all such homicides. Indeed strangulation is the commonest method of killing female victims regardless of the relationship of victim to suspect. Strangulation was the method of killing employed in 25 per cent of all female victims killed in 1991 compared with 7 per cent of male victims (*Criminal Statistics*, 1991, Table 4.3). The figures for 1992–94 show a marked similarity where strangulation accounted for 25, 27 and 28 per cent of female deaths and 6, 8 and 8 per cent of male deaths for the respective years (*Criminal Statistics* 1994, Table 4.3, p. 79). This method of abuse is routinely experienced by women victims. Notwithstanding, the lethality potential of this method of violence, the traditional response of police in dealing with complaints of this type of abuse where the victim survives is not to press charges in the absence of corroborative signs of injury. Such violence, surprisingly perhaps, frequently produces little or no forensic evidence even where a victim dies as a result. For the survivor of an attempted asphyxiation either by suffocation or traumatic asphyxiation where the aggressor may sit on top of the victim's chest, there may be no visible signs of injury whereas in other cases signs of petechial haemorrhage may be found on the upper eyelids and internally on the pleural surfaces of the lungs. (See Knight 1982, pp. 175–6). Likewise in attempted strangulation apart from reddening and bruising there may be little else. Those counselling women find that attempted strangulation and attempted asphyxiation are typically experienced by domestic violence victims. Examination of these cases alone suggests that men are driven by a will to possess and control and an absolute concept of possession and proprietorial right which persists even after a relationship has ended.

The tyranny of intimate relationships and patriarchal power may be so complete that no act of force or threat of force is necessary. In a case investigated by Greater Manchester police's domestic violence unit, it was discovered that an elderly woman who visited the local hospital had throughout her married been life looked in the coal shed when her husband went out to work. The case was investigated by police and social services and the woman herself had become so accustomed to this over 50 years of marriage that she considered it the norm (*The Independent*, 8 February 1992). So all this, then, is the reality of violence that is called 'domestic'.

Sexual violence: love, passion and hate

In recent years there has been a growing awareness of the extent to which sexual violence is an integral part of the exercise of control, power and male violence. Until recently, the institution of marriage, whilst denying women any legal protection under the law from rape perpetrated by a husband, has rendered husbands immune from criminal liability. A wife can refuse unreasonable demands, however, as in *Holborn* v *Holborn* [1947] 1 All ER 32, where a wife satisfied the justices that the husband's demands revolted her, or where a husband has venereal disease as in *Foster* v *Foster* [1921] 152 TLR 70. Until 1991, a wife could not refuse her husband's sexual advances; his right to sexual intercourse and, it seems, to perform and demand other sexual acts has been absolute. The presumption of male sexual privilege within the marriage contract has extended *de facto* if not *de jure* to unmarried couples, informed by the supposition that the sexual relationship outside marriage is in reality a quasi-informal marriage contract, and the notion that consent is once and for all. Thus, denial of protection has extended in practice to unmarried women where not only is the rape of a cohabitee, but also other forms of sexual assault, including forced fellatio and acts of buggery, regarded as a male proprietorial right and a woman's contention of non-consent is doubted especially where there is evidence of consent to these acts on prior occasions.

In 1991, a husband's legal immunity from the rape of his wife was extinguished, (see *R* [1991] 2 WLR 1065 at 1074; see Law Commission Paper No. 205; see also the chapter entitled, Sex Crime). The prelude to this historic ruling was charted by the conviction of the appellant for attempted rape and assault occasioning actual bodily harm, where he had tried to have sexual intercourse with his wife at the same time, squeezing her neck with both hands. Owen J, presiding at the Crown Court ruled:

> I accept that it is not for me to make the law. However, it is for me to state the common law as I believe it to be. If that requires me to indicate a set of circumstances which have not so far been considered as sufficient to negate consent as in fact so doing, then I must do so. I cannot believe that it is part of the common law of this country that where there has been withdrawal of either party from cohabitation, accompanied by a clear indication that consent to sexual intercourse has been terminated, then that does not amount to a revocation of that implied consent.

The Owen ruling was followed in *C* [1991] 1 All ER 755, where Simon Brown J declared that the concept of 'marital exemption' in rape was wholly misconceived. 'In my judgment, the position in law today is, as already declared in Scotland, that there is no marital exemption to the law of rape. This is the ruling I give.'. In *J* [1991] 1 All ER 759, however, a case which came before the courts only weeks after this judgment, the judge ruled in contradistinction that s. 1 of the Sexual Offences Amendment Act 1976 preserved the marital exemption. A further unreported case of S (15 January 1991), reached the same conclusion. Following Owen J's ruling in R the conviction was appealed before a five member division of the Court of Appeal (R [1991] 2 All ER 257), which held in a judgment delivered by Lord Lane CJ that, '... the husband's immunity ... no longer exists. We take the view that the time has now arrived when the law should declare that a rapist remains a rapist subject to the criminal law, irrespective of his relationship with his victim' and upheld the conviction. A final appeal was heard before the House of Lords on 23 October 1991, which in a historic ruling reversed the 350 year old dictum of Sir Matthew Hale in *A History of the Pleas of the Crown* (1836: 1971 edition at p. 636), 'But the husband cannot be guilty of a rape committed by himself upon his lawful wife, for by their mutual matrimonial consent and contract the wife hath given herself up in this kind unto her husband which she cannot retract' (R [1991] 4 All ER 481). The House of Lords was unanimous, in the opinion handed down by Lord Keith, that, '... in modern times the supposed marital exemption in rape forms no part of the law of England' (at p. 489).

Prior to 1991, whether a husband was immune from criminal liability for other unwanted sexual overtures excepting rape on a wife was a legal point considered in several cases. Where forced fellatio, accompanied by violence has taken place, the court has on occasion taken such incidents as evidence of indecent assault, and like rape in marriage or between intimates or ex-intimates it has been difficult for the victim to convince a jury of her lack of consent. In *Caswell* [1984] Crim LR 111, in the court of first instance, the estranged wife was attacked, kicked in the face and ribs and forced to suck her husband's penis, which was, as the editors of Criminal Law Review reporting the case added, '... activity they had performed consensually during cohabitation ...' In this case although a divorce petition was issued, the wife's consent was not negatived and the husband was thereby immune from criminal liability. The reasoning in *Caswell* was not followed by the Court of Appeal in *Kowalski* (1988) 86 Cr App R 339, [1988] Crim LR 124. Here, it was held that the legal presumption in marriage that intercourse does not require the consent of the wife cannot be extended to acts of fellatio merely because the parties are lawfully married. In *Kowalski* the appellant forced his wife to have oral sex and sexual intercourse by threatening her with a knife. In *Brown* (1993) 14 Cr App R (S) 434 at 435, the ex-partner kicked the front door in, ordered the ex-girlfriend to undress, forced oral sex upon her and raped her. She did not resist because she was frightened. Later, he kicked her about the head and body. Lloyd LJ described him as an 'unreconstructed chauvinist of the first order': probably an apposite description of all men who abuse women whom they believe to be their possession.

An analysis of cases of buggery perpetrated against partners, similarly reveals the insuperable difficulties women encounter in convincing jurors that they did not consent to the act complained of, even where it is accompanied by other acts of violence. The problematic nature of women's 'consent' and 'assent' in coercive relationships involving physical or mental violence and duress is all too apparent. In *T* v *T* [1964] P 85, [1963] 2 All ER 746 a husband persuaded a wife that sodomy was part of her matrimonial duty. She petitioned for a divorce on the grounds of behaviour. The trial judge dismissed her petition finding that there had been consent to sodomy. 'I am satisfied that this particular wife had complete freedom to choose whether she would permit sodomy or would not permit sodomy'. The wife appealed and the Court of Appeal found, '. . . the wife's consent to sodomy was not real consent, she had not complete freedom of choice'. In the words of Donovan LJ, 'What we have to consider is the quality of the wife's consent. Was it real consent or not?', concluding that she did not have freedom of choice and that her appeal should be granted. The quality of a woman's consent and the all too often conflation of her assent as consent, runs through the case law. In *Krause* (1989) 11 Cr App R (S) 360, a sentence of five years' imprisonment was upheld for buggery of a female cohabitee without her consent. Following a dispute, the appellant buggered the complainant twice after he had inflicted violence upon her. Mustill LJ, delivering the judgment of the court, is in no doubt about her subjugation and suffering. In his judgment he said, '. . . he told her to put on a pair of stockings and take all the rest of her clothes off. This requirement plainly had a sexual element . . . All of what she permitted to be done to her was without any true consent on her part. She was frightened of what he might do to her . . .'. In explaining the husband's behaviour the judge resorted only too readily to the alcohol theory, '. . . no doubt the origin of this offence was because you had been drinking all day . . . You came home violent and aggressive and you set about her. Not only did you treat her violently, you subjected her to the degradation of being buggered, and one only has to read her statement to see the distress which she must have suffered as a result . . .'. In *Stapleton* (1989) 11 Cr App R (S) 364, a sentence of five years' imprisonment was upheld for buggery of a female cohabitee on a number of occasions without her consent, in which he threatened violence with a knife, '. . . the first act of buggery which you committed was committed at knife point and thereafter over a period of several months you frequently committed acts of buggery against your partner and without her consent. She was in fear of you, and on many of those occasions you actually showed violence towards her or you threatened violence to her'.

Where charges of buggery and of rape have been preferred, women have had less success in bringing a prosecution. Where the defendant is acquitted of rape, it follows *ipso facto* that buggery is regarded as a consensual act. In the case of *Bush* (1989) 11 Cr App R (S) 295, a former cohabitee was admitted to the victim's house after he threatened to kick the door down. He was indicted for rape and buggery. Acquitting the man on the charge of rape, the court also took the view that the buggery had taken place with her consent. In *Cawley* (1988) 10 Cr App R (S) 452, a similar logic was applied where a man was charged with assault, rape and buggery of an ex-girlfriend. Reasonable and unreasonable belief in a woman's consent has also provided the aggressor with a defence and mitigated sentence. In *David Malcolm W* (1994) 15 Cr App R (S) 561, the appellant's sentence was varied on appeal to three months on the grounds that he thought the victim was consenting. Counsel submitted in his defence, '. . . she never demonstrated that she was not consenting and he honestly believed that she was consenting throughout'. On these occasions the wife bit her wrists in order to endure the pain of anal intercourse, submitting through fear. Counsel for the appellant explained the wrist biting thus, 'as a natural representation of how she was enjoying orgasm'. Where buggery has taken place on a number of occasions and the male cohabitee or husband has argued in his defence that he thought it was with her consent, then derisory sentences are granted normally of three months which is consistent with current sentencing practice for what is termed 'truly consensual buggery'.

No one working with victims of domestic violence can be in any doubt as to the ubiquity of this conduct in subjugating women. When a discussion of this point was delivered in a paper to an Annual Conference of the National Association for the Development of Work with Sex Offenders (NOTA), one of the female participants approached me afterwards recalling how her former husband had beaten her for twenty years, he had on most occasions put his hand over her mouth and tried to suffocate her. He took photographs of her in sexual poses to show to his workmates. She 'co-operated' to avoid further beatings and to protect her five children. She had left him eleven years before our meeting, her most distressing and enduring memory (and she cried as she recollected it) was her experience of going to the hospital to have her rectum sutured following his forced buggery of her. The Criminal Justice and Public Order Act 1994, s. 142, now classifies non-consensual heterosexual buggery as rape. It is likely that victims of anal rape will face the same gruelling inquisition as victims of vaginal rape. Convictions will be rare, although longer sentences will now be available to the courts where the victim is made. Current sentencing practice indicates that non-consensual buggery on a woman accompanied with violence attracts a five year sentence and buggery without violence, where the aggressor contends that he thought his victim was consenting, 3 months. The issue of consent is as problematic in the heterosexual context as it is in the homosexual context as previously discussed in the Chapter Gay Prohibition. In the case of *Wilson* (1996) *The Times*, 5 March) Court of Appeal where a husband had branded a wife's buttocks with the capital letters W and A, Lord Justice Russell in a reserved judgment said that intervening in apparently consensual activities between husband and wife in the privacy of the home was not a proper matter for criminal investigation or prosecution. The Court held that the trial judge Crabtree J had misdirected the jury when he said that the cases of *Donovan* and *Brown* [1993] 2 All ER 75 constrained him to rule that consent was no defence.

Mental violence

Domestic violence, both physical and mental, often results in psychiatric injury including fear, trauma, anxiety, hopelessness, low self esteem, shame and guilt. Psychiatric injury can induce physical illness, nervous shock, post-traumatic stress, paranoia and anticipation of violence and abuse, sleeplessness, phobias, peptic ulcers and mental illness including mental breakdown and including attempts to inflict self harm, often ordered or encouraged by the abusive partner. There is no legal redress for the effects of mental violence caused by the physically or mentally abusive partner. The House of Lords, in 1897, reviewing the case of *Russell* v *Russell* [1897] AC LR 395 held, 'There must be danger to life, limb, or health, bodily or mental, or a reasonable apprehension of it to constitute legal cruelty'. This position has remained relatively unaltered.

In recent years the Court of Appeal has recognised that psychiatric injury can constitute assault, and until *Burstow* (1996) (unreported) 5 March there had not been a successful conviction. In *Chan-Fook* [1994] 2 All ER 552, although the appeal against conviction was allowed on the ground that there was in fact no evidence of psychological injury to the complainant, the court reiterated the principle that assault occasioning actual bodily harm was indeed capable of including psychiatric injury. In *Gelder, The Times*, 9 July 1994, the defendant was convicted of grievous bodily harm following causing a woman psychiatric injury and sentenced to eighteen months' imprisonment, after subjecting her to a series of obscene telephone calls. The conviction was quashed on procedural grounds (see the chapter entitled, Sex Crime for further detail).

In *Burstow* the defendant had stalked a woman for three years who as a result was under psychiatric treatment. Burstow followed her, made phone calls, sent malicious mail, stole clothes from her washing line and watched her house. He was convicted of grievous bodily harm following the psychiatric injury he inflicted on his victim (*The Daily Telegraph*, 5 March 1996). Countless other victims will be unable to satisfy the standard of injury required and will be forced to rely on the existing civil law remedies in tort or the domestic violence injunctive relief (discussed later). See Bernstein 1993, Salame 1993, Woods 1993 for a discussion of stalking laws in the United States.

The effects of physical and mental violence on women's mental state are documented in the medical reports prepared on women who kill (see the chapter entitled, Unreasonable Women — Battered Woman Syndrome on Trial), and broadly, in the casework of psychiatrists and in research studies on battered women (see Walker 1989). Respondents in a study conducted in women's refuges, said that mental cruelty in the form of constant belittling, humiliation and indignities and mental cruelty of smashing the house to bits and threats of all kinds was experienced by many women (Edwards 1989a, p. 164). Indeed the effect of smashing furniture, fixtures and household property is underestimated in its effects on women and children at whom it is frequently directed. Duress and coercion is also a significant part. Southall Black Sisters describe the gamut of psychiatric injury experienced by women who seek their help:

... women arrive in varying stages of depression. They exhibit signs of confusion, guilt, shame and insecurity. The depression can sometimes be acute, bordering on mental illness. Some women actually suffer mental breakdown as a direct result of violence and harassment. A large number of them have actually contemplated or attempted suicide (Home Affairs Committee (1993), Minutes of Evidence, *Domestic Violence* 222).

In 1984, Krishna Sharma was found hanging in her own home. The coroner's verdict was one of suicide, a verdict disputed by the local community. She had for many years been subjected to her husband's violence, the police had been approached by her for assistance on numerous occasions, and on the night before she died police had advised her to contact a Citizens Advice Bureau, which had in fact been closed for eight years (Edwards 1987b).

This is the reality of the abuse that is called 'domestic'. Legal remedies similarly reflect the marginalisation and trivialisation of private violence both at the level of the legal remedy itself and its application. The analysis that follows focuses almost exclusively on the criminal law.

THE PUBLIC AND PRIVATE ORDERING OF LEGAL PROTECTION

The family is and always has been a private institution, one which the State has left relatively unfettered. As O'Donovan expresses it, 'Home is thought to be a private place, a refuge from society, where relationships can flourish untrammelled by public interference' (1985, p. 107). The presumption of non-intervention by the State has not merely acceded to the patriarchal authority of the family thereby tolerating male violence, but has placed violence against wives on the very lowest rung. The law has served to institutionalise domestic violence symbolically by elevating the principle of non-interference in family life and patriarchal authority as paramount, above the principle of protection of the wife. In addition, the legal construction of the marriage contract has furthered her vulnerability. The legal concept of 'one flesh', the unity of the interests of man and wife (Gilbert 1801, p. 136), and the principle of family privacy have all colluded in the emergence of a *laissez-faire* approach to domestic violence where the State has seen fit to intervene only as a last resort. Mill noted, 'The vilest malefactor has some wretched woman tied to him, against whom he can commit any atrocity except killing her, and if tolerably cautious, can do that without much danger of legal penalty' (1978, p. 35). The position of the male has been strengthened and legitimated by the legal power bestowed upon him under the rules governing chastisement and marital discipline of wives. In 1663, it was held in *Bradley* v *Wife* (1663) (cited in Cleveland 1896, p. 222), that a husband could not be bound over for wife beating because he had the power of castigation. Lady Leigh had judgment ruled in her favour by Lord Hale, who declared that *salva moderata castigatione* was not meant of beating but of admonition and confinement. Even in 1946, the case of *Meacher* v *Meacher* [1946] P 216, provides a salutary reminder of the extent of the law's ratification of patriarchal authority, where the court of first instance found in favour of a husband who was justified in assaulting his wife following her refusal to stop visiting her sister. The respondent assaulted her, hitting her in the stomach. Her application for a divorce was refused although reversed upon appeal. The power of the male has been consolidated in his absolute right to consortium until 1991 and the House of Lords in *R* [1991] 4 All ER 481.

In the criminal domain the initiation of criminal protection has been left to the woman, and in the rules governing evidence she could not be compelled, thus treating domestic violence even in the criminal courts as if it were a civil matter. In the civil law the key arena of conflict has been in respect of whether a woman's right to protection is paramount where proprietary interests of male partners provide the competing interest. The House of Lords in *Davis* v *Johnson* [1978] 1 All ER 1132 decided this conflict, finding in favour of protecting the injured party from violence. Subsequent statutes, *inter alia* the Matrimonial Homes Act 1983, have relegated the protection of victims from domestic violence, in so far as ouster orders are concerned, to its former position, that is in accordance with the 1983 Act, domestic violence is one of several factors to which the court must pay equal regard. It is unlikely that the Family Homes and Domestic Violence Bill [HL] 1995 (now the Family Law Bill) will remedy this situation. Indeed, with the new 'balance of harm' test as it applies to ouster injunctions and the consideration of such applications it will lead to competing claims for protection from violence versus rights to occupation.

Criminal remedies: it's only a domestic

The effectiveness of criminal remedies depends on implementation by police, the Crown Prosecution Service, the courts, and sentencers. This chapter proceeds with an analysis of each of these sequential stages in turn, together with an examination of the development of the law with regard to evidential issues with a view to discerning how far the nature of the law and the rules governing admission of evidence have assisted or thwarted women's efforts toward protection.

Victim reporting   Few women who experience domestic violence ever report it to the police. In fact, most studies have found that the police are often contacted only as the very last resort. Edwards found that 50 per cent of women in refuges had never contacted the police, many women tell no one at all. The motives for women's silence have been widely documented in the literature (see Radzinowicz and King 1978, p. 38). Women are deterred from reporting from feelings of shame and from a belief that the police will do very little to assist. In 75 per cent of cases reported to the police it is the victim who reports the incident. Witnesses/bystanders, accounting for the remaining 25 per cent, have been traditionally reluctant to interfere in 'disputes' between married couples and cohabitees in the 'private' domain. Kitty Genovese was murdered by her husband watched by bystanders who thought it was not their business, as it was instead just another domestic quarrel (see Mawby 1985, p. 461, Edwards 1985).

Police investigation   In the US (see Sherman et al 1984, Sherman et al 1990, p. 183), in Canada (see Jaffe, Wolfe, Telford, and Austin 1986), in Australia and New Zealand (Hatty 1989, Tolmie 1991) and in England and Wales (see Hanmer 1989, Mooney 1993, Grace 1995), studies suggest that significant improvements have been made in the policing of domestic violence. The Metropolitan Police in London have led the field in England and Wales in implementing new instructions issued to officers in a Force Order in June 1987. The Order emphasised that assaults which occurred in the home were to be considered as serious as assaults which occurred in public, stressing the importance of police support to victims, liaison with local agencies and reminding officers of their powers of arrest. In 1990, Home Office Circular 60/1990 was issued to all police forces in England and Wales advising police to ensure that, '... all police officers involved in the investigation of cases of domestic violence regard as their overriding priority the protection of the victim and the apprehension of the offender'. The Circular emphasised the importance of liaison with other agencies, the establishment of Domestic Violence Units, the reviewing of recording policy and ensuring that officers were aware of the power of arrest, and providing support to the victim. Undoubtedly, the Circular has been instructive in changing force policy especially with regard to introducing greater consistency of policing nationwide, although ACPO (the Association of Chief Police Officers) conceded in their evidence to the Home Affairs Committee '... some forces have not made the progress achieved by others ...' (ACPO's Evidence to the Home Affairs Committee on *Domestic Violence*).

The key policing deficiencies have been *inter alia*, ineffective handling of cases at the scene, (see Reiner 1985, Oppenlander 1982, Bell 1984), the predilection to decline charges, and a habituation of the practice of 'no criming' (see Buchan and Edwards 1991, Edwards 1989b, c). The pro-arrest guidelines contained in the 1987 Force Order for London and the Circular 60/90 give considerable support to officers in executing arrests. Research conducted by Edwards 1988 (1989c), in the London area indicated that arrests had risen since the Force Order of 1987 and later research by Buchan and Edwards (1991) indicated a rise after the 1990 Circular reversing the earlier trend of doing nothing. Such initiatives developed in this country after the success of American police pro arrest policies in Minneapolis (Sherman and Berk 1984) which indicated that early arrest intervention by police in domestic violence had a significant deterrent effect on repeated and more serious acts of violence. The study was replicated in six other cites. Jaffe, Hastings, Reitzel and Austin (1993) argue, contrary to Sherman and Berk, that it is not the arrest of the assailant per se which is the decisive factor but the pressing of charges (see Mitchell 1992, Sherman 1992). In the UK, the Home Office Circular of 60/1990 in giving guidance to police encouraged a quick and effective response arresting suspects if the protection of the victim required it. In a study conducted in Streatham, London in 1989 (Buchan and Edwards 1991), a total of 204 suspects were arrested (46 per cent) out of a total of 446 domestic violence related crimes. Of the 204 suspects arrested 105 (52 per cent) were charged, the decision on 66 was deferred (under the deferred caution scheme) for two months, a further 9 (5 per cent) the outcome was recorded as no further action. Following the introduction of the new policy at Steatham more offenders were arrested than in previous years (52 per cent) as compared to 30 per cent for 1988 of total domestic violence incidents recorded and more offenders were charged (27 per cent) as compared to 18 per cent.

The Domestic Violence Unit   As part of this broader initiative in changing police attitudes to domestic violence and the investigation and handling of cases, specialised units staffed with officers trained to deal with domestic violence have been instituted. The first Domestic Violence Unit (DVU) was established in Tottenham, North London in 1987. The aims of the DVUs are to give support to victims, to refer them to local agencies, where necessary to provide a chaperone in court, to keep victims apprised of the progress of the prosecution case, to provide follow up visits in all cases and to enhance the collation of information and intelligence on domestic violence. The protection of women has improved as bail conditions can now be attached by the police where a suspect is charged. Under the Criminal Justice and Public Order Act 1994, s. 27 gives power to the police to grant conditional bail. Research by Edwards (1989b, c, 1991), showed that the presence of a DVU on a police division resulted in a more positive police intervention at the scene and an increase in arrests and charges preferred. Home Office Circular 60/90 gave further impetus to the move towards establishing DVUs outside the Metropolitan Police area. Much debate has followed with regard to whether a specialised domestic violence unit is something which is needed long term or whether the additional police manpower is justifiable in the short term only. In a number of police divisions Chief Superintendents remain resolutely against setting up such units. In Southall, West London an area with a high immigrant population and where relations between police and the community, largely Asian, are strained, a DVU was not set up until 1995. Yet, such matters are ultimately a matter for Chief Superintendents. The deployment of officers and the implementation of the law is a matter for police discretion and a principle enshrined in law. The *locus classicus* is *Metropolitan Police Commissioner ex parte Blackburn* [1968] 1 All ER 763 at 769, where Denning MR opined:

> I hold it to be the duty of the Commissioner of the Police, as it is of every chief constable, to enforce the law of the land. He must take steps so to post his men that crimes may be detected; and that honest citizens may go about their affairs in peace. He must decide whether or no suspected persons are to be prosecuted; and, if need be, bring the prosecution or see that it is brought; but in all these things he is not a servant of anyone, save of the law itself. No Minister of the Crown can tell him that he must, or must not, keep observation on this place or that; or that he must, or must not, prosecute this man or that one ... It must be for him to decide on the disposition of his force and the concentration of his resources on any particular crime or area'.

And so whether to have a DVU or not is a matter for police discretion. The Metropolitan Police Service Working Party Report on Domestic Violence of 1993 further endorsed the importance of DVUs in improving the police response to domestic violence at both the level of victim support and in the prosecution of the offender. Research indicates an increase at stations with DVUs of 95 per cent in complainant reporting, 22 per cent in arrest rates, 21 per cent in cases reported to the CPS, and a 24 per cent reduction in the no crime rate as against the following figures for stations with no DVU at 65 per cent, 14 per cent, 13 per cent and 16 per cent respectively (Metropolitan Police Report 1993), although many of its recommendations are still to be implemented.

Crime recording The traditional police reluctance to record domestic violence as a crime, recorded on a crime sheet and entered into the crime statistics submitted to the Home Office for publication, arises from the conventional wisdom held by many officers that such cases are not 'real crimes,' and from the supposition that such cases are unlikely to proceed to prosecution. In a higher proportion of domestic violence cases compared to other crimes the incident is not recorded at the outset. As Chatterton (1976, p. 44, 1983) found, police officers considered that recording an allegation of domestic violence as a crime was a waste of time because women withdrew the complaint. Where domestic violence is initially recorded as a crime, the 'no crime' classification has been used all too frequently at the final classification stage thereby avoiding entry of the crime as uncleared into official statistics. The 'no crime' classification is reserved to enable police to write off those crimes that have been recorded erroneously. The theft of the pedal cycle that turned out to have been borrowed and later returned by a neighbour, provides an example of the legitimate use of the 'no crime' classification. The 'no crime' classification was never intended to write off stab wounds, bruises, and broken limbs, for no other reason than because a complainant is considered likely to withdraw the charge at some later point. The perennial problem for police which impacts on this abuse of the 'no crime' is that where the 'clear up' rate is regarded as a key performance indicator, and high clear up rates are considered a measure of police efficiency, then police are likely to ensure that the only crimes recorded are those they are certain of clearing. When a crime is recorded but does not proceed to prosecution, and depending on force policy may result in a 'not cleared' final classification, cases with a low prosecution potential result in a reduction in the clear up rate. Such an outcome is highly undesirable from a police point of view, for although an artificial and misleading measure of police performance, the clear up rate functions in the mind of both police and public as a barometer of police effectiveness.

Studies by Edwards (1986, 1989b, c), and by Buchan and Edwards (1991) found a staggeringly high proportion of offences of domestic violence 'no crimed'. For the period 1982-1986 Edwards found as many as between 80-90 per cent of cases 'no crimed'. Following the introduction in 1987 of the Force Order and a clear statement from the Metropolitan Police of its intention to address this problem, this fell to 65 per cent in 1988. Buchan and Edwards in the Streatham study 1989-1990, where a new pilot scheme involving the deferred cautioning of domestic violence first time offenders was being implemented, found that the 'no criming' levels dropped phenomenally to 30 per cent. However, the researchers found that the very same kinds of cases were still being no crimed. Consider the seriousness of the following 'no crimed' cases: case 1 — cuts and bruises to the head, cut on left hand, bite marks to the middle finger on left hand, attacked with milk bottle, hit with shoe; case 2 cut to back of head, victim found unconscious (1991, p. 49). The introduction of police policy has resulted in an improvement in crime recording, and is reflected in the rise in recorded crime for violence against the person in the Metropolitan Police District (MPD), and in turn is discernible in its impact on the national profile. In 1985, 20,242 offences of violence against the person were recorded in the MPD rising to 38,400 in 1993; in turn national figures on indictable recorded crimes of violence against the person have risen from 121,731 in 1985 to 205,102 in 1993 and 219,744 in 1994.

Police attitudes   Whatever changes are made in police policy in respect of recording practice or arrests, the changing nature of police attitudes to domestic violence is largely invisible and difficult to measure. Over the last decade Gary Armstrong and I have charted changes in police statements about domestic violence, in several Metropolitan Police divisions. We recognise, however, that these may only be signifying public methods of accounting and may not reflect any change in privately held attitudes. Nevertheless, police accounts of domestic violence have changed significantly over this period, and it is reasonable to assume that some attitudinal change may also have followed although we remain tentative in our drawing of that particular inference. In 1985 we conducted 44 interviews with officers at a North London and a West London police station (Edwards and Armstrong 1988), a further 20 interviews with officers from the Kent Constabulary in 1987 (see Bourlet 1990), in 1987 we conducted interviews with 30 police trainees at the Police Training School at Hendon, London (Edwards 1989b) and in 1990 we interviewed 53 serving police officers of all ranks at a South London police station (Buchan and Edwards 1991).

In the three studies prior to the 1987 Force Order we detected a remarkable consistency in the responses of serving police officers to domestic violence. Domestic violence was regarded as problematic and a waste of time, was trivial, and was rubbish work. With regard to the police operational response, arrest was rarely used and was not perceived as a viable means of dealing with the problem. On the occasions when the suspect was arrested it was invariably for breach of the peace even when evidence of criminal assault was indicated. 'We don't want to take action in these occasions anyway' said one officer (Interview 12, North London sample 1985). Police were concerned that the victim would be likely to withdraw the allegation. 'If she withdraws it goes down the drain that's the job' (Interview 13, North London sample). The public/private divide which so often characterises police response to 'domestics' was exemplified in this not untypical comment from a police officer. 'A husband and wife is treated exactly the same as any other assault. But with hindsight and experience they lead to great difficulties due to charges being dropped. If you were walking in the street and someone smashed you in the eye I would arrest. If you were walking in the street and your wife hit you, I wouldn't' (Interview 16, North London sample). Many officers believed that women were responsible for male violence, 'Because women have sharper tongues than men they go on and on' (Interview 20, North London).

The interviews we conducted in 1990, as part of an evaluation of a new divisional policy at Streatham (discussed above), provided an important opportunity to compare the nature of police accounting for domestic violence before and after the 1987 Force Order. The negative attitudes to domestic violence, the stereotypical approaches to victims and offenders we had earlier encountered were not so transparent. The operational response indicated a significant change from the response we found in studies we conducted in the mid 1980s. Officers now arrested in minor cases and stated they would even arrest in cases where women were fearful. Officers now displayed a heightened sensitivity and awareness although a small quorum of officers still expressed well worn and traditional stereotypes, 'it's grief', 'it's rubbish', 'it's not what police work should be but we've got to sort them out'. However views about the sanctity of marriage, who deserves to be protected, and 'just deserts' still introjected in police work influencing key decisions. The following case is instructive, 'We had one Irish fellow living with a black girl, she's got a baby by someone else, and now she's expecting his baby. She wanted to go out at night 'clubbing'. He objected. The house was a tip. I wiped my feet as I walked out. That's how bad it was. It's quite obvious she doesn't want to know. He whacked her and we didn't arrest . . . she was making his life Hell! Nothing to be gained from arresting him!' (Edwards and Buchan 1991, p. 85). A study of assault in Bristol (Clarkson, Cretney, Davis and Shepherd 1994), similarly confirmed the resilience and longevity of such traditional police attitudes; quoting one officer they wrote, '. . . crime's crime, that's good old black and white, you know what's wrong in that. But domestic, ooh . . .'. In the wake of significant police policy change in the US and legislative developments (the Violence Against Women Act 1994, see Klein 1995) research has shown that traditional attitudes to domestic violence are intransigent.

Pressing charges   Where there is evidence of violence, the traditional approach of the police has been not to press charges. This reluctance sprang, at least in the mid 1980s, from a view that women would be unlikely to proceed with the prosecution and would withdraw their complaint. Research is undecided on this point, some studies have indicated that this 'copping out' as Oppenlander (1982) has coined it, is more likely to be induced by the police themselves in their insensitive and unsupportive handling of the case and advice to complainants. Police justify this heavy handed inquisitorial strategy as merely testing the strength of the evidence and the resolve of the complainant. Research has also indicated that once charges are brought it is unlikely that women will withdraw charges. Dawson and Faragher (1977, p. 142), found that only one in ten charges were withdrawn at this stage. Wasoff (1982, p. 194), found withdrawals in 2 out of 59 cases. Whilst the recognition and recording of domestic violence as a crime has contributed to an increase in notifiable offences, it has not, however, meant a proportionate increase in the level of domestic violence cases prosecuted. Police are still reluctant to press charges in both the US and UK. Buchan and Edwards (1991) found that where arrests had been made any increase did not necessarily mean a proportionate increase in charges brought.

In the US following the relative success of the pro-arrest policy in Minneapolis where only three of the 136 offenders arrested went on to be prosecuted, yet subsequent domestic violence assaults were deterred, several states introduced legislation mandating arrest. In Indiana for example, where a man habitually assaults his partner the crime is considered more serious and what would if a single offence be considered a class A misdemeanour battery is instead considered as the more serious D felony which carries with it a four year instead of a one year sentence (see Ford and Regoli 1993, p. 129). But research is still unequivocal on the deterrent effects of arrest and counselling and diversion as compared to arrest and prosecution.

Whilst pro-arrest and pro-prosecution might have been the desired goal of the late 1980s, the handling of domestic violence is now affected by the general trajectory in North America and the UK towards diversion from prosecution evinced in cautioning projects and mediation initiatives.

Diversion from prosecution — cautioning   The presumption that once an allegation has been made and there is sufficient evidence to proceed with a prosecution that this will be the automatic course adopted, is fallacious. Many crimes are in fact dealt with by means of a police caution. The use of the caution in domestic violence cases has received a very mixed reception. On the one hand cautioning men for wife beating has been seen as symptomatic of the tendency to 'down crime' the seriousness of domestic violence cases; it is seen as a soft option. However, in the absence of any police response at all arguably a caution represents a substantial improvement. A caution is citable in the court for up to three years and depends upon the offender admitting guilt. In 1989, at Streatham police station in South London, a unique 'deferred caution' policy was in operation. Allegations of domestic violence were dealt with by arresting and removing the suspect and then deferring the decision to caution or prefer charges for two months. This allowed police to review the suspect's behaviour. The decision to caution was not mandatory but an option along with prosecution or no further action where cases met the set criteria, including: where the injury was of a minor nature, where the suspect admitted the offence and where the victim agreed to a caution. Where the victim wished the offender to be charged, where there was concern for the victim's safety, or where the offender had a previous conviction or caution for assaulting the victim, the deferred caution would be inappropriate. The researchers evaluating the policy found that cautioning offered police another option in dealing with domestic violence, heightened police awareness and ensured that doing nothing as an option was extinguished.

The Crown Prosecution Service: the tail that wags the dog

In many jurisdictions, e.g., England and Wales, North America and Australia, since the 1980s the police have consistently tried to improve the prosecution potential of domestic violence cases. In England and Wales since the Prosecution of Offences Act 1985, the Crown Prosecution Service (see *Crown Prosecution Service Annual Report* 1991–92, 1992–93) has taken over prosecutions and determines whether to prosecute in criminal cases. Prior to 1985 the police were both investigators and prosecutors. This conflation of roles and responsibilities gave rise to a number of criticisms. Police were said to lack independence. Cases were said to be poorly prepared. Too many cases before the courts were resulting in judge directed acquittals (see *Judicial Statistics*; Royal Commission on Criminal Procedure 1981, *The Investigation and Prosecution of Criminal Offences in England and Wales, The Law and Procedure*). In accordance with the Prosecution of Offences Act 1985, s. 23, it is the prosecutor who decides whether a case should be proceeded with and the nature of the charge or whether a case should be discontinued. There are two tests to be considered. In consideration of the first test the prosecutor must consider whether there is a sufficiency of evidence to afford a 'realistic prospect of conviction'. If that is decided in the affirmative the second test is then applied. In consideration of the second test the prosecutor must assess whether a prosecution is in the 'public interest'. Both these tests apply in cases of domestic violence as in any other crime. Prosecutors are guided in this task by the Code for Crown Prosecutors (see Blackstone's 1996 p. 2244), issued pursuant to the Prosecution of Offences Act 1985.

Evidential sufficiency   As is stated in the Code, 'The CPS does not support the proposal that a bare *prima facie* case is enough' (Blackstone's 1996 Appendix 5, p. 2244) and thus the *prima facie* test applied by the police and the 'realistic prospect of conviction' test applied by the prosecutor are markedly different. In assessment of the 'realistic prospect of conviction', in domestic violence cases in particular regard is placed on the credibility of the witness/victim, and reference in the 1991–92 Code was made to the significance of a change in a complainant's attitude with respect to proceeding.

> In some cases it will be appropriate for the Crown prosecutor to have regard to the attitude of a complainant who notified the police but later expresses a wish that no action be taken. It may be that in such circumstances proceedings need not be pursued unless either there is a suspicion that the change of heart was actuated by fear or the offence was of some gravity (Code for Crown Prosecutors 1991–92 CPB Annual Report, p. 51). It is not known how far this consideration influences the decision of prosecutors in 1996.

The Crown Prosecutor must draw on his own experience of how the evidence is likely to stand up in court. This raises particular questions where offences of domestic violence are being alleged (Blackstone's 1996 D1.63).

Public interest   Having established a sufficiency of evidence in order to proceed, the second stage requires the prosecutor to consider whether a prosecution is in the public interest. In 1989, in a case observed by the author at Streatham, where a paediatric surgeon had assaulted his wife, the papers were returned from the CPS marked, 'not in the public interest to prosecute'. In reaching a decision not to prosecute on public interest grounds, prosecutors' rules require consideration of the following factors *inter alia*, whether the sentence would be nominal, a small fine or a conditional discharge; whether the case is stale; whether the offender is young or old; and whether the complainant changes her attitude. Following much criticism of the prosecutors' role in domestic violence cases and the poor prosecution prognosis, the CPS in April 1993 introduced a new policy (*A Statement of Prosecution Policy: Domestic Violence*, 1993). The new policy emphasised amongst other concerns that where a victim wishes to withdraw a complaint regard should be had to the following procedure: (i) A prosecutor of Principal Crown Prosecutor level should be informed and supervise the case. (ii) Prosecutors should request that withdrawals be confirmed in writing. (iii) A written statement of withdrawal should be made. (iv) If the victim's first statement contradicts the later statement then consideration may be given to proceeding against the victim for an offence of public justice (waste of police time). (v) Prosecutors should consider the options for continuance: (a) is it necessary to call the victim? (b) should the victim be compelled? (c) could a victim's statement be adduced under s. 23, Prosecution of Offences Act 1985 (discussed below)? The object is to give consideration to the difficulties faced by victims. The CPS domestic violence policy document states, '. . . the more serious the offence the more likely it is that the public interest will require a prosecution'. The CPS goes on to state that there will be difficulties in finding this balance not least because it is recognized that there is one aspect of public interest which rightly condemns personal violence in any form, and another which recognises the benefit of preserving a family unit wherever possible:

> . . . in some cases where the victim wishes to withdraw the complaint, the public interest will not require a prosecution. Factors likely to be relevant to this decision are the seriousness of the offence, the likelihood of recurrence, any continuing relationship with the accused, and the effect which pursuing the prosecution in the face of the victim's wishes is likely to have on that relationship.

Despite the CPS initiative in respect of domestic violence their general approach to the public interest consideration works in contradistinction where the 1994–95 policy identifies these amongst a number of factors where a prosecution is less likely to be needed where the court is likely to impose a very small or nominal penalty where the loss or harm can be described as minor (see Blackstone's 1996, p. 2247).

It seems that there has been little retrenchment from the idea of preserving the family unit over and above the protection of the woman within it. Domestic violence is still to be interpreted as a crime between the victim and aggressor instead of a crime between the aggressor and the State, and there it seems is where public interest considerations lie, i.e., in an unwillingness to prosecute in essentially private matters.

Discontinuance   Cases are frequently terminated by the prosecutor. Discontinuance is classed as a 'performance indicator' in the CPS *Annual Report* of 1991–92 (at p. 20). 'Earlier decisions to discontinue cases will reduce unnecessary court appearances, and monitoring the timing will identify our progress.'. The power to withdraw or discontinue is found in s. 23, Prosecution of Offences Act 1985 and considered in *Cooke* v *DPP* [1992] Crim LR 746.

Here C was charged with a number of offences. Before committal, the s. 47, Offences Against the Person Act 1861 assault charges, which were offences triable either way, were substituted by the prosecutor with an offence under s. 51, Police Act 1964, triable summarily only. At an adjourned hearing the defendant's solicitor applied for the s. 47 charges to be reinstated. On an application for an order of *mandamus* it was argued that by purporting to withdraw the s. 47 charges in court and failing to serve a notice of discontinuance, the CPS was in breach of s. 27(3), Prosecution of Offences Act 1985, which provided the defendant with the right to insist that the case on s. 47 continue and be tried by a jury. Counsel argued that a prosecutor could sweep a charge away if there was no evidence but contended that was not the case here. The CPS argued that s. 23 was co-terminus with the pre-existing powers at common law to discontinue the proceedings. The court, dismissing the application, held that s. 23 might allow the CPS the right to withdraw a charge, discontinue proceedings and offer no evidence. The decisions of the CPS are unimpeachable, unless arrived at via an abuse of procedure (see *DPP ex parte Tamsin C* (1995) 1 Cr App R 136 discussed in depth in the chapter entitled, Sex Crime). In the context of domestic violence this has meant that neither a victim nor the police has a right of review against the prosecutor's decision not to proceed at all. Figures provided by the CPS for 1993 show a national average of cases discontinued at 13.3 per cent with a considerable variation in discontinuance rates between the 31 CPS areas in the period up to 1992 (since 1993 the CPS has reorganised into 13 areas). My own calculations derived from criminal statistics for the year 1992 suggest as many as one in five cases being dropped in London, Essex, Devon and Cornwall. It has been more expedient to drop cases at the onset than try to support prosecution witnesses who even if compelled may be hostile. In domestic violence cases *ipso facto* the case is perceived to be 'at risk'. Yet, the predilection of the CPS to discontinue cases is strongly resented by many victims (see Home Affairs Committee *Annual Report of the Crown Prosecution Service Minutes of Evidence* 1992, p. 21, para. 6.1). By 1993 the CPS's solution to the problem of high discontinuance is now to encourage police to refer cases to the CPS for advice and consultation prior to charging. Pre-trial advice referrals rose from 57,000 in 1987 to 73,337 in 1991. It is here especially that the Crown Prosecution Service is now determining the police's hand (see Crisp and Moxon 1994, Crisp, Whittaker and Harris 1995). Cretney and Davis (1996, p. 167), found that discontinuance figured in 29 per cent of non-domestic cases and in 38 per cent of domestic cases where the suspect and complainant were no longer cohabiting and in 60 per cent of cases where the parties were cohabiting.

Down criming   Alternate charging or down criming by both police and prosecutors has been discussed widely in the literature (see Steer 1980, Chatterton 1983, Reiner 1985, Sanders 1988, Bourlet 1990). In addition to discontinuing cases, the CPS routinely 'down crime' cases put before it by police. The power invested in the CPS to decide what charges to prefer is contained within the Prosecution of Offences Act 1985, ss. 10 and 23. Recent case law puts this power to the test. In the case of *Sheffield JJ ex parte DPP*

[1993] Crim LR 136, a common assault and battery charge under the Criminal Justice Act 1988, s. 39, was substituted for the more serious offence of assault under the Offences Against the Person Act 1861, s. 47 (triable by a jury in the Crown Court). The defendant claimed that this was abuse of process and argued that it would prejudice him since he could no longer elect for trial. The magistrates' court accepted this submission and stayed proceedings, the prosecutor responded and applied for judicial review. The High Court held that the charge was a matter for the discretion of the prosecutor and that the charge of common assault and battery was appropriate. The guidelines for prosecution state that a domestic background is not regarded as a factor reducing the seriousness of the charge. In making representations as to the most appropriate forum for trial, prosecutors must have regard to the *National Mode of Trial Guidelines* issued by the Lord Chief Justice in 1990, recently amended in accordance with the Criminal Justice Act of 1991, and as amended in the 1993 Act. The guidelines note that '... essentially offences should be tried summarily unless they include one or more of the features set out in the guidelines and magistrates consider powers of sentencing to be insufficient' (*National Mode of Trial Guidelines* [1990] 1 WLR 1439).

It is well known that domestic violence is routinely down crimed. First, it is cheaper for cases to be heard before a magistrates' court. Secondly, the down criming has been further facilitated by the introduction of s. 39 of the Criminal Justice Act 1988. Here common assault has been made a summary offence triable only before magistrates. Down criming is particularly likely to occur where a sentence of six months or less is considered likely. With the result that prosecutorial assessment of likely sentence becomes the dependent variable of charge reduction, the consequence follows that domestic violence assault with the habitual minor sanctions attached may routinely be reduced to s. 39 or not proceeded with at all if the public interest against prosecution in the Code for Crown Prosecutors prevails. Victims feel that their sufferings are not recognised and the aggressor is secure in the knowledge that he will be treated leniently, if even dealt with at all. The law's treatment of the offender conveys a symbolic message to potential victims deterring them from reporting at the outset.

Evidential evasion: a husband's immunity   It is not only at the level of process or practice and application of law that domestic violence is trivialised, the very ontology and method of law itself deeply embedded in the rules of evidence ensures that spouses receive a lesser justice. The doctrine of one flesh, the unity of husband and wife and their identity of interest has resulted in conferring a special evidential privilege on a spouse absolving them of the duty to give evidence against the other in criminal proceedings. Section 80(3)(a), Police and Criminal Evidence Act 1984, extinguished this fundamental principle of the common law overruling *Hoskyn* v *Commissioner of the Police for the Metropolis* [1979] AC 474. *Hoskyn* is instructive as it symbolises the common law approach to compellability and more specifically exposes the judicial attitude of the highest court in the land in which their Lordships were to reaffirm that domestic violence is a private and not a public matter, a civil or matrimonial rather than criminal wrong. In *Hoskyn* the defendant, who was an ex-boyfriend of the victim, called her out of a public house where she was having a drink with her mother so that he could speak with her. Agreeing to his request she went outside with him, within moments she returned having sustained multiple injuries which he had inflicted upon her, including two stab wounds in the chest, penetrating the outer lining of the lung on each side; a nine centimetre cut extending from the temple to her right ear; smaller cuts to her right lip and chin; and a four and a half centimetre cut to the left forearm. Two days before the trial commenced some several months after the assault, Janis Scrimshaw became Mrs Hoskyn. Rumour has it that she was advised that if they were married she could not be compelled to give evidence against him and the prosecution case would fold. The trial judge, Lane CJ, in interpreting the common law and following *Lapworth*, the only direct authority on the point, ruled that she was both competent and compellable to give evidence. She was put into the witness box and gave her evidence. The judge asserted:

> It must be borne in mind that the court of trial in circumstances such as this where personal violence is concerned (and this case is a good example where wounding with a knife is concerned) is not dealing merely with a domestic dispute between husband and wife, but it is investigating a crime. It is in the interests of the state and members of the public that where that is the case evidence of that crime should be freely available to the court which is trying the crime. It may very well be that the wife or the husband, as the case may be, is the only person who can give evidence of that offence. In those circumstances it seems to us that there is no reason in this case for saying that we should in any way depart from that ruling . . . in *Rex* v *Lapworth* [1931] 1 KB 117 . . .

Hoskyn was convicted. He appealed on the grounds that as his wife, Mrs Hoskyn was not a compellable witness and the judge had erred in law in compelling her to give evidence against him. The following point of law was certified as of general public importance: whether a wife is a compellable witness against her husband in a case of violence on her by him. The House of Lords like the trial judge considered *Lapworth* but instead took the course of distinguishing, which meant that the authority of *Lapworth* could be conveniently ignored and side-stepped altogether, allowing the House to reach their decision that a spouse was not compellable without overruling *Lapworth*. Their Lordships were informed by the common law principle of 'one flesh' and the necessity at all costs to support marital harmony. Lord Salmon declared, 'It seems to me altogether inconsistent with the common law's attitude towards marriage that it should compel such a wife to give evidence against her husband and thereby probably destroy the marriage' (p. 149). Lord Wilberforce asserted, '. . . to allow her to give evidence would give rise to discord and to perjury and would be, to ordinary people, repugnant' (p. 159). The solitary voice of Lord Edmund-Davies dissented from the majority in the interpretation of the common law and, focusing on the function of the criminal law, he wisely asserted:

Such cases are too grave to depend simply upon whether the injured spouse is, or is not, willing to testify against the attacker. Reluctance may spring from a variety of reasons and does not by any means necessarily denote that domestic harmony has been restored. A wife who has once been subjected to a 'carve up' may well have more reasons than one for being an unwilling witness against her husband. In such circumstances, it may well prove a positive boon (to) her to be directed by the court that she has no alternative but to testify. But, be that as it may, such incidents ought not to be regarded as having no importance extending beyond the domestic hearth. Their investigation and, where sufficiently weighty, their prosecution is a duty which the agencies of law enforcement cannot dutifully neglect (p. 159).

Throughout the 1980s several jurisdictions have similarly looked to ways of making spouses compellable witnesses, taking the view that making a spouse a compellable witness for the purpose of giving evidence and enforcing the compellability provision is an essential step towards ensuring her protection. In *Moran* v *Beyer* (1984) 734 F 2d 1245, 7th Circuit, an Illinois case, spousal immunity was declared unconstitutional in a suit brought by a wife against her husband for injuries inflicted during the course of their marriage. The object of immunity was to preserve and maintain 'family harmony'. Since this harmony no longer existed the court took the view that the doctrine of spousal immunity was unconstitutional.

In Canada, in the case of *McGinty* [1986] 52 C R (3d) 161, the court held that, '. . . a rule which leaves to the husband or wife the choice whether he or she will testify against his aggressor spouse is more likely to be productive of family discord than to prevent it'. In this case the victim was the husband of the accused and upon his evidence the accused was convicted (see Brownlee 1990, p. 107 at p. 111).

Since the coming into force of the Police and Criminal Evidence Act 1984, s. 80(3)(a), *Hoskyn* has been overruled. It has not as yet indicated any benefits to women, courts have been insensitive, obtuse and heavy-handed in the few cases where attempts at enforcement have been made (see Munday 1991). The most notorious error of enforcement occurred during the trial of *Williams* where the victim, Michelle Renshaw, was imprisoned for one week by Pickles J for contempt of court for refusing to give evidence (see *Renshaw* [1989] Crim LR 811, *The Times*, 23 June 1989). Renshaw had sustained beatings from her boyfriend, Michael Williams (unmarried partners are competent and compellable witnesses in accordance with the powers contained in s. 97, Magistrates' Courts Act 1980). When the case came before Pickles J, Renshaw said she was 'too frightened' to give evidence. Pickles J said, and quite rightly, 'I took the view that this was not a private dispute between her and the defendant but a matter between the Crown and the defendant' (*The Guardian*, 14 March 1989). This statement cannot be faulted, although the solution to the problem was wholly wrong in punishing the weak instead of the real contemnor, Michael Williams. The prison sentence was subsequently overturned by the Court of Appeal on the ground that the trial judge had not conducted the contempt proceedings in a fair manner and proper account had not been taken of the fact that the appellant claimed to have been threatened by her boyfriend.

In the case of *Earnshaw* [1990] Crim LR 53, Pickles J sentenced a wife beater to 18 months' imprisonment. He appealed on the grounds of remarks made by the judge to the media, in respect of the *Renshaw* contempt case, remarks which counsel for the appellant argued may have had a bearing on the instant case. The conviction was quashed.

Similar unwise decisions have been made in other jurisdictions faced with a frightened witness. In Canada, in 1984 Karen Mitchell was sent to prison for three months for refusing to testify. Some have objected to the new provisions on compellability arguing that it takes choice out of the woman's hand (see National Association of Victim Support Schemes, *Domestic Violence Working Party Report* 1991). The New South Wales Task Force on *Domestic Violence* is unequivocal, remarking in 1984, 'The placing of a choice in the hands of the woman herself is almost an act of legal cruelty, and it imposes upon her a tremendous burden which complainants in other cases do not face. It leads directly to the intimidation of the woman.... The temptation for him to 'heavy' 'her, either directly or indirectly, is very often not resisted' (1985, p. 55).

Whilst a spouse is now in law compellable to give evidence, this can only have an effect if victims are supported throughout the prosecution process. A victim who is merely compelled at the stage of giving evidence-in-chief, in the absence of support, is likely to be hostile to the proceedings and make a poor witness as a result. Compellability potentially offers the opportunity of taking the burden of the decision to prosecute away from victims of domestic violence, a burden which has, in the past, led to women being reluctant to press charges and report at the outset. Lord Edmund-Davies in *Hoskyn* summarised the function of law thus:

... the criminal law serves a dual purpose: to render aid to citizens who themselves seek its protection; and itself to take active steps to protect those other citizens who, though grievously in need of protection, for one reason or another do not themselves set the law in motion.

Frightened witnesses   Notwithstanding the compellability of spouses, both spouses and girlfriend victims of domestic violence are often frightened to give evidence. Even with the compellability provision in place women have refused to testify and cases have been dropped. Women's fear of their aggressor presents the main obstacle to successful prosecutions. This perception of witnesses has had an impact on the prosecutorial assessment of the prospect of conviction, influencing their decision to continue or discontinue proceedings at the outset. Victim reluctance (see Wasoff 1982, 1987, McLeod 1983), springs from fear but also from lack of support and there is much, albeit anecdotal, evidence that prosecutors and police rely on victim withdrawal as a justification for their own inaction. Recent legislation, at least in theory, allows for the prosecution witness under certain circumstances to be excused giving oral evidence (Munday 1991, p. 349). Section 23 of the Criminal Justice Act 1988 permits a statement made by a person in a document to be admissible as evidence of any fact of which direct oral evidence by that person would be admissible. Sections 23(3)(a) and 23(3)(b) are of relevance, '... that the statement was made to a police officer or some other person charged with the duty of investigating offences or charging offenders; and that the person who made it does not give oral evidence through fear or because he is kept out of the way.'. However, whether such statements may be admitted is entirely a matter for the magistrates or trial judge after consideration of all the circumstances and whether it is in the interests of justice to do so, and not prejudicial to the defendant (s. 26).

The Divisional Court has considered the meaning of s. 26 in two recent judgments. In *Acton Justices, ex parte McMullen & Others*; *Tower Bridge Magistrates' Court, ex parte Lawlor* (1991) 92 Cr App R 98, the applicants proceeded with applications for judicial review against the magistrates' decision to admit written statements of the witnesses in place of oral evidence. The applicants, McMullen and others, were charged in committal proceedings with aggravated burglary, violent disorder, malicious wounding and criminal damage. One of the witnesses refused to give evidence because of fear. In the case of *Lawlor*, who was charged with attempted murder, one of the prosecution witnesses, a young man of 16 also refused to give evidence because of fear. The Divisional Court upheld the magistrates' decision to admit evidence and ruled that the terms 'fear' and 'kept out of the way', could be treated disjunctively, dismissing their applications, and the defendants were committed for trial.

The first reported test case where this provision has had a direct application in domestic violence is the case of *Ashford Magistrates' Court, ex parte Hilden* [1993] 2 All ER 154, 96 Cr App R 92. Here, the applicant was charged with causing grievous bodily harm with intent and false imprisonment of his girlfriend. Police evidence indicated that the grievous bodily harm which formed the basis of the charge involved violence which was more akin to attempted murder than the charge preferred. Donna Terrace, the victim, sustained severe lacerations to the legs, a broken nose, broken teeth, and multiple wounding to the face and head. At the committal proceedings the complainant went into the witness box, but refused to give evidence through fear. The magistrates granted the prosecution's application for her written statement to be admitted in evidence. The magistrates had not read the statement but deposed that they would have reached the same conclusion even if its contents had been put before them. The applicant applied for judicial review of the magistrates' decision raising three grounds. First, that a witness's written statement was only admissible under s. 26, if the witness did not give any oral evidence at all, that is, refused to utter a single word. Secondly, that the witness herself actually had to say that she/he was not giving evidence through fear, and thirdly, that the magistrates were required to have read the statement before deciding whether it could be admitted or not. In consideration of the first point, the Divisional Court held that a refusal to give evidence meant a refusal to give 'evidence of significance'. On the second point the Court ruled that the fear experienced did not have to be explicitly stated by the witness in court and it was a matter that could be determined by the court. Thirdly, the Divisional Court held that a court was not required to have seen or read the witness's statement before making a decision to accept it. The application for judicial review was refused accordingly. Hilden was finally committed for trial on 22 December 1992, when he entered a not guilty plea to the charges. The complainant's statement was read and she made no reply, the judge responded by warning her that she was obliged to answer questions put to her. Notwithstanding s. 23(3)(b), the CPS took a decision to withdraw the charges against Hilden and the prosecution declined to offer evidence. And so it appears that s. 23 is not the panacea it was intended to be. Original fears that it would open up the floodgates to victims of violent crime and would be a positive boon to the frightened witness have not been borne out. All that the cases of *Lawlor*, *McMullen* and *Hilden* have established is the meaning of the wording of the section. The matter regarding the exercise of discretion as to admissibility of evidence depends on both magistrates at the committal hearing and the trial judge at trial, both magistrates at committal and judges at trial must be satisfied that the victim is in fear and the admission of the written statement is in the interests of justice. Cretney and Davis (1996, p. 169) found inconsistencies in the management of compellability and indeed withdrawal of complaints where some women wishing to drop charges were asked to go into the witness box to retract their original statement.

What is clear is that notwithstanding spousal compellability and this relaxation of the rules of evidence, the victim of domestic violence is still very much unprotected within the criminal process. The legal treatment of these cases resonates with the same misunderstanding about the victim of domestic violence as is found in this part of Lord Salmon's judgment in *Hoskyn* [1979] AC 74, '. . . if she does not want to avail herself of this protection, there is, in my view, no ground for holding that the common law forces it upon her'.

Magisterial and judicial sentencing and the penal question

For those victims who successfully negotiate the trial process, at the point of sentencing the law once again demonstrates a differential treatment of the domestic violence offender as compared with the non-domestic violence offender. Sentences in the domestic context compared with the non-domestic context have tended to be derisory. Little research has been conducted on the enforcement of the law in respect of sentencing the domestic violence offender. A study of sentencing in London in 1990 (see Buchan and Edwards 1991), found that in cases of assault the more typical sentence of the court was a fine, and even in the case of grievous bodily harm, very few offenders were committed to prison. Indeed, of a total of 105 suspects who were charged, 79 were remanded in custody. Four were charged with grievous bodily harm and 55 with the lesser offence of actual bodily harm. The remaining suspects were charged with a variety of other offences. Only two received prison sentences. Of the 55 cases, seven were withdrawn, seven dealt with by means of a fine and/or compensation order, five were bound over, 13 discharged or discontinued, four conditionally discharged, two received compensation orders, one probation, 10 outcome unknown, one received community service and two were committed to prison or to a young offender institution, with one receiving a mental health order.

In the sentencing process the courts give consideration to several mitigatory factors, e.g., the seriousness, dangerousness, likelihood of repeat offending, are all factors put forward into the bargaining forum. Other factors such as the woman's infidelity, her setting up in a new relationship, the man's respectability or the fact that the offence is 'out of character', or he is not 'a threat to the public', all function in reduction of sentence or on appeal or in upholding a decision to award at the lowest end of the scale. In sentencing negotiations, counsel for such appellants frequently invoke ideologies which promulgate a divide between domestic violence and other crimes of violence in minimalising the criminality and perceived dangerousness of their client. It is not surprising that the penal question has figured significantly in analyses of sentencing by feminists. The movement for harsher sentencing has been championed by both those on the left and on the right. Whilst the left have been traditionally wary of the zealousness of the State's response to sentencing (Garland 1990, Melossi and Pavarini 1981), feminists in pursuit of justice for victims call for harsher sentencing. As Nelken (1987) has identified 'critical writers, including those writing from a feminist perspective, now seem to be arguing for more rather than less use of criminal law.' (See Braithwaite and Pettit (1994) for a consideration of the debate in the United States.)

The Court of Appeal Although the Appeal Court, on occasion, has emphasised that domestic violence should be treated in the same way as any other crime of personal violence, such pronouncements of equality in sentencing are hard to find in the experience of the courts. In *Buchanan* (1980) 2 Cr App R (S) 13, where a husband stabbed a wife in the leg and on arrest said, '. . . I knew what I was doing, I was in complete control. I had the knife to do her in and I would have done it, if they hadn't pulled me off her,', Bridge LJ held that, 'The courts cannot regrettably be deflected from their duty of imposing sentences appropriate to the gravity of the offence when crimes of violence of this nature are committed against a domestic background'. In *Giboin* (1980) 2 Cr App R (S) 99, where the husband asked the wife to continue with their marriage and asked her to kiss him whilst stabbing her in the back and chest inflicting wounds some of which were three inches in depth, Ormrod LJ held:

> . . . assaults on wives are to be regarded as very serious matters, and not to be lightly brushed aside as due to emotional upsets or jealousy or anything else . . . Wives are the most vulnerable people when it comes to violent husbands, and there is no reason why a man should not be punished in the same way for assaulting his wife as he would be for assaulting any other person.

In *Cutts* [1987] Fam Law 311, *The Times*, 3 December 1986, the appellant, who was the estranged husband of the victim, visited her in a drunken state, struck her across the head, knocking her to the floor, causing a cut which required several stitches, kicked and punched her in the jaw, punched her on the nose causing it to break, forced her to have sexual intercourse during the course of which she blacked out. When she came round she tasted semen as he had ejaculated in her mouth whilst she was unconscious. According to the victim he then asked her to shake hands with him and forget about it and said that she deserved a good hiding each time she refused sex. Michael Davis J said:

In the view of this court it is high time that the message was understood in clear terms by courts, by police forces, by probation officers and above all by husbands and boyfriends of women, that the fact that a serious assault occurs in a domestic scene is no mitigation whatsoever and no reason for proceedings not being taken and condign punishment following in a proper case.

Since 1988, with the introduction of the Criminal Justice Act, where the sentence of the court has been considered overly lenient, the prosecution have been able to apply for its reconsideration on appeal although the court on appeal is reluctant to increase sentences unless they are plainly wrong. In *Attorney-General's Reference No. 13 of 1990 (Trevor Bailey)* (1990) 12 Cr App R (S) 578, a former husband had been found guilty of a knife attack on his wife, slashing her face a number of times, inflicting wounds requiring 40 sutures after she refused to go back and live with him. He formed the view that if he could not have her no one else would see her beauty. He said, 'I took the knife from home to cut her face'. The court considered the sentence of two years unduly lenient and increased it to three. In *Attorney-General's Reference No. 14 of 1992 (Austin Anthony Lindsay)* (1993) 14 Cr App R (S) 239, a sentence of two years was increased to four where a cohabitee hit the victim in the throat with a glass resulting in two lacerations 14 centimetres and five centimetres in length severing the jugular vein. In this case the woman suspected the man of having an affair as he returned home at 2 am in a car driven by another woman. An argument ensued and he assaulted her. In *Attorney-General's Reference No. 1 of 1993 (Horrigan)* [1994] 15 Cr App R (S) 367, where the offender shot an ex girlfriend through one leg the bullet lodging in the other, a sentence of three years was ordered. A sentence of five years was substituted on appeal under s. 2(2)(a) of the Criminal Justice Act 1991.

Where assaults on partners or ex partners are concerned it seems that the courts are unlikely, whatever the seriousness, to consider passing a longer than normal sentence, in the absence of mental illness and a history of assaults on other people, where the offender is not normally considered a threat to the public. In *Nicholas* [1994] Crim L R 77, the appellant attacked his wife and then, on a subsequent occasion, he attacked her again when she discovered he was seeing another woman. In this case a longer than normal sentence was passed under s. 2(2)(b) of the Criminal Justice Act 1991. The court held that a longer than normal sentence was not precluded for the protection of a single member of the public, and although it said that it had not heard full argument on the point, it substituted a sentence of three years.

It is not only that domestic violence is regarded as a private affair which impacts on the assessment of sentence, but the all too often tendency of the sentencer is to view it as an episodic event, the result of, e.g., drink, external stress factors such as unemployment and also on the basis of provocation that the victim in some way was to blame. Typically the courts seem particularly sympathetic towards the man who cannot accept that the relationship with the victim is over. Man's inexorable proprietorial, psychotic obsession is no doubt a product of his socialisation: the law only reaffirms and legitimates this in its approach to sentencing. In the case of *Reilly* (1982) 4 Cr App R (S) 288, where the appellant attacked his wife with an axe, she had ended their relationship and was having an affair with another man. May LJ acceded that the appellant, '. . . was not a man addicted to the use of violence at all . . . he was not a threat to the public', considering that 'the offence was out of character', although he dismissed the appeal against a six year sentence. In the case of *Beaumont* (1992) 13 Cr App R (S) 270, a ten year sentence for attempted murder of a girlfriend was reduced to eight years. The girlfriend wished to end their relationship, 'he was upset, and said that if he ever caught her with another man he would kill her'. He stabbed her in the neck, chest, and back and used more than one knife in perpetration of the violence. The court took into consideration that apart from stabbing his girlfriend he was 'a man of good character'. Again, the 'out of character' factor was accepted by the court in *Trevor Bailey* (above) as mitigation. In this case the judge had this to say in summing up, reflecting his acceptance of counsel's mitigation and adding some of his own. 'No doubt the incident when he discovered the man in the friend's house was the beginning of an emotional turmoil which came to a head in the café. No doubt remarks made by her in the café, which may have been justified but were undoubtedly cruel was the last straw so to speak . . .'.

It is not only judicial discretion and attitudes to domestic violence offenders that result in a differential treatment of domestic violence but statutory guidance on sentencing arguably gives way to this divide. The Criminal Justice Act 1991, concentrates sentencers' thinking on dangerousness and whether the defendant is a threat to the public. Section 1(2) states '. . . Subject to subsection (3) below, the court shall not pass a custodial sentence on the offender unless it is of the opinion — . . . (b) where the offence is a violent or sexual offence, that only such a sentence would be adequate to protect the public from serious harm from him'. This provision in the absence of guidance on statutory interpretation may well provide the official blessing to treating violence in the home differently from violence in the street. In *Oudkerk* [1994] Crim LR 700, the appellant approached a young woman waiting at a railway station, put her in a headlock and tried to drag her away, threatening to kill her. He bit her cheek and each of the arresting officers. He was sentenced to 30 months for the offence on the woman and 30 months concurrent for each of the assaults on the officers. The Court passed a longer than normal sentence under the Criminal Justice Act 1991, s. 2(2)(b). The plea had been tendered on the basis that the incident was a 'lovers tiff' rather than a random attack on a woman he did not know:

> It was not apparent that the judge had sentenced the appellant on the basis of the victim's version of the facts, but if the appellant's version was correct, this was not an attack made without rhyme or reason of the type which might properly entitle the sentencer to use powers under section 2(2)(b), but an attack arising out of a personal relationship which largely explained its nature and circumstances.

Negotiating sentence   Much has been said recently about the need for justice for victims particularly in their having a role in the sentencing process.

The right of victims to be heard in pre-sentence reports was established in the US following the Victim and Witness Protection Act 1982, particularly in respect of harm to the victim. In the US the victim/witness impact statements have for many years made a considerable impression on sentencing whereby the court will take into consideration, when sentencing, any information on the impact of the offence on the victim, and the wishes of the victim regarding the sentencing of the offender, although not without considerable controversy. In *Booth* v *Maryland* 482 US 496 (1987), the court noted that a number of States permit victim impact statements in some contexts, and expressed no opinion on their use in non capital cases (cited in Wright 1990, p. 23). The use of victim witness statements in capital cases was overruled in *Payne* v *Tennessee* 111 SCt 2597 (1991).

In Canada, the use of victim/witness statements has been restricted to sentencing and in South Australia and New Zealand its use has been confined to written statements (see Sebba 1994). The object is to acquaint the court with the victim's needs. It is clear that defence lawyers regard it as an opportunity to reduce sentence by placing justice for victims back in the family domain. Particular ethical problems are posed in the context of domestic violence, since sentencing should not be dependent on the degree to which the victim articulates the harm done. The particular problem posed for the victim who knows the offender is that duress is ever present and many victims may find that the burden they bear for the prosecution, and the outcome, is intolerable and only eased if they make pleas on the offender's behalf at the sentencing stage. My own concern is with the mitigating effect of forgiveness on the victim and the benefit this has for the offender's sentence. 'The mitigating effect of forgiveness on the part of the complainant in a sexual case must, as it seems to us, vary from individual case to individual case' (see Krause 363).

'Wonderfully forgiving wives'   Consider the following cases where victim impact statements have resulted in reduction of sentence on appeal. In *Ball* (1982) 4 Cr App R (S) 351, considerable weight was attached to the apparent forgiveness of the victim and the parties' intentions of reconciliation, in reducing the offender's sentence. '... in the circumstances as they have now developed and the state of the parties' minds towards one another being as they are'. In *Krause* (1989) 11 Cr App R (S) 360, 363 the court gave weight to the forgiveness of the wife:

What does make this case perhaps rather out of the ordinary is this. Not only had the couple been living together on terms of affection previous to the incident, but it seems that this degree of affection had continued thereafter. So far from being repelled by this man as a result of what he had done and wishing, because of what he had done, to have no more to do with him, she had, up to the moment when he came to be sentenced, corresponded with him on terms of real affection. Since his sentence was imposed and he has found himself in prison, the affectionate correspondence has continued. We have had the opportunity of seeing the letters. They are touching, and they do express what we believe to be genuine feeling for this man and a genuine longing to put together again the life of the couple and of the children upon release ... We accept that in the present case, the genuine affection between the couple is to be taken into account.

In *Stapleton* (1989) 11 Cr App R (S) 364, 365, it is not clear how far the fact that, as the report states, the complainant herself had written a letter to the court expressing her love for the offender affected the decision to reduce the sentence. In the case of *Houlahan* (see Edwards 1989d, p. 1740), where a husband had thrown his wife to the floor, punched her in the face, head and body and threatened to make a mess of her with a Stanley knife and then barricaded their home and kept her prisoner overnight, the victim withdrew the allegation because of fear. The prosecution went ahead, the defence pleaded not guilty alleging that the victim's injuries were self-inflicted (photographs showed her face to be unrecognisable). The offender was convicted and sentenced to a six month term of imprisonment. On 9 October 1989, his appeal against sentence was successful and a prison term was reduced to a suspended term. The judges of the Appeal Court took into consideration the fact that the wife had forgiven him and wanted him back with the family. Tucker J said that she was 'a wonderfully forgiving wife'. In the case of *Carr* (unreported 1990), a man who had tried to strangle his wife when she told him she was leaving, was put on probation. The judge said, 'Your wife has written to me begging me not to send you to prison'. In *Plater, The Guardian*, 7 January 1992, sentence was reduced from seven to five years for attempted murder. The man tried to throttle the woman with a belt, and stabbed her in the shoulder when she told him she was leaving. She wrote in a letter to the court. 'He has lost his home, me and the kids and that is enough for any man'.

In *Giboin* (above), the wife wrote to the court expressing her concern that the sentence was harsh and the court was also to hear that she had not given up hope of reconciliation. In *Buchanan*, Bridge LJ noted, 'Another striking feature of the case is that the lady is willing to have him back, has completely forgiven him, is willing to resume her life with him ... had written him a long and loving letter expressing her feelings and her forgiveness ...' (although sentence was not reduced). If, as some of these cases clearly indicate, the 'apparent' wishes of victims have a varying impact on the sentencing process in domestic violence, this is a most disturbing trend. Women are 'got at' by the men themselves, by their relatives and by their lawyers, the victims are encouraged to believe that only they can make a difference to the sentence. Women's sense of responsibility is absolute and overwhelming and women never escape from this cycle of duress.

Mediation: a contest between unequals   A further indication that domestic violence is being trivialised and privatised is the trend towards mediation in North America and in England and Wales. It is to be treated with caution since it too moves away from placing responsibility for male violence with the male perpetrator. Ideologically it is somewhat retrogressive in the wake of other efforts to protect battered women. Hilton (1991, p. 29–53) is clearly alarmed at this recent move towards mediation in the area of domestic violence.

Bootlegged from the divorce arena, mediation stands in contradiction and as an anomaly to everything that practitioners are trying to do in the field of domestic violence. There can be no mediation between unequals where one party is abusing another. Domestic violence is not about a difference of ideas or of approaches, it is about the abuse of a vulnerable person by another (see the Report of the New York Task Force on Domestic Violence, 1987 which is highly critical of mediation and the automatic truce in the domestic violence arena). Again, the move towards 'mutual protection orders' in the US requiring both parties to abide by the restraints, reflects the view that domestic violence occurs within a level playing field (see Klein, 1995, p. 268).

The dangers of mediation were made all too apparent when on 29 April 1991, a wife was murdered by a husband in a domestic violence unit at Stoke Newington Police Station in London. On this occasion the police provided a meeting place following a request for such a meeting by a case worker from the local women's refuge. The meeting between Janti Patel and his wife, Vandana took place as arranged at the police station and the couple were left alone to discuss their situation. Officers left the couple alone with the intervening door open. After a period of 25 minutes a brief check was made by the police, and because they appeared to be getting on well together they were then left for a further twenty minutes when a scream was heard. On entering the room police discovered Janti Patel holding a knife, with his wife lying on the floor having been stabbed (see *The Vandana Patel Enquiry*, an internal Metropolitan Police Report 1991; see Edwards, When Cruel Death Doth Them Part, *The Guardian*, 1992b).

The Family and Civil Committees of the Council of Her Majesty's Circuit Judges (1990) (20 Fam Law 225), in their response to the Law Commission's Working Paper on Domestic Violence suggested:

> In 1989, with the development of the concepts and practice of conciliation and mediation, we believe that domestic violence needs to be considered in a broader context than short term protection. In some cases which reach the courts a long-term chronic history of violence presents. Even in these cases our anecdotal experience shows that women quite often resume cohabitation after having obtained an injunction.

The document goes on to lay down some policy proposals favouring the approach of an automatic truce, and mutual undertakings.

THE CIVIL REMEDIES

Wives, cohabitees and partners disenchanted with the ineffectiveness of the criminal process, or for other reasons reluctant to commence with a criminal prosecution, may well decide instead to pursue a civil remedy. As Women's Aid Federation England explained in their evidence to the Home Affairs Committee:

> From the point of view of the woman experiencing the abuse, it may seem preferable to apply for protection in the civil courts rather than to give

evidence in a criminal prosecution of her partner. Firstly the process seems to be more under her control: she instructs the solicitor, who will represent her in court, or will instruct a barrister on her behalf. Secondly in most cases the hearing will be in a closed court or in the Judge's chambers, and there will be no publicity. Thirdly, her partner will not acquire a criminal record, which could hamper his employment prospects and hence indirectly affect the economic situation of the woman and her children. For all these reasons it is important that the process of obtaining injunctions or personal protection orders should be as straightforward as possible, and that the orders, once obtained, should be effective and, if breached, should be strictly enforced (see Home Affairs Committee 1993, p. xxxiv).

The existence of a specific civil legal remedy to address domestic violence outside the general arena of the remedy for assault in tort serves to reaffirm the belief that domestic violence is a civil and not a criminal matter. The civil remedies currently available to women experiencing violence are, as the Law Commission No. 207 (1992), notes, several and confusing. The main types of remedies offering protection take two forms, and are straddled across three statutes. One form of relief is provided by the non-molestation injunction granted to protect a spouse or common law spouse and/or children living with them where there is molestation (Domestic Violence and Matrimonial Proceedings Act 1976). There is in addition the injunction (personal protection order) granted against the spouse to protect the spouse and/or children of the family where there is physical violence or the threat of such violence (Domestic Proceedings and Magistrates' Courts Act 1978). The second type of relief is provided in the power to exclude a violent party from the matrimonial home for a short time, obtainable under both the aforementioned acts. The Matrimonial Homes Act 1983 provides for occupation rights and the protection of those rights for parties to a marriage where a re-entry or exclusion order can be granted.

The law offers protection to those who resemble or most closely conform to the legal institution of marriage or familial relationships, with little regard for the social family, thereby excluding many from its protection leaving girl-friends, non-cohabitees and those in a relationship or those who have terminated a relationship in a vulnerable position.

The Domestic Violence and Matrimonial Proceedings Act 1976

The Domestic Violence and Matrimonial Proceedings Act 1976 ('the 1976 Act'), ensured that wives and cohabitees could seek redress from violence without having to instigate divorce proceedings (see *Des Salles D'Epinoix* [1967] 2 All ER 539). The county courts and High Court provide redress only in so far as the parties are living with each other in the same household as man and wife (s. 1(2)). This stipulation excludes from its ambit married couples living separately where the marriage is in the process of breakdown, where one party has moved out or ex-spouses. It also excludes from protection partners who are living in separate households. In drawing the criteria so narrowly the

1976 Act provides a very restrictive view of the range of applicants eligible for protection and mirrors a concept of a legal rather than a social family. Curiously, the law and the categories of person for whom protection is afforded, run in contradistinction to the research findings on the categories of persons who experience domestic violence. Evidence shows that women are at considerable risk from partners both at the point of, and after separation (see Walker (1989, 1993) and the chapter entitled, The Gender Politics of Homicide). The terms 'man' and 'wife' ensure a specific and highly restrictive application depending on sexual intimacy, precluding those who live together but who may no longer be sexually active. The case of *Adeoso* v *Adeoso* [1981] 1 All ER 107 raised just such a limitation. Here the court took a broad view of the second requirement of 'man' and 'wife', in extending protection where the parties had not had sexual intercourse for 16 months. In *Davis* v *Johnson* [1978] 1 All ER 1132 in construction of the term 'living together' the court considered whether living together applied to the moment when the conduct was alleged or at the time of the application. Such a consideration has more recently featured in case law determining the time at which 'significant harm' to children is relevant under the Children Act 1989 (see the chapter entitled, A Betrayal of Trust, the Sexual Abuse of Children). Before granting a non-molestation injunction under s. 1(1)(a) or a s. 1(1)(c) ouster order, the court must be satisfied that molestation has occurred in the past (see *Spindlow* v *Spindlow* [1979] Fam 52). It is unclear whether or not the court must be satisfied that it is likely to occur again (see Foakes 1986, p. 7). In consideration of the nature of the conduct amounting to evidence of molestation, on occasions injunctions have been granted where there has been evidence of molestation but not of violence. In *Vaughan* v *Vaughan* [1973] 3 All ER 449, where the aggressor called at the victim's place of work and made a complete nuisance of himself, it was held that molestation could be construed more broadly than violence. In *Johnson* v *Walton* [1990] 1 FLR 350, it was held that molestation occurred where there was such a degree of harassment, that the courts' intervention was necessary. Harassment included with it an element of intent to cause distress or harm, where partially nude photographs of the plaintiff were sent to a national newspaper with the intention of causing her distress; *Smith* v *Smith* [1988] 1 FLR 179, 18 Fam Law 2.

> Common instances include persistent pestering and intimidation through shouting, denigration, threats or argument, nuisance telephone calls, damaging property, following the applicant about and repeatedly calling at her home or place of work . . . filling car locks with superglue, writing anonymous letters and pressing one's face against a window whilst brandishing papers was held to amount to molestation' (Law Com No. 207, p. 4, para. 2.3).

There is a considerable body of research evidence (Barron 1990) which indicates that non-molestation injunctions are seldom granted in the absence of physical violence or the threat of it.

The second type of remedy provided by the 1976 Act is the ouster injunction. Section 1(1)(c) gives the courts power to exclude a party from the matrimonial home and/or a specified area. When the Act was first passed it was uncertain whether ousters could be granted where the husband or common law husband had a proprietary interest in the matrimonial home. In *Davis* v *Johnson* [1978] 1 All ER 1132, the House of Lords held that a woman's interest in protection prevailed over her partner's proprietary interest. The appellant and respondent were joint tenants of a council flat. The respondent was frequently beaten by the appellant. In 1977, Brentford County Court granted Jennifer Davis's application for a non-molestation injunction, adjourning the application for an ouster until a later sitting when an ouster was granted. Following the decision of the Court of Appeal in *Cantliff* v *Jenkins* [1978] 1 All ER 836, where the court decided that where parties were joint tenants neither had the right to exclude the other, Johnson responded and successfully applied for an order rescinding the original ouster. The respondent Davis appealed to the Court of Appeal which restored the ouster (Denning, George Baker and Shaw LJJ (Goff and Cumming-Bruce LJJ dissenting)) on the grounds that *Cantliff* v *Jenkins* and *B* v *B* [1979] 1 All ER 821, had been wrongly decided and could not stand with the intention of parliament. Lord Denning was hailed as the darling of battered wives. The appellant (Johnson) appealed to the House of Lords that the judge had been wrong in law, that the 1976 Act did not give him the power to exclude a party from the premises of which he was a joint tenant: the decision of the Court of Appeal was upheld by a majority. Lord Diplock preferred a 'narrower interpretation of section 1', whilst Viscount Dilhorne spoke of 'That drastic inroad into the common law rights of property has now been made by the amendment of s. 1(2) of the 1967 Act by s. 3 of the 1976 Act'. Lord Kilbrandon said, 'The supposed protection of unmarried women under this Act according-ly turns out to be largely illusory since it amounts to no more than procedural advantages available to a woman who has the sole right of occupation, whether as owner or tenant, of what the statute calls her "matrimonial home". This, in the social conditions with which we are all familiar, must be a rare bird indeed'. Lord Salmon most clearly articulated what he regarded as the intention of Parliament, 'In my view, Parliament, in passing this Act, was concerned not with the preservation of proprietary rights but with affording protection to "battered wives" by giving them the chance of finding fresh accommodation in safety when the husband or paramour has made life in the matrimonial home intolerable, impossible or dangerous.'. Lord Scarman in echoing the sentiment expressed by Lord Salmon said that the Act was concerned to protect 'not property but human life and limb' and '. . . suspends or restricts the family partner's property rights . . .'. The courts have been extremely reluctant to grant ouster injunctions, granting them only in circumstances of extreme violence (see Table 13). The Bar Association recently noted that there should be great caution exercised in the grant of ousters (see Home Affairs Committee, 1993, p. xxxvii, para. 110). In practice, many applications for non-molestation are dealt with by one party giving an undertaking to the court. An undertaking is a promise to the court which can be enforced by committal. Undertakings have been frequently used in preference to injunctions. It is difficult to estimate how popular a course this has been for the courts in the absence of figures (see Barron 1990). Undertakings, like the use of cautions in criminal offences, have been regarded as the Cinderella to injunctions, although the perfunctory reputation of undertakings has been controverted by Butler-Sloss LJ in *Roberts* v *Roberts and Another* [1990] 2 FLR 111, at 113, declaring that, 'It is important for parties in matrimonial disputes to appreciate that an undertaking has all the force of an injunction', in a case where the husband remained in the family home and gave an undertaking not to molest, assault or interfere with the applicant and where he was in contempt by cutting off the services to her part of the matrimonial home. In securing immediate protection for the applicant, the court has the power to grant injunctions *ex parte*, where there is a 'real immediate danger of serious injury or irreparable damage'. The courts have been extremely reluctant to grant them, a resistance reflected in the attitude of the Council of Circuit Judges, '. . . it is a fundamental principle of natural justice that a court should not grant an order which involves a person's civil liberties and rights without giving them the opportunity to be heard' (see Home Affairs Committee 1993, p. xxxvii). The number of applications under the 1976 Act has increased in recent years from 14,510 in 1984 to 20,030 in 1989, to 20,462 in 1993 and 25,034 in 1994.

Table 13: Domestic Violence and Matrimonial Proceedings Act 1976

Year	Applications	Ousters	Non-molestation	Power of arrest
1981	7,110			1,774
1982	7,691			1,876
1983	10,820			2,501
1984	14,510			3,568
1985	13,531	3,818	9,202	3,314
1986	16,046	4,759	10,826	4,005
1987	16,474	4,903	11,081	4,623
1988	19,329	5,633	13,133	4,996
1989	20,030	6,180	14,239	5,870
1990	21,023			
1991	21,205			
1992	20,648			
1993	20,462			
1994	25,034	3,946	24,566	9,793

Source: Judicial Statistics 1981–1994 (Incomplete data reflects decision of Lord Chancellor's Department not to collect such information. Data incompleteness for 1992–1993 is due to a new category making comparisons impossible)

Domestic Proceedings and Magistrates' Courts Act 1978

The Domestic Proceedings and Magistrates' Courts Act 1978 ('the 1978 Act'), provided injunctive relief in the magistrates' court. This remedy was restricted to applicants who were married and living in the same household. The remedies under this Act are similar to those under the 1976 Act, they include the personal protection order and the exclusion order. Section 16(2) of the 1978 Act provides for the grant of an exclusion order where the respondent has used, or threatened to use violence. The difference is that the powers under the 1978 Act are much more restrictive: mental cruelty or molestation is not enough, it must involve threatening or using violence (s. 16(3)). Molestation was not included in the 1978 Act as magistrates were considered unable to adjudicate on matters requiring expert evidence (para. 3.12, Law Com No. 77, 1976). The threshold requirements depend on the use of violence or threats of violence. When exercising its powers to evict under s. 16(3), the court must place the interests of the child as paramount (s. 15). Expedited orders may be made in respect of applications for personal protection orders where the danger of physical injury is imminent. Again, like the *ex parte* order under the 1976 Act, magistrates are extremely reluctant to grant expedited orders. In 1984 8,480 orders were made for family protection/personal protection, in 1988 this fell to 5,510 applications, further declining to 3,450 in 1991, reflecting a steady decline in the use of the magistrates' courts as a place of protection.

Table 14: Family protection

Year	1983	1984	1985	1986	1987	1988	1989	1990	1991	1992	1993
Family protection or exclusion order	5,180	5,800	4,420	4,160	3,720	3,480	3,140	2,850	2,050	1,260	640
expedited order	2,560	2,680	2,350	2,190	2,040	2,030	1,860	1,810	1,400	940	496
Power of arrest protection or exclusion	830	860	820	840	670	650	740	610	750	310	197
expedited	1,190	1,230	1,150	1,190	1,110	1,130	980	890	730	480	280
MCA breach of family protection order	210	240	190	180	200	150	360	100	70	70	29
Total	7,950	8,720	6,950	6,530	5,960	5,660	5,340	4,760	3,520	2,260	1,642

Source: Domestic Proceedings England and Wales, Home Office Statistical Bulletin for the years 1983 to 1992

The Matrimonial Homes Act 1983

The Matrimonial Homes Act 1983 ('the 1983 Act'), s. 1(3) has assumed increasing importance in the arena of family violence. It provides yet another option of relief for parties who are married (s. 1(3)), that is where one spouse has either a right of occupation, or a beneficial interest, and the other does not, but the first spouse gives the non-owning spouse statutory rights of occupation. Where an applicant is seeking an ouster injunction and is married, she must proceed under this legislation following *Richards* v *Richards* [1984] AC 174, and, given the criteria to which the court must have regard, the battered wife may be disadvantaged. In considering whether to exercise its powers to 'prohibit, suspend or restrict the right of either spouse to occupy' the matrimonial home, or to 'require either spouse to permit the exercise by the other of that right' (ss. 1(2)(b)(c), 9(1)), the court must give consideration to all the circumstances of the case. Here in giving consideration to all the circumstances, the emphasis is shifted away from the protection of a party from violence, or the threat of it, as paramount, established in *Davis* v *Johnson* (above) where the parties were not married but joint tenants. The court may make such an order as it thinks, 'just and reasonable having regard to (a) the conduct of the spouses in relation to each other and (b) otherwise their respective needs and financial resources, (c) to the needs of any children and (d) to all the circumstances of the case' (s. 1(3)). Unlike under the 1976 Act following the House of Lords in *Davis* v *Johnson*, where rights to protection took precedence over proprietary interest, or under the 1978 Act where in consideration of an eviction order children's interests are paramount, under the 1983 Act consideration is to be given to all factors: none is to be regarded as paramount.

In *Richards*, the House of Lords held that where the applicant was a spouse and where the relief sought was an ouster, then s. 1(2) of the Matrimonial Homes Act was the appropriate remedy. In interpretation of the relevant section the court in *Richards* considered each of the four factors under s. 1(3). In so doing the court is to 'balance the hardship' to both of the parties, on the one hand the risk of harm and the need for protection, and on the other property rights and hardship. Yet it was these two 'hardships' so-called which were the very 'hardships' that their Lordships in *Davis* had concluded, in application of the 1976 Act, could not be balanced. The Matrimonial Homes Act 1983 and the decision in *Richards* insisted that the only proper course for an ouster application where couples were spouses was effectively to cut off the remedy of the 1976 Act as a form of relief and impose a new set of criteria which annulled the House of Lords judgment in *Davis* v *Johnson*.

In application of the Matrimonial Homes Act in *Dawe and Edwards* (see Lexis Enggen 3.2.89), an ouster application was refused, since in 'balancing the hardships' of the parties where the applicant had sustained a black eye, the court came to the conclusion that the risk and degree of violence is only one factor to be taken into account, although in *Brown* v *Brown* [1994] 1 FLR 233, the court was justified in making an order where the husband was strict, jealous and unyielding. In consideration of needs and resources the court will take into account who is to look after the children and where they are to reside as well as the husband's need for accommodation. Children's interests seem no longer paramount thereby effectively undermining the philosophy of the Children Act 1989, s. 1 (see *Gibson* v *Austin* [1992] 2 FLR 437) and the primacy of their needs will not even 'tip the balance' (see *G* v *J* *(Ouster Order)* [1993] 1 FLR 1008).

It is arguable that protection of battered women, at least for the married spouse who seeks an ouster injuction, has now reverted to a pre-*Davis* v *Johnson* state, where the court is required by statute to take into account broader ranging criteria. The Law Commission Working Paper, *Domestic Violence and*

Occupation of the Matrimonial Home conceded that the criteria do not give priority to the applicant's personal protection (para. 4.23). Following the introduction of the Matrimonial Homes Act and the decision in *Richards* there has been a decline in ousters granted under the 1976 Act (see Edwards and Halpern 1991, p. 101), and an increase in orders granted under the 1983 Act, at least for the years immediately following it, although from 1986 both the remedy of the 1978 Act and the 1983 Act decline rapidly in the number of applications made. The shadow of the law is clear and where prognosis is poor the spouse seeking an ouster is advised that the new criteria may mean that she will not succeed.

Enforcement

Just how effective are civil remedies in preventing violence? It has been said by many that an injunction or ouster without a power of arrest 'is not worth the paper it is written on' (Select Committee on Violence in Marriage 1975, Edwards 1989a). An additional problem with the civil remedies is the ineffectiveness of enforcement procedures. The means of enforcement since 1976 are twofold. First, the court can *post facto* attach a power of arrest to the injunctive order and secondly proceedings may be instigated for contempt where an injunction or undertaking has been breached. When an injunction is granted under the 1976 Act (s. 2(1)) and the 1978 Act (s. 2) in respect of an non-molestation injunction, personal protection order, ouster or eviction order, a power of arrest may be attached, although it may not be attached to an undertaking or an order under the 1983 Act. A power of arrest provides a *de facto* enforcement, giving police powers to arrest and to bring that person before the court if an injunction is breached. In attaching a power of arrest in accordance with s. 2(1) of the 1976 Act, the judge must be satisfied that actual bodily harm has been caused to the applicant and is likely to occur again. It is in essence a rather different test to that applied when an injunction is being considered. In *Lewis* v *Lewis* [1978] 1 All ER 729, the judge ruled that a power of arrest should not be a routine remedy (see *Practice Note* [1981] 1 WLR 27). In granting a power of arrest in accordance with s. 18 and s. 1 of the 1978 Act, magistrates must be satisfied that the man is likely to re-offend, so it is not simply a question of the seriousness of what he has done in the past but what he is likely to do in the future. Statistical evidence makes clear that there is a wholesale reluctance to attach a power of arrest, however, whether that is because of its quasi precognitive status before the event is uncertain. Circuit judges commenting on the power of arrest have regarded it as a major inroad into civil liberties. In evidence to the Home Affairs Committee they said, '. . . the attachment of a power of arrest, at least in relation to entry into a proscribed home or area, should continue to be granted only where the court finds that there is a likelihood of further violence or a breach of the peace' (see Home Affairs Committee, *Domestic Violence*, p. xxxviii). Case law shows that a power of arrest is attached only in cases of extreme violence. In *Kendrick* v *Kendrick* [1990] 2 FLR 107, a non-molestation application was adjourned upon an undertaking. The wife applied for a breach of the undertaking where the husband had 'repeatedly banged on the door, threatened to smash my face in, blow my kneecaps off and run away with the children'. The husband appealed on the basis that s. 2(1) of the 1976 Act required proof of actual bodily harm. Glidewell LJ concluded, 'I really do not think this husband has much merit . . . But for the general purposes of the law, I am confident that more must be proved than was proved in this case', taking the view that a person is assaulted if psychological harm is suffered. Mrs Kendrick's fear, however, was considered insufficient, the court deciding that there must be evidence of a real change in psychological condition. The injunction was rescinded. In addition, wide regional variations in the predilection to attach a power of arrest suggest that enforcement depends on the exercise of discretion of particular judges. The case law is littered with comment respecting individual judges and their application of discretion. For example in *Davis* v *Simpson* 13 November 1991 (unreported), 'The injunction was issued yesterday, but the judge refused to grant a power of arrest, declaring, so we are informed by counsel, that he is always reluctant to take that course ex parte'. Where an order has been breached, fines and imprisonment, either suspended or immediate, or granting no order at all, are the options open to the court. Rarely, if ever, are penalties of committal applied or enforced. An application may be made to the county court or High Court to commit a person for contempt of an order or contempt of an undertaking. Enforcement mechanisms are only activated in those cases where the injunction is continuously breached. The courts have also been reluctant to lay down any guidelines with respect to penalties. The Home Affairs Committee recognised the unsatisfactory nature of enforcement procedures although it proposed the use of sanctions other than imprisonment (see Home Affairs Committee, *Domestic Violence*, 1993, p. xi). A committal has been generally regarded as a sanction of last resort. First, the court must make a finding of contempt. In *Pidduck* v *Molloy* [1992] 2 FLR 202, where the defendant assaulted the complainant by threatening to get her and torch her car, there was no finding of contempt, but a further injunction was granted. There were further breaches and this time the court made a finding of contempt. In *McCann* v *Wright* [1995] 2 FLR 579, where there had been further violence and the applicant had breached the injunction he appealed on the ground that the judge had erred in ordering a three month suspended committal order, and attaching a power of arrest to an existing injunction. The Court of Appeal held that the sentence was not excessive and dismissed the appeal. Where there is a finding of contempt the use of committal seems to be rarely used. Again there are variations between regions depending on the views of breaches held by judges. Indeed in *Aubrey* v *Damallie* [1994] 1 FLR 131, Leggat LJ said, 'The heresy that there can in cases of domestic violence be what Lord Donaldson in *Jordan* v *Jordan* called "one free breach" was scotched in that case'. In *Buchanan* v *Buchanan* 1993 (unreported) the judge remarked that a practice has developed '. . . of suspending the committal in a case of first offence where there was no previous record of criminal offence' (see *Brewer* v *Brewer* [1989] 2 FLR 251). Butler-Sloss LJ remarked in *Roberts* v *Roberts* (1990) in respect of injunctions, 'It is all too easy for people to promise and all too easy for them to break that promise. Then they, quite rightly, have to face the wrath of the court for having made promises which were not worth the paper which they have signed' (p. 113).

Appeals against committal and power of arrest

Grounds for appeal are frequently provided to applicants either from an erroneous exercise of discretion or more typically from procedural irregularity. In *Loseby* v *Newman* [1995] 2 FLR 754, the Court of Appeal, allowed an appeal against a committal order suspending a three month prison sentence for one year. The Court held that it would not normally rectify a defective committal order unless there were exceptional circumstances. Procedural errors are frequently rendering the remedies invalid and as a result women are losing out on protection. Contemnors are appealing against committal on the grounds that the procedures are invalid: enforcement procedures are so complicated that many contemnors are successful. There is a litany of cases where men have escaped committal on the grounds of irregularity.

In *Banton* v *Banton* [1990] 2 FLR 465, where an ouster order and a non-molestation order were in force, the wife alleged breaches. The breaches were found and the husband was committed to prison for 28 days suspended. On appeal the court held that imprisonment was not the inevitable consequence of a breach of an injunction when a party is subject to a suspended committal. The court had the power to commit, impose a fine or make no order at all. There is clear conflict in the Court of Appeal as to how such irregularities should be approached. Lord Donaldson in *Smith* v *Smith* [1992] 2 FLR 841, for instance, was highly critical of cases where failure to comply with the procedural requirements would be considered fatal to the lawfulness of the committal. He asserted that in deciding such appeals the central principle to be considered is whether the contemnor has suffered any injustice. In absence of injustice he asserted that the committal order should stand subject to the necessary (procedural) amendments. One further issue has been the reluctance of the courts to commit someone accused of contempt to prison where criminal proceedings are pending. In *Keeber* v *Keeber* [1995] 2 FLR 748 where a district judge had adjourned a contempt proceeding pending the outcome of a criminal prosecution and the former wife appealed, Butler-Sloss LJ reaffirmed the separateness of the jurisdiction emphasising that the inherent jurisdiction of the court was quite separate remit and the matter was to be heard before a circuit judge.

Unprotected in civil law

The civil remedies are largely restricted to cohabiting and/or married couples: partners living apart and not under the same roof, ex cohabitees, ex spouses and girlfriends with the result that relationships are not protected by any of the aforementioned Acts not withstanding the remedies in tort. (Excluded parties can, however, pursue an action for damages for personal injury in tort). Definitional difficulties also arise in respect of the meaning of 'living together' where girlfriend/boyfriend relationships may entail parties spending some of the week cohabiting. The concept of the family as embraced by these provisions is outdated and incongruous. The General Household Survey for 1987 showed that 19 per cent of households were cohabiting. It is probably the case that more persons who experience domestic violence are actually excluded from the law's protection than those included. The Law Commission responded to these difficulties and problems in its report, *Domestic Violence and Occupation of the Matrimonial Home* acknowledging that the existing law is 'complex, confusing and lack[s] integration'.

Lord Donaldson in 1992 called for reform of the law on two occasions (see *Pidduck* v *Molloy* above, *Duo* v *Osborne* below). The Family Homes and Domestic Violence Bill 1995, amended by the Family Law Bill, incorporated some of these recommendations. But this new attempt at consolidation was challenged and provisions which sought to extend occupational rights to cohabitees revamped. Even in its amended form it will not improve the protection to victims of domestic violence. First, the original Bill extended the class of persons qualifying for protection yet was still founded on a legalistic construction of the family. 'Associated persons' as defined in clause 1 of the original Bill extended the categories of persons protected, but required the parties to 'live or have lived in the same household' (Family Law Bill c. 56(3)(c)) to qualify. Whilst this definition extends parties protected to include homosexual couples, and family relatives, for example grandparents, aunts and uncles, those who have had a relationship whether or not sexual in nature but have never lived together in the same household fall outside the ambit of protection of the law. A study in Streatham (Buchan and Edwards 1991) found that 52 per cent of domestic violence cases involved girlfriend/boyfriend relationships who would automatically fail the 'live or have lived in the same household' test. It is to be noted that the exclusion of such non-household relationships is contrary to the recommendation of the Law Commission (at paras. 3.36, 4.9). The restrictive category of persons for whom protection will be available was criticised by a wide range of individuals and organisations who gave evidence to the House of Lords Committee. Consider too that in *Duo* v *Osborne (formerly Duo)* [1992] 2 FLR 425, where there had been a breach of an undertaking and where the parties were no longer married and no longer living together, the court *per curiam* recognised, '. . . it is a serious defect that the Domestic Violence and Matrimonial Proceedings Act 1976 applies only so long as the parties are married or living together as a couple. The need for a non molestation injunction buttressed by a power of arrest is often greater when the parties have split up.'. This provision is contrary to the recommendation of the Law Commission (at paras. 3.18–3.26, 4.9). Secondly, one of the key problems has been the reluctance of the courts to make non-molestation orders in the absence of violence. The new test in the Family Law Bill providing the trigger for intervention is that of 'health, safety or well being' (clause 37(5)). Harassment, including pestering and obscene telephone calls, subjection to threats of all kinds which put a person in a constant state of fear, constant anxiety, trauma and duress, all are forms of molestation. The difficulty is that often in such circumstances there may be no evidence of threats of violence and yet the molestation may go on in perpetuity. If the Bill proposes to recognise such molestation under the heading of 'health, safety or well being', this should also, in order to provide consistency, be the standard when the courts come to consider attaching a power of arrest. The third concern arises in the attempt to balance different and competing concerns in considering ouster applications and the use of three different terms or standards *inter alia* 'harm' (c. 30(8)b, 31(8)b, 33(5)b); 'significant harm' (c. 30(8)b) to identify the standard required to consider intervention.

'Harm' when it applies to children conveys the same meaning as s. 31, Children Act 1989, for parties other than children 'harm' means 'ill-treatment or the impairment of physical or mental health'. 'Significant harm' when applied to children again follows the Children Act, whereas for adults there is no express definition clause. The terms contained in the Family Law Bill, clauses 7(6), 9(6), 17(3)(b) are terms to be employed when the court is considering occupation orders. When the courts are considering non-molestation orders, 'health, safety and well being' (clause 37(5)) is the trigger for intervention. The further reconstruction of this issue as a matter of competing interests and justice between the parties places the need for protection within the framework of a contest. Thus, the debate is recast on the basis of competing rights rather than on a basis of the recognition of the precedence of the right to protection from molestation. In our evidence to the Family Homes and Domestic Violence Bill (1995, pp. 18–20), Ann Halpern and I argued that there should be separate powers to deal with these two different claims and where molestation is at issue this right to protection should be given priority over and above rights of occupation. It is left to judges using the new 'balance of harm', test (although this term appears in the Explanatory Memorandum only), together with the concept of 'significant harm' imported from the Children Act. It is acknowledged that 'balance of hardship' was a consideration in several cases; see *Bassett* v *Bassett* [1975] Fam 76, where the courts considered the interests of the party to protection on the one hand and the interests of the respondent to proprietorial interest on the other. Balance of hardship cannot be substituted with balance of harm. This test will have direct application in the granting of occupation orders (clause 28(7)) and will result in the proliferation of litigation by respondents who will now be locked in contest trying to establish that the harm they will suffer from the granting of any order will be the greater.

The Family Law Bill 1995 Part III deals with improving enforcement by establishing a positive duty to attach a power of arrest (clause 42(2)(3)), although this duty is activated only where there is 'violence or the threat of it' and in this respect is consonant with the language and concepts of the legislation that precedes it (Domestic Violence Act 1976, s. 2(1)), rather than in conformity with the several terms employed in the Bill itself. The attachment of a power of arrest is much more restrictive whilst apparently widening the ambit of the ground upon which a non-molestation order may be granted. Unless there is clear guidance and training the proviso to clause 40(1) will allow courts not to attach a power of arrest if they are satisfied that the applicant or child will be adequately protected. Present practice indicates that the courts have overwhelmingly been of that view. This clause will do little to change that presumption.

The Family Law Bill will not significantly improve the protection of victims of domestic violence. The increasing trend towards rendering protection to those in cohabitation will place many non-cohabiting partners at risk.

Even where a person experiencing violence qualifies and satisfies the criteria few can afford the expense. Injunctions are very costly remedies and it is likely that only the rich or the very poor are able to avail themselves of this protection. Like the fear over Criminal Injuries Compensation Claims where the victim is living with the aggressor who may benefit, the same household concept also applies where legal aid is being considered. Where the aggressor lives in the same household his finances are taken into account which makes it impossible for the victim to get legal aid in an action against him. The Lord Chancellor's Department recognised that legal aid was the key to providing women with protection but could not say what could be done for a woman who was being battered but who did not qualify for legal aid and could not afford to consult a solicitor. The inevitable result is that the remedies of the civil court are effectively removed from a very large number of victims.

The final strategy in protection for the victim of violence or molestation in all its forms are the remedies available in tort. Given the stringent 'live together or have lived together' test which must be satisfied under the new Family Law legislation before any protection can be secured, many women who fail the cohabitation test will be forced to resort to the remedies in tort. On the whole these remedies have been largely ineffective.

The redress takes two forms. First a party may apply for injunctive relief. In *Khorasandjian* v *Bush* [1993] 3 All ER 669, where the plaintiff never cohabited with and never married the defendant, the plaintiff had to look to the common law to provide her with remedy in the form of an interlocutory injunction (s. 37(1), Supreme Court Act 1981) against the defendant. The defendant appealed, contending that the judge had no jurisdiction to restrain him from 'harassing, pestering or communicating with' the plaintiff, because these words did not reflect any tort known to the law. The appeal was dismissed.

In *Burris* v *Azadani* [1996] 1 FLR 266, the defendant was given a suspended sentence for breaching an interlocutory injunction granted under s. 37, Supreme Court Act 1981. The injunction prohibited the defendant from going within 25 years of the plaintiff's home.

Second, there is the remedy of damages for an action in tort where there is trespass to the person, assault and battery, and nuisance. In the arena on an action for assault and battery there must be proof of physical force. Such a provision is largely inadequate to deal with the problem of harassment, telephone calls, letters, pestering, abuse etc. In tort, an action for nuisance is defined as 'an unlawful interference with a person's use or enjoyment of land' and may include interference with comfort or convenience.

The law, its interpretation and application, is influenced at each and every stage of the process by two overriding public policy principles. One is that the family is private and that its sanctity takes precedence, the other is that violence by men on women in the family is a private matter not to be equated with public violence. The law is rarely invoked to protect women and the courts are reluctant to enforce existing law through sentencing the aggressor commensurately or else enforcing the orders of the civil courts. The net result is that the State through its laws, legal process and personnel, in its reluctance to invoke legal procedures or to effect them, symbolically condones male violence and creates and reproduces a wider cultural climate and supporting ideology in which violence against partners, unless it is of the most appalling gravity, is perpetuated.

SIX

Unreasonable women — battered woman syndrome on trial

This discussion examines the role of what has come to be regarded as 'battered woman syndrome' evidence, in defence of battered women on trial for the murder of their partners, in trials where the defence is one of duress or coercion, in trials of women for failure to protect a child and also as part of the prosecution case where women withdraw allegations of assault against men. The analysis draws heavily on case law outside the UK, since British psychiatry and psychology is currently in the process of identifying and diagnosing battered women syndrome and British courts remain largely impervious to the admission of such evidence (see Edwards 1990, 1992c). The 'battered woman syndrome' defence strategy has been developed by defence lawyers in North America and Australia, with a view to assisting the jury in understanding the state of mind of battered women who kill their abusers and in assessing the reasonableness of their actions. The presiding caveat is that whilst evidence of the 'syndrome' assists in acquainting the jury with the long term effects of persistent violence on the mental state, particularly the defendants' perception of imminence, this accommodation is achieved within a conceptual framework which stitches a woman right back into a pathological strait jacket focusing on her mind instead of the man's prior conduct. This medicalisation has given rise to several objections, principally that the success of the defence depends on fitting the defendant to the 'syndrome', when the aetiology of her defensive retaliation is more appositely a function of a reasonable response to male violence and duress than a manifestation of unreasonableness. Where the battered woman defence strategy is proposed, it is 'her' state of mind and personality which is 'on trial', and a defence which emerged out of a necessity to acquaint jurors with her specific predicament becomes metamorphosed into a mental health excuse.

THE BATTERED WOMAN SYNDROME DEFINED

The term 'battered woman syndrome' to define the battered woman's experience and predicament is profoundly misleading, connoting something more akin to an intrinsic condition of mental illness or disorder, rather than an acquired response, the result of the long term consequences of violent abuse, on the perceptions and judgment of the victim. Further confusion arises where some have regarded the 'syndrome' as characterising the morphology of violence, whilst others have taken the 'syndrome' to connote a severe 'stress reaction'. Lenore Walker, a clinical psychologist practising in the US, first coined the term 'battered woman syndrome' after observing the recurrence of a severe stress reaction in the many battered women she counselled. Devising the 'battered woman syndrome' as a working model to explain and document the more typical effects of battering on women, Walker analysed both the morphology of violence (objective evidence) and women's (subjective) reaction to it. Her thesis is that male violence against women follows a three phase programme. Her argument is as much an analysis of the narrative of male violence as it is an exposition of women's reaction.

The 'syndrome' provides, '. . . a psychological rationale for why the battered woman becomes a victim, and how the process of victimization further entraps her, resulting in psychological paralysis to leave the relationship' (Walker 1977, p. 525). The first stage involves a period of heightening tension, where in response to the escalation of male argument, verbal attack and 'explosions of acute violence', the woman adopts various strategies to pacify, appease and placate her aggressor. The male feeling contrite pleads for forgiveness with gifts and declarations of love, in an attempt to regain the territory which has been irrevocably spoiled. She forgives him and the cycle begins once again wherein she becomes an 'accomplice' (sic) in her own battering. Walker discovered that women develop a psychological stereotype which meshes with the batterer's regime. The second stage rests on the subjective experience of 'learned helplessness' which characterises the reaction of the battered woman to the violence. Explained by entrapment and inability to escape, accompanied by the internalisation of feelings of self-blame, low self-esteem, despair, depression and anxiety, the woman believes that there is nothing she can do to abort, halt or deflect the violence and that nothing and no one can help. Hence she develops what Walker calls a 'diminished perception of alternatives'. The third element is less well defined and perhaps the most controversial, characterising the battered woman's final desperate attempt at survival, which may lead her to kill.

This morphology of batterer and victim has been observed by many practitioners working with battered women who have identified fear, anxiety, apprehension and trauma as common elements. Dworkin describes the all consuming fear of the battered woman:

I remember withdrawing further and further into that open grave where so many women hide waiting to die — the house. I went out to shop only when I had to; I walked my dogs; I ran out screaming, looking for help and shelter when I had the strength to escape, with no money, often no coat, nothing but terror and tears. I met only averted eyes, cold stares and the vulgar sexual aggression of long, laughing men that sent me running home to danger that was at least familiar and familial. Home, mine as well as his. Home, the only place I had. Finally, everything inside crumbled. I gave up. I sat, I stared, I waited, passive and paralyzed, speaking to no one, minimally maintaining myself and my animals, as my husband stayed away for longer and longer periods of time, slamming in only to thrash and leave. No one misses the wife who disappears ... Wives after all, belong in the home. Nothing outside depends on them (cited in Jones 1991, p. 316).

Hilberman and Munson (1978), in their study of battered women referred to a mental health clinic found:

There was a chronic apprehension of imminent doom, of something terrible always about to happen. Any symbolic act or actual sign of potential danger resulted in increased activity, agitation, pacing, screaming and crying. They remained vigilant, unable to relax or sleep (cited in Gillespie 1989, p. 124).

Ewing (1987, p. 62), provides an alternative formulation of the effects of battering on women. Arguing that battered women who kill, do so in 'psychological self-defence', he contends that the battered woman kills when faced with a choice of killing or being reduced to a psychological state. For Ewing, once battering is recognised as a form of domestic or conjugal terrorism it becomes easier to identify with the psychological plight of the battered woman. He formulates the turning point for women as a conscious anticipation or dread described as 'disintegration anxiety'. Summarising this turning point he cites Ferraro and Johnson (1983) thus, 'most battered women eventually experience a turning point when the violence or abuse done to them comes to be felt as a basic threat, whether to their physical or social self, or both' (cited in Ewing at p. 65). He equates the battering experience with that of terrorism and uses the term 'conjugal terrorism' to describe it. The legal doctrine he proposes would not be limited to battered women or to battered spouses, it would also provide a defence for battered children who kill battering parents. In the UK psychiatrists and psychologists are yet to agree on how sustained abuse can affect the battered women. They are less inclined to follow the precise formulation identified by Walker. Sandra Horley who gave expert evidence in the trial of Sally Emery (discussed later) said, 'Women who suffer abuse are in a state of shock and trauma suffering stress as well as mental exhaustion, they are incapable of making informed choices.' (*The Independent* 4 November 1992). The precise formulation will be argued, debated and determined in the *Thornton* retrial in May 1996.

Critiquing the syndrome nomenclature

Criticism of the 'syndrome' nomenclature has centred on three aspects. First, there has been the rather more general objection that, yet again, women are psychiatrised and therapeutised in a too ready explanation of their criminality (see Coughlin 1994, Kennedy 1992). In this formulation, the action of the battered woman is considered more appositely a product of an inner predisposition rather than a result of the externalities of violence, entrapment and survival. The American Psychiatric Association in the *Diagnostic and Statistical Manual of Mental Disorders* DSM–111–R (1992), adds further affirmation of this medical nosography when it lists, 'battered woman syndrome' as a sub-category of post-traumatic stress disorder. 'The syndrome is a collection of thoughts, feelings, and actions that logically follow a frightening experience that one expects could be repeated' (see Walker 1993, p. 247). But it is not wholly from the definition of 'battered woman syndrome' in its original concept that this therapeutisation derives, but also the demands and rigours of expert testimony and the legally validated domain of the expert which assists in this configuration within the legal nosology of 'disease'. It is in the work of Coughlin (1994, p. 79), that the most extreme and vituperative critique of the battered woman syndrome theorisation is launched, reaching its zenith when she accuses Walker of constructing a misogynist defence.

> The answers that Walker ultimately derived from her empirical study are as disturbingly reductionist as the ideas of the nineteenth century physicians who offered findings about canine reproductive systems to prove, '. . . that women are not capable of doing what men do'.

Coughlin contends that the defence re-affirms that women lack the capacity for self-control that is possessed by men, and that such a defence is based on the notion that women *per se* are inadequate and childlike as a result of some innate defect and that the battered woman's syndrome recapitulates the same misogynist assumptions about women's helplessness to govern their lives, whilst later conceding, 'I emphasize that the failures of the battered woman syndrome defence really are not the product of feminism', yet continuing to lambast Walker's attempt to rescue women from the inherent masculinism of law's legal method. Coughlin fails to recognise that Walker's formulation of the battered woman syndrome is not the product of gender but the product of the social situation in which women find themselves. She fails to make the distinction between a theory which promotes the belief in an innate predeter- mined condition and a condition which emerges as the result of a socio- and psycho-political context induced in women by male violence. She fails too, to draw a distinction between the theory and its utilisation and transcription by the demands of evidence and the law. Coughlin's criticism is unremitting:

> Walker's project is not capable of producing a feminist theory of responsibil- ity because critical phases of her research, namely, the specific problems she defined as the object of her study and her interpretation of the data she collected, were informed, not by a feminist methodology or theory of epistemology, but by the same cognitive patriarchal categories that structure the two disciplines — law and psychology — that she sought to bridge.

Controversy has also centred and perhaps with rather more justification on the inherent inconsistency of the theory, explaining as it does women's 'learned helplessness' at one moment and her homicidal behaviour at another. Faigman (1986, p. 636) and Leader-Elliott (1993) are particularly sceptical about the capacity of this theory to explain how the 'learned helplessness' of the battered women allows her to use deadly force and what finally triggers this. Leader-Elliott asks what finally transforms 'an assertive act of self-defence into a manifestation of weakness and incapacity' (1993, p. 411). Yet, perhaps in reply to the critics, like the formulation of anger and passion necessary to a successful defence of provocation, objections about internal consistency are labouring under a masculinist construct of homicide and intent, whereas a feminist critique might align the homicidal reaction of a battered woman less with assertiveness and more with self-preservation and despair, which may then allow for a reading of consistency even with 'learned helplessness' (see Edwards 1985).

Transcending the way a masculinist legal system, legal method and legal structure constructs law and utilises feminist insights and attempts a prosthetic rather than a root and branch treatment of law, is one of the key feminist objections to engaging with the law at all. As Jones (1991, p. 361), Smart (1989), and Mossman (1986), concede, it is not enough to peel away the gendered basis of law. It is the very morphology and ontology which must of necessity be addressed.

INTO THE LEGAL ARENA

The placing of the syndrome in the hands of psychiatrists and psychologists in the courtroom transports the syndrome even further into the medical and therapeutic arena. This of course fits law's image of women, in particular law's typification of women who kill. Further objections have focused more specifically on two aspects. First, the battered woman syndrome defence functions as an 'excuse', instead of a 'justification', with the inevitable consequence that it is considered material to a plea of diminished responsibility or temporary insanity, rather than to a plea of provocation or self-defence. The strictures and limitations of an excuse based defence are well known, construed as *de facto* explanations of behaviour, locating explanations for criminal conduct within some debilitating intrinsic pathology. The use of such loosely defined 'mental health' defences erroneously locate women's motive for conduct within an abnormal state of mind rather than within a framework of reasonableness, necessity and duress. Second, Faigman (1986, p. 619), objects to the inevitable legal unfolding, in that the courts are expending too great an effort expounding the battered woman's psychological self and too little time explaining the justness of her action, focusing on her state of mind, and eclipsing the man's violence. Elizabeth Schneider, the New York feminist lawyer, is similarly concerned that:

Judicial willingness to find women's perspectives acceptable may relate to the fact that the perspective courts are hearing and to which they are responding is that of *damaged* women, not of women who perceive themselves to be, and may in fact be, acting competently, assertively and rationally in light of the alternatives (cited in Browne 1987, p. 177).

Given this particular construction of homicidal conduct as 'excuse' rather than as 'justification', many advocates have been reluctant to use the 'battered woman syndrome' for fear that women who are responding to present or future violence or threat of violence will be classified as mentally ill (see Blackman 1989, Mihajlovich 1987, Maguigan 1991, Mahoney 1991.

UK lawyers have expressed similar reservations. Helena Kennedy (1992, pp. 93–94), argues, 'It seems more sensible to avoid gender-specific labels like this because of the pathological cul-de-sac they create for women'. Nicolson and Sanghvi (1993, p. 734), concede, '... it will always actively shift the emphasis from the reasonableness of the defendant's action to her personality in a way which confirms existing gender stereotypes, silences battered women and conceals society's complicity in domestic violence.'. The invocation of the battered woman syndrome defence is one of several efforts to address the structural inequality enmeshed in the law, whilst it explains women's predicament it does little to address or challenge the inherent masculine bias of the law. The object of introducing evidence of battered woman syndrome into the trials of battered women is to bring about some redress, albeit limited, for women who kill violent partners, and to assist juries in their assessment of whether their behaviour was reasonable. The battered woman has a different perception of threats and an expert knowledge based on experience of the aggressor's likelihood of carrying them out; she is in a constant state of anticipation and fear knowing from past experience that anything or nothing at all may result in him assaulting or trying to kill her. Whilst self-defence relies on a subjective standard, it depends for its success on its reasonableness as assessed by others. But such evidence does not fit squarely with self-defence or a mental health or insanity defence. Simply, the battered woman syndrome is a strategy which attempts to address the law's intransigence and inflexibility regarding the interpretation of what a reasonable man would do and the interpretation of imminent.

This necessitates introducing objective evidence of men's violence, and expert evaluation of the effect of battering on such women, particularly with regard to how her assessment of his threats and her perception of the likelihood of him carrying out the threat might be affected. The purpose, argues Elizabeth Schneider, is to combat the masculinist model of self-defence and to 'equalise the positions of male and female defendants by recognising their differences' (1980, p. 640). Since:

> ... battered women have learned to be attentive to signs of escalating violence and to modify their behaviour in response to these danger signals in order to pacify violent husbands. Subtle motions or threats that might not signify danger to an outsider or to the trier of fact acquire added meaning for a battered woman whose survival depends on an intimate knowledge of her assailant (p. 634).

Walker explains its possibilities and limitations. The introduction of evidence as to the effects of battering on the state of mind of the defendant, eschews an attack on one aspect of the law's dominion, that is the subjective test in manslaughter, self-defence and duress pleadings. It cannot offer a critique on the construction of these categories or on the ingredients which must be satisfied. Any attempt to deconstruct law's masculinist empire must look to the morphology of law itself and not merely to the application of its rules by judges or the interpretation by juries of its facts. Schneider alludes to this predicament, 'The male assumptions contained in legal doctrine and the manifestations of those assumptions in court rulings . . . deny to women an opportunity equal to that of male defendants to present their claims of self-defence' (1980, p. 647).

Challenges to masculinist morphology and ontology of law

There have been feminist challenges other than that of the battered woman syndrome defence to this masculinist ontology. Such critiques have not resulted in any change to the law's inherent structure or legal method, but there have been some concessions to the argument through the exercise of judicial discretion in particular cases, obviating challenge to the defences, which is a course regarded as heresy. The overriding question has been in these challenges whether the law is inherently masculinist and whether this violates a woman defendant's right to equal protection. The case of *State* v *Wanrow* 88 Wash 2d 221, 559 P 2d 548 (1977), provides an example of the efforts to address the masculinist presumptions of law (for a further discussion of this point see the chapter entitled, The Gender Politics of Homicide). In *Wanrow*, the appellant shot a man whom she understood to have attempted to abduct her son. She pleaded self-defence. The court permitted the jury to consider the defendant's conduct through her subjective perception of the situation, conceding:

> . . . Woman defendant's right to equal protection of the law was violated in second-degree murder and first-degree assault by instructions on self-defence that suggested, by persistent use of male gender, that a woman's conduct in defending herself be measured against that of a reasonable male finding himself in the same circumstances . . . In our society women suffer from a conspicuous lack of access to training in and the means of developing those skills necessary to effectively repel a male assailant without resorting to the use of deadly weapons. Instruction No. 12 does indicate that the 'relative size and strength of the persons involved' may be considered; however, it does not make clear that the defendant's actions are to be judged against her own subjective impressions and not those which a detached jury might determine to be objectively reasonable . . . The second paragraph of instruction No. 10 not only establishes an objective standard, but through the persistent use of the masculine gender leaves the jury with the impression that the objective standard to be applied is that applicable to an altercation between two men. The impression created [is] that a 5' 4" woman with a cast on her leg and using a crutch must, under the law, somehow repel an assault by a 6' 2" intoxicated man without employing weapons in her defense.

The respondent was entitled to have the jury consider her actions in the light of her own pereceptions which were the product of our 'nation's long and unfortunate history of sex discrimination' (see Schneider 1980, pp. 641–42). There have been other attempts in the US to address the equal protection issue (see *Wilson* in the chapter entitled, The Gender Politics of Homicide). In *Easterling* v *State* 267 P 2d 185, 188 (1954), where the defendant was grabbed by the hair by the deceased, beaten and choked and where the defendant stabbed him, the court recognised that particular physical attributes of a defendant might justify her use of a dangerous weapon to repel an unarmed attacker. Where a battered woman tried to repel her husband with a pocket knife the court of first instance held that this was a simple assault and any degree of force to repel it was not justified, thereby convicting the accused of murder. Jones J in the appellate court reversed this decision and said:

> There may be such a difference in the size of the parties involved or disparity in their ages or physical condition which would give the person assaulted by fists reasonable grounds to apprehend danger of great bodily harm and thus legally justified in repelling the assault by the use of a deadly weapon. It is conceivable that a man might be so brutal in striking a woman with his fists as to cause her death.

Admissibility issues: universal knowledge v expert evidence

The only facts which are real in law are those which the law has so authorised either through claims that such knowledge is after all common sense and universally held, or else through expert knowledge which is the province of the experts. 'Law's knowledge is limited by the rules of evidence' writes O'Donovan (1993, p. 428). 'New ideas about the justifying or excusing of killings in particular circumstances are policed by definitions and rules from existing legal doctrine.' In the United States, the effects of battering have been considered as expert knowledge, outside the everyday comprehension and understanding of jurors. The original intention of expert testimony was to assist the judge and jury in assessing the defendant's responsibility and *mens rea* and understanding the reasonableness of a woman's actions. The objection which is all too apparent is that men's experience is common sense. Thus, the law as it defines self-defence, and in the UK provocation, is a matter of what we all know, believe in, subscribe to and share. Diminished responsibility by contrast is a matter for experts. In educating juries and trying to bring about social change in the law, an expert is required. Thus, knowledge about battered women and the effects of battering, becomes defined as expert knowledge. This has two consequences, it may imbue that knowledge with greater authority, but at the same time the status of that knowledge becomes reified and not part of the common domain. If knowledge about men is common sense and knowledge about women requires experts to speak to it, what does that say for the relative status of that knowledge and its relative ubiquity and exceptionality? O'Donovan objects to the presence of experts (1993, p. 431). Expert evidence labels women as 'unreasonable, incompetent, suffering from psychological impairment or just plain crazy'. Yeo (1993, p. 111) expresses a similar concern. 'The law's insistence on the use of expert witnesses has the effect of rendering domestic violence an exceptional and unfamiliar occurrence when the reality is that it is so common as to be the norm.' This concern is borne out in application. Expert knowledge on the 'battered woman syndrome' has been adduced both as a part of a mental health defence, as in insanity or temporary insanity and also as part of a self-defence strategy. Some State courts in the US have limited the expert to adducing a general statement on the effects of battering on a woman, leaving the matter of whether the defendant was so affected for the consideration of the jury.

The reception of battered woman syndrome evidence has been chartered by struggles and conflicts over admissibility. Under the rules of evidence, expert testimony may be admitted either as a rule of law, or at the trial judge's discretion. The rules governing admissibility differ from State to State and this has meant that justice for women, on this issue, has depended wholly on geography. As a rule of law, some States have provided, within the rules of evidence, for the reception of battered woman syndrome. For example, in California, the Evidence Code 1993, 1107 provides:

(a) In a criminal action, expert testimony is admissible by either the prosecution or the defense regarding battered women's syndrome, including physical, emotional, or mental effects upon the beliefs, perceptions, or behaviour of victims of domestic violence, except when offered against a criminal defendant to prove the occurrence of the act of abuse which forms the basis of the criminal charge, (b) The foundation shall be sufficient for admission of this expert testimony if the proponent of the evidence establishes its relevancy and the proper qualifications of the expert witness. Expert opinion testimony on battered women syndrome shall not be considered a new scientific technique whose reliability is unproven (Klis 1994, p. 134).

At the highest level, the United States Supreme Court has been petitioned but has refused to grant certiorari in at least four cases which rely on evidence of battered woman syndrome (see *Moran* v *Ohio* 83 L Ed 2d 285 (1984), *Thomas* v *Arn* 474 US 140 (1985), *Neely* v *Alabama* 488 US 1020 (1989), and *Willis* (1994) 38 F 3d 170, 19 June 1995). The Supreme Court has not validated battered woman syndrome as a defence worthy of express recognition thereby clarifying the admissibility question for all US states. In *Moran* v *Ohio* the appellant, Betty Moran, was convicted of the murder of her husband. She claimed that she acted in self-defence as a result of the repeated and brutal beatings she had suffered at her husband's hands. Substantial evidence was adduced that her husband repeatedly beat and brutalised her. In one incident it was alleged that he had her by the neck and held her by the throat and was hitting her with a gun. The petitioner's mother testified that she saw the husband, '. . . hit her and knocked her on the floor, and I seen him take his feet and was kicking her'. On 12 May 1981, he told her that he wanted some money that he thought she had saved, and, if she did not have the money ready for him by the time he woke up he would, 'blow [her] damn brains out'. She could not produce the money he demanded and while he was sleeping she fatally shot him. At her trial she pleaded self-defence, claiming she was a victim of battered woman syndrome and that the Ohio court system unfairly allocated burdens of proof with respect to her claim of self-defence. The jury at her trial was instructed that, 'The burden of proving the defence of self-defence is upon the defendant. She must establish such defence by a preponderance of the evidence'. The Court of Appeals affirmed the conviction, and the Ohio Supreme Court dismissed the appeal, 'for the reason that no substantial constitutional question exists'. She sought a writ of certiorari to vindicate her 14th Amendment right to have the state bear the burden of proof in a criminal prosecution. Certiorari was denied, although Brennan J and Marshall J dissenting would have granted certiorari. As Hanson (1993, pp. 42, 43), points out, had the Supreme Court granted certiorari they could have reversed her conviction and used the opportunity to discuss the battered woman's syndrome.

At a Federal Judicial Circuit level (13 circuits), it was the case of *Arcoren* v *United States* 929 F 2d 1235, 1242, 8th Circuit (1991), which was the first Federal appellate case to consider and to rule the battered woman syndrome relevant and admissible (discussed below). 'This court has held expert testimony admissible under Rule 702 in other circumstances where the expert's specialized knowledge would assist the jury to understand the evidence.' The court also held that there was no persuasive reason to limit this testimony to women who wished to use it in self-defence. At a State level, some States have ruled such evidence admissible as a rule of law, introducing legislation to ensure that women can as a rule of law adduce expert witness testimony. Missouri, Texas, Maryland and California introduced Bills in 1989 and 1990, and several States have passed laws recognising the battered woman syndrome. In 1992, Congresswoman Connie Morella from Maryland introduced federal legislation that would encourage all States to change their laws to mandate such testimony when a woman claims she has been the victim of violence (see Fair Justice Acts 1992, see Walker 1993, p. 253). In States where the reception of battered woman syndrome is not a rule of law, admissibility is a matter for the discretion of the trial judge.

In Canada, the admissibility of a battered woman syndrome defence has been of much more recent origin and enters exclusively as part of a self-defence strategy (*Lavallee* [1990] 55 CCC 3d 97 — see Sheppard 1991). In Australia, the battered woman syndrome is similarly recognised as a part of a self-defence strategy (see *Runjanjic* v *Kontinnen* [1991] 53 A Crim R 362, *Hickey* (1992) 16 Crim LJ 271; *Kontinnen* (1992) 16 Crim LJ 360; and see Yeo 1993, p. 111). In the UK, attempts to introduce this evidence have been both under the limb of a defence of provocation (Homicide Act 1957, s. 3) and diminished responsibility s. 2 as in *Ahluwalia* [1992] 4 All ER 889. Battered woman syndrome evidence under provocation was rejected as not having the necessary degree of permanence to constitute the 'notional characteristic' of the reasonable man, although such evidence was accepted as part of further evidence of diminished responsibility, submitted on appeal.

Evidence of battered woman syndrome in such trials has not been limited to heterosexual relationships, it has also been ruled admissible in lesbian battering cases (see West 1992, p. 249, Bricker 1993, p. 1379). New York legislature on this point restricted the application to heterosexual relations. The Penal Code, s. 243 applied to dating relationships but battered woman syndrome had never been introduced in cases involving homosexuals. Some male offenders have also raised a battered person syndrome defence. In *Commonwealth* v *Stonehouse* 555 A 2d 772 (1989), the court stated, 'We shall apply the rule pertaining to the syndrome to men as well as to women'. In *Commonwealth* v *Kacsmar* 617 A 2d 725 (1992), where a man was convicted of the voluntary manslaughter of a brother, evidence of the deceased's bullying and intimidation was admitted. The syndrome has also been admitted in cases involving children as in the battered child syndrome defence. In *State* v *Janes* 850 P 2d 495, 496 Wash (1993), a 17 year old was convicted of second degree murder when he killed his mother's cohabitee who had been abusing him for 10 years. In the UK, 'battered husband syndrome' evidence was admitted in a case where a husband killed his wife (*Irons* (1995) 16 Cr App R (S) 46). In the UK some have voiced a concern that battered woman syndrome may be present in other relationships, 'the features are also present in other relationships where there is a power imbalance: hostage and captor; battered child and abusive parent; cult follower and leader; prisoner and guard' (Kennedy 1992, p. 94).

Self-defence and admissibility

Under US law, a person is guilty of criminal homicide if he/she 'purposely, knowingly, recklessly or negligently causes the death of another human being' (see *Black's Law Dictionary*, 5th ed, 1979, p. 661, citing the Model Penal Code 210.1 (1962)). Homicide is divided into murder in the first degree and the lesser charge of murder in the second degree. Justifiable homicide (self-defence), by contrast involves an element of intent, but without an evil design. The rules that govern self-defence are the same as in the UK based on the subjective test (see the chapter entitled, The Gender Politics of Homicide), for example, in the US following *Wallace* v *United States* 162 US 466 (1896), the accused is generally allowed to admit evidence about what he thought the victim was going to do. Thus the standard relies on the perception of the accused. In the US there is no diminished responsibility defence in every State although some States have a diminished capacity defence (see Browne 1987, p. 159). The mental health defence that applies is one of temporary insanity. In order to utilise this defence it is not enough for the defence to say that a person is of weak mind (*Rogers* v *State* 57 SE 227 (Ga 1907)), it must be something more. There is also the defence of provocation/voluntary manslaughter, similar to provocation in UK law and involuntary manslaughter provides for accident. What lies at the heart of the problem for battered women in the US who plead self-defence is that they rarely kill in a classic situation of self-defence, i.e., that of physical confrontation, the threat to their life is not considered imminent and their use of deadly force is not regarded as reasonable (see Ewing 1987, p. 586, Tomkins, Kenning, Greenwald and Johnson 1993, p. 262). Women in pleading self-defence have often killed a sleeping man thereby negating the rigours of imminence and use of deadly force. In self-defence the requirement would be that the woman should wait and see what happens, this requires a woman to wait until the assault is underway (see *Lavallee* [1990] 55 CCC 3d 97). Battered women who kill more frequently plead guilty to lesser charges, the most common plea arrangement found (Browne 1987, p. 163), was one of voluntary manslaughter, which means that women have abandoned any claim that the killing was justified under self-defence.

In self-defence pleadings, the battered woman syndrome is used in legal argument to contend that the woman had a reasonable perception of imminent danger and was justified in using lethal force. The testimony is used to help establish whether a battered woman's perception of imminence is reasonable given her experience of prior battering (see *People* v *Torres* below, *People* v *Aris* 215 Cal App 3d, 1178 (Calif Ct App 1989) 264 Cal Rptr (2d) 167; *People* v *Day*, 2 Cal App 4th 405 (Calif Ct App 1992) 2 Cal Rptr (2d) 916).

In *Aris* the appellant killed a sleeping husband. Aris said '... he (sic) didn't think he was going to let me live till the morning'. She shot him five times in the back. Evidence of battered woman syndrome was statute barred. In *Day* an application was made for a retrial since the defence failed to present battered woman syndrome evidence. The court held that battered woman syndrome was not relevant in determining whether the defendant's actions were objectively reasonable. The Appeals Court held that counsel's failure to investigate and present battered woman syndrome was deemed to be prejudicial, reversing the original judgment and ordering a retrial.

Even where battered woman syndrome is admitted, it rarely results in a complete acquittal, instead the defendant may be convicted of murder in the first degree or more usually convicted of second degree manslaughter. The celebrated case of *Ibn-Tamas* v *United States* 407 A 2d 626 (1980) (1983) (cited in Walker 1989, p. 74), where a battered woman pleaded self-defence and was convicted of second degree murder following a second trial, is instructive in understanding this early struggle for admissibility. Beverly *Ibn-Tamas*, a licensed nurse, had suffered long term physical abuse at the hands of her husband, a neurosurgeon, violence including threats with a gun and repeated punching which caused her to lose consciousness. When she became pregnant the abuse continued, involving repeated kicking and punching, often aimed at her stomach. On the fatal morning of 23 February 1976, he hit her in the stomach and threatened to shoot her, pointing a .38 calibre revolver at her face saying, 'You are going to get out of here this morning one way or the other'. She struggled with him and shot him in the chest at point blank range, frightened he was going to get up and kill her, she shot him again. At her trial Lenore Walker's evidence on the battered woman syndrome was ruled inadmissible. The expert evidence was rejected as the prejudicial value outweighed the probative value. The state of scientific knowledge was considered insufficiently developed and so began a six year battle for admissibility of the battered woman syndrome. In cross-examination she was asked, 'Dr Walker, is the study of battered women a recognized diagnostic category in your profession, by that I mean does it appear in any of the typologies used to recognize mental health disorders'? As Walker (1989, p. 269) explains:

What a dilemma! If I answered affirmatively, Judge Stewart might allow my testimony; but, in that case, it would be for the purpose of labeling Beverly Ibn-Tamas mentally disturbed, not for the purpose of validating her reasonable perception of imminent bodily danger (the self-defence standard, and her defence attorney's preferred course of action). Battered women advocates were struggling to keep such a category out of the mental health classification system for just that reason.

Walker responded, 'No, there are no typologies or classification systems of which I am aware that currently list battered women as a category'.

The trial court refused to admit expert testimony on three grounds. First, it would go beyond that which a jury is entitled to hear about. Second, it would invade the province of the jury, who are the triers of fact, and third the fact that Dr Walker claimed that the deceased was a batterer, was a fact which was not on trial. Her testimony was not admitted on the basis that the psychological field of study was not sufficiently well developed to support expert opinion. Ibn-Tamas was convicted of second degree murder, her plea of self-defence failed. Unusually, if not uniquely, in such cases, the judge imposed a prison sentence of one to five years and Ibn-Tamas was released after two years (Walker 1989, p. 271). Notwithstanding, the battle for admissibility had only just begun. Ibn-Tamas's lawyers appealed on the basis that the judge had been wrong to exclude Walker's testimony and therein began a six year battle for admissibility. In 1979, in a preliminary ruling, the District of Columbia appellate court conceded that jurors need educating in this field, adding a further qualification that those providing expert testimony had to be qualified, sending the case back to the original trial judge who responded in affirming his original decision. Ferren J held that:

(1) expert testimony relating to 'battered women', which was given by clinical psychologist in support of defendant's claim of self-defense to killing of her husband, was not inadmissible on grounds that it would invade province of jury or that its probative value was outweighed by its prejudicial impact; however, record was insufficient for appellate determination with regard to its ultimate admissibility without remand for consideration of witness' qualifications and a determination as to whether witness methodology for identifying and studying battered women had attained general acceptance.

Ibn-Tamas's lawyers instituted a second appeal in 1983 when once again the decision of the original trial judge was upheld. The preliminary ruling in *Ibn-Tamas* recognising that jurors needed educating in this field, was instituted in several States (see *Smith* v *State* 247 GA 612, 277 SE 2d 678 (1981) in Georgia; *State* v *Anaya* 438 A 2d 892 (1981), in Maine; *People* v *Minnis* 455, NE 2d 209 (1983) in Illinois; *State* v *Allery* 682 P 2d 312 (1984) in Washington; *State* v *Kelly* 478 A 2d 364 (1984) in New Jersey; *People* v *Torres* 128 Misc 2d 129, 132; 488 NYS 2d 358, 361, Sup Ct (1985) in New York; *Hawthorne* v *State* 408 So 2d 801, 470 So 2d 770 (1985), in Florida; *Kentucky State* v

Hundley 693 P 2d 475 (1985) in Kentucky; *State* v *Green* 652 P 2d 697 (1982) in Kansas; *Commonwealth of Kentucky* v *Craig* 783 SW 2d 387 (1990) in Kentucky; *State* v *Hennum* 441 NW 2d 793 (1989) in Minnesota; *State* v *Baker* 424 A 2d 171 (1980) in New Hampshire; *State* v *Koss* 551 NE 2d 970 (1990) in Ohio; *Commonwealth* v *Stonehouse* 555 A 2d 772 (1989) in Pennsylvania; *State* v *Ciskie* 751 P 2d 1165 (1988) in Washington; *State* v *Kelly* 685 P 2d 564 (1984) in Washington; *State* v *Steele* 359 SE 2d 558 (1987) in West Virginia; *State* v *Pozier* 255 SE 2d 552 (1979) in West Virginia).

The test for admissibility was formulated by the Supreme Court of New Jersey in a landmark case in 1984; *State* v *Kelly* 478 A 2d 364 (1984). The court asserted:

> It is aimed at an area where the purported common knowledge of the jury may be very much mistaken, an area where jurors' logic drawn from their own experience may lead to a wholly incorrect conclusion, an area where expert knowledge would enable the jurors to disregard their prior conclusions as being common myths rather than common knowledge.

This was a case where a wife stabbed a husband with a pair of scissors after he had tried to choke her and where she was convicted of reckless manslaughter. In *State* v *Kelly*, the court ruled that an adjudication on whether the defendant suffered battered woman syndrome was to be determined by the jury (see Gousie 1993, p. 458), reversing and remanding for a retrial the reckless manslaughter conviction, as the court had erred in excluding expert testimony on battered woman syndrome. In *People* v *Torres* (1985) (above), where the defendant was charged with the second degree murder of her common law husband and proffered expert testimony of the battered woman syndrome, Bernstein J held such evidence admissible, adding '. . . It is the opinion of this court that the theory underlying the battered woman's syndrome has indeed passed beyond the experimental stage and gained a substantial enough scientific acceptance to warrant admissibility' (see Walker 1989, p. 363).

Some States during this period continued to ban expert testimony on the battered woman syndrome altogether (*Buhrle* v *State* 627 P 2d 1374 (Wyo 1981), *Fielder* v *State* 683 SW 2d 565 Tex App 2d Dist 1985, *Bechtel* (in Oklahoma City) see *Bechtel* v *State* 840 P 2d 1 (1992) cited in Walker (1989, p. 278)). In *State* v *Thomas* 423 NE 2d 137 (1981), the Ohio Supreme Court rejected expert testimony on the ground that the battered woman syndrome is not outside the understanding of the average juror (see Gillespie 1989, p. 167, Jones 1991, p. 310). This ruling was challenged six years later, in *State* v *Koss* 551 NE 2d 970, 974 (1990), where the court overturned Ohio's earlier ban on expert testimony. In *Koss*, the wife was indicted for murder and pleaded not guilty, claiming that her husband hit her as she was undressing and at the next moment she remembered a 'noise or something'. When asked if she had shot her husband she said 'No', and that she could not remember anything about killing him. Evidence was adduced that she had been beaten by her husband repeatedly. Expert evidence on the battered woman syndrome and the effects of that battering was excluded following the earlier ruling in *State* v *Thomas* 423

NE 2d 137 (1981). On appeal, Koss succeeded in challenging the ruling against the admissibility of battered woman syndrome. In a judgment written by Justice Alice Robie Resnick, (the only woman on Ohio's circuit), it was held:

> We overrule *State* v *Thomas* ... to the extent that it holds that expert testimony concerning the battered women syndrome may not be admitted to support the affirmative defense of self-defense, ... expert testimony concerning the syndrome may be admitted to assist the trier of fact in determining whether the defendant acted in self-defense.

Holmes J, in concurring, cited Rosen in his judgment (1986, pp. 11, 43):

> Most battered woman's defense cases involve situations in which the defendant was not, in fact, in imminent danger of death or serious bodily harm at her victim's hands. The defense relies on persuading the jury that defendant suffered from an identifiable psychological syndrome that caused her to assess the dangerousness of the situation in a different manner than an average, ordinary person — including a woman who does not suffer from battered woman syndrome. In other words, acquittal is dependent upon proving that defendant had ... a disability that caused a mistaken, but reasonable, belief in the existence of circumstances that would justify self-defense. *It is a theory of excuse rather than of justification.*

Hanson (1993, p. 48), in a critique of Holmes J's judgment, accuses him of 'riding the waves of neutrality'.

In Canada, the admissibility of battered woman syndrome evidence was considered by the Supreme Court of Canada in *Lavallee* [1990] 55 CCC 3d 97, where it was held in a most eloquently formulated and argued judgment that evidence of battered woman syndrome was admissible in a case of a woman who was charged with murder and relied on the defence of self-defence. Angelique Lavallee shot her cohabitee, Kevin Rust, in the back of the head as he was leaving her room after assaulting her and threatening her with the words 'wait till everybody leaves, you'll get it then'. A psychiatrist, called by the defence, gave evidence on battered-wife syndrome, arguing that the accused felt she would be killed unless she defended herself. Lavallee was acquitted. The Crown appealed to the Manitoba Court of Appeal for a re-trial, on the basis that the trial judge did not adequately instruct the jury with respect to the evidence of the psychiatrist and in particular did not properly instruct the jury as to the effect of hearsay evidence (conversations the psychiatrist had with Lavallee's mother). The Court of Appeal convicted. Lavallee appealed to the Supreme Court of Canada, where her appeal was allowed and the acquittal restored. The Court ruled per Wilson J (Dickson CJC, Lamer, L'Heureux-Dube, Gonthier and McLachlin JJ concurring), in a judgment described by Kennedy (1992, p. 93), as the finest legal exposition on domestic violence:

> Expert evidence is admissible to assist the trier of fact in drawing inferences in areas where the expert has relevant knowledge or experience beyond that

of the lay person. The evidence of the psychiatrist in this case concerning the battered-wife syndrome was relevant and necessary in the context of this case. The mental state of the accused could not properly be appreciated without such evidence. The battering relationship is subject to a large group of myths and stereotypes and as such it is beyond the experience of the average juror and thus is suitable for explanation through expert testimony.

Without this evidence the accused faces the prospect of being condemned by popular mythology about domestic violence, the trier of fact improperly concluding that she was not as badly beaten as she claims or she would have left the man long ago, or even if she was severely beaten that she stayed out of some masochistic enjoyment of it. Moreover, the expert testimony was relevant to specific elements of the defence of self-defence under s. 34(2) of the Criminal Code. Expert testimony relating to the ability of the accused to perceive danger from the deceased would go to the issue of whether she reasonably apprehended death or grievous bodily harm on the occasion in question. While s. 34(2) does not actually stipulate that the accused apprehend imminent danger before acting in self-defence, there is an assumption that it is inherently unreasonable to apprehend death or grievous bodily harm unless and until the physical assault is actually in progress at which point the victim can reasonably gauge the requisite amount of force needed to repel the attack and act accordingly. Expert testimony can cast doubt on these assumptions as they applied in the context of a battered wife's efforts to repel an assault. In particular, where evidence exists that an accused is in a battering relationship, expert testimony can assist the jury in determining whether the accused had a reasonable apprehension of death when she acted by explaining the heightened sensitivity of a battered woman to her partner's acts. Without such testimony it is doubtful that the trier of fact would be capable of appreciating why her subjective fear may have been reasonable in the context of the relationship. Thus in this case the 'reasonable man' might have thought that it was unlikely that the deceased would make good on his threat to kill the accused that night because they had guests staying overnight. The issue is not, however, what an outsider would have reasonably perceived but what the accused reasonably perceived, given her situation and her experience. The expert evidence would also be of assistance to the jury on the issue of whether the accused believed on reasonable grounds that it was not possible to otherwise preserve herself from death or grievous bodily harm. The question the jury must ask itself is whether, given the history, circumstances and perception of the accused, her belief that she could not preserve herself from being killed by the deceased that night except by killing him first was reasonable. To the extent that expert evidence can assist the jury in making that determination such testimony is both relevant and necessary. By providing an explanation as to why the accused did not flee when she perceived her life to be in danger, expert testimony may assist the jury in assessing the reasonableness of her belief that killing the accused was the only way to save her life. The trial judge therefore properly admitted the expert evidence. Ultimately, of course, it would be for the jury to decide whether in fact the accused's perceptions and actions were reasonable. Expert evidence cannot usurp the function of the jury. The jury is not compelled to accept the opinions proffered by the expert about the effects of battering on the mental state of victims generally, or on the mental state of the accused in particular. Fairness and integrity of the trial process, however, demand that the jury have the opportunity to hear such opinions. Further, the trial judge's charge to the jury concerning the use to be made of this evidence was adequate.

Expert opinion is admissible if relevant, even if it is based on second-hand evidence. This hearsay evidence is admissible to show the information upon which the expert opinion is based not as evidence going to the existence of the facts on which the opinion is based. Where psychiatric evidence is comprised of hearsay evidence the problem is the weight to be attributed to the opinion. Before any weight can be given to an expert's opinion, however, the facts upon which the opinion is based must be found to exist. In this case, the trial judge warned the jury that they could not decide the case on the basis of things that the witnesses did not see or hear which would include those matters which the expert neither saw nor heard. While it would have been preferable if the trial judge had specifically pointed out that his interview with the accused was a source of inadmissible evidence, when the charge was read as a whole it would be clear that the jury was to consider only admissible evidence. Provided there is some admissible evidence to establish the foundation for the expert opinion, the trial judge cannot subsequently instruct the jury to completely ignore the testimony. In this case, the psychiatrist had admissible evidence about the nature of the relationship between the accused and the deceased in the form of the accused's statement to the police and hospital records. There was substantial corroborative evidence provided at trial by other witnesses including a friend of the deceased who had described the several assaults that he had witnessed upon the accused. Where the factual basis of an expert opinion is a mixture of admissible and inadmissible evidence, the duty of the trial judge is to caution the jury that the weight attributable to the expert testimony is directly related to the amount and quality of admissible evidence on which it relies. In this case the trial judge performed his task adequately in this regard.

The impact of battered woman syndrome in Canada has not been as all pervasive as in the United States. The impact of *Lavallee* has been limited (see Coughlin 1994, p. 55, Sheppard 1991). Sheehy (1994), explores the impact of the judgment on later cases in the period following *Lavallee* to August 1993. In eight cases battered woman syndrome evidence was used in mitigation of sentence (discussed below), one resulted in an acquittal as a result of the *mens rea* and in one a defence of self-defence failed. In *Eagles* [1991] YJ No 147 (Yukon Terr Ct) the evidence was used unusually to make out a 'no *mens rea*' defence in a case where the defendant was charged with making a threatening telephone call to her husband. Lilles J also placed great emphasis on battered woman syndrome although the accused was no longer living at home and was seemingly not being threatened by him. Battered woman syndrome evidence has also been of importance in cases where the prosecution have dropped charges, as in the case against Roxanne Murray after evidence of a long history of violence (see MacQueen K, Justifiable Homicide, *The Ottawa Citizen*, 3 May 1991).

Admissibility: temporary insanity — diminished responsibility Battered woman syndrome evidence is introduced where the defence is one of temporary insanity/diminished responsibility. In the early days, evidence of battered woman syndrome was advanced as part of a mental health defence of temporary insanity, as in the case of Francine Hughes (1977) below (see Jones 1991, p. 299, Walker 1989, p. 187), who killed her husband by pouring gasoline around the bed whilst he slept. Her acquittal on the grounds of temporary insanity was regarded as a shallow victory, since an acquittal on the grounds of insanity, instead of on the grounds of a reasonable response to violence and tyranny, focused on the defendant as pathogenic rather than on the circumstances. Whether battered woman syndrome can, or should be adduced to support a mental health defence continues as an ongoing debate (see *State* v *Felton* 329 NW 2d 161 172–4 (Wis 1983)). Roxanne Gay, in December 1976, stabbed and killed a sleeping husband. The deceased had been extremely violent to her over the years and police records showed that she had called them numerous times in the three years previous to her arrest for his murder. A sanity hearing in March 1978 found insufficient evidence that she been a battered wife. Four psychiatrists found against her claims that she was a battered wife, instead finding that she was a suspicious and nervous wife. She was finally admitted into a psychiatric hospital for the insane and murder charges were dropped against her. She was diagnosed as a paranoid schizophrenic (Jones 1991, pp. 305, 306). Contemporary case law indicates that battered woman syndrome evidence is used in both self-defence and diminished responsibility/insanity pleadings.

The question arises in such cases whether battered woman syndrome follows on after the battering or is a pathological condition prior to the battering. The recent trial of Nikki Rossakis, *New York Law Journal*, 26 October 1993, raises the question of whether a defendant who seeks to present testimony on the battered woman's syndrome is a normal person whose actions can be explained by the syndrome, or a psychologically dysfunctional or mentally defective person. Rossakis had called police to her home and said that she had shot her husband in his sleep. In this case, the prosecution insisted on conducting its own examination. Linakis J noted that New York law precludes the introduction of psychological or psychiatric evidence at trial unless the defendant serves the prosecution with a written notice of intent to present such evidence. 'Since defendant is seeking to escape punishment for the alleged murder based upon her mental state, she is subject to use of established methods to determine her claim objectively.', Justice Linakis said. 'Fundamental fairness' required that Ms. Rossakis file the required notice for sentence reduction and the prosecution be permitted to conduct a psychiatric/psychological examination of her. The judge rejected Rossakis's contention that as the battered woman syndrome does not involve a mental disease or defect she was not required to file such a notice or undergo an examination. Thus in diminished capacity defences the prosecution may also conduct its examination to rebut the defence. However, as is pointed out later, this is not the case where battered woman syndrome evidence is admitted under a defence of self-defence or of provocation manslaughter.

In *United States* v *Johnson* 956 F 2d 894, 899 (1992), following a conviction for drug offences where the appellant with others pleaded duress acting under the coercion of a drug ring, the Court of Appeals held that, 'Battered woman's syndrome is not a gross, identifiable mental defect'. The court cited the Model Penal Code where, 'by the continual use of unlawful force, persons effectively break down the personality of the actor, rendering him [or her] submissive to whatever suggestion they make. They then, using neither force nor threat of force on that occasion suggest that he or she perform a criminal act;' (1d 2.09, 900). The court also cited Glanville Williams *Criminal Law*, 1961, p. 755–62 'in thrall to some person' and said that since her involvement in the crime was voluntary, a downward departure of sentencing was not available to her. The Court of Appeals disagreed, and argued that the lower court appeared to equate 'voluntary' with 'absence of duress'. They substituted their finding and remedied for downward departure (i.e., reduction of sentence) by reason of effect of incomplete duress'.

In *United States* v *Bell* 855 F Supp 239, 240 (1994), the court declared, '. . . battered woman's syndrome evidence seeks to establish that, because of her psychological condition, the defendant is unusually susceptible to the coercion' and therefore is a defence unrelated to a defendant's mental capacity. Here, the government filed for a mental examination because the defendant wanted to offer a defence of duress. The court took the view that the government were not entitled, as duress is not a diminished capacity defence. 'Here, the defendant's defense theory does not depend upon a diminished mental capacity. Rather it seeks to excuse a defendant from criminal responsibility for conduct she intentionally committed.'. The court continued, 'This court finds the Vega-Penarete decision unacceptable to a defense that does not focus on *mens rea* of crime', although, in *United States* v *Willis* 38 F 3d 170, 175 (1994), battered woman's syndrome was said to be a psychological condition. In this case the defendant appealed against the exclusion of battered woman evidence in a defence of duress. (Certiorari was denied on 16 June 1995.)

Adducing battered woman syndrome as part of a mental health defence is in conflict with the argument that the woman's response was reasonable. Gillespie argues (1989, p. 160):

> . . . it is important to understand that a defense based on the battered woman syndrome is in no way an insanity defense. This is sometimes misunderstood because the experts who are brought in to testify about the characteristics of battered women are often psychologists or psychiatrists, and the term 'syndrome' is often used to describe mental illness.

Turning attention away from the US courts to England and Wales, here the courts are reluctant to entertain self-defence and decidedly averse to admitting evidence relating to battered woman syndrome. In *Ahluwalia* [1992] 4 All ER

889, where psychiatric evidence relating to battered woman syndrome was admitted, the court said that it was are not convinced of the cogency of the evidence and ordered a retrial. Certainly the use of battered woman defence in women who kill is of very recent origin. Nicolson and Sanghvi (1993, p. 733), chart that emergence in the case of *Ahluwalia*. With reference to battered woman syndrome they write, '. . . its recognition by the Court of Appeal in relation to provocation was novel'. Kiranjit Ahluwalia was convicted of murder at Lewes Crown Court on 7 December 1989. She had been subjected to many years of violent abuse by her husband and so that, in her words, he could not run after her and hurt again, 'I set fire to the bedding . . . I didn't intend to kill him or cause him really serious injury'. She was convicted of murder, a defence of provocation having failed. On appeal, counsel raised three grounds. The first two grounds related to the trial judge's direction to the jury on provocation (already discussed in the chapter entitled, The Gender Politics of Homicide). Counsel for the appellant argued that Devlin J's direction in *Duffy* was wrong, and since it preceded the Homicide Act 1957, s. 3, the statutory provision had the greater authority (see Lord Diplock's argument in *DPP* v *Camplin* [1978] AC 705). Counsel submitted, in relying on expert evidence not before the trial judge, that women who have been subjected frequently over a period to violent treatment may react to the final act or words by what he calls a 'slow burn' reaction rather than an immediate loss of self-control. The second ground of appeal raised the question of the treatment of the appellant's characteristics, that is the fact that she was a battered woman and that this was material and should have been considered as a notional characteristic of sufficient permanence to allow for assimilation within the notion of reasonable man. On this point, the judge's direction to the jury contained this passage: 'The only characteristics of the defendant about which you know specifically that might be relevant are that she is an Asian woman, married, incidentally to an Asian man, the deceased, living in this country.'. The ground of appeal turned on the very characteristic the judge ignored, that is, the evidence of battering as a notional characteristic, and the effects of battering as in battered woman syndrome, which could, it was submitted, be embraced as a characteristic within Lord Diplock's formulation in *Camplin*. The third ground of appeal related to diminished responsibility and the new evidence based on psychiatric reports. The Court of Appeal responded in quashing the conviction for murder and substituting one of manslaughter/diminished responsibility on the basis of fresh medical evidence of diminished responsibility which was introduced enabling the court to conclude that there may have been an arguable defence which was not put forward at the original trial. It was the first time that the Court of Appeal had admitted evidence of battered woman syndrome in an appeal against a conviction for murder. Yet the fresh evidence of battered woman syndrome was considered not under the limb of provocation as a notional characteristic of the accused, but under the limb of diminished responsibility. This gave rise to objections that the assimilation of evidence of battered woman syndrome focused on her state of mind rather than his violence (see Edwards 1990, 1992c; see also the chapter entitled, The Gender Politics of Homicide).

Provocation and admissibility In the UK, in recent months, several Court of Appeal decisions have contributed to the expansion of the concept of the reasonable man. Since *Dryden* and *Humphreys* the Court of Appeal has shown for the first time a willingness to entertain mental characteristics as relevant to a defence of provocation. Battered woman syndrome evidence has entered this expansion as a mental characteristic of sufficient permanence to which the court must have regard. In *Ahluwalia* battered woman syndrome evidence was introduced within a plea of diminished responsibility but was rejected as not having a sufficient degree of permanence required of a mental disease or condition. In *Dryden* [1995] 4 All ER 987, the characteristics of obsessiveness and eccentricity were considered to be characteristics relevant to the assessment of the reasonable man. In *Humphreys* [1995] 4 All ER 1008, the appeal was successful where the trial judge was held to have wrongly excluded expert psychiatric evidence from the jury's consideration. Hirst LJ, 'It is common ground that the judge was ... explicitly directing the jury, as a matter of law, not to attribute to the reasonable young woman, in her situation, any of the seriously abnormal characteristic described by Dr Tarsh, including her attention-seeking trait through her tendency to wrist cutting'. (at p. 1014).

A further expansion was indicated in *Thornton (No. 2)* [1995] where the court adduced for the first time that battered woman syndrome could be a relevant characteristic for the jury's consideration in a defence of provocation in a murder trial. In a reserved judgment Lord Taylor CJ, Mr Justice Hidden and Mrs Justice Ebsworth asserted:

> The severity of such a syndrome and the extent to which it might have affected a particular defendant would no doubt vary and was for the jury to consider ... it might be relevant in two ways. (1) It might form an important background to whatever triggered the actus reus. A jury might more readily find there was a sudden loss of control triggered by a minor incident if the defendant had endured abuse over a period, on the 'last straw' basis. (2) Depending on the medical evidence, the syndrome might have affected the defendant's personality so as to constitute a significant characteristic relevant to the second question the jury had to consider in regard to provocation.

The two lines of argument on which the retrial will rely have been explicated. What is far from clear however is what, for the purposes of psychological definition, categorisation and diagnosis, constitutes a dependent personality disorder and battered woman syndrome.

What is clear is that women who live with violent men do suffer from a mental crisis characterised by several features ranging from depression and low self esteem, to anxiety fear, trauma, anticipation, desire to please etc. and that these characteristics or some of them follow on from living in fear of a partner's violence and intimidation. However, this does not mean that there is unanimous agreement in the UK regarding battered woman syndrome — nor is there belief that it's components are fixed. The question which remains for British psychiatry and British courts is precisely how defence experts will define it and how prosecution experts will challenge the definition and find ways of suggesting that a woman does not fit the syndrome. The *Thornton* retrial in 1996 will be as much a trial of her *mens rea* as of psychiatric evidence and noslogy.

Only if the cap fits   Whilst admissibility of battered woman syndrome has been one long and monumental legal battle for battered women defendants in most US States, dependent severally upon the court's acceptance of the theory, of the experts and their credentials and status, and the belief that battered woman syndrome is beyond the experience of the average juror, the battered woman's struggle is by no means over, for she must show that she fits the category in every respect if it is going to assist her. And, as expert evidence on the effects of sustained violence and abuse on women is admitted in courts in the UK, the same problems will arise. This qualification has presented the major impediment to admissibility of battered woman's syndrome. As Yeo (1993, p. 111) concedes, '. . . by giving the syndrome such a prominent role, the courts have created a real danger of the law denying the experiences of many battered women who do not manifest the clinical symptoms of the syndrome.'. At the heart lies the conceptual incongruity of the fit of the notion of 'learned helplessness' in explaining a woman's response at the point of killing her spouse. It is this apparent quantum leap from passivity to assertive defensive action which lies at the heart of the conundrum presented in fitting women who kill to the designated 'pathology'. The difficulty in reconciling this apparent contradiction arises as a result of the masculinist construction of the defensive act of violence as one of assertiveness or anger and rage, when instead for the battered woman it is more appositely an expression of reactive despair and an act of self-preservation. This conceptualisation brings the syndrome somewhere in the hiatus between a mental health defence and a Ewing's formulation of psychological self-defence (discussed above). The success of the prosecution argument depends upon rebutting the relevance of the syndrome. Walker never intended that each element of the 'syndrome' so-called would of necessity be present in order that a woman be considered to suffer the psychological effects of battering. Yet the law's pursuit of exactitude and scientific certainty requires that a woman claiming battered woman syndrome, must prove the presence of each element before she can avail herself of its debatable 'benefits'. It is precisely this conundrum which constitutes the basis of feminist criticism of engaging with law (see Mossman 1986).

In consideration of whether the components of battered woman syndrome are satisfied, one might ask whether this same degree of precision is required in a defence of provocation under UK law, and ask why provocation has not been subject to the same scrutiny as a matter for experts instead of part of common experience. Certainly, whether the courts accept the precise Walker formulation or not, or whether they should be persuaded to accept a more general formulation, battered women assume certain common characteristics notably living in fear in the continuous present (discussed above). Whilst the defence team are trying to establish a defence by utilising the syndrome, the prosecution are engaged in trying to show both how she does not fit the criteria of the legal defence and how she does not fit battered woman syndrome.

Where evidence of battered woman syndrome is admissible but the defendant's profile falls outside the strictures of the syndrome, expert evidence is excluded. In *Aris* (above), (cited in Klis 1994, p. 133), the defendant killed a sleeping man in self-defence. On the night of the killing he had beaten and threatened to kill her when he awoke. She shot him in the back five times. She was convicted of second degree murder and sentenced to a prison term of 15 years to life. The Court of Appeals affirmed the decision of the trial court despite the appellant's claim that battered woman expert testimony had been excluded.

For the battered woman to succeed in achieving a complete acquittal on the grounds of self-defence she must fulfil the standards demanded by the legal defence. It is precisely because battered women have been unable to satisfy the test of imminence and proportionate retaliation, that evidence of the effects of battering on her perception of imminence has been quintessential. Where women have pleaded self-defence, they must persuade the jury first that they thought (subjective test) that an attack was imminent and second that the degree of force they used to repel it was reasonable. The battered woman is unable to satisfy the imminence stricture. In understanding what is imminent to the defendant, battered woman syndrome is of importance in acquainting the jury with the reality of the perceptions of the battered woman where shock, trauma, fear and heightened anticipation colour their perception of what is imminent. Paradoxically, some States have only considered battered woman syndrome where there is evidence of self-defence. Protagonists of battered woman syndrome contend that such evidence must precede, not post date, that evaluation. Without the benefits of the admission of expert testimony to the assessment of whether her behaviour was reasonable and to whether in her view her death or serious injury was imminent, women who plead self-defence are doomed to fail.

> Such a woman's past experiences with her assailant and her firsthand knowledge of his violence and his willingness to inflict injury on her, inevitably influence the reasonableness of her assessment of the likelihood that he is about to seriously injure or kill her and whether or not she can prevent that from happening without seriously injuring or killing him first (Gillespic 1989, p. 123).

In the face of the exclusion of such evidence, women are convicted of first degree or second degree murder.

In *Lumpkin* v *Ray* 977 F 2d 508 (1992), the petitioner who had been convicted of the first degree murder of her husband (*Lumpkin* v *State* 683 P 2d 985, 987 (1984), petitioned for a writ of habeas corpus on the basis of equal protection rights violation, on the grounds that evidence of battered woman syndrome was barred, since she failed to satisfy other elements of self-defence. At the original trial, illustrating the problems that surround the admissibility of this expert evidence, the very issue to which the evidence was relevant was the issue of imminence and yet in some States expert evidence is precluded unless imminence is satisfied. In *Lumpkin* three lay witnesses and a physician were not permitted to give evidence as to her fear of her husband and the extent of his violent behaviour. She argued that as a battered woman she was in a discrete class of persons, 'who as a group are disadvantaged by the imminence requirement'. In argument she claimed, 'that the cyclical trap of the "battered woman syndrome" sets the battered woman apart from others who have financial and other resources and support, including reasonable access to police and courts, to supplement their smaller physical size and lack of ability to defend themselves.'. She argued that 'the "battered woman" should have an opportunity to show the jury that her actions were based on a subjectively reasonable apprehension of imminent bodily harm and therefore at least excusable if not justifiable.'. Lumpkin argued that the policy underlying the imminence requirement is to limit self-defence to circumstances in which the defendant has no alternative to prevent the threatened harm but to use violence. Failing the imminence requirement of Oklahoma's self-defence law meant that she could not adduce battered woman syndrome and yet paradoxically it is precisely in respect of this deciding on imminence question that juries need educating if they are to comprehend the perceptions of the battered woman which results in her specific perception of imminence. Her conviction was affirmed.

In *Burton* v *Johnson* 948 F 2d 1150 (1991), the defendant pleaded self-defence and was, like Lumpkin, convicted of first degree murder. Burton admitted that on 14 August 1983 she shot her husband, claiming in her defence that she had done so because she believed that she and her children were in imminent danger of great bodily harm, sexual abuse and death. Evidence from the accused and from her children supported the danger and bodily harm to which they had been subjected in the past. Although in her case evidence was adduced that she suffered from battered woman syndrome, there was also evidence that the daughter had been raped by the father. The wife travelled 70 miles to obtain a gun, returned home, walked through the patio doors and he said, 'If you are going to use that thing, use it.'. She shot five times. Even with the benefit of battered woman syndrome evidence her conduct was not considered to be a response to an imminent threat from the deceased and her behaviour failed to satisfy a defence of self-defence, resulting in a conviction for murder. On appeal, she contended that she had been denied a fair trial on the grounds that members of the jury were not impartial and that one member in particular had failed to respond to the *voir dire*. One of the jurors, Mrs G, had been a victim of domestic violence of a similar kind to the defendant. Mrs G at the *voir dire* was asked questions about domestic violence and child abuse. Even after the trial she feared that her husband would find out about her testimony and harm her or her family and though the *voir dire* was *in camera* she was struggling in fear, on the basis that Mrs G might have treated the accused more harshly given that she may well have taken the view, 'I put up with a violent husband, why couldn't she?' and 'would judge the defendant in this case more harshly than would a juror without personal experience'. A new trial was ordered which affirmed her original conviction. Not only must the battered woman show that she fits self-defence in respect of the demands of imminence and the legal strictures, she must also show that she conforms to the battered woman syndrome. Diagnosis is crucial to the fit of the battered woman syndrome. And so legal debates have centred around whether the characteristics of the defendant are in fact congruous with the stereotype. The courtroom is transformed into a trial within a trial, where both syndrome and defendant are 'on trial'. In order to succeed, prosecuting counsel must show that the defendant simply does not fit the syndrome.

The case of *DiDomenico* 985 F 2d 1159 (1993), is illustrative of prosecutorial attempts to demolish the syndrome defence. The defendant was convicted of fraud and transportation of stolen property, she had stolen computer equipment from a professor's office at Yale University. A psychiatrist was called to testify that the defendant had a 'dependent personality disorder with narcissistic features'. Evidence was adduced that the defendant idolised her boyfriend and showed, 'susceptibility to being duped by the boyfriend'. Cabranes J granted the government motion, relying on:

> The fact that certain personality traits or conduct may be identified or characterised by the psychiatric profession . . . does not necessarily make the traits or conduct a mental disease or mental disorder that can be the basis of the defence of insanity . . . Expert evidence on this relatively commonplace experience is simply inappropriate. This so-called disorder is surely one of 'the host of attitudes and syndromes that are part of daily living'.

In fitting the category, she must conform to the passivity and fragility of the women in the stereotype. She must, in addition, endear the jury to her. As Ewing notes:

> Acker and Toch point out, 'jurors may acquit some battered women defendants not so much because they sympathise with these women or conclude that these killings were committed in self-defence, but because they believed the deceased batterer deserved to die'. 'The killing of a battering husband could be "justified" in the juror's minds not because it was necessary that a battered woman act with responsive deadly force when she was threatened with death or serious bodily injury by her mate but because it was a fitting act of retribution directed at a member of a sadistic fraternity who had finally reaped his just deserts' (Acker and Toch 1985, pp. 147, 148).

In this respect there is also an inherent contradiction for the battered woman in a situation of self-defence where the defendant and the deceased are engaged in fighting, since this suggests that she is assertive and not passive and is taken as a rebuttal of the contention that she is suffering from 'learned helplessness'.

In *United States* v *Wilson* (unreported) Lexis 4584 2 February 1993 the defendant pleaded self-defence and was found guilty of involuntary manslaughter. Evidence of battered woman syndrome was introduced at the trial at the discretion of the trial judge. The prosecution argued that Wilson's conduct showed that she was not passive and therefore did not conform to the battered woman syndrome notion of passivity and helplessness. '. . . ladies and gentlemen . . . this is a case of a defiant wife who went home . . . minutes after having been satisfied by another person, who then walked in and got into an argument with her husband'.

In *United States* v *Whitetail* 956 F 2d 857 (1992), where the defendant was indicted for second degree murder, she alleged self-defence in killing her cohabitee, and told the police that she had stabbed because he was about to beat her. Evidence was adduced from several witnesses and two experts that she was indeed a battered woman. Several witnesses testified that they had seen her with bruises, black eyes, and a broken nose. The expert concluded that she was suffering from battered woman syndrome, 'A woman who experiences battered woman syndrome, according to these experts, would feel trapped, desperate, isolated, ashamed, and hopeless, would have a low self esteem, and would tend to be submissive and passive.'. In attempt to rebut that she suffered from battered woman syndrome, the prosecution adduced evidence that she did not fit the stereotype. In disclosing that she had fights with her husband, the prosecution successfully persuaded the expert for Whitetail on cross-examination to state that fighting was inconsistent with battered woman syndrome. In addition, the prosecution skilfully extracted the damning detail from the mouth of the defendant herself.

Q. 'You like to fight, don't you?'

A. 'Yes.'

Q. 'In fact, you fight with your brothers and sisters, don't you?'

A. 'Yes.'

Q. 'In fact, you start some of those fights, don't you?'

A. 'Well, they push their limit where I have to defend myself with them.'

Q. 'And you defend yourself with a knife usually?'

A. 'No, I don't. Not with them.'

The jury rejected her claim of battered woman syndrome after hearing this evidence of her capacity for violence. Her conviction was affirmed on appeal. Simply, she did not fit the syndrome. Neither did she endear the jury towards her, although battered woman syndrome was accepted in mitigation of sentence on appeal indicating a different standard of proof required at the level of defence and the level of mitigation, or a difference between jury and judicial perception on the matter.

It would appear that women are more likely to fit the model of battered woman syndrome where they are non-assertive and passive and conform to the legitimate victim stereotype. Thus it is also a particular type of woman who is more likely to avail herself of a defence of self-defence or a finding of manslaughter: paradoxically it is not a woman who displays evidence of assertiveness, although it is to be noted that this was not the approach adopted in Canada in the case of *Bennett (No. 2)* [1993] OJ No. 892 (Ont. Prov. Court) where the judge asserted:

> I have no difficulty accepting that the real Jocelyne Bennett is both: a woman who for reasons of emotional dependence, love and low self esteem was brutally abused by Lonnie Shaw, yet also a woman who is a player in the underworld of this city, capable of being aggressive and reckless ... All victims of abuse, not only those who are sweet, meek and conform to the stereotyped acceptable behaviour for a female, are deserving of the same compassion and an opportunity to break the cycle through rehabilitation and counselling (cited in Sheehy 1994).

The approach in *Bennett* seems exceptional. Crocker (1985) argues that battered woman syndrome is establishing a new stereotype, that of the bona fide battered woman. As Gillespie points out (1989, p. 180):

> There have already been a number of court opinions that have relied on deviations from this battered-woman stereotype — that a woman was not absolutely passive but fought back in the past, that she was not economically dependent but held a good job, that she owned or knew how to use a pistol, that her husband left her rather than her being unable to leave her husband, or that she was hit only once before the final assault — to uphold trial judges' exclusion of expert testimony on battering.

McColgan (1993, p. 524) sums up the predicament thus:

> Where such evidence has been admitted it has frequently been used to construct a stereotypical battered woman, rather than to counter the male 'perceptions of danger, immediacy and harm [which] inform the perception of what constitutes a reasonable physical response' and to 'explain why a battered woman might reasonably perceive danger, use a deadly weapon, or fear bodily harm under circumstances in which a man or non-battered woman might not'.

And so, whilst women might experience years of battering and abuse, it is not this fact that is up for scrutiny but whether she fits the Walker formulation of battered woman syndrome. The question which inevitably arises is whether the syndrome perpetrates injustice against women who deviate from the syndrome's mould, accommodating only those women who conform to the stereotype and thus diverting attention away from the extent of their victimisation onto the demands of a fixed psychological reaction to it.

Coercion/duress

The recognition that a woman may kill to survive has also led to the realisation that battered women may commit crimes under the duress of a violent or coercive partner. The syndrome has been admitted in support of a defendant's claim of duress in criminal trials involving a range of offences from robbery to drug conspiracies, thus shifting the dynamics from self-defence to coercion. Under the UK common law there was a rebuttable presumption that a wife who committed a crime in the presence of her husband did so under marital coercion; the presumption was abolished by the Criminal Justice Act 1925, s. 47. Recent efforts to accommodate her predicament under duress have less to do with any innate predisposition or 'psychological deficit' and more to do with a recognition of the external forces acting upon her, namely his will, dominion and force. In a climate which gives recognition to the ubiquity of male violence, it would be inconsistent not to consider the fact that threats of further violence do influence women's behaviour and strategies for survival in significant ways, not least, in their apparent co-operation and compliance with the batterer's demands. The issues facing the courts mirror those discussed in the context of murder, *inter alia* admissibility, whether the defendant 'fits' the syndrome, and the stringent requirements of a duress defence which require proof of an immediate threat of death or severe bodily injury, or a well grounded fear that the threats will be carried out with no opportunity to escape.

The principles apply generally throughout common law jurisdictions. Where duress is pleaded threats must be of death or grievous bodily harm, although threats can be made to a third party (see *Hurley* [1967] VR 526 (Australia); *Ortiz* (1986) 83 Cr App R 173 (United Kingdom)). Threats made to a homosexual partner were accepted in *Graham* [1982] 1 WLR 294. Where the accused joins a criminal gang or organisation, thereby voluntarily exposing himself to threats, duress cannot be pleaded, but the line here is rather blurred and it has forced courts in the UK to make a distinction between types of gangs. Thus in *Sharp* [1987] QB 853, duress was no defence and in *Shepherd* (1987) 86 Cr App R 47 the Appeal Court said that the trial judge had wrongly withdrawn the defence of duress from the accused solely on the basis of voluntary involvement. Arguably the law fails to recognise other forms of pressure placed on women by their partners from physical violence, mental violence and threats to leave (see Yeo 1993, p. 107).

Where coercion is the plea, threats of physical force or actual physical force are not required. The principle is re affirmed in *Shortland* [1996] 1 Cr App R 116, 119, where in her statement she said '... if I disagree with him he torments me, he keeps on and on at me until I've had enough and I agree with anything he says'. This case, where a wife made a false statement to procure a passport was quashed where the Court of Appeal held that to establish a defence of marital coercion a jury had to be satisfied on the balance of probabilities that the will of the defendant was overborne by her husband.

The strictly gendered defence of marital coercion is of dubious help. It is difficult to distinguish from duress although arguably broader, where it is a defence to prove that the crime was committed in the presence and under the coercion of the husband. This defence is regarded as an anachronism, and in the UK the Law Commission (1977) (No. 83) Defences of General Application, recommended its abolition. Yet, in this new climate of heightened awareness of domestic violence and the subtler kinds of pressure which can be exerted on the weaker party, attention should be focused on his dominion and control rather than on an antecedent presumption of her complicity and obedience which underlies the historical origin of the defence.

Again, the overriding difficulty facing women is that any expression of assertive behaviour on a woman's part weakens both her claim to be suffering from battered woman syndrome and her claim as to duress since assertion presupposes voluntary action. In the case of *McMaugh* v *State* 612 A 2d 725 (1992) (see Gousie 1993, p. 446), a husband and wife were convicted of murder and conspiracy and sentenced to life imprisonment. The wife petitioned for post conviction release in an appeal against sentence on the grounds that she was a battered woman. A psychologist testified to the effect that she was indeed a battered wife and suffered from battered woman syndrome and this was supported by three psychiatrists. The trial judge decided that the testimony of the experts was 'not worthy of any weight' (see Gousie, p. 467), and the court concluded that she was not subject to duress because she displayed 'assertive behaviour' during the course of the trial. This reaffirms the feminists' concerns that to qualify for a finding of battered woman syndrome women must conform to the stereotype. The trial judge concluded that the '[t]estimony at the post-conviction hearing fell lamentably short of presenting any facts sufficient to raise the defense of coercion or duress or any fact relevant to the absence of malice' (Gousie 1993, p. 466). The judge concluded that she exhibited no evidence of battered woman syndrome, she was articulate, well oriented, skilful; and 'contradicted the portrait of the battered woman' post conviction relief, 'Today we acknowledge that this court does recognise that battered women's syndrome is a mental or an emotional condition that can affect women and that it does have certain legal consequences.'. Simply she was not seen to fit the model of the battered woman:

It is well established that battered women have several common personality traits. These traits include low self-esteem, traditional beliefs about the home, the family, and the female sex role, tremendous feelings of guilt that their marriages are failing, and the tendency to accept responsibility for the batterer's actions ... The presence of these characteristics leads to the stereotype of the battered woman as fragile, haggard, fearful, passive, lacking job skills, and economically dependent on her batterer. Nevertheless, the existence of this list of traits does not mean that all battered women look and act the same. Although some battered women may have some of or all these characteristics, it is entirely possible for a battered woman not to evidence any of these characteristics.

On appeal the court held that she was indeed a battered woman and remanded her case for a new trial. In the event McMaugh entered into a plea agreement to a charge of involuntary manslaughter. In *United States of America, Plaintiff* v *Lisa Gregory, Defendant* (No 88 CR 295 United States District Court for the Northern District of Illinois, Eastern Division 988 US Dist Lexis 2 September 1988) the court rejected Gregory's argument that she was a battered woman, since in their view she did not meet the burden, that is, conformity to all the characteristics of the syndrome, because she was free to come and go, maintained employment and communicated with friends (Gousie 1993, p. 479).

A different view is taken of the defendant who commits the crime involuntarily (see *State* v *Lambert* 312 SE 2d 31 (W Va 1984)) and the defendant who commits the crime voluntarily (*United States* v *Homick* 964 F 2d 899 (9th Circ 1992)). In *United States* v *Sebresos* (unreported, US Lexis 17757 14 January 1992), even after years of physical and mental torment the defendant failed to establish coercion because she said that her involvement in the crime was involuntary. The conundrum here is that a coercion defence requires the defendant to act voluntarily. Many have argued that women commit crimes under duress in order to meet their batterer's demands (see Coughlin 1994, p. 57). In *United States* v *Santos* 932 F 2d 244 (1991), on appeal, the defendant contended that at trial there was a failure by the judge to submit her defence of duress to the jury accurately and completely. Santos was convicted on seven counts of cocaine related activity for distributing half an ounce of cocaine. Following her arrest she agreed to assist the FBI in exchange for leniency. Duress could be established against her and against her children since she claimed that her common law husband, Ramos threatened both her and her children with knives and guns and beat them, so that she had to obtain protection at a home for battered women in Philadelphia. John O'Brien was called to give expert testimony on battered woman syndrome and the effects of this on duress. He said that she was acting in response to an immediate threat of death; that she had a well grounded fear that the threats would be carried out; and that she had no reasonable opportunity to escape from him. The judge said:

> Certainly an abusive husband is no license to become involved in transactions, half pound or half ounce or kilo transactions of narcotics ... In order to make out a case for duress, there must be an immediate threat of death or serious bodily injury. Secondly, a well-grounded fear that the threat will be carried out; and third, a lack of reasonable opportunity to escape the threat of harm.

Santos's case failed and both sentence and conviction were upheld. The decision was something of a triumph as it concluded that evidence of battered woman syndrome as part of a self-defence theory was relevant to duress.

In Australia, battered woman syndrome is similarly admissible to assist the jury in assessing the reasonableness of a woman's acts or whether she was acting under duress. The Victorian Crimes Act 1958, s. 336, provides a complete defence of duress where there is pressure, physical, mental, financial or 'in any other form'. In *Runjanjic* v *Kontinnen* [1991] 56 SASR 114, before the Supreme Court of South Australia, two women charged with false imprisonment and causing grievous bodily harm advanced a defence of duress. Both appellants claimed that they had been under the influence of a man named Hill who had beaten them and detained them against their will, and had beaten another woman with a shotgun in front of them breaking her arm.

The admission of expert evidence of patterns of behaviour of normal human beings even in abnormal situations or relations is fraught with danger for the integrity of the trial process. The risk that by degrees, trials, especially criminal trials, will become battle grounds for experts and that the capacity of juries and courts to discharge their fact-finding functions will be thereby impaired, is to be taken seriously (1991, p. 53 Crim R 362, 369).

The evidence of battered woman syndrome was excluded as inadmissible on the ground that the test was objective and that expert evidence of the state of mind of the appellants was therefore irrelevant. On appeal, the judge found that that was not a sound basis for excluding the evidence as it ignored their subjective assessment of the threat. The conviction was set aside and a new trial ordered (see Yeo 1993, p. 111; *Hickey* (1992) 16 Crim LJ 271; *Kontinnen* (1992) 16 Crim LJ 360; (O'Donovan 1993, p. 436). In the case of *Winnett* v *Stephenson* (unreported 19 May 1993 cited in Easted, Hughes and Easter (1993)), where a woman was charged with Social Security frauds, battered woman syndrome was adduced in general terms to acquaint the magistrates with the circumstances of the defendant which included death threats and violence from her ex-spouse.

Fear and recantation

In some cases battered woman syndrome evidence has been used to assist a jury in understanding conflicting statements from a witness where a former statement has been recanted. It is well known that women allege assault against partners only to deny this later (see the chapter entitled, All in the Name of Privacy — Domestic Violence). In *Arcoren* v *United States* 929 F 2d 1235, 1242 (1991), in a case involving several charges of assault against a husband, expert testimony on battered woman syndrome was adduced to assist the jury in determining the credibility of two conflicting statements made by the wife, the later statement denying the previous statement . . . certiorari denied. The wife had separated from her husband. Later that day she returned home to find her husband having intercourse with a 15 year old girl. The husband then pulled his wife into the room and forced both women to have sexual intercourse. The wife managed to escape and notified police officers. At the trial she recanted her previous statements. In this case it was the prosecution who called for battered woman syndrome testimony under Rule 702 of the Federal Rules of Evidence. The defence objected, but the court admitted evidence of an expert witness who said 'the syndrome is a psychological condition, which leads a female victim of physical abuse to accept her beatings because she believes that she is responsible for them and hopes that by accepting one more beating, the pattern will stop'.

In *United States* v *Whalen* (unreported, US App Lexis 23993 (1995)), the appellant was arrested on charges of having assaulted his wife. In her original statement she claimed that the appellant kicked her and closed the car door on her leg and hip as she tried to escape. Christina Whalen, in testimony, recanted her prior written statements. She testified that she believed that Archie Whalen had not intentionally tried to injure her on 26 October, and that the bruises on her leg resulted when he accidentally closed the car door on her leg. She said that she had been out of control that evening, and had even told the defendant and her daughter that she wanted to kill herself. She testified that she had made up the story about being assaulted and as for the defendant's attempt to telephone her on 27 October in violation of a court order, she testified that she had given the defendant permission to call, because her son, Robert wanted to talk to him. The court concluded that her sworn statements were not rendered unreliable and relied on a growing body of academic evidence that many women change their minds about pressing charges out of fear of further violence. In *United States* v *Gordon* 812 F 2d 965 (1987), a wife who was sexually and physically abused filed a motion to suppress the oral and written statements she had made to investigators. Coughlin (1994, p. 40), argues that '... the predominant rationale for the marital coercion excuse was the belief that married women suffered from a volitional disability'. It remained nonetheless a defence. On the one hand, it is regarded as an anachronism and many have called for its abolition. Coughlin regards it as misogynist since it shows that:

> women suffer from special psychological deficits that make them incapable of resisting illegal pressures exerted by men ... This feature of the battered woman syndrome defense is most objectionable if we believe that criminal punishment acts to deter conduct that the community finds abhorrent. The defense discourages wives from resisting their subordination. Women who manifest the capacity for independence are punished, while those who prove that their husbands controlled their behaviour are excused.

In *McA Ontario Court of Justice* 1994 Ont Ct Lexis 625 (unreported), the issue to be decided was whether the complainant continued the relationship with the accused out of fear of further injury. In this case battered woman syndrome evidence was inadmissible largely because the personality profile of the complainant did not conform to that of a woman under duress. Salhany J found that the complainant was a mature and articulate woman who was quite capable of explaining herself and why she did not complain earlier.

In mitigation of sentence

Evidence of battered woman syndrome has also played a role in mitigation of sentence. In the US sentence reduction is referred to as 'downward departure'. In *United States of America* v *John Gable Jr*, *United States of America* v *John G. Thomas*, *United States of America* v *Mary Ann Funderburk* (1994) US App Lexis 7 March, the appellant was charged with money laundering, interstate transportation for the purposes of prostitution and Travel Act violation. Funderburk made an application for a downward departure on the basis of coercion and duress, arguing that she was entitled to a retrial so that she could raise the defence of duress. Battered woman syndrome has also been taken into account when assessing the effect upon the victim of the crime. In *United States* v *Merovci* ((unreported) US App Lexis 20235, 1993), the appellant appealed against his conviction and sentence on the grounds that his offence had been varied upwards on the basis of the victim's vulnerability. The letters which he mailed to his girlfriend whilst in prison read:

> Jennie please I don't want to get out of here angry mad and crazy and then come and look for you and him and blow your [expletive deleted] heads off ... I will make it here but you are gonna pay for it ... I don't want to get out of here MAD Because if I do, we both gonna Die.

The guidelines on sentencing authorise a 'two level increase in the base offence level' where a defendant 'knew or should have known that a victim of the offense was unusually vulnerable due to age, physical or mental condition, or that a victim was otherwise particularly susceptible to criminal conduct' and the court responded in affirming the increase.

In *United States* v *Ezeiruaku* (unreported) (Crim Action No. 94–42 (Jei) United States District Court for the District of New Jersey 1995 US Dist Lexis 6037 2 May 1995), on 7 February 1994, defendant Mildred Akiagba and co-defendant Vincent Ezeiruaku were indicted for conspiracy to distribute and to possess with the intent to distribute heroin. On 7 October 1994, she sought leave to file notice out of time of an intent to introduce expert testimony regarding her mental condition from a cultural expert and an expert on battered wife syndrome who would both testify that Okuzu, Akiagba's estranged husband, coerced her into dealing with heroin and she requested consideration of these facts of duress or coercion in mitigation/downward departure of sentencing. Dr Okechukwu Ugorji, an expert on Nigerian, and particularly Igbo, culture, testified that within the Igbo culture, the man plays the dominating role, and that Igbo marital relationships often contain physical abuse of the wife and forced sex. He concluded that in conformance with this cultural profile, Akiagba was very dependent upon Okuzu. If the defendant committed the offence because of serious coercion, blackmail or duress, under circumstances not amounting to a complete defence, the court could decrease the sentence below the applicable guideline range. The court ruled that the cases cited by the defence (see *United States* v *Johnson* 956 F 2d 894, 902 (9th Cir 1992) (remanding for resentencing where defendants were abused by 'a manipulative, violent, brutal drug lord'); *United States* v *Nelson* 740 F Supp 1502, 1517 (D Kan 1990) (finding that defendant was 'under the spell and influence' of her husband); *United States* v *Naylor* 735 F Supp 928, 929 (D Minn 1990) (court decided where defendant's paramour 'used his romantic relationship with Naylor and his age to exert substantial influence on Naylor and to manipulate her'), to be distinguishable, finding Akiagba's argument based on her cultural upbringing unconvincing. In citing *United States* v *Gaviria* 804 F Supp 476, 479 (EDNY 1992), however, the court recognised that the defendant was 'a victim of systematic physical and emotional abuse'.

In Canada, Sheehy's analysis of cases post *Lavallee* indicates that in several cases evidence of battered woman syndrome has been influential in mitigation of sentence (see *Bennett (No. 2)* [1993] OJ No. 892 Ont Prov Court; *Phillips*

[1992] OJ 2716 (Ont Ct J Gen Div); *Bradbury* [1992] NWTJ No. 178). The Supreme Court of Tasmania in *The Queen* v *Gunnarsson-Wiener* 13 August 1992, Lexis, where a wife obtained fiancial advantage via deception and committed other offences in connection with breach of company legislation because in her words she would do anything to placate him and avoid confrontation, said in sentencing that instead of immediate imprisonment the term would be suspended on the basis of battered woman syndrome as evidence of marital coercion. In the UK, evidence of battered woman syndrome was introduced for the first time in mitigation in the appeal of Janet Gardner who was convicted of manslaughter and jailed for five years for stabbing her brutal and bullying ex-lover. Leggatt LJ, sitting with Rougier and Sedley JJ, in the Appeal Court said the trial judge had not had the advantage of the detailed psychiatric report on Gardner which had since been prepared. The report by Dr Gillian Mezey of St George's Hospital, Tooting, London into Mrs Gardner's state of mind now and at the time of the attack, found the mother-of-three was showing classic signs of 'battered woman syndrome'. The court took the view that the expert evidence had given fresh insight into the circumstances, showing she was suffering from battered woman syndrome — a state of hopelessness and depression, following unremitting physical and verbal attacks. Helena Kennedy QC, commenting on the case, said, 'Courts have had a problem realising the woman's powerlessness and inability to leave because of a psychiatric paralysis. This decision is a victory of knowledge over a failure of understanding.' (*The Guardian*, 30 October 1992).

Women's silence — women's compliance

In the UK, duress has been pleaded in cases where women 'fail to act' in circumstances where their children are abused and killed by their partners excepting the case of *Boyce* (unreported) (1995) *Legal Action*, 13 December, in which expert evidence on a history of battery was admitted where a woman faced drug related charges. Such cases raise questions about the capacity and complicity of the mothers of these children, who apparently colluded with their demise. The mothers of Jasmine Beckford, Tyra Henry and Kimberley Carlisle were portrayed as evil, wicked, cruel and demonised. In *Beckford and Lorrington* 28 March 1985, *Dietnam* v *London Borough of Brent* (1988) IRLR 299 Maurice Beckford was found guilty of the manslaughter of his four year old stepdaughter whilst Beverley Lorrington was convicted of ill treatment and neglect. The report of the guardian *ad Litem* on Beverley Lorrington explained that when she tried to protect the children from Beckford he would hit her and tell her that she did not know how to look after the children because she was stupid. She felt frightened of Beckford (*A Child in Trust* 1985, pp. lxxii-lxxiii). In the case of Tyra Henry (*Whose Child?* 1987 LB of Lambeth), who died at the age of 21 months, 50 bite marks were found on her body. The father was convicted of her murder. The mother of Kimberley Carlisle was also abused by her boyfriend who was responsible for killing the child (Lyon and de Cruz 1993, p. 31).

The courts were unable to understand the plight of these women, or the duress they were under. Of Beverley Lorrington, Dr Hugh Jolly, honorary consultant paediatrician said, 'Miss Lorrington has already had relationships with two violent men and I would expect her to choose similar men in the future because this pattern is seldom broken.'. Of Kimberley Carlisle's mother, the report said, 'A woman such as Mrs Carlile, fatally attracted to violent co-habitees, was highly vulnerable to the acuter problems of child rearing' (cited in Lyon and de Cruz, p. 32).

It was in the case of Susan Poole in July 1988, who pleaded guilty to the manslaughter of her son, that a different picture of these women emerged. Her partner was charged and convicted of murder and sentenced to life imprisonment. The reports on Susan Poole revealed a woman totally controlled by the child's father, although even in this case Owen J said, 'When one thinks of the extraordinary maternal sacrifice and care shown by lower animals one has to wonder at her apparent selfishness'. Notwithstanding, the Appeal Court in reducing her sentence began to acknowledge that failure to act arose out of duress and fear and not complicity.

Sally Emery (1993) 14 Cr App R (S) 394 stood trial with her boyfriend, Brian Hedman for cruelty to a child. She was acquitted of occasioning actual bodily harm, but convicted of failure to protect. She was the mother of a child who died at the age of 11 months. The child was found to have many injuries, including fractured ribs and a rupture of the bowel, the result of several weeks of severe physical abuse. Emery said in evidence that Brian Hedman had routinely abused her daughter and herself and fear of Hedman rendered her unable to protect her daughter. At the conclusion of her evidence an application was granted allowing her to call expert evidence in support of her defence, which was one of duress. Two experts were called, namely Dr Stuart Turner, a psychiatrist who specialised in response to serious trauma of various kinds, including domestic violence, and Sandra Horley, who had some 13 years' experience working with abused women and was director of 'Refuge'. This was the first trial where evidence of battered woman syndrome was introduced to explain why and how a woman could do nothing to help her child. Emery gave evidence of how she was beaten and raped and how Hedman had tried to strangle her. Horley argued that the degree of violence was sufficient to induce a state of helplessness such that Emery might be incapable of protecting her child. This evidence was rebutted by medical evidence for the prosecution which stated that the level of violence she sustained was insufficient to induce a state of helplessness. The jury acquitted her of assault occasioning actual bodily harm, but rejected her defence of duress. She was convicted of failure to protect and sentenced to four years' imprisonment. Astill J said, 'It is difficult to understand how it is possible for you to have stood by and watched the agony, day by day, of your small child. You allowed her to die and you had much opportunity to prevent it.'. On appeal sentence was reduced on the grounds that the judge, in passing sentence, paid insufficient regard to the relationship between these two appellants, and in particular to the medical evidence as to the effect of that relationship on the mental state of Emery. Helena Kennedy QC said that the judge in passing sentence had paid insufficient regard to the relationship between these two appellants, and in particular, to the medical evidence as to the effect of the relationship on Emery.

The court suggested that experts should confine themselves to a description of post traumatic stress disorder and not express a view as to whether the woman was battered, this being an issue for the jury (private communication with Emery's lawyers, 10 November 1992). In trials where the defence is one of duress expert testimony is admissible. In this case the prosecution contested the application to admit expert testimony, on the grounds that the evidence proposed was within the juror's experience. Mackay and Coleman (1996, p. 940) make a plea for the admissibility of expert testimony in duress cases and support clause 42(3)(b) of the Criminal Code Bill, which if implemented would rid the law of the objective test which is currently the standard and would thereby allow for admission of expert psychological and psychiatric evidence in cases which fall short of mental disorder but nevertheless involve mental conditions which are not understood by jurors — battered woman syndrome being one such example. The problem persists in trials where the defence is one of duress. For such evidence to be admitted, the objective test is applied — would a person of reasonable firmness have been overborne? However, the courts consider quite differently the will of a woman who is subjected to violence and is in terror and is not of reasonable firmness: this is in conflict with the duress requirement.

Hedda Nussbaum watched as her child was beaten to death by her partner. He was a god. He could do anything and she had to wait, until he said she could summon help (see *People* v *Steinberg* 595 NE 2d 845 (1992); see also Susan Brownmiller's controversial account, *Waverley Place* (1989), Kirkwood 1993, p. 4). Hedda Nussbaum was undoubtedly a victim of battered woman syndrome when she was called as a prosecution witness to testify against Joel Steinberg, her nose was visibly broken, her face scarred and battered, the result of prior beatings. One law in Minnesota provides a defence where '... at the time of the neglect there was a reasonable apprehension in the mind of the defendant that acting to stop or prevent the neglect would result in substantial bodily harm to the defendant or the child in retaliation' (see Davidson 1993, p. 365).

Is battered woman syndrome truly a panacea for masculinism in the law or does it further psychiatrise women and by doing so exclude many women from having their battering background considered by the court? How far does the syndrome merely pathologise, leaving legal method intact and excluding women who fail to fit? Battered woman syndrome addresses only one aspect of the law's injustice to women: what is required is a root and branch treatment. Battered woman syndrome can only be effective in introducing evidence of the background of battering and assessing the effect this background might have had on the state of mind of the defendant in relation to imminence in self-defence pleas, instability in mental health pleas and cumulative provocation in provocation pleas. The problem persists that battered woman syndrome does not fit squarely into any of the existent defences. It is regarded largely as a prosthesis attached to a system whose legal constructs of reasonableness remain resolutely intact. In the US the lack of direction from the Supreme Court has resulted in a piecemeal approach in Federal Circuits and State Courts. The feminist critique of law must not be content with the piecemeal and highly controversial 'gains' achieved by the admissibility of battered woman syndrome. It must strive for a more holistic revision of the law's legal method. At the same time even a holistic change cannot provide the panacea for a sexist society which legitimates and authenticates only masculinist constructions. The assimilation of women's experience into the law in this way has been achieved by way of grafting this new knowledge onto the same masculinist body (see Mossman 1986, Martin 1992), leaving the body intact and impervious to the female perspective. The dilemma is whether reception of battered woman syndrome evidence is an anachronism or whether this heightened awareness of women's subordination and violent experience at the hands of partners should be adduced to protect and defend women. The difference between battered woman syndrome evidence today and the precepts underlying the doctrine of marital coercion is that the latter is bound by a masculinist view of inherent female fragility and frailty, whereas the former turns the focus on the ubiquity of male violence and society's reluctance to intervene in violence against women. This is arguably the difference that feminist critique makes to the masculinism of the law where women's coercion and duress is the product of social experience rather than something inherently biological. Emphasis should be placed more on the experience of being battered and less on establishing whether a defendant meets with a pre-determined construction of the effects of battering on women.

As expressed by Pat Cervelli, a counsellor in the field of domestic violence in *People* v *Day* 2 Cal Rptr (2d) 916 (at p. 921), 'In my 13 years experience working with battered women, I have seen many different types of women, many of them 'docile, submissive, humble, etc. . . . many battered woman are not 'docile, submissive, humble, etc.' Many of the over 500 women I have worked with are what I might call 'aggressive'. It is a great myth that a battered woman must be passive to be so categorised. What defines a woman as being 'battered' is the fact that she is the victim of violence perpetrated by her partner, and that she remains in the relationship after repeated violent incidents'. Clearly, battered women respond to the abuse experienced in a variety of ways some of which may not meet with the requirements of the battered woman syndrome typology. In *State* v *Kelly* 685 P 2d 564 (1984), the judge supported the State's rebuttal testimony concerning the defendants prior acts of aggression towards her husband, and neighbours suggestions that she did not, in fact, live in a crippled state of 'learned helplessness'. Easteal (1992, pp. 10–11), more appropriately chooses to focus less upon fixed characteristics and more on the evidence of violence 'what can be the results for someone living in this situation? Quite simply, she may become a hostage in her own home. Unlike a political hostage who is kept behind doors without the physical means of escape, the woman develops the psychological inability to unlock the door. . . . Over time the woman's self-esteem plummets as the emotional abuser tells her clearly, 'It's all your fault'. She may become isolated as battering is still a shameful and private action in our culture. And, most importantly, her life becomes full of terror. She never knows when the violent partner will strike. Life is centred on survival, walking on egg shells, trying to please him'.

SEVEN

A betrayal of trust — the sexual abuse of children

Some children die at the hands of their parents. Some children suffer repeated abuse from those who care for them. Whilst child sexual abuse prevention programmes educate children and young people to be wary of strangers, it is those who care for them who are more likely to perpetrate abuse, betraying their unconditional trust. At the level of international child rights, what do we do to protect children? Principle 2 of the *Declaration of the Rights of the Child* (1959) states:

> The child shall enjoy special protection, and shall be given opportunities and facilities, by law and by other means, to enable him to develop physically, mentally, morally, spiritually and socially in a healthy and normal manner and in conditions of freedom and dignity. In the enactment of laws for this purpose, the best interests of the child shall be the paramount consideration.

Principle 9 of the Declaration provides, 'The child shall be protected against all forms of neglect, cruelty and exploitation' (Ghandi 1995, p. 39). At a domestic level, recent legal reforms have improved the protection of children from abuse, facilitated children in giving evidence in court (see Criminal Justice Acts 1988, 1991, Criminal Justice and Public Order Act 1994) and standardised procedures in the investigatory stages (*Memorandum of Good Practice*, 1992). These legal developments have taken place in a context of competing rights calling on the one hand for a more pro-active, pre-emptive role of social work agencies and the police in child protection, and calling on the other for protection of the family from state intervention, unwarranted surveillance and accusation (see Frost 1990, p. 25).

In this chapter this tension between legislative efforts to protect children and the competing parental rights is explored. It is the intention of this chapter to explore the extent of the problem of child sexual abuse, its recent discovery and the criticism all too often made of professionals that they are inventing the problem, and to consider the extent of the 'double victimisation' of the child in the legal process.

DEFINING CHILD ABUSE

Child abuse is only formulated within that which is politically and legally recognised as abuse and depends upon who has the power to name and to identify certain acts as abusive (Dworkin 1989). Until the 20th century child abuse was considered not to exist simply because it lacked official recognition (Parton 1985). The increasing awareness of child abuse as a problem parallels children's increasing legal status and the emergence of the child as an individual with rights and the diminution of and challenge to the hegemony of parental authority. Child abuse embraces child pornography, the abuse of children in sex tourism, the use of children in child prostitution, including sexual and physical abuse by family members. Child abuse can take a variety of forms, including physical abuse, emotional abuse, neglect and sexual abuse. Physical abuse of children becomes an offence if the violence used extends beyond 'moderate and reasonable' punishment. Hall and Martin (1993) refer to the guidelines used by the medical profession in evaluating whether corporal punishment constitutes abuse:

> Any injury that requires medical treatment is outside the range of normal corrective measures. One bruise may be inflicted inadvertently; however, old and new bruises, bruises on the face, or bruising in a child less than one year of age represents abuse. In addition, any punishment that involves hitting with a closed fist or an instrument, kicking, inflicting burns, or throwing the child obviously represents child abuse regardless of the severity of the injury sustained as a result.

The Report of the Panel of Inquiry into the Circumstances surrounding the Death of Jasmine Beckford (1985), revealed the extreme physical abuse perpetrated by a stepfather. Jasmine died after sustaining cerebral contusions and subdural haemorrhage. Prior to her death she was emaciated and had been subject to battering over a period of time, made evident by the multiple old scars found on her body (1985, p. 2). In the United States, Joel Steinberg was convicted of the manslaughter in the first degree of his adoptive daughter, Lisa Nussbaum (see *People v Steinberg* (1991) 170 AD 2d 50, (1992) 595 NE 2d 845), who sustained long term physical abuse and died of injuries following chronic abuse. Children are tortured by parents. Lord Taylor CJ upheld an eight year term of imprisonment on *Brian Anthony J* [1996] 1 Cr App R (S) 20 who had burned his six year old stepson on the nose, chin, thigh and penis.

Children suffer all forms of emotional abuse from constant verbal abuse, emotional coldness, aloofness and rejection. It may involve demanding that a child perform certain tasks beyond that of which he is capable, constantly placing unachievable goals which lead to the child's continual and inevitable failure, or it may involve the deliberate setting of low achievements for the child in order that the child may be ridiculed and derided (see *Child Abuse Issues and*

Answers, 1986, Dept of Social Services, San Mateo County Ca 94403, cited in Hall and Martin 1993, p. 4). Emotional abuse also includes unfairness in discipline and punishment, inequitable treatment of siblings and scapegoating, threats of violence and attempts to frighten the child often with leaving or sending the child away. Emotional abuse involves exposure to domestic violence between parents and an unhappy and warring atmosphere (see Edwards and Halpern 1988, p. 111). Kellmar Pringle berated the traditional approach to this problem, 'Remarkably little attention has so far been paid to the likely psychological consequences of child abuse compared with the considerable and still expanding literature on the problems and needs of their parents' (see 1980, p. 204). The significance of her remarks underpins the courts' lack of uniformity and ambivalence in approaching this question. In the case of *Bassett* v *Bassett* [1975] Fam 76, [1975] 2 WLR 270, Cumming-Bruce LJ acknowledged:

> ... the court must be alive to the risk that a spouse may be using the instrument of an injunction as a tactical weapon in the matrimonial conflict ... Where there are children whom the mother is looking after, a major consideration must be to relieve them of the psychological stresses and strains imposed by the friction between their parents, as the long-term effect upon a child is liable to be of the utmost gravity. This factor ought to weigh at least as heavily in the scales as the personal protection of the parent seeking relief.

This was cited with approval in *Walker* v *Walker* [1978] 1 WLR 533, 538–539), although in *Summers* v *Summers* [1986] 1 FLR 343, an order was set aside where the harm to the child was considered as only one among a number of factors for consideration of the court.

In other cases the evidence required to show that children are harmed may be onerous. In *Wiseman* v *Simpson* [1988] 1 All ER 245, a father appealed against an ouster order removing him from the home. The original order was granted after the court had taken into consideration the effect on the child of the altercation between the parties. The mother had asserted that the continual arguments between the parties adversely affected the child's development. The court held that there was a lack of substantive evidence on this point and allowed the father's appeal. On occasion the harm to the child of an argumentative atmosphere may be considered less harmful than a father's absence from the matrimonial home. The decision in *Richards* v *Richards* [1984] AC 174, where a remedy was sought under the Matrimonial Homes Act 1983, indicated that notwithstanding an altercative atmosphere between the parties, the court might not grant an ouster injunction on the grounds that a child's interests might best be served by the father remaining in the home (see the chapter entitled, All in the Name of Privacy — Domestic Violence for further discussion).

In recent years the psychological effects of domestic violence on children of the family are finally being recognised (see Hester and Radford 1992, Hester 1995; National Children's Home Survey December 1994, Mullender and

Morley eds., cited in Family Homes and Domestic Violence Bill [HL] 71). The Children Act 1989, s. 1 (1), now places the welfare of the child as, 'the court's paramount consideration' where matters of upbringing or the administration of property or the application of income are concerned. However, the Court of Appeal has not seen fit to interpret s. 1(1) of the Children Act 1989 as overruling *Richards*, as was made apparent by the decision of the court in *Gibson* v *Austin* [1992] 2 FLR 437, where, in deciding the issue of the appropriateness of an ouster injunction, the court cited with approval the decision in *Richards* not to accord paramountcy to the needs of children. The court in rejecting the argument for the father, said that the argument that the Children Act had overridden *Richards* was a 'hopeless one'. Here, the father applied for an ouster against the mother where she went through the motions of attacking him, 'threatening him although not determinedly . . . and I suspect that it is more a gesture than a serious threat . . .'.

Child abuse includes the failure to provide the physical necessities of life, i.e., medical care, adequate nourishment, etc., and may in law amount to a finding of neglect. The move away from making moralistic judgments about poor families with a low but adequate standard of living, which characterised social work practice in the 1970s is to be welcomed. Yet, the non-interventionist stance of the State in child welfare in recent years and the reluctance to require an objective standard of care has led inevitably to tragedies (see Freeman 1994, p. 17). In the Beckford case cited above, an aspect of the inquiry which generated concern was the placement for fostering of an Afro-Caribbean child with an Anglo-Indian foster father and English foster-mother and the propriety and efficacy of trans-racial fostering. In addition, much criticism was made of the choice of the key social worker; a woman of Swedish origin supervised by a white American trained social worker. The social workers involved explained their lack of intervention by the adherence to a liberal practice and non-judgmentalist approach with poor and ethnic minority families. Channer and Parton (1990, p. 105), ask whether it is 'possible to judge absolute standards of family care and functioning while also understanding the different approaches to rearing children within different cultures.'. They argue that whilst, 'black families may be subject to inappropriate and heavy handed interventions, leading to an over-representation of black children in care, recent public inquiries and research suggest the opposite may be happening in child abuse cases.'.

As the Beckford case showed, it was precisely such an approach which left families such as this vulnerable. Maurice Beckford (Jasmine's stepfather) was found guilty of murder and Beverly Lorrington (Jasmine's mother) of cruelty.

DEFINING CHILD SEXUAL ABUSE

The sexual abuse of children can take a number of forms. The National Society for the Prevention of Cruelty to Children (NSPCC), defines child sexual abuse as:

the involvement of children in sexual activities they do not truly comprehend, to which they are unable to give informed consent, or which violate the social taboos of family life, or are against the law.... The term relates to abuse by parents or care givers, or their failure to protect children from abuse. It includes not only incest as legally defined, but also sexual relationships with others, such as adopted children and stepchildren. The term includes intercourse, buggery, fondling, mutual [sic] masturbation, the involvement of children in pornographic activity, and in prostitution (see Hall and Martin 1993, p. 7).

Sexual assault can be as traumatic as incest. Yet, it is also the case that children may be touched so unobtrusively that they may not be aware anything sexual is happening. It is also the case that adults and the courts may minimise the effects of abuse on young children. In *C* v *C* *(Child Abuse: Access)* [1988] 1 FLR 462, where a six year old child spoke of physical contact with the father, which the court described of an intimate or inappropriate nature, and where there was inappropriate behaviour by the child including exposing herself and making unsuitable physical approaches to adults, the court considered that the father's conduct 'fell short of abuse' and granted supervised access. The child in interview had said, 'This is Daddy's game'. Latey J said, 'In my judgment, there is no room for doubt that R has been sexualised' (*sic*). Of the child's allegation and recollections he said, 'There is room for fantasizing. There is plenty of room for exaggeration or distortion in her descriptions or for notions to have been planted in her mind unwittingly. There is plenty of room for honest misunderstanding and misinterpretation.'. The judge later said '. . . the father had indulged in crude, raucous (as he puts it) horseplay which has stimulated R sexually — sexualised her.' (*sic*). This judgment betrays an obtuseness and *naïveté* about the exploitation of children by adults akin to Lord Lane's approach in a case involving an eminent paediatrician where he described the defendant's obsession with child pornography as something akin to collecting cigarette cards in olden times (cited in the chapter entitled, Freedom from Pornography in an Age of Sexual Liberalism) (see Tate 1991, p. 261). It is more commonly the case that sexual abuse of children is accompanied by force, either physical or emotional, including making threats, threatening to tell others, especially the mother or other persons the child loves most. The child frequently 'complies' to protect herself and others. In *David John D* (1993) 14 Cr App R (S) 639, in order to secure a daughter's 'compliance' to rape, the father would turn her upside down, put her head and upper body into a cold bath of water and would say to her, 'Are you going to let me do it now?'. Curtis J concluded that, '. . . there was a regime of fear and physical intimidation to both girls to enforce their silence, and the torture of one girl to enforce her compliance'. In *David James N* (1992) 95 Cr App R 256, where the appellant indecently assaulted and attempted to rape his daughter, 'She complied because he smacked or struck her with a stick if she did not'. Other examples of duress, coercion and intimidation to enforce compliance were revealed in the *Report of the Inquiry into Child Abuse in Cleveland 1987* (1988). One mother wrote, 'These are the things she has told me: — she was told, somebody will come and take her away, people would hit her for telling lies, Mammy will cry if you tell her' (1988, p. 7, para. 19). In addition to compliance and silence fear also results in children psychologically distancing and disassociating themselves from what is happening. In *Michael D* (1993) 14 Cr App R (S) 489, 490, when the stepfather began to abuse the stepdaughter she pretended to be asleep until it was over. Research studies provide further support to the evidence that children comply out of fear and intimidation. In a study conducted by the Harborview Medical centre, in Seattle, during the period 1977–1979, 16 per cent of children had been made to submit by the use of a weapon, 63 per cent were coerced by adult authority and 3 per cent by tangible enticement. Children are terrorised and out of fear of the aggressor are sometimes convinced of the truth of otherwise objectively fantastic and unlikely stories and so assent. In *Hollies* [1995] Crim LR 171–2, a 43 year old male pleaded guilty to six counts of rape of his female cohabitee's daughters. He had acquired their assent after telling them that he was required to rape them by a criminal organisation. In *Re W (Minors) (Child Abuse: Evidence)* [1987] 1 FLR 297, 304, in an interview with a member of Dr Bentovim's child abuse team, the child was asked, 'What does Daddy think would happen if you told someone else?', she answered, 'They would take me away.'. The fact that children delay reporting their abuse often affects the perceived credibility of their stories. In *C* v *R*, Supreme Court of Australia, 18th August 1993, Lexis, the child's delay in reporting the abuse and her continued visits to her abusive father cast doubt on the veracity of her allegation of incest against him. Courts are now beginning to educate jurors through expert testimony in understanding why children are silent and helping jurors towards realising that delay is not inconsistent with molestation but instead part of a psychological response on the part of the victim which ranges from silence and delay in reporting to accusation followed by recantation (see *R* v *J* (FE) 1990 74 CR 3d 269, *R* v *R (S)* (1992) 73 CCC (3d) 225, both are Canadian cases).

THE PERPETRATORS

Child sexual abuse is the systematic abuse of children by adult men, which is both ahistorical and cross cultural. Women by contrast, rarely abuse children, when they do it is usually in the capacity of accomplice where their role is passive, and their co-operation ensured through fear and powerlessness. The NSPCC found in a study of actual registrations in 1989 (Research Briefing No. 11), that 78 per cent of sexual abuse victims were girls. The perpetrator was recorded in 89 per cent of the sexual abuse registrations where natural fathers were suspected in 25 per cent of cases, father substitutes in 20 per cent, brothers and other relatives in 23 per cent, mothers in 2 per cent, both parents in 3 per cent and others in 17 per cent of cases (p. 6).

Waterhouse, Dobash and Carnie (1994) found that of the interview sample of 53 child sexual abusers, 48 per cent were related to or responsible for the child whilst 52 per cent were abused by non-family members. The researchers found that men committing offences within the family tended to to be charged with the more serious offences of rape and incest whilst those committing offences outside the family were charged with indecent assault or lewd and libidinous practices. Child sexual abuse is inexorably gendered   a male crime committed against children.

All in the family: grandfathers, fathers: stepfathers

Nawal Saadawi (1980, 1983), Maya Angelou (1984, p. 75) and Alice Walker (1983), are some of a breed of feminist writers who provide further support for the thesis of the family as the primary site of sexual abuse. Sadaawi, practising as a doctor in Cairo, was told by a patient (1980, p. 17):

> Like the rest of my family . . . I feared my grandfather . . . he would call me in a voice that was a little less harsh than usual: 'Come let us pick some flowers from the garden'. He would hand me a few red and yellow flowers and when I had become engrossed in their petals and colours, seat me on his lap, and start caressing me, or singing to me until I closed my eyes, like one going to sleep. But I never fell asleep, because each time I could feel his hand creeping tenderly and stealing under my clothes, and his finger disappearing to a hidden spot in my knickers.

In *John Francis C* (1993) 14 Cr App R (S) 562, the appellant, a man of 79 years of age, committed a series of offences upon his grandchildren including buggery, indecency and rape. The offences came to light when one of the grandchildren was in psychotherapy as an adult suffering from the trauma of childhood memories of abuse. The grandchildren ranged from 15 to 32 years of age when the case came to trial. A sentence of eight years was upheld on appeal. Abuse of this kind by older men on grandchildren is not, however, rare. In 1993, 13.4 per cent of convictions for incest, and 7.3 per cent of convictions for gross indecency with children involved men aged 60 and over (see Table 15 which shows the age of defendants convicted of child sexual abuse for 1993).

Table 15: Age of defendants convicted in 1993

	Incest	Gross indec with child	USI girl under 13
Age			
10–14	0	0	0
14–u18	2	0	5
18–u21	6	9	11
Total 21 +	81	113	51
21–u25	2	10	13
25–u30	1	17	5
30–u40	16	34	15
40–u50	35	25	12
50–u60	15	18	5
60 +	12	9	1

Source: Criminal statistics Supplementary Tables vol. 2 1993

In *David John D* (1993) 14 Cr App R (S) 639, over a period of 19 years a father committed a series of rapes on one of his daughters. He indecently assaulted another daughter from a young age and then raped her until she was 21. These rapes were accompanied by perverse acts (see also *Peter O'S* (1993) 14 Cr App R (S) 632, for a similar case). Stepfathers frequently abuse stepsons and daughters. In the case of *Michael D* (1993) 14 Cr App R (S) 489, a stepfather indecently assaulted his 13 year old stepdaughter by rubbing her breasts and vagina, lying on her and ejaculating between her legs. He had previously been cautioned for indecent assault on the same stepdaughter (see also *Lewis* (1983) 76 Cr App R 33). In *David Edward Clayton* (1994) 15 Cr App R (S) 69, the appellant smacked a 14 year old girl, the daughter of his girlfriend, on her bare bottom under the pretence of chastisement. An 18 month sentence was reduced to nine months.

Wives on rare occasion, act as accomplices, although more usually under duress. This is provided for in the Criminal Justice Act 1925, s. 47, '... on a charge against a wife for any offence other than treason or murder it shall be a good defence to prove that the offence was committed in the presence of, and under the coercion of, the husband' (see the chapter entitled, Unreasonable Women — Battered Woman Syndrome on Trial for further discussion of duress). In *Terence Patrick J* (1993) 14 Cr App R (S), the entire family, including the grandparents, systematically abused a young child. The father was convicted of sexual intercourse with a girl under 13 and of aiding and abetting buggery. The child concerned was between four and eight years when these offences were committed. There were co-accuseds. One was his wife, Susan J, another the child's grandmother. In addition, several adults watched and participated in the abuse. The mother gave evidence at the trial which spared the daughter a further ordeal, and was sentenced to six years' imprisonment. A sentence of life imprisonment on Terence Patrick was reduced on appeal to a prison term of 12 years.

On occasion women act independently as in *Maureen S* (1993) 14 Cr App R (S) 768, where a mother was found guilty of indecent assault on her young sons. The abuse included playing with the older boy's penis and fellating him from the age of five years. She also admitted having intercourse with them. She tried to commit suicide and finally went to the police and wrote letters to her sons telling them to tell anyone who inquired of the whole story.

Contrary to public perceptions of the child sex abuser, teenagers also commit sexual abuse against young children. Young boys who are sexually inexperienced will use younger siblings to experiment, often not realising the seriousness of their actions. In *Cuddington* [1994] Crim LR 698, the appellant was 15 or 16 at the time of the offence. He was convicted of indecency with a child and indecent assault on a female. The offences occurred when he baby sat for his niece. It was alleged that the appellant had persuaded the children to masturbate him and suck his penis. See *Re G* 5 January 1993 CICB London, 1462 CLY 1993. Under duress children may also be used in abuse. In *Pickford* [1995] 1 Cr App Rep 420, a stepfather compelled his stepson to have sexual intercourse with his mother forcing his stepdaughter to watch.

Sexual abuse by strangers

Sexual abuse on children is also committed by strangers. The stranger may abduct the child for the primary purpose of sexual molestation, this abduction may result in the death of the child as part of the abuse (see *Brady and Hindley*, 6 May 1966 Chester Assizes (for a full account of the trial see Goodman 1986); *Black* [1995] Crim LR 640; *Barrell and Others* (1992) 13 Cr App R (S) 646, the Jason Swift case)), or in order to conceal the crime. The sexual abuse of children rarely leads to their murder. In the case of *Cole* (1993) 14 Cr App R (S) 668, the appellant stopped a 10 year old girl who was walking home and asked her if she would like to go to the shops to buy some sweets. She said she would not and ran indoors distressed. The appellant was subsequently apprehended in his car, the zip of his trousers was undone, on the passenger seat were chocolates and in the back of the car was a video and a polaroid camera. In interview he admitted that he had been looking for a young girl to take to a secluded spot to interfere with sexually and to take photographs. A sentence of four years was reduced to one of two years (see *Jackson* (1987) 9 Cr App R (S) 294). In the case of *Fisher* [1995] Crim LR 173, the appellant approached two girls 8 and 10 and offered them money to allow him to kiss their bottoms. A few days later he approached a four year old girl and indecently assaulted her. The interrelation between the sexual abuse of children and the use of child pornography and the use of children for the purpose of making child pornography is frequently underestimated. In many cases including *Black* (above) and *Cole* (above), the taking of photographs of the abuse is a part of the abuse, rebutting arguments which promulgate the view that the collection of child pornography is merely fantasy. Indeed, the collection of child pornography is often a prelude to exhibitionism, genital manipulation, cunnilingus, fellatio, mutual masturbation, manual manipulation of the children's vagina or anus, anal intercourse and/or vaginal intercourse (see Renvoize 1983, p. 26).

HOW EXTENSIVE IS CHILD SEXUAL ABUSE?

It is only very recently that it has been possible to gather statistics on the problem of child sexual abuse. This has been largely due to political, public and professional recalcitrance. Without acknowledgment, support and protection and in the absence of legal remedies and the will to apply them, children have been isolated and their unquestioning trust and loyalty in those that are entrusted to care for them, betrayed. The same motives that induce children's compliance with the perpetrator also prevent children from telling. Fear, powerlessness, a desire not to hurt those whom the child loves, a desire not to break up the already shaky fabric of the family, repression and disassociation are some of the several motives for silence and survival strategies that prevent children from speaking out (La Fontaine 1990, p. 45). Samantha's story to the *Report of the Inquiry into Child Abuse in Cleveland* (1988), is revealing, 'I thought an adult would not believe me — they would think I was making up a story . . . I didn't know what might happen. For my brother's sake I didn't want my family split up. I loved my father so much. I respected him as a father. But I was confused, didn't understand. I wanted it to stop. I hated that part of it so much' (1988, p. 9 para. 34). Adler (1987, p. 13), in a personal interview with a child sexual abuse victim, records this experience:

> I felt I couldn't do anything. I knew what I had to do, but I felt that if I did, I would hurt my mother. So for a long time I didn't say anything. I'm not the only one who went through it, not the only stepchild, I know of two others. And for a long time, I felt really guilty about it. I thought if I had done something about him, he wouldn't have hurt anyone else. But even when I told my mother what was going on, she didn't believe me. She said nothing, she just didn't do anything or say anything. No reaction at all, none whatsoever. She didn't believe me until one day, I'm not sure how old I was, she saw him.

Children often decide not to report because they consider that no one will believe them. In the *Cleveland Inquiry*, a girl of 12 told the Official Solicitor that her stepfather had told her that no one would believe her (p. 7 para. 19). In *David John D* (above), the case law report itself alludes to the difficulty children have in convincing others of what has occurred, reporting, '. . . when finally the children were believed'. Fear and powerlessness results in sealing their silence. One girl aged five said that she had kept quiet because 'my daddy told me I would lose my voice if I told anyone' (*Cleveland* 1988, p. 7, para. 19). Children also experience guilt and feel that they are in some way responsible. In the case of *David John D* the daughter who had been subjected to rape and sexual perversions for 19 years felt she was to blame.

Quantitative indicators of child sexual abuse are gleaned largely from *inter alia*, the National Society for the Prevention of Cruelty to Children data of children on Child Protection Registers (see below); orders granted under the Children Act 1989 following a finding by the court of 'significant harm' which includes, amongst other forms of abuse, sexual abuse (see Table 17); criminal statistics of those proceeded against for criminal offences (see Table 18); and in addition from a range of research studies. Taken together, such information provides a glimmer of knowledge on the extent of the problem, although it is acceded that it is only the tip of the iceberg. In respect of the first source of information, the NSPCC's studies, these have focused research on those children who are placed on Child Protection Registers. The 1989 study covered some 10 per cent of children living in England and Wales. NSPCC data showed that in 1988, 597 children were registered owing to sexual abuse and in 1989 this rose to 621. From these base figures their research estimated that this would account for a registration incidence of 5,400 of 0–14 age group, 6,400 of 0-16 in 1988, and 5,850 and 6,600 respectively for 1989 (*Research Briefing* 1989 No. 11, p. 2).

Table 16: Child Protection Registration by category

	1991	1992	1993	1991	1992	1993
Total	28,300	24,500	24,700	45,300	38,600	32,500
Neglect	3,300	3,800	6,000	6,800	7,700	8,500
Phys Inj	6,700	7,000	9,800	10,600	10,700	11,900
Sex Abuse	3,900	4,200	6,400	6,000	6,600	8,300
Emot Ab.	1,300	1,700	2,500	2,600	2,800	3,500
Grave con.	14,100	8,800	1,800	21,100	12,900	2,700
Percentages						
	1991	1992	1993	1991	1992	1993
Neglect	12	15	24	15	20	26
Phys Inj	24	29	40	23	28	37
Sex Abuse	14	17	26	13	17	26
Emot Ab.	5	7	10	6	7	11
Grave con.	50	36	7	47	34	8

Source: Children Act Report 1993 Table 3.4

Table 17: Disposal of selected applications in public law proceedings 1993–4

No. of Applications	Withdrawn (a)		Refused (b)		No order (c)		Granted (d)		% No order as a % of (c) and (d) (e)	
	1993	1994	1993	1994	1993	1994	1993	1994	1993	1994
care	379	562	47	80	123	162	3,249	4,169	3.6	3.7
contact with child in care	168	209	131	117	104	67	1,419	1,719	6.8	3.7
discharge of care	147	152	77	43	14	17	996	795	1.3	2.0
refusal of care/contact	42	62	26	23	11	28	703	883	1.5	3.0
emergency protection order	122	130	81	64	27	24	2,282	2,754	1.1	0.9
secure accommodation	127	165	12	14	18	31	1,106	1,240	1.6	2.4
supervision	116	102	9	4	33	45	1,203	1,320	2.7	3.3
supervision order/discharge	8	7	3	7	4	—	66	70	5.7	0
section 8										
residence	75	134	76	71	25	17	1,470	1,496	1.7	1.1
contact	40	49	67	31	26	25	937	885	2.7	2.7
prohibited steps	36	7	9	2	3	3	542	299	0.5	0.9
specific issue	6	3	2	—	2	—	93	43	2.1	0

Source: Judicial Statistics 1993 and 1994 derived from Table 5.2

Table 18: Persons sentenced at all courts by offence and age of victim

	England and Wales 1988									
Sex offences	under 5		5–9		10–14		15–16		total	
	no	0%	no	0%	no	0%	no	0%	no	0%
rape			1	2	7	4	1	1	9	2
indecent ass	7	16	23	55	56	33	22	17	108	28
unl sex int	1	2	4	10	15	9	3	2	23	6
gross indecency	3	7	3	7	3	2			9	2
buggery	2	5	1	2	14	8	7	5	24	6
other sex off			4	10	9	5	3	2	16	4
all sexual off	13	30	36	86	104	61	36	28	188	49

Source: Home Office Statistical Bulletin 1989/42 Criminal Proceedings for Offences of Sex and Violence Against Children, Table 4, 5 December 1989.

With regard to the second source of quantitative information on child sexual abuse, under the Children Act 1989, s. 31, a finding of significant harm which may indicate physical or sexual abuse or neglect, may result in an order for care or supervision or indeed an order under s. 8 for residence or contact. It is not possible to determine in what proportion of these orders child sexual abuse is indicated, although the overall picture is provided in Table 17 together with figures on the number of 'no orders' where the court decides, following a finding of 'significant harm', that it is better for the child not to make an order at all (a point to which I return later). The third, albeit limited, source of information on the extent of child sexual abuse is provided in criminal statistics of offences of abuse reported to the police and recorded as 'notifiable offences' and the number of persons finally sentenced for sex offences against children (see Table 18). Few cases initially recorded in this way ever go to trial. The *Report of the Advisory Group on Video-Recorded Evidence* chaired by His Honour Judge Thomas Pigot QC, reported that there were 3,229 prosecutions for offences against children in 1983 rising to 3,723 in 1987. The main criminal categories under which child sexual abuse is subsumed include incest, and gross indecency against a child; it is only within these specific categories that the number of prosecutions for child sexual abuse can be accurately determined. Whilst there are also prosecutions for offences of rape, indecent assault on a female, indecent assault on a male, buggery, unlawful sexual intercourse on a girl under 13, unlawful sexual intercourse on a girl under 16, it is not possible to ascertain what proportion of these offences, excepting unlawful intercourse on a girl under 13, are actually committed against children. The crime of incest involves the abuse of a female by 'intercourse' by a father, grandfather or brother (see Rook and Ward 1990, p. 90; Blackstone's 1996 B3.62). Section 10(1) of the Sexual Offences Act 1956 provides, 'It is an offence for a man to have sexual intercourse with a woman whom he knows to be his granddaughter, daughter, sister or mother'. The alternative verdicts are unlawful sexual intercourse with a girl under 13 (Sexual Offences Act 1956, s. 5), unlawful sexual intercourse with a girl under 16 (s. 6) or indecent assault (see Blackstone's B3.65). Gross indecency with children is provided for by the Indecency with Children Act 1960, s. 1(1) 'Any person who commits an act of gross indecency with or towards a child under the age of 14, or who incites a child under that age to such an act with him or another, shall be liable on conviction on indictment to imprisonment for a term not exceeding 2 years' (Blackstone's B3.111). Examples of gross indecency are masturbation, oral/genital contact as in *Speck* [1977] 2 All ER 859, *Morley* [1989] Crim LR 566 and *Francis* (1989) 88 Cr App R 127. Buggery is prosecuted under s. 12(1), Sexual Offences Act 1956 where, 'It is an offence for a person to commit buggery with another person.'. It involves the anal penetration of a child and is punishable with life imprisonment as a maximum. When a father commits an offence of anal penetration against his young son, this is buggery not incest. In 1993, only 73 per cent of those sentenced for this offence received a custodial sentence. Seven years seems to be the average sentence, and is discussed later in this chapter (see *Simpson* (1981) Cr App R (S) 345, Blackstone's 1996 B3. 72) (see Table 19).

Table 19: Unsuspended sentences of imprisonment 1993

	incest	gross indec with child	USI girl under 13
total trial	78	77	46
under 4 mth	4	3	2
4 to 6 mth	1	6	2
6 mth to 1 yr	2	22	6
1 yr to 18 mth	6	30	5
18 mth to 2 yr	6	15	1
2 yr up to 3 yr	9	1	3
3 yr up to 4 yr	18		8
4 yr up to 5 yr	13		3
5 yr up to 7 yr	9		8
7 yr up to 10 yr	8		8
over 10 yr	2		
Life	0		

Source: Criminal Statistics Supplementary Tables 1993, Vol 2, Table S2.6

An act of indecent assault can be committed upon a male or a female. Both offences are punishable with a maximum of ten years' imprisonment (see Rook and Ward 1990, p. 5, Blackstone's 1996 B3.68). In *Court* [1988] 2 WLR 1071, the appellant spanked a girl 12 times on her bottom over her shorts. When asked to explain why he had done this, he said to the police, 'I don't know — buttock fetish'. The House of Lords held that an assault is either inherently indecent or rendered indecent by the surrounding circumstances. The surrounding circumstances included the appellant's comment to the police indicating his secret motive (see *Clayton* above), although evidence of any secret motive is only admissible on the issue of indecency if right minded persons consider the assault indecent (see *Beal* v *Kelly* (1951) 35 Cr App R 128). Note the contrast with child pornography and the decision in *Graham-Kerr* [1988] 1 WLR 1098 (see the chapter entitled, Freedom from Pornography in an Age of Sexual Liberation) where, when indecent photographs are considered, any evidence of secret motive is immaterial. Indecent assault is an alternate verdict to incest. In addition, there are the offences of unlawful sexual intercourse with a girl under 13 (see s. 5, Sexual Offences Act 1956), and unlawful intercourse with a girl under 16 (s. 6(1)). Both these charges include those cases where the female consented and those where there was no consent but an alternate charge was considered to fail. Unlawful sexual intercourse is an alternate verdict to incest (see Rook and Ward 1990, p. 153, Blackstone's 1996 B3.65). The defendant may also be charged with rape. In *Howard* [1966] 1 WLR 13 a conviction was upheld where there was a misdirection by the trial judge who directed the jury that consent did not arise because as a matter of law a child could not consent to intercourse (see Rook and Ward 1990, p. 49). The court relied on *Harling* [1938] 1 All ER 307, when Humphreys J said:

> It is desirable that this court should restate the law, which is not subject to doubt, but which it may perhaps be useful to repeat, that while a girl under the age of sixteen is perfectly capable of consenting, and, as everyone knows who tries these cases, frequently does consent to an act of sexual intercourse with a man, the law has provided that such consent affords no defence to men on a charge of carnal knowledge of a girl under sixteen; but there is no provision as to the crime of rape. In every case of rape it is necessary that the prosecution should prove that the girl or woman did not consent and that the crime was committed against her will.

This again further illustrates the considerable ambiguity in law in respect of the protection of children. Rapes by family members would, however, come under incest and so those proceeded against for rape are likely to be strangers or acquaintances, not family members. As few cases are reported, or recorded, and even fewer offenders prosecuted or care proceedings instituted, such statistics provide a very incomplete picture of the extent of the abuse of children. As La Fontaine (1990, p. 45), indicates, 'The difficulties of establishing anything like an accurate assessment are seldom given serious consideration and they are formidable.'.

WICKED FAIRY TALES

Child sexual abuse has been and continues to be disavowed. A problem of relatively recent origin, allegations of sexual abuse made by both children, and by adults in recalling their childhood experience were deemed hardly credible. In the 19th and 20th centuries the dominant discourse of psychoanalysis has lent support to the denial and refutation of such allegations. Freud's theory on infantile sexuality after 1898 provided much of the intellectual and pedagogic justification for this negation. The adult patient who recalled childhood experiences of incest was disbelieved and discredited. The child talking of current abuse was fantasising. As Freud wrote when he laid the foundation for decades of denial, 'I was at last obliged to recognise that these scenes of seduction had never taken place, and that they were only fantasies which my patients had made up' (see Masson 1984, p. 11).

The idea that children made false accusations of sexual abuse gained widespread support. During the 19th century physicians from psychiatry, mental health and medicine including *inter alia* Lawson Tait, Flint, Smith, Dixon Mann, Routh, Taylor and Norman, reported on the extent of false accusations of sexual abuse which they claimed to have encountered in clinical practice (see Edwards 1981, pp. 126, 142, see also Masson 1984). Dr Tait, a practising police surgeon, reported on nearly 100 cases of allegations of sexual assault yet advised prosecution in only six. 'Two dirty little wretches of ten and twelve, who had been thrashed by their father for stealing, promptly turned round on him with a charge of having seduced them' (1894, p. 232). Those who challenged the psychoanalytical orthodoxy were soon silenced and deemed heretical. Sandor Ferenczi's contribution to the early struggle for recognition and validation of child sexual abuse was received with such hostility that its publication was effectively obstructed for several years. In 1932, in his seminal paper '*Confusion of Tongues Between Adults and the Child*', read before the International Psycho-Analytic Congress he asserted:

> Even children of respected, high-minded puritanical families fall victim to real rape much more frequently than one had dared to suspect. Either the parents themselves seek substitution for their lack of [sexual] satisfaction in this pathological manner, or else trusted persons such as relatives (uncles, aunts, grandparents), tutors, servants, abuse the ignorance and innocence of children. The obvious objection that we are dealing with sexual fantasies of the child himself, that is, with hysterical lies, unfortunately is weakened by the multitude of confessions of this kind, on the part of patients in analysis, to assaults on children (see Masson 1984, pp. 288–289).

He went on to say, 'I believe, should all this prove true, that we shall be obliged to revise certain chapters of the [psychoanalytic] theory of sexuality and of genitality'. Such a fundamental attack on psychanalysis had to be silenced: Ferenczi's work was not published and he was declared mad. Freud said he was suffering from pseudologia phantastica and was paranoid. Masson has the final say, 'The lies came from Freud and the whole psychoanalytic movement. Ferenczi, in 1932, was the one man who would have no part of the lie.'. Yet, there was a wealth of post-Freudian loyalist psychoanalysts, notably Deutsch, to keep the fire of refutation of the child's accusation burning. Deutsch wrote, 'Girlish fantasies relating to rape often remain unconscious, but evince their content in dreams, sometimes in symptoms, and often accompany masturbatory actions' (see Edwards 1981, p. 105). This seemingly impenetrable orthodoxy of psychoanalytical purism, writes Alice Miller (1985, p. 4):

> ... is obliged to regard everything patients tell about their childhood as fantasy and as their own desires projected onto the external world. Thus, in terms of the drive theory, patients do not actually abuse their children in order to fulfil their own needs, but children supposedly fantasise this abuse, repressing their own aggressive and sexual (instinctual drives) and experiencing these desires — through the mechanisms of projection — as being directed against them from the outside.

Psychoanalysis and the judicial process

The consequences of this orthodoxy that child sexual abuse is fantasy, and that children are sexual and provocative, are ideas that have influenced medical jurists, the public, politicians, practitioners as well as the judiciary. Children were, and are still considered to make false allegations and to be a seat of unbridled sexuality. These two constructions of the child have had an impact on rules of evidence, a point considered in some depth by Edwards (1981, pp. 100–114, 130–135). Wigmore (1940, pp. 459–460), perhaps the most influential Anglo-American jurist, wrote:

> Modern psychiatrists have amply studied the behaviour of errant young girls and women coming before the courts in all sorts of cases. Their psychic complexes are multifarious, distilled partly by inherent defects, partly by diseased derangements or abnormal instincts, partly by bad social environment, partly by temporary physiological or emotional conditions. One form taken by these complexes is that of contrary false charges of sexual offences by men. The unchaste (let us call it) mentality finds incidental but direct expression in the narration of imaginary sex-incidents of which the narrator is the heroine or the victim.

This fallacious assertion still appears in the 1972 Chadbourn Revision read by both students and practitioners of law.

The belief in false allegations made by adolescent girls still resonates throughout medical jurisprudence (see Williams 1963, p. 159, Hughes 1962, Knight 1972, p. 167–72, Polson and Gee 1973, p. 500, Paul 1975, p. 156). Bernard Knight wrote:

> There is a particular risk in medicine and dentistry of unfounded allegations of indecent assault, either through malice or through confusion following an anaesthetic for dental or minor operations.... Though the majority of allegations of sexual interference are unfounded especially where young teenage girls are concerned.

These and other similar views have influenced the police and the courts when called upon to consider the validity of such allegations and so a credence has been given to the false accusation theory. Sutcliffe J, in a trial at the Old Bailey in April 1976, is reported to have said, 'It is well known that women in particular and small boys are liable to be untruthful and invent stories' (see Pattullo 1983, p. 18). Salmon LJ said:

> ... in cases of alleged sexual offences it is really dangerous to convict on the evidence of the woman or girl alone. This is dangerous ... because human experience has shown that girls and women do sometimes tell an entirely false story which is very easy to fabricate but extremely difficult to refute. Such stories are fabricated for all sorts of reasons, which I need not now enumerate, and sometimes for no reason at all (*Henry and Manning* (1969) 53 Cr App R 150, 153).

In the case of *Hunt* [1995] Crim LR 42, a newsagent was convicted of a number of assaults on different young girls he employed on news rounds. The judge directed the jury that the evidence of each girl was potentially corroborative of each other girl, but only if they could reject the defence suggestion that the girls had put their heads together to invent the story, although this proposition was not accepted by the Court of Appeal. Not only is there the view that children bring false allegations, there is also the view that they are responsible for their demise and as seductresses and temptresses to whom adult males fall victim. This notion has been exploited considerably in defence argument and is a popular mitigatory strategy of defence counsel at the point of sentencing. It is a vein which has been given authority in recent years by Lord Lane's guidelines on sentencing in incest cases (see *Attorney-General's Reference (No. 1 of 1989)* [1989] 3 All ER 571).

Overzealous professionals

By the 1960s the problem of child sexual abuse was finally being recognised by medical, social work and psychiatric professionals and there was a rising concern that child sexual abuse was not being taken seriously enough. In North America, Europe and in the UK, however, there was a backlash too, and social work professionals and paediatricians who began to diagnose child sexual abuse faced a barrage of criticism and were labelled 'moral zealots', identified as orchestrators of an unprecedented 'moral panic' about child sexual abuse. Professionals in their credo of child protection have, some allege, become overzealous. This backlash of refutation is characterised by two concerted phases of resistance. The first is manifested in the 1980s in response to the child sexual abuse allegations arising out of Cleveland, Orkney and elsewhere. The second phase of resistance emerges in the 1990s in response to allegations of recovered memories as false memory syndrome which promises to undermine the credibility of allegations of child sexual abuse.

The strength of the belief in professional hysteria in the first phase is reflected in a headline from a Dutch newspaper reporting on allegations of multiple child sexual abuse on children at a day care centre in Rotterdam, 'Preference for one's mother above jam is regarded as a signal' (see Edwards and Soetenhorst 1994, p. 109). Similarly, the identification of child sexual abuse in the Cleveland, Rochdale, Orkney and Ayrshire cases was said to be no more than a heightened 'moral panic' about the extent of child sexual abuse. It resulted too in a concern with the unbridled power of the State to intervene and dislocate family life on a 'whiff' of suspicion.

Cleveland (England)   In January 1987, Marietta Higgs arrived in Cleveland. The wave of moral panic began when many cases of child sexual abuse (specifically ano-rectal abuse), were diagnosed at Middlesbrough General hospital, Cleveland. By May of that year it was clear that the number of detected cases of child sexual abuse had reached epidemic proportions, far beyond what social services, the police and the caring professionals had the resources to deal with.

In total 125 children were diagnosed as sexually abused between February and July 1987: 66 became wards of court. In the wardship cases, 27 were dewarded and went home with the proceedings dismissed; 24 went home on conditions as to medical examination of the children, and two went home on interim care orders. Nine children who are wards of court remain in care of the County Council and away from their families. Of those not made wards of court, 27 were the subject of place of safety orders. In all, 21 children remain in care. We understand that out of the 121 children, 98 are at home. (Cleveland Inquiry, Cm. 412, 1988, p. 12.)

At the onset of the investigation children were forcibly removed from their homes in 'dawn raids' under place of safety orders, and the diagnosis of child sexual abuse rested on the highly questionable and contentious evidence of 'anal dilatation' as the definitive sign. The children at the centre of the allegations had initially presented to hospital following a range of complaints including constipation, failure to thrive, an itchy bottom, urinary tract infections, bruised perineum, soiling, bowel problems, weight loss, tonsillitis, fits and asthma (Cleveland Inquiry, p. 19 para. 43). Campbell in defence of the Cleveland diagnoses (1988, p. 2), argues that the symptoms were all connected with sexual abuse. A diagnosis of sexual abuse followed in many cases. Press reports sided for the main part with the accused parents whom they cast in the role of victim. The sexual abuse epidemic was portrayed as the creation of overzealous professionals. Some newspaper reports, in efforts to discredit, suggested links between militant feminism and the diagnosis of abuse. Campbell documents how the female paediatrician at the centre, Dr Marietta Higgs, was transformed through media representation into a symbol, a metaphor of militant feminism. Children were removed from homes, parents' rights to information and to challenge and children's rights to have a voice, were disregarded.

As a result, on 9 July 1987, the Secretary of State for Social Services ordered that a statutory inquiry should be established to look into the arrangements for dealing with suspected cases of child abuse in Cleveland from 1 January 1987 in response to the unprecedented rise in child sexual abuse diagnosis. The Right Honourable Lord Justice Butler-Sloss, as she was then known, was appointed to chair the inquiry. In its conclusions the inquiry expressed concern over the diagnosis of sexual abuse, the management of these cases and the 'double victimization' or secondary abuse of the children concerned. The inquiry did not find that there had been an unjustified diagnosis of child sexual abuse although the major area of contention and criticism raged over the presumption of anal dilatation as a valid and sole method of diagnosis. Raine Roberts, the police surgeon involved, reported that forceful separation of the buttocks may trigger the anal reflex and this was not of itself a useful diagnostic tool. Her opinion was supported by the Association of Police Surgeons who in giving evidence to the judicial inquiry reported that anal dilatation was not pathognomic of sexual abuse but it should give rise to suspicion. Campbell states that in only 18 cases was anal dilatation the sole method of diagnosis (1988, p. 2).

The handling of these cases by the medical professionals was heavily criticised. Children were transported some 100 miles away to enable a colleague of Dr Higgs to confirm her dilatation diagnosis. They were photographed in the ano-genital areas by police photographers, who soon refused to co-operate further, as children were showing obvious signs of distress. Children reported to social workers that they were terrified of the medical investigations and of the police. One girl said that Dr Wyatt, the colleague of Dr Higgs, had turned her over and wanted 'to go into her front'. She said that Dr Wyatt was 'talking not very nice', he was shouting and she was afraid. Children said of police surgeons, 'one child was held in a head lock while being examined' (Cleveland Inquiry 1988, p. 40). Children spoke of being 'grilled' (p. 15 para. 13).

Parents were not consulted nor their consent to examinations obtained, access was restricted or denied altogether (1988, p. 36). The inquiry drew up a series of recommendations for the future diagnosis and management of such cases, to be followed in subsequent child abuse investigations, emphasising the need for training, experience and aptitude of interviewers, open minds and open ended questions, a presumption against multiple interviews, and the need for meticulous recording of interviews. The Children Act 1989 provides for the making of a pre-emptive strike in order to protect the child whilst at the same time allowing for consultation and communication with parents and for parents to communicate with children unless prohibited by the court in both emergency protection orders and child assessment orders. The impact which the Higgs 'demonisation' and the witchhunt of the professionals has had upon future preventative diagnosis is uncertain. Reported cases arising out of Cleveland include *Cleveland County Council* v *W and Others*; *Cleveland County Council* v *B and Others* [1989] Fam Law 17, *Re W and Others (Ward) (Publication of Information)* [1989] 1 FLR 246).

Meanwhile, Dr Higgs, at the centre of the epidemic, was scapegoated and singled out for a disciplinary hearing. Efforts to sack her continued until the summer of 1989 when she was finally reinstated but not in a paediatric capacity, accepting a post in a special baby care unit. Marietta Higgs pursued an unsuccessful damages action, *Higgs* v *Northern Regional Health Authority, The Times*, 7 April 1989, for breach of contract. In an interview for a programme on child sexual abuse in June 1989, she said that the child sexual abuse diagnosed represented only 1 per cent of her total caseload. Whatever the rights and wrongs of the case the protection of children took a knocking, rather than making a pre-emptive strike, professionals returned to waiting to see what would happen, when it was then too late. After Cleveland, Higgs herself was accused of being overly cautious, and criticised in 1993 for failing to recognise the symptoms of battering, when she concluded that injuries were 'found to be consistent' with the story of how they occurred and were diagnosed to be accidental as a result (*Daily Mail*, 1 October 1993).

De Bolderkar, Rotterdam (Holland)   The extent of diagnosis in Cleveland was not an isolated phenomenon. In Europe and in North America the extent of child sexual abuse was being realised and, as in Cleveland, the press and the public refused to believe the wave of diagnoses, demonising the professional who dared to speak the name and dislocate happy families. In

1988 in Vlaardingen, a suburb of Rotterdam, in a day care centre for 'problem' children, staff were suspected of sexual abuse in 25 per cent of day care admissions. This preliminary diagnosis was based on family information, the child's behaviour in the group, medical investigation, and intensive observation of the child over a two week period. In cases where sexual abuse was suspected the anatomical doll method was one of the procedures used during this period of observation. This resulted in nine children being placed in a children's home, two following allegations of sexual abuse, and seven following an order of the juvenile court. The remaining six cases were reported to police for subsequent prosecution. On appeal some of these verdicts were overturned, and in one case a father received damages equivalent to £10,000 for a wrongful conviction. In a further case parents protested about the accusation that they had abused their child and the intervention of social workers to remove the child without consultation with the parents. On appeal the removal of the child was upheld although the court recognised that the emergency procedures involved in preserving the child's welfare were far from ideal. The De Bolderkar story was reported in the press thus, 'Vlaardingen in the grip of incest cases'. Parents campaigned collectively and the press responded by portraying the parents as victims, the caring professionals as orchestrators of a moral panic about child sexual abuse; and branding the director of the day care centre as a moral zealot. The De Bolderkar investigation was followed by an inquiry, whose report was made public in April 1989 and which criticised the methods of diagnosis (largely the anatomical doll method), intervention of social workers and the response of the courts. The inquiry established similar procedures to those in Cleveland for the management of suspected child sexual abuse cases (see Edwards and Soetenhorst 1994). In these and in other inquiries the need for proper procedures to protect children, including the consideration of all parties and including the parental right to consultation, is paramount.

Manchester (England)   Social workers in Manchester in the late 1980s were alerted to the possibility of child sexual abuse following interviews with several children, which led them to believe that 'a ring or network of abusers, probably carried out in a ritual or ceremonial setting, and possibly in connexion with satanic rites' was in existence. In *Re C and L (Child Abuse: Evidence)* [1991] FCR 351, a number of children were identified as victims of child sexual abuse. The allegations were made by social workers, not by the children themselves, with the result that five applications were made in wardship in respect of 13 children who were all members of the same family. Medical examination showed that two of the sisters had been sexually abused. They were taken into care and fostered. Ten further children were also taken into care and were made wards of court. All of the children except for one were subject to prolonged interviews. Holling J ruled that the social workers were obsessed with the belief that they were investigating ritualistic satanic abuse, and that in almost every respect the Cleveland guidelines had been breached. There were, he said, 'serious faults in the way the children were interviewed'. The court acknowledged that interviews must be carried out with care and expertise (see

Cleveland County Council v *E* [1988] FCR 625, *Re Z (Minors) (Child Abuse: Evidence)* [1989] FCR 440), and that leading questions are to be avoided (*Re M (A Minor) (Child Abuse: Evidence)* [1989] FCR 433). The court held that there was no evidence to justify a care order in respect of seven of the children and no evidence of satanic ritualistic abuse although the making of a care order in respect of five of the children was justified. After the hearing eight of the children were returned home, five remained in care (see Lyon and De Cruz 1993, p. 57), indicating that the concern for the children was grounded in evidence of abuse.

Rochdale (England)   In November 1989 in a school in Manchester teachers reported to the Social Services that a boy of six had started talking about ghosts. This resulted in an investigation into what teachers and social workers believed amounted to ritualistic abuse. Twenty children from six families were made wards, the majority being removed from their homes. The allegations were that they had been subjected to, or were at risk of satanic or ritual abuse. According to social workers, 'B talked of ghosts in the house who took him from his home, or being given drinks that made him fly and of the killing of babies.'. The social workers involved surmised that A and B had been given hallucinogenic drugs and had been subjected to ritual abuse, although there was no evidence of sexual abuse against the children. Place of safety orders were obtained for all four children of that family (now emergency protection order, Children Act 1989 s. 44). Wardship was obtained for children in the other five families. Children were then fostered. The court found:

> The overall gist of what the children had been saying, or apparently saying, was that serious sadistic abuse had been committed on them and other children when some or all of the seven children had been present at gatherings in certain buildings, confusingly described and never safely identified, and their abuse had been by adults, some of them parents, or other adults unknown. There was quite evidently a great deal of fantasy and misleading replies to leading questions or otherwise in response to improper techniques.' (*Rochdale Borough Council* v *A* [1991] 2 FLR 192).

The children were all eventually returned home although children of certain families remained wards of court (see Lyon and de Cruz 1993, p. 54–56).

Orkney (Scotland)   In November 1990, following allegations by one of the children of a family, referred to as the W family, seven younger siblings of that family were removed and a further nine children from families referred to as the B, H, M, and T families were subsequently removed in February 1991. The children of the W family were removed to the mainland of Scotland and the children from the other families were flown to placements in the Highlands and Strathclyde Regions. The father of family W had already been sentenced to seven years' imprisonment for various offences of sexual abuse (*Report of the Inquiry into the Removal of Children from Orkney in February 1991* (1992)). The children were removed at dawn, access between them was refused, access by

relatives was refused. Excessive interviews were conducted by police and
RSSPCC staff. The allegations were made by one child who was not claiming
to be a victim of the abuse. Sheriff Kelbie dismissed the case on 4 April 1992
on the grounds that the earlier hearings had been fatally flawed (Lyon and De
Cruz 1993, p. 59). The report of the inquiry criticised the Social Work
Department and its failure to follow adequately the guidance issued in the
Cleveland Report, it also stated that the methodology of interviews was open to
question and that there was failure at several levels of intervention.

Ayrshire (Scotland)   In 1990, following allegations of ritual child sexual
abuse, eight children were removed from their families. A mother asked a
doctor to check whether her three sons had been sexually abused. A police
investigation was set up involving 70 adults and children. No charges were
brought. However, four boys and four girls were removed from their homes
under place of safety orders. Sheriff Neil Gow at the original hearing found
evidence of 'sadism, ritualism and torture'. The children were made subject to
supervision orders and spent five years in care until their return to their parents
in February 1995 ordered by Sheriff Miller. The children made no allegations,
there was no corroboration and the investigation was instigated following one
incident where a father, in a drunken state, got up during the night and fell
asleep on the children's bed. When Mr F returned to bed Mrs F found her son
lying face down in bed with his pyjama trousers down and reported the matter.
Sheriff Miller criticised social workers, care workers and the police for their
handling of the case particularly in respect of the way in which interviews were
conducted. Sheriff Miller said 'The interviewers pursued a single hypothesis to
the exclusion of all other explanations.'. The families at the centre of the
allegations were three related families from the travelling communities. Sheriff
Miller in his report concluded:

> I am also conscious that at the time in 1990 there is evidence to the effect that
> there was a fashion to seek out sexual abuse and in particular abuse of a ritual
> or satanic nature. I am aware that nearly five years later the climate has
> reversed and it is as is shown by the Professor La Fontaine report now
> fashionable to find there is nothing at all to justify allegations of such a nature
> in the vast majority of cases . . . I am left with the feeling . . . that it is possible
> that this has been a case of child sexual abuse but any evidence of it has been
> so ineptly collected and so contaminated for all the reasons that I have
> accepted from the experts and all as I have argued in relation to each witness
> in this case, with the end result that it is not possible for me to conclude
> whether or not the statements of fact which the Reporter prays in aid of his
> grounds of referral have been proved on the balance of probabilities.

In accepting the report the Lord President said.

> It is however clear, from what the Sheriff has told us, that a tragedy of
> immense proportions has occurred in this case . . . in this very difficult
> situation the welfare of the child must be our prime consideration and we are

conscious that speed may be as or even more damaging to their best interests as delay. (*Scots Law Report*, 21 April 1995, Court of Session, *The Times*, 21 April 1995.)

New battlegrounds

In the 1980s and 1990s and in the US especially, a spate of civil actions for damages alleging sexual abuse in childhood were brought by adults against parents (see Bannon 1994, Ernsdorff and Loftus 1993, Cote 1992–3, Spikes and Rud 1995, Roseman 1992). What is especially significant about these claims is that the knowledge of abuse had only recently been discovered by the victims under hypnosis. These adults are supposed to develop 'psychogenic amnesia', and early abuse is dealt with by protective dissociation. Professional bodies including the American Psychiatric Association, the American Medical Association, the British Medical Association remain, as yet, undecided, whilst many psychiatrists argue that repressed memories are objectively false (see Goldstein 1992, Cote 1992–3, p. 427). There is the additional problem in that the therapists unearthing these repressed experiences are not always qualified. Ofshe remarks, '[r]ecovered-memory therapy will come to be recognized as the quackery of the 20th century' (cited in Bannon 1994, p. 846). There is also the allegation that some therapists facilitate, invent and even implant such ideas into the mind of an unhappy patient. It is considered that poor techniques, including the asking of leading questions, can result in false memories being produced to please the interviewer (see Bannon 1994, p. 844). In response to this problem of pleasing the interviewer with the answer he or she seems to want, experts interviewing children in the UK are bound by the *Cleveland Guidelines* (discussed above), although no similar good practice guidelines exist for interviewing the adult victim of sexual abuse as a child. Recovered memory has resulted in an orchestrated litigation where parents and children are locked in battles which are played out in the courts, not only at the level of the abuse but at the level of the credibility of the therapist. Some therapists have been sued by wrongfully accused parents, some therapists have been sued by patients for the additional trauma this realisation has caused them and some therapists have been sued by patients for implanting such ideas. The 'repressed memory syndrome' threatens to pour discredit and suspicion on all adults bringing cases against abusers whether memory is repressed or not.

The phenomenon of 'repressed memory evidence' together with the phenomenon of adults recognising adult trauma as a product of early abuse has led some States to make amendments to existing civil statutes in respect of the discovery rule, incorporating this into the Statute of Limitation (see Donaldson 1993). Prior to the introduction of statute, plaintiffs were encountering difficulties in bringing actions for damages against alleged abusers, such claims being statute barred. In *Tyson* v *Tyson* 727 P 2d 226 (Wash) (1986), where a daughter brought an action against a father following recent recovery of memories of child sexual abuse under hypnosis, the court held that such action was barred by the discovery rule, although Pearson J, dissenting, asserted, 'I believe it is unfair to deny adult survivors of childhood sexual abuse a legal remedy'. In the case of *Mary D* v *John D* 264 Cal Rptr 633 (1989), the plaintiff filed a suit nearly 20 years after the abuse perpetrated by her father had occurred, and over three years after the Statute of Limitations had expired, following recovered memories repressed for years. The court, on appeal, sought to make a distinction between cases which have recently come to light as a result of repressed memory and cases in which the victim has only recently made the connection between the abuse and the psychological injury (see Ernsdorff and Loftus 1993, p. 129). This distinction creates a double standard for the victim of repressed memory compared with victims who, whilst not repressing the memory and realising the abuse, have only recently made a connection between their childhood abuse and psychological damage. In *De Rose* v *Carswell* 242 Cal Rptr 368, 373 (1988), where a plaintiff alleged that her stepgrandfather had sexually abused her, the ground for a delay of 13 years before bringing the claim was because she was not aware of the relationship between the abuse and her psychological injury. The court did not find that she had repressed memories but that she had become aware instead of the connection between the abuse and her present psychological state. The trauma sometimes prevents survivors of incest from understanding their emotional injuries until they receive appropriate therapy. The court took the view in applying the discovery rule that if *De Rose* could and did allege that she repressed her memories of the sexual assaults until one year before filing her complaint, she might be able to invoke the delayed discovery rule. She was effectively denied redress.

The injustice heaped on victims of psychological trauma barring them from any remedy has resulted in some States reviewing existing civil statutes. In 1989 Washington was the first State to provide civil relief:

> All claims or causes of action based on intentional conduct brought by any person for recovery of damages for injury suffered as a result of childhood sexual abuse shall be commenced within the later of the following periods: (a) Within three years of the time of the act alleged to have caused the injury or condition; (b) Within three years of the time the victim discovered or reasonably should have discovered that the injury or condition was caused by said act; or (c) Within three years of the time the victim discovered that the act caused the injury for which the claim is brought (Wash Rev Code Ann 4.16.340 (1992)).

At least 20 other States have now enacted similar legislation and some have gone further and abolished the Statute of Limitations for actions arising from childhood sexual abuse, notably Illinois in 1993, allowing plaintiffs to bring a cause of action where the time period runs from the time of 'discovery' rather than the time of the actual abuse itself. Both those cases where an abused child recently discovers the causal connection between adult psychiatric problems and the original (non-repressed) abuse have benefited.

Returning to the problem of repressed memory as opposed to merely delayed discovery, there is a real concern for the defendant, since accusatory evidence is based wholly on details which emerge between patient and therapist under hypnosis. Litigation by parents against therapists has followed in cases where parents and relatives consider that they are the victims of false accusations. Some States and courts have recognised that the therapist owes a duty to third parties, (see California Supreme Court in *Tarasoff* v *Regents of the University of California* 551 P 2d 334 (Cal 1976), where the court held that a university doctor had a duty of care where a patient represents a serious danger to another). The Colorado Court of Appeals held in *Montoya* v *Bebensee* 761 P 2d 285 (1988), that the therapist has a duty of care to the parent and the parent has a valid claim for negligence and emotional distress. The Supreme Court of Texas concluded that the psychologist had no professional duty to a third party 'to not negligently diagnose' (Bannon 1994, p. 849 in reference to *Bird* 868 SW 2d 767 (Tex 1994)). In *Bird*, a child's father sued the child psychologist for an incorrect diagnosis. Although the court held that a therapist held no duty, it went on to say that the judgment '. . . should not be read as conferring a grant of absolute immunity upon mental health professionals . . . false accusations of child abuse can be devastating'. In *Vineyard* v *Kraft* 828 SW 2d 248, 252 (Tex Ct App 1992) it was held that a doctor had no duty to third persons. In *Ramona* v *Isabella* Napa Ct, Cal, 13 May 1994 (cited in Spikes and Rud 1995, and in *Farris* v *Compton* 652 A 2d 49 (1994)), a father pursued an action in damages against his daughter's therapists who were responsible for unearthing in her repressed memories of child sexual abuse. He was awarded $500,000 in damages. The case of *Sullivan* v *Cheshier* 846 F Supp 654 (1994), has taken litigation on this matter a stage further in that the court concluded, in an action for damages brought by the parent against the therapist, that a jury could infer that memories were intentionally or recklessly implanted.

Patients are also bringing claims against therapists. Lynn Gondolf felt coerced in therapy, so too did Steven Cook (see Bannon 1994, pp. 844–5). Concern, in such cases, has also centred on the academic and clinical status of 'repressed memory', the validity of the theory, the pseudo-scientific status of the technique including the several questionable methods employed to facilitate or free memory. In the case of *Joyce-Couch* v *DeSilva* 602 NE 2d 286 (Ohio Ct App 1991), punitive damages initially of $125,000, were awarded against a psychiatrist who had administered between 141 and 171 sodium pentothal injections to aid a patient in recovering the lost memory. Dr De Silva advised the appellant that her problems were caused by information she had been repressing in her subconscious. (Subsequent appeals made were: 585 NE 2d 835, 1992, and to the Supreme Court of Ohio, 632 NE 2d 522 1994.)

Critics of 'repressed memory syndrome' refer to this phenomenon as False Memory Syndrome [FMS], providing fresh ammunition for child sex abusers and defence teams to discredit child sexual abuse victims and rebut their allegations, thus bringing us full circle once again to the denial and refutation of child sexual abuse, as a problem of the narrative of false allegation. The repressed memory syndrome has produced a spate of litigation between child and parent, and parent and therapist. Wherever the truth lies, there are inevitably some adults who have suffered sexual abuse in childhood, many have 'normalised' what has happened to them as a way of coping with an abusive childhood. Therapy and counselling of the right kind undoubtedly empowers and enables such adults to make choices which they were unable to make as children. Their consciousness is raised about their right to protection and validation and as with many cases which come to court it is psychotherapy and counselling which has given these adults the courage to speak (see *Stubbings* v *Webb* [1993] 1 All ER 322 (action for damages); *John Francis C* (criminal action) (above). In both these cases the reality of what had happened to them as children was neither repressed nor forgotten. But as UK law stands they were denied damages because of the expiry of the statutory limitation period. In the UK, a social worker was sacked from a children's charity because her daughter had said, following treatment for depression, that her mother abused her (*The Times*, 22 December 1994). The new battleground will be fudged by polarising the positions of the two camps rather than listening to their valid claims and criticisms. Already, those willing to entertain repressed memory allegations are said to be anti-family and feminists bent on the destruction of the family. The spread of the phantom memory thesis amongst defence lawyers is particularly worrying as it lends further credence to the all too familiar strategy to discredit child sexual abuse allegations.

LEGAL PROTECTION

Both civil and/or criminal remedies are available to protect a sexually abused child. Whilst civil proceedings are often preferred, avoiding, at the present at least, the necessity of lengthy examination and cross-examination of the child, there are serious problems and difficulties with the criminal justice system which militates against prosecution, and with civil justice the standard of proof is higher in child sexual abuse cases than in other civil proceedings (see *Re H and R (Child Sexual Abuse: Standard of Proof)* [1995] 1 FLR 643), significant harm is difficult to prove, and where proven an order does not automatically follow since the court is obliged to consider making no order. Once an allegation of abuse is made, or there are grounds for suspecting that a child is at risk, the police have a duty to investigate and to prosecute the suspect where there is sufficient evidence, although since the level of proof required in criminal trials is beyond reasonable doubt, criminal proceedings may not be instituted. Under the Children Act 1989, the local authority is also under a duty to investigate and to institute civil proceedings as appropriate. Evidence, or reasonable suspicion of significant harm is the threshold test which must be satisfied, before any order for child assessment (s. 43(1)), or emergency protection (s. 44(1)), and the compulsory 'public' orders of care or supervision under s. 31 can be granted.

The first stage of any investigation involves checking the Child at Risk register to determine whether a child or member of the child's family is already on the register. For the purpose of registration, 'risk' falls into four categories: neglect, physical injury, emotional injury and sexual abuse (see *Working Together* 1991, para. 6.40). Until 1991, there was a further category of 'grave concern' where, 'social and medical assessments indicate that there is significant risk of abuse'. Since 1991, this category has been withdrawn and cases reclassified amongst existing registrations from that date (see *Children and Young People on Child Protection Registers* 1994, p. 9). At 31 March 1994, fewer children and young people were on child protection registers in England than in 1991, 34,900 compared with 45,300 (*Children Looked After by Local Authorities*, DoH 1995, p. 2, see Table 16). This was hailed at the time as indicating the success of the Children Act 1989, indicating co-operation and partnership between local authorities and families.

The next stage is the convening of a child protection conference within eight days of referral of a child, to decide whether or not there is any foundation for the suspicion of abuse. Even at this stage harm must be determined in accordance with the statutory principle of significant harm. The child and the parents are both encouraged to be present at the conference in order to facilitate maximum communication and again this stage is underpinned by the concept of 'partnership'. The Child Protection Conference decides whether a child should be placed on, or removed from, the Child At Risk register. In 1994, of the 45,800 children who were the subject of an initial child protection conference, 28,500 were subsequently registered (*Children Looked After by Local Authorities*, DoH 1995, p. 3). Further investigations are necessary and in specific circumstances of non-co-operation by the parents (see Bainham 1993, pp. 422–425) an application for a child assessment order (Children Act 1989, s. 43(1)), which empowers the court to examine and assess the child may be made. The standard here is that the applicant has 'reasonable cause to suspect' that the child is suffering or likely to suffer significant harm. It is an order of short duration (seven days) which allows an assessment of the child. The second limb of protection for an abused child is provided by the emergency protection order (s. 44(1)) replacing the former 'place of safety order', which is operative for 15 days as a maximum upon extension. It may be sought by anyone and is intended to provide immediate protection to a child and may be granted *ex parte* although Hollings J, in *Re A*, emphasises that an order should only be made ex parte if there is an immediate apprehension of emergency. Once an emergency protection order has been granted it may not be necessary to remove a child from the home although this may in fact be the usual course. Importantly and uniquely, hearsay evidence, for example the evidence of a police officer to the effect that a child told him that she had been abused even though normally excluded, is permissible. (The Civil Evidence Act 1968 allows the use of hearsay.) The emergency protection order confers on the applicant parental responsibility for the duration of the order, where contact with parents may be maintained, although this is subject to the court's power to give direction and the court may prohibit contact altogether. The child must normally be allowed to return home the moment that it appears to the applicant that it is safe to do so (s. 44(10), (11)). This decision is final and there is no right of appeal.

In 1994, of those children registered on Children At Risk registers, 7,500 were looked after by local authorities and 200 were under emergency protection orders (*Children and Young People on Child Protection Registers*, DoH 1995/13). In March 1993, of children who started to be looked after by local authorities, 1,300 children were subject to emergency protection orders, compared with 630 for 1992 (*Children Looked After by Local Authorities*, 1995 Table K 42, 52). This trend suggests that at the outset more children are receiving immediate emergency protection. Where all these 'compulsory' orders are sought, parents have already demonstrated non-co-operation to make such an approach necessary, nevertheless the philosophy of partnership continues to underpin the provisions of these orders as in all others. The emphasis on partnership is indicated by giving notice to parents and to the child, in the case of the child assessment order, and allowing reasonable contact in both the child assessment order and emergency protection order. This approach is markedly different from the pre Children Act period of emergency protection dogged by 'dawn raids', where children were dragged away under a 'place of safety order' lasting for up to 28 days and denied access to parents, as was the experience of children in the cases of Cleveland, Orkney, and Rochdale (see *Re A and others (Minors) (Wardship: Child Abuse: Guidelines)* [1992] 1 All ER 153), and also in the Ayrshire case (see Sheriff Miller's Report 1995, *The Times*, 21 April 1995, Bainham 1993, p. 416, Frost 1990, p. 25). In *Re A*, Hollings J criticised the early morning removals of the children. The Cleveland investigation resulted in 276 applications for orders and 174 were heard by a single magistrate at home (see *Cleveland Report*, Cm. 412, p. 173 para. 10.9). The Carlile Report, *A Child in Mind: Protection of Children in a Responsible Society* (1987) which reported on the circumstances following the death of Kimberley Carlile, considered that there should be other mechanisms for obtaining access in cases where there may be suspicion of abuse but insufficient evidence to justify the grant of 'a place of safety order'. The new orders of child assessment and emergency protection under the Children Act reflect this need for balance.

Although compulsory orders are regarded as the last resort, the preferred procedure is for a child to be received on a voluntary basis for the purpose of investigation. In *Re A (A Minor) (Care Proceedings)* [1993] 1 FCR 824, an emergency protection order was obtained after the birth of the child. In *Re G and R (Minors)*, CA Transcript, 14 March 1995, an emergency protection order was granted in a case which became known as the South Pembrokeshire cases where following an allegation of sexual abuse made by a young boy against his father, a number of adults were arrested and a paedophile investigation instituted. In this particular case the child was placed immediately with foster parents and the interim care order renewed. Once proceedings for care or supervision of a suspected abused child are underway, it may be necessary to safeguard the child by granting an interim care order or interim supervision order under s. 38(1)(b), or to remove the child from the home under a voluntary agreement. Voluntary agreements reflect the partnership principle and the minimal intervention principle, underscoring the Children Act. The idea of the non-interventionist State in child welfare and protection is further underscored by the anticipation that arrangements for child protection may be made with parents on a voluntary basis (s. 20, Children Act 1989). The number of children looked after by voluntary agreement increased from 17,500 in 1992 to 20,000 in 1993 (Children Act 1993, s. 34) indicative of the 'success' of the application of this partnership principle. A study by Plotnikoff and

Woolfson (1994), however, has shown alarmingly that cases were taking a long time to reach a conclusion and that this delay has worsened since the introduction of the Act. This is clearly reflected in the increasing number of interim orders made. In 1993, of children who started to be looked after, 1,000 were under s. 38 interim care orders, compared with 400 in 1992 (*Children Looked After by Local Authorities*, DoH 1995 Table K). These interim orders depend in most cases on removing the child victim from the home. (See *Re W (A Minor) (Interim Care Order)* [1994] 2 FLR 892 *Re R and G (Minors) (Interim Care or Supervision Order)* [1994] 1 FLR 793.)

The Children Act made no provision for removing the suspect abuser from the family home. The solution to child protection in the removal of children from the home rather than the suspect abuser has been widely criticised by family lawyers and those working with children (see Bainham 1993, pp. 434–5). In 1992, the Law Commission responded to this concern and considered proposals for the removal of the suspect abuser. In their report *Domestic Violence and Occupation of the Family Home* (1992 No. 207), they recommended a short term ouster order with the power to attach a power of arrest (paras. 6.15–6.22).

There are obviously cases where a child needs immediate and guaranteed protection from risk of serious harm which can only be given by removal from home. There are other cases where instant removal is not obviously the answer, but there are serious concerns and it is difficult to know whether the trauma to the child of a hasty or unjustified removal will be greater than the hazards of leaving him at home pending further investigations. Sudden removal from home, whatever its deficiencies, always carries some risk to the child's welfare, varying with the age of the child and how the removal is done (para. 6.16).

In an attempt to circumvent this obvious lacuna in the Children Act, s. 54 has been used by local authorities, albeit unsuccessfully, to remove suspect abusers from the family home. In *Nottingham CC v P* [1993] 2 FLR 134, the local authority attempted to oust the father from the home via a 'prohibited steps order' under s. 8. Sir Stephen Brown in his judgment, said that the step taken to oust a father via the route of a prohibited steps order was 'wholly inappropriate', but he clearly shared the concerns of the local authority, '. . . at the absence of any power to direct [the] authority to take steps to protect the children'. Likewise, a specific issue order under s. 8, was applied for in the case of *Pearson v Franklin* [1994] 2 All ER 137, where a mother wished to remove the father from the house. Here the court said that the purpose of such an order is for determining a specific question in relation to an aspect of parental responsibility and it was not to be used to oust 'since a right of occupation would be interfered with' (per Nourse LJ). In *Re S (Minors) (Inherent Jurisdiction: Ouster)* [1994] 1 FLR 623, the local authority sought an order under the inherent jurisdiction of the court to oust a stepfather following allegations of sexual abuse, the threshold conditions were satisfied and where an order under s. 38(2) was and s. 34 was not deemed appropriate.

In response to these concerns the Family Homes and Domestic Violence Bill [HL] 1995, now incorporated in the Family Law Bill [HL] 16 November 1995, provides for the removal of an alleged abuser, but only where the courts have granted an emergency protection order or an interim care order. As already indicated, very few emergency protection orders are in fact granted and they are considered the last resort where parents refuse to co-operate and where the child is in immediate danger. Second, fewer interim care orders are granted where child protection is resolved wherever possible by voluntary agreement. Arguably, the new provision of ousting the alleged abuser is limited in its practical application and will not be available to many children who might need it. Clause 47 Sch. 6 amends s. 38(1) and provides the power to include an exclusion requirement in interim care orders and an exclusion requirement in emergency protection orders (s. 44A(1)). Furthermore, and equally worrying, the court may also accept undertakings in lieu of exclusion orders in both these circumstances.

The new provisions, now contained within the Family Law Bill, will not provide the much needed panacea for child protection since the duration of the emergency protection order is limited to 15 days, allowing the alleged abuser to return after this very short period. Local authorities will now be mandated to apply for one or the other of the orders of interim care or emergency protection as a prerequisite of removing the alleged abuser, procedures which are exorbitantly expensive. Local authorities, in pursuing an interim care order as it confers custody on the local authority, may also find that many more cases are contested by parents and relatives on this basis which will result in considerable financial implications. Whilst the ousting of the suspect abuser is important, the procedures to achieve this result may have undermined its potential efficacy.

Care proceedings

In safeguarding the protection of children, the philosophy of promoting partnership between parents and/or the local authority is premised on an idealistic vision of family autonomy, free from State interference. In promoting this approach the principle of facilitating the upbringing of children within the family so long as it is safe to do so is emphasised (s. 17(1)). This statutory objective was stated by the Court of Appeal in *Re M* [1994] 3 All ER 298, where the father killed the mother with a meat cleaver. The court asserted that weight had to be given to the principle of:

> The availability of an extended family carer is only one of the factors that has to be considered, albeit a very weighty one, but which in this case, in my judgment correctly, has been considered to be outweighed by accumulation of other factors to which I have referred. Of course, as was accepted, there are always risks in adoption: the task a local authority and a guardian and, in the last resort, a court has is to carry out a balancing of the risks on either side (cited in *Oldham* [1994] 1 FLR 574).

The partnership concept emerged partially in response to the overwhelming public concern over the methods employed by local authorities following Cleveland where intervention by the State is regarded as a last resort and voluntary agreement encouraged as between the State and those exercising parental responsibility. The non-interference lobby will be further fuelled by Sheriff Miller's report on the Ayrshire case where children were removed for up to five years and parents denied all contact. It is agreed that where the private orders under s. 8, of contact, residence, prohibited steps and specific issue are being considered then partnership is appropriate and important, but where significant harm /abuse is suspected, attempts to tread the path of partnership are ill founded and likely to be detrimental and potentially dangerous for the child concerned. Bray argues, 'One of the most tragic weaknesses in the Act is that it apparently fails completely to take into account what we as a society already know about the characteristics of people, parents or otherwise, who abuse their children, in physical, emotional and sexual ways' (1994, p. 60). Freeman (1994) has similarly indicated that partnership is largely illusory. This is not the view of all child care experts, Masson (1994, p. 173), for example, is of the view that the House of Lords decision in *Re M* (above), has weakened the position of the family, arguing, 'The protection of the child will be less a matter of partnership between the family and the state and more a matter for local authority policy'. In *Re M* a relative was able to care for a child under a residence order but the local authority preferred a care order. Where a local authority applies for a compulsory order, a care or a supervision order may be made. The effect of a care order under s. 31(1)(a) of the Act, is to place a child under the care of a local authority with parents, others, in children's homes or with foster parents (see *Children Looked After By Local Authorities*, DoH 1995, p. 35), and a supervision order (s. 31(1)(b)), places a child under the supervision of a local authority or probation officer, where the child is placed usually at home or with those exercising parental responsibility. In March 1993 as few as 40 supervision orders carried a residence requirement (*Children Looked After by Local Authorities*, DoH 1995, p. 47). Both these orders may be made in relation to a child who has reached the age of 17 years. Very few orders for care or supervision are in fact made for 16 and 17 year olds, this age group accounting for only 40 people who started to be looked after in 1992 and 40 in 1993 under s. 31, and only 10 supervision orders with residence for both 1992 and 1993 respectively (*Children Looked After by Local Authorities*, DoH, Table FK). Under s. 38, for 1993, 40 16 and 17 year olds were the subject of an interim care order, and 290 were the subject of a care order under s. 31(1)(a). Under the Children Act 1989, s. 31(3) care or supervision orders may not be made where the child has reached 17 although there were 430 deemed care orders (resolutions made prior to 14 October 1991). The fact is that for 17 year olds provision is inadequate (see Lowe (1989) 139 NLJ 87). This leaves older children in a totally unsupported vacuum where protection is suspended. Children must wait until 18 for their rights to provision of a roof provided by the local authority and the provision of income support (Social Security Act 1986, s. 4(1)) and presumably must take action on their own behalf against an alleged abuser. In furthering the endeavour towards enhancing the relevance of the child's views, s. 10(8) provides the child with the right to be given leave to start or join in family proceedings thereby making an application on its own behalf. Notwithstanding, the courts have been reluctant to accede to children making applications, on grounds that they are not competent (see Lyon and Parton 1995). The State, in this way, has covertly manipulated the problem of adolescent vulnerability.

When considering an application for either care or supervision (s. 31), the court must also consider the alternative of a s. 8(1) order, referred to as the private orders or arrangements made for children including residence and contact order, and orders for specific issue and prohibited steps. It may be the case that a private law order, such as a residence order, can be used to protect a child adequately from abuse as where a child may be placed with a relative or grandparent without the need of a care or supervision order. A residence order is an order 'settling the arrangements to be made as to the person with whom a child is to live' (s. 8(1)). The new order accommodates a much wider set of living arrangements than the old law, for example residence can be made in favour of two persons who do not live together. It can be made to a person who does not have parental responsibility as, for example, a relative, as a result that person will acquire parental responsibility by virtue of the order (s. 12(2)). It is for a fixed period (s. 11(7)(c)). Anyone who is entitled to apply for a s. 8 order can also apply for a variation or discharge (s. 8 (2)) of the order. In the period 1992–1993 a s. 8 order for residence or contact was granted in public law proceedings in 2,398 cases (see *Children Act Report* 1993, p. 20).

A contact order is an order 'requiring the person with whom a child lives . . . to allow the child to visit or stay with the person named in the order' (s. 8(1)). This replaces the old order for access. Prior to the Children Act there was a conflict between whether contact was the right of the parent or the right of the child (although in *M* v *M (Child Access)* [1973] 2 All ER 81, it was perceived as the right of the child). It is formulated rather differently under the Children Act in that it does not provide for the non-custodial parent to have access to the child but for the child to visit and in many cases stay with the parent, reflecting the independent claims of the child. Contact is rarely denied by the courts. So in *Re B (Minors Access)* [1992] 1 FLR 142, where the father was eccentric and bizarre, on one occasion having walked down the road with a plastic bag on his head, and on another occasion attempting to set fire to grass where the children were sitting, the court said that it ought not to deprive the father of defined access (now contact) provided there was no suggestion of violence or verbal aggression nor that there was a risk that he might use access to undermine the children's feelings towards their mother. A child's request for 'no contact' was acceded in *Re F* [1993] 1 FCR 945, where the children aged 12 and 9 wanted no contact with a transsexual father. It is child abuse, physical or sexual which may result in the court denying contact (see *C* v *C (Child Abuse: Access)* [1988] 1 FLR 462; *Re R (A Minor) (Child Abuse: Access)* [1988] 1 FLR 206). Even where there is abuse, contact may be allowed in 'appropriate' cases (see *H* v *H (Child Abuse: Access)* [1989] 1 FLR 212, where there had been sexual abuse on a five year old girl. In *L* v *L (Child Abuse: Access)* [1989] 2 FLR 16, where a finding of sexual abuse had been made, contact was not ruled out on the grounds that a close bond existed and the children were socially adjusted).

As part of the purpose of empowering children, a child may make an application for a residence order (see *Re SC (A minor) (Leave to seek residence order)* [1994] 1 FLR 96). Here S sought a residence order to allow her to leave the children's home and live with a friend who would assume parental responsibility. S's mother opposed the application for leave. The court were satisfied that S had a sufficient understanding of the situation to enable the court to grant her leave to make an application. In *Re AD (A Minor) (Child's Wishes)* [1993] Fam L 43, a child applied for an order under s. 8 to obtain a residence order so that she could live with her boyfriend's parents. Given the difficulty in securing a care or supervision order, parents might be persuaded to resolve problems for their children by making use instead of these private orders.

Statutory interpretation: significant harm

There has been considerable debate too over the legal construction of the term 'significant harm' which, where proven, provides the trigger for orders. Sexual abuse, physical abuse, emotional abuse and neglect must be subsumed within the legal construct of significant harm. Section 31(2) provides:

> a court may only make a care order or supervision order if it is satisfied: (a) that the child concerned is suffering, or is likely to suffer, significant harm; and (b) that the harm, or likelihood of harm, is attributable to: (i) the care given to the child, or likely to be given to him if the order were not made, not being what it would be reasonable to expect a parent to give to him, or (ii) the child's being beyond parental control.

Arguably it is the lack of precise definition which allows the court considerable flexibility and margin to intervene in a wide range of harmful or potentially harmful circumstances. The definition embraces both an objective and a subjective test of harm, including evidence of harm (objective) and the effect and impact of the harm on the child concerned (subjective). Thus harm may be considered significant regardless of the perceived effect on the child: it is not necessary therefore to assess degrees of damage to the child in emotional, psychological or other terms. This objective/subjective divide is indicated in the *Guidance to the Act* (para. 3.19), where significant harm may be derived from '... the seriousness of the harm or in the implications of it', and adds that it will be a 'finding of fact for the court' (para. 3.19).

What is harm?   The meaning of significant harm is contained in s. 31(9) amounting to 'ill treatment or the impairment of health or development'. When looking to satisfy the criterion of harm, the court may be satisfied that any one of three elements, i.e., 'ill treatment', 'impairment of health' or 'impairment of development' is present. It is not necessary to establish evidence of all three (see the guidance offered by the Department of Health, *The Children Act 1989 Guidance and Regulations*, Vol. 1, Court Orders, 1991). As Bainham (1993) notes, the construction of this section of the Act was bound to give rise to ambiguity and litigation. In the case of *Newham London Borough Council* v *AG* [1993] 1 FLR 281 at 289, the court emphasised that whilst the wording of the Act was to be considered, the words were not intended to be unduly restrictive. This point was affirmed by Thorpe J in *Re A (A Minor) (Care Proceedings)* [1993] 1 FCR 824, where in interpreting this section he said 'On the application of the check-list did the risk of harm to this child outweigh the obvious advantage to any child of natural parenting?'.

Harm is to be set against a comparator and s. 31(10) provides 'that could reasonably be expected of a similar child'. The DHSS *Review of Child Care Law* stated:

> Having set an acceptable standard of upbringing for the child, it should be necessary to show some substantial deficit in that standard. Minor shortcomings in the health and care provided or minor defects in physical, psychological or social development should not give rise to any compulsory intervention unless they are having, or likely to have, serious and lasting effects upon the child (para. 15(15)).

Difficulties have arisen however over what is meant by 'impairment' and what can be expected of 'reasonable'. The court has held that it must be judged by looking at what might reasonably be expected of a child with similar characteristics. The courts have wrestled with the 'similar child' construct. In its consideration of *Re O (A Minor) (Care order: Education Procedure)* [1992] 2 FLR 7, the court was dealing with a young girl who had been truanting from school. The local authority justified its application for a care order rather than an education supervision order, on the basis that all that could be achieved by an education supervision order had been unsuccessful (NB: under the Children Act there is no power to commit a child to care for truancy, therefore the only route into care is via s. 31). The ingredient focused on was 'impairment of intellectual or social development'. The issue for the court's consideration was whether she had suffered significant harm and that judgment could only properly be made by comparison with a similar child. Ewbank J held:

> In my judgment, in the context of this type, a child of equivalent intellectual and social development, who has gone to school and not merely an average child who may or may not be at school. In fact what one has to ask oneself is whether this child suffered significant harm by not going to school. The answer in my judgment, as in the magistrates' judgment, is obvious.

Fortin (1993), comments that it does not appear that there was any attempt to consider evidence about the progress of a similar child. The evidence of the *guardian ad litem* and the educational psychologist did not make any comparison with a 15 year old girl who had not attended school. In fact the educational psychologist said:

O was a girl of average general ability; she had a good vocabulary, she reads novels for pleasure; her writing is neat and legible, spelling good, she writes at a good speed; her mental arithmetic ability is slightly below average for her age, which probably reflects missing school; she is numerate and has no specific difficulty with mathematics (see Fortin 1993, p. 152).

Thus, it would appear that development does not have to be the best that can be expected but reasonable, and any deficit has to be substantial. Fortin writes (p. 151), 'It is particularly regrettable that none of the doubts surrounding s. 31(10) were properly considered in *Re O (A Minor)(Care order: Education Procedure)* [1992] 2 FLR 7.' Harm may also embrace bizarre and frightening behaviour as in *Re J (a minor)* 11 June 1994 Lexis where the teenage mother was said to have a severe personality disorder, emotional problems and the local authority wished to place the nine month old baby boy for adoption.

On the boundaries of harm   Yet, whilst eliminating the problem of State intervention often based on bourgeois moralism about childrearing practices and standards of home care has also led in some cases to exposing children to great harm and neglect resulting in death. Again the resiling from bourgeois moralism has influenced the construction of what is a 'similar child', with the result that the child ought to be one with the same innate characteristics rather than one from the same social, economic or cultural background. This is to avoid any discrimination against children who are from impoverished, disadvantaged backgrounds since we might be arguing that treatment of a disadvantaged child would be reasonable whilst the same treatment received by a middle class child might be considered unreasonable. As Hoggett (1993, p. 181), notes '... It may be difficult to tell the difference'. Freeman (1994) notes the dangers and raises the problem of the extent to which cultural pluralism should be taken into account, raising the question whether the hypothetical reasonable parent has to be located within the dominant white English Christian culture. Childrearing practices may vary and the problem is illustrated by the judgment of the court in *Re H* [1987] 2 FLR 12, where a Vietnamese mother's chastisement practice was judged against '... reasonably objective standards of the culture in which the child is brought up' (see Newson and Newson in Frude).

The Act offers no definition of 'significant', that is the 'degree' of perceived harm, save in the context of the child's health or development. Case law has interpreted 'significant' to imply 'considerable, noteworthy or important'. In *Humberside CC v B* (1993) below, Booth J accepted the local authority's submission that a dictionary definition should be used. The result was that the definition of 'significant' turned upon whether the harm was 'considerable, noteworthy or important,' and that the harm should be considered in the context of the child's future. The *DHSS Review of Child Care* (Law 1985, para. 15.15), considered that having decided what might be reasonable it would be necessary to show a 'substantial deficit'.

Harm when?   The interpretation of the phrase, the child 'is suffering or is likely to suffer' has led to some extraordinary flights of interpretation. The current position after some wrangling is found in *Re M (A Minor) (Care Order: Threshold Conditions)* [1994] 2 FLR 577, where Lord Mackay said:

> ... there is much to be said for the view that the hearing that Parliament contemplated was one which extended from the time the jurisdiction of the court is first invoked until the case is disposed of and that was required to be done in the light of the general principle that any delay in determining the question is likely to prejudice the welfare of the child. There is nothing in s. 31(2) which in my opinion requires that the conditions to be satisfied are to be disassociated from the time of the making of the application by the local authority. I would conclude that the natural construction of the conditions in s. 31(2) is that where, at the time the application is to be disposed of, there are in place arrangements for the protection of the child by the local authority on an interim basis which protection has been continuously in place for some time, the relevant date with respect to which the court must be satisfied is the date at which the local authority initiated the procedure for protection under the Act from which these arrangements followed. If after a local authority had initiated protective arrangements the need for these had terminated because the child's welfare had been satisfactorily provided for otherwise, in any subsequent proceedings, it would not be possible to found jurisdiction on the situation at the time of initiation of these arrangements.

The preceding case law betrays confusion and conflict concerning whether the relevant time is at the time of the application or at the time of the hearing. The relevant case law on this point commences arguably with *Re D* [1987] AC 317, where Lord Goff said, 'The words "is being" are in the continuous present. So there has to be a continuum in existence at the relevant time, which is when the magistrates consider whether to make a place of safety order.'. According to this interpretation the child must be suffering at the time of the court order. In contradistinction, Lord Brandon said, '... the court, in considering, as at the point of time immediately before the process of protecting the child is concerned is first put into motion ... must look both at the situation as it is at the point of time and also at the situation as it had been in the past.'.

In *Northamptonshire County Council* v *S* [1993] Fam 136, the meaning of 'is suffering or is likely to suffer' was held to refer to the situation and circumstances before the legal process of protecting the child began, thus following Lord Brandon in *Re D*. This case involved two children, a girl, E aged 6 and a boy, C aged two and a half. The family proceedings refused the paternal grandmother's application for a residence order and made care orders in respect of both children and ordered a contact order in favour of the father. The court on appeal rejected the father's argument that the court should not have made a care order because of the use of the present tense in s. 31(2). Ewbank J held that the meaning of 'is suffering' applies to the period immediately before the action commenced. The principle that suffering in the past is a guide to the future 'likely to suffer', was affirmed in *Re B (A Minor) (Care Order: Criteria)* [1993] 1 FLR 815, where Douglas Brown J seemed to ally himself with the Brandon view in *Re D*, when he held that the court was not confined to facts only existing at the date of the hearing. In *Re M* [1994] 1 FLR 73, the Court of Appeal, in an extraordinary ruling, declared this line of argument to be wrong, and overruled all previous case law on the point, requiring instead evidence of present or future harm at the actual date of the hearing. In this case, the father murdered the mother when the child was four months old and the mother's cousin later applied for a s. 8 residence order. The father and the *guardian ad litem* appealed against the decision and supported the making of a care order. The original order of Bracewell J, following *Northamptonshire* (above) was overruled in the application of the test to the period immediately before the process of protecting the child was put into motion. The Court of Appeal substituted a residence order in favour of the mother's cousin and held that the harm must be suffered at the relevant time, i.e., when the court makes its decision, reaching the conclusion that the reasoning in *Re D* was incorrect and concluded in the absence of a sensible alternative that the court should make a residence order. Balcombe LJ said:

> The use of the present tense in the first of these alternatives — 'is suffering' — makes it clear that the harm must be being suffered at the relevant time, which is when the court has to be satisfied of the fulfilment of the threshold conditions, i.e., when it decides whether or not to make a care order ... Of course, this does not mean that the child must be suffering significant harm at the precise moment when the court is considering whether the threshold conditions are satisfied: it is sufficient if there is a continuum in existence at that time.

The Court of Appeal in making a residence order in favour of the father's cousin did, however, achieve one principle of the Act, namely, the endeavour to keep families together wherever possible.

In *Re M* [1994] 2 FLR 577 Lord Templeman, in returning statutory purpose to some stability, said that the decision of the Court of Appeal was an illustration of the tyranny of language and the importance of giving effect to the spirit rather than the letter of the Act.

Risk of harm: 'likely'   Before making any care or supervision order, to protect a child from abuse, the court must be satisfied on the balance of probabilities that the child is suffering or is likely to suffer significant harm (s. 31(2)(a)) embracing the opportunity for a pre-emptive strike before a child is harmed. There has been considerable ambiguity in the correct test to be applied and where the courts are considering present harm versus future harm, whether a different level of proof should be required.

In assessing 'likely to suffer', it is enough that there is a 'real' risk of the harm occurring and the guiding principle has been whether there is a significant change.

In *Re F (Minors) (Wardship jurisdiction)* [1988] 2 FLR 123 Hollis J said, 'only a real possibility of abuse had to be shown and not a probability' although this was criticised by Purchas J for being less than a balance of probabilities. In *Re G (A minor) (Child abuse: standard of proof)* [1987] 1 WLR 1461, 1466, Sheldon J said:

> ... a higher degree of probability is required to satisfy the court that the father has been guilty of some sexual misconduct with his daughter than would be needed to justify the conclusion that the child has been the victim of some such behaviour of whatever nature and whoever may have been its perpetrators.

In *Newham London Borough Council* v *AG* [1993] 1 FLR 281, where the child was cared for by the grandmother because of the mental illness of the mother, Sir Stephen Brown P argued that 'likely' did not have to be strictly construed:

> Clearly that is not the meaning which could or should be given to the term 'likely to suffer'. The court is not applying a test to events which have happened in the past and deciding on the evidence, on the balance of probabilities, which is the standard of civil proof, whether such an event has in fact happened. That is not what is involved in this case.... You can prove that a past event has happened.

Sir Stephen Brown P quoted with approval the ruling in *Davies* v *Taylor* [1974] AC 207, where Lord Reid said, '... but you cannot prove that a future event will happen and I do not think that the law is so foolish as to suppose that you can. All that you can do is to evaluate the chance. Sometimes it is virtually 100%: sometimes virtually nil. But often it is somewhere in between.'. The Court in *Newham* concluded that, '... in looking to the future the court has to assess the risk. Is this child likely to suffer significant harm?'. The likelihood of future harm exercised the consideration of the court in *Re H (A Minor) (Section 37 Direction)* [1993] 2 FLR 541, Scott Baker J emphasised that:

> the likelihood of harm is not confined to present or near future but applies to the ability of a parent or carer to meet the emotional needs of a child in the years ahead ... I am not limited ... to looking at the past and immediate future. If a court concludes that a parent, or a carer, is likely to be unable to meet the emotional needs of a child in the future — even if years hence — my view is that the condition in s. 31 (2) would probably be met.

In *Re H and R (Child Sexual Abuse: Standard of Proof)* [1995] 1 FLR 643, the court adopted a two stage approach to the standard of proof, which it argued in sexual abuse cases must be proved to a standard beyond a mere balance of probability. The court rejected the submission of counsel, 'Parents and families also have to be protected from unwarranted interference by the State and one purpose of the threshold criteria is to strike a balance.', although Kennedy LJ, interpreting s. 31(2)(a) dissented and held that a lower standard of proof may be appropriate where the courts are considering '. . . is suffering, or is likely to suffer, significant harm'.

> But I, for my part, do not accept that if the evidence relates to alleged misconduct on the part of, for example, a man who is or is about to become a member of the child's household, that misconduct must itself be proved on a balance of probabilities before the evidence can be used to satisfy the criteria in s. 31(2)(a).

The position seems to be that the standard of proof required for both 'is suffering' or 'is likely to suffer' is pitched at a higher level than in other cases. The decision of the appeal court was upheld by the House of Lords (*Re H and R (Child Sexual Abuse: Standard of Proof)* [1996] 1 FLR 80, although the House of Lords conceded that a court could conclude that there was a real possibility of suffering harm in the future even though harm in the past had not been established. Lord Browne-Wilkinson, parting company with the majority, said he was 'anxious that the decision of the House in this case may establish the law in an unworkable form to the detriment of many children at risk'. *(Re B (Child Sexual Abuse: Standard of Proof)* [1995] 1 FLR 904).

Re H and R [1995] returns us to an overly cautious interpretation in line with earlier cases, rejecting the view in *Re H* [1993] thereby defeating the purpose of the Act in providing for a pre-emptive strike.

No orders   Where in the court's view, the threshold criteria are not satisfied they may refuse the application. In 1993, 'refusals' constituted 1.4 per cent of all care order applications, 0.8 per cent of supervision orders, 3.3 per cent of emergency protection orders. (*Children Act Report*, 1993, (1994) Table 3.1). Where the threshold criteria are satisfied then there is the presumption against a court order which applies during marriage and also on divorce and also in cases involving harm. The balance to be struck is whether the risk of harm to the child outweighs the obvious advantage to the child of natural parenting (*Re A* above). Section 1(5) of the Act introduces the novel presumption that a court will only make an order if doing so would be better for the child than making no order at all. 'Where a court is considering whether or not to make one or more orders under this Act with respect to a child, it shall not make the order or any of the orders unless it considers that doing so would be better for the child than making no order at all.' This places the burden on the person wanting to make the order to explain to the court why an order is better than leaving things as they are. In consideration of whether to make an order or not, the court must place the child's welfare as the paramount consideration (s. 1(1)). In making any orders under s. 8 or a care or supervision order the court must have regard to the criteria specified in s. 1(3) which include amongst others, the wishes of the child. Section 1(3) provides, 'A court shall have regard in particular to (a) the ascertainable wishes and feelings of the child concerned (considered in the light of his age and understanding'. When considering these orders the child's welfare, and child's rights for the first time may supersede the parental right. So how have the child's interests been balanced in the consideration of the making of an order? The decision in *Birmingham CC* v

H (No. 2) [1993] 1 FLR 883, highlights the uncertainty and ambivalence in the application of this principle, where the Court of Appeal held that neither the interests of the child nor the interests of the mother should be given priority in a case involving contact between a mother and her son. The percentage rate of no orders in public law proceedings at 3.6% of care orders granted (see Table 17) is to be contrasted in cases where orders under s. 8 are being sought. Here the tendency is to leave things as they are to a much greater extent (see Table 20).

Table 20: Disposal of selected applications in private law proceedings 1993–1994

nature of application	withdrawn		refused		no order		granted		% no order as a % of (d) and (c)	
	(a)		(b)		(c)		(d)		(e)	
	1993	1994	1993	1994	1993	1994	1993	1994	1993	1994
parental responsibility										
s. 8	2,068	2,499	509	545	392	372	3,412	3,885	10.3	8.7
residence	4,720	5,503	972	1,004	2,239	2,436	22,264	24,012	9.1	9.2
contact	7,962	8,943	1,956	2,113	4,044	4,166	27,780	31,506	12.7	11.7
prohibited steps	1,214	1,202	317	316	483	453	6,631	5,974	6.8	7.0
specific issue	308	401	137	154	174	202	1,563	1,810	10.0	10.0

Source: Judicial Statistics Annual Report 1993/1994 (derived from Table 5.3)

It is clear from the 1993 figures that in an increasing number of cases on divorce 'no order' orders are made presumably with the intention of preserving joint parental responsibility. The spirit behind the 'no order' rule is that parents should try to agree with each other and/or Social Services about what is best for children. This represents a significant de-legalisation where the Children Act '... marks a radical and restrictive view of the right of the state to interfere in private arrangements' (Dewar 1993, p. 349). Dewar argues that this is evidence that the law, 'is in retreat in relation to intervention in family life. The emphasis moves away from compromise between the interests or rights of parent versus child, it moves away from striking a balance between parents and child to a position where the emphasis is on the child's interests.'. But what does this presumption achieve for child protection? It means that even where significant harm is found an order will not automatically follow. The justification cannot be based on the principle of letting parents sought out matters when clearly one or both parents have forfeited that right by their conduct. How can the extension of this no order principle carte blanche be sustained? Freeman suggests it may be because, 'There is too much foster care breakdown and too much abuse in care for anyone to believe that a care order is any kind of panacea' (1994, p. 29). This hardly seems a reason for sending children back into abusive families.

In *Re M (A Minor) (App No. 2)* [1994] 1 FLR 59, where the local authority applied, there was evidence of both neglect and physical abuse, a duodenal haematoma, the child was underweight and emaciated, and there was evidence of multiple bruising to the shins, knees, buttocks, face, chest and back, which were denied by the mother and boyfriend. The judge was not prepared to find that the mother or the stepfather had beaten or starved the child and did not make any order. He went on to consider s. 1(5), concluding that he would 'give the parents a chance', and the child was returned to the mother. The court had heard that the child had told her foster mother, 'On Christmas Day I could not finish my dinner. Daddy started kicking me and punching — then Mummy' and had told her *guardian ad litem* that she did not want to live with her mother and wished to live with her grandparents. This evidence was not admitted since it only tended to confirm the view that the child was ambivalent about returning home to her parents. This case well illustrates the problems posed by the standard of proof in such cases detailed earlier. Spencer sums up the problem thus:

> The consequence of finding that the parents nearly killed their child when they did not will be that the child will be removed from them. The consequence of wrongly finding they did not do it when they did is likely to be the refusal to make a care order, and the child being returned to the people who nearly killed her.

Since the court is required to consider the 'ascertainable wishes and feelings of the child', this provides another example of where the courts are prepared to override children's wishes. In the year up to September 1993, where the court considered a care order application, taking orders granted, and applications refused, in 3.3 per cent an order of 'no order' was made. This compared to an order of 'no order' in 3.7 per cent of supervision orders sought and 1.0 per cent in emergency protection order applications (see *Children Act Report*, 1993, Table 3.1) (see Table 23 above for similar rates in 1993–4). This must mean that more children are being abused and not, as the government would have us believe, fewer.

Case law reflects the considerable judicial ambiguity and ambivalence over the correct procedure to follow. It is clearly a two stage process where once significant harm is established the second test is to consider whether to make an order or not. Some courts on a finding of significant harm have *ipso facto* made an order, whilst others in applying s. 1(5) have considered whether to make an order or not. In *Northamptonshire CC v S and others* [1993] 1 FLR 554, Ewbank J's interpretation of s. 1(5) stated that the correct procedure was:

> The fact that the threshold test is met does not mean that the family proceedings court has to make a court order ... the justices have the choice once the threshold conditions are met of making a care order, of making a supervision order, or of making any other order under the Children Act 1989.

In *Humberside CC v B* [1993] 1 FLR 257, where the parents were diagnosed schizophrenics and there was bruising to a six month old child, Booth J held:

> The court, on being satisfied as to the criteria, is then required to have regard to the welfare of the child, and the matters set out in s. 1 of the Act. In my

judgment it is at that stage that the court is determining a question with respect to the upbringing of the child so that the child's welfare must be the court's paramount consideration. Section 1 (4) enjoins the court in considering whether or not to make, vary or discharge either a s. 8 order or an order under Part IV of the Act, the Part under which these proceedings were founded, to have regard in particular to the matters set out in s. 1(3).

However, in *Kent CC* v *C* [1993] 1 FLR 308, where an application was being contested, the court took a rather different approach. Ewbank J said, 'The mother and the *guardian ad litem* agreed that the conditions were met and accordingly there was *no contest* on the question of whether a care order should be made'. This approach begs the question whether judges are more likely to ignore this second stage of the 'no order' presumption, where applications for care orders are uncontested. If this is the case then courts are applying the balancing act as between the competing interests of local authorities and families, rather than what is best for the child itself and the application of the welfare principle.

Interpretation of national care trends   How far has the Children Act been successful in protecting children? In making an assessment, rather than focusing exclusively on the appeal court and statutory construction, the answer lies in considering what is happening on the ground. What is of immediate significance and of enormous concern is the decline in orders for care and supervision since the introduction of the Act. In 1992, 54,500 children were looked after by local authorities, by 1993 this had fallen to 52,000. A total of 29,100 children started to be looked after in the year ending March 1993 compared with 29,400 children in 1991. The proportion of children under care orders constituted 67 per cent (36,300) of all local authority cases in 1992 and 60 per cent (31,700) in 1993. Most of these children were the subject of deemed orders, that is orders made prior to the Children Act coming into force.

In 1993, 2,200 children started to be looked after under emergency protection orders and 1,000 children were admitted under interim care orders. Overall, however, it is to be noted that in 1982, 88,663 children were in care compared with 52,000 in 1993 (see *Children Looked After by Local Authorities*, Table D, 1995). By contrast, the number of children looked after by voluntary agreement (s. 20) represented 29 per cent (17,615) of all orders at March 1991, 32 per cent of orders (17,500) at March 1992, and 37 per cent at March 1993 (19,800) (see Table 4.1 *The Children Act Report*, reproduced here as Table 21).

Table 21: Children looked after or cared for by local authorities

Legal Status	1991	1992	1993
all children looked after		54,800	54,000
all children looked after			
excl. cats. not in care prior to CA 1989	59,834	54,400	52,000
CARE ORDERS	41,638	36,300	31,700
interim orders		2,300	1,700
full care orders		860	3,000
deemed care orders		32,600	26,900
interim orders CYPA 1969		600	100
interim wardship		1,000	
criminal care orders		530	
on remand or detained in la accommodation	581	410	300
emergency protection orders		90	100
other excl. s. 20 CA		130	400
accommodated under s. 20	17,615	17,500	19,800
s. 20 CA short term placements			
episodes recorded		400	400
agreement recorded			1,300

Source: The Children Act Report, 1993, Table 4.1

What do these trends mean for child protection? The government has consistently, since the inception of the Act, interpreted this inverse relationship as evidence that the partnership approach to child care is working and that children are remaining with the family, State intervention operating only as a very last resort. The decrease in children under care or supervision orders cannot simply be hailed as a success since, if there is no evidence of change in the behaviour of parents and families towards children in their care, we can assume that an equally valid conclusion to be drawn is that an increasing number of children are left with abusing adults. In addition, if one of the objectives of the Act is to provide for the opportunity of removing a child where significant harm 'is likely', i.e., the notion of pre-emptive strike, then extending the circumstances under which intervention is legal would *ipso facto* produce an increase not decrease in orders. The number of 'no orders' and 'refusals' has cast its shadow on local authorities seeking protection for children. It is undoubtedly the case that the shadow of the law is impacting on applications made and on withdrawals. In applications in public law proceedings over 30 per cent are withdrawn.

Fortin (1993, p. 155) argues, 'it is widely suggested that it is the "no order" principle contained in section 1(5) which is responsible for the considerable drop in applications for care orders, rather than the difficulty of satisfying the court on the requirements of section 31.'. Evidence suggests that where the family are 'co-operating' then a 'no order' would be most likely to apply, in an attempt to acknowledge the partnership principle. Whatever the competing arguments, many agree with consternation that the only interpretation is that some children are being left in abusive homes (Bray 1994, p. 71).

PROTECTING CHILD SEX ABUSERS

Few child sexual abusers face court proceedings and fewer still are convicted, '... it is widely agreed that parents and guardians are often unwilling for children to give evidence and that when children do testify these difficulties sometimes inhibit the giving of a full account and, on occasion, prevent the courts from receiving coherent evidence at all ... this leads to some unjustifiable acquittals ...' (Pigot 1989, p. 17, para. 2.15). The prosecutor's 'realistic prospect of conviction' test has proved to be an almost unsurmountable hurdle to criminal proceedings, and in civil law the standard of proof in cases of sexual abuse is higher than in any other (see Re G [1988] 1 FLR 314, 320, 321; Re H and Re K [1989] above). In addition, until the 1989 Children Act, the evidence of children had to be sworn. The judicial obstructions are compounded further by the fact that many child sexual abusers deny the abuse. In a study in Bexley, as many as 86 per cent of suspects denied the allegations made against them. In addition, children have variously been considered too young and too unreliable to give evidence and thus have been excluded. Presumptions about young children infect the legal process, for example, children make poor witnesses because their memories are unreliable, they are highly suggestible, they do not understand the duty to tell the truth in court and above all they make false accusations and often lie about such matters (see Spencer and Flin 1993, Hedderman 1987, p. 3).

The view that the legal process is undoubtedly harmful and doubly victimises the child is shared by all practitioners working in the field. This led, in 1984, to the 15th report of the Criminal Law Revision Committee, to recommend that the prosecution of child sexual abusers should be a last resort.

Both we and the Policy Advisory Committee consider that the intervention of the criminal law should be as limited as possible in practice and principally directed to ending the relationship and protecting any younger children of the family. The institution of criminal proceedings and the punishment of those involved may cause added distress to, and even harm, the very persons whom the law is seeking to protect ... (Cmnd. 9213, p. 72, para. 8.43).

The 1980s has witnessed concerted efforts by those working with children and within the legal process to reform the rules of evidence in order to provide support and assistance to children in the giving of evidence. Legislative changes have allowed for children to give evidence unsworn, without the need for corroboration of material substance, provided children with the opportunity to give evidence from behind a screen to lessen their trauma and abolished the necessity of the old style committal which meant that children were cross-examined both at the magistrates' court as well as the Crown Court. In addition, there is a greater willingness shown by the CPS to prosecute suspects several years after the event (*Wilkinson* [1996] 1 Cr App R 81).

Evidential obstructions — competence requirement

It has been an erstwhile presumption of evidence that young children are not considered competent largely because they do not understand the oath and because children are considered unreliable witnesses (see Spencer and Flin 1993, p. 285). After a concerted campaign by the NSPCC, children were permitted under the Criminal Law Amendment Act 1885, s. 4, to give unsworn evidence, although this applied only to trials for unlawful sexual intercourse with girls under 13, and was introduced in response to the problems of the white slave traffic and juvenile and child prostitution. The Children and Young Persons Act 1933, s. 38(1), enabled children to give unsworn evidence in all criminal trials where the trial judge was satisfied that he or she was of sufficient intelligence, if, 'in the opinion of the court, he [or she] is possessed of sufficient intelligence to justify reception of the evidence, and understands the duty of speaking the truth.'. Arguably, this gave judges a very wide discretion, yet case law shows that they have interpreted this provision with exceeding caution. Moreover, the standard for assessing whether the child is competent, that is understands the duty of speaking the truth, a standard which is that of 'beyond reasonable doubt', is based on a test which at best is variable and at worst capricious, including questions varying from asking the child what she understands about God, and about lying. In *Hampshire* [1995] 2 All ER 1019, the Court of Appeal ruled that where a judge considered it necessary to investigate a child's competence to give evidence he should do so in open court in the presence of the accused. In any event there has been a presumption against admitting the evidence of young children. In *Wallwork* (1958) 42 Cr App R 153, a man was convicted of incest (rape) of his five year old daughter. The child had complained to her grandmother, 'Daddy hurt my botty and my privates and made me bleed'. This was corroborated by a doctor. The girl was called as a witness, but said nothing. Lord Goddard acceded to the appellant's grounds of appeal that there had been material irregularities in the admission of hearsay evidence of the child to the grandmother. He said:

> The court deprecates the calling of a child of this age as a witness.... The jury could not attach any value to the evidence of a child of five; it is ridiculous to suppose that they could. Of course, the child could not be sworn. There must be corroborative evidence if a child of tender years and

too young to understand the nature of an oath is called, but in any circumstances to call a little child of the age of five seems to us to be most undesirable, and I hope it will not occur again.

The judge, however, upheld the conviction by means of the proviso. It remains a matter for the judge to decide whether the child may be said to be of 'tender years' or not (see *Campbell* [1956] 2 All ER 272).

The rulings in these cases had their obvious repercussions.

At Winchester Crown Court [X] denied assaulting the girl, then aged six, in Southampton between Sept 2 and 5. Mr David Jenkins, prosecuting counsel, asked Judge Joanne Bracewell if she would hear the girl's evidence. He said he made the application in view of recent Appeal Court decisions which had criticised the use of evidence by little girls. . . . Judge Bracewell said she was 'troubled by the tender age of the witness' and needed time to consider the matter. She retired for ten minutes before ruling: 'This little girl is too young to be called as a witness in this case.' . . . [X], married with a child, was formally found not guilty and released (*Daily Telegraph*, 10 May 1989, Spencer and Flin 1993, p. 55).

As one child care expert remarking on the state of the law at that time said, 'the law as it stands allows paedophiles to molest and photograph children under ten virtually unfettered. One offender actually told me that provided he and his like play safe and stick to even younger children they will be OK because no court will allow children to testify' (see Tate 1990, p. 253).

By 1990, there had been a marginal retreat from the Goddard ruling, in the case of *Re B, The Times*, 1 March 1990, where Lord Lane in the Court of Appeal said that although there was no rigid age limit, a child of five would rarely satisfy the competency test, '. . . It might be very rarely that a child aged five would satisfy the requirement of section 38(1) . . .'. This presumption that a child would, 'rarely satisfy the competency test' was followed in *Wright and Ormerod* (1990) 90 Cr App R 91, where the appellants, who were convicted of indecent assault on a six year old girl, appealed on the grounds that the judge had erred in allowing her to give evidence, where she had testified that they had 'hurt her in the back'. The court in quashing the conviction held, 'In our view, it must require quite exceptional circumstances to justify the reception of this kind of evidence'. Again, in *Z* [1990] 2 QB 355, the appellant was convicted of incest against his five year old daughter but appealed on the grounds that she should not have been allowed to give evidence. Lord Lane in upholding the conviction said there was no arbitrary age below which children's evidence must be rejected, although he went on to comment that a child of five would be competent only very rarely.

It seems to us that Parliament, by repealing the proviso to section 38(1), was indicating a change of attitude by Parliament, reflecting in its turn a change of attitude by the public in general to the acceptability of the evidence of very young children and of an increasing belief that the testimony of young children, when all precautions have been taken, may be just as reliable as that of their elders. For these reasons we would be reluctant in any way to fetter the discretion of the judge set out in section 38(1), save to say, which scarcely needs saying, as already expressed, the younger the child the more care must be taken before admitting the child's evidence.

In *Selby*, 24 May 1991, No. 90/1925/X4, the judge allowed evidence of a four year old child to be admitted (see Spencer and Flin, p. 54). In *CAZ* (1990) 91 Cr App R 203, there was no arbitrary limit imposed by reason of age which should prevent a child from giving unsworn evidence. In *David James N* (1992) 95 Cr App R 256, a conviction for attempted rape and indecent assault by a male cohabitee on a woman's six year old daughter was upheld, the Court of Appeal held that the trial judge had '. . . directed himself on the basis that the case was one of those "rare and exceptional" cases where, notwithstanding the child's age, the evidence should be put before a jury'. In *Norbury* [1992] Crim LR 737, the appellant was convicted of attempted rape and indecent assault on a six year old girl and appealed on the grounds that the trial judge was wrong to have allowed her to give evidence. The Court of Appeal dismissed the appeal concluding that, despite the very young age of the complainant, her evidence was correctly admitted under s. 38(1), Children and Young Persons Act 1933. The Court of Appeal held that s. 34 of the Children and Young Persons Act, as amended by the Criminal Justice Acts of 1988 and 1991 made it possible for unsworn evidence to be admitted and a conviction to follow, notwithstanding the lack of corroborative evidence. There is some concern that although the court is no longer under a duty to inquire into the competence of a young witness, it may still decide that a young child is incompetent under the common law. Spencer and Flin (1993, p. 63) argue that the scheme is flawed since it allows a judge to stand down a child witness if that witness appears not to communicate intelligibly, which now sets children to be judged by the same general standard as adults. Spencer and Flin write, 'There is, unfortunately , a real risk that the provision will indeed be interpreted as preserving or even raising the competency requirement.'.

The corroboration requirement and the duty to warn in cases where evidence is uncorroborated, have further obstructed the prosecution of child sex abusers. Child sexual abuse is perpetrated behind closed doors, out of public gaze, to one or to several children in succession or in concert. Indeed, even when the corroboration requirement was abolished, what amounts to corroboration is restrictive given the rule against cumulative corroboration. In *McInnes* (1990) 90 Cr App R 99, the court accepted that a child's evidence that she was kidnapped and indecently assaulted was corroborated by the fact that she described the features of the interior of the car of which she could not have been aware unless she had been inside it. The insuperable difficulty was acceded in *Campbell* (1956) (above), where Lord Goddard said:

> . . . courts have always warned juries of the danger of convicting on the uncorroborated evidence of a child of tender years, the evidence of such a child could not amount to corroboration unless his or her evidence was also

corroborated. From this, it would seem to follow that a child's evidence would never be corroborated, for if the evidence of the corroborating child had in turn to be corroborated by a person of more mature years it would follow that it would be the latter's evidence that affords the corroboration.

Whilst the 1933 Children and Young Persons Act, s. 38 allowed children to give unsworn evidence in all criminal trials such evidence could only be admitted with the proviso that it had to be corroborated by 'other material evidence'. This stringent requirement was not repealed until the Criminal Justice Act 1988, s. 34(1) repealed the earlier stipulation which required corroboration of a child's unsworn evidence and the ruling (see *Director of Public Prosecution* v *Hester* [1973] AC 296) that the evidence of one child could not corroborate the evidence of another. This meant that where abusers had assaulted several children, if they were too young to take the oath, i.e., give sworn evidence, then after 1988 corroboration was not necessary . This was further amended by the Criminal Justice Act 1991, s. 52 which effectively abolished sworn evidence by children altogether. Section 52(1) of the 1991 Act inserts the following section in the 1988 Act:

33A (1) A child's evidence in criminal proceedings shall be given unsworn. (2) A deposition of a child's unsworn evidence may be taken for the purposes of criminal proceedings as if that evidence had been given on oath. (3) In this section 'child' means a person under fourteen years of age.

Section 52(2) states:

... accordingly the power of the court in any criminal proceedings to determine that a particular person is not competent to give evidence shall apply to children of tender years as it applies to other persons.

In *Whitehouse* [1996] Crim LR 50, where an appeal was dismissed the Court of Appeal said that the evidence of one boy was capable of corroborating the evidence of another. In *R* v *H* (1995) *The Times*, 25 May the House of Lords held that where a defendant had been charged in the same indictment with sexual offences of a similar nature upon an adopted daughter and a step-daughter the judge was entitled to rely on the evidence of each of the complainants as similar fact.

A second modification relates to the duty to warn the jury in cases where evidence was sworn and also in any case involving an allegation of a sexual nature. Judges were provided with a set incantation including the word 'dangerous'. The Criminal Justice Act 1988, s. 34 abolished the judge made rule requiring a warning about the dangers of convicting on uncorroborated evidence of children sworn or unsworn. However these amendments do nothing whatsoever for the victim of child sexual abuse, since all allegations of sexual offences were relegated to a special category or status. Victims of sexual offences, including children, continued to be bound by the special rules regulating corroboration. The rules of evidence historically have targeted particular groups: children and women and madmen. The specificity of this rule of evidence is rooted in a history which has regarded children's testimony and the testimony of women as less worthy than the testimony of men (Heydon (1975)). The practical application of the duty to warn in sexual offence allegations has led to the exposure of some deep seated prejudices. Such ideologies are held widely beyond the realms of the judicial mind. The authors of Blackstone's *Criminal Practice* (1996 F5. 20), write, 'It is in sexual cases that the dangers of acting on the uncorroborated evidence of children have always been most acute, because of the *risks of hysterical invention, childish imagination and collusion*' (emphasis supplied). Modification of the rule does not influence what a judge may say or how he may say it, that is, whether he may read the incantation alone or add his own personal gloss to it. Modifications to the competency requirement have resulted in the status of uncorroborated evidence moving from a duty to warn, to a matter of judicial discretion and how that warning is given is a matter for judges. The Criminal Justice and Public Order Act 1994, s. 32(1) abolished this obligation to warn in sexual offences cases involving adults or children:

> Any requirement whereby at a trial on indictment it is obligatory for the court to give the jury a warning about convicting the accused on the uncorroborated evidence of a person merely because that person is — (a) an alleged accomplice of the accused, or (b) where the offence charged is a sexual offence, the person in respect of whom it is alleged to have been committed, is hereby abrogated.

Section 32(2) states, 'In section 34(2) of the Criminal Justice Act 1988 (abolition of requirement of corroboration warning in respect of evidence of a child) the words from "in relation to" to the end shall be omitted.'. In *Makanjuola* and *Easton* (1995) *The Times*, 17 May, the court laid down guidelines to assist the jury about convicting on uncorroborated evidence. The court said that the wording of 'merely' in s. 32(1) Criminal Justice and Public Order Act 1994, did not mean that where the complaint was of a sexual nature a warning should be given automatically. The basis of the appellants case was that there had been a misdirection or non-direction on corroboration and that a proper direction to the jury should include within it guidance that 'it is dangerous to convict on uncorroborated evidence'. The court of appeal did not agree and held that the judge is not required to conform to any formula.

Clearly, these changes will have significant benefits to the child victim. The impact on the prosecution mentality of the necessity for corroboration has meant that cases have not been proceeded with. The NSPCC research 1983–1987 found that prosecutions were proceeded with in only 9 per cent of the physical abuse cases and in 28 per cent of the sexual abuse cases (see Report of the Advisory Group on Video-Recorded Evidence (Pigot Committee), 1989, para. 1.6). In the case of the abuse of the Northdown House children, the mother of Rachel, the first victim to disclose, said:

There has never been any question but that these children were sexually abused, but the police's attitude is that without adult corroboration there can be no proceedings. I think that is terrible. We took our children away, but the playschool remained open. Rachel is adamant that she was abused at the school, and the other children say the same. But I and a lot of other parents were made to feel as if we were to blame we felt the finger was pointing at us. A lot of us were frightened that we would lose our children.

However, this does not mean in considering general principles of justice that judges will refrain from offering a warning, simply that they are released from a strait-jacket of recitation of a set form of words, but what they say may amount to the same thing.

Screens and video testimony

A further obstacle to the prosecution of child sex abusers has been the problem that child welfare is not being served by the court inquisition, especially by having to face an abuser in court, nor by excluding hearsay evidence. Judges cognisant of the first problem for the child victim have in the past rearranged the court so that the child witnesses could avoid any visual confrontation with the accused. In *Smellie* (1919) 14 Cr App R 128, the defendant was asked to sit out of sight of the child when she gave her evidence. Judges have also asked children to give evidence out of the witness box as in a trial in 1986 (*The Times*, 9 December 1986) where the child sat next to the judge. Easing the burden of the trial itself for children has resulted in reforms relating to the abolition of committal proceedings, the use of screens and live television links. The Criminal Justice Act 1988, s. 33 (substituting s. 103, Magistrates' Courts Act 1980) precluded calling a child witness for the prosecution in committal proceedings and statements made by the child were admissible in place of oral testimony, but the effect of this provision was limited since the defence could and would routinely object in order to try to get the case thrown out. The use of screens was first introduced by Pigot J in the trial of *X*, *Y*, *Z* at the Old Bailey in 1987. The accused appealed ((1990) 91 Cr App R 36), on the grounds that the use of the screen was unfair and prejudicial to the defendants. This was rejected by the Court of Appeal on the basis that they also had a duty to see that the system operated fairly in the case of victims and the Court of Appeal endorsed their use in subsequent hearings. The Lord Chief Justice said:

It had become apparent from experience that children in cases such as this, not surprisingly, were shown to be reluctant to give evidence at all. Again we are told that there had been cases which had collapsed simply because the child was unwilling or unable to speak ... Consequently it seemed to the court, upon representations one imagines by the Crown Prosecution Service, that steps ought to be taken in order if possible to remedy the situation, if that could be done without unfairness to the defendants.

Morgan and Plotnikoff (1990) found that, following the Criminal Justice Act 1988 provisions, screens were used at the Old Bailey in 100 cases. In 1991, the

Criminal Justice Act extended the use of screens to those giving evidence under 17 years of age. It is the job of the prosecutor to apply for evidence to be admitted with the use of the screen and a matter for the judge as to whether the use would be in the interests of justice (see Re Z (Minors) (Child Abuse: Evidence) [1989] FCR 440).

If the court does not possess live linked facilities then the 1991 Act provides for the hearing to be moved to a court that does. In addition to the use of screens in court, since the Criminal Justice Act 1988, s. 32(1), a child witness under the age of 14 has been able to give evidence through a live television link (amended by s. 55(7), Criminal Justice Act 1991, to abolish the age limitation). A video link can be made available to children, from a room outside the courtroom, or by satellite link where the witness is outside the UK. This means that the child need not be in the courtroom at all. There are limitations, however. Such facilities are available only at certain Crown Court centres and the child is not spared cross-examination. None of the reforms outlined change or alter one jot the nature or manner of cross-examination.

The second major change relates to modifications to, and some would say inroads into the rule against hearsay. One of the most significant changes is provided in the Criminal Justice Act 1991, s. 54, which amends s. 32A of the 1988 Criminal Justice Act and has made admissible pre-recorded interviews with child witnesses in place of live evidence-in-chief. This development extends the exceptions to the rule of hearsay. The Children and Young Persons Act 1933, ss. 42 and 43 already permitted hearsay evidence where the giving of evidence posed a serious danger to the child's life or heath. More recently s. 23(3)(b) of the Criminal Justice Act 1988 allows for a child's statement to be given in court in place of oral evidence where that child is in fear or kept out of the way. The new development represents the move to a more child centred approach to evidence. It is a matter for the judge to decide whether it should be admitted. Leave of the court must be given; it will not be granted if the child will not be available for cross-examination. In accordance with s. 32(10) video recording is admissible at all stages of the proceedings in trials at the Crown Court and youth courts. A video recording, however, is admissible only where: the child is not the accused; the child is available for cross-examination; rules of court, requiring disclosure of the circumstances in which the recording was made, have been properly complied with.

Earlier investigative interview recordings are not admissible as a matter of course; they must first be seen by a judge who has the power to deem them admissible. Again, it is a matter for the judge to grant leave and left to the judge's discretion there can be a difference, although Herrod J, in Guy 21 December 1989 (see Flin p. 105), laid down these guidelines in a written ruling:

(a)   A judge should not grant permission for the live link automatically, but should balance the risk of harm to the child against the risk of creating prejudice against the defendant by allowing the live link to be used.

(b)   In principle, if the prosecution want the live link to be used it is up to them to produce some evidence that it is likely to be harmful to this particular child to give evidence in the traditional way.

(c)   In the case of a very young child, however 'there must come a time when the very fact of a child's age is almost sufficient in itself to show that it would be detrimental for the child to have to give evidence in open court and to be cross-examined in the usual way'.

In a Home Office study 98 per cent of applications were granted (Davis and Noon 1991, p. 30).

However, neither pre-recorded video testimony, nor testimony via television link eradicates the ordeal for children. In *R v Rawlings, R v Broadbent* [1995] 1 All ER 580, Rawlings appealed by certificate of the trial judge against a conviction for buggery and indecent assault, Broadbent appealed with leave against conviction for gross indecency to a child. In each case evidence-in-chief was given by playing the jury a video recording of an interview with the child in accordance with s. 32A of the Criminal Justice Act 1988 as amended. In both cases this evidence had been replayed. Rawlings's grounds for appeal on a point of law were, 'Whether, when a complainant's evidence in chief has been given by means of a video tape pursuant to section 32A(2) of the Criminal Justice Act 1988, it is permissible for the jury to view the video recording again after they have retired to consider their verdict and, if so, upon what terms and conditions.'. The Court of Appeal in consideration of this point ruled:

> If the judge does allow the video to be replayed, he should comply with the following three requirements. (a) The replay should be in court with judge, counsel and defendant present. (b) The judge should warn the jury that because they are hearing the evidence-in-chief of the complainant repeated a second time well after all the other evidence, they should guard against the risk of giving it disproportionate weight simply for that reason and should bear well in mind the other evidence in the case. (c) To assist in maintaining a fair balance, he should, after the replay of the video, remind the jury of the cross-examination and re-examination of the complainant from his notes, whether the jury asked him to do so or not.

Despite the obvious advantage of the screen and the use of live video link, the advantages of pre-recorded interviews with children must not be exaggerated since these innovations do nothing whatsoever to limit or change the nature of the cross-examination (McEwan 1990). The overwhelming criticism is that the witness still must face evidence at the trial, both remedial examination-in-chief and cross-examination. Screens or live links do not alter the tone of cross-examination and the questioning may be no less intimidating. The result is that children will not be removed from the adversarial arena and traumatisation continues relatively unabated (see Birch 1992).

Conviction and sentence

As with other criminal cases, appeals against conviction frequently succeed because of technicalities or failures in the trial process, which may be unrelated to the guilt or innocence of the accused. The proviso in s. 2, Criminal Appeal

Act 1968, allows the Court of Appeal to uphold a conviction even where the grounds of appeal succeed, if the court is of the view that the jury would have come to the same verdict had the irregularities not occurred and there is no miscarriage of justice. On the whole, sentences in cases of child sexual abuse have been overly lenient, both at the point of sentencing and also on appeals against sentence. Lord Lane in the case of an eminent paediatrician (detailed in the chapter entitled, Freedom from Pornography in an Age of Sexual Liberalism) reduced a 12 month sentence to six months, on appeal, and regarded the collection of child pornography as not serious, making a clear separation between this kind of behaviour as fantasy as distinct from sexual abuse as reality. Experts on paedophiles, however, regard such behaviour as a strong indicator of the likelihood of a connection between fantasy and reality. Adler (1987, p. 3), reports on the inability of judges to grasp the seriousness of such offences. 'In December 1983, an Old Bailey judge, commenting on a man who had had intercourse with a friend's 7 year-old daughter, said that this struck him as 'being one of the kind of accidents that could almost happen to anyone'. Judge Ian Starforth-Hill commented that an eight year-old victim of a sexual attack was 'not entirely an angel' (*The Guardian*, 10 June 1993).

Charlotte Mitra's (1987) study of sentencing in cases of father-daughter incest is instructive. She examined a sample of 63 appeals against sentence during the period 1970-1980. Sixty two of the offenders received immediate custodial sentence. The Court of Appeal reduced sentence in 38 of those cases and it substituted a non-custodial sentence in 11 cases. The appeal was dismissed in 14 cases. Mitra found that the most frequently imposed sentence length was four years, providing further evidence of the inconsequential treatment incest has received. Mitra's work more importantly reveals the stereotypes of the male offender and female child victim which inform the law and shape judicial discretion. Fathers were generally regarded as committing incest episodically, as a response to stress or to the failure of the wife for whatever reason to meet his sexual needs. The victims were often regarded as contributing to their own demise. Whilst the provisions in the Criminal Justice Act 1988, ss. 35 and 36 have addressed the overly lenient sentence by providing for the opportunity of appeal by the prosecution to the Attorney-General who may refer the case to the Court of Appeal, attitudes to child sexual abusers within the family which seek to normalise the abuse and transfer blame persists. In *Attorney-General's Reference No. 1 of 1989* (under Criminal Justice Act 1988 section 36) [1989] 3 All ER 571, where a daughter had been raped by her father for four years since she was 11, a three year prison sentence was imposed for the incest and 18 months for the indecent assault. This was increased to six years, at the same time providing a clear example of the resistance of judicial ideology to changes in sentencing. Lord Lane laid down guidelines to be followed in similar cases of incest. First, where the girl is over 16, a sentence of three years is regarded as the maximum. This depends upon the degree of force used, the need to minimise family disruption, the harm to the girl, and the degree to which she was willing, or was an instigating party, or was corrupted. Secondly, where the girl is 13 to 16 years, the maximum sentence is three to five years. The principles guiding the exercise of discretion previously outlined are also to be applied here, 'though the likelihood of corruption increases in inverse proportion to the age of the girl.'. Thirdly, where the girl is under 13 years then the sentence ranges from six years. Aggravating features, irrespective of the age of the girl, include, age, harm both physical and psychological, time scale and duration of abuse, perversions, threats and violence, pregnancy, and multiple victimisation. *Attorney-General's Reference No. 4 of 1989* [1990] 1 WLR 41, cites with approval Lord Lane's guidelines. Of particular concern is the inclusion of mitigatory factors which transfer blame from the adult to the child including, 'her previous sexual experience' which is always really referring to her previous victimisation and abuse. Further blaming of the child victim is found in mitigation 'where she had made deliberate attempts at seduction'. The credence the Lane guidelines have given to erroneous constructs such as the precociousness of children is a thread that runs throughout cases involving sexual abuse of children. In the rape cases of both *SMS* [1992] Crim LR 310, and *Said* [1992] Crim LR 433, such presumptions led to the quashing of the convictions on the ground that past moral character had been improperly excluded (see the chapter entitled, Sex Crime). This notion that children provoke their own demise resonates throughout sentencing decision making. Thomas (1970, pp. 119–122) notes that where the daughter has had previous sexual experience with a third party this may result in sentence reduction. In *Hadigate* (1986) 8 Cr App R (S) 273, a mitigating factor was that the girls had had previous sexual experience. In *T* (1944) 15 Cr App R (S) 871, in mitigation the court heard that the girl had gone to the man, and had had previous sexual relationships with other men. Similarly in *P* (1994) 15 Cr App R (S) 116, the incest was said to have happened at the instigation of the complainant. Mitra found in her study that blame transference from perpetrator to child is common. In 16 per cent of cases the fathers claimed that there was an element of responsibility by the daughter who was variously described as 'a willing partner', and of another victim 'the offence came from her initiative' (Mitra, p. 136). In the case of a girl who was not a virgin, the court held 'this girl, first, was not a virgin, secondly, she was somewhat precocious in her appearance . . . she appears to have — I will not say led him on, but certainly not discouraged him' (Mitra, p. 136). In *Moores* (1980) 2 Cr App R (S) 317 the sentence was mitigated because of the 'deeply promiscuous daughter'. In *Taylor and Others* (1977) 64 Cr App R 182, the court referred to the wantonness of the teenage girls involved. In this respect the Lane guidelines here are a complete travesty relying on transference of blame for the offence onto the child victim, returning thinking on child sexual abuse to the 1890s.

Perpetrators also try to allocate blame to social and other family factors, unhappy marriages, unemployment, stresses and strains and alcoholism. In *Buckham* (1979) 143 JP 696, 'the motivation in this case was not any form of sexual perversion, nor that there was any desire to replace an unattractive wife by an attractive daughter as sometimes happens', said the court, betraying what they conventionally regard as motives. Sir Harold Cassels's infamous remarks following the sexual assault of a 13 year-old stepdaughter led to a public furore: 'Pregnancy leads to a lack of sexual appetite in the lady and considerable problems for a healthy young husband'. In *Smith* [1980] Crim LR 391, the incest with the daughter was understood as the result of marital strife. In *Wilson* (1974) 58 Cr App R 304, although the father had threatened the daughter in order that he could commit incest, the court heard that he had turned to his daughter because the wife had starved him of affection. Other attempts at exoneration have included drink wherein . . . 'it was a straightforward case of a man drinking too much and losing control of himself' (see *Buckham*). In *Cole* (1993) 14 Cr App R (S) 670, the court held that the man was considered a danger to children, but it was only 'an attempt' and not the full offence of abduction. In the event no harm came to the child, he was a man of good character, he had no previous offences and so the six year sentence was reduced to four years. It was not because of his conscience, however, that the crime was only one of attempt but because of the actions and speedy reporting by the child and reaction of police involved.

In mitigation of sentence the courts have also considered the effect on the victim and the willingness of the family, invariably the wife, to stand by him. In *Peter O'S* (1993) 14 Cr App R (S) 632, the ground of appeal against sentence was whether the sentencer was entitled to assume that incest had had a damaging effect on the victims in absence of the evidence. The sentencer had said that the offences had resulted in serious damage to the girls who had been indecently assaulted, and this presumption (although reasonable) resulted, on appeal, in a reduction in sentence. In the case of *Anthony Hobstaff* (1993) 14 Cr App R (S) 604, counsel in opening the case on a plea of guilty made reference to the effect on the victims. In this case the appellant assaulted the young daughters of his neighbour aged between five and eight including masturbation and fellatio. Counsel for the prosecution had this to say:

> The pleas were accepted on the last occasion on the basis that the children did not encourage any of these acts. The effects of these assaults on the children have been quite horrific. R suffers from extreme nightmares and she wakes up screaming. Mrs A. has to get up to see to her. R has also taken to sleepwalking. When she suffers these attacks she is drenched in sweat. Both children have had to see a child psychologist. The psychologist has found that R in particular is suffering from mixed emotions of anger, disgust and distress which have damaged her relationship with her mother. She is withdrawn and extremely frightened.

The sentence was reduced on the basis that, 'it was based in significant part upon material which ought not to have sounded in the sentencing exercise at all', resulting in a reduction in sentence of four to three years. (One might wonder then why the comments of battered wives to the effect that they have forgiven their batterers have been accepted in some court cases in mitigation of sentence (see the chapter entitled, All in the Name of Privacy — Domestic Violence).

Where wives are willing to stand by their partners in the face of sexual abuse, the abuse is redefined as an episodic rather than long term problem. In *John M* (1992) 14 Cr App R (S) 286, where the appellant had committed incest with his daughter over five years since she was 14 years old, mitigation of his guilty plea, an hysterical conversion disorder and a compassionate wife all seemed to be considered in the reduction of sentence.

Claims for compensation and for damages have also been dogged by presumptions about the degree to which children are responsible for their demise. Under the current rules (1995) compensation is available to those who have suffered buggery, indecent assault, and incest among other sex offences and the injury must be physical or mental. 'Trivial' injuries are excluded where the amount ordered is likely to be below £1,000. There is a time limit of three years since the incident, which like the damages rule (see *Stubbings* v *Webb* above) operates against many victims of abuse who need to live independent lives away from the abuser before they can speak out without fear. A criminal conviction is not necessary, but the Criminal Injuries Compensation Board must be satisfied on the balance of probabilities that the events took place. Where applications are made on behalf of a minor it must be made by a person who has parental responsibility for the child. Children who are wards must obtain permission from the court of wardship (see *Re G (A Ward) (Criminal Injuries: Compensation)* [1991] 1 FLR 89, [1993] 1 FLR 103). Claims for compensation for child sexual abuse have historically been excluded from the scheme due to the 'under the same roof' principle although since 1979 it is possible for compensation to be payable even if living as a member of the same family. These changes to the rules in 1979 are not retrospective and so those whose abuse occurred before 1979 could not claim. In *CICB ex parte P and another* (1995) 1 All ER 870, the Court of Appeal upheld the decision of the Divisional Court that an adult who was the victim of child abuse was not entitled to compensation under the 1990 scheme because victims of family violence were excluded at the time of the abuse. P made allegations of sexual abuse which occurred between 1967–1976. In 1988 she reported the case to police. Her application for compensation was refused because the 'same roof' principle was in force until October 1979. P applied for judicial review challenging the legality of this refusal. The Divisional Court rejected her claim for compensation in respect of offences prior to 1978. G also appealed and her similar claim was rejected.

Financial awards for cases involving abuse of children including sexual intercourse, buggery, oral sex, and digital penetration have an upper limit of £17,500, see *Re E J K and D* [1990] CLY 1596, *Re AP (female)* [1991] CLY 1363, suggests that the upper bracket may be £20,000 although in *Re V* [1991] CLY 1370, the buggery award was fixed at £12,000. *Re E J K and D* involved young children of five to eleven years who were regularly abused by their mother, father, grandfather and other adults, the children were significantly disturbed as a result. In *AM and T* [1994] CLY 1579, three sisters were subjected to sexual abuse by the father, grandfather and two other men for several years. In the case of A and M the abuse had included everything excepting buggery. The abuse of T had also included buggery. All the children suffered post-traumatic stress syndrome, helplessness, powerlessness, loss of the capacity to trust, loss of self esteem, they were frightened of their father, and they suffered from sleep disturbances. A and M were awarded £15,000 each and T £20,000. By 1995 the level of award was increased to £25,000 at the upper end of the scale of severity (see *Re Y* [1995] CL September Monthly Digest, p. 42 and see Denyer 1993, p. 297).

Freeman (1994) argues rather cynically that there is no evidence that suggests children are better off removed from the home, since the standard of care in local authority homes is open to criticism and children may well suffer all forms of abuse. In *Re G* [1993] CLY 1460, the claimant had been in care of the local authority from the age of eight because of a combination of family circumstances and educational disadvantage, at the age of 15 she was in the care of a children's home. The proprietor of the home and a male teacher systematically sexually and physically abused her for four years, including intercourse and extreme forms of degradation, being tied up, urinated on, and having objects inserted inside her. She developed urinary tract infections and anal spasms. Following disclosure, a close relative murdered the adult abusers. The girl was so traumatised that she tried to commit suicide by swallowing glass, self-electrocution, and self-strangulation. The total award was £59,200.

The sexually abused child faces a social construction of child sexual abuse which denies the reality and a legal system which perpetrates further violence. The ideology of the family as a safe haven from the demands of the public world continues to resist the reality of abuse. It is not a masculinist construction of child sexual abuse *per se* but a construction of the sanctity and implacable sanctuary of family life and the indelible, universal truth of parents as protectors which are the precepts that need continually to be challenged.

EIGHT

Sex Crime

Women speak of a wide range of sexual assault, from the experience of indecent exposure in the park, countryside and on the street, to finding pornographic messages and images transmitted onto the office computer (Merchant 1993, 1995, Braithwaite 1995). Whilst women are in the main the victims, the domain of sexual assault has been nevertheless largely defined by men, and masculinist legal definitions have circumscribed what conduct constitutes sexual assault for legal purposes. It has been part of the task of contemporary feminist critique to define sexual assault from women's experience, and to recognise and include conduct, some of which has been traditionally unrecognised by law or marginalised in its seriousness. Such conduct includes obscene telephone calls, frotteurism (touching, rubbing or pressing against a person), indecent exposure or 'flashing', stalking, to the all pervasive 'assault' on many women who work in a sexually intimidating environment where nude pictures of women, for example, are commonplace (see *Lois Robinson* v *Jacksonville Shipyards Inc* 760 F Supp 1486 (1991) (discussed below). Some feminists have regarded 'feminist methodologies' as central to this reconstruction and these definitions (Hanmer and Saunders 1993, Kelly 1988, Wise and Stanley 1987). Rather than a specific feminist methodology, the impetus for such an approach is derived from the symbolic interactionist endeavour of the 1960s which relies on the importance of letting the subject speak and 'tell it like it is' (see Lemert 1951, Garfinkel 1967, Segal 1988). Part of the feminist critique has championed a retreat from biologism and essentialism in the understanding of the aetiology of 'sex crimes' hitherto exclusively a problem of psychopathology, of testosterone or instinctual drive, to embrace instead the role of social constructionism and the legitimation of violence in the creation of a dangerous masculinity (see Scully 1990, p. 46, Miedzian 1992). This emphasis is not exclusive to feminism, some male social theorists and therapists concerned with masculinity and violence have similarly identified the importance of social constructionism in this analysis (Metcalf and Humphries 1990, Stoltenberg 1990, Giovannoni 1989). This chapter specifically explores the nature and extent of the sexual abuse of women and the negotiation of legal defences by perpetrators. It examines the presumptions about rape especially and the competing sexualities in which these presumptions are grounded, all of which are attitudes which shape the common law and the interpretation of statute and considers how this interpretative framework constructs rape and indecent assault as a question of consensual sex and how the legal method in rape reflects the masculinist proprietorial presumptions enshrined in law.

THE NATURE OF SEXUAL ABUSE

The sexual abuse of women has been traditionally regarded in the literature as if it is degendered. Early studies of sexual abuse from within criminology have talked about sexual assault of women in a vacuum, stripped of the gender of perpetrator and victim. Rape, and indecent assault involving as it does the systematic abuse of children and women by men, curiously and unconscionably has ignored the obvious gender divide of victim and perpetrator. It is only through feminist scholarship that the obvious has been articulated and challenged. Indecent assault is committed by both acquaintances and strangers and spans a wide range of behaviours, from conduct involving no physical contact with the victim to assault which falls short of rape. The presumption is that indecent assault is trivial in consequence. And so the forcible insertion of broomhandles, knives, bottles into the anus or vagina of women, as an indecent assault, has been rendered less serious than rape (see *Re G* 12 March 1993, CICB, London; CLY 1993, 1460).

Buggery is yet another means by which men inflict force, violence and dominion over women, this crime in the domestic context is discussed in the chapter entitled, All in the Name of Privacy — Domestic Violence. Presented as an aberration, Ferguson and Webster (1994) report that of the rape victims in their study one quarter of women were also buggered by the perpetrator. Lloyd and Walmsley (1989, p. 21) in their 1973 study found that 107 cases of rape also involved additional sexual acts and 5 per cent included buggery. In the 1985 sample of 228 rape victims buggery was reported in 11 per cent. Other sexual acts included fellatio 15 per cent in 1973, 29 per cent in 1925, cunnilingus in 5 per cent in 1973, 11 per cent in 1985, victim forced to masturbate offender in 10 per cent in 1973 and 9 per cent in 1985 and insertion of a finger into the victim's vagina in 26 per cent and 25 per cent of cases respectively. Further sexual acts included ejaculation over the victim, insertion of object into the vagina, insertion of object or finger into the anus and breasts sucked. The use of physical violence found in Lloyd and Walmsley is represented in Table 22.

Table 22: Rape and additional acts of violence

	1973		1985	
	no	0%	no	0%
some threat or use of physical violence	200	85	365	90
threat of manual violence	55	24	65	16
threat of use of knife	34	15	90	22
threat of use of gun	4	2	13	3
threat of use of another weapon	7	3	11	3
threat of death	63	27	97	24
hand over mouth	78	34	123	31
physical restraint	197	84	283	70
gagging/tying up	12	5	24	6
punching/kicking/choking	65	28	116	29
use of weapon not endangering life	8	3	9	2
use of weapon endangering life	2	1	8	2

Source: Lloyd and Walmsley 1989 Table 6.1

Jill Saward's rape was accompanied by further acts of degradation, 'Now the worst is happening but it is not in the dark alleyway I have always imagined it is here in my own home ... The man is pulling down his trousers, pushing me to my knees in front of him ... What this man is telling me to do is even more disgusting ... My body has become an object. A machine. It must stay like that if I am to survive. ... Man 2 ... tells me to turn on my stomach. Apologising for what he is about to do. This is worse. Far worse. I did not think such things were possible. Words won't ever explain how I feel' (Saward and Green 1990, p. 30). This kind of assault on women becomes an increasingly typical element in men's violence against women.

Indecent exposure or 'flashing', that is the exposure of the penis, involves no physical contact with the object of the 'indecency'. It is similarly portrayed as a rare event with little or no consequences for its victim. By contrast, many women talk of having experienced this at some time or other in their lifespan and with rather more serious consequences (see *British Crime Survey* 1983, Hough and Mayhew, 1985, Hough and Mayhew, 1988, Mayhew, Elliott and Dowds, 1992, Mayhew, Aye Maung and Mirrlees-Black; *Islington Crime Survey* 1986 Jones, MacLean and Young, *The Second Islington Crime Survey* 1990 Crawford). When I was about 11 or 12 years old, I was walking to high school. It was a winter morning and not fully light. I took my usual route, a well-used short cut through an alleyway between residential houses which backed onto one another. At the halfway point stood a man exposing himself. I don't remember his face or anything else for that matter. I considered turning back as I approached him, but thought that I should deal with my fear and decided instead to walk on by. When I was a first year student at university I spent some considerable time in the city reference library on a regular basis. On one occasion a man with whom I had spoken but a few words on a previous occasion struck up a conversation, as he was doing so he began masturbating, rubbing his hand over his clothes. I sat there for a short while dissociating, pretending it wasn't happening, until I could regain some control of the situation and edged the conversation round to a point at which I could leave. I didn't report this incident, it was far too embarrassing and anyway I thought the fact that he had behaved in this manner and that I did not leave immediately would reflect on me in some way. Having just completed a Master's degree I went holidaying to stay with friends in Belgrade. I had decided to visit parts of the city on my own. I was spending a perfect afternoon reading on the banks of the River Dunav when the calm was interrupted by a man who emerged from behind the bushes and exposed himself. I left immediately, this time furious at the vile intrusion. I didn't report it, my Serbo-Croat was limited and what would the police have done anyway? Indecent exposure such as this is rarely perceived as an assault, although it is clearly an act of indecency towards another person. In the first example the exposure involved indecency towards a child, and is provided for by the Indecency with Children Act 1960, s. 1(1), 'with or towards a child under the age of fourteen'. It would appear that a different view is taken of the flasher who directs his indecency towards adult women. Here, the Vagrancy Act 1824, s. 4 provides that 'every person wilfully, openly, lewdly and obscenely exposing his person with intent to insult a female shall be deemed a rogue and vagabond'.The Public Order Act 1986, s. 5(1) which prohibits threatening, abusive, insulting behaviour likely to cause alarm or distress, is now used to prosecute such behaviour. Sentencing ranges from three months, or in the Crown Court up to one year (see Rook and Ward 1990, p. 321), although in the absence of violence the penalty is unlikely to be a sentence of imprisonment. In the 1824 Act 'person' means penis; *Evans* v *Ewels* [1972] 1 WLR 671. In this case the appellant openly, lewdly and obscenely exposed his person with intent to insult a female, contrary to s. 4 of the Vagrancy Act 1824, and was ordered to pay a fine of £15. The conviction was quashed on appeal since person means 'penis' and not a v-shaped area of stomach that was exposed.

Women have also had to endure the insult in everyday life of men pressing themselves against them. Such conduct described as a fetish by nineteenth century psychiatry (see Krafft-Ebing 1901) is in fact today commonplace. Macpherson J, the trial judge in *Chagan* (1995)16 Cr App R (S) 15, remarked, 'Cases of this kind are usually dealt with in the magistrates' court. Simply for example again, in crowded places such as Wimbledon week and on tube trains, these things do occur ...'. Saward (1990, pp. 27, 28) writes, 'The first time, aged nine, I was with my brother and sister at London Zoo. I was watching the seals being fed, when a fat man came and stood behind me, pushing his hand inside my clothes and breathing heavily.... The second time I had just left college, but I was still petrified when a man started to follow me through Walpole Park. He kept chatting, asking me to go out with him or kiss him. The third incident happened on my way to work early one morning. As I began my daily walk along the alleyway two Asian lads in school uniform were coming towards me. Suddenly one ran at me and grabbed my chest as he passed. I turned round in utter amazement. He stood there, some distance away, rubbing his penis through his trousers with a big grin on his face.'. In *Chagan* (1995), the appellant rubbed his body against a woman on the underground. He moved his groin towards her pelvic area. The police had already been alerted to his behaviour. Notwithstanding what appeared to be overwhelming evidence, it was suggested to the complainant in cross-examination that her evidence was inaccurate. The court on appeal, not considering this a serious matter, reduced the defendant's sentence to 12 days' imprisonment. In *Townsend* (1995) 16 Cr App R (S) 553, a man was convicted under similar circumstances for rubbing against women on the underground and was sentenced to six months' imprisonment for indecent assault, reduced to three months. He was seen by police officers at a London Underground station to follow a young woman onto a train; he stood behind her, rubbing his groin against her bottom, and followed her when she moved away. He was arrested by the police officers shortly afterwards. Having been convicted by the jury, the appellant was released on bail and saw two female members of the jury near the court building. He stared at one of them, and made a gesture by drawing his hand or finger across his throat. He then saw a third female member of the jury on a bus which he had boarded; he pushed past her twice, and then stood in front of her, staring at her. (See Table 23.)

Table 23: Crimes on London Underground — indecent assaults

Year:	1986	1987	1988	1989	1990	1991	1992	1993	1994/5
Number:	146	166	201	305	276	214	262	258	246

Source: British Transport Police, London Underground

Several years ago I was returning home after a day's teaching in Central London. Embarking on the train at Piccadilly Circus I was relieved to see one empty seat and struggled past the standing passengers and through an alcoholic haze of expired fumes which increased in pungency as I approached the vacant seat. The man who was sitting next to me was drunk, so too were his two companions. He started to rub his hand over the outside of my thigh over my clothes passing some inaudible remarks as he did so. I did nothing, said nothing, waiting and hoping that he would soon be leaving the train. After a few stops he and his companions left the train amid comments of revelry to women passengers. Their departure brought relief to me and to the Asian woman sitting opposite who had also had to endure the verbals from the drunk sitting next to her. But freedom from harassment was shortlived and I had been naïve. With momentary relief I remarked audibly with indignation for others around in the crowded train who had been all too aware of what was happening, but did nothing at all to assist us, 'And he was feeling my leg!'. To which a 'gentleman' dressed in an expensive suit, clean shaven and sober, remarked (no doubt he thought as a compliment), 'Well, if you don't mind me saying, I don't blame him.' (*sic*). It would seem that the desire to 'feel a woman' is commonplace and where such behaviour is not accompanied by physical violence is frequently neutralised as male fun and a good joke. In *Lyons* (1994) 15 Cr App R (S) 460, a rather more serious view was taken where a woman who was walking her dog was grabbed by the appellant and pulled to the ground. The appellant tried to unzip her coat and then ran off giving himself up to the police. In his statement he admitted that, although he was not able to effect his purpose, he had intended, in his words, to 'feel the woman'. He was convicted of indecent assault in the light of his declared 'secret motive'.

The menace of obscene telephone calls has been the dread, fear and reality for many women, until recently they have not been regarded seriously, if at all. Pease (1985) in an analysis of data from the British Crime Survey found that 10 per cent of women with access to a private telephone receive obscene phone calls every year. A summary offence under the British Telecommunications Act 1981, s. 49, Telecommunications Act 1984, s. 43(1), it has been regarded as trivial. As Pease notes it has been regarded as an offence which its victim can end at any time. Yet, Pease found the fear of crime arising from this form of 'assault' is immeasurable, fear ranging from burglary, to sexual assault, to being watched. The Criminal Justice and Public Order Act 1994, s. 92(1) in recognition of the serious impact this form of assault can have on people's lives increases the penalty for this offence to six months' imprisonment, amending the Telecommunications Act, 1984 s. 43(1). In 1992–3 there were 1,101 prosecutions or cautions for malicious telephone calls rising to 2,383 for the years 1993–4 and 2,800 for the years 1994–5. Of these calls 60 per cent were silent, 15 per cent were threatening or abusive and 15 per cent were obscene (BT 2 August 1995, *News Release*; see also Buck, Chatterton and Pease 1995, pp. vi–vii).

Some obscene telephone calls have been considered so seriously harmful to victims that charges of assault have been preferred. In *Gelder, The Times*, 9 July 1994, a bank clerk was convicted of grievous bodily harm after subjecting a woman to a series of obscene telephone calls over a period of nine months. On 16 December 1994, Lord Taylor LCJ quashed his conviction after a trial judge's misdirection on whether a normal person would have foreseen that obscene telephone calls would have harmed the victim, when the direction to the jury should have been to consider whether a person like the defendant would have foreseen the consequences. In *Wadland* (1994) 15 Cr App R (S) 543, the appellant made telephone calls to 270 women. He told them that he had kidnapped their child or husband and would harm them unless they complied with his demands, or he would ring women up and say that he and his colleagues were enjoying themselves with the woman's daughter. Demands for money were made and demands that the women mutilate themselves by setting fire to their pubic hair and sticking pins through their nipples. Twelve women injured themselves in order to comply with his demands hoping that their loved ones would go unharmed as a result. The trial judge said, 'Your victims included a 14 year-old girl, a pregnant woman and a woman whose husband came home to find her naked having been forced by her terror into self mutilation and setting fire to herself.'. In conversation with his probation officer, the appellant said that he found the telephone calls thrilling and that they gave him a sense of power. The appellant was convicted of threats to kill and a sentence of five years was upheld. In the case of *Onyon* (1994) 15 Cr App R (S) 663, the appellant pleaded guilty to eight offences of threatening to kill and asked for 145 similar offences to be taken into consideration. He had telephoned a number of women and told them that he had kidnapped their daughter and threatened to kill the daughter, unless the woman performed sexual acts including masturbation, demanding that they bring money and jewellery to him whilst they were wearing a raincoat with no clothes on underneath. The appellant terrorised and humiliated 21 women and one child. A sentence of six years' imprisonment was reduced to five.

Women have endured, and often without complaint until very recently, various forms of sexual harassment. In the workplace, in school, in college and in everyday public life women have been intimidated and made to feel uncomfortable as a hostile environment is created around them (see MacKinnon 1979, Wise and Stanley 1987, Pattinson 1991, Collier Rohan 1995). Most forms of harassment have been so institutionalised as part of everyday life that women who have objected have faced a wall of resistance, portrayed as childish, immature or women who cannot accept a bit of harmless male fun. Male fun has meant that women have suffered embarrassment, discomfort, loss of dignity in enduring the pin-ups in the office, in the factory, in fact everywhere, except in the ladies' room. Institutionalisation of sexual harassment as acceptable male behaviour begins within the school where the sexual intimidation of girls is learnt behaviour as part of growing up from boy to man. My 13 year-old daughter, attending a mixed sex school, relayed the story of one of the boys in her class who had collected a bag full of 'page three' semi-nude pin-ups which he showed to the girls in his class who experienced a range of reactions and emotions from embarrassment, intimidation and shock to hurt. The male geography teacher upon discovering this behaviour dealt with it by treating it as some kind of boys' club joke and laughing said, 'what would your mother say?', thus reaffirming that such behaviour was after all quite amusing. Challenges to such institutionalised behaviour get met with further insult and resistance.

Sexual harassment in the work environment, as legally recognised, depends on the effect of the behaviour on women's working conditions. The European Commission's Code of Practice defines sexual harassment as behaviour recognised as unacceptable and offensive and is a condition imposed upon the recipient (see Equal Opportunities Commission *Sexual Harassment Guide* 1994, Lester 1993, Matthews 1992). Sexual harassment is institutionalised and widespread: low reportage is not an indicator of the absence of harassment. Russell (1984, p. 270), reported that 42 per cent of all female employees reported varying degrees of sexual harassment. Research shows that the effects can be quite devastating, 86 per cent of those experiencing sexual harassment said that it had an adverse effect on their work (COHSE Survey 1991 cited in

Collier, p. 8). In the police service, Her Majesty's Inspectorate of Constabulary (1993), found that one woman in ten had considered leaving because of sexual harassment. Terri Pattinson recounts how Brenda Dean, General Secretary of the Society of Graphical and Allied Trades (SOGAT), was sitting at a table when the man next to her started fondling her thigh; she was so amazed that she ignored it (Collier Rohan 1995, p. 21). In *Porcelli v Strathclyde Regional Council* [1986] IRLR 134 CS, Mrs Porcelli won her case of sexual harassment against two male colleagues who had run a campaign of trying to get rid of her which included sexual remarks and brushing up against her. She complained that this conduct was contrary to s. 6(2)(b) of the Sex Discrimination Act. In *Johnstone v Fenton Barns (Scotland) Ltd* (1990) (cited in Rohan Collier, pp. 54–55), Mrs Johnstone won her case of sexual harassment following colleagues' continual references to sex, menstruation and masturbation. In *Cann v Unilift Ltd* (1992) (cited in Collier Rohan, pp. 55–56), Mrs Cann lost her case because she had not made it clear to the harasser that his behaviour was unwelcome.

In the United States the sexual assault of women includes sexual harassment, which invades a woman's sense of self and worth and undermines a woman's sense of equality and safety. In *Lois Robinson v Jacksonville Shipyards Inc* 760 F Supp 1486 (1991), pursuant to Title VII of the Civil Rights Act 1964, the plaintiff asserted that the defendant had created a sexually hostile and intimidating environment. This environment included pictures of nude and partially nude women throughout the workplace in the form of plaques, photographs on the wall calendars supplied by advertising tool companies including, amongst others, a picture of a woman, breasts and pubic areas exposed, a picture of a black woman, pubic hair and labia exposed (see *De Angelis v El Paso Municipal Police Officers Association* 51 F 3d 591 (1995) and *Burns v McGregor Electronic Industries* 955 F 2d 559 (1992)).

In *Singh-Marwa* (1995) 16 Cr App R (S) 537, a 21 month prison sentence was reduced to 15 months where a man indecently assaulted a young woman who came for an interview for a job. He pulled up her shirt, fondled her breasts and offered her money to perform indecent acts upon him. Part of the creation, maintenance and passive acceptance of this hostile environment ensures that men control it and women's only resort is to retreat back into the 'safety' of the home (see chapter entitled, All in the Name of Privacy — Domestic Violence). When women challenge this hostility around them they may be transformed into 'she devils' (see *Halford v Sharples and others* [1992] 3 All ER 624). All this sexual assault, and this level of tolerance of sexual assaults against women and this predilection to make women responsible for their demise, leads to creating a climate of fear which affects the nature and quality of women's lives. Research has shown the way in which fear of sexual attack limits women's lives and freedom, from going out alone, to staying in doors etc., to learning self-defence, to dressing down, to learning survival strategies. *The Standing Conference on Crime Prevention* (1989, p. 17), found that women were more fearful of crime than men at the rate of 3–1. Asian women's fear was even greater than for white women (see Grade Report 1909, Aharbanel 1986, Bart and O'Brien 1985). But as research indicates it is not just a structural but a psychological curfew that is placed on women's lives (see Hanmer and Saunders 1984, Stanko 1985, Da Silva 1995). Some women's fear becomes a lived reality. Jill Saward whose assault became public property in the Ealing Vicarage Rape case (Saward and Green 1990) wrote, 'He is facing me with a knife. Ordering me to undress . . . This is the fear every woman has grown up with from the time we are old enough to be warned not to talk to strangers.'. In some cases the rapist goes on to kill his victim (see Cameron and Frazer 1987, Caputi 1987, Holmes and De Burger 1988, Russell and Radford 1992). In the extreme case of the so-called 'Yorkshire Ripper', Peter Sutcliffe raped and murdered many of his victims (see Craft and Craft 1984, Boulos 1983).This is the gamut of sexual assaults on women and this is the extent of women's experience.

RAPE

The response of the law to sexual assaults on women has been weak, from the recognition or lack of recognition of some of this conduct as crimes to the rules of evidence and procedure which place the victim and her *mens rea* as much on trial as the *mens rea* of the defendant. Fundamental assumptions about male and female sexuality are played out in rape law, the legal method governing rape, and the conduct of the cross-examination of the complainant in the rape trial, such that the law perpetrates a further and ultimate violation on complainants.

Friends or strangers

Susan Estrich (1987, p. 1), in her autobiography, writes:

> In May 1974 a man held an ice pick to my throat and said 'Push over, shut up, or I'll kill you'. I did what he said, but I couldn't stop crying. When he was finished I jumped out of my car as he drove away. I ended up in the back seat of a Boston police car. I told the two officers I had been raped by a man in my own parking lot (and trying to balance two bags of groceries and kick the car door open). He took the car, too. They asked me if he was a crow (a black man).

In *W* v *Meah, D* v *Meah and another* [1986] 1 All ER 935, Miss D brought an action against the defendant, Christopher Meah claiming damages for personal injuries sustained as a result of the defendant's intentional assault and battery on her, Miss D was raped and stabbed in the chest by Meah and received £10,250 damages. Mrs W suffered great trauma, violence and oral sex was forced upon her. She was awarded £6,750 damages. Meah by contrast was awarded £45,000 in damages for his change of personality as a result of a road traffic accident; *Meah* v *McCreamer* (No. 2) [1986] 1 All ER 943.

Whilst accounts of stranger rape as these cited above confirm the public stereotype of rape, it is intimates and acquaintances and men placed in positions of authority and trust who are, in the main, the offenders. Paul Hickson was sent to prison for a succession of indecent assaults, including forced oral sex and rape, on young women over a period of years, whom he was training in his capacity as Olympic swimming coach (*The Times*, 28 September 1995). This was conduct which he normalised, along with many other lecturers, teachers and those in similar positions of authority (see the chapters entitled, A Betrayal of Trust — the Sexual Abuse of Children, and All in the Name of Privacy — Domestic Violence). Wright (1980), found that acquaintance rape constituted 60 per cent of all reported rapes. Chambers and Millar (1983) in their study of rape in Scotland reported similar rates. Smith (1989, p. 17), in a study of rape in two London Boroughs, Islington and Lambeth in 1984–1986, found that of 4,521 reported cases of rape, 39 per cent of cases involved men well known to the victim, 29 per cent involved men who were brief acquaintances and 32 per cent involved strangers. Research by Channel 4's *Dispatches* programme and the University of North London found that six out of seven women were raped by men they knew. Of these more than half were friends, colleagues, neighbours and casual acquaintances, men with whom they had never had consensual sex (see Ferguson and Webster 1994). Grace, Lloyd and Smith (1992) found that 70 per cent of rapes were perpetrated by acquaintances or by men well known to the victim. American research by Koss et al (1987) found the figure to be 84 per cent; and Russell (1984, p. 61) 83 per cent. The ubiquity of acquaintance rape has led many commentators to use the term 'date rape' (see Reeves Sanday 1981) to emphasise that the reality of rape is that the rapist is someone we know. It is precisely this 'acquaintance' factor which provides the most insurmountable obstacle to rape cases going to trial, and where such cases go to trial, to success in rape prosecutions. Ferguson reports in the Channel 4 study cited above that only 36 per cent of acquaintance rapes resulted in a conviction compared with 100 per cent conviction rate in cases involving stranger rapes. It is this 'acquaintance' factor which also allows the defence to reconstruct rape as a matter of consent and a matter of sex. Even in cases where violence is present, and where parties are known, rape becomes reconstructed within the sexual discourse of pain and pleasure, of masochism and sadism, rather than within the discourse of violence, domination and tyranny.

The extent

The official record of rape depends upon women's willingness to report and police to record such incidents as notifiable offences. Women have been reluctant to report sexual assault for a variety of reasons (see Radzinowicz and King 1977, p. 38, Winkel and Vrij 1993, Hall 1985, London Rape Crisis Centre 1984, Russell 1984, Temkin 1987, p. 11, Adler 1987, p. 4). This reluctance to report to the police arises because of fear of retaliation, shame, distrust of the reaction of family and friends, lack of confidence in the police and in the court process. Low levels of reporting are similarly found in Canada (Begin 1987), in the US, in Australia and New Zealand. The US National Crime Survey in 1986 suggested that only half of all rapes are reported to the police (US Department of Justice Sourcebook of Criminal Justice Statistics, 1988). In addition, widely publicised rape acquittals in particular, have a significant impact on women's perception of the criminal justice system, and the likely prognosis affects their decision to report rape and/or to prefer charges at the onset. Even where convictions are secured, judicial comments on the prudence or otherwise of women's behaviour further erode and undermine women's already tenuous confidence in the system of justice and in judicial attitudes which have a considerable impact in sentencing. In *R v Campbell* (unreported) where the accused was convicted of rape, the trial judge, Bell J, in passing sentence admonished the victim when he said, 'I regard her invitation to come to her bedroom when she was scantily clad, as opposed to asking you to wait downstairs until she was more suitably dressed, as an amber light' (*The Times*, 28 January 1995). Improvements in police response to rape have led commentators to assume that women are now more likely to report rape than before (see Chappell and Riedel 1976, p. 9). But there is no empirical evidence for this presumption; the reluctance to report may be as fragile as before and rape remains a hidden crime for most of its victims.

Recording practices

There is no doubt that there have been significant changes in the recording of rape by police in recent years, following Home Office Circular 69/1986, requiring police to record all rapes reported to them unless they are false or malicious (see Table 15). Chambers and Millar (1983, p. 39–40), found that police in Scotland considered one quarter of reported rapes to be false or malicious. How far policy has influenced police perceptions of false allegations is uncertain. Traditional police recording practice prior to 1986, where it was anticipated that the complainant would withdraw the allegation or showed a reluctance to proceed, had been to declassify the initial crime sheet record by writing the offence off as a 'no crime' (see Chambers and Millar 1983, Blair 1985), thereby removing reported rapes before the notifiable stage which leaves figures open to public scrutiny. The impact of the new police recording initiative is reflected in the increase of offences recorded and a decline in the use of the 'no crime'.

Table 24: Notifiable Offences of Rape in England and Wales

Year	1983	1984	1985	1986	1987	1988	1989	1990	1991	1992	1993	1994
Number	1,334	1,433	1,842	2,288	2,471	2,855	3,305	3,391	4,045	4,142	4,589	5,039

Source: Criminal Statistics 1994, Cm 3010, Table 2.16

Smith (1989) observed a 'no crime' rate of 61 per cent in 1984, 44 per cent in 1985 and 38 per cent in 1986 in her study of Islington and Lambeth. Table 16 shows how recorded rapes in the Metropolitan area rose significantly following Home Office Circular 69/1086 and the impact of Blair (1985) (a Metropolitan Police inspector's research on Metropolitan Police policy). By contrast, Grace et al (1992, pp. 5–6), a study of all police forces excluding the Metropolitan

Police for the second quarter of 1985 yielded 335 recorded rapes or attempted rape relating to 302 complaints and 327 suspects. Twenty four per cent of the complainer sample withdraw the allegation which was subsequently recorded as a 'no crime'. Arguably changes in the Metropolitan Police policy have had the greatest impact on the national profile for recorded rapes.

Table 25: Notifiable offences of rape in the Metropolitan Police Area

Year	1980	1987	1988	1989	1990	90–91	91–92	92–93
Number	249	732	806	896	981	1,032	1,149	1,199

Source: Report of the Commissioner of the Police of the Metropolis

Prosecuting practices

Concern has always been expressed over the low levels of prosecution in rape offences. It is difficult in the absence of research to discern the reasons for these levels (see Chambers and Millar 1986, Brown, Burman and Jamieson 1993). What is abundantly clear from an examination of criminal statistics is that, expressed as a proportion of recorded rapes (notifiable offences), the prosecution of rape has declined in recent years.

Table 26: Rape for trial as a percentage of notifiable offences

Year	1983	1984	1985	1986	1987	1988	1989	1990	1991	1992	1993	1994
Number of cases	451	451	565	590	646	793	924	911	954	931	891	936
Percentage of notifiable offences	33.8	31.4	30.6	25.7	26.1	27.7	27.9	26.8	23.5	22.4	19.2	18.6

Source: Criminal Statistics England and Wales for the years 1983–1994, Criminal Statistics Supplementary Tables vol. 2, for the years 1983–1994

This national decline may be the product of an increasing number of rapes being recorded where a prosecution is unlikely rather than a change in police or prosecutors' willingness to proceed with rape cases. Smith (1989, p. 25) argues that the changes pressed for in Home Office Circular 69/1986 and the Metropolitan Police Working Party have caused the decline, but it might also be the result of the Crown Prosecution Service declining to prosecute in all but watertight cases which are likely to yield convictions. What we know about rape would lead to the assumption that rape convictions in the absence of excessive violence and where parties are known are exceedingly unlikely. This is because, unlike other crimes, rape is turned into a matter of sex by the defence, i.e., that the complainant consented.

The second assault of the woman is perpetrated by the criminal justice process; this second abuse reaching its zenith in the trial where her assault becomes pornography, as defence counsel must, if they are to succeed, construct the defendant's account as a matter of consensual sex — controverting the woman's account of non-consensual violence (see Estrich 1987, p. 13). The Crown Prosecution Service advise against prosecution in para. 8.6. of the Code,

(a) Whenever two or more persons have participated in the offence in circumstances rendering both or all liable to prosecution, the Crown Prosecutors should take into account each person's age, the relative ages of the participants and whether or not there was any element of seduction or corruption when deciding whether, and if so in respect of whom, proceedings should be instituted. (b) Sexual assault upon children should always be regarded seriously, as should offences against adults, such as rape, which amount to gross personal violence. In such cases, where the Crown Prosecutor is satisfied as to the sufficiency of the evidence, there will seldom be any doubt that prosecution will be in the public interest.

This was cited in *DPP ex parte Tasmin C* (1995) 1 Cr App R 136, 139 discussed below), although the evidential sufficiency criteria are measured thus, 'is there a realistic prospect of conviction, bearing in mind the evidence available and those lines of defence which are plainly open to, or have been indicated by the accused?'. (*Ex parte Tamsin C* (1995) at 138.) Where victims feel aggrieved at a *nolle prosequi* decision, the options are to pursue a claim for civil damages in tort where the burden of proof is on the 'balance of probabilities', or to pursue a private prosecution, although the Crown Prosecution Service still have authority to halt private proceedings.

The power to review a CPS decision against prosecution is rarely used. In *ex parte Tasmin C* (1995), the only challenge in the past ten years to a decision against prosecution made by a service which, on its own admission, discontinued 11 per cent of cases in 1994, it was held that the Divisional Court has the power to review a decision of the DPP not to prosecute. In this case the complainant was buggered on several occasions by her police officer husband, the buggery being accompanied by violence. The DPP decided against a prosecution. The applicant applied for judicial review which was allowed and the case was remitted to the DPP for further consideration. The Divisional Court cited Lawton LJ in *Selvarajan* v *Race Relations Board* [1975] 1 WLR 1686 at 1697, 'As far as I know, the courts have never interfered with the exercise of the Director's discretion; but it does not follow that they could not do so if he refused or failed to perform his public duties or acted corruptly or unfairly.'. The court went on to identify three conditions which would result in its intervention: where a policy was unlawful; where the DPP failed to act as stated in the Code; and where a decision was perverse. Mr Naunton for the CPS had said in his evidence 'I concluded that in all the circumstances the complainant's grievance could be more appropriately dealt with in the matrimonial court, and that the public interest did not require the institution of criminal proceedings.'. When the case was finally heard the jury were unable to reach a verdict. Following a retrial, the defendant was acquitted of all charges. The final outcome went unnoticed and so one of the most important constitutional challenges of the decade was buried.

It is the decision of the prosecutor declining prosecution, that is discontinuing a case, which has led to some litigants pursuing instead a private prosecution. The question is whether such private proceedings expose the shortcomings of the public prosecutor or merely defend the rights of the citizen. Carol X was brutally attacked and raped by three Glasgow youths who with a razor inflicted innumerable slashes on her face and body, leaving her for dead. The respondents were indicted in the High Court in October 1980 and in 1981, following a second indictment, for a variety of reasons were not called. One of the reasons was that the complainant failed to go ahead with a prosecution because she was too traumatised and there were fears that she might attempt suicide (see Hansard 21 January 1982 col. 423). Later a private prosecution was instituted when the complainant saw no option but to give evidence. On 28 May 1992 the first respondent was convicted of rape and assault and received a sentence of twelve years whilst the other respondents were convicted of indecent assault and placed on a deferred sentence for a year (see *X* v *Sweeney, Sweeney and Thompson* SCCR (1982) 161, 181) (see Harper and McWhinnie 1983). A private prosecution was not followed in the case of Jill Cook, however, who was gang raped in her own home (see Bonnington 1995). There have been other similarly contentious private prosecutions. On 20 September 1995 (*The Guardian*, 21 September 1995), a man was jailed for 14 years following a private prosecution brought by two prostitutes, paid for by women's rights groups, after the CPS had decided against a public prosecution. Such instances indicate a prosecution service which is moving in a direction against prosecutions and ultimately against justice for victims.

RAPE ON TRIAL

The masculinist assumptions about female and indeed male sexuality that have crafted the common law continue to inform the construction of statutory rape. The Sexual Offences Act 1956, s. 1(1) states, 'It is a felony for a man to rape a woman', now amended by the Criminal Justice and Public Order Act 1994, s. 142, which recognises male buggery by force as male rape and buggery of a woman without consent as rape. Under UK law non-consensual acts between men will be a treated as anal rape. The offence of buggery will be retained for those offences where there is consent in fact but not in law, including offences against men under 18, since it will be necessary to define those cases where in law consent is prohibited, as where buggery is committed in a public lavatory or where more than two persons are present, although there may be consent in fact. Forced buggery of a woman will constitute rape for the purposes of the amendment. Other jurisdictions, notably Canada (Begin 1987) and some States in the US, notably Michigan (Caringella-MacDonald 1991, Dauvergne 1994), have reformulated rape in similar gender neutral terms. Notwithstanding these reforms the genderedness of rape stereotypes cannot be erased by legal fiat. Caringella-MacDonald found in a recent survey that rape acquittals led to a reduction of the charge, that past sexual history still emerges in court and that prosecutors continue to intimate culpability to victims.

Actus reus

It is the absence of consent which is arguably the only element, following the decision in *R* v *R* [1991] 4 All ER 481 and the amendments in the Criminal Justice and Public Order Act 1994, s. 142. The Sexual Offences (Amendment) Act 1976, s. 1(1), for the first time defined in statute the constituent elements of the *actus reus* and *mens rea* of the offence of rape, 'a man commits rape if (a) he has unlawful sexual intercourse with a woman who at the time of intercourse does not consent to it; and (b) at the time he knows that she does not consent to the intercourse or is reckless as to whether she consents to it.'. This definition followed the Heilbron Committee's recommendations on the Law of Rape (1975) and was later amended by the Criminal Justice and Public Order Act 1994, s. 142(2)(a), omitting the term 'unlawful' so as to remove ambiguity in the statutory wording following the recognition in *R* v *R* of rape in marriage. Prior to *R* v *R*, the marital rape exemption reflected the masculinist proprietorial interests driving the law. Hale (1971) wrote, 'But the husband cannot be guilty of a rape committed by himself upon his lawful wife, for by their mutual matrimonial consent and contract the wife hath given up herself in this kind unto her husband, which she cannot retract.'.

What are the essential ingredients of the actus reus? To constitute rape, it has long been recognised that it is proof of penetration: if penetration is not proven, a defendant may be convicted of attempted rape. Penetration *per anum* is now included under the 1994 Act, s. 142 amendments. Emission is irrelevant. Sexual intercourse is also considered a continuing act. In *Kaitamaki* [1985] 1 AC 147, a decision of the Privy Council from the Court of Appeal of New Zealand, the appellant was convicted of rape, on the grounds that he acknowledged that on the second occasion of rape he was aware that she did not consent but he did not desist. The Privy Council held that if consent was withdrawn during the act, then from that point thereafter the act could be deemed rape, '... Sexual intercourse is a continuing act which only ends with withdrawal'. The Court of Appeal in *Cooper and Schaub* [1994] Crim LR 531, reaffirmed this principle in ruling that a trial judge had been correct in directing the jury that 'penetration' is a continuing act, in responding to the jury who had asked the question, 'If we find initially that there was consent to intercourse and this was subsequently withdrawn and intercourse continued, does this by law constitute rape?'. In *Brookes* (1993) 14 Crim App R (S) 496 three years for rape was upheld where the defendant was not aware at the outset that the complainant did not consent but pleaded guilty on the basis that he *continued* with the intercourse knowing that she was not consenting. Interestingly, this logic of making men liable throughout the intercourse runs contrary to the orthodoxy on male sexual arousal, i.e., that men are seething volcanoes of sex and, like taps, once turned on are difficult to turn off. This continuous act construction places the onus on men for self-control, although it is acceded that in practice where a complainant claimed that she stopped consenting during the act, having consented prior to the act, it is unlikely given such circumstances that her story would be considered credible.

Against her will v 'Does not consent'

The concern to shift the vortex of interpretation on rape as conduct 'against her will' to a matter of 'does not consent' has been central to feminist politics on rape (Brownmiller 1975). In the early days of research and male academic debate on rape, rape was referred to as forcible rape (see Amir 1970, MacNamara and Sagarin 1977). Masculinist assumptions about precisely how and when this lack of consent must be manifested, determine law shaping its rules and the circumstances considered relevant to proof. Under the common law, injury to the body was not always sufficient, it had to be accompanied by injury to the genitalia (Edwards 1981, pp. 130–133). Glaister's *Medical Jurisprudence* (1945), states that the victim must maintain resistance to the last, giving up only when overcome by, 'unconsciousness, complete exhaustion, brute force or fear of death. This thinking resonated throughout every text on medical jurisprudence and is the same thinking that persists today *de facto* if not *de jure*. Under the common law, consent could only be vitiated or negatived where there was evidence of force or resistance, fraud or fear. 'Before the middle of the nineteenth century, judges would direct juries that rape was sexual intercourse against a woman's will by force, fear or fraud' (see Edwards 1981, p. 38). Otherwise 'a healthy scepticism as to the truth of her statement should be displayed' (Glaister 1945, cited in Edwards 1981, p. 130). In *Camplin* (1845) 1 Den 89, ER 169, 163, where the complainant had been drugged with alcohol, the court ruled that rape was ravishing a woman, 'without her consent and not against her will'. Lord Denman CJ said 'It is put as if resistance was essential to rape; but that is not so, although proof of resistance may be strong evidence in the case'. But the ruling in *Camplin* has been as fanciful to the ontology of rape in the nineteenth century as the ruling in *Olugboja* [1981] 3 All ER 443 (discussed below) to rape in the post 1980s.

This presence or absence of physical injury in modern times influences reporting by victims, police recording practices and prosecutorial discretion to prosecute. MacKinnon (1987, p. 88), writes, 'Finders of fact look for "more force than is usual" during the preliminaries.'. Mike Tyson expressed a universal male presumption when he said to his appeal lawyers, 'If I had all my weight on her [Desiree Washington] she'd have been black and blue, but she had no bruises. If she had no bruises then it couldn't have happened the way she said it happened' (in Reekie and Wilson 1993, p. 146). In practice force is essential to a rape prosecution and conviction. Kalven and Zeisel (1966) in examining the effect of this one factor on juries, found that rape in the absence of violence, otherwise known as 'simple rape', resulted in 60 per cent jury disagreement, the jury convicting in only three out of 42 cases. Smith (1989, p. 13) found that of 507 reported cases analysed actual violence was used in 36 per cent of cases, threats of violence in 17 per cent of cases and no indicator of violence in 47 per cent of cases. In under one fifth of all reported cases, 19 per cent involved the use of weapons accounting for over one half of all cases involving actual violence. Lloyd and Walmsley (1989, p. 18), in a study of rape convictions, compared two samples, one in 1973 and the other in 1985. With regard to physical violence there was a slight proportionate increase. In 1973, 85 per cent of cases involved some threat or use of physical violence; in 1985 this amounted to 90 per cent.

It is absence of consent and not fraud which is the key element of the *actus reus*. In *Linekar* [1995] Crim LR 320, the appellant was convicted of rape. On appeal the conviction was quashed, where the appellant had sex with a prostitute and later declined to pay the previously agreed sum of £25. The Court reaffirmed the principle that it was absence of consent, not the existence of fraud, which makes conduct rape. Major confusion arose in the nineteenth century where consent or submission had been obtained because of fraud. A deception as to the nature of the sexual act itself will not give rise to valid consent. In *Flattery* [1877] 2 QBD 410, it was held that there was no consent where a woman had been induced to believe that the defendant was performing a surgical operation. In *Williams* [1923] 1 KB 340, a man who had intercourse with a girl after falsely pretending that his acts were a method of training her voice, was properly convicted of rape.

In *Saunders* (1990) (cited in McMullan and Whittle 1994, pp. 38–39) the court convicted a transsexual female to male of indecent assault on two women. The women had consented to sexual intercourse on the basis that they believed the defendant was a man: he achieved intercourse via the use of a strapped on penis. They claimed they would not have consented had they known he was a woman. Consent was obtained via fraud as to the sexual act and the identity of the perpetrator. Saunders could not be charged with rape, since rape is an offence that can only be committed by a man and the court took the view that, as he was a female at birth then he was indeed a female, notwithstanding surgical intervention (see the chapter entitled, Transsexuals: In Legal Exile).

Paradoxically, in circumstances where the complainant thought the person was her husband and thereby consented, a woman's consent has been held to be a defence (see *Jackson* (1822) Russ and Ry 487, CCR ER 168, 911, *Barrow* (1868)11 Cox CC 191. Such frauds have been provided for in the Criminal Justice and Public Order Act 1994, s. 142, albeit restricted to marriage, which provides, 'A man also commits rape if he induces a married woman to have sexual intercourse with him by impersonating her husband.'. In *Elbekkay* [1995] Crim LR 163, where the appellant was convicted of rape the court took a broader view. He had stayed the night with the complainant and her boyfriend. All three had been drinking. During the course of the night the complainant was awakened by a man in bed with her whom she assumed was her boyfriend. She felt a penis enter her and then realised the man was not her boyfriend. A submission of no case to answer was made out on the basis that impersonation applied only to a husband, not a boyfriend. The submission was rejected and the defendant convicted. The appeal was dismissed.

To use the precise wording of the statute, 'does not consent' is a question of fact for the jury. The burden is on the prosecution to prove that at the time of the 'sexual intercourse' the woman 'does not consent'. There is no statutory definition of consent, or lack of it, whether it means words, gestures or conduct. The court has relied upon the common law construction and all that that has been taken to imply, including how the lack of consent has been manifested and communicated. The introduction of 'does not consent' is a monumental step forward, promising to take the qualification and requirement of resistance out of rape.

The case of *Olugboja* [1981] 3 All ER 443, centred on the interpretation of s. 1(1)(b) of the Sexual Offences (Amendment) Act 1976, and established for modern case law the legal principle that lack of consent does not have to be accompanied by resistance, evidence of a struggle, violence or threats. The appellant, a Nigerian student, had intercourse with Jayne who was 16 years of age, at the bungalow of the co-defendant, Lawal. Jayne and her friend Karen had been offered a lift home as a deliberate trick on the part of Lawal to get them to go to Lawal's bungalow. Jayne had already been raped by the co-defendant. Both girls had made some attempt to get out of the car and did not want to go into the bungalow. Jayne said to the appellant, 'Why can't you leave me alone?'. She removed her trousers, she did not struggle, she did not scream, and she made no resistance. She said she did not struggle because she was afraid. She was certainly intimidated. Olugboja was convicted and appealed on a question of law whether, to constitute the offence of rape, it is necessary for the consent of the victim of sexual intercourse to be vitiated by force, the fear of force, or fraud, or whether it is sufficient to prove the victim did not consent. Whilst juries are responsible for determining the meaning of consent, it is the judicial direction on consent which remains central. Dunn LJ said:

> We do not think that the issue of consent should be left to a jury without some further direction. What this should be will depend on the circumstances of each case ... [The jury] should be directed that consent, or the absence of it, is to be given its ordinary meaning and if need be, by way of example, that there is a difference between consent and submission; every consent involves a submission, but it by no means follows that a mere submission involves consent.... In the less common type of case where intercourse takes place after threats not involving violence or the fear of it ... we think that an appropriate direction to a jury will have to be fuller. They should be directed to concentrate on the state of mind of the victim immediately before the act of sexual intercourse, having regard to all relevant circumstances, and in particular the events leading up to the act, and her reaction to them showing their impact on her mind. (pp. 448–49)

The trial judge in *Olugboja* had used the words 'constraint' and 'duress' in directing the jury, both terms were criticised by Dunn LJ on appeal. But clearly such terms were required, in my view, to acquaint the jury with the nature of Jayne's predicament and her experience of it as a highly sexually intimidating situation in which she felt entrapped.

The construction of s. 1(1)(b) of the Sexual Offences (Amendment) Act 1976 in *Olugboja* was met with widespread criticism. First, because it appeared to pave the way for convictions for rape committed by acquaintances however tenuous, in the absence of threats, violence and struggle. The Report of the Criminal Law Revision Committee in 1984, *Sexual Offences*, in a direct challenge to the Court of Appeal's interpretation of 'does not consent' proposed a statutory provision which would allow the vitiation of her consent only where there were threats of violence:

> ... The offence of rape should arise where consent to sexual intercourse is obtained by threats of force, explicit or implicit, against the woman or another person, for example, her child: but that it should not be rape if, taking a reasonable view, the threats were not capable of being carried out immediately. If, for example, a woman is confined by a man for the purpose of sexual intercourse, there may well be an express or implied threat of force to be used against her should she try to escape. If so, the man should be open to conviction for rape should sexual intercourse occur under such duress. In other cases the threats may be capable of being carried out only at some time in the future, and that should not lead to liability for rape. (para. 2.26–2.29).

Secondly, Smith and Hogan (1988, p. 434) in a veiled criticism of the proposals that consent was a jury matter commented:

> It is doubtful if the bounds of the crime of rape can be satisfactorily drawn by a distinction between consent and submission. Second, a lesser criticism focused on the fact that construction of consent was said to be wholly a jury question (see Williams 1983, p. 551) and *Olugboja* seemed to justify judicial direction especially in these difficult cases arguably in such cases replacing a judicial version of consent. It is so vague ...

Williams (1983, p. 554), in responding rather more robustly said that it was wholly inappropriate to leave the matter to the jury. In truth, whilst *Olugboja* stands as Court of Appeal authority on the circumstances under which consent can be considered negated, its effect on future rape cases is minimalised. Where women have submitted in circumstances of similar psychological duress and entrapment, in the absence of threats, and where the parties are acquainted or 'dating', the reality is that the CPS would be unlikely to proceed. Case law merely states that rape is possible where there is submission and lack of consent. As Temkin has noted, '... *Olugboja* is unlikely to become a complainant's charter' (1987, p. 66). Experience has shown that its impact has been limited. However, the lack of struggle or lack of resistance characterised by a submission yet not necessarily a consent, characterises many situations in which women submit but do not consent to rape.

Hickson (see above) had been raping and indecently assaulting young girl swimmers in his charge since one of them was 13 and these were young women who put all their trust in him. For the girls who were abused swimming was their life and this man had the power to drop them from the team. The Law Commission in the consultation paper on *Consent and Offences Against the Person*, 1994, No. 134 acceded to the possibility of consent being obtained through the misuse of power (see Vega 1988). In their second consultation paper on consent, *Consent and the Criminal Law No. 139*, 1995 (hereafter) (*Consent No. 2*), the Law Commission proposed a new offence distinguishable from rape where sexual intercourse is secured by non-violent theats (para. 6.45, p. 70). Such a proposal devalues much that has been emphasised about rape as an issue of non-consent and overrules the decision in *Olugboja*.

Prosecuting rape — men's *mens rea*

The constituent elements of the *mens rea* for rape are the intent to have sexual intercourse knowing that the woman does not consent or else recklessness in relation to whether she consented or not (s. 2(2) Sexual Offences Act 1956). Section 1(2) of the 1976 Act, as amended by the Criminal Justice and Public Order Act 1994, Sch. 10, para. 35, is relevant, 'It is hereby declared that if at a trial for a rape offence the jury has to consider whether a man believed that a woman or man was consenting to sexual intercourse, the presence or absence of reasonable grounds for such a belief is a matter to which the jury must have regard, in conjunction with any other relevant matters, in considering whether he so believed.'. This formulation follows the House of Lords ruling in *DPP* v *Morgan* [1975] 2 All ER 347, and the recommendations of the Heilbron Committee which was convened precisely to, '. . . provide the opportunity to clarify existing law and in particular to bring out the importance of recklessness as a mental element in the crime. Such a definition would also emphasise that lack of consent (and not violence) is the crux of the matter.'.

In *Morgan*, the mental element in rape was considered by the House of Lords. Here Morgan, an RAF pilot, and three of his male friends had intercourse with Morgan's wife. The prosecution case was that she protested and struggled and cried out 'No' throughout. The defence claimed, wholly incompatibly, that the three men believed she was consenting because Morgan had told them that she was 'kinky' and liked the additional thrill of a struggle. The trial judge directed the jury that the defendants should be acquitted if they considered that the men honestly believed that the woman consented and their belief in her consent was 'reasonable'. On the basis of this direction the three men were convicted. They appealed against conviction to a single judge who dismissed their appeal ([1975] 1 All ER 15), although the judge certified that a point of law of general public importance was involved because the trial judge had misdirected the jury on reasonableness by wrongly directing the jury that the belief in her consent had to be based on reasonable grounds. The House of Lords, acceding the point in the defendants' favour, held that it was not necessary that the grounds for their belief must be reasonable. The House of Lords held, however, that their belief, reasonable or unreasonable, was not honestly held and reinstated the conviction by applying the proviso (Criminal Appeal Act 1968, s. 2 which allows a conviction to be upheld under certain circumstances '. . . provided that the court may, notwithstanding that they are of the opinion that the point raised in the appeal might be decided in favour of the appellant, dismiss the appeal if they consider that no miscarriage of justice has actually occurred' (now amended by the Criminal Appeal Act 1995, s. 2)). Lord Cross explained it thus:

That any jury which thought that the grounds for a belief in consent put forward by the appellants which if truly held would have been eminently reasonable, were in fact never entertained by them at all, should in the same breath hold that they may have an honest belief in consent based on different and unreasonable grounds is inconceivable.

Prior to the ruling in *Morgan*, in order for a mistake to provide a defence, it had to be based on objectively reasonable grounds. Lord Hailsham said:

> Once one has accepted, what seems to me abundantly clear, that the prohibited act in rape is non-consensual sexual intercourse, and that the guilty state of mind is an intention to commit it, it seems to me to follow as a matter of inexorable logic that there is no room either for a 'defence' of honest belief or mistake, or of a defence of honest and reasonable belief of mistake (p. 316).

What might be considered to amount to an honest belief in a woman's consent, notwithstanding that its unreasonableness is shaped and bound by unwritten assumptions, codes and conventions of behaviour which shape and mould the male belief about what might indicate a willingness to sex? Whilst not a rule of law, her behaviour, sociability, attitude, willingness to go to his home or invite him to her home, are factors all of which are assessed for the impact each may have on the formulation of his beliefs.

The second element of considerable difficulty in assessing a man's *mens rea* relies upon a consideration of whether or not he was reckless and explores the state of mind of the man who could not care less whether she consented or not and, somewhat paradoxically, also the man who had not even considered whether she was consenting or not. Mistaken belief is often equated with recklessness and in the middle ground the two overlap. Lord Hailsham's deliberations on this point in *Morgan* are illustrative of the conflation:

> I am content to rest my view of the instant case of the crime of rape by saying that it is my opinion that the prohibited act is and always has been intercourse without consent of the victim and the mental element is and always has been the intention to commit that act, or the equivalent intention of having intercourse willy-nilly not caring whether the victim consents or no (p. 362).

In the years following the 1976 Act, the courts were unclear as to the appropriate direction to juries on recklessness in rape. In *Pigg* (1982) 74 Cr App R 352, where two girls aged 15 and 17 experienced a horrifying ordeal of attempted rape by a stranger who seized and attacked them, girls subjecting them to a catalogue of indignities, one of the several grounds of appeal related to the trial judge's direction to the jury on recklessness. Lord Lane held that the Diplock ruling of recklessness in criminal damage could not, '. . . be lifted bodily and applied to rape' and modified it to apply it to rape. He asserted:

... so far as rape is concerned, a man is reckless if either he was indifferent and gave no thought to the possibility that the woman might not be consenting in circumstances where if any thought had been given to the matter it would have been obvious that there was risk she was not, or, that he was aware of the possibility that she might not be consenting but nevertheless persisted regardless of whether she consented or not (p. 362).

It was held that if anything the judge's direction was in fact too favourable to the defendant. Judges found difficulty with applying a direction which did not make clear whether it should have been obvious to the defendant, or to a reasonable man, whether or not she was consenting (Rook and Ward 1990, p. 55). Jurisprudentially, this formulation also gave rise to a lack of logic since in assessing *mens rea* it was considered untenable to find a man possessing the necessary *mens rea* even though he had not considered the question at all.

Further difficulties arise as to the appropriate test to apply. A subjective test is based on the defendant's perceptions and assessment of the situation, whilst an objective test is based on what a reasonable man would have considered or perceived to be the situation. Given the options, the defence is likely to be one of mistaken belief relying on the subjective test, where however unreasonable the defendant's belief, he can plead that he genuinely thought she was consenting. The prosecution may challenge the mistaken belief claim on the grounds of recklessness, whether the defendant was reckless as to her consent or not is to be determined by the jury who must consider whether he ought to have considered whether she consented. The *Pigg* ruling introduced some conflict with the ruling in *Morgan* as *Pigg* did not settle whether the test was objective or subjective, whereas *Morgan* had made it clear that the test was subjective. There have been problems in the test to be applied in reckless rape which have led to the Court of Appeal quashing a string of convictions for rape on the basis of a misdirection on whether the test to be applied is a subjective or objective one. In *Bashir* (1983) 77 Cr App R 59, where the defendant appealed against a conviction for rape on the basis that the direction to the jury embraced both an objective and subjective component, the court took the view that the test to apply in rape was whether the defendant acted recklessly (subjective test), not whether a reasonable man acted recklessly (objective). The court stated that in their view *Pigg* was based on a subjective interpretation and in support of *Pigg*, 'It will be noted that that definition allows none other than a subjective approach to the state of mind of a person of whom it is said he acted recklessly in committing a crime.'. In *Bashir*, two girls went back to the home of a former boyfriend, The upshot was that the man said they wanted intercourse and had it. The defendant said he could not remember anything. The conviction was quashed on the grounds that the judge had misdirected the jury.

In *Satnam S, Kewal S* (1984) 78 Cr App R 149, the Court of Appeal accepted the ambiguity in the *Pigg* ruling regarding the test to be applied, which they stated was *obiter*, and went on to distinguish reckless rape from criminal damage and recklessness, finally laying to rest any ambiguity, Bristow J said, 'Any direction as to the definition of rape should ... be based upon section 1 of the 1976 Act and upon *DPP* v *Morgan* without regard to *R* v *Caldwell* or *R* v *Lawrence*. . . . In the case of rape the foreseeability is as to the state of mind of the victim', (p. 154) thereby reaffirming that the test was one of whether the belief in her consent was considered to be honestly held or whether he was reckless. It would appear that absence of belief in consent has been equated with recklessness. Has the *Satnam* ruling assisted the negotiation of this legal terrain? In subsequent cases recklessness has been further clarified along the lines of the Hailsham ruling in *Morgan*. In *Taylor* (1985) 80 Cr App R 327, 332, Lord Lane giving the judgment of the court said, 'Was the defendant's attitude one of "I could not care less whether she is consenting or not, I am going to have intercourse with her regardless"?'. The appeal was dismissed. In this case the complainant was getting ready to go out with her friend and her friend's children. As it turned out her friend went out on her own and the complainant stayed at the friend's house and cooked a meal for her friend's husband who then proceeded to rape her. In his statement he said, 'Well she did not exactly agree but she did not exactly say no either.'. In addition, he had said to a friend, 'I gave her one.'. A sentence of two years was upheld. In *Gardiner* [1994] Crim LR 455, Lexis Transcript, in a case of attempted rape, an absence of direction by the trial judge that the burden of proof was on the Crown to disprove a defence of 'mistaken belief' in consent led to quashing the conviction, although the other grounds of appeal were rejected. The trial judge directed the jury on recklessness thus:

> However, it must be borne in mind, and Mr. Poole stresses this because he says this is an important aspect of this case: whether or not she consents, the Prosecution have to establish another element . . . either that he knows she is not consenting . . . or else he is reckless as to whether she is consenting or not — reckless as to whether she is consenting or not. What does that mean? He must be reckless in a sense he never gave it a thought, or he was aware that she might not be consenting but goes on just the same. It is very simple, put it this way: 'I couldn't care less whether she's consenting — I'm going to have intercourse with her.' That would be the element of recklessness. Do you understand that, ladies and gentlemen? 'I couldn't care less whether she was consenting — I'm going ahead.'

He went on to make a further reference to the questions of consent and knowledge and he said this: 'In the last analysis what is in his mind is what counts, but when you are deciding that you are entitled to have a look at the reasonable grounds for belief or lack of it. Do you understand that ladies and gentlemen?' Then the judge said:

> All those indicate that he was believing she was consenting by the fact that he did not have to use any force to her — he did not use any force to her — he did not have to get her clothes off as opposed to taking them off gently, and whether he might have been nervous or not, or 'scared', as he put it, by the presence of his housekeeper — that he was scared because she might catch them in the act rather than anything else . . . In that context if the defence is that he believes that she consented and the defence here is that he believes

she consented, the presence or absence of reasonable grounds for his belief is a matter to which you are entitled to have regard.

This ruling was not faulted although the conviction was quashed on the grounds that had been an inadequate direction on burden of proof.

In *Larter and Castleton* [1995] Crim LR 75, where a 14 year old girl had been raped, but was drunk and insensible at the time and unable to give her consent, the accused said, 'Well she must have been game to go with John, that sort of thing'. 'I didn't know how old she was. I knew nothing.' He was asked later on, 'You just assumed she wanted it, didn't you, basically?'. To which his answer was 'Yeah'. He did not suggest at any stage that he obtained her consent. The judge's direction was held on appeal to be perfectly adequate:

The question is did she at the material time understand her situation and was she then capable of exercising a rational judgment?'... are you sure she did not consent and if you are sure that she did not consent when you are considering the case of each defendant you then go on to consider whether the defendant whose case you are considering knew that she was not consenting or could not care less as to whether she was consenting or not.

In *McFall* [1994] Crim LR 226, the appellant was charged with the rape and kidnapping of a woman with whom he had been cohabiting, in fear and terror of him she faked consent to intercourse and further pretended that she was enjoying the experience. She believed that this was necessary to preserve her life. He appealed on the ground that he believed she had consented. The Court of Appeal upheld the jury's conviction. This case raises the difficulty that women do not assent because of fear but may well assent and fake enjoyment to ensure their safety.

Recklessness was an issue in the case of *State* v *Tyson* (1992) (unreported), *The Washington Times*, 27 March 1992 and the conviction for rape was affirmed on appeal in *Tyson* v *State* 619 NE 2d 276 (1994). In this case Tyson and the victim, Desiree Washington, met briefly on 18 July 1991. At about 1.30 a.m. Tyson telephoned the victim and invited her to go around Indianapolis with him. She initially refused as she was already in bed, Tyson persisted and said that it would be the only opportunity to see him as he was leaving Indianapolis in the morning. The victim got dressed and took a camera with her and she joined him in the limousine. Tyson then went to his room as he said he wanted to get something and the victim accompanied him. After fifteen minutes of talking, the conversation was turned to sexual innuendo, then Tyson pushed the victim on the bed, told her not to resist and restrained her. The jury did not support the giving of an honest and reasonable mistake of fact instruction. Tyson appealed on the ground that past moral character was excluded. The appeal court upheld the conviction on the grounds that past moral character was properly excluded. Reckless rape, however, is difficult to establish where the defence is claiming that the woman consented or that the man's belief is mistaken and a conviction on the basis of recklessness would arise only in those cases where the proprietorial right and expectation of sex was blatantly manifest.

PAST MORAL CHARACTER AND WOMEN'S MENS REA 'ON TRIAL'

The law has defined and organised issues of consent and rules of evidence around ideologies about women's desire for sex, rather than around the masculinist presumption of proprietorial right to sex. Where consent is advanced as a defence the trial focuses on the state of mind of the victim as Bristow J stated in *Pigg* 'the foreseeability is as to the state of mind of the victim'. Where the defence is one of consent the rape is presented as a sex parody, a pastiche of soft pornographic representation, where even violence is reconstructed by the defence as a manifestation of sex to allow for the maximum opportunity for acquittal (see MacKinnon 1987, Smart 1989, Lees 1992). Hodge Jones and Allen, solicitors and Bindman and Partners, solicitors, have in the past refused to represent clients charged with rape where the defence is one of consent. Today Hodge Jones and Allen say that each case would 'be looked at on its merits', Bindman's have said they would not act for a man charged with rape where consent is an issue, unless it had been agreed by the partners of the firm.

The key objections and problems raised in this critique are threefold. First, although s. 2 of the Sexual Offences (Amendment) Act 1976 generally prohibits questions as to past moral character, it seems that where judges are persuaded that such questions are considered critical to the issue of consent then such character evidence is admitted. This is the mischief of s. 2 (see *Larter* above). Secondly, defence counsel persuade the court, even in the presence of violence, that the conduct was above all sexual which then rebuts the woman's allegation of non-consent. Thirdly, there seems to be little restriction placed on the tactics of defence counsel once such character evidence is deemed admissible. Where the defence is one of consent, then in assessing the woman's state of mind, rules of evidence have developed and are derived from the common law. The presumptions defending the relevance of her sexual past to the issue of consent in rape are derived from the common law and have a pedigree dating back to Hale who insisted (1971, p. 633):

> The party ravished may give evidence upon oath, and is in law a competent witness, but the credibility of her testimony, and how far forth she is to be believed, must be left to the jury, and is more or less credible according to the circumstances of fact, that concur in that testimony. For instance, if the witness be of good fame, if she presently discovered the offence and made pursuit after the offender, shewd circumstances and signs of the injury ... these ... give greater probability to her testimony.

Mounting objection to this 'free rein' cross-examination resulted in the Report of the Advisory Group on Rape, the Heilbron Committee, recommending, 'We have reached the conclusion that the previous sexual history of the alleged victim with third parties is of no significance as far as credibility is concerned and is only rarely likely to be relevant to issues directly before the jury.'. Restricting the ambit of cross-examination as to previous sexual experience with other men, and as to general moral character, was finally provided by s. 2 which provides:

(1) If at a trial any person is for the time being charged with a rape offence to which he pleaded not guilty, then, except with the leave of the judge, no evidence and no question in cross-examination shall be adduced or asked at the trial, by or on behalf of any defendant at the trial, about any sexual experience of a complainant with a person other than the defendant. (2) The judge shall not give leave in pursuance of the preceding subsection for any evidence or question except on an application made to him in the absence of the jury by or on behalf of a defendant; and on such an application the judge shall give leave if and only if he is satisfied that it would be unfair to that defendant to refuse to allow the evidence to be adduced or the question to be asked.

Whilst the Sexual Offences (Amendment) Act 1976, s. 2, limits the introduction of sexual history evidence in cross-examination with third parties, research has shown that this rule is relaxed in the majority of cases, and once relaxed the nature of cross-examination proceeds without limit. Adler's 1987 study showed that of 45 cases that went to trial, an application under s. 2 was made in 40 per cent of these cases (1987, p. 73). Where the defence is one of consent, 60 per cent of defendants made such an application. In 75 per cent of all applications the judge took the view that exclusion of the evidence would be unfair to the defendant (1987, p. 75). Temkin (1987, p. 7) writes, 'The law permits only relevant evidence to be adduced in criminal trials. In rape cases, they appear all too often to have given defence counsel free rein'. Temkin argues that the section is being given an increasingly narrow interpretation (1993, p. 2). Whilst many counsel make applications to the judge under s. 2, Adler found that others ignore it and besmirch the character of the complainant by innuendo (1982, p. 673). It is a matter for the trial judge to decide where there is an application for leave to cross-examine, whether the proposed questions are relevant and whether the exclusion of such matters would be prejudicial to the defendant. In considering this matter the judge must consider whether the evidence to be adduced will go to credit or is relevant to an issue in the case. The test is whether the exclusion of such evidence would be unfair to the defendant.

Whilst some judges have held that past moral character is immaterial to the issue of consent and material only to credit, others have held that past moral character goes to the very heart of the issue. It is very difficult to see where this line of reasoning, i.e., whether past moral character goes to credit or goes to consent, starts and finishes. It is *de jure* a matter of law. However, it seems that whether past moral character is a function of credit or consent depends upon how bad a woman's past sexual history appears to be, so although deemed a question of law, it is in practice determined by fact.

The primary purpose of s. 2 is thereby negated, since after all, the point is that however bad the sexual history, such matters should have no bearing on the case before the court. Whilst in the UK this matter is left to judges to decide, Temkin points out that legislation in other countries is far stricter (1993, p. 4). Improper exclusion of character evidence can result in the appeal court quashing the conviction. The Court of Appeal has taken a back seat approach to delineating the parameters of when past moral character can be included or excluded. It would appear from the case law that the tendency is to quash convictions where an application on appeal is made on the grounds that past moral character was improperly excluded. If the Court of Appeal casts a shadow over the strategies of defence counsel, the obvious strategy would be to make an application to the trial judge for past moral character to be admitted. If this fails, then an appeal on the basis that past moral character was wrongly excluded should be made. It is much more difficult for the Court of Appeal when presented with such an appeal to reason why such evidence was appropriately excluded. In so doing the Court of Appeal lays down guidelines which circumscribe the uncircumscribable, given that issues to credit and issues to consent do not seem to be at opposite ends of the continuum, but in practice interchangeable.

Although said to be a matter of law (see Archbold 1995, vol. 1, 7–68) it appears that the Court of Appeal merely replaces its discretion on the matter for that of the trial judge, such that the appeal court continuously contributes to the sabotage and dismantling of s. 2. In *Lawrence and Another* [1977] Crim LR 492, when considering whether or not to allow an application under this section, May J formulated the test thus:

> The important part of the statute which I think needs construction are the words 'if and only if he [the judge] is satisfied that it would be unfair to that defendant to refuse to allow the evidence to be adduced or the question to be asked'. And in my judgment, before a judge is satisfied or may be said to be satisfied that to refuse to allow a particular question or a series of questions in cross-examination would be unfair to a defendant he must take the view that it is more likely than not that the particular question or line of cross-examination, if allowed, might reasonably lead the jury, properly directed in the summing-up, to take a different view of the complainant's evidence from that which they might take if the question or series of questions was or were not allowed (p. 493).

May J added that cross-examination designed to say that 'this is the sort of girl she is' is not relevant to credit. That is the whole point, i.e., that juries may take a wholly different view of the evidence upon hearing what kind of girl she is, not because it necessarily has a bearing on the instant case. In *Mills* (1979) 68 Cr App R 327, in an appeal against a trial judge's refusal to allow cross-examination under s. 2 where the defence had wanted to cross-examine the complainant as to sexual experience with third parties, the Court of Appeal held that such matters were properly excluded. However, in *Viola* [1982] 3 ALL ER 73, the appellant knocked at the complainant's door, alleging that he had thrown his car keys into her doorway because police were after him. The complainant let him in to the house so that he could look through the window to see if the police were still looking for him. He became violent and raped her.

The Court of Appeal here decided that cross-examination had been improperly disallowed. The appeal rested on two main grounds of appeal where cross-examination had been disallowed. First, the presence of two men in the house before the appellant arrived, where a heavy drinking session took place and the complainant made sexual advances to one of the men. Secondly, that a friend who had come to pick up the complainant's son to take him to school found a man lying naked on the sofa. Lord Lane CJ set out some guidelines for judges in consideration of s. 2 in subsequent cases:

> On (the) one hand evidence of sexual promiscuity may be so strong or so closely contemporaneous in time to the event in issue so as to come near to, or indeed to reach the border between mere credit and an issue in the case. Conversely, the relevance of the evidence to an issue in the case may be so slight as to lead the judge to the conclusion that he is far from satisfied that the exclusion of the evidence or the question from the consideration of the jury would be unfair to the defendant (p. 77).

In this case the court said that the questions went to the issue and not just to credit. Thus, the blurring of where issues of past moral character go to credit or to the case itself remains unclear and ambiguous. This ambiguity has facilitated defence argument that past moral character issues go to the heart of the case. It is curious how sexual promiscuity may be so strong 'or so closely and contemporaneous in time to the event' that it is said to bring the case to the borderland of credit or issue. Is there in fact a difference at all, or is it merely a strained distinction at centile points on a continuum? The Lord Chief Justice in *Viola* conceded, 'Inevitably in this situation, as in so many situations in law, there is a grey area which exists between the two types of relevance, namely relevance to credit and relevance to an issue in the case.'.

So what is improper exclusion? The position seems to be that in the majority of cases where consent is the issue, past moral character is admitted; where it is not and the point is argued on appeal, the appeal court rarely upholds the trial judge's refusal. All in all the vast majority of cases result in admitting past moral character either at trial or by ruling it improperly excluded on appeal. The amplification of admission of past moral character occurs as a result of the weakness of the Court of Appeal in its overly cautious approach. The watershed provision of admitting past moral character in exceptional circumstances is only replaced by admission of past moral character almost by rote.

The present position indicates a departure from *Lawrence* where past sexual character is considered almost always to go to the issue. In *Redguard* [1991] Crim LR 213 the complainant said that she would not allow anyone to stay in the flat, let alone allow anyone to have sex with her. The judge refused to allow an application where the line of questioning sought to cross-examine her on the fact that she had had a sexual encounter with another man who stayed in her flat two weeks previous to the incident in question. The judge said that the purpose of such a line of questioning was irrelevant and intended to besmirch. On appeal the court said that such evidence was improperly excluded and stated that these facts were relevant both to credit as well as to consent. In

Barnes [1994] Crim LR 691, where a stepfather had raped a stepdaughter and the trial judge had excluded cross-examination as to sexual history, the convictions were quashed and a retrial ordered. The judge had refused to allow cross-examination regarding sexual experience with other males and on the vibrator that was found in her room (it is difficult to see what a vibrator has to do with sexual consent or whether a stepfather had raped his stepdaughter). The Court took the view that her sexual background went to the issue and not merely to credit. A similarly staggering decision was made in *SMS* [1992] Crim LR 310, where past moral character of the complainant was considered relevant to consent. Here, a male aged 26, with one hand and a false eye, was charged with raping a 14 year old girl. The rape took place in extremely squalid circumstances. The defence made an application to cross-examine to ascertain whether she had had intercourse with any others before the alleged rape since she said she was a virgin. The trial judge refused. The appellant appealed on the basis that the judge had wrongly excluded cross-examination and the appeal court considered that the question of the girl's past sexual experience went to consent and that it was not a matter of discretion but a matter of judgment. The conviction was quashed on the basis that past moral character had been improperly excluded. In *Said* [1992] Crim LR 433, yet another extremely worrying decision, the complainant, a 14 year old girl, alleged rape; she too said she was a virgin. In this case cross-examination was excluded. The appeal was allowed on the basis that past moral character had been wrongly excluded and such evidence went to the credit of her story and would have assisted the jury in determining whether she consented. It would have determined whether her story about her virginity was true or false.

The difficulty is explained by the authors of Blackstone's with reference to the case of *Funderburk* (1990) 90 Cr App R 466: 'Where the disputed issue is a sexual one between two persons in private, the difference between questions going to credit and questions going to the issue is reduced to vanishing-point' (Blackstone's 1996 F7.19, p. 1872) and '... there is a grey area between the two types of relevance (F7.15, p. 1863). The authors of Archbold 1996, Vol. 2, paras. 20–34a, similarly assert that, '... the dividing line is extremely fine' and it is submitted that this is exactly the sort of reasoning that the Act of 1976 was intended to outlaw. In *Funderburk*,

> It seems to us that on the way the prosecution presented the evidence the challenge to the loss of virginity was a challenge that not only did the jury desire to know about on the basis that it might have affected their view on the central question of credit, but was sufficiently clearly related to the subject matter of the indictment for justice to require investigation for the basis of such a challenge (p. 476).

Where the case turns on similar fact evidence then the argument for admitting past sexual character seems even more compelling. Defence counsel seem to take particular advantage of this. Adler 1982 cites a case from her study where the defence claimed that because the complainant had had sexual intercourse in the past with 'coloured' men, she was similarly not averse to coloured men having sex with her on waste ground. Judges are not implacable on this point and on occasion resist the over stretching of similar fact: in this case the judge felt unable to concede the argument, 'Are you saying that a girl of 15 who has had sexual intercourse before is necessarily more likely to consent, lie on the filthy ground and have sexual intercourse with complete strangers?'.

Where the complainant is a prostitute this is highly likely to be regarded as relevant to the issue of consent rather than merely to credit, indicating again that the question is not one of judgment or of law but depends on the strength of the facts. The common law has taken the general view that prostitute women, *ipso facto* are unlikely to tell the truth. The difficulty for the unchaste victim of rape was addressed by Lord Coleridge CJ in *Hallett* (1841) ER 173, 1038.

> It has been held that evidence to shew that the woman has previously had connection with persons other than the accused, when she has denied that fact, must be rejected, and there are very good reasons for rejecting it. It should in my view be rejected, not only upon the ground that to admit it would be unfair and a hardship to the woman, but also upon the general principle that it is not evidence which goes directly to the point at issue at the trial ... It is obvious, too, that the result of admitting such evidence would be to deprive an unchaste woman of any protection against assaults of this nature.

The prostitute, as the notoriously sexually bad girl, is going to find that as a matter of course past sexual moral character is admitted with the consequence that the jury are inevitably going to be prejudiced and her way of life will cloud the issue (see Lees 1989, 1993). The fact remains and it has been voiced in many quarters, that as long as past moral character is regarded as of relevance to consent, it will be impossible to freebase it from consent and indeed improper to exclude it. The Criminal Law Revision Committee in its 1984 report on Sexual Offences commented:

> It seems that some people, and in particular some women's organisations, think that these statutory provisions are proving ineffective for the protection of complainants because many judges, so it is alleged, grant leave to cross examine about a complainant's previous experience upon being asked to do so. Critics do not seem to appreciate that a complainant's previous sexual experience may be relevant to the issue of consent (p. 25).

SEXUALISING FORCE

The 1990s has opened up a new approach to constructing violence and abuse. In the name of sexual liberalism the comments made by the courts indicate that what otherwise might have been considered in the domain of the violent is now considered part of the sexual.

Defence strategies

The second problem arises where violent rape is reconstructed as a question of sex by carefully playing on contemporary discourses of sexual violence and bizarre sex as irrevocably consensual. Frequently, defence counsel seek to normalise the violence as part of consensual sex, not as an expression of force and resistance. In the face of wholly incompatible accounts, defending counsel must present the rape as a matter of consensual sexual intercourse, must exploit popular mythology and appeal to rape stereotypes so as to transform rape into consensual sex. In *Holdsworth, The Economist* 25 June 1977, the defendant, a Coldstream Guardsman, was convicted of attempted rape and grievous bodily harm. He had wrenched out the victim's earrings, broken one or two ribs, dug his fist into her kidney and inserted a ringed hand into her vagina in an assault at a bus stop. The defendant had 'allowed his enthusiasm for sex to overcome normal good behaviour', said Wien J whilst the appeal court reduced his three year sentence to six months, 'The only reason we are taking this course is that we do not want to see your career in ruins for ever, richly as you deserve that three-year sentence'.

Adler, in her study of rape trials at the Old Bailey, found this reconstruction of violence as sex, of 'no' as meaning 'yes', a common defence strategy (1987, pp. 92, 115, 116). Edwards (1981, p. 166) discovered how easy this reconstruction of violence as sex is and how effective, in empirical research on rape trials conducted in 1980. On 26 February 1980 in Birmingham two brothers were charged, one with rape, the other with assault. The complainant suffered bruising, abrasions and a cut to the lip. Defending counsel accepted that the complainant had been hit. The prosecution's presentation was that she had been raped and assaulted. The defence version was that she had asked to be hit with the hackneyed and unlikely words, 'Hit me, hit me, I'm kinky'. In another case observed by the author in an adjacent court the prosecution described how the complainant had been held down by the arms and raped, forensic evidence showed she had bruising to the forearms and to the thighs. The prosecution explained that she had been forcibly pinned down by the arms and the weight of the somewhat overweight man on top of her. The defence version did not dispute that she had been held by the forearms but explained that this had occurred after consensual sex had taken place, in an effort by the defendant to calm and quieten an hysterical woman who, racked with guilt after having had sex, began to cry uncontrollably. The defence counsel, in cross-examination of the forensic witness as to the bruising on the thighs, asked whether it was possible to distinguish between bruising and suction marks occasioned by a love bite. The forensic expert, inexperienced in courtroom defence tactics, after a series of excusatory, reductionist questions by the defence, uttered the compelling words which the defence had so skillfully engineered, 'Yes, it is possible that the marks of a bruise and love bite are similar'. Upon this the judge withdrew the case from the jury by ordering an acquittal.

In *Boyea* [1992] Crim LR 574, the defendant was convicted of indecent assault. The defendant had inserted his hand into the complainant's vagina causing injuries. The judge in directing the jury said that if they were satisfied that his actions were likely or intended to cause bodily harm, whether she consented or not was not a relevant consideration since the extent of violence inflicted went beyond the risk of minor injury. The defendant appealed on the ground that the jury should have been directed on the subjective formulation, i.e., 'did the defendant know or should it have been obvious to him that bodily harm might result?'. The Court of Appeal in dismissing the appeal upheld the direction of the trial judge. What is interesting about this case is that the issue consent was not raised by the defence. On the contrary, the defence relied on the fact that he passed out and remembered nothing. The victim alleged non-consent and said that she passed out after the incident. It was the judge who introduced consent in his summing up:

> In some cases where an indecent assault is alleged whether the person complaining of the assault consented to what was done becomes a crucial issue in the case because in many cases where an indecent assault is alleged consent to what was done by the person complaining of the assault is a complete defence. In a case where consent is a complete defence to the charge it is for the prosecution to satisfy the jury that the person complaining of the indecent assault did not consent; it is not for the defence to prove that there was consent by the complainant.

It was the Court of Appeal which added, 'The court must take into account that social attitudes have changed over the years, particularly in the field of sexual relations between adults. '. . . As a generality, the level of vigour in sexual congress which is generally acceptable, and therefore the voluntarily accepted risk of incurring some injury, is probably higher now than it was in 1934. . . .' Since the question of consent was neither raised by defence nor by the prosecution it is curious that it was raised at all by the judge and later by the Court of Appeal who placed an entirely new impression on this case. The result is that *Boyea* is cited as authority for later cases on the question of consent.

Where the dead cannot speak, such as the victims in *Slingsby* [1995] Crim LR 570, and *Williamson* (1994) 15 Cr App R (S) 364, what might the deceased's story have revealed, if we could have heard it? In *Slingsby* the deceased died of septicaemia. The appellant had sexual intercourse with the victim, buggered her, penetrated her vagina and rectum with his hand, all of which he said were consensual acts. She suffered cuts but did not realise her injuries were potentially very serious. Counsel for the Crown held that she could not have consented. The judge ruled that, notwithstanding the tragic consequence of what happened, the count of manslaughter could not be sustained given that the act of inserting a hand into the vagina did not constitute an unlawful act (this goes against *Boyea*).

In *Williamson* the appellant's four year sentence was reduced to three for manslaughter. The appellant had accidentally killed the victim during consensual, 'essentially pseudo-masochistic' sexual intercourse. The defendant claimed that each held the other's neck in order to heighten the thrill of sex, and the deceased put a pillow over her face, as she had done before, to muffle the sounds that she made. He later went to the police station and gave an account of what had happened. The availability of a discourse on sexual stimulation and partial asphyxia allowed his account to be rendered credible. The Crown's pathologist said that sexual practices involving mutual asphyxiation were recognised in the medical profession and the defence expressed the same view.

The defence described their relationship in endearing terms, 'these two had been deeply attached to one another'. The appellant, however, had a string of convictions for offences of violence including wounding with intent, common assault, actual bodily harm and assault on the police. He was undoubtedly a very violent man; he had in addition taken heroin and cannabis. Williamson was released in October 1993 when he went to live with an ex-girlfriend and was later arrested for an attack on her. He then went to live with his mother whom he stabbed to death. The judge said, 'This man's past shows the public needs the maximum protection from him in his current mental state.'. This construction of violence as consensual sex affects both the interpretation of fatalities involving women in the heterosexual as well as the homosexual context (as the case of *Billia* [1996] 1 Cr App R (S) 39, illustrates. How far consent is now going to invidiously infect future defence strategies in such cases remains to be seen.

Rape as sex in courtroom language

Matoesian (1993) talks of the domination of the defence in the court room particularly given the freedom of cross-examination. The defence must suggest not merely that she is lying but convince the jury that the conduct is sex. Once it is regarded as sex then the construction of her account as lies follows. Where the defence is one of consent no restrictions are placed on the line of questioning and although deprecated this is a well established style of cross-examination. In *Hutchinson* (1986) 82 Cr App R 51, where the appellant had been convicted of three murders and a rape, this was the way in which the cross examination of the victim was approached.

DC 'I suggest that you went to your bedroom and he followed you, and you put on some music.'

Victim 'No.'

DC 'The two of you danced together.'

Victim 'No.'

DC 'You Kissed.'

Victim 'No.'

DC 'You petted.'

Victim 'No.'

DC 'You stripped.'

Victim 'No.'

DC 'Sexual intercourse took place.'

Victim 'No.'

(*The Times*, 6 September 1984.)

As this example from Matoesian (1993, p. 117) indicates, although the prosecution alleges violence, the defence must reconstruct the incident as sex if they are to succeed.

District Attorney 'Do you know what that feels like?'

Victim 'Yes.'

District Attorney 'To have somebody climax in you?'

P.A. 'Objection, your honour.'

Judge 'Objection sustained.'

District Attorney 'Your Honour, I'm not delving into this woman's past sexual history.'

There is the problem too of the way in which the offence of rape is recorded in law reports, and cases are summed up by judges. *Hopkins* (1994) 15 Cr App R (S) 373, provides a typical summing-up of a rape case. 'He first tried to penetrate her with his finger, and then with his penis. He was unsuccessful because her vagina was dry. Accordingly, he seized a piece of soap, put it in under the tap and managed to generate sufficient lather to rub on her vagina and facilitate penetration' (per Lord Taylor CJ).

The third problem arises in respect of the relatively free rein given to defence counsel in cross-examination and the tactics employed once cross-examination as to past sexual experience is allowed. It is not known whether judges have now begun to apply Bar Council rules, or indeed whether there is any change in interpretation of such rules. There are general rules regulating conduct in cross-examination, but counsel may ask leading questions (see Adler 1987, p. 46).

Defence Counsel 'Would you agree that your evidence, as to the detail hasn't been the same on each occasion?'

Victim 'I am somewhat confused as to the details.'

Defence Counsel   'I suggest to you that Joe did not come back after leaving the bedroom.'

Victim   'He did.'

The judge is placed under a duty to restrain unnecessary cross examination, (see Archbold 1995, Vol. 1, pp. 8–99). Researchers who have made empirical observations on the rape trial find it hard to find any cases where this duty has been exercised. Witnesses may be asked questions about antecedents, associations or mode of life which, although irrelevant to the issue, would be likely to discredit their testimony. However, such cross-examination must be within the limits prescribed by the rules laid down by the Bar Council, restated in 1990. In *Sweet-Escott* (1971) 55 Cr App R 316, Lawton J, in consideration of this question asked, 'How far back is it permissible for advocates when cross-examining as to credit to delve into a person's past and to drag up such dirt as they can find there?'. In a case I observed in 1975 a conviction for prostitution some twenty years old was dredged up in court. Old attitudes die hard and although without foundation the belief that women bring false accusations persists with intransigence. Home Office Circular 25/1983 states, 'Although in some cases it may be subsequently established that a complaint is without foundation. . .'. Similarly, the 1984 Report of the Criminal Law Revision Committee states (para. 2.7), 'By no means is every accusation of rape true . . .' A false accusation may, for example, be made by a girl who has had sexual intercourse with consent but who, on being challenged by her mother, who is suspicious about the state of her daughter's clothing excuses herself by claiming that she has been raped' (pp. 5–6), (see *Ellen Smith* (1993) 14 Cr App R (S) 762; *Gregson* (1993) 14 Cr App R (S) 85; *Goodwin* (1989) 11 Cr App R (S) 194; *Kyriakou* (1990) 12 Cr App R (S) 603). And it is the false accusation concern that has fuelled the necessity for the corroboration ruling. The Criminal Justice and Public Order Act 1994, s. 32 abolished the requirement of the obligatory corroboration rules. However, this simply means that the obligation to give a warning is abolished, it does not mean, however, that judges are prevented from giving a warning if they deem it appropriate, neither will it curb those judges who want to embellish it. (Archbold 1995, Vol. 1, pp. 16–36).

PLEAS, CONVICTION, MITIGATION, SENTENCE

Despite the increase in notifiable offences, the actual proportion of prosecutions for rape has declined dramatically over the years. (see Table 18). This means that either the Crown Prosecution Service is less willing to prosecute in such cases, or that more cases are being recorded by police where prosecution is unlikely. In 1993, of 4,589 offences of rape recorded in England and Wales, 19 per cent went for trial, this compares with a higher rate of 34 per cent in 1983 (see Table 28). This high attrition rate is supported in case studies of rape, e.g., Wright (1980) found of 204 arrested suspects, 22 (11 per cent) were found guilty of rape. In a recent study of rape in Scotland, in 1992 of 63 rapes that went to court, 18 defendants were found not guilty, in 11 cases the charge was not proven and in 34 cases the defendant was found guilty (*Daily Record*, 14 September 1994).

Table 27: Persons proceeded against for offences of rape

	Year								
	1979	1980	1981	1982	1983	1984	1985	1986	1987
proceeded against at mc	657	697	587	709	648	657	844	927	1,048
committed to Crown	596	633	539	643	585	583	758	804	867
for trial at Crown	491	564	426	543	453	454	569	593	649
acquitted at Crown	117	144	117	143	144	127	140	175	221
acquittal rate (%) of those acquitted at Crown after trial at Crown as a proportion of for trial	24	26	27	26	32	28	25	30	34
sentenced at all courts	382	433	321	403	312	335	430	403	425
sentenced as a % of those originally proceeded against	58	62	55	57	48	51	51	43	41

Source: Home Office Statistical Bulletin, Table 3: Rape Issue 4/89

Table 28: The attrition of rape from notifiable offences to conviction

	Notifiable Offences (a)	for trial		acquitted		found guilty	
		No (b)	% of (a)	No (c)	% of (b)	No (d)	% of (b)
1983	1,334	451	34	144	32	306	68
1984	1,433	451	31	127	28	321	71
1985	1,842	565	31	140	25	418	74
1986	2,288	590	26	175	30	398	67
1987	2,471	646	26	218	34	423	65
1988	2,855	792	28	291	37	497	63
1989	3,305	924	28	337	36	584	63
1990	3,391	911	26	363	40	538	59
1991	4,045	954	24	408	43	536	56
1992	4,142	931	22	427	46	492	50
1993	4,589	891	19	411	46	462	51
1994	5,039	936	19	486	52	432	48

Source: Compiled from Criminal Statistics England and Wales Supplementary Tables vol. 2 1983–1993 (shortfall accounted for by defendants not tried)

Pleas

It is suggested that in the majority of rape cases the defence is one of consent. Regrettably criminal statistics do not record information on plea. However, case studies shed some light on plea patterns in rape. Grace, Lloyd and Smith (1992) in their study found that 36 per cent of the sample pleaded guilty, 4 per cent with a late guilty plea, 41 per cent pleaded not guilty and 23 per cent pleaded not guilty to the principal charge but guilty to a lesser charge.

This compares with the findings of Adler (1987) who found that of the 81 trials involving 112 men against 102 complainants, 29 per cent pleaded guilty to rape or a lesser charge and a significant number of guilty pleas came from men charged with raping more than one female. Lees (1989), (1993) examined records of 52 cases heard between June and September 1988 and found that 10 men pleaded guilty, 42 pleaded not guilty (80 per cent) and of those who pleaded not guilty, 9 (21 per cent) were convicted of rape.

Acquittal rate

There is considerable concern, given that women are also on trial and that past moral character very much prejudices a jury in the defendant's favour, that rape is likely to have a higher acquittal rate than any other offence. National figures allow only an examination of the number acquitted as expressed as a percentage of the total for trial. It is not possible to discern what proportion of defendants pleaded not guilty in order to derive the true rate of acquittal (see Tables 18 and 19). Nevertheless these acquittal figures do reveal some important pointers.The acquittal rate, expressed as a percentage of the total for trial, shows a dramatic increase from 25 per cent in 1985, rising to 36 per cent in 1989, 43 per cent in 1991, and 46 per cent in 1993 (Table 28). This rise suggests one of two possible changes: either more defendants are pleading not guilty to rape and being acquitted at the same rate as in previous years, or else the same proportion of defendants are pleading guilty but juries are more likely to quit than before (Adler, pp. 47, 121).

Lees showed that of ten rape cases observed at random, in seven the verdict was an acquittal, one was abandoned and two were found guilty (see 1989, p. 10). In the Grace study above, of those proceeded against, 41 per cent were convicted of the principal offence, 20 per cent were convicted of a lesser charge, 23 per cent were convicted of an alternate or lesser charge only and 16 per cent were acquitted. If juries are more likely to convict, this tendency is the result of the Court of Appeal interpretation of s. 2 together with the impact of longer sentences on jury decision making. Whilst the *Billam* [1986] 1 All ER 985 guidelines were hailed as the way ahead in sentencing in rape cases in stating five years as the normal starting point, research needs to be established to discover the extent to which *Billam*, with its starting point of a sentence of five years for a rape, has contributed to this downward prosecutorial trajectory and upward acquittal profile.

Mitigation

Sexual assaults are perpetrated largely by men upon women. Whilst we all prefer to believe that such men are if not physically identifiable then identifiable by personality traits, it is often the case that rapists are neither mentally ill nor psychopathic. That is not to deny that some rapists are profoundly disturbed but hormonal treatment or chemical therapy is not the universal panacea for rape. Sexual conduct is often an aberration in an otherwise normal man. In *Wadland* (1994) 15 Cr App R (S) 543, where a man threatened to kill a number of women and made phone calls to 270 women, 66 character letters were submitted on his behalf. The judge in passing sentence said, '. . . it is quite clear that apart from these offences you are a man who people are pleased to know, pleased to have as a friend'. In mitigation of sentence a number of accounts have developed with greater or lesser cogency, shedding light less, however, on motivation and more perhaps on social and legal constructions of sexual motive.

Mitigatory models in sexual assault and rape cases cluster around the following six main areas: (1) breakdown in mental functioning, i.e., blackout; (2) an inner impulse whereby he was compelled to act; (3) accident, mistake, defective social skills; (4) emotional stress; (5) alcohol; (6) mistake, but complainant's conduct ambiguous. In mitigation, the inner impulse or drive reduction theory is based on a model of normal masculinity and continues to inform sentencing. In 1983, Judge Brian Gibbens told a 35 year old builder who had sex with a neighbour's seven year old daughter that this was 'one of those kinds of accidents that could almost happen to anyone' (*The Guardian*, 10 June 1993). In a case where a man indecently assaulted his 13 year old stepdaughter Sir Harold Cassel said that it was the result of a man needing to satisfy normal urges when his wife was pregnant.

So far as the accident, mistake, defective social skills mitigation is concerned. men excuse their behaviour relying on a range of rationales from 'I don't know what came over me', to, 'I couldn't control myself', to, 'it was a mistake'. Some of these excusatory rationales have been grounded in law as a defence to rape, whilst others have occupied a central place in mitigation. In *Fenton* (1992) 13 Cr App R (S) 85, 87, where a man had broken into a flat and raped a woman and threatened her it was said, 'He admitted to the rape at once. He said he had lived in the flats for three and a half months and had spoken to the complainant but could not pluck up the courage to ask her out.'.

The retreat from psychopathology has charted the feminist response to understanding the perpetrators. Such men are considered inadequate and facing masculinity crises. The feminist contribution to an understanding of sex crime significantly located this specific manifestation of violence as violence against women rooted in patriarchy, misogyny and for others in masculinity pressures. Giovannoni's work on sex offenders found that power and masculinity was a vital component.

Dworkin (1989) argues that there is a conflation of sex with violence in the social construction of masculinity, and a hatred of women is normalised within our culture. Rape is not a violation of social order then but a reinforcement of gender relations. As in the words of Eldridge Cleaver 'Rape is an insurrectionary act' (Cleaver, *Soul on Ice*).

Groth (1979, p. 17) in his study of rapists found, 'Rape is a pseudosexual act, a pattern of sexual behaviour that is concerned much more with status, hostility, control and dominance than with sensual pleasure or sexual satisfaction. It is sexual behaviour in the primary service of non-sexual needs.'. Judicial insensitivity in interpretating male motivation in rape and the role the victim's willingness to forgive should play in sentencing decisions, has led to considerable controversy. In cases where the parties are known to one another *Henshall* (1995) 16 Crim App R (S) 388, 390 where the victim was raped with a knife 'Observations on the willingness of the victim to forgive the offender ... and 'The forgiveness of the victim and the desire of the victim not to pursue the matter is a factor which should be taken into account in mitigation, but it could not be the only consideration'. The defendant said in threatening the victim with a pair of scissors pointed at her breasts and between her legs 'You fucked my life up and now I am going to fuck you to see how you like it'.

Not only do defendants offer neutralising mitigatory accounts, judges are also willing to accept certain motivatory rationales. A commonly utilised excusatory rationale is: 'I thought she was consenting'. In *Allen* (1982) unreported (see Edwards 1982), the judge said,'The circumstances of this case do not disclose any particular intention to rape this lady rather a lecherous hope that she would have sex with you.'. Other judicial clangers included the insensitive compensation order, telling the victim to go and have a holiday. Judge John Prosser ordered a 15 year old to pay his victim £500 for a good holiday (*The Times*, 15 June 1993). Judicial perceptions of male sexuality and the impact of rape on the victim are in themselves a fascinating area of study. As with domestic violence, there is a concern that, where the victim is trying to put her life together and minimise the trauma, her courage, strength and tenacity and above all forgiveness work in favour of mitigation of sentence. It is interesting that principles of punishment, retribution, deterrence and reparation ... also embrace a new principle in mitigation, that of victim survival and compassion. In *Fleming* [1994] Crim LR 541, the court noted, 'There was no specific evidence of any continuing psychological effect on the victim, but the experience must have been quite horrifying.'. In the Ealing rape case according to the judge (Mr Justice Leonard) the trauma suffered by the victim 'was not so great' (Saward 1990, p. 133).

Sentencing

In sexual assault as elsewhere, the length of sentence depends largely on the presence or absence of prior relationship. A clear distinction is nearly always made between stranger and acquaintance rape, even where the complainant is a child. In sentencing a man who pleaded guilty to the rape of his 14 year old stepdaughter in exchange for the dismissal of charges of sexual assault against his 12 year old stepson, a Michigan trial judge gave vent to popular stereotypes commenting:

On your behalf, there are many things that you are not. You are not a violent rapist who drags women and girls off the street and into the bushes or into your car from a parking lot; and I have had a lot of these in my courtroom. . . . You are not a child chaser, one whose obsession with sex causes him to seek neighbourhood children or children in parks or in playgrounds, and we see these people in court. You are a man who has warm personal feelings for your stepchildren, *but you let them get out of hand*, and we see a number of people like you in our courts. (emphasis supplied) (*People* v *Gauntlett* [1984] 352 NW 2d 310, 313.)

Sentencing in rape cases is dealt with largely by means of a custodial sentence. Of those 462 defendants found guilty in 1993, 1 per cent were dealt with by way of a probation order, 90 per cent were sentenced to terms of immediate imprisonment, 0.2 per cent received an absolute discharge, 2 per cent were in receipt of a hospital order and 4 per cent of defendants were detained under s. 53(2), Children and Young Persons Act 1933. This profile compares with 1991, where 93 per cent of convicted rapists, both adult and young offenders, received custodial sentences. In 1991, of those 430 adults sentenced to prison, 52 per cent received prison sentences of more than five years (excluding lifers who constituted an additional 3 per cent), leaving the remaining 45 per cent in receipt of prison sentences up to five years. This sentencing profile is an advance over the pre-*Billam* sentencing predilection for 1985 where only 26 per cent of offenders received prison sentences of five years. This difference cannot be interpreted as the product of a year in which offenders were more brutal or rapes more serious, but an indication of changes in sentencing patterns.

The public concern over lenient sentences is reflected in *Roberts* [1982] 1 All ER 609, where the Court of Appeal emphasised that rape is always a serious crime which calls for an immediate custodial sentence other than in wholly exceptional circumstances. The guidance in *Roberts* was in part a response to the variability in sentencing already in that year Bertrand Richards J had fined a man £2,000 for rape which prompted a review of sentencing (see Edwards 1982). Later in 1986 17 cases were listed together to give the Court of Appeal the opportunity to restate sentencing principles. In *Billam* [1986] 1 All ER 985, 986–7, guidelines for sentencers were clearly established where rape, in the absence of aggravating features, should be dealt with by a five year sentence. Where a rape is committed by more than one person, or where a house is broken into by the defendant, or where the person is in a position of responsibility or trust, or where there is abduction, the starting point should be eight years. Where there is a campaign of rape, a sentence of 15 years or more may be appropriate. Where the defendant has manifested perverted psycho-pathic tendencies or a gross personality disorder and is a danger to women, a life sentence will not be inappropriate. 'Aggravated' means the use of weapon, attempt to frighten or wound, where the victim is subjected to indignities, and finally the effect on the victim.

The outstanding concerns are these. First, whilst sentencing and *Billam*, together with the Attorney-General's sentencing review in the Criminal Justice

Act 1988, can address the problem of lenient sentences, *Billam* does not address nor does it attempt to address rapes committed in the absence of violence or aggravating features save to say that the starting point should be five years. Setting any rape at five years, whilst it had the vision of making it clear that rape was always a serious offence, will have repercussions for the more difficult rape cases. The five year minimum in my view is one of the factors that has contributed to an increase in acquittals, since juries are loath to convict where they may take the view, 'well it was rape but it doesn't warrant five years'. Secondly there is the problem that guideline judgments do not always 'calibrate' by specifying the range of normal variation around the guideline. Thirdly, whilst *Billam* has no doubt had an impact on stranger rapes and rapes between acquaintances where there is violence, acquaintance rapes in the absence of violence remain without exegesis. Whilst we can turn to appropriate sentences in the post-*Billam* era, equally there are sentences which fall far short (see Table 20). Where courts have applied the *Billam* guidelines but still arrived at an overly lenient sentence, then sentences have been increased via the Attorney-General. In *Attorney-General's Reference No. 7 of 1989* (Paul Anthony Thornton) (1990) 12 Cr App R (S) 1, here the defendant was convicted of rape upon his former cohabitee. Lord Lane CJ said that once cohabitation had ceased, there was no licence for a man to have sexual intercourse with the girl willy nilly. In *Attorney-General's Reference No. 1 of 1991* (Eric Stephen Hughes) (1992) 13 Cr App R (S) 134, the victim was a woman in her mid sixties who worked as a bereavement counsellor and invited the offender, who posed as a distressed widower, to her home. A sentence of five years was increased to seven. In *Attorney-General's Reference No. 28 of 1993* (Sean Cawthray) (1995) 16 Cr App R (S) 103, a sentence of six and a half years was increased to eight for a man with a previous conviction of rape.

Table 29: Rape sentencing post Roberts 1982 and post Billam 1986

year convicted	prison	0% prison	up to 5yr	% under 5 yrs	over 5yr–7yr	over 7yr–10yr	over 10yr +	Life
1980	339		287	85	31	14	3	4
1981	247		204	83	22	10	2	9
1982	309		229	74	39	22	5	14
1983	227		166	73	36	11	2	12
1984	196		171	87	11	8	0	6
1985	268		199	74	34	20	6	9
1986	291		157	54	74	42	6	12
1987	323	94	126	32	105	63	17	12
1988	378	92	175	46	91	74	27	11
1989	449	92	209	46	112	84	32	12
1990	410	91	201	49	98	71	30	10
1991	430	93	195	45	125	71	26	13
1992	394	91	162	41	119	74	27	10
1993	380	90	158	42	102	79	28	13
1994	369	92	130	1	101	93	33	12

Source: Criminal Statistics Supplementary Tables vol. 2 1980–1994

Now that this offence applies also to men who rape men, it will mean that male complainants will receive the same shoddy treatment as women, although presumptions about male sexuality will no doubt be implied only where the complainant is homosexual, and precisely what stereotypes and presumptions about male homosexuality will be played out in court we have yet to witness. In cases of heterosexual and homosexual anal rape, problems will arise regarding the issue of consent and whether sexual experience with the person accused and, or with, persons other than the appellant will be necessary to prove evidence of past buggery. The question of past moral character or previous experience of buggery was raised in *Ahmed and Khan* [1994] Crim LR 669. Here, the appellants admitted buggery. The complainant was walking home, the appellants previously known to her as school 'colleagues', picked her up and drove to an address. She refused intercourse. They threatened her with a knife and she was buggered by them in turn. In court, this young woman was then subjected to cross-examination as to sexual experience relating to buggery, since it had been held that restrictions on cross-examination without leave under s. 2 did not cover buggery. On appeal the judge ruled that issues of buggery and past moral character were not relevant, considering that the real reason for seeking to adduce such evidence was to 'sling as much muck at the complainant as possible'. The appeal was dismissed. In *Attorney-General's Reference No. 25 of 1994* (Robert John B) (1995) 16 Cr App R (S) 562, 30 months' imprisonment for buggery of a young woman by a stepfather was increased to five years in a case where a stepfather buggered a 17 year old stepdaughter and terrified her. The defence was that there had been other forms of sexual behaviour between them to which he alleged she had consented. Following the amendments introduced by the 1994 Act, it remains to be seen whether leave will have to be sought before questions as to previous acts of buggery will be admitted, since non-consensual buggery now constitutes rape for the purposes of the Sexual Offences (Amendment) Act 1976. Apart from changes affecting the class of persons who now have a remedy in law, the law remains as it was in 1976. Past moral character becomes an issue throughout, from police protection to the trial and beyond, where the victim's story is monitored for the extent to which her behaviour deviates from chaste femininity. Even at the point of compensation this factor is a key consideration. In 1977, Marcella Claxton, one of Peter Sutcliffe's surviving victims, made a claim to the Criminal Injuries Compensation Board. Her application was refused since her character and way of life indicated that she was in some way responsible. She was, however, paid £17,500 in 1982. She had been struck on the head with a hammer eight or nine times and needed 52 stitches. Claxton denied that she had ever been a prostitute (*Daily Telegraph* 25 May 1989). Later in *Re A* 21 July 1992 CICB Leeds, 1603 CLY 1992, an 11 year old girl was raped by a neighbour who was found guilty of two counts of unlawful sexual intercourse. The child's application was initially refused on the grounds that she was a 'willing, consenting and at least to some extent, an enthusiastic party as to the sexual exploits which occurred'.

In *Criminal Injuries Compensation Board Ex Parte S* [1995] 2 FLR 615, a woman of 30 was raped in an alleyway and assaulted with a screwdriver which was forced into her vagina. As a result of the attack she was so deeply traumatised that she was unable to speak to anyone fully about the incident for six weeks. She could not leave her house, was unable to go to work and could not relate the full details of the incident to her work manager, her close friends her vicar, victim support and the several other people who tried to support and comfort her. When she finally made a statement to the police and an application for compensation, the Criminal Injuries Compensation Board turned down her application on the grounds of delay. In her application she tried to relate the experience to the Board. 'I lay on the ground for a while, although I don't know how long. I was listening to see if he was coming back. I was petrified. I didn't know what to do. I remember wishing the man had killed me, because surely being dead felt better than the way I felt then ... I was aware that telling the police would involve me in going into every graphic detail and possibly having to stand up in court and tell everyone present what he had done to me ... one afternoon two policewoman called. I remember screaming and shouting for them to go away. I was too frightened of having to relive that night' (pp. 616, 619). The High Court, Sedley J presiding, granted *certiorari*.

Blame, transference of responsibility from offender to victim, where a woman's right to protection must be earned by her conduct and where the right of protection is held out as a gleaming star only to those who can truly earn it are all attitudes that can be detected in rape cases. Feminist engagement with rape has been directed at the way in which ideologies of sex and consent continue to inform and construct the violent event. The focus has been on the ideologies informing rape and more recently on the application of the trial judge's discretion in the admission of past moral character evidence. The legal method of rape allows for evidence to credit to be read as evidence to issue, thus tilting the balance in favour of a reading of consent, so that the rape is transformed into 'sex' and the defendant's version of events prevails.

NINE

The gender politics of homicide

The critique in recent years of homicide law and its application has been dominated by a concern with the battered woman who turns defendant but finds difficulty in availing herself of homicide defences, and the comparative ease with which men who kill spouses successfully plead provocation and diminished responsibility on the basis of her conduct. In an attempt to acknowledge her response to his violence as a self-defensive reaction — the pre-emptive strike of a frightened woman — the battered woman syndrome debate is now focusing on her state of mind often to the exclusion of his violence. It is argued that whilst claiming impartiality, neutrality and objectivity, the law is saturated and entrenched with a gendered vision of what constitutes manslaughter, provocation in particular, and what constitutes self-defence.

The quintessence of homicide law is 'male', the authoritative definitions of the legal rules that define it and interpretation of these principles have been prescribed by men and have addressed what men do. In consequence the law exonerates men absolutely and eclipses the predicament and experience of women. Struggles in and around the law on this issue alone have resulted in lawyers trying to match women's accounts to the immutable and unyielding masculinist legal categories. In the short term such negotiations have been expedient, in the long term in efforts to conform to law's standard universal subject, women's accounts are distorted. Feminist lawyers and jurisprudents have raised these concerns throughout common law jurisdictions (Fiora-Gormally 1978, Schneider 1980, Rittenmeyer 1981, Scutt 1981, Bacon and Lansdowne 1982, Wasik 1982, Durham 1984, Edwards 1985, Taylor 1986). The essence of women's legal predicament in provocation is identified by Horder (1992, pp. 188–189):

> Many battered women do not lose their self control immediately prior to the killing of the batterer. Following long term abuse, some battered women appear to have taken a calculated decision to kill that was not triggered by any very recent provocation; still others appear to have acted in the face of

recent provocation, but with more or less deliberation at or close to the moment of the fact. They are thus not given the benefit of a direction to the jury on the issue of provocation, and because they did not appear (or do not claim) to be mentally abnormal they do not plead or do not succeed in a plea of insanity or diminished responsibility. Such women are convicted of murder and hence receive a mandatory life sentence . . .

Augmenting and extending the existing rules of provocation and self-defence so as to accommodate women's reactive response is regarded by judges and some academics as legitimating a woman's licence to kill. Yet, such a licence already exists and has been habituated in law where male conduct is almost without exception considered 'reasonable' (provocation) or if unreasonable (diminished responsibility) then his abnormality of mind is the result of the victim's conduct. What judges and juries consider constitutes justification for provocation and self-defence, whilst being hailed as an objective legal standard making claims to neutrality and universality, is instead a masculinist constructs encapsulated within a legal form. There is a further insidious problem that those very same justifications for provocation which rely on the bad conduct of the deceased, are invoked as excuses where defendants plead abnormality of mind, such that his 'jealousy' and depressive illness becomes the excuse for killing her. It is the endeavour of this critique to deconstruct the iconography of these several defences and reveal the process in which and by which these legal constructs are produced, reproduced and expanded to embrace what men do, eliding women within this. In this discussion, I propose to evaluate the problems raised above through a review of the empirical evidence of the extent of spousal homicide, the *modus operandi* of killing, the legal disposition and final outcome and the moment in these relationships when the killing occurs. Secondly, the intention is to consider the common law and statute as it defines homicide, through an examination of the legal principles, their development and application. Thirdly, I will consider the practical availability of these defences for women and by contrast for men who kill.

THE FACTS OF SPOUSAL KILLINGS

The extent

Spousal homicide defines the killing of a partner, wife/husband, cohabitee/ ex-cohabitee. In England and Wales this constituted the second largest category of victims of homicide. Figures for 1992 show that there were 89 female and 20 male victims of spousal homicide, whilst a further 18 females and 11 males were killed by lovers or former lovers or their lovers' spouses or partners. Figures for 1993 show that of 606 homicides, 77 (13 per cent) involved female spouses and 9 (2 per cent) male spousal victims whilst the lover or former lover category included 14 female and 9 male victims (*Criminal statistics* (1993), Table 4.4). In 1994 (latest figures available), 81 female spouses were killed and 18 male spouses, 20 female lovers and former lovers and 16 male lovers and former lovers (*Criminal statistics* (1994), Table 4.4). This 1992-4 profile is consistent with earlier years where throughout the 1980s, on average 19 per cent of homicide was spousal (see Table 30). Studies by McClintock (1963), and Blom-Cooper and Morris (1964), discerned a similar profile.

Table 30: Spousal homicide currently recorded expressed as a percentage of total homicide victims by year

Homicide	Year								
Victims	1983	1985	1987	1989	1990	1991	1992	1993	1994
(a) spouse	103	115	96	117	98	121	109	86	99
(b) all	482	536	600	523	556	625	584	574	677
(a) as % of (b)	21	21	16	22	18	19	19	15	15

Source: *Criminal Statistics, England and Wales 1994 Table 4, p. 80.*

In Canada, not unlike England and Wales, spouses constitute the second largest category of homicide victim. Figures for 1992 show that 14.4 per cent and 2.7 per cent of all homicide involves female spouses as victims and male spouses as victims respectively (*Homicide Survey Policy Service Program*, Canada Centre for Justice Statistics, July 1993, Table 19). Consistency is demonstrated for earlier years in a study conducted by Wilson and Daly (1994), for the years 1974–1992, who found that of all female homicide victims (1,435), 38 per cent were spouses. By contrast, of all males killed, spousal homicide was indicated in only (451), 6 per cent of all. In the United States in 1992, whilst the homicide rate per 100,000 population is considerably higher than elsewhere, spousal homicide expressed as a proportion of all homicide is lower than elsewhere. Of a total of 22,540 homicides, 6.35 per cent were perpetrated against wives and girlfriends and 2.76 per cent against husbands and boyfriends (see *Sourcebook of Criminal Justice Statistics — 1993* Table 3.125). In 1993 (latest figures available) of 23,271 homicides, 3.9 per cent were perpetrated against wives, 1.2 per cent against husbands, 1.1 per cent on boyfriends and 2.5 per cent on girlfriends. (*Sourcebook of Criminal Justice Statistics 1994, p. 334*). Other studies by Wolfgang (1958), Willbanks (1983), Dawson and Langan (1994) found similar rates. This 'relative equity' of male to female spousal homicide at a ratio of 1:3 has resulted in battered women who kill constituting a powerful lobby critiquing the law and the legal treatment of women who kill in these circumstances. Whilst spousal homicide committed against wives/girlfriends constitutes a smaller proportion of the total US homicide profile than in England and Wales, nevertheless the role of spousal is at least three times greater, at 0.58 per 100,000 population in the US compared with 0.18 in England and Wales.

In a study of homicide in Victoria, Australia conducted by the Law Reform Commission (1991, p. 5), of the 259 victims studied in the years 1981–1987, 45 were spouses (14.1 per cent) and of those, 32 were females and 11 males (*Homicide Prosecutions Study* 5). A similar spousal profile is observed in a study of homicide in New South Wales ('1988 *Homicide*), almost one quarter of all cleared homicides in NSW were spouse killings and 73 per cent were committed by men. In a study of homicide in 1989–1992 in Australia, over a two year study period of 513 homicides, 150 or 29 per cent were spousal (see Easteal 1993a, pp. 26–27; see for further discussion Easteal 1993b, c and 1994). Given that in many jurisdictions spousal homicide is high it is perhaps surprising that only in recent years has debate at a public and political level focused on the relative treatment by the criminal justice system of men and women who kill spouses.

Spousal killing: modus operandi

The legal relevance of modus operandi in the construction of intent is glossed over in favour of an analysis of method by gender preference and the relationship of method to the relative size and strength of the sexes. The method of killing female spouses is distinctive, showing a higher rate of strangulation and asphyxiation, than in the general female homicide victim population. In 1993, of female spousal victims, 29 per cent were killed with a sharp instrument, 12 per cent with a blunt instrument, a further 10 per cent were killed by hitting and kicking, 29 per cent by strangulation and asphyxiation, and 16 per cent by shooting. Clearly, in a significant proportion of cases where men kill female spouses, the body is used as deadly force, where the killing is committed by the use of hands, fists or feet. Body force of several kinds was employed in 44 per cent of female spousal killings in 1992 and 39 per cent in 1993. Women by contrast are incapable of killing by using the body as a deadly force and must of necessity resort to the use of weapons. In 1993, of males killed by female spouses, 40 per cent were killed with a sharp instrument, 20 per cent with a blunt instrument, 20 per cent were strangled or asphyxiated and 20 per cent were shot (see Table 31). When women used strangulation or asphyxiation this was after the man had been incapacitated by drink, sleep or by the use of a weapon to immobilise him (see *Ahluwalia* [1992] 4 All ER 889, *Gardner, Sunday Times*, 8 November 1992 discussed below). The *modus operandi* of spousal homicide in the US, where firearms constitute the principal method of killing in both male on female and female on male nevertheless still shows a gender divide in the use of brute force (hands, feet, asphyxiation). In 1992, of male spouses killed, 95 per cent were killed with a weapon (firearms 53 per cent, knives 40 per cent and blunt instruments two per cent) whereas female spouses were killed with a weapon in 87 per cent of cases (firearms 66 per cent, knives 17 per cent and blunt instruments four per cent). Where brute force constituted the *modus operandi*, two per cent of males were killed by hitting, kicking or strangulation compared with 11 per cent of females (Zawitz 1994, p. 10).

Table 31: Offences currently recorded as homicide of a spouse by apparent method of killing, by sex of victims

Apparent method	1989		1990		1991		1992		1993	
	No	0%	No	0%	No	0%	No	0%	No	0%
sharp instrument										
male victim	11	65	4	40	3	60	8	73	2	40
female victim	31	45	15	26	19	26	17	31	15	29
blunt instrument										
male victim	0	0	1	10	2	40	1	9	1	20
female victim	10	14	12	21	13	18	5	9	6	12
hitting/kicking										
male victim	0	0	0	0	0	0	0	0	0	0
female victim	3	4	4	7	6	8	4	7	5	10
strangulation										
male victim	2	12	2	20	0	0	1	9	1	20
female victim	17	25	19	33	16	22	20	37	15	29
shooting										
male victim	0	0	1	10	0	0	1	9	1	20
female victim	6	9	6	11	10	14	6	11	8	16
burning										
male victim	3	18	2	20	0	0	0	0	0	0
female victim	1	1	1	2	5	7	0	0	1	2
drowning										
male victim	1	5	0	0	0	0	0	0	0	0
female victim	1	1	0	0	0	0	1	2	0	0
motor vehicle										
male victim	0	0	0	0	0	0	0	0	0	0
female victim	0	0	0	0	1	1	0	0	0	0
other										
male victim	0	0	0	0	0	0	0	0	0	0
female victim	0	0	0	0	1	1	0	0	0	0
not known										
male victim	0	0	0	0	0	0	0	0	0	0
female victim	0	0	0	0	1	1	1	2	1	2

Source: Home Office statistics provided for the author as at 5 August 1994

The *modus operandi* of spousal homicides in Canada displays a marked similarity with the England and Wales profile (excepting that a higher proportion of female victims were beaten to death by partners). Women victims of spousal homicide were shot in 42 per cent of cases, stabbed in 21 per cent, strangled in 11 per cent, killed with a blunt instrument in 1 per cent, 21 per cent were beaten and 3 per cent of victims were killed by 'other' methods, including being electrocuted, and doused with petrol. When women killed spouses, 27 per cent stabbed their partners, 27 per cent shot them, 8 per cent beat their victims, 3 per cent strangled their victims, 2 per cent used a blunt instrument and 3 per cent used other methods (Wilson and Daly 1994, p. 5, Table 32). Again, men were far more likely than women to use their bodily strength to perpetrate the killing: in 32 per cent of cases for men compared with 11 per cent for women.

In Australia, in the Victoria study cited above, men killed spouses with firearms in 41.2 per cent of cases, a sharp instrument in 26.5 per cent of cases, a blunt instrument in 2.9 per cent of cases, fists and feet in 17.6 per cent of cases and strangulation in 11.8 per cent of cases. When women killed spouses, 56.3 per cent did so using a sharp instrument, 31.3 per cent using a firearm. Overall, women used bodily force in 6.2 per cent of killings compared with 29.4 per cent for men (*Homicide Prosecutions Study* and see Table 32). In a study of *modus operandi* of spousal homicides in Australia, men killed spouses with firearms in 29.8 per cent of cases, a sharp instrument in 29.8 per cent of cases, a blunt instrument in 5.8 per cent of cases, following an assault in 20.7 per cent of cases, and strangulation in 7.4 per cent of cases. Females killed male spouses by firearms in 27.6 per cent of cases and by sharp instruments in 62.1 per cent of cases (Easteal 1993a, p. 33, Table 5).

Table 32: Modus operandi in spousal homicide (Australia)

Method	Relationship of victim to suspect	
	Male on Female	Female on Male
Firearm	14	4
Sharp instrument	9	6
Blunt instrument	1	1
Fist	6	0
Strangulation	4	0
Burning	0	0
Other	0	0
Total	34	11

Source: Homicide Prosecutions Study 1991

Whilst men utilise superior physical strength, i.e., killing through the use of brute force, women's physical incapacity means that they will often resort to a weapon to effect their purpose. The law's response to women's innate and conditioned incapacity is to deem certain methods of killing to be more or less indicative of heinousness and cold blooded intent and other methods to indicate passion and loss of self-control. Modus operandi, although not a rule of law, has important implications for defence strategies as it is considered an integral part of the general circumstances to which the court must have regard in determining intent. The implications of *modus operandi* for defence strategies are explored in depth later in this chapter.

Legal disposition and final outcome

Throughout all common law jurisdictions, writers, lawyers and critics have expressed concern that women are more likely to be convicted of murder or manslaughter (diminished responsibility) and less likely to be convicted of manslaughter (provocation) when compared with their male counterparts (see Fiora-Gormally 1978). Whilst in Australia legal efforts have attempted to redress the inbuilt imbalance and bias (see Homicide Law Amendment Act 1982), in England and Wales the official response has been a refutation of bias in legal method and/or in the application of the law to women who kill. In 1991, in response to speculation that women were more likely to be charged and convicted of murder and manslaughter (diminished responsibility) than men, Sir John Wheeler asked the Secretary of State for statistical information on the acceptance of defences to murder in domestic homicide cases and their treatment by the courts (see *Hansard*, 17 October 1991, Vol. 196 eds 189–191.). The Home Office responded providing detailed information on indictments and final disposal in such cases. The figures were widely hailed and interpreted as scotching the supposition that the law treated women un-favourably, indeed on the contrary, women were portrayed as the law's darlings, the law's favourites. Regrettably, few have attempted any rigorous interpretation and critique of those figures (excepting Bandalli 1992, p. 716). Whilst it is conceded that a superficial examination of the statistical evidence might tend to allay the immediate concerns of gender bias in the law, the conclusions drawn by the Home Office are erroneous and highly misleading.

Two discrete areas provide the focus for this critique of the Home Office figures on indictment and those on final disposition. First, in turning to indictments (the initial charge), this showed that for the years 1982–1989, 164 women and 753 men were indicted for murder, and 13 women and 32 men for manslaughter (see Tables 33 and 34). Manslaughter indictments constituted 7 per cent of all females proceeded against compared with 4 per cent of all males indicted. From this raw data, the Home Office concluded, over-simplistically, that women were nearly 'twice as likely' (sic) to be indicted for manslaughter as were men. Yet the issue is not and never has been about a crude comparison of figures. The debate is about whether certain facts are more or less likely to result in a successful defence of provocation. In comparing the two base samples, where different sample sizes are being compared, any conclusions are fraught. Setting aside problems of measurement, any comparison would demand isolation of the cases at the outset which indicated provocation and the proportion of these cases in which provocation was conceded for the purpose of indictment and/or final outcome. Attention should have been directed towards an analysis of any differences in the treatment of the male and female cases according to their facts, rather than the statistical end product of these highly problematic and discretionary processes. Issues of discretion regarding decisions as to appropriate indictments, which shape the numerical outcomes were neither raised nor noted, as being of relevance. Hence, the Home Office's stark conclusion that 'women were nearly twice as likely as men' to be indicted for manslaughter (Bandalli 1992, p. 716), would only be valid, if at the outset the male/female, and female/male homicide were strictly comparable on the facts. Whilst the circumstances surrounding the killing of male spouses by women are likely to be characterised by the abuse of the defendant over a long period, the killing of female spouses, is, by comparison, characterised by an escalating trajectory of violence by the defendant which culminates in the killing. The two distinctly different imprints of circumstances surrounding the homicide are not comparable.

Table 33: Domestic homicide convictions (women)

England and Wales	number of persons								
Conviction	1982	1983	1984	1985	1986	1987	1988	1989	Total
Women									
Murder	3	2	1	4	1	7	4	5	27
Section 2	3	10	4	3	5	2	4	5	36
Other	8	4	11	8	9	9	10	11	70
Lesser offence					3			1	4
Acquit/unfit to plead	4	5	6	4	4	6	7	4	40
Total	18	21	22	19	22	24	25	26	177

Manslaughter as a percentage of murder and manslaughter

	79	88	94	73	93	61	78	76	80

Source: Home Office: Hansard, 17 October 1991, Vol. 196, cols. 189–192

Table 34: Domestic homicide convictions (men)

England and Wales	number of persons								
Conviction	1982	1983	1984	1985	1986	1987	1988	1989	Total
Men									
Murder	34	28	29	29	43	26	38	51	278
Section 2	44	31	31	31	33	22	20	27	239
Other	27	27	26	33	33	29	30	20	225
Lesser offence		2					1	3	6
Acquit/unfit to plead	5	1	9	5	6	6	3	2	37
Total	110	89	95	98	115	83	92	103	785

Manslaughter as a percentage of murder and manslaughter

	68	67	66	69	61	66	57	48	63

Source: Home Office: Hansard, 17 October 1991, Vol. 196, Vols. 189–192

The second trawl of statistical evidence relied upon by the Home Office as a further indicator of the law's equal if not favourable treatment of women is found in their interpretation of statistics on final disposition, that is, the outcome of spousal homicide cases after processing by the courts. This data shows that 20 per cent of all women indicted were found guilty of murder, compared with 37 per cent of all men, and 80 per cent of all women indicted were convicted of manslaughter, compared with 63 per cent of men. Of the manslaughter convictions, 53 per cent of women and 30 per cent of men were convicted of other manslaughter (including involuntary manslaughter, the result of lack of intent or provocation). Again, the objection to the Home Office's conclusions rests on the fact that male on female and female on male homicides are not comparable as to the facts since there is the absence of a level playing field at the outset. The conclusions also take no account of the several stages in the judicial process of the role of plea acceptance by the prosecution, or jury decision making. As Bandalli (1992, p. 719), points out, there is the additional problem that the statistics do not record whether the manslaughter is the result of a trial or plea nor of whether the issue of provocation was raised. She suggests that these figures eclipse what lies at the heart of the debate and that is:

... that whenever the issue of provocation becomes a tried issue ... the woman will generally not succeed because the pressures on her and her subsequent behaviour are not within those recognised as relevant in the gendered legal concept of provocation. The cases where provocation does succeed in trials seem to have distinct elements of self-defence.

Proof of parity of access to the law and to its defences would demand that, given the facts, the majority of women should have access to a defence of provocation or self-defence. By contrast, males who kill females would find that their conduct only rarely allowed them to avail themselves of this defence. If this proposition is accepted, then the marginally 'more favourable' final dispositions for women who kill compared with men, cannot make out the case for the conclusion which the Home Office all too readily draws. The Home Office figures cannot provide an answer as to why men who kill women for moving the mustard pot are successful with a defence of provocation (as in *Corlett* reported in *The Lawyer*, 29 August 1995), (see *Joseph McGrail* whose wife, the judge remarked, 'would have tried the patience of a saint', Birmingham Crown Court, 31 July 1991), whilst women who kill men after years of physical beatings are not able to avail themselves of a provocation defence (*Thornton* below) and face a murder conviction.

The successful appeals of *Ahluwalia* [1992] 4 All ER 889, *Humphreys* [1995] 4 All ER 1008 , and *Thornton (No. 2)* [1995] NLJ Rep 1888, on grounds which it has to be acceded suggest a considerable stretching of both appeals procedure (in *Ahluwalia* and *Thornton*) and legal categories (in *Humphreys*) indicate a concern amongst appeal court judges and the Lord Chief Justice, that in doing law, the law may not be doing justice.

At risk when?

Women kill men usually when they are drunk or incapacitated through sleep, frequently following threats to kill. The evidence of the crisis point when men kill women is more extensively documented. Walker (1992) found that women were more at risk to the person after separation. Statistics for England and Wales for the years 1986 and 1987, show that one third of all the spousal homicides of females were perpetrated when the parties were separated (see Easteal 1993a, Tolmie 1991). Wilson and Daly (1994, pp. 1, 7) found that the rate of husbands killing wives was elevated in the aftermath after separation, where 23 per cent of homicides on female spouses occurred where the couples were separated. In Australia, Wallace (1986), found that 98 of 217 of women slain (43 per cent), were separated or in the process thereof. In addition, women are stalked by their partners and where women have escaped a partner's violence in the home, they are later stalked and killed by that partner when they have moved to a refuge (Bourlet 1990). In *People* v *Wood* 391 NE 2d 206 (1979), where a husband killed his wife, the children testified that in March 1976, holding a shotgun to her head, he said, 'I swear if you ever leave me, I'll follow you to the ends of the earth and kill you'. In September 1976 one month after their divorce he killed her. As Gillespie (1989, p. 151) argues, men who batter are desperately emotionally dependent on the women in their lives.

> In some cases, the threat is reported to be a potential or actual desertion. In other cases, the threat is the denial of the right that the eventual killer believed he had to dominate his wife and exercise control over her actions . . . the threat of separation is usually the trigger for violence in these cases.

THE LEGAL METHOD OF HOMICIDE DEFENCES

In this section I will review the law as it pertains to homicide, focusing on the general rules applying to murder, involuntary manslaughter — no intent, voluntary manslaughter — provocation, diminished responsibility and self-defence, providing a flat statement of what the law is, in readiness for the critique which follows in the subsequent discussion. A conviction for murder carries with it the full weight of the law and a mandatory life sentence, the ultimate crime should carry the ultimate sentence. The House of Lords Select Committee on Murder and Life Imprisonment (1989), recommended the abolition of the mandatory life sentence for murder in 1989. Lord Taylor, the Lord Chief Justice, and his predecessor, Lord Lane, have both said it should go. That sentence is a matter for the trial judge; see (s. 1(1), Murder (Abolition of Death Penalty) Act 1965 for those 21 and over, the Criminal Justice Act 1982, s. 8 for those under 21, and the Children and Young Persons Act 1933, s. 53(1) for those under 18 years. In practice, the length of sentence is arrived at following a recommendation from the Parole Board and in consultation with the Home Secretary and the Lord Chief Justice, although the sentencer is required to state the minimum period (s. 1(2), 1965 Act, see Emmins 1993, pp. 138–156) In November 1995 the High Court ruled that the Secretary of

State's interference in setting the time to be served in prison for mandatory lifers was without authority. The harshness of the law is mitigated by the responsibility of the offender and whether there are grounds for justification or excuse. The Homicide Act 1957, s. 1(1) states:

> Where a person kills another in the course or furtherance of some other offence, the killing shall not amount to murder unless done with some malice aforethought (express or implied) i.e. with intent to kill or cause grievous bodily harm as is required for a killing to amount to murder when not done in the course or furtherance of another offence.

The convicted person is considered wholly responsible for the commission of the crime.

Murder is distinguished from manslaughter by the *mens rea*, which is an intention to kill or to cause grievous bodily harm (see *Moloney* [1985] AC 905, *Hancock and Shankland* [1986] AC 455; *Cunningham* [1982] AC 566 HL). The presence or absence of intent is a matter for the jury (*Bryson* [1985] Crim LR 669, *Purcell* (1986) 83 Cr App Rep 45). In applying the dual test provided by the Criminal Law Act 1967, s. 8:

> A court or jury, in determining whether a person has committed an offence, — (a) shall not be bound in law to infer that he intended or foresaw a result of his actions by reason only of its being a natural and probable consequence of those actions; but (b) shall decide whether he did intend or foresee that result by reference to all the evidence, drawing such inferences from the evidence as appear proper in the circumstances.

However, a conviction for murder is not only restricted to cases where the harm occasioned is likely to endanger life (see *Cunningham* [1982] AC 566). This has caused considerable consternation, Lord Edmund-Davies remarked, 'I find it passing strange that a person can be convicted of murder if death results from, say, his intentional breaking of another's arm, an action, which, while calling for severe punishment, would in most cases be unlikely to kill'. Whilst murder is a crime requiring specific intent and while foresight may be evidence of intention, it is not to be equated with it (see *Moloney* [1985] AC 905, explaining *Hyam* v *DPP* [1975] AC 55). This question of whether the defendant foresaw the consequences of his actions has been refined further in *Nedrick* [1986] 1 WLR 1025, where the court held that the standard for the jury in determining whether the accused intended to kill was whether death or grievous bodily harm was a 'virtual certainty' and that the defendant appreciated that this was the case. This principle was somewhat expanded by the Court of Appeal in *Walker* (1990) 90 Cr App R 226, where the court upheld a judge's direction that 'a very high degree of probability' although arguably at a much lower level than virtual certainty, would suffice. As we will go on to see, the line between murder and other manslaughter for the purpose of intention is in practice often blurred and it would seem that the prosecution and the jury in accepting alternate pleas to murder are applying morality to the facts rather than law.

Involuntary manslaughter

By contrast, a conviction for involuntary manslaughter recognises that the defendant was only partially responsible for his or her actions, where the accused has some blameworthy mental state not amounting to intention to kill or to cause grievous bodily harm, yet through recklessness, gross negligence, or an unlawful act, kills. A person can be guilty of involuntary manslaughter through a reckless act, an act of gross negligence or through omission; *Seymour* [1983] AC 493, *Adomako* [1994] 3 WLR 288, *Holloway, The Times,* 21 May 1993, or through an act which is unlawful and dangerous; *Lamb* [1967] 2 QB 981, *Cato* [1976] 1 WLR 110, *Newbury* [1977] AC 500. In cases of gross negligence, and recklessness the courts are largely concerned to regulate the conduct of professionals where a breach of duty results in death. The concern of the author rests with manslaughter occasioned as the result of an unlawful and dangerous act. The courts have considered pleas of involuntary manslaughter (no intent) where, in the course of a fight, the deceased, following a punch, falls back and hits his head on the pavement. For accidental killing as a result of an intention to cause injury but not an intention to kill, and not in circumstances in which foreseeability of death was likely, see *Wesson* (1989) 11 Cr App R (S) 161, where a man in cleaning his gun shot his wife, *Lamb* (1967) 51 Cr App R 417, where a man shot a friend, *Turner* (1990) 12 Cr App R (S) 202, where a man punched another in a pub argument and *Scarlett* (1994) 98 Cr App R 290 where a man, following eviction from a pub, fell down the stairs. There is also some evidence of cases of domestic homicide where there has been a history of violence being successfully pleaded as no intent/manslaughter (see Thomas 1970, p. 118). In *Cenci* (1989) 11 Cr App R (S) 199, a female cohabitee, in an attempt to escape further violence from her boyfriend, smashed a window with an iron in order to escape and fell to her death. His plea of involuntary manslaughter was accepted. (See *Morgan* (1990) 12 Cr App R (S) 504.) In *Slingsby* [1995] Crim LR 570 the killing was considered to have arisen from an act which was not unlawful. The Crown offered no evidence and a plea of not guilty was entered. It is the harshness of the mandatory sentence following a conviction for murder that has led to some quite extraordinary bending of the rules, which seem to become excessively malleable especially in circumstances of men killing wives, which will be explored in the subsequent section.

Voluntary manslaughter — provocation

Considerable debate in recent years has revolved around the formulation of the rules governing provocation and their application, criticism has been virtually unanimous that this defence is more consonant with the male experience (see Taylor 1986, Edwards 1984, 1987b, Dressler 1982). The ingredients necessary to establish a successful defence of provocation are similar in all common law jurisdictions. There must be evidence of provocation sufficient to provoke the reasonable man (otherwise known as the objective test or condition) and that this provocation resulted in the accused losing self-control (the subjective test or condition). The Homicide Act 1957, s. 3 provides:

> Where on a charge of murder there is evidence on which the jury can find that the person charged was provoked (whether by things done or by things said or by both together) to lose his self-control, the question whether the provocation was enough to make a reasonable man do as he did shall be left to be determined by the jury; and in determining that question the jury shall take into account everything both done and said according to the effect which, in their opinion, it would have on a reasonable man.

The burden of proof is on the prosecution to prove beyond all reasonable doubt that the case is not one of provocation.

Statutory interpretation: the subjective test   In applying the subjective test, the court must consider the state of mind of the defendant, as indicated by his reaction to the alleged provocation. The standard provided by the common law is derived from the formulation expounded by Devlin J in *Duffy* [1949] 1 All ER 932n, where a wife killed a brutal husband.

> Provocation is some act, or series of acts, done by the dead man to the accused which would cause in any reasonable person, and actually causes in the accused, a sudden and temporary loss of self-control, rendering the accused so subject to passion as to make him or her for the moment not master of his mind.

Although this is not the standard required by the Homicide Act 1957, s. 3 which instead refers merely to 'loss of self control', it is the *Duffy* formulation which is preferred, (excepting Lord Taylor's formulation in *Ahluwalia* discussed below). The first element of this test is the formulation of 'suddenness', construed to denote the relationship in time between the provocative act and the reaction, i.e., the immediacy, spontaneity, reflexivity, rather than the acute nature or explosiveness of the reaction. In detailing the elements Devlin J in *Duffy* asserted:

> The first of them is whether there was what is sometimes called time for cooling, that is, for passion to cool and for reason to regain dominion over the mind. That is why most acts of provocation are cases of sudden quarrels, sudden blows inflicted with an implement already in the hand, perhaps being used, or being picked up, where there has been no time for reflection.

In deciding the question the court will take into account, '... the nature of the act by which the offender causes death, to the time which elapsed between the provocation and the act which caused death, to the offender's conduct during that interval, and to all other circumstances tending to show the state of his mind' (Stephen's *Digest of the Criminal Law*, art. 317, cited in *Mancini v DPP* [1942] AC 1, 9). In observance of the *Duffy* 'suddenness' there have been several permutations on what is an acceptable time lapse. The morning of the killing was approved in principle as an acceptable time span in *Brown* (1972) 56 Cr App R 564, where a husband killed his wife with a razor severing the carotid artery, the jugular veins, the windpipe and the gullet, although the jury rejected the defence of provocation and convicted of murder. In *Ibrams and Gregory* (1982) 74 Cr App R 154, a seven day time lapse between the last act of provocation and retaliation resulted in the trial judge withdrawing the defence of provocation from the jury and the Appeal Court ruling that the judge had not misdirected the jury. In cases where the trial judge has taken a more rigid view and applied a more restrictive time lapse, the Court of Appeal has not seen fit to interfere, although there is some evidence in contradistinction that in cases involving domestic killings, the trial judge has on occasion let the case go to the jury even where there has been a substantial time interval between the provocation and the reaction (see *Wyatt* (unreported) 21, 22 November 1984, observed by author, discussed below). This suggests that a generous view of the time lapse is occurring covertly and largely invisibly at the court of first instance and not in the Court of Appeal, thus avoiding the expansion of the legal principles by the Court of Appeal, whilst allowing trial judges discretion in the court of first instance. In *Ahluwalia* [1992] 4 All ER 889, where a battered wife killed a violent and bullying husband, the time lapse hurdle was circumvented whereby the Court of Appeal gave to the word 'suddenness' a new emphasis whilst retaining the wording. No longer regarded axiomatic upon the provocation, suddenness becomes a quality of the nature and manifestation of the loss of self-control. The Court said:

> ... it is open to the judge, when deciding whether there is any evidence of provocation to be left to the jury and open to the jury when considering such evidence, to take account of the interval between the provocative conduct and the reaction of the defendant to it ... In some cases such an interval may wholly undermine the defence of provocation; that, however, depends entirely on the facts of the individual case and is not a principle of law ... We accept that a subjective element in the defence of provocation would not as a matter of law be negatived simply because of the delayed reaction in such cases, provided that there was at the time of the killing a 'sudden and temporary loss of self control'.

The Court of Appeal in *Thornton* [1992] (above), similarly retains the language of the *Duffy* direction and indeed a little more of its spirit. Beldam J, in dismissing the appeal on the grounds that there was no evidence of 'sudden and temporary loss of self-control', said, 'the essential feature [is] that provocation produces a sudden or impulsive reaction leading to a loss of self-control', and later added, '... there is no suggestion that she reacted suddenly and on the spur of the moment ... to the provocative statements made by the deceased'.

The reluctance of the Court of Appeal to abandon the *Duffy* formulation and its emphasis on this element of 'suddenness' arises because of a concern that the Homicide Act 1957, s. 3, is drawn too widely, and if applied without reference to the common law would lead to circumstances otherwise amounting to murder, coming instead within the ambit of provocation merely because, at the time of the killing, there was a 'loss of self-control', thus rendering virtually indistinguishable cases involving the loss of self-control from frenzied killings to killings for revenge or planned killings.

What expressions or manifestations have come to signify what passes for 'loss of self-control', although not a rule of law, are arguably of extreme importance in assessment of the subjective condition. Case law has constructed a very specific and definite typology, characterised by outwardly visible manifestations and changes in the mental and physical state of the accused, where outbursts of anger, or passion justified by moral indignation (see Horder 1992) pass for the requisite 'loss'. An enormous significance attaches to the words used by the defendant to describe the state of mind at this moment. Defendants successfully pleading provocation have described this critical moment as, 'the last straw', 'snapping' (see *Warner, Guardian*, 1 May 1982, *Wyatt*, 22 November 1984 observed by author), 'cracked' (*Wheeler*, 25 September 1986), 'exploded' *Hinton, Daily Telegraph*, 26 March 1988 and see Horder 1992, p. 109), although availing oneself of the linguistic orthodoxy is in itself not enough. In *Phillips* [1969] 2 AC 130, 138, the defendant explained, '. . . I spin round quickly was to punch her with my hand (sic)', and in *Brown* (1972), the defendant said he 'blacked out'. Such cases are indicative of manipulation of linguistic devices to assist a defence strategy, rather than accurately reflecting a state of emotion. Sara Thornton, in contrast said, 'there was no loss of self control' (*Thornton* [1992] (above)), and by failing to explain herself in the appropriate linguistic terminology, she negated the second element of the subjective test necessary for a successful defence of provocation.

The second element of the subjective test relies on the question of precisely how much loss of self-control is required to satisfy the test. In *Phillips* [1969] 2 AC 130, where the appellant killed his mistress with a machete, Lord Diplock rejected the argument of Louis Blom-Cooper for the appellant that, '. . . loss of self-control is not a matter of degree but is absolute; there is no intermediate stage between icy detachment and going berserk', asserting that, 'This premise . . . is . . . false. The average man reacts to provocation according to its degree with angry words, with a blow of the hand, possibly if the provocation is gross and there is a dangerous weapon to hand, with that weapon'. Courts have held that self-control must not be lost completely, i.e., so that he did not know what he was doing, since that would denote a lack of responsibility, more congruous with a permanent state of instability than that permitted of a 'reasonable' man. In *Richens* [1994] 98 Cr App R 43, 44, on appeal against conviction for murder, the Court of Appeal held that the trial judge's direction to the jury that loss of self-control amounted to, 'a complete loss so as not to know what he was doing' was a misdirection. But it is not just a matter of loss of self control, but what is considered to constitute a loss. The role of the judge in directing the jury on this question has been expanded in *Stewart* [1995] 4 All ER 999. Here, where a husband killed a wife and raised the defence of accident, the Court of Appeal said that where the judge as a matter of law must leave provocation to the jury he should indicate to them what evidence might support the conclusion that the appellant had lost his self control. The trial judge did not direct on the matter and the Court of Appeal said that this amounted to a non-direction. Following *Stewart* it would appear that judges will be required to give direction to the jury on the subjective test and what may constitute loss of self control. Judges will then become the exponents, arbiters and gatekeepers of traditional notions of what constitutes loss of self control. Loss of self control as it is bound by a masculinist construction is seen reflected in rage and anger rather than in despair, exhaustion, isolation and hopelessness. The *Stewart* guidance will be of little benefit to expanding the understanding of what might be a loss of self control in cases where battered women kill.

Objective tests and standard legal subjects The second condition necessary to a defence of provocation turns on what kinds of conduct are accepted as likely to elicit a 'loss of self-control'. Under the common law this question was a matter for the judge and where the judge considered there to be insufficient evidence he withdrew the defence of provocation from the jury. Broadly speaking, it had to be things done to the accused by the deceased, although in *Holmes* v *DPP* [1946] AC 588, where a husband had been unfaithful and killed his wife after she said, 'I have been untrue to you ...', in considering whether there was any exception to the general rule, the court conceded that words could not constitute provocation, '... except in circumstances of a most extreme and exceptional character'. The test to be applied has rested with the 'reasonable man' construct, requiring jurors to consider how a reasonable man presented with the same facts might have reacted. The reasonable man claims an objective standard. This construct has sanctioned the indignation, fury and anger of men at a wife or lover's adultery, her leaving him and pursuing a new relationship as being the common standard. Thus, within the objective test judges have evolved and developed a degree of judicial subjectivity on the matter, allowing the development of a number of reasonable men according to the circumstances, such that a loss of self-control was considered 'reasonable' under circumstances of the wife's betrayal. In *Bedder* v *DPP* [1954] 2 All ER 801, in a case where a prostitute had jeered at the appellant and he claimed that his loss of self-control was reasonable, taking into account his impotence, the House of Lords held that the test was not one of a 'reasonable impotent man'. Judges have also rejected the argument that a drunken man can claim that his drunkenness provided special circumstances (see *McCarthy* [1954] 2 QB 105), rejecting also pugnacity as in *Lesbini* [1914] 3 KB 1116. The effect of *Bedder* was twofold. First it finally laid to rest the automatic presumption that evidence of a wife's adultery was sufficient exculpation for a defence of provocation. Indeed there had been a litany of cases preceding it where such evidence was sufficient argument; see *Rothwell* [1871] 12 Cox CC 145, *Jones* [1908] 72 JP 215, or where a husband suspected a wife and killed a brother in law, *Birchall* (1914) 9 Cr App R 91, *Ellor* (1920) 15 Cr App R 41, *Hall* (1928) 21 Cr App R 48, *Woolmington* v *DPP* [1935] AC 462, 472, 480. Second, it closed the door to any other flexibility on the objective standard.

Since the 1957 Act, it is for the judge to direct the jury on what ingredients of the objective test, i.e., what amounts to reasonableness, may be present, not merely on a statement of what the law is. Although no longer a judicial but a jury question, the legacy of what amounted to provocation as decided by judges under the common law, lingered on. Jurors will be influenced by the content, nature and tenor of the direction given by the trial judge. Whilst the standard claims objectivity, there have been attempts to soften the test on the basis that it is inappropriate and misleading for a jury to apply the test of how an ordinary Englishman might react where the defendant is black, or, indeed, is a woman who is battered. In assessing reasonableness any characteristic of the accused might be relevant in attempts to assess the gravity of the provocation. It was not until the House of Lords in *DPP* v *Camplin* [1978] 2 All ER 168, that the court began to develop a softening of the reasonable man standard in accommodating certain characteristics of the accused where they bore a relationship to the provocation, in assessing the gravity of the provocation. They held, in a case where the appellant was 15 years of age, that age was indeed a relevant characteristic of the accused in assessing the gravity of the provocative conduct. The court held, 'It seems to me that the courts are no longer entitled to tell juries that a reasonable man has certain stated and defined features ... If an impotent man was taunted about his impotence the jury would not today be told that an impotent man could not be a reasonable man as contemplated by the law'. Lord Diplock was of like mind, '... the unqualified proposition accepted by this House in *Bedder* that for the purposes of the "reasonable man" test any unusual physical characteristics of the accused must be ignored requires revision as a result of the passing of the 1957 Act' and in approving Lord Simonds LC's proposition in the Appeal Court, '... it would be plainly illogical not to recognise an unusually excitable or pugnacious temperament in the accused as a matter to be taken into account but yet to recognise for that purpose some unusual physical characteristic, be it impotence or another'. The House of Lords relied upon the New Zealand case of *McGregor* [1962] NZLR 1069, which had taken the first step in expanding upon the characteristics of the reasonable man. North J held:

The characteristic must be something definite and of sufficient significance to make the offender a different person from the ordinary run of mankind, and have also a sufficient degree of permanence to warrant its being regarded as something constituting part of the individual's character or personality ... The word 'characteristic' in the context of this section is wide enough to apply not only to physical qualities but also mental qualities and such more indeterminate attributes as colour, race and creed ... Moreover, it is to be equally emphasised that there must be some real connection between the nature of the provocation and the particular characteristic of the offender by which it is sought to modify the ordinary man test. The words or conduct must have been exclusively or particularly provocative to the individual because, and only because of the characteristic.

McGregor has been widely accepted but its spirit infrequently applied. This formulation was cited with approval in *Newell* (1980) 71 Cr App R 331, where the Appeal Court stated that it represented both New Zealand and English law in an 'impeccable passage'. Although the court, faced with the problem of chronic alcoholism, concluded that this might well be a characteristic, the condition did not bear a direct relationship to the provocation and the words by which he was provoked and was a condition of a transitory nature not satisfying the required test of permanency. The courts have been hesitant to develop any allowance of notional characteristics since this would shift an objective test into considering the subjective.

It was precisely on this point of the interpretation of what constitutes a 'characteristic' and its effect on the gravity of the provocation that *Ahluwalia* (above) appealed. She had endured a long course of violence directed against her by the deceased. In applying the ruling in *Camplin* [1978] (above), the judge in directing the jury on this point said, 'The only characteristics of the defendant about which you know specifically that might be relevant are that she is an Asian woman, married, incidentally to an Asian man, the deceased, living in this country'. This direction excluded any reference to the fact that the characteristic of relevance had less to do with her legal marriage and more to do with the fact that being battered over a long period of time had resulted in inducing within her chronic fear, anxiety expectation and morbid anticipation of imminent attack. She was a battered woman. On appeal, it was argued that the experience of being battered (subjective) and evidence of being battered (objective) was a relevant characteristic of the accused such as to require a jury to consider not a reasonable man, but whether a reasonable battered woman could or would have reacted in the same way. The Court of Appeal rejected the point, deeming the effects of battering not a 'characteristic' with the necessary degree of permanence. Perhaps then it was an extraordinary leap of faith when in *Humphreys* [1995] 4 All ER 1008 an abnormal state of mind, including immaturity and attention seeking behaviour; was regarded as a notional characteristic of the reasonable man, and cumulative provocation given greater authority and recognition than hitherto. Here, the Court of Appeal conceded that the trial judge should have taken these characteristics into account in assessing whether a person with those characteristics might have reacted in the same way. Humphreys became a prostitute at 16, the deceased was a drug addict 16 years older. He controlled her. He beat her. The appellant had a history of cutting her wrists to gain attention in order to show him how far he had driven her. On the day in question she cut her wrists. The deceased responded with cruel goading, saying that she had not made a very good job of it. She responded and stabbed him with a knife. At her trial in 1985 she pleaded provocation and was convicted of murder. In 1995 she appealed on the ground that the trial judge had been wrong not to direct the jury to take into account the abnormal mentality evidence of the consultant psychiatrist as a characteristic of sufficient permanence of the reasonable person and on the ground that the judge did not detail the background to the provocation in his summing-up and direction to the jury. A further expansion of the reasonable man is found in *Morhall* (1995) 3 All ER 659, where in reversing the finding of the Court of Appeal ((1994) 98 Cr App R 108), that a self-induced glue sniffer would not be more or less vulnerable to provocation than a non self-induced glue sniffer or a non glue sniffer, glue sniffing was deemed to be a characteristic of the accused. The House of Lords found that references to glue sniffing, drug taking etc. could constitute provocation provided that the glue sniffer or drug taker or alcoholic who was provoked was not in a state of intoxication or addiction at the time of the killing. Here, in *Stewart* the Court of Appeal has held that where as a matter of law the judge is required to leave the issue of provocation to the jury, the judge should indicate to them what evidence might support the conclusion that the accused had lost self control.

A further expansion of principles is noted in *Dryden* [1995] 4 All ER 987. Here the accused appealed on the ground that in directing the jury on provocation the judge had failed to put for their consideration an obsessional personality and eccentricity as characteristics of the reasonable man. The Court held on appeal that these psychological traits were indeed relevant (at p. 998).

In assessing whether the reasonable man might have reacted in the same way, the background circumstances have been held to be of varying import. 'Background', according to the *Duffy* formulation, 'where there was a long course of cruel conduct', was said to be irrelevant. In more recent years, however, the relevance of the background has become of increasing import-ance. Widgery LJ, in *Davies* [1975] QB 691, in assessing the conduct of a wife's lover, held, '. . . the background is material to the provocation as the setting in which the state of mind of the defendant must be judged'. In domestic assault cases where the defendant has suffered continual violence, the background or history of violence is now considered of relevance where the last act of provocation is slight. The headnote to *Thornton* [1992] 1 All ER 306, 307 states, *inter alia*:

> Provocative acts in the course of domestic violence over a period of time which did not cause sudden and temporary loss of self-control did not amount to provocation in law, but might be considered by a jury as part of the context or background against which the accused's reaction to provoca-tive conduct has to be judged.

Humphreys [1995] 4 All ER 1009, further extended this principle of cumulative provocation when the Court of Appeal ruled:

> In a case where the provocative circumstances comprised a complex history with several distinct and cumulative strands of potentially provocative conduct which had built up over time until the final encounter, the judge ought to give guidance to the jury in the form of a careful analysis of these strands so as to enable them too understand their potential significance. Having regard to the appellant's tempestuous relationship with A over the long term, prior to the events of the night in question, it was clear that the judge should have given such an analysis and that a more historical recital of the facts devoid of any analysis or guidance was insufficient.

The modus operandi and construction of intent A further element relevant to this assessment of the state of mind (*mens rea*) and loss of self-control, although as stated earlier not a rule of law, is the weapon used. The relevance is explained by the editors of Archbold 1996 (Vol. 2, 19–62):

> Various matters which formed the basis of the old authorities, in particular whether there was a 'cooling-off interval' between the provocation and the killing, the kind of weapon and the degree of force used in proportion to the degree of provocation, may properly be mentioned to the jury ... but care should be taken to avoid giving the impression that they result in any binding presumptions or rules of law.

The court in *Mancini* v *DPP* [1942] AC 1, 9, in applying the test of whether a reasonable man would have been provoked said it is of importance to '... take into account the instrument with which the homicide was effected, for to retort ... by a simple blow, is a very different thing from making use of a deadly instrument ...'. Whilst following the 1957 Act it was no longer a requirement that the mode of resentment be proportionate to the provocation, since words alone could be sufficient to constitute provocation, whether the body or a weapon is used to perpetrate the violence is still a consideration which has some bearing on assessment of intent (see Lord Diplock in *Phillips* [1969] 2 AC 130, 138). The reasoning behind this is that using a weapon is considered likely to extend the time lapse between the provocation and the killing as compared with the use of bodily force. Sara Thornton did not plead provocation at her original trial. The judge, however, did put provocation as an alternative before the jury for their consideration as he was placed under a duty to do so. Provocation in the alternative failed. One of the reasons for that failure was because Thornton went into the kitchen to fetch a knife. Kiranjit Ahluwalia's plea of provocation similarly failed because she carried paraffin and a taper upstairs to the bedroom where her husband slept.

Provocation — a jury challenge   Since the 1957 Act judges can no longer withdraw a defence of provocation from the jury and where the defence are not relying on provocation, or indeed, where provocation is contrary to the defence case, the judge is placed under a duty to put provocation to the jury if there is some evidence of it. It seems that the only ground on which provocation may be withdrawn is when the judge considers that there is no evidence of loss of self-control. Some cases have succeeded on appeal simply because the judge at trial considered the evidence of loss of self-control to be insufficient, whereas the Court of Appeal took a different view. It is uncertain what strength of evidence of provocation gives rise to the duty. This point was considered by Taylor LCJ in *Cambridge* (1994) 99 CR App R 142, when he queried, 'But what sort of evidence gives rise to the duty? ... There must be some evidence but of what strength?'. In *Bullard* (1957) 42 Cr App R 1, the Court of Appeal made it clear when it said it was, 'any evidence ... fit to be left to a jury'. Lord Diplock in *Camplin* (above) said, 'however slight' and in *Rossiter* (1992) 95 Cr App R 326, this was confirmed with the words, it was 'evidence however tenuous'. It is not clear, however, whether in these cases the court had been referring to evidence of loss of self-control (subjective test) as acting on the duty, or evidence of provocative conduct (objective test). In *Camplin* and *Rossiter* the reference was made in respect of the strength of the provocative words or acts themselves, rather than on the entirety of the defence as a whole, i.e., the strength of the response to provocation.

In advancing what is and what is not reasonable, judges, when directing juries, frequently let their own impressions filter through. In *Thornton* [1992] whilst the judge was under a duty to put the defence of provocation to the jury, at the same moment in his direction he indicated a veiled rejection of the reasonableness of her actions, thus suggesting his own rejection of provocation. Some judges have interpreted this duty as predicated on the provocative acts (objective test), whilst others have looked to the totality of the case. In *Doughty* (1986) 83 Cr App R 319, the Court of Appeal quashed a murder conviction and substituted one of manslaughter provocation on the ground that the judge deprived the accused of the opportunity of having this point considered by the jury. Where the defence does not plead provocation, the judge must still put provocation as an alternative, if there is material evidence. In *Burgess and McLean* [1995] Crim LR 425, a conviction for murder was quashed and manslaughter substituted where the appellants had both alleged provocation from the victim. B said she had quarrelled with the victim over the victim's assertion that she had slept with her husband and M said she had lost her temper following remarks about her mother and ex-husband. Counsel had submitted that the matter should not go to the jury, the fact that the judge did not place it before the jury resulted in quashing the conviction. This judicial requirement is problematic for the defendant and the case prognosis, since where defence counsel decides not to put provocation as a defence, but then in consequence imposes a duty on the judge to place provocation before the jury, provocation entering by this postscript route is more likely than not to be rejected by them, since it can hardly be said that they have heard persuasive argument on the point. The mere recanting by the judge of this duty is of dubious benefit to the defendant. Indeed in *Thornton* [1992] the judge's direction to the jury on provocation, in the absence of defence counsel adducing such evidence, was positively damaging. The Court of Appeal held the trial judge's ruling on the law on provocation to be impeccable. Certainly as a flat statement of current law it was, yet the tone, tenor and manner of it was unhelpful.

> It is my duty to mention this to you, members of the jury, [because] you will notice that [counsel] did not address you on the basis of provocation and it will I think be obvious to you why in a moment when you have heard what I have to say to you about it ... The first question is whether the provocative conduct, such as it was, if there was any, caused the defendant to lose her self-control ... The defendant herself asserts that there was no sudden loss of self-control. Members of the jury, that no doubt is why [counsel] did not address you and invite you to consider provocation.

The trial judge proceeded to invite the jury to consider the evidence for the second ingredient, having detailed her action, he said:

... it may be very difficult to come to the conclusion that that was, and I use the shorthand, a reasonable reaction. There are ... many unhappy, indeed miserable, husbands and wives. It is a fact of life. It has to be faced, members of the jury. But on the whole it is hardly reasonable, you may think, to stab them fatally when there are other alternatives available, like walking out or going upstairs.

That the jury did not accept provocation was not altogether surprising. An issue of provocation put by the judge like a full blown defence put by counsel, once placed before a jury and rejected, closes off a possible avenue of appeal, leaving flagrantly incompetent advocacy or fresh evidence as the only avenues. Provocation must also be put as an alternative in pleas of self-defence. In *Rossiter* (1992) 95 Cr App R 326, where self-defence was pleaded unsuccessfully, the fact that the judge failed to leave the issue of provocation to the jury resulted in the Court of Appeal quashing the conviction.

Diminished responsibility

A defence of diminished responsibility is provided by the Homicide Act 1957, s. 2(1):

> Where a person kills or is party to the killing of another, he shall not be convicted of murder if he was suffering from such an abnormality of mind (whether arising from a condition of arrested or retarded development of mind or any inherent causes or induced by disease or injury) as substantially impaired his mental responsibility for his acts and omissions in doing or being a party to the killing.

The burden of proof is on the defence and the required standard is on the balance of probabilities. There are three ingredients. First, the accused must be suffering from an 'abnormality of mind'. In *Byrne* [1960] 2 QB 396, a case involving a sexual 'psychopath', it was held that abnormality of mind meant a state of mind 'so different' from the normal state. In *Brown* [1993] Crim LR 961, where a 17 year old had strangled his girlfriend in a fit of temper because she told him she no longer loved him, the Court reaffirmed a broader definition that abnormality of mind was not restricted to mental illness or insanity but embraced perception, understanding, judgment and will. In *O'Connor* (1994) 15 Cr App R (S) 473, where the defendant brutally attacked and sexually mutilated a woman with whom he had been on intimate terms, when he was drinking and taking drugs, the court ruled that an 'abnormality of mind' may not be a mental disorder and may not be treatable. In *Woollaston* (1986) 8 Cr App R (S) 360, medical evidence submitted that the appellant suffered from an anxiety state or depression as a result of the behaviour of the deceased. The effects of battering, 'battered husband syndrome', were said to constitute an abnormality of mind in *Irons* (1995) 16 Cr App R (S) 46, where the psychiatric evidence found, 'Irons was suffering from such an abnormality of mind, namely chronic reactive depression (induced by disease) and battered husband syndrome (induced by injury)'. The expansion of the abnormality is clear from serious to something mild. How much 'abnormality of mind' is required is somewhere on the continuum between 'trivial and total impairment' (see Dell 1984, p. 33).

Secondly, the abnormality must arise from 'arrested or retarded development disease or injury', although it need not have existed from birth (soft determinism). This has been taken to embrace a broad range of conditions or causes, including extraneous factors which have some bearing on the 'mental' condition, although it is suggested by the editors of Blackstone's (1995) B1.16, that where a husband is jealous and kills a wife, s. 2 was designed precisely to exclude such causes. Indeed this principle was asserted in *Vinagre* (1979) 69 Cr App R 104, where, whilst Lawton LJ was unhappy about the nomenclature, he felt unable to interfere with the verdict. Yet, as I show in some detail later, the evidence runs contrary to this noble intention. Indeed, in many cases of wife killing where jealousy is said to cause depression and is described in disease nosology, successful diminished responsibility pleas are fast becoming the norm. Indeed, the trajectory seems to be that the mere labelling or naming of conduct in disease terms brings that conduct firmly within the section. Thirdly, the abnormality of mind must have substantially impaired the accused's mental responsibility. It is on this point that juries must make an assessment. Some psychiatrists are, quite rightly, reluctant to make a judgment on this final ingredient as they are of the opinion that this is a moral and not a medical question. Yet it is clear that the question of substantial impairment is being hammered out by psychiatrists. As in *Dryden* (above) what is not a matter for the expert has now been transformed into a major area of their battleground. The trial judge said

> Now, let us look ... finally at the evidence of Dr McClelland which differs from that of Dr Wood and differs significantly from Dr Burton. Dr McClelland's view is that the defendant has a diminished responsibility for what he did because of an abnormality of mind and because he was depressed, but that it does not significantly impair his responsiblity. He differs from Dr Burton and Dr Wood in the degree of impairment; it is not such as to diminish his responsibility? (at p. 995).

This conflict of expert opinion on the question of substantial impairment was significant in *Thornton* where whilst there was agreement as to the psychiatric evidence, Dr Bullard and Prof. Brandon believed her responsibility was substantially impaired. Dr Brockleman did not (at p. 311). Where the medical evidence is unequivocal and uncontradicted, the trial judge should direct the jury to accept a plea of diminished responsibility (see Archbold 1995, Vol 2, paras. 19–76).

Pleas and diminished responsibility   Research conducted by Dell (1984) indicates that pleas of diminished responsibility are accepted by the prosecution in about in 80 per cent of cases, with the result that judges direct the jury to accept the plea notwithstanding the fact that the third element of whether the accused's state of mind is 'substantially impaired', is a matter for them alone. A defence of diminished responsibility is only put to proof where there is conflict between prosecution and defence. Dell found that in only 13 per cent of cases did prosecution doctors challenge. In 64 per cent of cases the jury rejects the evidence and convicts on the murder charge. However, where the judge considers the case borderline, even though both defence and prosecution are in agreement on the evidence of abnormality, if there are 'other' circumstances, the medical evidence must be considered in the light of them, as was asserted in *Sanders* (1991) 93 Cr App R 245. Here two psychiatrists were to play a prominent part in the trial; one was produced by the Crown and the other by the defence. Both of them were called by the defence. Their evidence as between one another was uncontroversial. They both agreed that this appellant was at the material time suffering from an abnormality of mind induced, so one said, by disease, and the other, by reason of inherent causes. They further agreed that the abnormality, which was a form of reactive depression, substantially impaired the appellant's responsibility for his actions. Clearly if that evidence had been accepted by the jury they would certainly have come to the conclusion that the appellant was not guilty of murder but guilty of manslaughter by reason of diminished responsibility. The plea to manslaughter was offered by the defence to the Crown; the offer was not accepted. It is not altogether clear what the nature of these 'other circumstances' is, nor how weighty they must be before the matter goes before the jury. Even where defence and prosecution are in agreement as to medical evidence, the judge may still insist on a trial of facts if 'other circumstances allow him to do so'.

At the trial of Peter Sutcliffe for the murder of 13 women and the attempted murder of seven others (see Boulos 1983, *Sutcliffe*, *The Times*, 23 May 1981), both prosecution and defence agreed that Sutcliffe was suffering from an abnormality of mind. He had heard voices telling him to kill prostitute women.

Peter Sutcliffe: 'I was attempting to kill her.'

James Chadwin: 'Why?'

Peter Sutcliffe: 'Because it was what I had to do: it was my mission.'

James Chadwin: 'Why?'

Peter Sutcliffe: 'Because I had been told they were the scum of the earth and had to be got rid of.'

James Chadwin: 'Who had told you?'

Peter Sutcliffe: 'God.'

There was agreement that Sutcliffe was suffering from schizophrenia. The judge was not convinced and put the matter before the jury who rejected the psychiatric finding of diminished responsibility (see Spencer 1984, p. 88).

Where a jury has rejected unanimous medical evidence, it seems that the Court of Appeal may still substitute a verdict of diminished responsibility (see *Matheson* [1958] 1 WLR 474), if the evidence is perversely rejected, although the Privy Council in *Walton* [1978] AC 788, refused to interfere with the finding of the court of first instance. So precisely when the Court of Appeal will intervene is unclear, depending very much on the facts of the individual case. Where diminished responsibility is not considered at the trial, unlike provocation, the judge has no power to raise this as an alternative defence and attempts on appeal to have a second bite at the forensic cherry and introduce diminished responsibility where it was not introduced at trial, are not permissible. In *Straw* [1995] 1 All ER 187, the defendant was charged with the murder of her husband but refused to instruct counsel on diminished responsibility even though the prosecution was willing to accept such a plea as medical evidence was unanimous. Her appeal against a conviction for murder failed.

Self-defence

The fourth contentious area of law's legal defences, generating much debate especially with regard to battered women who kill, is the defence of self-defence. In accordance with the Criminal Law Act 1967, s. 3(1):

> A person may use such force as is reasonable in the circumstances in the prevention of crime, or in effecting or assisting in the lawful arrest of offenders or suggested offenders or of persons unlawfully at large.

The essential ingredients of a self-defence plea are that the person believes he is under imminent threat of attack, and that the degree of force used to repel an attack or anticipated attack is reasonable. The onus is on the prosecution to prove that it was not self-defence. The standard governing self-defence, is that of reasonable force. The burden of negativing the defence rests on the prosecution. In *Beckford* v *The Queen* [1988] AC 130, where a police officer killed a man whom he believed to be a dangerous gunman, the Privy Council said, 'the test to be applied for self-defence is that a person may use such force as is reasonable in the circumstances as he honestly believes them to be in the defence of himself or another'. Unlike provocation, in self-defence the retaliation or force used must be proportionate to the attack. The reasonableness of the force used is based on the accused's belief (subjective test) that the degree of force was necessary (see *Shannon* (1980) 71 Cr App R 192, 197). The jury must consider what the accused thought. Lord Morris in *Palmer* [1971] 55 Crim App R 223, said, 'Was this stabbing within the conception of necessary self-defence judged by the standards of common sense, bearing in mind the position of the appellant at the moment of stabbing; or was it a case of angry retaliation or pure aggression on his part?' Ormrod LJ, in the Court of Appeal, said that as this consideration was precluded by the trial judge, the conviction for manslaughter would be quashed.

The test was further expounded in *Williams* (1984) 78 Cr App R 276, 281, where the Lord Chief Justice said:

where self-defence or the prevention of crime is concerned, if the jury came to the conclusion that the defendant believed, or may have believed, that he was being attacked or that a crime was being committed, and that force was necessary to protect himself or to prevent the crime, then the prosecution have not proved their case. If however the defendant's alleged belief was mistaken and if the mistake was an unreasonable one, that may be a powerful reason for coming to the conclusion that the belief was not honestly held and should be rejected.

As with provocation, the accused's perception of the imminence of the anticipated attack is a factor to be taken into consideration, where 'imminent' is based on reasonable grounds and honest belief (see *Chisam* (1963) 47 Cr App R 130, 134). In *Beckford* (above), however, a man about to be attacked does not have to wait for his assailant to strike the first blow or fire the first shot. Thus a person can use force to ward off an anticipated attack but not if the anticipation of the attack is unspecified as any time in the future. The difficulty lies in the fact that someone who thinks he is about to be attacked is likely to be alarmed or terrified, and it is difficult in such a state of apprehension to assess the precise degree of force that would be required to repel the impending attack. Lord Morris of Borth-y-Gest was one of a few who recognised the uncertainty; in *Palmer* [1971] 55 Crim App R 223, 242 he said, '. . . it will be recognised that a person defending himself cannot weigh to a nicety the exact measure of his necessary defensive action'. Ormrod LJ in *Shannon* (1980) 71 Cr App R 192, 194 suggested:

a bridge between what is sometimes referred to as 'the objective test', that is what is reasonable judged from the viewpoint of an outsider looking at a situation quite dispassionately, and 'the subjective test', that is the viewpoint of the accused himself with the intellectual capabilities of which he may in fact be possessed and with all the emotional strains and stresses to which at the moment he may be subjected.

CRITIQUING THE MASCULINISM OF HOMICIDE'S LEGAL METHOD

The law is a distillation of judicial reasoning applied to a set of facts, where judgments are realised and reified in formal rules or precedents (Mossman 1986, Forell 1992). Law's logic and law's method is a proclamation of the hegemony of the scientific method of induction. Yet, these facts are indefatigably 'social' and 'historical' which in the process of assimilation into legal rules lose their social facticity and acquire the guise of truths which have authority *sui generis*. A deconstruction of legal rules precipitates questions about the nature and content of rules and how legal rules are interpolated as general or universal typifications about social conduct. Thus, some conduct is imbued with authority and therefore universalised (the conduct of men), whilst other conduct (conduct of women) is without authority and particularised (de Beauvoir 1974).

In homicide law certain social facts are transposed into legal rules such that the subject is male and the *actus reus* and *mens rea* is about what men do and about what they intend and how their actions may be excused and/or justified. This process implies that legal discourse constructs for itself a standard human subject. That standard human subject is inexorably male. Two specific problems have emerged in this discussion on homicide defences. First, the gender selectivity in deeming certain accounts of motive and intent as the authority and secondly, the consequence of the inductive logic of the law for the perpetuation of particular constructs and concepts as universal legal standards. Thus through this process the law passes from singular statements, such as accounts of the results of observations, to universal statements such as theories or more specifically legal principles. How far in any event we are justified in inferring universal statements from particular ones is not a problem peculiar to law (see Popper 1968, p. 28). Although inductive logic itself is not inherently gendered, legal method unwittingly perpetuates a masculinist, 'a priori valid' conceptualisation through the application of the standard legal subject. That is to say, the law builds on individual cases to principles, elevating particularities into universal truths. The empirical basis is selective, it is not haphazard or arbitrary, some particulars become the universal experience, other particulars remain just that. Social facts are then given a 'thing like facticity' considered general through society (see Durkheim 1966, p. 13).

In applying these insights to homicide defences the singular or particular statements are derived from male empiricism. The force of the argument that there is a gender politics of homicide has centered around the issue that a successful voluntary manslaughter/provocation defence is particularly difficult for women as a group or class to argue and that this is particularly the case for the battered woman who kills. Home Office figures referred to earlier merely disguise the process of case mortality and attrition which selectively exclude women from provocation and self-defence. Any attempt to reformulate law to accommodate women's experiences must begin with outlining the evidence of its masculinist bias. Whilst some feminists have attempted to engage in a reformulation of the law, many are of the opinion that 'legal method is structured in such a way that it is impervious to a feminist perspective' (Mossman 1986).

The intent of 'no intent-manslaughter'

Pleas of involuntary manslaughter/no intent, once reserved for the pub brawl, where intention to kill or to cause grievous bodily harm are notoriously difficult to prove, are being pleaded successfully in cases of domestic homicide where there has been a history of violence by the accused towards the deceased and where the last act is one in a trajectory of deliberate violence. In the development of the defence case, the killing is portrayed as a tragic accident following a marital argument where the accused had no intention of causing death or grievous bodily harm. Such fatalities are located within a context of marital strife, constructed in defence accounts as 'stormy', 'tempestuous' or 'on the rocks' and where the accused's violence is minimised and the part played by both parties equalised. The prosecution engage in a strategy of capitulation. They are willing to accept these highly dubious pleas without contest, where there is evidence of intent evinced both in a history of violence against the deceased and the final *modus operandi*. In *Williams* (unreported, Inner London Crown Court) 7 July 1994 (Transcript), where there had been evidence of past violence, bruising had been seen on the deceased by friends, family and work colleagues, the defendant entered a plea of manslaughter/no intent which was accepted by the prosecution. The victim sustained injuries following what the defence alleged was an accident, where the defendant hit the deceased and she fell against a wall radiator causing it to fall from the wall. It was the prosecution in accepting the plea who said:

> Your Honour, one is confronted time and time again, sadly, with cases in which a punch, classically the pavement case where somebody is punched, falls over and cracks the back of their head on the pavement and then dies. In such circumstances, and in the absence of the use of a weapon or boot, it is really not open to the Crown to say to a jury that from a punch alone there is intent to cause really serious injury. Having considered it with care, that is all there is in this case. . . .

The blow to the back of the neck was said to cause the fatal cervical spine injury, wherein the defendant explained that he pushed her back against the radiator. There was controverting evidence. The defendant was possessive and jealous, although these character traits were minimised by the defence description of their relationship as 'stormy', with its 'ups and downs'. Previous assaults upon the deceased were also marginalised by the defendant, who said, 'Well I might have hit her once or twice but like everybody argues' (*sic*). The judge for his part acceded that the death was fortuitous. In *Palmer* (1990/1991) 12 Cr App R (S) 585, the husband lost his temper and in his defence said that he fetched a knife from the kitchen with which to frighten her, and he stabbed the deceased in the heart. The deceased had told the appellant that she and her family wished him to leave but he did not want to. Mann LJ remarked, 'The marriage was a tempestuous one punctuated by bouts of argument, drink and financial problems . . . Her absences provoked argument'. By contrast Mrs Thornton had also presented a similar line of defence, *inter alia* that the knife she used was intended to frighten, the stabbing also an accident. It seems that such an alibi from the lips of a woman approximately 8 stones in weight and 5 feet 2 inches in height, is more credible since such a small frame would hardly be capable of doing anything more than to frighten: the court did not believe her.

The defence of involuntary manslaughter/no intent is stretched to the limits in *Murphy* (1992) 13 Cr App R (S) 717. Here, where there had been a history of violence the husband said, 'Where the fucking hell have you been?', dragged her by the hair, swung her round and started banging her head against the concrete in front of the house. He attacked her with a dagger, hit her on the head, stabbed her four times with a knife with a 6 inch blade. The appellant admitted bringing the knife from his own house and stabbing his wife while she was on the ground. The jury accepted the defence of involuntary manslaughter/

no intent, concluding that it was a tragic accident. On the face of it seems unconscionable that a jury could find no intent. The fact that the husband thought that the wife had been out with another man may well have persuaded them that the morally correct verdict was manslaughter and not murder. Not content with a manslaughter conviction Murphy appealed against his sentence. Lane LCJ, in refusing to reduce the sentence of the trial judge and distinguishing the case from *Palmer* above expressed a rather different view, 'I repeat, this was an unlawful act of violence resulting in death, not an accidental stabbing'. On occasion women who kill spouses enter a plea of involuntary manslaughter/ no intent, as was the main line of defence in *Ahluwalia* above. Her case was that she had no intention either of killing her husband or of doing him really serious harm, only to inflict some pain on him. The jury, unconvinced, convicted of murder which was subsequently quashed on appeal.

On occasion, it is not merely a level playing field of domestic disharmony which results in manslaughter/no intent conviction but a belief in a level playing field of consensual sexually dangerous acts. In *Williamson* (1994) 15 Cr App R (S) 365, a defence of manslaughter/no intent was accepted where his partner died following what he alleged was the practice of mutual partial asphyxiation for the purpose of heightening sensation during sexual intercourse (see the chapter entitled, Sex Crime for further detail). In *Slingsby* [1995] Crim LR 570, a conviction of manslaughter/no intent was returned in the court of first instance where the deceased died of septicaemia, following the penetration of her vagina and rectum with the accused's hand which caused injury. The accused also had sexual intercourse with the victim, and buggered her. The court held that violence with consent, even for the purposes of sexual gratification, is not lawful even if the person suffering the harm consents (*Donovan* [1934] 2 KB 498, *Boyea* [1992] Crim LR 574, *Brown* [1994] 1 AC 212). It was held that consent to injury did not arise, however, because all they were considering at the time was 'vigorous sexual activity' (*sic*). The judge ruled that the defendant could not be found guilty since 'fisting' was not an unlawful or dangerous act (contrast *Boyea*).

The masculinism of provocation

'The problem with provocation is its masculinism. First, the standard legal subject is predicated on what men do and how they react (subjective test). Secondly, the objective test allows for almost any male behaviour which, when it is claimed by the defendant, wounds pride and results in a loss of control, then conduct is deemed *de facto* as provocative.' The nature of the reactive outburst considered likely to satisfy the first limb of the subjective test for provocation, i.e., evidence of a sudden and temporary loss of self-control, is a response particularly permitted of, and consonant with, the experience of men. As Scutt (1981, p. 11) points out:

> ... the man's social conditioning and physique enable him to lash-back and to come within the bounds of a mitigating defence. The woman's social conditioning and physique preclude her from reacting in the same way, and thus tend to preclude her from gaining the benefit of that rule of mitigation.

Women fail to react immediately and fail to conform to the male standard. Women's failure is rooted in biology and aculturisation. The female constitution militates against an immediate response. Women are smaller, physically weaker than their aggressors, generally less able to engage in physically defensive or retaliatory strikes. For the battered woman in particular, the general debilitation may be even more acute, compounded by the fact that she must contend with an acquired psychology and knowledge of the potential and limits of her aggressor, whilst she is experiencing a morbid state of chronic terror and anxiety, with the continual and heightened expectation and foreboding of further violence and threats. Where there has been a time delay and provocation has succeeded, it has been restricted to those cases where, at the time of the killing itself, there is evidence of a sudden and temporary loss of self-control. There is some evidence that cases before the Crown Court have arguably allowed flexibility in the time lapse requirement. Pauline Wyatt was tried for the murder of her husband at Manchester Crown Court (21, 22 November 1984 observed by the author). She had five children from 8 months to 12 years. On the night of 17 February 1984, he had made threats to kill her and the children. She went upstairs, took a shotgun from the cabinet, loaded it and shot her husband. Acquitted of murder, she was found guilty of manslaughter (provocation) and placed on probation for three years. He had subjected her to years of violence. His last words were, 'I'm like a stick of dynamite, when the fuse is lit, I'll explode and then you will know what has happened to that little dog you had. I'm going to kill the baby the same way . . . Then the kids . . . you will watch, then you are next.' 'I said "You are not going to do that", he has hit them in the past and has threatened them. I then went and got the gun out of the cabinet, he was laughing. I brought it into the bedroom, put the cartridge in and lifted it up, and it went off. I had never used it before. I didn't even think I had got him , I didn't realise what I had done . . . He had branded me, he did up the electrical wires with a blow lamp and burned me on my private parts. He hit me with slippers so that I couldn't recognise myself in the mirror, and that is only a bit of it. About the kids, he said he would wring the baby's neck like he did to the dog . . . talking to him this morning, he said he would kill the kids, he twisted the pup's neck round about two years ago, he said he would make me watch what he did to the kids and then it would be my turn' (author's own verbatim notes). Similarly, in the case of *Ratcliffe*, *The Times*, 13 July 1980, where the husband had been violent over a period of years and where the defendant killed him six days later, although there was no provocation immediately prior to the attack, a defence of provocation was accepted by the prosecution on the basis of the violent history. Whilst there is some evidence of relaxation of the immediacy principle in the lower courts, the visibility and scrutiny of judgments made by the Court of Appeal results in a judicial reluctance to extend these principles which would allow non domestic cases an opportunity for a successful provocation plea.

Although not a rule of law, loss of self-control is acknowledged through rage, anger, passion and indignation. By contrast, there is no accommodation of a concept of loss of self-control through fear, panic, hysteria and trauma, emotions which may not necessarily manifest themselves in the typified explosive outburst. Women who kill violent men, kill not in rage but in their words, in self-defence, in an effort to escape. Kiranjit Ahluwalia explained, 'to stop him running after me' (*Ahluwalia*, above). The reaction of such women is often characterised by inertia, inability to act, a period of endurance and restraint and then followed by a loss of self-control in a final effort to survive. If loss of self-control along the lines of frenzy and passion is the only standard satisfying provocation, then since the battered woman's final action is often devoid of frenzy or passion, women fail to meet the standard required of the reactive response. Mrs Ahluwalia's lack of apparent sudden and temporary loss of self-control was such to defeat any provocation defence, carrying as she did the fuel up the stairs, lighting the taper and pouring it around the bed as her husband slept. The requirement of immediacy, and the loss of self-control, only gives legitimate excuse to those who fight back and not to those who endure a partner's violence in perpetuity and then finally defend their lives in a mood of despair (see Nicolson 1995).

The 'objective test' of provocation is also gendered. The things said or things said and done, which are authorised as likely to provoke the reasonable man are based on a masculinist empiricism i.e., the behaviour or conduct that men have claimed has resulted in their loss of self-control. Why certain conduct is acceded as provoking a man to lose self-control, is a moral question and one explored by Horder. Horder (1992), takes as his starting point Austin's (1961) distinction between provocation as an excuse, and provocation as a justification for action. In the former, the provocation functions to exempt the person from responsibility, such that he was unable to control himself. In the latter, the justification for conduct depends on how strong is the sense of moral outrage. In provocation, not only is there a sense of moral outrage but outrage becomes legitimated under certain defined circumstances relating largely to the experiences of men. Austin prefers to think of justifiable provocation as stemming from innate reflexive motivation, rather than as a purely linguistic device which facilitates the conduct and grounds the excuse. In truth, in provocation 'motive' is less about some innate, impulsive, psychological or mental precursor to action and more about the way in which particular scenarios tried and tested provide both a facilitation and justification for conduct.

An exegesis on the morphology of social action has been advanced by Weber (in Gerth and Mills 1970, p. 112) and Schutz (1972), and it is important to examine these contributions to the argument that motive may more properly be regarded as a linguistic device. Weber's argument is that motivation is not a prior antecedent but arises instead in the process of action itself. This point is further developed and explored by Becker (1973) who argues that, 'deviant activity springs from motives which are socially learned', thereby opening up the possibility that motive does not simply crudely and deterministically precede the action but exists before the action is constructed. Gerth and Mills engaged in the same project explain 'motives are acceptable justifications for present, future, or past programs of conduct. But to call them "justification" is not to deny their efficacy; it is merely to indicate their function in conduct'. Schutz (1972, p. 91) delineates two kinds of motives which he defines as 'in order to' motives and 'because of' motives. He explains the distinction in this way:

Suppose I say that a murderer perpetrated his crime for money. This is an in-order-to statement. But suppose I say the man became a murderer because of the influence of bad companions ... the in-order-to motive explains the action in terms of the project, while the genuine because-motive explains the project in terms of the actor's past experience.

The contribution of phenomenology to this analysis then is to suggest that the accused's account of his action is not simply reducible to some innate pre-given physiological response but is a response and an articulation which is learned in order to fulfil the legal requirement. Of course, in most homicides perpetrated by men on wives, accounts fall into the 'because of' category whereas women who kill in terms of self-defence or self-preservation would fall into the 'in order to' category. It is clear then, that the structure of the criminal law paradoxically invites the individual to neutralise his normative attachment to it (see Matza 1964, p. 61).

Applying these insights to the elements of a defence of provocation assists in understanding how justifications for conduct are social constructs. Whatever the process or the moral questions it is the jurors, as triers of fact, who must determine whether the 'things said or things done or both' amount to provocation based on their perception of how they think the 'reasonable man' would have reacted. The law concedes that there is a recognisable range of provocative conduct which may result in a reasonable man losing his self-control. It is framed as monocausal and prospective, where the provocative conduct causes the loss of self-control. Yet this is a rationalisation after the event *de facto*, where a loss of self-control becomes justified under certain conditions, e.g., a wife's infidelity where, and it is then and only then, the behaviour is deemed provocative. Where provocation is alleged, juries may set different standards for men and women, according to what men and women are expected to tolerate and endure, thus creating a different standard of reasonable men and reasonable women. Only certain grounds for provocation are given authority, such that a series of background expectancies shape and define what passes for provocation. These archetypal scenarios serve to exculpate men, and such accounts are reproduced in law thereby becoming 'authority' in a reified form in two ways. Those social accounts given legal authority are then evolved in a process as a function of the actor rather than of the action itself. There is very little that is ontologically sound about which excuses, rhymes and reasons rendered are to be given authority. Authority is derived from a process of interaction with the actor rather than an inherent property of the action itself. That is to say, accounts rendered by males for killing spouses are given social and legal authority. By contrast, women's accounts for killing men who batter them are not material. Women's accounts for homicide in contrast to men's, have neither social nor legal authority. Consequently, several archetypal rationales and excuses have become habituated in what the law deems acceptable. Men who kill learn to utilise and articulate the more socially acceptable and legally enshrined rationalisations in their own defence. Men's pleas and defences are negotiated in the knowledge of the nature of legal rules and precedents, being guided by defence lawyers.

Constructing the case for the prosecution is designed to achieve as much evidence as possible to point to understandable and justifiable moral outrage. Several typical linguistic devices are utilised and in advancing a defence of provocation the defendant is depicted as a man, teased and taunted by an adulterous and flirtatious wife. The deployment of such typified metaphors assists the jury in understanding the moral outrage (objective condition) and loss of self-control (subjective condition). It is the moral outrage of men that shapes the construction of provocation. In 1983, Richard Turner was found guilty of manslaughter by reason of provocation. His wife had 'taunted him' about her lovers. He had hit and strangled her (*Turner, The Times*, 5 November 1983). Such evidence functions in both the construction of the defence and in mitigation. Gordon Asher who killed his wife at a party, where he strangled her whilst guests stood by thinking he 'only' punched her out cold. He carried her home only to bury her dead body in a gravel pit. At the trial the model of victim precipitation was advanced and she was portrayed as a two timing flirt. He was convicted of manslaughter provocation and received a derisory six month suspended sentence (Radford 1992, p. 254). In the trial of Mutaz Biag, the defence claim was one of the wife's adultery, this seemed to justify his provocation (see Lees 1992, p. 273), thereby indicating the notion of victim precipitation which often underlies a provocation defence (see Clarkson and Keating 1994, pp. 647–648).

Loss of male self-control through moral outrage is also legitimated where the female spouse has contributed to her own demise by being a troublesome wife (see Lees 1992). In the trial of *Blewis, The Times*, 13 September 1983, the defendant killed his senile wife when, as he claimed, the strain of her nagging became unbearable. The court accepted the plea of provocation. The judge meted out another derisory sentence of two months in prison with eighteen months suspended for two years. In the case of *Bandy, The Times*, 9 July 1983), a man killed his domineering wife after her mental and physical deterioration had begun. This deterioration included the removal of one leg from bone cancer. The 'total' humiliation of the husband began, this included being pushed down the stairs, said his defence. The judge agreed that he had suffered more than any man should have to bear. In the trial of *Wilkes, The Scotsman*, 9 October 1984, the husband was put on probation for two years after strangling his wife of whom the judge said, 'The wife insulted, abused, threatened, lied and goaded her husband for many months and on re-entry to the family home on that fateful night the threats and taunts were the last straw that broke the camel's back.'.

There is a litany of cases where the less than model acquiescent wife is murdered, and the loss of control alleged by the defendant receives the court's empathy. *Nicolas Boyce*, The Daily Telegraph, 14 February 1989, strangled his wife, cut her body up and put part of it in plastic bags which he left in various places in London, and, part of it he cooked. He was said by his counsel to have been the subject of '. . . a non stop form of humiliation and degradation which drained every bit of self respect from a grown man' (see Lees 1992, p. 277). James Miskin J said, 'a man of reasonable self-control might have been similarly provoked and might have done what you did' (Edwards 1987). In *Simpson*

[1957] Crim LR 815, the defendant killed his wife by strangulation because, in his words, of her constant nagging and threats. He had been kept awake by his wife's shouting at him whenever he fell asleep. In 1987 Corlett was given three years for strangling his wife on the grounds of provocation because she moved the mustard. Judge Gerald Butler said that Corlett was a hard working man of impeccable character who snapped after skivvying after his wife for years. In the case of *Singh-Bisla* (Central Criminal Court, unreported) 29 January 1992 Transcript, the defendant claimed that he intended to stop his wife shouting at him. Judge Denison in his summing up said:

> What he did was first to strangle his wife with his hands. Then he obtained a ligature — that is the turquoise string, cord, call it what you like — and put that around the front of her neck. Then, probably standing above her as she lay face downwards, he pulled it tight until she died ... There are really two questions ... First: you must decide, did the defendant, subjected as he was to a prolonged torrent of abuse from his wife, subjected as he had been to a miserable existence, did he suddenly snap and temporarily lose his self control? ... If you decide that he did, then the second question is this, using your common sense and your knowledge of human behaviour: would a reasonable man, similar to the defendant, same sort of age, some sort of background, same sort of characteristics, faced with the situation with which he was faced, would that reasonable man have reacted as the defendant did, ...? The cause of the trouble, you may think, was the behaviour of the wife. She was domineering ...

The jury acquitted of murder, convicting of provocation. And so it would appear that almost any kind of behaviour on the part of the wife from infidelity, desiring to leave, challenging his authority, to recalcitrance may constitute provocation in law. Notwithstanding the negation of victim precipitation in *Duffy*: 'you are not concerned with the blame attaching to the dead man', it is precisely victim precipitation which becomes the dramatic focus when men kill.

By contrast, when wives kill husbands, their reasons for killing are not given a voice. The law provides no legal category that assimilates 'her' motives and indeed there is no rhyme or reason which can justify or exculpate her treason. The reasonable man (woman) test is not judged on the same footing as it is for men, with the result that women who kill are never regarded as defending their honour, being motivated by an affront to their pride, justifiably morally outraged, or even less defending themselves (Forell 1992, Minow 1988). So, whilst his access to excuses and exculpations, rhymes and reasons is absolute, her action is construed as verging on heresy. Women's reasons for killing do not fit into the standard moral/legal categories and conventional normative legal constructs. Women must negotiate the law by fitting their reasons into the existing legal categories which may then work to their advantage. Unlike men who kill, the cohort of women who kill is constituted largely from women who kill in self-defence, or self-preservation in the face of physical violence. Women rarely kill husbands because they are unfaithful, or because they are goading or because they have challenged the wife's dominion or authority or because they are outraged by a husbands' behaviour.

The only partial defence to murder is provocation or diminished responsibility. This means that women must fit into the pre-given category with its associated rhymes and reasons if they are going to succeed. Motives for murder become linguistic devices in the arena of developing a defence to murder. Such accounts will be more or less at variance with the socio-legal accounts depending upon the degree to which the available partial defences are congruent with provocation. Where husbands are adulterous and wives are provoked, this rarely constitutes sufficient grounds for a defence of provocation, where husbands are domineering, bullying and make life a misery, rarely are these considered sufficient reasons for killing them. The law cannot be applied in the same way when there is no level playing field. The image of the troublesome husband does not exist within society and the comparator for the adulterous female or the nagging wife in the adulterous husband or the nagging husband does not have the same cultural meaning and is not considered in society or in law to be imbued with the same degree of provocation such as to make killing understandable or justifiable. And so where women have been provoked where, for example, men have been two-timing flirts, either a defence of provocation has not been advanced or else it has failed. Howard in *Australian Criminal Law* (see Scutt 1981, p. 11), surmises that the provocation defence would be applicable to a wife finding her husband in adultery and killing him in passion, for '. . . there is no reason to suggest itself why a wife would not be as annoyed by adultery as her husband', however, he points out that there has never been a case of that type. Scutt suggests that perhaps wives have not found husbands in an acts of adultery or if they do, then they react differently. Or perhaps when women respond in a similar way defence lawyers consider a diminished responsibility defence has a better chance of succeeding than one of provocation. Pamela Megginnson was provoked by her lover's involvement with another woman. Since 1970, Pamela had lived with her lover, Alec Hubbers. He became infatuated with a woman half his age. He was 79 years old and Pamela 65 years. One night in bed he told her, 'I don't want you'. She responded to these taunts by hitting him over the head with a champagne bottle, killing him. She appealed against the conviction for murder. The Court of Appeal upheld the conviction on the grounds that taunts, rejection for a younger woman and the deceased's conduct did not amount to provocation (see Kennedy 1992, p. 217). In the majority of cases where women kill it is not in defence of a sense of pride or honour, but in defence of their lives.

The Court of Appeal until *Humphreys* [1995] has rejected a history of battering as constituting a ground for provocation, it has also rejected cases as constituting provocation where there is a time delay even though this must be inevitable where the wife is the recipient of physical violence. In May 1979, June Greig was jailed for six years for killing her husband. Greig inflicted the fatal blow as her husband was incapacitated through drink. She claimed provocation. Lord Dunpark instructed the jury:

> In the normal case of murder, provocation only operates when the accused is either attacked or is so alarmed by the violent conduct of the other person as to be reasonably apprehensive of his or her immediate safety — and I

emphasise 'immediate' . . . But if one day the worm turns, if I may use that phrase, not under the immediate threat of violence, but by taking a solemn decision to end her purgatory by killing her husband, is she not to be found guilty of murder? There are many expedients open to a woman like you but a licence to kill is not one of them.

Casting women's self-defensive reaction as a licence to kill was the phrase used by Crown counsel in *Thornton* when it was maintained rather than an act of survival that an acquittal would be providing like minded women with a killing licence. In the context of victim precipitation in homicide it is women as a class who are regarded as naggers, taunters, adulterers; men, frequently, have good sound moral reasons for being provoked, reasons which earn a status within the very fabric of defences and mitigation. When building up the case for the defence the scene constructed must be one capable of convincing a jury of the congruence between social and legal accounts. Women become the provokers and men the victims who defend their sexual prowess, reputation and honour in a drama which takes on Grecian qualities of melodrama and archetypes, and so the very legal requirements of the homicide defence require evidence to be adduced which goes to provocation. As O'Donovan (1991, pp. 226) notes, 'the judiciary has been willing to broaden the standard of reasonableness but has retained a male oriented view of provocative behaviour'. Case law enshrines this gender bias and moral indignation is permitted of attacks on male pride, and honour. This bias is being acceded by some. 'From the beginning, the legal standard of reasonableness has referred to one sex only — and to idealised members of that sex' (Taylor 1986, p. 1687). Thus, physical violence or the detection of the female spouse in the act of adultery was considered to typify the classic scenario of provocation, revealing genderedness rather than neutrality (*Maddy* (1671) 2 Keb 829). This antiquated relic of construction was somewhat modified in *Holmes* v *DPP* [1946] AC 588, 590, where it was held that a confession of adultery alone could not justify a verdict of manslaughter. Viscount Simon expressly put an end to such bias asserting, '. . . as society advances, it ought to call for a higher measure of self-control' and further, 'In my view, however, a sudden confession of adultery without more can never constitute provocation of a sort which might reduce murder to manslaughter', rejecting the argument for the appellant that 'The effect of such a confession cannot be timed with a stop-watch'.

The problem with diminished responsibility

A defence of diminished responsibility is considered in popular conception to be more congruous with a woman's defence, conflating with perceptions of women as inherently unstable and certainly so when they come to kill (Allen 1987). But just below the surface of the popular stereotype is another quite separate scenario, that is, in domestic cases, where a husband kills the wife, diminished responsibility is frequently the defence, and the standard of 'sickness' required is exceeding low, in stark contrast to the standard required for women who kill and the standard required of men who kill strangers. In addition, the prosecution is willing to accept a low standard of abnormality and the excuses of jealousy or depression even in cases where there is a history of violence perpetrated against the deceased by the defendant. Where jealousy, infidelity and her leaving him are material, the line between diminished responsibility and provocation defences become increasingly blurred, under- mining the essential distinction between the two of unreasonable/reasonable. It appears that diminished responsibility pleas are predicated on the same facts as provocation. Where men plead diminished responsibility in the domestic context the accused is usually said to be suffering from jealousy possessiveness, inability to let his wife go, revenge and bitterness. All these emotions are considered to contribute to his abnormality of mind characterised usually by 'reactive depression' (see *Foster* Nottingham Crown Court, 5 July 1995 (unreported) Transcript, *Harvey* Lincoln Crown Court (unreported) 27 January 1995, Transcript, *Parry* Shrewsbury Crown Court (unreported) 23 February 1995, Transcript), or else chronic reactive depression (see *Seers* (1984) 79 Cr App R 261, *Irons* (1995) 16 Cr App R 46, or a pre-existing fragile mental state (see *Smith* Maidstone Crown Court (unreported) 26 June 1995, Transcript).

In cases where there is evidence of a wife leaving or infidelity on her part, evidence of his reactive depression to these events seems to be accepted readily by the prosecution as a defence rather than as mitigation. In this sense the mitigation precedes the construction of the defence where jealousy and revenge are pathologised such that the sickness is considered to diminish the responsi- bility. What permits a distinction to be made between provocation and diminished responsibility is that in the former the man is reasonable whilst the circumstances are not, in the latter the man is unreasonable and so the different defences purportedly go to the essence of responsibility. What this means in effect is that the law and psychiatry are together condoning and legitimating male killing of women by letting provocation in through the side door and by validating the dubious excuse that women's conduct makes men ill. Dell (1984, p. 11), found that 38 per cent of diminished responsibility pleas were wife and girlfriend killings. The majority of these cases arose from amorous jealousy, where possessiveness and proprietorial rights over women are recognised as a sickness in pathological jealousy. This is notwithstanding that the intention of s. 2, Homicide Act 1957 was to preclude the jealous husband pleading her conduct in his defence, reaffirmed by Lawton LJ in *Vinagre* (above), where the Appeal Court said that jealousy was 'a kind of conduct against which wives ought to be protected'. Contrary to the sentiment in *Vinagre* it is clear that the medicalisation of the s. 2 defence, through pathologising male power and presumptions of a proprietorial right to women, has exonerated men who kill in the domestic context by increasingly applying disease nosology. It is evident that the same facts admitted under provocation, instead of the reason for loss of self-control now become the reason for abnormality of mind. This allows for the very essence of the conditions of provocation, *inter alia* her infidelity, her leaving him, and her conduct, entering the arena this time as grounds for diminished responsibility. In *Russell-Jones*, Chester Crown Court (unreported) 30 July 1992, the defendant explained his violent outburst as a result of his jealousy and depression. He stabbed and strangled his wife and then tried to commit suicide. Mr Justice Phillips in sentencing him said. 'We have heard that you suspected her of infidelity whilst she was living with you but the only basis for such suspicion seems to have been that because you were having other sexual relations you, without any justification, though she might be doing the same'. Whichever way, reasonable man or unreasonable man, essentially what we have in this defence is moral culpability wrapped up in psychiatric nosology where instead anger, and rage and jealousy are the sickness. Whilst jealousy on occasion figures in cases where women kill husbands who have been unfaithful, it is not clear that this factor allows them to succeed on provocation or on diminished responsibility. The courts have also evinced a certain sympathy in cases where men have killed because the man could not accept losing the woman and the courts have accepted a plea of diminished responsibility. The net result is that diminished responsibility becomes a category utilised where deceased wives are deemed responsible, in a model of victim precipitation, for their husbands' sickness. This suggests that certain excuses exonerate responsibility and that these excuses are linked to particular emotions which are gendered. So, wives may also be jealous or unable to cope following a relationship breakup rarely is this considered to excuse murder through her diminished responsibility.

In domestic killings where the husband seems unable to cope with the breakup of a relationship or of a marriage, a defence of diminished responsibility is often accepted by the prosecution. In *Sanders* (1991) 93 Cr App R 245, where an ex-cohabitee killed his partner with a hammer, a successful appeal against a conviction for murder reduced it to manslaughter. She had begun to consort with another man. The appellant contemplated suicide and could not lose her. Watkins LJ, in summarising the evidence said, 'The loss of Mrs Sadlier was something he could not bear ... she told him that she had been with the other man that weekend. She seemed to flaunt the fact and taunt him with it.'. The medical evidence of the defence talked of a 'reactive depression'. The Crown saw the case somewhat differently as premeditated killing by a man overwhelmed by bitterness. In *Seers* (1984) 79 Cr App R 261, where a husband killed an ex-wife the conviction was reduced from murder to diminished responsibility where he was said to be suffering 'chronic reactive depression' following the breakup of the marriage. Several witnesses had heard that he had threatened to kill his wife some days previous to the killing, the defence interpreted this evidence as going to abnormality of mind arguing that no normal person would announce such an intention. (Contrast the court's treatment of his announcement of his intent to kill with Thornton, where her announcement 'I will kill him' was taken as evidence of intent.) In *Gussman* (1994) 15 Cr App R (S) 440, a man killed his cohabitee's ex partner, and stabbing him 131 times said to the police, 'Sorry lads, I just couldn't live without her'. In *Chambers* (1983) 5 Cr App R (S) 190, a sentence of ten years was reduced to eight where a man had been convicted of manslaughter/ diminished responsibility. The victim had left him and had formed another relationship. He subsequently attempted suicide claiming, 'I just didn't want to lose her.'

A feature in all these cases is that the men are portrayed as victims of flighty wives or else as poor vulnerable souls who are unable to live without the one they love. The defence invariably allocate blame to both parties, the marriage is portrayed as 'stormy' or 'tempestuous', reducing the man's violence to an 'acceptable' level, suggesting that either party might have been victim. Such a presentation is rarely challenged by the prosecution notwithstanding *Sanders* where if there is 'any other evidence', that is part of the background against which evidence of diminished responsibility is to be assessed. On occasion not only the prosecution but the judge identifies with the defendant's plight. In *Smith* (above), where the wife was thought to be having a relationship with another man, the defendant went into the kitchen and picked up a knife and stabbed her. The judge said, in summing-up, that the facts might with reason, 'disturb any man'.

There is, however, another often untold story, and far from the accused being the victim of a flirtatious wife, there is evidence that the deceased has been the victim of violence for many years. In *Jewsbury* (1981) 3 Cr App R (S) 1, a jealous husband was considered to suffer from depression as a result of his wife's behaviour. He was sentenced to three years. The court were to hear how she had had four affairs, whilst by contrast he was portrayed as the model husband. The Lord Chief Justice said that his depressive illness intensified due to the fact that he found some empty contraceptive packets in his wife's handbag. 'This sort of situation of the stable, reliable husband and the flighty wife is not a rare one'. In *Sanderson* (1994) 98 Cr App R 325, the appellant killed a girl most brutally with whom he was on intimate terms, suspecting her of infidelity. He pleaded diminished responsibility on the basis of a 'paranoid psychosis' causing him to form an abnormal belief, which was the result of upbringing and drug use. On appeal, the murder conviction was quashed and diminished responsibility substituted on the basis that 'paranoid psychosis' could come within the definition of s. 2. The medical evidence was challenged by the prosecution. The victim had been subject to his violence over a period. He inflicted 100 blows upon her in killing her, the defence describing their relationship 'as stormy'. In addition to violence to the deceased there was also evidence of violence to other women in the past. In *Vinagre* (1979) 69 Cr App R 104, the appellant killed his wife because he thought she was having a relationship with another man. He was described as suffering from the 'Othello syndrome' and 'morbid jealousy'.

> The case would seem to hinge on whether indeed Mrs Vinagre was being unfaithful to her husband by having sex relationships with the plain clothes policeman Michael. If there was no such liaison then the possibility of a jealous spouse or Othello syndrome may be raised whereby the accused became so overwhelmed by his jealous suspicion that after having not slept the night before and only two hours that morning, later that day after a violent argument with his wife he attacked her with fatal consequences.

Yet, following the stabbing the wife called out to the children, 'Quick I am not dead yet; dial 999'. The appellant said 'Oh well I will kill you then'.

In many cases, however, it seems that the killings are clear cases of revenge where men exercise their right to the body of the woman as if she were a possession. In *Norman* (1981) 3 Cr App R (S) 377, where the deceased and the appellant were separated, the accused considered that there was still some chance of reconciliation, he kissed her and strangled her. Something 'snapped in him' when she said that she did not want a reconciliation. A case bearing the hallmarks of revenge was treated instead as diminished responsibility and on appeal the sentence was reduced to five years, although the trial judge conceded, 'I think this case was absolutely next door to murder'. In *Andrew* (1989) 11 Cr App R (S) 309, where the accused who could not accept that the relationship was over killed his ex partner brutally, Auld J, in sentencing, referred to the case as being 'in the provenance of the despair of the jilted lover. She had bruises on her neck, arms and thighs and near her knees. A tooth had been knocked out. She was only partly dressed . . .' and a sentence of seven years was upheld. In *Collins* (Southwark Crown Court, 8 February 1995, Transcript) there had been a history of violence in a revenge attack on a wife for preferring rape charges against him and for instituting injunctive proceedings. The accused battered the deceased around the head with a tyre wrench. She was said to have been so badly beaten around the head as to be unrecognisable. A post-mortem revealed lacerations, abrasions and bruises, the result of a mixture of punches, kicks, stamps and blows which were inflicted with moderate to severe force required for the smashing of bones. The court accepted although not without some difficulty his plea of diminished responsibility. In *Foster* (above) where the prosecution rejected the original defence plea of no intent contending that the case should go before a jury, a plea of diminished responsibility (reactive depression) was entered in a final effort at 'plea bargaining', a plea accepted by the prosecution. The judge was not it seems entirely happy but in the light of the prosecution's acceptance of the plea was obliged in the absence of strong objections to accept it. The plea was not placed before the jury. The accused had forcibly gripped the victim's neck for 30 seconds following an argument; he said, 'I suppose I shook her'. The victim died of vagal inhibition, although nail clippings from the deceased suggested a fairly violent struggle had occurred. In mitigation of sentence the focus shifted, as it so often does, onto the conduct of the deceased. The husband had received letters from the solicitor indicating the wife's intention to divorce. The defence said in mitigation, 'it is not a case of asphyxia or of lengthened strangulation or anything like that' and the judge in passing sentence said 'I am prepared to accept that the violence in this case was not extreme'.

Men are getting away with murder, the stricture of the mandatory life sentence as the option means that defence counsel and prosecution negotiate in a world of plea acceptance as a means of getting trials 'done'. In *Sanders* (1991) (above) the prosecution said that it was a premeditated killing by a man overwhelmed by bitterness and jealously. In *Vinagre* (above) the prosecution painted a picture of hatred and revenge. In *Ellis* (1992) (above) the killing was the result of 'morbid jealousy' where, because the wife had instituted divorce proceedings, the husband decided to kill her, obtaining a stout piece of cord, cancelling the milk and the order for coal. The judge imposed a life sentence, in the case of *Parry* (above), where the husband said, as he shot his wife twice at point blank range, 'If I can't have you nobody can'. This problem has not escaped the scrutiny of Lawton LJ who said in *Robinson* (1979) Cr App R (S) 108, 109, 'We think Parliament would have been very surprised indeed to be told that the Homicide Act would be used as an excuse for relieving men of their responsibility for killing their wives because their tolerance to bad matrimonial behaviour had been lowered by drink.'. This was a case where there was evidence of a history of violence including an injunction against the husband and where he had spoken of killing his wife.

In the very few cases where the prosecution is not prepared to accept the plea, or else the judge is emphatic that he has worries about the evidence, then the matter is placed before a jury for their consideration. In borderland cases, the concerns of the judge are also reflected in sentencing, which becomes both a tool of confirming the abnormality where a medical disposal is the outcome and also a means of confirming disapproval or ambiguity concerning the plea. In domestic homicide cases very rarely is a medical disposal the outcome.

By contrast women who kill spouses where diminished responsibility is pleaded must satisfy a much higher level of abnormality of mind. Very rarely is 'reactive depression' sufficient. This is not, however, only a function of the application of legal categories, but also of the willingness of juries who seem less willing to convict women of diminished responsibility where low levels of diminished responsibility prevail. Battered women who kill whilst seeking to avoid a conviction for murder would at the same time wish to avoid a conviction for manslaughter/diminished responsibility, since such a defence focuses attention on the woman's abnormal state of mind, instead of the man's battering of her. In *Thornton* (above) counsel put forward a defence of diminished responsibility, three psychiatrists, two for the defence and one for the prosecution, agreed that she was suffering from a 'personality disorder' which amounted to an abnormality of the mind and that this was due to retarded development or her personality or due to inherent causes. The Crown, however, did not take the view that the abnormality was such as substantially to impair her mental responsibility at the time of the killing. As has already been said, this is not a question for the medical expert but one for the jury. The jury rejected diminished responsibility and the alternative of provocation put to them by the judge and convicted Thornton of murder. On appeal, the court held that the decision of the appellant's legal advisers to concentrate her defence on diminished responsibility did not raise any 'lurking doubt' that she had suffered injustice nor that the conviction was unsafe and unsatisfactory.

Where women are convicted of diminished responsibility in the domestic context their cases usually reveal considerable provocation but their reaction to that provocation fails the masculinised standard reaction. The case of *Christine English, The Guardian*, 8 May 1995, is instructive. Her lover told her that he was having an affair and put two fingers up at her. She snapped and drove into him with a car. Her defence lawyers did not put up a provocation defence which would have been the obvious choice had English been a man. The plea entered was instead one of diminished responsibility. In addition, to strengthen her case, evidence of pre-menstrual tension was discovered and adduced and the court considered it to have played a part. In the case of *Davis, The Times*, 29 July 1985, the accused said that she was provoked when her husband told her that he had another woman and wanted to leave her. Despite the obvious element of provocation she too put forward a plea of diminished responsibility which was accepted. Beulah Birch was convicted of the manslaughter of her husband on the grounds of diminished responsibility. He too was having a relationship with another woman at the time. She was described as being intensely jealous. She stabbed her husband and shot him in the course of an argument. Birch was sentenced to a hospital order with restriction under the Mental Health Act 1983, s. 41. Section 41 can only be made if it is 'necessary for the protection of the public from serious harm'. On appeal the s. 41 restriction order was quashed, the hospital order under s. 37 remained.

If the Home Office figures referred to at the outset of this chapter suggest that men are less likely to succeed with a defence of provocation than women, and are more likely to succeed with diminished responsibility, the evidence from these cases suggests that, whether it is provocation or diminished responsibility that men plead, the facts and the reasons for killing are almost identical. Men kill women as an expression of their dominion over them in a history of violent encounters.

The problem with self-defence

Battered women who kill uniquely inhabit a legal hiatus somewhere between provocation and self-defence. Even where there is *de facto* evidence of self-defence such pleas fail. In *Rossiter* (1992) 95 Cr App R 326, the defendant maintained that she was defending herself in stabbing her husband following a struggle. The Court of Appeal held that there was no misdirection in the judge's direction to the jury, and a finding of no evidence as to self-defence was supported. 'No one, not even she, suggests that she struck with that knife or that in doing so to defend herself. Do you understand?' (sic) The Court of Appeal also dismissed self-defence as a viable proposition although it found that the judge failed to leave provocation to the jury. Schneider (1980, p. 647) argues, 'The male assumptions contained in legal doctrine and the manifestations of those assumptions in court rulings . . . deny to women an opportunity equal to that of male defendants to present their claims of self-defence'.

In *People* v *Garcia* 54 Cal Ap 3d 61 (1977), the defendant appealed against a conviction of second degree murder. On appeal the interpretation of imminence was extended beyond the immediate time period of the assault, and established that it was reasonable to believe that she was in imminent danger some hours after. Equal force presumes that there are two males involved of equal or roughly equal strength. The issue was raised in *State* v *Wanrow* 88 Wash 2d 221, 559 P 2d 548 (1977), where the trial judge directed the jury that a reasonable person 'has no right to repel a threatened assault with naked hands, by the use of a deadly weapon, in a deadly manner . . .'. The Supreme Court responded and granted a new trial, 'in our society women suffer from a conspicuous lack of access to training in and the means of developing those skills necessary to effectively repel a male assailant without resorting to the use of deadly weapons'. The court directed that self-defence instructions would ensure that women have the right to have those differences taken into account (see Browne 1987, p. 173).

Women taking self-defensive action frequently avail themselves of a pre-emptive strike, this is largely because their fear of violence is in the continuous present. Women's language in the situation of domestic violence suggests a motive of survival or self-defence. Rarely, if ever, are self-defence pleas attempted. Again, such pleas are wholly incongruous with women's actions. Satisfying the requirement of imminent danger is predicated upon the notion of the other person being prepared upon that moment for combat by strangers in an episodic violent encounter. There is no place for the realisation of an accused facing chronic repeated violence or the need to defend oneself from violence in the future. The accommodation of the pre-emptive strike is acceded only where that strike is imminent and does not consider the accused's perception of that strike at any time in the future. (The law in other areas accommodates a notion of evidence of past harm as being sufficient to warrant action to prevent present or future harm, see the chapter entitled, A Betrayal of Trust — The Sexual Abuse of Children). Women lose out on the strictures of proportionality and immediacy once again. The self-defence plea entered by Carol Peters failed. She suffered domestic violence and fought back. 'The history of domestic violence was minimised in the defence ... for fear that its full disclosure would arm the Crown with the powerful weapon of motive ... Despite a well-fought defence and an exemplary summing-up by the judge, the jury convicted' (see Kennedy 1992, pp. 214, 215). Emilia Rossiter (discussed above) entered a plea of self-defence. The judge directed the jury on self-defence, provocation was not raised and the appeal succeeded on the basis that the judge should have put the issue of provocation to the jury. In the case of Janet Clugstone (*Chicago Tribune*, 1 October 1987, *The Guardian*, 6 October 1981) she was raped and killed her rapist in self-defence as she was unable to scream out because her larynx had been removed following cancer. Judge Hazan instructed a jury to acquit her saying that she had acted in self-defence.

The case of *Wang* [1990] 2 NZLR 529, is instructive in that it illustrates the difficulties of relying on self-defence. Here, the appellant was found guilty of provocation and sentenced to five years in prison. The ground of her appeal was that the judge had wrongly refused to put to the jury the defence of self-defence. She killed her husband whilst he was in a drunken sleep. Immediately prior to falling asleep he had made threats to her that he would kill her and her sister. The question arises as to when the defence of self-defence should be put to the jury. The judge took the view that self-defence was plausible, but that if there were other courses of action open, then it would not be reasonable to make a pre-emptive strike. In the circumstances the defence was not open as she killed him, stabbing him four times in his sleep and there was no immediacy to the threat to kill. In respect of the appeal against sentence the court said:

... it was not a case in which there had been a sudden rebuke, insult, or discovery of an adulterous situation causing an immediate surge of passion;

but rather one of a weakening of the accused's ability to reason leading to a situation where in her own perception she was in a desperate situation with an apparent absence of alternatives.

The case was further weakened by the modus operandi. She tied two or three bathrobes round him, attempted to strangle him with a cord, stabbed him in the stomach several times, then put a pillow over his face. This passage from police evidence of her statement is instructive:

> What happened this morning? This morning he said 'I want to kill you, and I'll make it look like you hang yourself'. He asked my sister to give him US$300,000. He said if she didn't he'd make my sister go to jail because she helped someone get out of China, that's bad in China. This is my sister that lives in Hong Kong. Is that why you stabbed him, because he wanted money from your sister? Yeah. Also because he said maybe I die or all my family die. (at p. 532).

In giving evidence the accused described her reaction to her husband's demand for money and threats in this way:

'What was it that you were asking him not to do?'

'I ask him not to blackmail my sister, not to create any trouble for my sister, and also don't go to Hong Kong to kill my sister and her family.'

'Where did this conversation take place?'

'We were walking back into the bedroom.'

'Did you go into the bedroom together?'

'Yes.'

'Did you leave the bedroom?'

'Yes.'

'Where did you go?'

'When he lie down I left. He was going to vomit.'

'Did he get up to do that or not?'

'He was vomiting along the corridor, and (also) vomiting beside the bed, and he was lying down, he couldn't get up.'

'What did you do?'

'I had never been so angry and I'd never been so frightened, and I really hated him.'

'How did you feel?'

'I felt that my head was going to explode.'

'Have you ever felt like that before?'

'No. It was too bad.'

'Then what did you do?'

'I had to kill him, there was no other way.'

'Yesterday, and at the police station, you told the police officers how that happened, was that how it did happen, the sequence of events?'

'Yes.'

'Approximately how long after the end of the phone call and the conversation that you had with your husband did the events happen?'

'About 30 to 40 minutes.'

'How did you feel after it was all over?'

'I felt that I was free and I was a human being again.'

(at p. 535).

Wang appealed against conviction for manslaughter on provocation on the basis that her defence of self-defence was withheld from the jury. The court held that the judge had applied the correct test, i.e., the subjective test as to what the accused believed was imminent.

Even where women closely conform to the legal requirement of self-defence they still seem to fail. Janet Gardner (*Sunday Times*, 8 November 1992, *Independent*, 30 October 1992), was actually being strangled, when she grabbed a knife from the kitchen wall and stabbed her partner. She was convicted of manslaughter and not of self-defence. She had been stalked for months by her lover who attacked, beat and punched her. She had never lived with him but was under his brutal domination. She had described many violent incidents over the years, including throttlings in which she lost consciousness, a knife cut to her neck, an assault while on holiday in Spain after which she attempted suicide and various instances of him punching about the head and body. During an argument at her home in September 1990, he grabbed her by the back of the neck and banged the side of her head against a door frame. She grabbed a knife from the kitchen wall and stabbed him. She then called the police.

In *Oatridge* (1991) 94 Cr App R 367, the defence was threefold: (i) that the offender lacked the necessary intent; (ii) that she acted in self-defence; and (iii) she acted under provocation. The court rejected self-defence although on the facts on the night of the offence the victim was drunk and abusive and had uttered threats to kill her. He had seized her throat and squeezed it. In the belief that he was attempting to kill her the appellant picked up a kitchen knife and stabbed him. In summing-up the trial judge, in dealing with the question of self-defence, gave the conventional direction on the need for proportionality between the force used and the nature of the attack, but he did not give a direction on mistaken belief. On appeal the conviction was quashed and a conviction of manslaughter provocation substituted. In the case of Elizabeth Line (*Daily Telegraph*, 4 February 1992) where the defendant was beaten, raped and abused by a husband who said, 'Which knife shall I use to cut your throat?', the defendant stabbed him seventeen times in self-defence. The court accepted provocation. Similarly, in a case which showed an overlap of self-defence and provocation the court was willing to accept provocation. In *The Queen* v *R* (1981) 28 SASR 321, where the appellant killed her husband with an axe while he was sleeping following her discovery that he had sexually abused the children of the marriage, 'that the provocation is not negatived where' the act or omission causing death was not an act or omission done suddenly'. Here the defence of provocation was not left to the jury which resulted in the Supreme Court setting aside a conviction for murder. Yet, her case was more akin to self-defence since she saw her action as protecting herself and her children from his violence. The court recognised in *Brennan* (1994) 15 Crim App R (S) 874, where there was a quarrel and the deceased had a knife against her stomach when she said she was pregnant she told the police that there had been a massive fight — it would have been 'me or him'. The central issue for battered women is that they know the offender, he has hit them before, he has threatened them and their anticipation of attack is grounded in empirical experience. In defending themselves they lose out since the court is not satisfied that the attack is imminent (see Browne 1987, p. 163).

Modus operandi: a gendered question

In both defences of provocation and self-defence, women are disadvantaged because rather than using bodily force they use a weapon to effect their purpose. In assessing *mens rea* the criminal law attaches a different significance to these methods. Using the body as a weapon is a legitimate response to provocation, men are trained from childhood to box, spar, land a good punch, in essence to use their body as a vehicle of their power, strength and dominance, of their presence, of their self. Women very rarely use the body as deadly force, for reasons rooted in biology and in culture. Women's socialisation is deliberately disabling, the acquisition of defensive skills is discouraged, and the use of the body in defence of self and others is negatively sanctioned in order to define and determine her subordination within patriarchy. The scenario of provocation and self-defence for women is to retreat and then to obtain a weapon for defence. A disapproval of weapons was clearly evident in

Brown (1972) 56 Cr App R 564, 570, where a husband killed an unfaithful wife. Talbot J in the Court of Appeal affirmed the judgment of the trial judge, who said:

> Members of the jury, it is often said, and rightly said, that in considering an issue of provocation you must look for some proportion between acts which provoke and the reaction which resulted from provocation. It may be that one set of circumstances could amount to provocation, to provoke a man to strike his wife a blow with his fist which might cause her death, or to grab her round the throat and throttle her in a moment of anger. But where, as here, a legal weapon in the form of a razor has been used, and used in acts which objectively regarded must have been, you may think, of great savagery, then you may think it would not be right to say that a reasonable person would have been provoked to that reaction unless the provocation was very grave.

Men who use the body to perpetrate deadly force, find that the method itself serves to obscure and conceal the 'intent' for practical legal purposes. Where the body becomes the instrument and weapon of violence, the several stages between (i) the provocative conduct (objective condition), (ii) being provoked or experiencing provocation (subjective), (iii) fetching a weapon, (iv) responding to provocative conduct, are stages which become conflated, but is it any less an action of intent merely because the fist or hands are the weapons of aggression particularly in those cases of strangulation, asphyxiation and vagal inhibition already mentioned in the consideration of involuntary manslaughter?

Women's use of weapons *ipso facto* indicates intent. Sara Thornton was initially convicted of murder for killing a brutal husband, a conviction upheld on appeal. She retreated, went into the kitchen and in her words sharpened the kitchen knife, returned to the lounge and pointed it at her husband, fully expecting him to push it away, accidentally in stabbing him she killed him. She claimed to have sharpened the knife which seems wildly improbable, unlikely and absurd. It was nevertheless regarded as a vital aspect of the prosecution case and considered compelling evidence of her intention to kill. Her conduct prior to the killing was not considered as 'drama', as part of a 'see what I am doing' and 'see what you have made me do' scenario, as she had no doubt intended that it should be. As Sara Thornton herself said, 'I didn't walk in there with the intention of stabbing him. I just wanted to show him how far he had driven me'. Her remarks to a friend some months previously, 'I am going to kill him' were not treated as mere surplusage, or an expression of exasperation (or as an indication of diminished responsibility) but in the light of the fatal event were constructed as further indication of her intent. Dorothy Smith in her seminal paper, 'K is Mentally Ill' (1978, pp. 23–53), provides an analysis of how a person, through a study of events as they were seen as relevant to reaching a decision about the character of those events, comes to be defined as mentally ill. Similarly, in the construction of the case for the prosecution, Sara Thornton's utterances and theatrics were regarded as indicators of a real intent which assisted in the construction of a murder conviction. As Nicolson (1995, p. 197) concedes:

Many people make similar threats without intending to carry them through. Yet, not only did Beldam LJ fail to mention Sara's denial of the alleged threat, he gave it the following gloss (made more dramatic by appearing in a new paragraph): 'But for subsequent events Mrs Thomas might well have dismissed this as no more than an expression of exasperation'.

In this retrospective construction, certain other conflicting versions such as the fact that Malcolm Thornton had been charged with criminal assault against her and was waiting to appear in court, were excluded. The fact that she used a weapon, that there was a time delay, that she failed to display frenzy and loss of control at the critical moment meant that she could not fit the strictures of a provocation defence. Yet her telephone conversation with the 999 crew whom she phoned for assistance is clearly indicative of shock and trauma and diminished responsibility.

Operator: 'Ambulance emergency.'

Sara: 'Hello, good afternoon. I've just killed my husband. I have stuck a six-inch carving knife in his belly on the left-hand side.'

Operator: 'Where are you, love?'

Sara: 'Bring an ambulance and the police round straight away.'

Operator: 'Where are you?'

Sara: 'I'm at 73 Church Walk, Atherstone, Warwickshire. My name is Mrs Sara Thornton, my husband is called Mr Malcolm Thornton, and I think he's dead.'

Operator: 'Yes, darling, your name is Mrs Thornton?'

Sara: 'Thornton. Shall I pull the knife out or leave it in?'

Operator: 'Leave it where it is, darling.'

Sara: 'Leave the knife in?'

Operator: 'That's right.'

Sara: 'Thank you. Goodnight.'

(Miller, *Sunday Times*, 2 May 1993).

Notwithstanding evidence pointing away from intent, it was that walk to the kitchen, the fetching of the knife and its sharpening which secured the fatal conviction. The legal presumption of a relationship between modus operandi and intent has been the subject of recent criticism and constitutional challenge in the United States on the basis of equality. In the US in *United States* v *Wilson* (No. 92–10346 (1993) (unreported) US App Lexis 2 February), the appellant contended that the provision in section 2A2.2 of the Sentencing Guidelines, authorising an increase in the base offence level for use of a dangerous weapon, unconstitutionally discriminated against women. Wilson reasoned that women needed to resort to the use of a weapon to defend themselves against men, but men can inflict the same deadly force against women without resort to a weapon. Wilson claimed that penalising women for obtaining through a weapon the same deadly force that is inherent in a man's fists constitutes gender discrimination in violation of the Equal Protection Clause. The court did not regard her claim as meritorious. It follows a line in legal thinking where the use of a weapon is considered more heinous than the use of brute force. Gillespie (1989, pp. 54–7), documents a litany of cases where women in self-defence have been convicted of murder where they use a weapon to repel brute force. In *Easterling* v *State* 267 P2d 185 (1954) the judge instructed the jury that, 'no person has the right to use a dangerous weapon merely to repel a simple assault without a weapon'. The accused was punched, beaten on her head, choked and fearing for her life she stabbed him with a pocket knife. The Appeals Court held that the self-defence instruction was erroneous and ordered a retrial. Similarly, in the Tasmanian case of *Cornick* (1987) (unreported) noted by Tolmie (1991, pp. 70–71), the Court of Criminal Appeal seemed to base their judgment on the assumption that an attack with fists is *per se* less threatening. Tolmie noted (at p. 71):

> ... the court appeared to be influenced by the fact that the deceased was only using his fists in finding that there was no threat of serious harm and that an armed response was not reasonably proportionate. Cox J stated that, 'on the best view of the evidence [the appellant] did what she did to protect her son from the threats of an *unarmed* man' *(emphasis supplied)*.

It is not only modus operandi but also and more subtly the cause of death which has a bearing on the formulation of intent. Killings of women in the domestic context are typically the consequence of asphyxiation following on from strangulation. The method is manual or mechanical strangulation which produces asphyxiation as cause of death. Pressure to the neck can produce vagal inhibition which brings on death. Vagal inhibition is distinguishable from cases of manual or mechanical strangulation in that death may occur very quickly after the onset of pressure. Whilst death by vagal inhibition can occur within 30 seconds, mechanical ligature strangulation over a period of five minutes may not of necessity result in death (see *Dearn* (1990) 12 Cr App R (S) 527 discussed in the chapter entitled, All in the Name of Privacy — Domestic Violence). In cases where the deceased dies as a result of vagal inhibition, the defence will make a fine distinction between the intent required in manual or ligature strangulation and the lack of intent where vagal inhibition follows. In *Walker* (1992) 13 Cr App R (S) 474, the prosecution accepted the plea of involuntary manslaughter/no intent, on the grounds that it was, 'not a case of strangulation but vagal inhibition involving pressure on the neck which triggers off the vagal nerve and the heart stops beating'. (See *Foster* (unreported) 5 July 1995, Transcript for a case of vagal inhibition and diminished responsibility.) In *Clarke* (1990) (unreported, 20 December) death was caused by vagal inhibition and electrocution where the defendant head butted the victim, grabbed her throat, lifted her on her toes with her heels off the ground and let go and again pressed with both hands on her neck and then electrocuted her by placing wire from an electric lamp in her mouth. He was convicted of murder. Where vagal inhibition is the cause of death it usually follows that such cases are considered to involve a lower level of intent and attract as a consequence a lower sentence. It is not merely the method of killing but the cause of death which seem to have an important bearing on the question of intent.

Reformulating the object of concern

In addressing the inherent bias within legal method, especially as it relates to provocation and to self-defence, there have been attempts to reformulate the law. First, there have been developments around the concept of provocation especially relating to the introduction of the concept of cumulative provocation. Secondly, the introduction of battered woman syndrome intended to acquaint the jury with the experience and effects of battering and the knowledge of the likely action of men who batter, has been considered and applied in several jurisdictions (this is considered in the chapter entitled, Unreasonable Women — Battered Woman Syndrome on Trial). Women who kill violent partners, it is argued, experience cumulative provocation, that is provocation extends over a period, it is a chronic rather than acute manifestation. Women react suddenly following on the last act of provocation, but that in itself is not always sufficient if the last act of provocation is slight and the history of battering is considered not material. Attempts to expand the common law notion of sudden and temporary loss of self-control following *Duffy* (above) have straddled two positions. First, attempts have been made to argue that 'sudden and temporary loss of self-control', should not be the standard and provocation is not negatived merely because of a delay between the last provocative act and the response. Lord Lane in *Ahluwalia* (above) for example was receptive to this idea and treated the time lapse between the deceased's last act and the killing as a matter of evidence not as a rule of law. Secondly, there have been attempts to argue that the experience of some battered women and those trapped in abusive relationships is that of a slow continuous provocation or 'slow burn' (see Wasik 1982). Case law has regarded the only reading of time, as 'cooling off' time. The presumption has been that the delay between the last act of provocation and the response allows the person to cool off. The question is whether this accurately describes people who are living continually with the aggressor, who are always fearful of future attack. The argument advanced by counsel in *Ahluwalia* and *Thornton* [1992] was that this presumption is erroneous. For battered women fearful of and anticipating violence, the inability to act, after battering and or threats of violence, is experienced as a time of fear, anticipation, slow burn, simmering etc. The last act of provocation for such persons is experienced at the moment of the last encounter, for this is the retrospective/prospective moment in which they are reminded of what was done to them in the past and the harm they are going to experience in the future. For those who live constantly with this fear of impending attack, this cumulative provocation is not episodic but is continuous. The fear and threat of violence is in the continuous present, a construction which is understood in child law and the construction of 'significant harm'. Fiora-Gormally (1978) explains the life of the battered woman is '... replete with prior provocation, continuing apprehension and the constant threat of impending anger'. In addition, the background once of no relevance at all is now material. This development has been crucial for the battered woman, since what marks off and separates the battered woman defendant from all other defendants is the history of violence she has sustained. This past history of violence is arguably as important an aspect of the battered woman's response and retaliation. In *Duffy*, 'severe nervous exasperation or a long course of conduct causing suffering and anxiety are not by themselves sufficient to constitute provocation in law'. In *Thornton* the past history of violence was also considered of relevance, but past history, however violent, is never so great as to negate or weaken the importance of immediacy of retaliation, functioning only to lessen the grip of the objective test of what amounts to provocation, to a greater emphasis on the subjective test. Although Thornton's appeal [1992] failed, it did nevertheless advance somewhat the concept of cumulative provocation in domestic homicide cases. A long history of violence was given some consideration although the court remained resolute in the construction of 'sudden and temporary', for the further away this violence and provocation was from the fatal retaliatory act the more likely the sudden and temporary stricture of a provocation defence would become impossible to satisfy.

In Australia, the rules governing provocation have developed to embrace the notion of cumulativeness. The Crimes (Homicide) Amendment Act 1982, removes the emphasis from the events immediately prior to the killing and therefore the *Duffy* stricture and focuses on the past conduct of the deceased which was regarded as not material in *Duffy*. Section 23(2) provides, that the provocative conduct of the deceased is relevant whether such conduct 'occurred immediately before the act or omission causing death or at any previous time'. In *Hill* [1980] 3 A Crim R 397, and in *R* [1981] 4 A Crim R 127, the case law was already moving towards a recognition of the reality of cumulative provocation for women trapped in domestic violence. In addition, Australian law has modified the reasonable man to embrace the concept of the ordinary man. The change in language although not helpful does allow for the battered woman's response to be assessed without the stricture of the reasonable man test. The test of ordinary person with the permanent characteristics of the accused relies on *Camplin* and shows a greater willingness to embrace the wide range of characteristics which the House of Lords indicated might be accommodated. Anne Edwards (1987) argues that this move forward is still problematic since at the very end of the day modification of the provocation defence to accommodate battered women who kill might result in the battered woman being automatically defended via provocation. As has been argued throughout this chapter the experience and language of the battered woman is more consonant with the defence of self-defence and it is an expansion of these principles which would address what lies at the heart of her 'crime'.

WHOSE LICENCE?

The sentencing experience is evidence of further discrepancies on gender lines. In both provocation and in diminished responsibility where men kill women, her conduct and his otherwise impeccable behaviour functions to mitigate sentence. In diminished responsibility the average sentence is four years. In provocation it is on average six years.

Any evidence of a woman's bad conduct real or imagined is milked to the full in pleas of mitigation and it seems to result in leniency. In *Townsend* (1979) 1 Cr App R (S) 333, a case of attempted murder, Donaldson LJ, on appeal, reduced the sentence by a third on the basis of the domestic context, 'The real question is whether, bearing in mind the domestic nature of this offence, contrasted with, for example, an armed robbery leading to the same result, it is possible to take a rather more merciful view ...'. This was a case where the husband said to the wife, 'If any of you come any nearer, it's the morgue she'll want, not an ambulance'.

The mixing of pleas in domestic homicide cases is interesting and of course illogical since at one point the man's state of mind is claimed to be abnormal and at the next declared normal. The case of *Porter* (1993) 14 Cr App R (S) 650, is illustrative. Where a wife had a relationship with another man the husband killed both the wife and the lover. The husband was convicted of provocation for killing the wife and a four year sentence was imposed although the killing of the lover was the result of diminished responsibility attracting a nine year sentence. The husband was suffering from a depressive illness and as a result of her affair he had neglected himself and was suicidal. In killing the lover the husband went to the lover's house where he and his wife were entertaining two other couples. He kept them under siege and killed the lover in front of them. The court said, 'Whilst I do not consider that Mr Porter is of great risk to society in general, he clearly has the propensity to react violently when under great emotional stress'. In *Taylor* (1989) 9 Cr App R (S) 175, where a wife had gone out with another man and the husband killed her, a seven year sentence was reduced to five.

When men kill, judges apply the same reasoning that domestic homicide is serious and have responded with prison sentences of on average four years. Much consideration is given to the deceased wife's conduct (see *Smith* (1995) (unreported) 26 June, Transcript, *Foster* (above). At the point of mitigation of sentence defence counsel in Foster turned the entirety of the focus of attention on the wife's conduct. 'It is quite plain that this marriage was on the rocks ... that each of them had their interests elsewhere ... one of those cases where they had got to a stage where they were not communicating properly'. And in *Smith* in mitigation counsel said, 'I am conscious that Mrs Smith is dead and cannot speak for herself ... she paid the ultimate price'.

When women kill, it is only when the wife kills the violent husband that mitigation or exoneration is adduced, no other circumstance seems to qualify.

In *Ratcliffe, The Times,* 13 May 1980, where a woman killed a husband with a carving knife following his burning of her with a lighted cigarette on the breasts, she was given a two year probation order.

Although there is plenty of evidence pointing to a harsher treatment, Lord Wheatly, Lord Justice Clerk said in *Paterson, The Guardian,* 27 July 1983, 'There are so many occasions when wives are subjected to the kind of treatment to which you were subjected. The difficulty is that I cannot establish a precedent to give a licence to wives to take the law into their own hands. Lord Dunpark in *HM Advocate* v *Greig* (1979) High Court, unreported (see Gane and Stoddart 1981, pp. 364, 365), where a special plea of self-defence was tabled although the judge withdrew this from the jury, said:

Now, there is evidence before you that the deceased was a drunkard, if you like, not an alcoholic but a drunkard in the general sense, that is he was a bully, that he assaulted his wife from time to time and that he made her life a misery. But, hundreds, indeed thousands of wives in this country, unfortunately, suffer this fate. The remedy of divorce or judicial separation or factual separation is available to end this torment. But if one day the worm turns, if I may use that phrase, not under the immediate threat of violence but by taking a solemn decision to end her purgatory by killing her husband, and by doing that very thing, is she not to be found guilty of murder? If you are satisfied beyond reasonable doubt that this is what this woman did then you would find her guilty of murder. If, on the other hand you can find some evidence, which I frankly cannot, that the accused was provoked in the sense in which I have defined it you could return a verdict of guilty of culpable homicide . . .

On appeal, Lord Wheatly, Lord Chief Justice dismissing her appeal in 1979 said, 'Here was a woman with a large carving knife who told her children, "I am going to kill him" and then a quarter of an hour later goes into the room and plunges the knife through the heart of her husband sitting in a chair watching television'.

The same reasoning was applied by the court in approaching *Thornton* [1992] 1 All ER 306. 'There are ... many unhappy, indeed miserable, husbands and wives. It is a fact of life. It has to be faced, members of the jury. But on the whole it is hardly reasonable, you may think, to stab them fatally when there are other alternatives available, like walking out or going upstairs.' (at p. 312). Whether at the point of defences or at the point of sentencing, the accommodation of women can be likened to a poor prosthesis. Women can only succeed if they behave more like men, exploding in the heat of the moment. And if women did so behave and bludgeoned men to death because of men's extra marital affairs, womens' experience in the legal process would still not achieve justice and would most possibly be considered to be vituperative. Women cannot fight back where men are often twice as strong and, because they canot attack on the spur of the moment, self-defence is beyond the grasp of most women.

In the UK a number of recent decisions by the Court of Appeal has indicated that the judiciary, or at least some of them, are not wholly convinced that battered women should be serving life sentences for murder. The recent successful appeals of *Ahluwalia, Thornton* [1995] and *Humphreys* suggest that the Court of Appeal and the Lord Chief Justice are at least cognisant of women's predicament. In *Ahluwalia* the Court of Appeal took an 'exceptional course' in admitting evidence under s. 23(1) of the Criminal Appeal Act 1968, in the interests of justice, although the defence had not been raised in the court of first instance and was therefore contrary to general principles enunciated in *Jones* v *Powis and Sons Ltd* (1980) Lexis Enggen, 28 January by Roskill LJ:

> We have often said in this court that where a question, and in particular a question of the admissibility of evidence, is deliberately not raised at the trial it is only in rare cases that we will allow the matter to be raised in this court for the first time. To allow otherwise would be to encourage counsel to keep points of this kind up their sleeve and then reserve them for the Court of Appeal and thus have a second bite at the forensic cherry.

Such a discretion to admit evidence not raised at trial is used only in exceptions (see *Kooken* (1981) 74 Cr App R 30). In *Thornton* [1992] the Court of Appeal had already looked at the case and decided that there was nothing they could do: they had applied the law, and the jury had rejected the evidence. An appeal via the Home Secretary under s. 17 of the Criminal Appeal Act 1968, is usually reserved for miscarriages of justice where the accused was wrongfully convicted on false confessional evidence, police malpractice or because of non-disclosure by the prosecution (see *Kiszko* (1978) 68 Cr App R, 18 February 1992 (unreported), the Guildford Four case, (see Conlon 1993), the Birmingham Six *McIlkenny and Others* [1992] 2 All ER 417, *Ward* [1993] 2 All ER 577, *Raghip, Silcott, Braithwaite* Lexis 5 December 1991 (unreported)).

In the *Thornton* [1992] case, this mechanism (i.e., an appeal under s. 17 now abolished and amended by Criminal Appeal Act 1995, ss. 3, 5) is being used to address an injustice inherent in the law. Political pressure resulted in the case coming before the Court of Appeal once again following a s. 17 referral. Section 17 references are not the vehicle for exposing the injustice of the substantive law. Section 17 is used on exceedingly rare occasions, only 25 referrals against conviction were made using s. 17 in the period 1982–1991. Often conflict is indicated between the Home Secretary and the Court of Appeal. In March 1991, a question was tabled to ask the Secretary of State for the Home Department how many representations he had received regarding the conviction of Kiranjit Ahluwalia: Mr Patten replied 'Forty-nine representations have been received about the conviction . . . we have considered these very carefully but have concluded that they do not provide any information that would justify the intervention of my right Hon. friend the Home Secretary in this case' (*Hansard* HC Vol 187 col 82, 5 March 1991). *Ahluwalia* was subsequently granted leave to appeal on 12 September 1991 and the Court of Appeal quashed her conviction on 31 July 1992. The law has been clearly reaffirmed in respect of battered women and provocation in *Ahluwalia*.

In looking further to this problem the Court of Appeal in *Humphreys* conflates the two defences of diminished responsibility and provocation in order to do justice first and law second. It remains to be seen what will be the outcome of this growing unease. The Home Office's line is to avoid the law and to turn a blind eye. Yet, the Home Secretary in consideration of probably his last s. 17 appeal as that function is taken over by the Criminal Cases Review Authority (Criminal Appeal Act 1995, ss. 3, 5), has been drawn further into this debate in *Thornton* and the Court of Appeal is currently struggling to do justice rather than doing law, in respect of the battered woman who kills who, to date, has been the subject of the ultimate miscarriage of justice. In *Thornton (No. 2)* the Court of Appeal ordered a retrial considering that further medical evidence raised in relation to provocation pointing to two characteristics which were not available at the original hearing. The first characteristic relates to a '[personality disorder]'. The second characteristics considers the effect of the deceased abuse over a period of time on her mental make up (battered women syndrome evidence). Following the House of Lords in *Morhall* [1995] and *Humphreys* [1995] it is now the case that mental characteristics can be taken into account as part of a defence of provocation. Following *Thornton (No. 2)*, a judge should give directions to the jury on what evidence was capable of amounting to a relevant characteristic. Again like the direction regarding what amounts to loss of self control in *Dryden* this direction promises to expand on the concept of the reasonable man but it is still judges who will determine what is and what is not capable of amounting to a characteristic.

The Court of Appeal in *Thornton (No. 2)* has made the decisive judgment concerning the admissibility of battered woman syndrome evidence within a defence of provocation. It is now a matter for the jury to decide whether the defendant lost her self control and how far they consider that her loss of self control was, given the characteristics of a battered woman and her perception of 'immediate', indeed related in time to his last act of provocation. Notwithstanding the interjection of battered woman syndrome in cases where women kill men who batter them masculinist assumptions continue to pervade at each and every level in statute, in the application of law, in the construction of legal categories and in legal method itself. Meanwhile, law authorises the particular statements of the male experience and the construction of reasonableness which it elevates into precedents, largely impervious to the experiences of women which are now beginning to challenge, if not falsify, the masculinist universal truths upon which the homicide heresy is built.

Bibliography

Abarbanel, G. (1986) Rape and Resistance, *Journal of Interpersonal Violence*, Vol. 1, No. 1, pp. 100–105.

Abrams, K. (1991) Feminist lawyering and legal method, *Law and Social Inquiry*, Vol. 16, pp. 373–404.

Acker, J. and Toch, H. (1985) Battered Women, Straw Men, and Expert Testimony: A Comment on *State* v *Kelly*, *Crim L Bull*, Vol. 21, pp. 125–55.

Adler, Z. (1982) Rape — the intention of Parliament and the practice of the courts, *Modern Law Review*, Vol. 45, pp. 664–75.

Adler, Z. (1987) *Rape on Trial*, Routledge.

Aguilar (1989) cited in De Dios (see below) at p. 5.

Allen, H. (1987) *Justice unbalanced: gender, psychiatry and judicial decisions*, Open University Press.

Allport, G. (1954) *The Nature of Prejudice*, Cambridge MA: Addison Wesley.

Althusser, L. (1971) Ideology and Ideological State Apparatuses (Notes towards an Investigation), in *Lenin and Philosophy and Other Essays* by Louis Althusser, Monthly Review Press, pp. 127–86.

Amir, M. (1971) *Forcible Rape*, University of Chicago Press.

Anderson, C. L. (1982) Males as sexual assault victims: multiple levels of trauma, in *Homosexuality and Psychotherapy*, Haworth Press, pp. 145–63.

Angelou, M. (1984) *I Know Why the Caged Bird Sings*, Virago.

Anleu, S. L. R. (1992) Critiquing the Law: Themes and Dilemmas in Anglo-American Feminist Legal Theory, *Journal of Law and Society*, Vol. 19, No. 4, 1992, pp. 423–40.

Archbold (1995) Criminal Pleading, Evidence and Practice, Vol. 1, Sweet and Maxwell.

Archbold (1996) *Criminal Pleading, Evidence and Practice*, Vol. 2, Sweet & Maxwell.

Arnup, K. (1989) Mothers Just Like Others: Lesbians, Divorce and Child Custody in Canada, *Canadian Journal of Women and the Law*, Vol. 3, Winter–Spring, pp. 18–32.

Ashworth, A. (1975) Sentencing in Provocation Cases, *Crim LR*, pp. 552–63.

Assister, A. and Avedon, C. (1993) *Bad Girls and Dirty Pictures, The Challenge to Reclaim Feminism*, Pluto.

Atoki, M. (1995) unpublished work on 'Prostitution' (University of Buckingham).

Attorney-General, Canada (1985) Report of the Special Committee on *Pornography and Prostitution*, Vols. 1 and 2, Canadian Government Publishing Centre, Ottawa, Canada.

Attorney-General, US Report on *Pornography and Prostitution* (1986) Final Report, July, Vols. 1 and 2. Washington DC: US Department of Justice.

Austin, J. L. (1961) A Plea for Excuses, in *Philosophical Papers*, 2nd edn, Oxford University Press, pp. 124–152.

Bacon, W. and Landsdowne, R. (1982) Women who Kill Husbands: The Battered Wife on Trial, in *Family Violence in Australia*, O'Donnell and Craney, J. (eds), Melbourne, Penguin, pp. 67–93.

Bailey, S. H., Harris, D. L. and Jones, B. L. (1991) *Civil Liberties: Cases and Materials*, Butterworths.

Bainham, S. and Cretney, S. (1993) *Children: The Modern Law*, Family Law, Jordans.

Baldwin, M. (1992) Split at the root: prostitution and feminist discourses of law reform, *Yale Journal of Law and Feminism*, Vol. 5, pp. 47–120.

Bandalli, S. (1992) Provocation from the Home Office, *Crim LR*, pp. 716–20.

Bannon, C. (1994) Recovered Memories of Childhood Sexual Abuse: Should the Courts Get Involved When Mental Health Professionals Disagree? *Arizona State Law Journal*, Vol. 26, No. 3, pp. 835–56.

Barnard, M. A. (1993) Violence and Vulnerability: Conditions of Work for Streetwalking Prostitutes, *Sociology of Health and Illness*, Vol. 15, No. 5, pp. 681–7.

Barron, J. (1990) *Not Worth the Paper...?* Women's Aid Federation, England.

Barry, K. (1984) *Female Sexual Slavery*, New York University Press.

Barry, K. (1995) *The Prostitution of Sexuality*, New York University Press.

Barry, K., Bunch, C. and Castley, S. (1984) *International Feminism: Networking Against Female Sexual Slavery*, International Women's Tribune Centre Inc., UN Plaza.

Bart, P. B. and O'Brien, P. H. (1985) *Stopping Rape: Successful Survival Strategies*, New York, Pergamon Press.

Bartlett, K. T. (1990) Feminist Legal Method, *Harvard Law Review*, Vol. 103, pp. 829–88.

Becker, H. (1973) *Outsiders*, Glencoe, Free Press.

Beckford, Jasmine: The Report of the Panel of Inquiry into the Circumstances surrounding the Death of Jasmine Beckford, *A Child in Trust*, London Borough of Brent, 1985, Brent Town Hall, Middlesex.

Begin, P. (1987) Rape Law Reform in Canada: Evaluating Impact; paper delivered to the Fourth International Institute on Victimology, Tuscany, Italy, 9–15 August 1987, in *Crime and its Victims*, Viano, E. (ed), Hemisphere Publishing Corporation, pp. 153–68.

Bell, D. J. (1984) The Police Response to Domestic Violence: An Exploratory Study, *Police Studies*, Vol. 7, No. 3, pp. 23–30.

Bell, V. (1991) 'Beyond the "Thorny Question"': Feminism, Foucault and the Desexualisation of Rape, *International Journal of the Sociology of Law*, Vol. 19, pp. 83–100.

Bendig, B. (1993) Images of men in feminist legal theory, *Pepperdine Law Review*, Vol. 20, pp. 991–1052.

Benjamin, H. (1971) Should Surgery be Performed on Transsexuals? *American Journal of Psychotherapy*, Vol. 25, pp. 74–82.

Benson, C. and Matthews, R. (1995) *National Vice Squad Survey*, Middlesex University.

Berger, P. (1987) *Ways of Seeing*, Penguin.

Berger, P. and Luckmann, T. (1971) *The Social Construction of Reality*, Penguin.

Bernstein, S. E. (1993) Living under seige: Do Stalking Laws Protect Domestic Violence Victims? *Cardozo Law Review*, Vol. 15, pp. 525–567.

Bibbings, L. and Alldridge, P. (1993) Sexual Expression, Body Alteration and the Defence of Consent, *Journal of Law and Society*, Vol. 20, No. 3, pp. 356–70.

Billings, D. B. and Urban, T. (1982) The Socio-Medical Construction of Transsexualism: An Interpretation and Critique, *Social Problems*, Vol. 29, No. 3, pp. 266–82.

Binney, V., Harkell, G. and Nixon, J. (1981) *Leaving Violent Men*, Women's Aid Federation, England.

Birch, D. J. (1992) The Criminal Justice Act 1991: (4) Children's Evidence, *Crim LR*, pp. 267–76.

Blackman, J. (1989) *Intimate Violence*, Columbia University Press.

Blackstone's (1996) *Criminal Practice*, Blackstone Press.

Blair, I. (1985) *Investigating Rape: A New Approach for Police*, Croom Helm and Police Foundation.

Blom-Cooper, L. and Morris, T. (1964) *A Calendar of Murder*, Michael Joseph.

Bonnington, A. (1995) Private prosecutions, *New Law Journal*, 21 July, Vol. 145, No. 6705, pp. 1105–1106.

Boulos, B. (1983) *The Yorkshire Ripper: A Case Study of the Sutcliffe Papers*, Occasional Paper No. 11, University of Manchester, Department of Sociology.

Bourlet, A. (1990) *Police Intervention in Marital Violence*, Open University Press.

Box, S. (1987) *Recession, Crime and Punishment*, Macmillan.

Bradney, A. (1987) Transsexuals and the Law, *Family Law*, Vol. 17, pp. 350–53.

Braithwaite, J. and Pettit, P (1994) Republican Crimonology and Victim Advocacy, *Law and Society Review*, Vol. 28, No. 4, pp. 765–76.

Braithwaite, N. (1995) Defamation on the Internet, 11 August, *New Law Journal*, Vol. 145, No. 6708, pp. 1216–18.

Brannon, R. (1993) Torturing Women as Fine Art: Why Some Women and Men are Boycotting Knopf, in *Making Violence Sexy*, Russell, D. (ed.), Open University Books, pp. 239–44.

Bray, M. (1994) Child Sexual Abuse, Family Life and the Children Act, in *Re Focus on Child Sexual Abuse*, Levy (ed.), pp. 59–72.

Brett, P. (1970) The Physiology of Provocation, *Crim LR*, pp. 634–40.

Bricker, D. (1993) Fatal Defense: An Analysis of Battered Women's Syndrome Expert Testimony for Gay Men and Lesbians who Kill Abusive Partners, *Brooklyn Law Review*, Vol. 58, pp. 1379–1437.

Brockman, J. (1992) Social Authority, Legal Discourse, and Women's Voices, *Manitoba Law Journal*, Vol. 21, pp. 213–36.

Brophy, J. (1985) Child care and the growth of power: the status of mothers in child custody disputes, in *Women and the Law*, Brophy, J. and Smart, C. (eds), Routledge, pp. 97–116.

Brown, B., Burman, M. and Jamieson, L. (1993) *Sex Crimes on Trial*, Edinburgh University Press.

Browne, A. (1987) *When Battered Women Kill*, New York, Free Press.

Brownlee, I. D. (1990) Compellability and Contempt in Domestic Violence Cases, *Journal of Social Welfare Law*, pp. 107–15.

Brownmiller, S. (1975) *Against Her Will*, Secker and Warburg.

Brownmiller, S. (1989) *Waverley Place*, Chatto and Windus.

Bruce, E. E. (1987) Prostitution and Obscenity: A Comment Upon the Attorney-General's Report on Pornography, *Duke Law Journal*, pp. 123–40.

Buchan, I. and Edwards, Susan, S. M. (1991) *Adult Cautioning for Domestic Violence*, Police Requirements Support Unit, Home Office Science and Technology Group, June.

Buck, W., Chatterton, M. and Pease, K. (1995) *Obscene, Threatening and other Troublesome Telephone Calls to Women in England and Wales*, Research and Planning Unit Paper 92, Home Office.

Buijs, H. W. J. (1987) Vrouwenhandel, *Justitiele Verkenningen*, Vol. 13, No. 1, pp. 93–109, cited in Van der Poel (see below).

Byassee, W. (1995) Junction of Cyberspace: Applying Real World Precedent to the Virtual Community, Vol. 30, *Wake Forest Law Review*, pp. 197–220.

Cahn, N. R. (1992) The Looseness of Legal Language: The Reasonable Woman Standard in Theory and Practice, *Cornell L Rev*, Vol. 77, pp. 1398–446.

Cain, P. (1989–90) Feminist Jurisprudence: Grounding the Theories, *Berkeley Women's Law Journal*, Vol. 4, pp. 191–214.

Cameron, D. and Frazer, E. (1987) *The Lust to Kill*, Polity.

Cameron, J. (1992) Abstract Principle v. Contextual Conceptions of Harm: A Comment on *R v Butler*, *McGill Law Journal*, Vol. 37, pp. 1136–57.

Campbell, B. (1988) *Unofficial Secrets, Child sexual abuse — the Cleveland case*, Virago Press.

Caputi, J. (1987) *The Age of Sex Crime*, Women's Press.

Caringella-MacDonald, S. (1991) An Assessment of Rape Reform; Victim and Case Treatment Under Michigan's Model, *International Review of Victimology*, Vol. 1, No. 4, pp. 347–61.

Carlile Report, *A Child in Mind: Protection of Children in a Responsible Society*, 1987).

Carrington, K. (1994) Postmodernism and Feminist Criminologies: Disconnecting Discourses? *International Journal of the Sociology of Law*, Vol. 22, No. 3, pp. 261–78.

Carter, A. (1977) *The Sadeian Woman*, Virago Press.

Carter, V. (1992) Abseil Makes the Heart Grow Fonder: Lesbian and Gay Campaigning Tactics and Section 28, in *Modern Homosexualities*, Plummer, K. (ed.), Routledge, pp. 217–26.

Chambers, G. and Millar, A. (1983) *Investigating Sexual Assault*, Scottish Home and Health Department, Edinburgh, HMSO.

Chambers, G. and Millar A. (1986) *Prosecuting Sexual Assault*, Scottish Home and Health Department, Edinburgh, HMSO.

Channer, Y. and Parton, N. (1990), Racism, Cultural Relativism and Child Protection, in *Taking Child Abuse Seriously*, The Violence Against Children Study Group, Routledge, pp. 105–120.

Chapman, R. and Rutherford, J. (1988) *Male Order Unwrapping Masculinity*, Lawrence and Wishart.

Chappell, D. and Riedel, M. (1976) *Issues in Criminal Justice*, New York, Praeger.

Chatterton, M. (1976) Police in Social Control, in *Control Without Custody*, King, J. (ed.), University of Cambridge Press.

Chatterton, M. (1983) Police Work and Assault Charges, in *Control in the Police Organisation*, Punch, M. (ed.), Cambridge, Mass., MIT Press, pp. 194–200.

Children Act Report 1993 (1994) Department of Health Cm. 2584, London, HMSO.

Children and Young People on Child Protection Registers Year Ending 31 March 1994, England, Department of Health, Personal Social Services, Local Authority Statistics, A/F 94/13 Government Statitical Service.

Children Looked After by Local Authorities 14 October 1991 to 31 March 1993, Department of Health, Personal Social Services, Local Authority Statistics, AF 93/12, Government Statistical Service, 1995.

Chimbos, P. (1978) *Marital Violence*, San Francisco, CA, R & E Research Associates.

Clapham, A. and Waaldijk, K. (eds) (1993) *Homosexuality: A European Community Issue* International Studies on Human Rights, Martinus Nijhoff.

Clapham, A. and Weiler, J. H. H. (1993) Lesbians and Gay Men in the European Community Legal Order, in *Homosexuality: A European Community Issue*, International Studies on Human Rights, Martinus Nijhoff, pp. 7–70.

Clark, C. D. L. (1961) Obscenity, the Law and Lady Chatterley I, II *Crim LR*, pp. 156–163, 224–33.

Clark, C. D. L. (1961) Obscenity, the Law and Lady Chatterly II, *Crim LR*, pp. 224–233.

Clarke, S. and Hepworth, D. (1994) Effects of reform legislation on the processing of sexual assault cases, in *Confronting Sexual Assault*, Roberts, J. and Mohr, R. (eds), University of Toronto Press, pp. 113–35.

Clarkson, C. M. V., Cretney, A., Davis, G. and Shepherd, A. (1994) Assaults: the relationship between seriousness, criminalisation and punishment, *Crim LR*, pp. 4–20.

Clarkson, C. M. V. and Keating, H. M. (1994) *Criminal Law*, Sweet and Maxwell.

Cleaver, E. (1968) *Soul on Ice*, New York, Dell-Delta. Ramparts.

Cleveland, A. R. (1896) *Women under English Law*, Hurst and Blackett.

Code for Crown Prosecutors, London, Crown Prosecution Service

Cohen, D. A. (1994) Compensating pornography's victims: a first amendment analysis, *Valparaiso University Law Review*, Vol. 29, pp. 285–96.

Cohen, S. (1978) *The Law and Sexuality*, Grass Roots Books.

Coleman, F. and McMurtrie, S. (1993) Too Hot to Handle, *New Law Journal*, 8 January, Vol. 143, pp. 10–11.

Collier, R. (1991) Masculinism, Law and Law Teaching, *International Journal of the Sociology of Law*, Vol. 19, pp. 427–51.

Collier, R. (1995) *Combating Sexual Harassment in the Workplace*, Open University Press.

Collins, P. H. (1993) Pornography and Black Women's Bodies, in *Making Violence Sexy*, Russell, D. (ed.), Open University Press, pp. 97–104.

Colvin, M. with Hawksley, J. (1989) *Section 28*, Liberty, NCCL.

Confederation of Health Service Employees (COHSE) (1991) *An Abuse of Power: Sexual Harassment in the NHS*, Banstead, Surrey.

Conlon, G. (1993) *Proved Innocent* (Penguin).

Cooper, D. and Herman, D. (1991) Getting the 'family' right: legislating heterosexuality in Britain, *Canadian Journal of Family Law*, Vol. 10, pp. 41–78.

Cotc, I. (1992–93) False Memory Syndrome: Assessment of Adults Reporting Childhood Sexual Abuse, *Western State University Law Review*, Vol. 20, pp. 427–33.

Cotton, D. (1986) Note *Ulane v Eastern Airlines*, Title VII and Transsexualism, *Northwestern University Law Review*, Vol. 80, No. 4, pp. 1037–65.

Coughlin, A. M. (1994) Excusing Women, *California Law Review Journal*, 1994, Vol. 82, No. 1, pp. 1–87.

Coulter, J. (1973) *Approaches to Insanity*, Martin Robertson.

Coward, R. (1982) Sexual Violence and Sexuality, *Feminist Review*, Vol. II, pp. 9–22.

Cox, J. (1994) Judicial enforcement of moral imperatives: is the best interest of the child being sacrificed to maintain societal homogeneity? *Missouri Law Review*, Vol. 59, pp. 775–806.

Craft, M. and Craft, A. (1984) *Mentally Abnormal Offenders*, Baillière, Tindall.

Crane, P. (1982) *Gays and the Law*, Pluto, London.

Crawford, A. (1990) *The Second Islington Crime Survey*, Middlesex Polytechnic Centre for Criminology.

Criminal Law Revision Committee (1984) Fifteenth Report, *Sexual Offences*, Cmnd 9213, HMSO.

Criminal Law Revision Committee (1985) Seventeenth Report, *Prostitution Off Street Activities*, Cmnd. 9688, HMSO.

Criminal statistics England and Wales (1982), Cm 9048, (1983) Cm 9349, (1984) Cm 9261, (1985) Cm 10, (1986) Cm 233, (1987) Cm 498, (1988) Cm 847, (1989) Cm 1322, (1990) Cm 1935, (1991) Cm 2134, (1992) Cm 2410, (1993) Cm 2680, (1994) Cm 3012, London HMSO.

Crisp, D. and Moxon, D. (1994) *Case Screening by the Crown Prosecution Service: How and Why Cases are Terminated*, Home Office Research Study 137, HMSO.

Crisp, D., Whittaker, C. and Harris, J. (1995) *Public Interest Case Assessment Schemes*, Home Office Research Study 138, HMSO.

Crocker, P. L. (1985) The meaning of equality for battered women who kill men in self-defense, *Harvard Women's Law Review*, Vol. 8, pp. 121–53.

Crown Prosecution Service, *Annual Report* 1990–91, 1992–93 London, CPS.

Crown Prosecution Service, *A Statement of Prosecution Policy: Domestic Violence* (1993), Policy Group, April.

Cumberbatch, G. and Howitt, D. (1993) *A Measure of Uncertainty*, John Libbey.

Daly, M. and Wilson, M. (1988) *Homicide*, New York, Aldine De Gruyter.

D'Amato, A. (1990) A New Political Truth: Exposure to Sexually Violent Materials Causes Sexual Violence, *William and Mary Law Review*, Vol. 31, pp. 575–605.

Da Silva, C. F. (1995) *Evaluation of the Effects of the Relationship on Women's Self-Reported Successful Defence Strategies*, Centre for Extra Mural Studies, Birkbeck College, University of London.

Dauvergne, C. A. (1994) Reassessment of the Effects of a Constitutional Charter of Rights on the Discourse of Sexual Violence in Canada, *International Journal of the Sociology of Law*, Vol. 22, pp. 291–308.

Davidson, H. A. (1995) Child Abuse and Domestic Violence: Legal Connections and Controversies, Family Law Quarterly, Vol. 29, No. 2, pp. 357–373.

Davis, G. and Noon, E. (1991) *An Evaluation of the Live Link for Child Witnesses*, Home Office.

Davis, K. (1937) The Sociology of Prostitution, *American Sociological Review*, Vol. 2, pp. 746–55, reprinted in *Deviance*, Dinitz, S., Dynes, R. and Clarke, A. (1969) Oxford University Press.

Dawson, B. and Faragher, T. (1977) Battered Women's Project: Interim Report, Keele, Department of Sociology, University of Keele.

Dawson, J. M. and Langan, A. (1994) *Murder in Families*, Bureau of Justice Statistics Special Report, US Deprtment of Justice, Office of Justice Programs, Bureau of Justice Statistics.

De Beauvoir, S. (1969) An Androgynous World, in Roszak and Roszak (eds), (see below), pp. 148–59.

De Beauvoir, S. (1974) *The Second Sex*, Penguin.

De Dios, J. A. (1991) Struggle Against Sexual Exploitation and Prostitution: A Philippine Perspective, a paper delivered to *An International Meeting of Experts, Days Inn State College, Pennsylvania*, 8–10 April.

Delgado, R. and Stefanic, J. (1992) Pornography and harm to women: 'no empirical evidence?', *Ohio State Law Journal*, Vol. 53, pp. 1037–55.

Dell, S. (1984) *Murder Into Manslaughter*, Institute of Psychiatry, Maudsley Monographs, Oxford University Press.

Denyer, R. (1993) The Abused Child and the Quantum of Damages/ Compensation, *Family Law*, Vol. 23, pp. 297–300.

Department of Health and Social Security (1985) *Review of Child Care Law*, Report to Ministers of an Interdepartmental Working Party, HMSO.

Department of Health, the guidance offered by the Department of Health, *The Children Act 1989 Guidance and Regulations*, Vol. 1, Court Orders, 1991, HMSO.

De Sade, M. (1991) *Juliette*, Random House.
Dessaur, C. I. (1979) De Staat als pooier *Delikt en Delinkwent*, Col. 9, No. 5, pp. 293–97.
Dewar, J. (1993) *Law and the Family*, Butterworths.
Devlin, P. (1959) *The Enforcement of Morals*, Oxford University Press.
Devlin, P. (1962) Law, Democracy and Morality, *University of Pennsylvania Law Review*, Vol. 110, No. 5, pp. 635–49.
Diagnostic and Statistical Manual of Mental Disorders (1992) (DSM III R), American Psychiatric Association.
Dobash, R. E. and Dobash, R. (1980) *Violence Against Wives*, Open Books.
Dobash, R. E. and Dobash, R. (1992) *Women, Violence and Social Change*, Routledge.
Douglas, M. (1973) *Rules and Meanings*, Penguin.
Downs, D. A. (1989) *The New Politics of Pornography*, University of Chicago Press.
Dressler, J. (1982) Rethinking Heat of Passion: A Defense in Search of a Rationale, *Journal of Criminal Law and Criminology*, Vol. 73, pp. 421–70.
Dunford, F. W., Huizinga, D. and Elliot, D. S. (1990) The Role of Arrest in Domestic Violence: The Omaha Police Experiment, *Criminology*, Vol. 28, No. 2, pp. 183–206.
Dunhill, C. (ed.) (1989) *The Boys in Blue*, Virago.
Durham, A. (1984) Death of a Battered Mother, *New Statesman*, 21 September.
Durkheim, E. (1966) *The Rules of Sociological Method*, Glencoe, Free Press.
Dworkin, A. (1982) Interview with Elizabeth Wilson, *Feminist Review*, Vol. 11, pp. 23–9.
Dworkin, A. (1985) Against the Male Flood: Censorship, Pornography and Equality, *Harvard Law Journal*, Vol. 8, pp. 1–29.
Dworkin, A. (1986) Personal Testimony to the Attorney-General, *Report on Pornography and Prostitution*, Washington DC: US Department of Justice.
Dworkin, A. (1989) *Pornography, Men Possessing Women*, New York, E. P. Dutton.
Dworkin, A. (1993) Living in Terror, Pain: Being a Battered Wife in *Violence Against Women*, Bart, P. B. and Moran, E. G. (eds), Sage, pp. 237–41.
Dworkin, R. (1977) *Taking Rights Seriously*, Duckworth.
Dworkin, R. (1986) *Law's Empire*, Fontana.
Easteal, P. (1992) Gender Inequity in Australian Courts, April–May, *Criminology (Australia)*, pp. 10–11.
Easteal, P. (1993a) Homicide Between Adult Sexual Intimates in Australia: Implications for Prevention, *Studies on Crime and Crime Prevention*, pp. 24–40.
Easteal, P. (1993b) Homicide Between Adult Sexual Intimates: A Research Agenda, *Australia and New Zealand Journal of Criminology*, Vol. 26, pp. 3–18.
Easteal, P. (1993c) Sentencing Those who Kill Their Sexual Intimates: An Australian Study, *International Journal of the Sociology of Law*, Vol. 21, pp. 189–218.

Easteal, P. (1994) Homicide-Suicides Between Adult Sexual Intimates: An Australian Study, *Suicide and Life-Threatening Behaviour*, Vol. 24(2), pp. 140–51.

Easteal, P., Hughes, K., and Easter, J. (1993) Battered women and duress, Vol. 18, No. 3, *Alternative Law Journal*, pp. 139–140.

Eckersley, R. (1987) Whither the Feminist campaign?: An evaluation of feminist critiques of pornography, *International Journal of the Sociology of Law*, Vol. 15, No. 2, pp. 149–78.

Edwards, A. (1987) Male Violence in Feminist Theory: An Analysis of the Changing Conceptions of Sex/Gender Violence and Male Domination, in *Women, Violence and Social Control*, Hanmer, J. and Maynard, M. (eds), pp. 13–29.

Edwards, S. S. M. (1979) *Female Sexuality, the Law and Society: Changing Socio-Legal Conceptions of the Rape Victim in Britain since 1800*, University of Manchester, Doctorate Thesis.

Edwards, S. S. M. (1981) *Female Sexuality and the Law*, Martin Robertson, Oxford

Edwards, S. S. M. (1982) 'Rape: A Consideration of Contributory Negligence, The Mandatory Sentence and Police Procedures', *Justice of the Peace*, 20 February, pp. 108–10.

Edwards, S. S. M. (1984) *Woman on Trial*, Manchester University Press.

Edwards, S. S. M. (1985) A Socio-Legal Evaluation of Gender Ideologies in Domestic Violence Assault and Spousal Homicides, *Victimology*, Vol. 10, No. 1–4, pp. 186–205.

Edwards, S. S. M. (1986) *The Police Response to Domestic Violence, in London mimeo 1986*, The Polytechnic of Central London.

Edwards, S. S. M. (1987a) 'The Kerb Crawling Fiasco', *New Law Journal*, 25 December, p. 1209.

Edwards, S. S. M. (1987b) Provoking Her Own Demise: From Common Assault to Homicide, in Hanmer, J. and Maynard, M., (eds) *Women, Violence and Social Control*, Macmillan.

Edwards, S. S. M. (1989a) Protecting the Honour of Innocent Men, in Dunhill (ed.), pp. 193–204.

Edwards, S. S. M. (1989b) *Policing Domestic Violence,* Sage.

Edwards, S. S. M. (1989c) *An Evaluation of the Impact of Police Policy on Police Response to Domestic Violence Calls*, A Final Report for the Police Foundation, Police Foundation.

Edwards, S. S. M. (1989d) 'What shall we do with a Frightened Witness?', *New Law Journal*, 17 November, p. 1740.

Edwards, S. S. M. (1990) Battered Women who Kill, *New Law Journal*, 5 October 1990, p. 1380.

Edwards, S. S. M. (1991a) A Plea for Censorship, *New Law Journal*, p. 1478.

Edwards, S. S. M. (1991b) 'Prostitution Whose Problem', Report for the Safer Cities, Wolverhampton.

Edwards, S. S. M. (1991c) 'The Law on the Kerb', *The Guardian*, 4 October.

Edwards, S. S. M. (1992a) Pornography: A Plea for Reform, *Denning Law Journal*, pp. 41–64.

Edwards, S. S. M. (1992b) When Cruel Death Doth Them Part, *The Guardian* 11 March.

Edwards, S. S. M. (1992c) Battered Woman Syndrome, *New Law Journal*, 2 October, p. 1350.

Edwards, S. S. M. (1993a) Selling the Body, Keeping the Soul, in *Body Matters*, Scott and Morgan (eds), Falmer Press, 1993, pp. 89–II, 104.

Edwards, S. S. M. (1993b) 'Prostitution in England and Wales', in *Prostitution: An International Handbook on Trends, Problems, and Policies*, Davis, Nanette J. (ed.), Greenwood Press, Westport.

Edwards, S. S. M. (1994) From Victim to Defendant: The Life Sentence of British Women, *Case Western Reserve Journal of International Law*, Vol. 26, No. 2–3, pp. 261–293.

Edwards, S. S. M. (1995) Suffer the little children — the Government's proposals on child pornography, *Child and Family Law Quarterly*, Vol. 7, No. 2, pp. 49–58.

Edwards, S. S. M. and Armstrong, G. (1988) 'Policing Prostitution: A Profile of the SOS', *Police Journal*, July–Sept, pp. 209–19.

Edwards, S. S. M. and Halpern, A. (1988) 'Conflicting Interests: Protecting Children or Protecting Title to Property', *Journal of Social Welfare Law*, pp. 110–24.

Edwards, S. S. M. and Halpern, A. (1991) Protection for the Victim of Domestic Violence: Time for Radical Revision?, *Journal of Social Welfare and Family Law*, pp. 94–109.

Edwards, S. S. M. and Soetenhorst-de Savornin Lohman, J. (1994) The Impact of Moral Panic on Professional Behaviour in Cases of Child Sexual Abuse: An International Perspective, *Journal of Child Sexual Abuse*, Vol. 3, No. 1, pp. 103–26.

Ellis, B. (1991) *American Psycho*, Picador.

Emmins, C. and Wasik, M. (1993) *Emmins on Sentencing*, Blackstone Press.

Engels, F. (1986) Reprint, *The Origin of the Family, Private Property and the State*, Penguin.

Equal Opportunities Commission (1994) Sexual Harassment Guide, in *Equal Opportunities Review*, November–December 1994, Pt. 58, pp. 35–38.

Ernsdorff, G. M. and Loftus, E. F. (1993) Let Sleeping Memories Lie? Words of Caution about Tolling the Statute of Limitations in Cases of Memory Repression, *Journal of Criminal Law and Criminology*, Vol. 84, No. 1, pp. 129–73.

Estrich, S. (1987) *Real Rape*, Cambridge, Mass.

Ewing, C. P. (1987) *Battered Women Who Kill*, Lexington Books, D. C. Heath and Company.

Faigman, D. (1986) The Battered Woman Syndrome and Self Defence: A Legal and Empirical Dissent, *Virginia Law Review*, Vol. 72, pp. 619–647.

Family Homes and Domestic Violence Bill [H.L.]. House of Lords, Paper 55, London, HMSO.

Fairweather, E. (1982) The Law of the Jungle in King's Cross, *New Society*, 2 December, pp. 375–7.

Feinberg, J. (1986) *The Moral Limits of the Criminal Law Vol 3, Harm to Self*, Oxford University Press

Ferguson, L. and Webster, J. (1994) Getting Away with Rape, *The Times*, 16 February.

Ferraro, K. G. and Johnson, J. M. (1983) How Women Experience Battering: The Process of Victimization, *Social Problems*, Vol. 30, No. 3, pp. 325–39.

Fine, S. (1992) In Anticipation of Violence, *The Globe and Mail*, 31 October.

Fineman, M. and Thomadsen, N. S. (1991) (eds) *At the Boundaries of Law*, Routledge.

Finlay, H. (1980) Sexual Identity and the Law of Nullity, *The Australian Law Journal*, Vol. 54, pp. 115–26.

Finlay, H. (1989) Transsexuals, Sex Change Operations and the Chromosome Test: *Corbett* v *Corbett* Not Followed, *Western Australia Law Review*, Vol. 19, pp. 152–57.

Finstad, L. and Hoigard, C. (1993) Norway (Prostitution in), in *Prostitution: A International Handbook on Trends, Problems, and Policies*, Davis, N. J., (ed.) Greenwood Press, Westport, Connecticut, London, pp. 204–24.

Fiora-Gormally, N. (1978) Battered Wives who Kill, *Law and Human Behaviour*, Vol. 2, No. 2, pp. 133–65.

Fiss, O. M. (1994) What is Feminism? *Arizona State Law Journal*, Vol. 26, pp. 413–28.

Foakes, J. (1984) *Family Violence*, Hemstel.

Ford, D., Regoli, M. (1993) The Criminal Prosecution of Wife Assaulters in Hilton, N.Z., pp. 127–164.

Forell, C. (1992) Reasonable Woman Standard of Care, *University of Tasmania Law Review*, Vol. 11, pp. 1–16.

Forna, A. (1992) Pornography and Racism: Sexualizing Oppression and Inciting Hatred, in *Pornography*, Itzin, C. (ed.), Oxford University Press, pp. 102–12.

Fortin, J. (1993) Significant harm revisited, *Journal of Child Law*, No. 4, pp. 151–56.

Foucault, M. (1978) *Herculine Barbin* dite Alexina, B., Gallimard.

Freeman, J. (1989–90) The feminist debate over prostitution reform: prostitutes' rights groups, radical feminists, and the (im)possibility of consent, *Berkeley Women's Law Journal*, Vol. 5, pp. 75–109.

Freeman, M. D. A. (1994) Legislating for Child Abuse: The Children Act and Significant Harm, in *Re Focus on Child Abuse*, Levy, A. (ed.), Hawksmere, pp. 17–42.

Freud, S. (1974) *New Introductory Lectures*, Hogarth Press.

Frost, N. (1990) Official Intervention and Child Protection: The Relationship Between State and Family in Contemporary Britain, in *Taking Child Abuse Seriously*, The Violence Against Children Study Group, Routledge, London, pp. 25–40.

Frude, N. (ed.) (1980) *Psychological Approaches to Child Abuse*. Batsford (ed.).

Frug, M. J. (1992) A postmodern feminist legal manifesto (an unfinished draft), *Harvard Law Review*, Vol. 105, p. 1045–83.

Fung, R. (1991) Looking for my Penis: The Eroticised Asian in Gay Video Porn, in *How do I Look: Queer Film and Video*, edited by Bad Object Choices, Bay Press, Seattle, pp. 145–60.

Fuss, D. (1989) *Essentially Speaking Feminism, Nature and Difference*, Routledge.

Gallo, J. J., Mason, S. M., Meisenger, L. M., Robin, K. D., Stabile, G. D., Wynne, R. W. (1966) The Consenting Adult Homosexual and the Law: An Empirical Study of Enforcement and Administration in Los Angeles Courts, Vol. 13, *UCLA Law Review*, pp. 643–830.

Gane, C. H. and Stoddart C. N. (1981) *Casebook on Scottish Criminal Law*, Green and Sons.

Gardiner, S. (1990) Reckless and Inconsiderate Rape, *Crim LR*, pp. 172–179.

Gardner, T. (1980) Racism in Pornography and the Women's Movement, in *Take Back the Night: Women on Pornography*, Lederer, L. (ed.), William Morrow and Company, pp. 105–114.

Garfinkel, H. (1967) *Studies in Ethnomethodology*, Prentice-Hall.

Garland, D. (1990) *Punishment and Modern Society*, Oxford University Press.

Garvey, J. H. (1993) Black and White Images, *Law and Contemporary Problems*, Vol. 56, pp. 189–216.

Gavigan, S. (1993) Paradise lost, paradox revisited: the implications of familial ideology for feminist, lesbian, and gay engagement to law, *Osgoode Hall Law Journal*, Vol. 31, pp. 589–624.

Gerth, H. and Mills, C. W. (1970) *Character and Social Structure*, Routledge.

Gessen, M. (1993) The Year in Review, *The Advocate*, 12 January.

Ghandi, P. R. (1995) Blackstone's *International Human Rights Documents*, Blackstone Press.

Gilbert, G. (1801) *The Law of Evidence* (London).

Gillespie, C. K. (1989) *Justifiable Homicide*, Ohio State University Press.

Gilligan, C. (1982) *In a Different Voice: Psychological Theory and Women's Development*, Cambridge, Mass.

Gilman Sander, L. (1985) Black Bodies, White Bodies: Toward an Iconography of Female Sexuality in Later Nineteenth-Century Art, Medicine, and Literature, *Critical Inquiry*, Vol. 12, No. 1, pp. 205–242.

Giobbe, E. (1990) Confronting the Liberal Lies about Prostitution, in *The Sexual Liberals and the Attack on Feminism*, Leidholdt, D. and Raymond, J. (eds).

Giovannoni, J. (1989) Sexual Victimization: Man's Struggle with Power, in *Crime and its Victims*, Viano, E. (ed.) Hemisphere.

Glaister, J. (1945) *Medical Jurisprudence and Toxicology*, 8th edn, London, E & S Livingstone.

Glazer, R. N. (1992) Women's body image and the law, *Duke Law Journal*, Vol. 43, pp. 113–47.

Goff, R. (1988) The Mental Element in the Crime of Murder, *Law Quarterly Review*, Vol. 104, pp. 30–59.

Golding, B. (1992) Policing Prostitution, *Policing*, Vol. 8, No. 1, pp. 60–72.

Goodman, J. (1986) *The Moors Murders: The Trial of Myra Hindley and Ian Brady*, Magpie Books.

Gorham, D. (1978) 'A Maiden Tribute of Modern Babylon re-examined: Child Prostitution and the Idea of Childhood in Late Victorian England', *Victorian Studies*, Vol. XXI, pp. 353–425.

Gousie, M. M. (1993) From Self Defense to Coercion: *McMaugh* v *State* Use of Battered Woman's Syndrome to Defend Wife's Involvement in Third-Party Murder, *New England Law Review*, Vol. 28, pp. 453–481.

Grace, S. (1995) *Policing Domestic Violence in the 1990s*, Home Office Research Study No. 139, HMSO.

Grace, S., Lloyd, C. and Smith, L. (1992) *Rape: from recording to conviction*, Research and Planning Unit Paper 71, Home Office.

Grade Report (1989) Standing Conference on Crime Prevention, Home Office Report on the Working Group on the Fear of Crime, 11 December 1989.

Graff, S. (1988) Battered Wives, Dead Husbands: A Comparative Study of Justification and Excuse in American and West German Law, *Loyola of Los Angeles International and Comparative Law*, Vol. 10, pp. 1–55.

Graycar, R. and Morgan, J. (1992) *The Hidden Gender of Law*, The Federation Press.

Grbich, J. E. (1991) The Body in Legal Theory, in *At the Boundaries of Law*, Fineman, M. A. and Thomadsen, N. S. (eds), Routledge, pp. 60–76. (See also the version in *University of Tasmania Law Review* (1992), Vol. 11, pp. 26–58.)

Green, R. (1992) *Sexual Science and the Law*, Harvard University Press.

Greenberg, D. and Tobiason, T. H. (1993) The new legal puritanism of Catharine MacKinnon, *Ohio State Law Journal*, Vol. 54, pp. 1375–424.

Gross, W. (1986) Judging the Best Interests of the Child: Child Custody and the Homosexual Parent, *Canadian Journal of Women and the Law*, Vol. 1, pp. 505–xx.

Groth, A. N. (1979) *Men who Rape: the psychology of the offender*, New York, Plenum Press.

Groth, A. N. and Burgess, A. W. (1980) Male Rape: Offenders and Victims, *American Journal of Psychiatry*, Vol. 139, pp. 967–70.

Guillaumin, C. (1995) *Racism, Sexism, Power and Ideology*, Routledge.

Gunning, J. and English, V. (1993) *Human In Vitro Fertilization*, Dartmouth.

Haag, J. S. and Sullinger, T. L. (1982) Is He or Isn't She Transsexualism: Legal Impediments to Integrating a Product of Medical Definition and Technology, *Washburn Law Journal*, Vol. 2, pp. 342–376.

Hale, Matthew (1971) edition *A History of the Pleas of the Crown*, (1836), London Professional Books.

Hall, G. (1992) Victim Impact Statements: Sentencing on Thin Ice, *New Zealand Universities Law Review*, Vol. 15, pp. 143–162.

Hall, G. J. and Martin D. F. (1993) *Child Abuse Procedure and Evidence*, Barry Rose.

Hall, R. (1985) *Ask Any Woman*, Bristol, Falling Wall Press.

Hamilton, J. R. (1987–88) Sodomy Statutes, The Ninth Amendment, and the Aftermath of *Bowers* v *Hardwick*, *Kentucky Law Journal*, Vol. 76, pp. 301–324.

Hanmer, J. (1989) Women and Policing in Britain, in *Women, Policing, and Male Violence*, Hanmer, Radford and Stanko, Routledge.

Hanmer, J. and Saunders, S. (1984) *Well Founded Fear*, Hutchinson and Co.

Hanmer, J. and Saunders, S. (1993) *Women, Violence and Crime Prevention: a West Yorkshire Study*, Aldershot.

Hanson, D. W. (1993) Battered Women: Society's Obligation to the Accused, *Akron Law Review*, Vol. 27, pp. 19–56.

Harper, R. and McWhinnie, A. (1983) *The Glasgow Rape Case*, London: Hutchison.

Hart, H. L. A. (1991) *Law, Liberty and Morality*, 1963 edn., Oxford University Press.

Hatty, S. E. (1989) Policing and Male Violence in Australia, in *Women Policing and Male Violence International Perspectives*, Routledge, pp. 70–89.

Hedderman, C. (1987) *Children's Evidence: The Need for Corroboration*, Research and Planning Unit, Paper 41, Home Office London.

Heffernon, L. (ed.), *Human Rights: A European Perspective*, Round Hall Press, Dublin.

Heidensohn, F. (1985) *Women and Crime*, Macmillan.

Helfer, L. (1990) Finding a Consensus on Equality: The Homosexual Age of Consent and the European Convention on Human Rights, *New York University Law Review*, Vol. 65, pp. 1044–1100.

Hernton, C. C. (1970) *Sex and Racism*, Paladin.

Hester, M. and Radford, J. (1992) Domestic Violence and access arrangements for children in Denmark and Britain, *Journal of Social Welfare Law*, Vol. 1, pp. 57–70.

Hester, M. (1995) Child Contact and Domestic Violence, *Magistrate*, 51(9), pp. 210, 222.

Heydon, J. H. (1975) *Cases and Materials on Evidence*, Butterworths.

Hilberman, E. and Munson, K. (1978) Sixty Battered Women, *Victimology*, Vol. 2, No. 3/4, pp. 469–471.

Hilton, Z. N. (1991) Mediating Wife Assault: Battered Women and the New 'Family', *Canadian Journal of Family Law*, Vol. 9, pp. 29–53.

Hodgson, D. (1995) Combatting the Organized Sexual Exploitation of Asian Children; recent developments and prospects. *International Journal of Law and the Family*, 9(1), pp. 23–53.

Hoggett, B. (1993) *Parents and Children*, Sweet and Maxwell.

Hoigard, C. and Finstad, L. (1992) *Backstreets Prostitution, Money and Love*, Polity.

Holmes, R. M. and De Burger, J. (1988) *Serial Murder*, Sage.

Home Affairs Committee (1992) *Annual Report of the Crown Prosecution Service Minutes of Evidence*.

Home Affairs Committee (1993) Minutes of Evidence, *Domestic Violence: report together with the proceedings of the committee*, HC 245, Session 1992–93, HMSO.

Home Affairs Committee (1994) First Report, *Computer Pornography: report, together with the proceedings of the committee, minutes of evidence and appendices*, HC 126, 1993/94, HMSO.

Home Affairs Committee (1994) Fourth Report *Video Violence and Young Offenders: report, together with the proceedings, minutes of evidence and memoranda*, HCP 514, 1993/94, 29 June 1994, HMSO.

Home Office (1989) *Statistics on Offences of Rape 1977–87*, Statistical Bulletin No. 4, 1989, Home Office.

Home Office (1989) *Criminal Proceedings for Offences of Violence Against Children 1989*, Statistical Bulletin No. 42, Home Office.

Home Office *Domestic Proceedings in the Magistrates' Courts, England and Wales*, Statistical Bulletin.

Home Office Circular (1983) Investigation of Offences of Rape, No. 25, Home Office.

Home Office Circular (1986) Violence Against Women, No. 69, Home Office.

Home Office Circular (1990) Domestic Violence, No. 60, Home Office.

Homicide Crime and Justice Bulletin (1993) Attorney-General Department, New South Wales, Contemporary Issues in Crime and Justice, No. 5.

Homicide Survey (1993) Policy Service Program, Canada Centre for Justice Statistics, July 1993.

Horder, J. (1989) Sex Violence and Sentencing in Provocation Cases, *Crim LR*, pp. 546–554.

Horder, J. (1992) *Provocation and Responsibility*, Clarendon Press.

Horley, S. (1988) *Love and Pain*, Bedford Square Press.

Hough, M. and Mayhew P. (1983) *The British Crime Survey*, HMSO.

Hough, M. and Mayhew P. (1985) *Taking Account of Crime: Key Findings from the Second British Crime Survey*, HMSO.

House of Lords Select Committee on Murder and Life Imprisonment. Chairman, the Rt. Hon Lord Nathan, H.L. Paper, 78–1, July 1989.

Hughes, G. (1962) Consent in sexual offences, *Modern Law Review*, Vol. 25, pp. 672–86.

Humphreys, L. (1970) *Tearoom Trade*, Duckworth.

Hunter, J. S. C. (1992–93) Homosexuals as a New Class of Domestic Violence Subjects under the New Jersey Prevention of Domestic Violence Act of 1991, *University of Louisville, Journal of Family Law*, Vol. 31, No. 2, pp. 557–627.

Hunter, N. D. (1992) A Rapist's Exculpation Act, unpublished manuscript, on file with *Virginia Law Review* cited in Sherman, at p. 667 (see below).

Illich, I. (1975) *Medcial Nemesis*, Calder and Boyars.

Inglis, A. (1975) *The White Woman's Protection Ordinance*, Sussex University Press.

Island, D. and Letellier, P. (1991) *Men Who Beat the Men Who Love Them*, Harrington Park Press, Haworth Press.

Itzin, C. (1992) (ed.), *Pornography*, Oxford University Press.

Jackson, E. (1992) Catharine MacKinnon and Feminist Jurisprudence, A Critical Appraisal, *Journal of Law and Society*, Vol. 19, No. 2, pp. 195–213.

Jackson, S. and Rushton, P. (1982) Victims and Villains: Images of Women in Accounts of Family Violence, *Women's Studies International Forum*, Vol. 5, No. 1, pp. 17–28.

Jaffe, P., Wolfe, D. A., Telford, A. and Austin G. (1986) The Impact of Police Laying Charges in Incidents of Wife Abuse, *Journal of Family Violence*, Vol. 1, pp. 37–49.

Jaffe, P., Hastings, E., Reitzel, D. and Austin, G. (1993) The Impact of Police Laying Charges in Hilton, N.Z. (ed.), pp. 62–95.

Jaget, C. (1980) (ed.), *Prostitutes: Our Life*, Falling Wall Press.

James, J. (1987) The Prostitute as Victim, in *The Victimisation of Women*, Chapman, J. R. and Gates, M. (ed.), Beverly Hills.

Jeffreys, S. (1994) *The Lesbian Heresy*, The Women's Press.

Johnson, E. G. (1992) A comparison of sexual privacy rights in the United States and the United Kingdom: why we must look beyond the Constitution, *Columbia Journal of Transnational Law*, Vol. 30, pp. 697–718.

Jones, A. (1991) *Women Who Kill*, Victor Gollancz.

Jones, T., MacLean B. and Young, J. (1986) *The Islington Crime Survey: Crime, Victimization and Policing in Inner-City London*, Gower.

Joseph, G. (1981) The incompatible *ménage à trois*: Marxism, feminism and racism in *Women and Revolution*, Sargent, L. (ed.), Boston, South End Press.

Judicial Statistics, Annual Report, 1987 Cm 428, 1988 Cm 745, , 1989 Cm 1154, 1990 Cm 1573, 1991 Cm 1990, 1992 Cm 2268, 1993 Cm 2623, 1994 Cm 2891. Lord Chancellor's Department, London.

Kaite, B. (1988) The Pornographic Body Double: Transgression is the Law, pp. 151–168, in *Body Invaders: Sexuality and the Postmodern Condition*, Kroker, A. and Kroker, M., Macmillan.

Kalven, H. and Zeisel, H. (1966) *The American Jury*, University of Chicago Press.

Kappeler, S. (1986) *The Pornography of Representation*, Polity.

Kaufman, M. (1987) (ed.), *Beyond Patriarchy: Essays by Men on Pleasure, Power and Change*, Toronto, Oxford University Press.

Kaufman, T. and Lincoln, P. (1991) (ed.), *High Risk Lives, Lesbian and Gay Politics after the Clause*, Prism Press.

Kaufman, S. (1974) *The Philanderer*, Secker Warburg.

Kellmar Pringle, M. (1980) Towards the Prediction of Child Abuse, in *Psychological Approaches to Child Abuse*, Frude, N. (ed.), Batsford Academic and Educational Ltd, pp. 204–19.

Kelly, L. (1988) *Surviving Sexual Violence*, Polity.

Kendall, C. N. (1993) 'Real Dominant, Real Fun!': Gay Male Pornography and the Pursuit of Masculinity, *Saskatchewan Law Review*, Vol. 57, pp. 21–58.

Kennedy, H. (1992) *Eve Was Framed: Women and British Justice*, Chatto and Windus.

Kennedy, I. and Grubb, A. (1994) *Medical Law*, Butterworths.

Kettle, M. (1977) *Salome's Last Veil: the libel case of the century*, Hart-Davis MacGibbon.

King, D. (1987) Social Constructionism and Medical Knowledge: The Case of Transsexualism, *Sociology of Health and Illness*, Vol. 9, No. 4, pp. 351–77

King, D. (1993) *The Transvestite and the Transsexual*, Avebury, Aldershot.

King, M. B. (1992) Male Sexual Assault in the Community in *Male Victims of Sexual Assault*, Mezey, J. and King, M. B. (eds), Oxford Medical Publications, pp. 1–12.

Kingston, J. (1994) Sex and Sexuality under the European Convention on Human Rights L. Heffernon (ed.), pp. 179–195.

Kinnell, H. (1989) *Prostitutes, their Clients and Risks of HIV infection in Birmingham*, Occasional Paper, Department of Public Health Medicine, Central Birmingham Health Authority, July.

Kirkwood, C. (1993) *Leaving Abusive Partners*, Sage.

Klein, C. F. (1995) Full Faith and Credit: Interstate Enforcement of Protection Orders Under the Violence against Women Act of 1994, Family Law Quarterly, Vol. 29, No. 2, p. 253–373.

Klein, D. (1982) in interview with Andriesson, M. (1982). 'We moeten de realiteit van vrouwenlevens leren begrijpen.' Interview met Doris Klein. (We must learn to understand the reality of women's lives.) *Tijdschrift voor Criminologie*, Vol. 24, No. 131–44.

Klis, D. A. (1994) Reforms to criminal defence instructions: new patterned jury instructions which account for the experience of the battered woman who kills her battering mate, Vol. 24, *Golden Gate University Law Review*, pp. 131–168.

Knight, B. (1972) *Legal Aspects of Medical Practice*, London, Churchill Livingstone.

Knight, B. (1976) Forensic problems in practice VIII, sexual offences, *The Practitioner*, Vol. 217, No. 1298, pp. 288–89.

Kollontai, A. (1978) Prostitution and Ways of Fighting it, in *Sexual Relations and the Class Struggle*, London, Alison Busby.

Koss, M. P. (1989) Hidden Rape: Sexual Aggression and Victimization in a National Sample of Students in Higher Education, in *Violence in Dating Relationships*, Pirog-Good, M. and Stets, J., Praeger, New York.

Krafft-Ebing, W. von (1901) *Psychopathia Sexualis*, Rebman Limited.

Lacan, J. (1994) *The Four Fundamental Concepts of Psychoanalysis*, Harmondsworth, Penguin.

Lacey, N. (1989) Feminist Legal Theory, *Oxford Journal of Legal Studies*, Vol. 9, pp. 383–94.

Lacey, N. (1993) Theory into Practice? Pornography and the Public/Private Dichotomy, *Journal of Law and Society*, Vol. 20, No. 1, pp. 93–113.

La Fontaine, J. (1990) *Child Sexual Abuse*, Polity.

La Fontaine, J. (1994) *The Extent and Nature of Organised and Ritual Abuse*, Department of Health, HMSO.

Lahey, K. A. (1991) Reasonable Women and the Law, in *At the Boundaries of Law: Feminism and Legal Theory*, Fineman, M. A. and Thomadsen, N. S. (eds), Routledge, pp. 3–21.

Langan, P. A. and Innes, C. A. (1986) *Preventing Domestic Violence Against Women*, Bureau of Justice Statistics, Washington DC, US Department of Justice.

Law Commission (1977) No. 83, Criminal Law: *Report of Defences of General Application*, London, HMSO.

Law Commission (1992) No. 205, *Criminal Law; Rape Within Marriage*, HC 167, HMSO.

Law Commission (1992) No. 207, *Domestic Violence and Occupation of the Family Home*, London HMSO.

Law Commission (1993) No. 218, *Legislating the Criminal Code: Offences Against the Person and General Principles*, HMSO, London.

Law Commission (1994) Consultation Paper No. 134, *Criminal Law: Consent and Offences Against the Person*, HMSO.

Law Commission (1995) Consultation Paper No. 139, *Criminal Law: Consent in the Criminal law*, London HMSO.

Law Commission (1989) Working Paper No. 113, *Domestic Violence and Occupation of the Family Home*, HMSO.

Law Reform Commission of Victoria (1991) *Homicide Prosecutions Study*, Appendix to Report No. 40, Melbourne.

Leader-Elliott, I. (1993) Battered but not beaten, *The Sydney Law Review*, Vol. 15, pp. 403–60.

Lederer, L. (1980) *Take Back the Night*, William Morrow and Company Inc.

Lee, M. and O'Brien R. (1995) *The Game is Up*, The Children's Society, London.

Lee, S. (1989) *Judging Judges*, Faber and Faber.

Lees, S. (1989) Trial by Rape, *New Statesman and New Society*, 24 November, pp. 10–13.

Lees, S. (1992) Naggers, Whores and Libbers: Provoking Men to Kill, in *Femicide*, Russell and Radford (eds.), pp. 267–88.

Lees, S. (1993) Judicial Rape, *Women's Studies International Forum*, Vol. 16, No. 1, pp. 11–36.

Leidholdt, A. and Raymond, J. (1990) *The Sexual Liberals and the Attack on Feminism*, Pergamon.

Leigh, L. H. (1976) Sado-Masochism, Consent, and the Reform of the Criminal Law, *Modern Law Review*, Vol. 39, pp. 130–146.

Lemert, E. (1951) *Social Pathology: A Systematic Approach to the Theory of Sociopathic Behaviour*, New York, McGraw-Hill.

Leng, R. (1994) 'Consent and Offences Against the Person: Law Commission Consultation Paper No. 134', *Crim LR*, pp. 480–88.

Leonard, A. (1994) Lesbian and gay families and the law: a progress report, *Fordham Urban Law Journal*, Vol. 21, pp. 927–72.

Lester, T. P. (1993) The EEC Code of Conduct on Sexual Harassment, 1993, *New Law Journal*, Vol. 143, Pt. 6621, pp. 1473–74.

Levy, A. (1994) (ed.), *Re-Focus on Child Abuse*, Hawksmere, London.

Littleton, C. A. (1989) Women's Experience and the Problems of Transition: Perspectives on Male Battering of Women, *University of Chicago Legal Forum*, pp. 23–57.

Lloyd, C. and Walmsley, R. (1989) *Changes in rape offence and sentencing*, Home Office research study No. 119, HMSO.

London Borough of Lambeth (1987) Whose Child? *The Report of the Panel Appointed to Inquire into the Death of Tyra Henry*.

London Rape Crisis Centre (1984) *Sexual violence: the reality for women*, Women's Press.

Longino, H. (1980) Pornography, Oppression and Freedom: A Closer Look, in Lederer (ed.) (see above), pp. 40–54.

Lothstein, L. M. (1982) Sex Reassignment Surgery: Historical, Bioethical, and Theoretical Issues, *Am J Psychiatry*, Vol. 139, No. 4, pp. 417–26.

Love, J. C. (1992) Tort Actions for Hate Speech and the First Amendment, *Law and Sexuality*, pp. 29–35.

Lowe, N. (1989) Caring for Children, 139 *New Law Journal*, pp. 87–89.

Lyon, C. and De Cruz, P. (1993) *Child Abuse*, Bristol, Family Law.

Lyon, C. and Parton, N. (1995) Children's rights and the Children Act 1989, in *The Handbook of Children's Rights*, Franklin, B., Routledge, pp. 40–55.

Mackay, R. D. and Colman, A. M. (1996) Equivocal Rulings on Expert Psychological and Psychiatric Evidence: Turning a Muddle into a Nonsense, *Crim LR*, pp. 88–95.

MacKinnon, C. A. (1979) *Sexual Harassment of Working Women: A Case Study of Sex Discrimination*, Yale University Press.

MacKinnon, C. A. (1982) Feminism, Marxism, Method, and the State: Towards a Feminist Jurisprudence, *Signs: Journal of Women in Culture and Society*, 7 No. 3, pp. 515–44, reprinted in *Violence Against Women*, Bart P. B. and Moran E. G., Sage, pp. 201–28.

MacKinnon, C. A. (1984) Not a Moral Issue, *Yale Law and Policy Review*, Vol. 11, No. 2, pp. 321–45.

MacKinnon, C. A. (1985) Pornography, Civil Rights, and Speech, *Harvard Civil Rights — Civil Liberties Law Review*, Vol. 20, No. 1, pp. 1–70.

MacKinnon, C. A. (1987) *Feminism Unmodified*, Harvard University Press.

MacKinnon, C. A. (1989) *Towards a Feminist Theory of the State*, Cambridge, Harvard University Press.

MacKinnon, C. A. (1990) Liberalism and the Death of Feminism, in *The Sexual Liberals and the Attack on Feminism*, Leidholdt and Raymond (eds), Pergamon Press, pp. 3–13.

MacKinnon, C. A. (1994) *Only Words*, Harper Collins.

MacLean, B., Jones, T. and Young J. (1986) *The Islington Crime Survey: crime, victimization and policing in inner-city London*, Gower.

MacNamara, D. E. L. and Sagarin, E. (1977) *Sex, Crime and the Law*, New York, Free Press.

Maguigan, H. (1991) Battered Women and Self Defense: Myths and Misconceptions in Current Reform Proposals, Vol. 140, *U Pa L Review*, pp. 379–486.

Mahoney, K. E. (1992) *R v Keegstra*: A Rationale for Regulating Pornography? *McGill Law Journal*, Vol. 37, pp. 242–69.

Mahoney, K. E. (1985) Obscenity: Morals and the Law: A Feminist Critique, *Ottawa Law Review*, Vol. 17, pp. 33–71.

Mahoney, M. R. (1991) Legal Images of Battered Women: Redefining the Issue of Separation, *Michigan Law Review*, Vol. 90, No. 1, pp. 38–93.

Mailer, N. (1991) Children of the Pied Piper, *Vanity Fair*, March, p. 124.

Manchester, C. (1995a) Criminal Justice and Public Order Act 1994: Obscenity, Pornography and Videos, *Crim LR*, pp. 123–31.

Manchester, C. (1995b) Computer Pornography, *Crim LR*, pp. 546–55.

Martin, S. L. (1992) Women as Lawmakers, *Alberta Law Review*, Vol. 30, No. 3, pp. 738–46.

Masson, J. (1984) *The Assault on Truth*, Faber and Faber.

Masson J. (1994) Social Engineering in the House of Lords: Re M, *Journal of Child Law*, Vol. 6, No. 4, pp. 170–174.

Mather, V. M. (1988) The Skeleton in the Closet: The Battered Women Syndrome, Self-Defense and Expert Testimony, *Mercer Law Review*, Vol. 39, pp. 545–61.

Matoesian, G. M. (1993) *Reproducing Rape: Domination through talk in the courtroom*, Polity Press.

Matsui, Y. (1984) 'Why I oppose Kisaeng Tours', in *International Feminism: Networking Against Female Sexual Slavery*, Barry K., Bunch, C. and Castley, S. (eds), pp. 64–72, International Women's Tribune Center, 777 UN Plaza, N.Y.

Matthews, P. (1992) Compensation in Sexual Harassment Claims, *Legal Action*, October, pp. 21–2.

Matza, D. (1964) *Delinquency and Drift*, John Wiley.

Mawby, R. (1985) Bystander Responses to the Victims of Crime: Is the Good Samaritan Alive and Well? *Victimology*, Vol. 19, No. 1–4, pp. 461–77.

Mayhew, P., Aye Maung, N. and Mirrlees-Black, C. (1993) *The 1992 British Crime Survey*, HMSO.

Mayhew, P., Elliott D. and Dowds, L. (1989) *The 1988 British Crime Survey*, HMSO.

McColl, Kennedy, I. (1973) Transsexualism and the Single Sex Marriage, *Anglo American Law Review*, Vol. 2, pp. 112–19.

McClintock, A. (1992) Screwing the System: Sexwork, Race, and the Law, *Boundary*, Vol. 2, Pt. 19, pp. 70–95.

McClintock, A. (1993) 'Maid to Order', in *Social Text*, No. 37 Duke University Press.

McClintock, F. (1963) *Crimes of Violence*, Macmillan.

McColgan, A. (1993) In Defence of Battered Women Who Kill, *Oxford Journal of Legal Studies*, Vol. 13, No. 4, pp. 508–529.

McEwan, J. (1990) In the box or on the box? The Pigot Report and Child Witnesses, *Crim LR*, pp. 363–370.

McKenzie, Norrie, K. (1988) Symbolic and Meaningless Legislation, *Journal of the Law Society of Scotland*, Sept, p. 310–314.

McLeod, E. (1982) *Women Working Prostitution Now*, Croom Helm.

McLeod, M. (1983) Victim Non Co-operation in Domestic Disputes, *Criminology*, Vol. 21, No. 3, pp. 395–416.

McMullan, M. and Whittle, S. (1994) *Transvestism, Transsexualism and the Law*, The Beaumont Trust, The Gender Trust.

McMurtrie, S. (1996) Pornography and Rights: The Theory of the Practice of Control, in Gearty, C. and Tomkins, A. (ed.) *Understanding Human Rights*, Mansells, pp. 507–525.

Melossi, D. and Pavarini, M. (1981) *The Prison and the Factory*, London, Macmillan.

Mercer, K. (1991) Skin Head Sex Thing: Racial Difference and the Homoerotic Imagery, in *How do I Look*, edited by Bad Object Choices, Bay Press, pp. 169–210.

Merchant, V. (1993) *Computer Pornography in Schools*, Report of a National Conference at the University of Central Lancashire.

Merchant, V. (1995) Computers and Pornography paper presented to the *European Forum on Child Welfare, Child Pornography and Sexual Exploitation Seminar*, National Council of Voluntary Child Care Organisations, March, London.

Merleau-Ponty, M. (1967) What is Phenomenology? in *Phenomenology*, Kockelmans, J. (ed.), New York, Anchor Books.

Metcalf, A. and Humphries, M. (1990) *The Sexuality of Men*, Pluto Press.

Metropolitan Police, Annual Report of the Commissioner of the Police for the Metropolis 1989, 1990, 1991.

Metropolitan Police, Force Order, Domestic Violence, 23 June 1987, OG/11/86/243, (TO30), Metropolitan Police, London.

Metropolitan Police: *Report of the Working Party on Domestic Violence*, Metropolitan Police London, May 1993.

Metropolitan Police (1994) Submission to The House of Commons All Parliamentary Group on *Prostitution TO9* (Crime and Divisional Policing Policy Branch).

Mezey, G. (1992) Treatment for Male Victims of Rape, in *Male Victims of Sexual Assault*, Mezey, G. and King, M. B., Oxford Medical Publications, pp. 131–44.

Mezibov, M. and Sirkin, H. L. (1992) The Mapplethorpe Obscenity Trial, *Litigation*, Vol. 18, pp. 12–15.

Miedzian, M. (1992) *Boys Will be Boys: Breaking the Link Between Masculinity and Violence*, Virago.

Mihajlovich, M. (1987) Does Plight Make Right: The Battered Woman Syndrome, Expert Testimony and the Law of Self Defense, Vol. 62, *Ind Law J*, pp. 1253–82.

Mill, J. S. (1869) *The Subjection of Women*, 1978, MIT Press, Cambridge.

Mill, J. S. (1859) *On Liberty*, 13 (Shields, C. (ed.) 1958), (1st edn. 1859).

Miller, A. (1985) *Thou Shalt Not Be Aware: Society's Betrayal of the Child*, Pluto.

Miller, E. M., Romenesko, K. and Wondolkowski, L. (1993) 'The United States', *Prostitution: An International Handbook on Trends, Problems and Policies*, Davis, N. J. (ed.), pp. 300–26.

Miller, R. (1993) Murderers, *Sunday Times*, 2 May.

Millet, K. (1973) *The Prostitution Papers*, Paladin.

Millns, S. (1992) Transsexuality and the European Convention on Human Rights, *Public Law*, pp. 559–66.

Minow, M. (1988) Feminist Reason: Getting It and Losing It, *Journal of Legal Education*, Vol. 38, pp. 47–60.

Miralao, V., Carlos, C. and Santos, A. (1990) *Women Entertainers in Angeles and Olongapo: A Survey Report*, Women's Education Development Productivity and Research Organisation and Katipunan ng Kababaihan para sa Kalayaan Quezon City Phillipines.

Mitchell, D. (1992) Contemporary Police Practices in Domestic Violence Cases: Arresting the Abuser: Is it Enough? Vol 83, *Journal of Criminal Law and Criminology*, pp. 241–249.

Mitra, C. (1987) Judicial Discourse in Father-Daughter Incest in Appeal Cases, *International Journal of the Sociology of Law*, Vol. 15, No. 2, pp. 121–48.

Mnookin, R. M. and Kornhauser, L. (1979) Bargaining in the Shadow of the Law: The Case of Divorce, *Yale Law Journal* (1979), Vol. 88, pp. 950–97.

Montgomery Hyde, H. (1964) *A History of Pornography*, Four Square, London.

Moon, R. (1993) *R v Butler*: The Limits of the Supreme Court's Feminist Re-Interpretation of Section 163, *Ottawa Law Review*, Vol. 25, No. 2, pp. 361–84.

Mooney, J. (1993) *The hidden figure: domestic violence in North London*, Islington's Police and Crime Prevention Unit.

Monahan, J. and Walker, L. (1994) *Social Science in Law: Cases and Materials*, Westbury, New York, The Foundation Press.

Moran, L. J. (1995) Violence and the law: The Case of Sado-Masochism, *Social and Legal Studies*, Vol. 4, No. 2, pp. 225–52.

Morgan, J. and Plotnikoff, J. (1990) Children as Victims of Crime: Procedure at Court, in Spencer, J., Nicholson, G., Flin, R. and Bull, R. (eds) *Children's Evidence in Legal Proceedings: An International Perspective*, Cambridge, University of Cambridge, Law faculty.

Morley, R. and Mullender, A. (1994) *Preventing Domestic Violence to Women*, Home Office Police Department.

Morris, J. (1987) *Conundrum*, Penguin.

Mossman, M. J. (1986) Feminism and Legal Method: The Difference It Makes, *Australian Journal of Law and Society*, Vol. 3, pp. 30–52, reprinted in Fineman and Thomadsen (see above) pp. 283–300.

Mountbatten, J. (1994) Transsexuals and Social Security Law: The Return of Gonad The Barbarian, *Australian Journal of Family Law*, pp. 166–77.

Mullender, A. (1995) *Children Living with Domestic Violence*, Whiting and Birch.

Munday, R. (1991) Hostile Witnesses and the Admission of Witness Statements under Section 23 of the Criminal Justice Act 1988, *Crim LR*, pp. 349–360.

National Association of Victim Support Schemes (1991) *Domestic Violence Working Party Report*, London.

National Society for the Prevention of Cruelty to Children (1989) *Research Briefing*, No. 11. London.

Nelken, D. (1987) Critical Criminal Law, *Journal of Law and Society*, Vol. 14, No. 1, pp. 105–17.

Newson, J. and Newson, E. (1980) Parental Punishment Strategies with Eleven Year-old Children in Frude, N. ed., Psychological Approaches to Child Abuse, Boston Academic and Educational Ltd.

New South Wales Task Force on *Domestic Violence* 1984 (1985) Canberra, New South Wales.

New York Task Force on *Domestic Violence* 1987, New York.

Nicolson, D. (1995) Telling Tales: Gender Discrimination, Gender Construction and Battered Women Who Kill, *Feminist Legal Studies*, Vol. 111, No. 2, pp. 185–206.

Nicholson, D. and Sanghvi, R. (1993) Battered women and provocation: the implications of *R v Ahluwalia*, *Crim LR*, pp. 728–38.

O'Donovan, K. (1985) *Sexual Divisions in Law*, Weidenfeld and Nicolson.

O'Donovan, K. (1991) Defences for Battered Women Who Kill, *Journal of Law and Society*, Vol. 18, No. 2, pp. 219–40.

O'Donovan, K. (1993) Law's Knowledge: The Judge, The Expert, The Battered Woman, and Her Syndrome, *Journal of Law and Society*, Vol. 20, No. 4, pp. 427–437.

O'Grady (1994) *ECPAT. To End Child Prostitution in Asian Tourism.*

Ohse, U. (1984) *Forced Prostitution and Traffic in Women*, West Germany, Human Rights Group.

Oppenlander, N. (1982) Coping or Copping Out, *Criminology*, Vol. 20, Nos. 3–4, pp. 449–465.

Orff, J. L. (1995) Demanding Justice without Truth: The Difficulty of Postmodern Feminist Legal Theory, *Loyola of Los Angeles Law Review*, Vol. 28, pp. 1197–1250.

Ormerod, D. (1994) Consent and Offences against the Person: Law Commission Consultation Paper No. 134, *Modern Law Review*, Vol. 57, No. 6, pp. 928–40.

Pace, P. (1983) Sexual Identity and the Criminal Law, *Crim LR*, pp. 317–21.

Pacillo, E. (1994) Getting a feminist foot in the courtroom door: media liability for personal injury caused by pornography, *Suffolk University Law Review*, Vol. 28, pp. 123–52.

Pannick, D. (1983) Homosexuals, Transsexuals and the Sex Discrimination Act, *Public Law*, pp. 279–302.

Parton, N. (1985) *The Politics of Child Abuse*, MacMillan.

Pateman, C. (1989) *The Sexual Contract*, Polity.

Pattinson, T. (1991) *Sexual Harassment*, Futura.

Pattullo, P. (1983) *Judging Women*, NCCL.

Paul, D. M. (1975) The medical examination in sexual offences, *Medicine Science and Law*, Vol. 15, No. 3, pp. 154–62.

Pauly, I. B. (1965) Male Psychosexual Inversion: Transsexualism, *Archives of General Psychiatry*, Vol. 13, pp. 172–81.

Pearsall, R. (1969) *The Worm in the Bud*, Penguin.

Pease, K. (1985) Obscene Telephone Calls to Women in England and Wales, *The Howard Journal*, Vol. 24, No. 4, pp. 275–281.

Penn State Report, Rapport de Penn State en anglais et français (1991), International Meeting of Experts on Sexual Exploitation, Violence and Prostitution, State College, Pennsylvania, USA, April 1991. A Publication of UNESCO and Coalition Against Trafficking in Women.

Perkins, R. and Bennett, G. (1985) *Being a Prostitute*, Sydney Allen and Unwin.

Pheterson, G. (ed.) (1989) *A Vindication of the Rights of Whores*, Seal Press, Seattle.

Pizzey, E. and Shapiro, J. (1982) *Prone to Violence*, Hamlyn.

Plummer, K. (ed.) (1992) *Modern Homosexualities*, Routledge.

Plotnikoff, J. and Woolfson, R. (1994) *The Children Act 1989 Time Tabling of Interim Care Orders Study*, DH SSI Publications.

Polikoff, N. D. (1989–90) The Child Does Have Two Mothers: Redefining Parenthood to Meet the Needs of Children in Lesbian-Mother and Other Nontraditional Families, *Georgetown Law Journal*, Vol. 78, pp. 459–75.

Polson, C. J. and Gee, D. J. (1973) *The Essentials of Forensic Medicine*, Pergamon Press.

Popper, K. R. (1968) *The Logic of Scientific Discovery*, Hutchinson.

Posner, R. A. (1992) *Sex and Reason*, Harvard University Press.

Pringle, K., Kaufmann, T. and Lincoln P. (1991) Clause 28 in Practice, in Kaufman and Lincoln (eds) (see above), pp. 4–12.

Radford, J. (1982) Marriage Licence or a Licence to Kill? Woman Slaughter in the Criminal Law, *Feminist Review*, Vol. 11, pp. 88–96.

Radzinowicz, L. and King, J. (1977) *The Growth of Crime*, London, Penguin.

Rawls, J. (1971) *A Theory of Justice*, Oxford University Press.

Raymond, J. (1981) *The Transsexual Empire*, The Women's Press.

Raymond, J. (1992) Pornography and the Politics of Lesbianism, in *Pornography*, Itzin, C. (ed.), Oxford University Press, pp. 166–78.

Reekie, G. and Wilson, P. (1993) Rape Resistance and Women's Rights of Self-Defence, *Australian and New Zealand Journal of Criminology*, Vol. 26, pp. 146–54.

Rees, M. (1995) *Dear Sir or Madam: The Autobiography of a Female-to-Male Transsexual*, Cassell.

Reeves Sanday, P. (1981) *Female Power and Male Domination*, New York, Cambridge.

Reiner, R. (1985) *The Politics of the Police*, Harvester.

Renvoize, J. (1983) *Incest*, Routledge.

Report of the Advisory Group on the Law of Rape (1975), Cmnd 6352 (Heilbron Committee), Home Office, London, HMSO.

Report of the Advisory Group on Video-Recorded Evidence (Pigot Committee), Home Office, December 1989.

Report of the Committee on Homosexual Offences and Prostitution (1957), Cmnd 247 (Wolfenden Committee).

Report of the Inquiry into Child Abuse in Cleveland (1987), July 1988, Cm 412, HMSO.

Report of the Inquiry into the Removal of Children from Orkney in February 1991, 1992, HMSO.

Review of Child Care Law, Department of Health and Social Security (1985), London, HMSO.

Rhode, D. (1994) Feminism and the State, *Harvard Law Review*, Vol. 107, pp. 1181–208.

Rights of Women, Lesbian Custody Group (1986), *Lesbian Mothers' Legal Handbook*, The Women's Press Handbook Series.

Rice, M. (1990) Challenging orthodoxies in feminist theory: a black feminist critique, in *Feminist Perspectives in Criminology*, Gelsthorpe, L. and Morris, A. (eds), Open University Press, pp. 57–69.

Ritchie, M. E. (1975) Alice Through the Statutes, *McGill Law Journal*, Vol. 21, pp. 685–707.

Rittenmeyer, S. D. (1981) Of battered wives, self defence and double standards of justice, *Journal of Criminal Justice*, Vol. 9, pp. 389–95.

Roberts, N. (1986) *The Front Line*, Grafton.

Robertson, G. (1979) *Obscenity*, Weidenfeld and Nicholson, London.

Robertson, G. (1991) *Freedom, The Individual and the Law*, Penguin.

Rodgerson, G. and Wilson, E. (1991) *Pornography and Feminism: the case against censorship*, Lawrence and Wishart.

Rook, P. and Ward, R. (1990) *Sexual Offences*, The Criminal Law Library, Waterlow Publishers, Pergamon Press.

Roseman, M. E. (1992) Adult Survivors of Childhood Sexual Abuse Litigation: Repressed Memories and Tolling the Statute of Limitations, *Western State University Law Review*, Vol. 20, pp. 81–101.

Rosen, C. J. (1986) The Excuse of Self-Defence: Correcting an Historical Accident on Behalf of Battered Women who Kill, *American University Law Review*, Vol. 36, pp. 11–56.

Roszak, B. and Roszak, T. (1969) *Masculine/Feminine*, Harper Row.

Royal Commission on Criminal Procedure (1981), *The Investigation and Prosecution of Criminal Offences in England and Wales, The Law and Procedure* Cmnd. 8092–1, London, HMSO.

Rumney, N. S. and Morgan-Taylor, M. P. (1996) Sentencing for Male Rape, *New Law Journal*, Vol. 146, p. 266.

Russell, D. E. H. (1984) *Sexual Exploitation: Rape, Child Sexual Abuse and Workplace Harassment*, Beverly Hills, California.

Russell, D. and Radford, J. (1992) *Femicide*, Open University Press.

Saadawi, N. (1980) *The Hidden Face of Eve*, Zed.

Saadawi, N. (1983) *Women at Point Zero*, Zed.

Sagarin, E. (1976) Prison homosexuality and its effect on post-prison sexual behaviour, *Psychiatry*, Vol. 39, pp. 245–57.

Salame, L. (1993) A National Survey of Stalking Laws: A Legislative Trend Comes to the Aid of Domestic Violence Victims and Others, *Suffolk University Law Review*, Vol. 27, pp. 67–111.

Samaras, C. (1993) Feminism, photography, censorship and sexually transgressive imagery: the work of Robert Mapplethorpe, Joel-Peter Witkin, Jacqueline Livingston, Sally Mann and Catherine Opie, Vol. 38, *New York Law School Review*, pp. 75–93.

Sanders, A. (1988) Personal Violence and Public Order: The Prosecution of Domestic Violence in England and Wales, *International Journal of the Sociology of Law*, Vol. 16, pp. 359–82.

Sanders, A., McConville M. and Leng R. (1991) *The Case for the Prosecution*, Routledge.

Sanders, D. (1994) Constructing Lesbian and Gay Rights, *CJLS*, Vol. 9, No. 2, pp. 1–45.

Sanders, D. (1996) Getting Lesbian and Gay Issues on the International Agenda, *Human Rights Quarterly*, Vol. 18, No. 1, pp. 67–106.

Saward, J. and Green, W. (1990) *Rape: My Story*, Bloomsbury.

Schapira, K., Davison, K., Brierly, H. (1979) The assessment and management of transsexual problems, *British Journal of Hospital Medicine*, pp. 63–9.

Scheler, M. (1960) *Die Wissensformen und die Gessellschaft*, Bern, Francke.

Scherer, D. (1992) Tort Remedies for Victims of Domestic Abuse, *South Carolina Law Review*, Vol. 43, pp. 543–79.

Schneider, E. (1980) Equal Rights to Trial for Women: Sex Bias in the Law of Self-Defence, *Harvard Civil Rights-Civil Liberties LR*, Vol. 15, pp. 623–47.

Schneider, E. M. (1986) Describing and Changing: Women's Self-Defence Work and the Problem of Expert Testimony on Battering, *Women's Rights Law Report*, Vol. 9, pp. 195–97.

Schneider, E. M. (1992) Particularity and generality: challenges of feminist theory and practice in work on woman-abuse, *New York University Law Review*, Vol. 67, pp. 520–68.

Schur, E. (1965) *Crimes without Victims*, Englewood Cliffs, New Jersey.

Schutz, A. (1972) *The Phenomenology of the Social World*, Heinemann Educational Books.

Schwarzenbach, S. (1990–91) Contractarians and feminists debate prostitution, *New York University Review of Law and Social Change*, Vol. 18, pp. 103–30.

Scraton, P. (1990) Scientific knowledge or masculine discourses? Challenging patriarchy in criminology, in *Feminist Perspectives in Criminology*, Gelsthorpe, L. and Morris, A. (eds), Open University Press, pp. 10–25.

Scully, D. (1990) *Understanding Sexual Violence: A Study of Convicted Rapists*, Unwin Hyman.

Scutt, J. A. (1981) Sexism in the Criminal Law, in Scutt and Mukherjee, see below, pp. 1–21.

Scutt, J. A. and Mukherjee, S. (eds) (1981) *Women and Crime*, Australian Institute of Criminology, in association with George Allen.

Sebba, L. (1994) Sentencing the Victim and the Aftermath of Payne, *International Journal of Victimology*, Vol. 3, No. 1/2, pp. 141–165.

Segal, L. (1988) *Is the Future Female: Troubled Thoughts on Contemporary Feminism*, Virago.

Segal, L. and McIntosh, M. (eds) (1992) *Sex Exposed: Sexuality and the Pornography Debate*, Virago.

Selby, H. (1987) *Last Exit to Brooklyn*, Paladin.

Select Committee on Violence in Marriage (1975), Report 1974–75, HMSO.

Sharpe, A. (1995) The Failure to Degenderise the Law of Rape: the Criminal Justice and Public Order Act and the Transsexual Victim, *Crim Law*, Vol. 53, pp. 7–8.

Sheehy, E. (1994) Battered Woman Syndrome: Developments in Canadian Law After *R v Lavallee* in *Women, Male Violence and the Law*, Stubbs, J. (ed.), The Institute of Criminology Monograph Series No. 6, Sydney, Australia.

Sheppard, A. F. (1991) The Supreme Court of Canada and Criminal Evidence Reform: Recent cases on Sexual Abuse of Children and Spousal Murder, *Canadian Journal of Family Law*, Vol. 9, No. 2, pp. 11–27.

Sheppard, A. T. (1992) Lesbian Mothers 11: Long Night's Journey into Day, *Women's Rights Law Reporter*, Vol. 14, pp. 185–212.

Sherman, L. W. (1992) The Influence of Criminology on Criminal Law: Evaluating Arrests for Misdemeanor Domestic Violence, *The Journal of Criminal Law and Criminology*, Vol. 83, No. 1, pp. 1–45.

Sherman, L. W. (1995) Love Speech: The Social Utility of Pornography, *Stanford Law Review*, Vol. 47, pp. 661–705.

Sherman, L. W., Lawrence, W. and Berk, R. A. (1984) The Specific Deterrent Effects of Arrest for Domestic Assault, *American Sociological Review*, Vol. 49, No. 2, pp. 261–72.

Sherman, J. G., Lawrence, W. and Cohn, E. G. (1990) The Impact of Research on Legal Policy, The Minneapolis Domestic Violence Experiment, *Law and Society*, Vol. 23, pp. 117–44.

Shirer, W. L. (1968) *The Rise and Fall of the Third Reich*, Book Club Associates, London.

Singer, B. L. and Deschamps, D. (1994) *Gay and Lesbian Stats: A pocket guide of facts and figures*, The New Press, New York.

Smart, C. (1989) *Feminism and the Power of the Law*, Routledge.

Smart, C. (1995) *Law, Crime and Sexuality*, Sage.

Smith, D. (1978) K is Mentally Ill: The Anatomy of a Factual Account, *Sociology*, Vol. 12, pp. 23–53.

Smith, D. K. (1971) Transsexualism, Sex Reassignment Surgery and the Law, *Cornell Law Review*, Vol. 56, pp. 963–1009.

Smith, L. J. F. (1989) *Concerns About Rape*, Research Study No. 106, HMSO.

Smith, J. C. and Hogan, B. (1988) *Criminal Law*, Butterworths.

Sourcebook of Criminal Justice Statistics 1986, 1993, 1991, 1994, Bureau of Justice Statistics, US Department of Justice.

Southall Black Sisters (1989) Two Struggles: Challenging Male Violence and the Police, in *The Boys in Blue*, Dunhill, C. (ed.), pp. 38–44.

Spaulding, C. (1989–1990) Anti-Pornography Laws As A Claim for Equal Respect: Feminism, Liberalism and Community, *Berkeley Women's Law Journal*, Vol. 4, pp. 128–65.

Spelman, E. (1988) *Inessential Woman: Problems of Exclusion in Feminist Thought*, Boston, Beacon Press.

Spencer, J. R. (1994) Evidence in Child Abuse Cases — Too High a Price for Too High a Standard? *Re: M (A Minor) (Appeal) No. 2*, *Journal of Child Law*, Vol. 6, No. 4, pp. 160–161.

Spencer, J. R. and Flin, R. (1993) *The Evidence of Children*, Blackstone.

Spencer, S. (1984) Homicide, Mental Abnormality and Offence, in *Mentally Abnormal Offenders*, Craft and Craft (see above), pp. 88–115.

Spikes, L. B. and Rud, A. L. (1995) 'Restored Recollections', Claims Based on Repressed Memories of Abuse, *Defense Counsel Journal*, pp. 89–94.

Stanko, E. (1985) *Intimate Intrusions: Women's Experience of Male Violence*, Routledge.

Steer, D. (1980) *Uncovering Crime: The Police Role*, Royal Commission on Criminal Procedure, Research Study 7, HMSO.

Steinem, G. (1980) Erotica and Pornography: A Clear and Present Difference, in Lederer (see above).

Stephen, J. F. (1877) *Digest of Criminal Law*, Sweet and Maxwell (1926, 7th ed.).

Stoller, R. (1968) *Sex and Gender*, Science House.

Stoller, R. (1975) *The Transsexual Experiment*, Hogarth.

Stoltenberg, J. (1990) *Refusing to be a Man: Essays on Sex and Justice*, Meridian.

Stoltenberg, J. (1991a) Pornography and Freedom, in *Men Confront Pornography*, Kimmell, M. (ed.) Meridian.

Stoltenberg, J. (1991b) Gays and the Propornography Movement: Having the Hots for Sex Discrimination, in *Men Confront Pornography*, Kimmell, M. (ed.), Meridian, pp. 248–62.

Stoltenberg J. (1992) Pornography, Homophobia and Male Supremacy, in Itzin (see above), pp. 145–65.

Stone, R. (1986) Obscene Publications: The Problems Persist, *Crim LR*, pp. 139–145.

Storr, A. (1964) *Sexual Deviation*, Penguin.

Straus, M. and Gelles, R. J. (1986) Societal change and family violence from 1975 to 1985 as revealed by two national surveys, *Journal of Marriage and the Family*, Vol. 48, pp. 465–79.

Strossen, N. (1993) A Feminist Critique of 'The Feminist Critique of Pornography', *Va L Rev*, Vol. 79, pp. 1099–1157.

Stubbs, J. (1994) *Women, Male Violence and the Law*, Institute of Criminology Monographs.

Stubbs, J., Sheehy, E. A. and Tolmie, J. (1992) Defending battered women on trial: the battered woman syndrome and its limitations, *Criminal Law Journal*, Vol. 16, pp. 369–94, Series No. 6, Sydney.

Stychin, C. F. (1992) Exploring the Limits: Feminism and the Legal Regulation of Gay Male Pornography, *Vermont Law Review*, Vol. 16, pp. 857–900.

Szasz, T. (1980) *Sex Facts, Frauds and Follies*, Basil Blackwell.

Tait, L. (1894) An Analysis of the Evidence in Seventy Consecutive Cases of Charges Made Under the New Criminal Law Amendment Act, *Provincial Medical Journal*, Vol. 13, pp. 226–33.

Taitz, J. (1988) Transsexuals and Sexual Identity, *Modern Law Review*, pp. 502–508.

Tatchell, P. (1990) *Out in Europe*, Channel 4 Television, London.

Tatchell, P. (1992) Equal Rights For All: Strategies for Lesbian and Gay Equality in Britain, in Plummer (ed.) (see above), pp. 237–48.

Tate, T. (1990) *Child Pornography*, Methuen.

Taylor, L. J. (1986) Reason in Men and Women: Heat-of-Passion Manslaughter and Imperfect Self-Defense, *UCLA LR*, Vol. 33, pp. 1679–735.

Temkin, J. (1987) *Rape and the Legal Process*, Sweet and Maxwell.

Temkin, J. (1993) Sexual History Evidence — the ravishment of section 2, *Crim LR* pp. 3–21.

Thayer, J. B. (1980) Judicial Notice and the Law of Evidence, *Harvard Law Review*, Vol. 3, No. 7, pp. 285–312.

Thomas, D. A. (1970) *Principles of Sentencing*, Heinemann.

Thomas, P. and Costigan, R. (1990) *Promoting Homosexuality, Section 28 of the Local Government Act 1988*, Cardiff Law School.

Thompson, B. (1994a) *Sado Masochism*, Cassell.

Thompson, B. (1994b) *Soft Core*, Cassell.

Thornton, M. (1989) Hegemonic Masculinity and the Academy, *International Journal of the Sociology of Law*, Vol. 17, pp. 115–30.

Tolmie, J. (1991) Provocation or Self Defence for Battered Women Who Kill, in *Partial Excuses to Murder*, Yeo, Melbourne, Federation Press.

Tomkins, A. J., Kenning, M. K., Greenwald, J. P. and Johnson, G. R. (1993) Self-Defence Jury Instructions in Trials of Battered Women Who Kill Their Partner, in Hilton NZ (ed.), pp. 258–285, *Legal Responses to Wife Assault*.

Tucker, S. (1991) Radical Feminism and Gay Male Pornography, in *Men Confront Pornography*, Kimmel, M. (ed.), Crown Publishers Inc., New York, pp. 263–76.

Tully B. (1992) *Accounting for Transsexualism and Transhomosexuality*, Whiting and Birch Ltd, London.

Unikel, R. (1992) 'Reasonable' Doubts: A critique of the reasonable woman standard in American Jurisprudence, *Northwestern University Law Review*, Vol. 87, No. 1, pp. 326–75.

Van Der Poel, S. (1995) Solidarity as Boomerang: The Fiasco of the Prostitute's Rights Movement in the Netherlands, *Crime, Law and Social Change*, Vol. 23, No. 1, pp. 41–65.

Van Dijk, P. (1993) The Treatment of Homosexuals under the European Convention on Human Rights, in *Homosexuality: A European Community Issue*, Waaldijk, K. and Clapham, A., Nijhoff.

Vega, J. (1988) Coercion and Consent: Classic Liberal Concepts in Texts on Sexual Violence, *International Journal of the Sociology of Law*, Vol. 16, pp. 75–89.

Walker, A. (1983) *The Colour Purple*, The Women's Press.

Walker, A. (1984) Coming Apart: in *You Can't Keep a Good Woman Down*, New York, Harcourt Brace Jovanovitch, pp. 41–53.

Walker, G. and Daly, L. (1987) *Sexplicitly Yours: The Trial of Cynthia Payne*, Penguin.

Walker, L. E. (1977) Battered Women and Learned Helplessness, *Victimology*, Vol. 2, pp. 525–26.

Walker, L. E. (1979) *The Battered Woman*, Harper Row.

Walker, L. E. (1989) *Terrifying Love*, Harper Row.

Walker, L. E. (1993) Battered Women as Defendants in Hilton NZ, (ed), pp. 233–57.

Walkowitz, J. (1977) The Making of an Outcast Group: Prostitutes and Working Women in Nineteenth-Century Plymouth and Southampton, *Widening Sphere*, Vicinus, M. (ed.), Methuen, pp. 72–93.

Wallace, A. (1986) *Homicide: The Social Reality*, NSW Bureau of Crime Statistics and Research, Research Study No. 5.

Walmsley, R. and White, K. (1979) *Sexual Offences, Consent and Sentencing*, Research Study No. 54, HMSO.

Wasik, M. (1982) Cumulative Provocation and Domestic Killing, *Crim LR*, pp. 29–37.

Wasoff, F. (1982) Legal Protection from Wife-Beating: The Processing of Domestic Assaults by Scottish Prosecutors and Criminal Courts International, *Journal of the Sociology of Law*, Vol. 10, pp. 187–204.

Wasoff, F. (1987) Prosecutor's Discretion in Court Allocation in Domestic Violence Cases, paper presented to the *British Criminology Conference*, at the University of Sheffield, 12–15 April 1987.

Waterhouse, L., Dobash, R. P. and Carnie, J. (1994) *Child Sexual Abuse*, Central Research Unit, The Scottish Office.

Wesson, M. (1991) Sex, Lies and Videotape: The Pornographer as Censor, *Washington Law Review*, Vol. 66, pp. 913–36.

West, A. (1992) Prosecutorial Activism: Confronting Heterosexism in a Lesbian Battering Case, *Harvard Women's Law Journal*, Vol. 15, pp. 249–271.

Whitaker, E. M. (1993) Pornographer Liability for Physical Harms Caused by Obscenity and Child Pornography: A Tort Analysis, *Georgia Law Review*, Vol. 27, pp. 849–901.

Whitehouse, M. (1993) *A Most Dangerous Woman?*, Lion.

Wigmore, J. H. (1940) *A Treatise on the Anglo-American System of Evidence in Trials at Common Law*, Vol. III, Boston, Little Brown.

Willbanks, W. (1983) The Female Homicide Offender in Dade County Florida, *Criminal Justice Review*, Vol. 8, No. 2, pp. 9–14.

Williams, G. (1961) *Criminal Law*, Steven and Sons.

Williams, G. (1962) Consent and Public Policy, *Crim LR*, pp. 74–78.

Williams, G. (1963) *The Proof of Guilt*, Stevens.

Williams, G. (1983) *Textbook of Criminal Law*, Stevens.

Williams, L. (1993) A Provoking Agent: The Pornography and Performance Art of Annie Sprinkle, *Social Text*, Vol. 37, Duke University Press, pp. 117–33.

Wilson, M. and Daly, M. (1994) *Spousal Homicide*, Vol. 14, No. 8, Juristat Service Bulletin, Canadian Centre for Justice Statistics.

Wilson, R. (1984) Life and Law: The Impact of Human Rights on Experimenting with Life, *Australian Journal of Forensic Sciences*.

Wilson, W. (1994) Is Hurting People Wrong? *Journal of Social Welfare and Family Law*, pp. 338–397.

Winkel, F. W. and Vrij, A. (1993) Rape Reporting to the Police: Exploring the Social Psychological Impact of a Persuasive Campaign on Cognitions, Attitudes, Normative Expectations and Reporting Intentions, *International Review of Victimology*, Vol. 2, No. 4, pp. 277–94.

Winkelman, S. J. (1993) Making a woman's safety more important than peep shows: A Review of the Pornography Victim's Compensation Act, *Washington University of Urban and Contemporary Issues*, Vol. 44, pp. 237–63.

Wise, S. and Stanley, L. (1987) *Georgie Porgie: Sexual Harassment in Everyday Life*, London, Pandora.

Wolfgang, M. E. (1958) *Patterns of Criminal Homicide*, New York, John Wiley.

Working Together under the Children Act 1989 (1991) Home Office, Department of Health, Department of Education and Science, Welsh Office, HMSO.

Woods, L. (1993) Anti-Stalker Legislation: A Legislative Attempt to Surmount the Inadequacies of Protective Orders, *Indiana Law Review*, Vol. 27, pp. 449–473.

Wright, A. (1995) Indecent Exposure on the Information Superhighway: Regulating Pornography on Integrated Broadband Telecommunications Networks, *Georgia State University Law Review*, Vol. 11, pp. 465–493.

Wright, M. (1990) *Justice for Victims and Offenders*, Open University Press.

Yates, C. (1990) A Family Affair: Part I — Sexual Offences Sentencing and Treatment 1989, *Journal of Child Law*, pp. 70–76.

Yeo, S. (1993) Resolving Gender Bias in Criminal Defences, *Monash University Law Review*, Vol. 19, No. 1, pp. 104–16.

Zawitz, M. W. (1994) Selected Findings, *Domestic Violence, Violence Between Inmates*, November, Bureau of Justice Statistics, US Department of Justice.

INDEX

Self-defence — *continued*
    Canada 241-4
    USA 237-41
  burden of proof 236
  imminent danger perception
    238-9, 241, 242, 249-50
  perception of accused 237
  psychological 229
  see also Diminished responsibility
  homicide 366, 389-90, 406-10
    female licence to kill 400
    imminence of danger 390
    pre-emptive strikes 407
  imminence of danger 238-9, 241, 242,
    249-50, 390
Sentences
  child sex abuse 275, 277, 316-21
    mitigation 317-19
    victim contributing to own demise
      317-18, 320
    wives forgiving partners 319-20
  domestic violence 207-12
    Court of Appeal 208-10
    'forgiving wives' 211-12
    mediation 212-13
    negotiations 210-11
    'out of character' 210
    victim statements 210-12
  pornography 112
  rape 360-4
  see also Mitigation
Sex
  violence as 94-5, 96, 323, 351-6
    partial asphyxia 354
    pseudo-masochistic sex 353-4
Sex offences 323-64
  buggery 187-9, 323, 335
    homosexuals 61-2
  flashing (indecent exposure) 323, 324-5
  gross indecency
    homosexuals 61
    prosecutions 64, 65-6
    public behaviour 63-4
  harassment 328-9
  indecency towards a child 325
  indecent assault 277-8
    pressing against victim 325-7
    transsexual victims 33
  indecent exposure 323, 324-5
  masculinist definitions 323
  obscene telephone calls 327-8
  pressing against 325-7
  rape *see* Rape
  transsexuals 25-34
    failure to disclose status change 26
    female to male offender 25-6
    gender specific offences 25

Sex offences — *continued*
  importuning 27, 28
  indecent assault 33
  living on immoral earnings 31-2
  loitering 27
  prostitution *see* Prostitution
  rape, transsexual victims 33
  soliciting 27
  victims 33-4
  see also Child prostitution; Child sex abuse;
    Prostitution
Sex shops 174
Sex tourism 144-7, 265
  prosecution for acts abroad 147
Sexual harassment 328-9
Sheehy Report (1993) 195
Soliciting 27, 61, 66-7, 150, 153-4
  outraging public decency 67
Southall Black Sisters 190
Stalkers 190
Strangulation 185
Supervision orders 290, 295-6, 301

Telephone calls, obscene 327-8
Threats
  battered woman syndrome and 232, 254
  domestic violence and 183-6
  to kill 183, 185
Transsexuals 8-51
  androgeny
    constructed 9, 11
    natally occurring 9, 40
  birth registration change 14, 39-40, 41,
    43-4
  criminal liability 25-34
    see also sex offences
  definition required 10
  as deviant 9
  diagnosis of transsexualism 44-5, 48
  employment protection 34-6
  equal pay 36
  European Union 40-4
  failure to disclose status change 26
  family law *see* marriage; parenting
  female to male offender 25-6
  gender specific offences 25
  hermaphrodites 9
    marriage 15
  human rights 34
    document name changes 39-40
    European Court 40-4
    family life 21-3, 41
    marriage 39, 40, 42-3
    privacy 41
    to be a man 40-2
    to be a woman 42-4
    to post-operative sex 39-44

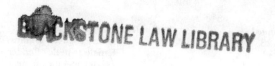